# Late Victorian Holocausts

# Late Victorian Holocausts

## El Niño Famines and the Making
of the Third World

$\blacklozenge$

MIKE DAVIS

Verso
London • New York

This paperback edition first published by Verso 2002
© Mike Davis 2002
First published by Verso 2001
© Mike Davis 2001

3 5 7 9 10 8 6 4

**Verso**
UK: 6 Meard Street, London W1F 0EG
USA: 180 Varick Street, New York, NY 10014-4606
www.versobooks.com

Verso is the imprint of New Left Books

ISBN 1-85984-382-4

**British Library Cataloguing in Publication Data**
A catalogue for this book is available from the British Library

**Library of Congress Cataloging-in-Publication Data**
A catalog for this book is available from the Library of Congress

Designed and typeset by Steven Hiatt
San Francisco, California
Printed in the USA by R. R. Donnelley & Sons

## Offended Lands

… It is so much, so many
tombs, so much martyrdom, so much
galloping of beasts in the star!
Nothing, not even victory
will erase the terrible hollow of the blood:
nothing, neither the sea, nor the passage
of sand and time, nor the geranium flaming
upon the grave.

–Pablo Neruda (1937)

# Contents

# Acknowledgements

An ancient interest in climate history was rekindled during the week I spent as a fly on the wall at the June 1998 Chapman Conference, "Mechanism of Millennial-Scale Global Climate Change," in Snowbird, Utah. Listening to the folks who mine environmental history from the Greenland Ice Sheet and the Bermuda Rise discuss state-of-the-art research on climate oscillations was a truly exhilarating experience, and I thank the organizers for allowing a mere historian to kibitz what was intended to be a family conversation.

The outline for this book was subsequently presented as a paper in September 1998 at the conference "Environmental Violence" organized at UC Berkeley by Nancy Peluso and Michael Watts. Vinayak Chaturvedi, Tom Brass and Gopal Balakrishnan generously offered expert and luminous criticisms of this project in its early stages. Kurt Cuffey spruced up some of the physics in Chapter 7. Dan Monk and Sara Lipton, Michelle Huang and Chi-She Li, and Steve and Cheryl Murakami provided the essential *aloha*. The truly hard work was done by Steve Hiatt, Colin Robinson, Jane Hindle and my other colleagues at Verso Books, while David Deis created the excellent maps and graphics and Tom Hassett proofread the galleys with care. A MacArthur Fellowship provided unencumbered opportunities for research and writing.

The real windfalls in my life, however, have been the sturdy love and patience of my *compañera*, Alessandra Moctezuma; the unceasing delight of my children, Jack and Roisín; and the friendship of two incomparable rogue-intellectuals and *raconteurs*, David Reid and Mike Sprinker. David took precious time off from 1940s New York to help weed my final draft. Mike introduced me to the impressive work of South Asian Marxist historians and provided a decisively important critique of the book's original conception. His death from a heart attack in August 1999, after a long and apparently successful fight against cancer, was simply an obscenity. He was one of the genuinely great souls of the American Left. As José Martí once said of Wendell Phillips: "He was implacable and fiery, as are all tender men who love justice." I dedicate this book to his beloved wife and co-thinker, Modhumita Roy, and thank her for the courage she has shared with all of us.

# Preface

The failure of the monsoons through the years from 1876 to 1879 resulted in an unusually severe drought over much of Asia. The impact of the drought on the agricultural society of the time was immense. So far as is known, the famine that ravished the region is the worst ever to afflict the human species.

—John Hidore, *Global Environmental Change*

It was the most famous and perhaps longest family vacation in American history. "Under a crescendo of criticism for the corruption of his administration," the newly retired president of the United States, Ulysses S. Grant, his wife Julia, and son Jesse left Philadelphia in spring 1877 for Europe. The ostensible purpose of the trip was to spend some time with daughter Nellie in England, who was married (after the fashion that Henry James would celebrate) to a "dissolute English gentleman." Poor Nellie, in fact, saw little of her publicity-hungry parents, who preferred red carpets, cheering throngs and state banquets. As one of Grant's biographers has put it, "much has been said about how Grant, the simple fellow, manfully endured adulation because it was his duty to do so. This is nonsense." Folks back home were thrilled by *New York Herald* journalist John Russell Young's accounts of the "stupendous dinners, with food and wine in enormous quantity and richness, followed by brandy which the general countered with countless cigars." Even more than her husband, Mrs. Grant – but for Fort Sumter, a drunken tanner's wife in Galena, Illinois – "could not get too many princely attentions." As a result, "the trip went on and on and on" – as did Young's columns in the *Herald*.[1]

Wherever they supped, the Grants left a legendary trail of gaucheries. In Venice, the General told the descendants of the Doges that "it would be a fine city if they drained it," while at a banquet in Buckingham Palace, when the visibly uncomfortable Queen Victoria (horrified at a "tantrum" by son Jesse) invoked her "fatiguing duties" as an excuse to escape the Grants, Julia responded: "Yes, I can imagine them: I too have been the wife of a great ruler."[2] In Berlin, the Grants hovered around the fringes of the great Congress of Powers as it grappled with the "Eastern Question" as a prelude to the final European assault on the uncolonized peoples of Africa, Asia and Oceania. Perhaps it was the intoxication of so much imperialist hyperbole or the vision of even more magnificent receptions in oriental palaces that prompted the Grants to transform their vacation into a world tour. With James Gordon Bennett Jr. of the *New York Herald* paying the bar tab and the US Navy providing much of the transportation, the ex–First Family plotted an itinerary that would have humbled Alexander the Great: up the Nile to Thebes in Upper Egypt, back to Palestine, then on to Italy and Spain, back to the Suez Canal, outward to Aden, India, Burma, Vietnam, China and Japan, and, finally, across the Pacific to California.

## Vacationing in Famine Land

Americans were particularly enthralled by the idea of their Ulysses in the land of the pharaohs. Steaming up the Nile, with a well-thumbed copy of Mark Twain's *Innocents Abroad* on his lap, Grant was bemused to be welcomed in village after village as the "King of America." He spent quiet afternoons on the river reminiscing to Young (and thousands of his readers) about the bloody road from Vicksburg to Appomattox. Once he chastised the younger officers in his party for taking unsporting potshots at stray cranes and pelicans. (He sarcastically suggested they might as well go ashore and shoot some "poor, patient drudging camel, who pulls his heavy-laden hump along the bank.") On another occasion, when their little steamer had to pull up for the night while the crew fixed the engine, Grant's son Jesse struck up a conversation with some of the bedouin standing guard around the campfire. They complained that "times are hard," forcing them far from their homes. "The Nile has been bad, and when the Nile is bad, calamity comes and the people go away to other villages."[3]

Indeed the Grants' idyll was soon broken by the increasingly grim conditions along the river banks. "Our journey," reported Young, "was through a country

Figure P1  The Grants in Upper Egypt

that in a better time must have been a garden; but the Nile not having risen this year all is parched and barren." Although so far the Grants had only basked in the warmth of peasant hospitality, there had been widespread rioting in the area south of Siout (capital of Upper Egypt) and some of the *fellahin* had reportedly armed themselves and headed into the sand hills. At the insistence of the governor, the Americans were assigned an armed guard for the remainder of their journey to Thebes and the First Cataract. Here the crop failure had been nearly total and thousands were dying from famine. Young tried to paint a picture of the "biblical disaster" for *Herald* readers: "Today the fields are parched and brown, and cracked. The irrigating ditches are dry. You see stumps of the last season's crop. But with the exception of a few clusters of the castor bean and some weary, drooping date palms, the earth gives forth no fruit. A gust of sand blows over the plain and adds to the somberness of the scene."[4]

Young, who had become as enchanted with Egypt's common people as with its ancient monuments, was appalled by the new British suzerains' contemptuous attitude toward both. "The Englishman," he observed, "looks upon these people as his hewers of wood and drawers of water, whose duty is to work and to thank the Lord when they are not flogged. They only regard these monuments [meanwhile] as reservoirs from which they can supply their own museums and for that purpose they have plundered Egypt, just as Lord Elgin plundered Greece." Young noted the crushing burden that the country's enormous foreign debt, now policed by the British, placed upon its poorest and now famished people. The ex-President, for his part, was annoyed by the insouciant attitude of the local bureaucrats confronted with a disaster of such magnitude.[5]

A year later in Bombay, Young found more evidence for his thesis that "English influence in the East is only another name for English tyranny." While the Grants were marveling over the seeming infinity of servants at the disposal of the sahibs, Young was weighing the costs of empire borne by the Indians. "There is no despotism," he concluded, "more absolute than the government of India. Mighty, irresponsible, cruel ..." Conscious that more than 5 million Indians by official count had died of famine in the preceding three years, Young emphasized that the "money which England takes out of India every year is a serious drain upon the country, and is among the causes of its poverty."[6]

Leaving Bombay, the Grant party passed through a Deccan countryside – "hard, baked and brown" – that still bore the scars of the worst drought in human memory. "The ride was a dusty one, for rain had not fallen since September, and the few occasional showers which usually attend the blossoming of the mango, which had not appeared, were now the dread of the people, who feared their coming to ruin the ripening crops."[7] After obligatory sightseeing trips to the Taj Mahal and Benares, the Grants had a brief rendezvous with the viceroy, Lord Lytton, in Calcutta and then left, far ahead of schedule, for Burma. Lytton would later accuse a drunken Grant of groping English ladies at dinner, while on the American side there was resentment of Lytton's seeming diffidence towards the ex-president.[8] Grant's confidant, the diplomat Adam Badeau, thought that Lytton had received "instructions from home not to pay too much deference to the ex-President. He believed that the British Government was unwilling to admit to the half-civilized populations of the East that any Western Power was important, or that any authority deserved recognition except their own." (Grant, accordingly, refused Badeau's request to ask the US ambassador in London to thank the British.)[9]

A magnificent reception in China compensated for Lytton's arrogance. Li Hongzhang, China's senior statesman and victor over the Nian rebellion (which Young confused with the Taiping), was eager to obtain American help in difficult negotiations with Japan over the Ryukus. Accordingly, 100,000 people were turned out in Shanghai to cheer the Grants while a local band gamely attempted "John Brown's Body." (Chinese enthusiasm, however, was mainly official. This was not Egypt. Young earlier noted the young mandarins who from the windows of their homes in Canton "looked upon the barbarian with a supercilious air, contempt in their expression, very much as our young men in New York would regard Sitting Bull or Red Cloud from a club window as the Indian chiefs went in procession along Fifth Avenue.")[10]

En route from Tianjin to Beijing, the Americans were wearied by the "fierce, unrelenting heat" compounded by depressing scenery of hunger and desolation.[11] Three years of drought and famine in northern China – officially the "most terrible disaster in twenty-one dynasties of Chinese history" – had recently killed somewhere between 8 million and 20 million people.[12] Indeed nervous American consular officials noted in their dispatches that "were it not for the possession of improved weapons mobs of starving people might have caused a severe political disturbance."[13] In his conversations with Li Hongzhang, Grant lectured with some insolence that railroads might have prevented such a catastrophe: "In the matter of famines, of which he had heard so many distressing stories since he came to China, it would be a blessing to the people to have railway communications. In America, there could be no famine such as had recently been seen in China, unless, as was hardly possible in so vast a territory, the famine became general. If the crops failed in one State, supplies could be brought from others at a little extra expense in money and time. We could send wheat, for instance, from one end of the country to another in a few days." Li Hongzhang responded that he was personally in favor of railways and telegraphs but unfortunately "his opinions on this were not shared by some of his colleagues."[14] The great Qing leader, of course, was engaging in heroic understatement.

## The Secret History of the Nineteenth Century

After Beijing, Grant continued to Yokohama and Edo, then home across the Pacific to a rapturous reception in San Francisco that demonstrated the dramatic revival of his popularity in light of so much romantic and highly publicized globe-trotting. Throat cancer eventually precluded another assault on the White House and forced the ex-president into a desperate race to finish his famous *Personal Memoirs*. But none of that is pertinent to this preface. What is germane is a coincidence in his travels that Grant himself never acknowledged, but which almost certainly must have puzzled readers of Young's narrative: the successive encounters with epic drought and famine in Egypt, India and China. It was almost as if the Americans were inadvertently following in the footprints of a monster whose colossal trail of destruction extended from the Nile to the Yellow Sea.

As contemporary readers of *Nature* and other scientific journals were aware, it was a disaster of truly planetary magnitude, with drought and famine reported as well in Java, the Philippines, New Caledonia, Korea, Brazil, southern Africa and the Mahgreb. No one had hitherto suspected that synchronous extreme weather was possible on the scale of the entire tropical monsoon belt plus northern China and North Africa. Nor was there any historical record of famine afflicting so many far-flung lands simultaneously. Although only the roughest estimates of mortality could be made, it was horrifyingly clear that the million Irish dead of 1845–47 had been multiplied by tens. The total toll of conventional warfare from Austerlitz to Antietam and Sedan, according to calculations by one British journalist, was probably less than the mortality in southern India alone.[15] Only China's Taiping Revolution (1851–64), the bloodiest civil war in world history with an estimated 20 million to 30 million dead, could boast as many victims.

But the great drought of 1876–79 was only the first of three global subsistence crises in the second half of Victoria's reign. In 1889–91 dry years again brought famine to India, Korea, Brazil and Russia, although the worst suffering was in Ethiopia and the Sudan, where perhaps one-third of the population died. Then in 1896–1902, the monsoons again repeatedly failed across the tropics and in northern China. Hugely destructive epidemics of malaria, bubonic plague, dysentery,

## Table P1
### Estimated Famine Mortality

| India | 1876–79 | 10.3 million | Digby |
|---|---|---|---|
| | | 8.2 million | Maharatna |
| | | 6.1 million | Seavoy |
| | 1896–1902 | 19.0 million | *The Lancet* |
| | | 8.4 million | Maharatna/Seavoy |
| | | 6.1 million | Cambridge |
| India Total | | 12.2–29.3 million | |
| China | 1876–79 | 20 million | Broomhall |
| | | 9.5–13 million | Bohr |
| | 1896–1900 | 10 million | Cohen |
| China Total | | 19.5–30 million | |
| Brazil | 1876–79 | 0.5–1.0 million | Cunniff |
| | 1896–1900 | n.d. | |
| Brazil Total | | 2 million | Smith |
| Total | | 31.7–61.3 million | |

Source: Cf. William Digby, *"Prosperous" British India,* London 1901; Arap Maharatna, *The Demography of Famine,* Delhi 1996; Roland Seavoy, *Famine in Peasant Societies,* New York 1986; *The Lancet,* 16 May 1901; *Cambridge Economic History of India,* Cambridge 1983; A. J. Broomhall, *Hudson Taylor and China's Open Century, Book Six, Assault on the Nine,* London 1988; Paul Bohr, *Famine in China,* Cambridge, Mass. 1972; Paul Cohen, *History in Three Keys,* New York 1997; Roger Cunniff, "The Great Drought: Northeast Brazil, 1877–1880," Ph.D. diss., University of Texas, Austin 1970; and T. Lynn Smith, *Brazil: People and Institutions,* Baton Rouge, La. 1954. Chapters 3 and 5 have detailed discussions of these estimates.

smallpox and cholera culled millions of victims from the ranks of the famine-weakened. The European empires, together with Japan and the United States, rapaciously exploited the opportunity to wrest new colonies, expropriate communal lands, and tap novel sources of plantation and mine labor. What seemed from a metropolitan perspective the nineteenth century's final blaze of imperial glory was, from an Asian or African viewpoint, only the hideous light of a giant funeral pyre.

The total human toll of these three waves of drought, famine and disease could not have been less than 30 million victims. Fifty million dead might not be unrealistic. (Table P1 displays an array of estimates for famine mortality for 1876–79 and 1896–1902 in India, China and Brazil only.) Although the famished nations themselves were the chief mourners, there were also contemporary Europeans who understood the moral magnitude of such carnage and how fundamentally it annulled the apologies of empire. Thus the Radical journalist William Digby, principal chronicler of the 1876 Madras famine, prophesized on the eve of Queen Victoria's death that when "the part played by the British Empire in the nineteenth century is regarded by the historian fifty years hence, the unnecessary deaths of millions of Indians would be its principal and most notorious monument."[16] A most eminent Victorian, the famed naturalist Alfred Russel Wallace, the codiscoverer with Darwin of the theory of natural selection, passionately agreed. Like Digby, he viewed mass starvation as avoidable political tragedy, not "natural" disaster. In a famous balance-sheet of the Victorian era, published in 1898, he characterized the famines in India and China, together with the slum poverty of the industrial cities, as "the most terrible failures of the century."[17]

But while the Dickensian slum remains in the world history curriculum, the famine children of 1876 and 1899 have disappeared. Almost without exception, modern historians writing about nineteenth-century world history from a metropolitan vantage-point have ignored the late Victorian mega-droughts and famines that engulfed what we now call the "third world." Eric Hobsbawm, for example, makes no allusion in his famous trilogy on nineteenth-century history to the worst famines in perhaps 500 years in India and China, although he does mention the Great Hunger in Ireland as well as the Russian famine of 1891–92. Likewise, the sole reference to famine in David Landes's *The Wealth and Poverty of Nations* – a magnum opus meant to solve the mystery of inequality between nations – is the erroneous claim that British railroads eased hunger in India.[18] Numerous other examples could be cited of contemporary historians' curious neglect of such portentous events. It is like writing the history of the late twentieth century without mentioning the Great Leap Forward famine or Cambodia's killing fields. The great famines are the missing pages – the absent defining moments, if you prefer – in virtually every overview of the Victorian era. Yet there are compelling, even urgent, reasons for revisiting this secret history.

At issue is not simply that tens of millions of poor rural people died appallingly, but that they died in a manner, and for reasons, that contradict much of the conventional understanding of the economic history of the nineteenth century. For example, how do we explain the fact that in the very half-century when

# PREFACE

PREFACE

9

peacetime famine permanently disappeared from Western Europe, it increased so devastatingly throughout much of the colonial world? Equally how do we weigh smug claims about the life-saving benefits of steam transportation and modern grain markets when so many millions, especially in British India, died alongside railroad tracks or on the steps of grain depots? And how do we account in the case of China for the drastic decline in state capacity and popular welfare, especially famine relief, that seemed to follow in lockstep with the empire's forced "opening" to modernity by Britain and the other Powers?

We not are dealing, in other words, with "lands of famine" becalmed in stagnant backwaters of world history, but with the fate of tropical humanity at the precise moment (1870–1914) when its labor and products were being dynamically conscripted into a London-centered world economy.[19] Millions died, not outside the "modern world system," but in the very process of being forcibly incorporated into its economic and political structures. They died in the golden age of Liberal Capitalism; indeed, many were murdered, as we shall see, by the theological application of the sacred principles of Smith, Bentham and Mill. Yet the only twentieth-century economic historian who seems to have clearly understood that the great Victorian famines (at least, in the Indian case) were integral chapters in the history of capitalist modernity was Karl Polanyi in his 1944 book *The Great Transformation*. "The actual source of famines in the last fifty years," he wrote, "was the free marketing of grain combined with local failure of incomes":

> Failure of crops, of course, was part of the picture, but despatch of grain by rail made it possible to send relief to the threatened areas; the trouble was that the people were unable to buy the corn at rocketing prices, which on a free but incompletely organized market were bound to be a reaction to a shortage. In former times small local stores had been held against harvest failure, but these had been now discontinued or swept away into the big market.... Under the monopolists the situation had been fairly kept in hand with the help of the archaic organization of the countryside, including free distribution of corn, while under free and equal exchange Indians perished by the millions.[20]

Polanyi, however, believed that the emphasis that Marxists put on the exploitative aspects of late-nineteenth-century imperialism tended "to hide from our view the even greater issue of cultural degeneration":

The catastrophe of the native community is a direct result of the rapid and violent disruption of the basic institutions of the victim (whether force is used in the process or not does not seem altogether relevant). These institutions are disrupted by the very fact that a market economy is foisted upon an entirely differently organized community; labor and land are made into commodities, which, again, is only a short formula for the liquidation of every and any cultural institution in an organic society.... Indian masses in the second half of the nineteenth century did not die of hunger because they were exploited by Lancashire; they perished in large numbers because the Indian village community had been demolished.[21]

Polanyi's famous essay has the estimable virtue of knocking down one Smithian fetish after another to show that the route to a Victorian "new world order" was paved with bodies of the poor. But he simultaneously reified the "Market" as automata in a way that has made it easier for some epigones to visualize famine as an inadvertent "birth pang" or no-fault "friction of transition" in the evolution towards market-based world subsistence. Commodification of agriculture eliminates village-level reciprocities that traditionally provided welfare to the poor during crises. (Almost as if to say: "Oops, systems error: fifty million corpses. Sorry. We'll invent a famine code next time.")

But markets, to play with words, are always "made." Despite the pervasive ideology that markets function spontaneously (and, as a result, "in capitalism, there is nobody on whom one can pin guilt or responsibility, things just happened that way, through anonymous mechanisms"),[22] they in fact have inextricable political histories. And force – *contra* Polanyi – is "altogether relevant." As Rosa Luxemburg argued in her classic (1913) analysis of the incorporation of Asian and African peasantries into the late-nineteenth-century world market:

Each new colonial expansion is accompanied, as a matter of course, by a relentless battle of capital against the social and economic ties of the natives, who are also forcibly robbed of their means of production and labour power. Any hope to restrict the accumulation of capital exclusively to "peaceful competition," i.e. to regular commodity exchange such as takes place between capitalist producer-countries, rests on the pious belief that capital ... can rely upon the slow internal process of a disintegrating natural economy. Accumulation, with its spasmodic expansion, can no more wait for, and be content with, a natural internal disintegration of non-capitalist formations and their transition to commodity economy, than it can wait for, and be content with, the natural increase of the working population. Force is the only solution open to capital; the accumulation of capital, seen as an historical process, employs force as a permanent weapon....[23]

The famines that Polanyi abstractly describes as rooted in commodity cycles and trade circuits were part of this permanent violence. "Millions die" was ultimately a policy choice: to accomplish such decimations required (in Brecht's sardonic phrase) "a brilliant way of organising famine."[24] The victims had to be comprehensively defeated well in advance of their slow withering into dust. Although equations may be more fashionable, it is necessary to pin names and faces to the human agents of such catastrophes, as well as to understand the configuration of social and natural conditions that constrained their decisions. Equally, it is imperative to consider the resistances, large and small, by which starving laborers and poor peasants attempted to foil the death sentences passed by grain speculators and colonial proconsuls.

## 'Prisoners of Starvation'

Parts I and II of this book, accordingly, take up the challenge of traditional narrative history. Synchronous and devastating drought provided an environmental stage for complex social conflicts that ranged from the intra-village level to Whitehall and the Congress of Berlin. Although crop failures and water shortages were of epic proportion – often the worst in centuries – there were almost always grain surpluses elsewhere in the nation or empire that could have potentially rescued drought victims. Absolute scarcity, except perhaps in Ethiopia in 1889, was never the issue. Standing between life and death instead were newfangled commodity markets and price speculation, on one side, and the will of the state (as inflected by popular protest), on the other. As we shall see, the capacities of states to relieve crop failure, and the way in which famine policy was discounted against available resources, differed dramatically. At one extreme, there was British India under viceroys like Lytton, the second Elgin and Curzon, where Smithian dogma and cold imperial self-interest allowed huge grain exports to England in the midst of horrendous starvation. At the other extreme was the tragic example of Ethiopia's Menelik II, who struggled heroically but with too few resources to rescue his people from a truly biblical conjugation of natural and manmade plagues.

Seen from a slightly different perspective, the subjects of this book were ground to bits between the teeth of three massive and implacable cogwheels of modern history. In the first instance, there was the fatal meshing of extreme events between the world climate system and the late Victorian world economy. This was one of the major novelties of the age. Until the 1870s and the creation of a rudimentary international weather reporting network there was little scientific apprehension that drought on a planetary scale was even possible; likewise, until the same decade, rural Asia was not yet sufficiently integrated into the global economy to send or receive economic shock waves from the other side of the world. The 1870s, however, provided numerous examples of a new vicious circle (which Stanley Jevons was the first economist to recognize) linking weather and price perturbations through the medium of an international grain market.[25] Suddenly the price of wheat in Liverpool and the rainfall in Madras were variables in the same vast equation of human survival.

The first six chapters provide dozens of examples of malign interaction between climatic and economic processes. Most of the Indian, Brazilian and Moroccan cultivators, for example, who starved in 1877 and 1878 had already been immiserated and made vulnerable to hunger by the world economic crisis (the nineteenth century's "Great Depression") that began in 1873. The soaring trade deficits of Qing China – artificially engineered in the first place by British *narcotraficantes* – likewise accelerated the decline of the "ever-normal" granaries that were the empire's first-line defense against drought and flood. Conversely, drought in Brazil's Nordeste in 1889 and 1891 prostrated the population of the backlands in advance of the economic and political crises of the new Republic and accordingly magnified their impact.

But Kondratieff (the theorist of economic "long waves") and Bjerknes (the theorist of El Niño oscillations) need to be supplemented by Hobson, Luxemburg and Lenin. The New Imperialism was the third gear of this catastrophic history. As Jill Dias has so brilliantly shown in the case of the Portuguese in nineteenth-century Angola, colonial expansion uncannily syncopated the rhythms of natural disaster and epidemic disease.[26] Each global drought was the green light for an imperialist landrush. If the southern African drought of 1877, for example, was Carnarvon's opportunity to strike against Zulu independence, then the Ethiopian famine of 1889–91 was Crispi's mandate to build a new Roman Empire in the Horn of Africa. Likewise Wilhelmine Germany exploited the floods and drought that devastated Shandong in the late 1890s to aggressively expand its sphere of influence in North China, while the United States was simultaneously using drought-famine and disease as weapons to crush Aguinaldo's Philippine Republic.

But the agricultural populations of Asia, Africa and South America did not go gently into the New Imperial order. Famines are wars over the right to existence. If resistance to famine in the 1870s (apart from southern Africa) was overwhelmingly local and riotous, with few instances of more ambitious insurrectionary organization, it undoubtedly had much to do with the recent memories of state terror from the suppression of the Indian Mutiny and the Taiping Revolution. The 1890s were an entirely different story, and modern historians have clearly established the contributory role played by drought-famine in the Boxer Rebellion, the Korean Tonghak movement, the rise of Indian Extremism and the Brazilian War of Canudos, as well as innumerable revolts in eastern and southern Africa. The millenarian movements that swept the future "third world" at the end of the nineteenth century derived much of their eschatological ferocity from the acuity of these subsistence and environmental crises.

But what of Nature's role in this bloody history? What turns the great wheel of drought and does it have an intrinsic periodicity? As we shall see in Part III, synchronous drought – resulting from massive shifts in the seasonal location of the principal tropical weather systems – was one of the great scientific mysteries of the nineteenth century. The key theoretical breakthrough did not come until the late 1960s, when Jacob Bjerknes at UCLA showed for the first time how the equatorial Pacific Ocean, acting as a planetary heat engine coupled to the trade winds, was able to affect rainfall patterns throughout the tropics and even in the temperate latitudes. Rapid warmings of the eastern tropical Pacific (called El Niño events), for example, are associated with weak monsoons and synchronous drought throughout vast parts of Asia, Africa and northeastern South America. When the eastern Pacific is unusually cool, on the other hand, the pattern reverses (called a La Niña event), and abnormal precipitation and flooding occur in the same "teleconnected" regions. The entire vast see-saw of air mass and ocean temperature, which extends into the Indian Ocean as well, is formally known as "El Niño-Southern Oscillation" (or ENSO, for short).

The first reliable chronologies of El Niño events, painstakingly reconstructed from meteorological data and a variety of anecdotal records (including even the diaries of the conquistadors), were assembled in the 1970s.[27] The extremely pow-

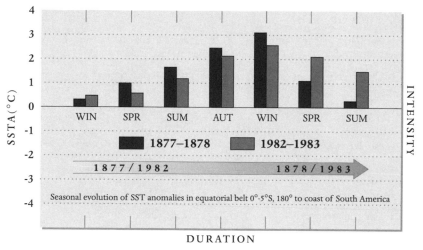

Figure P2  Comparison of the 1877–78 and 1982–83 El Niño Events

erful 1982 El Niño stimulated new interest in the history of the impacts of earlier events. In 1986 two researchers working out of a national weather research laboratory in Colorado published a detailed comparison of meteorological data from the 1876 and 1982 anomalies that identified the first as a paradigmatic ENSO event: perhaps the most powerful in 500 years (see Figure P2).[28] Similarly, the extraordinary succession of tropical droughts and monsoon failures in 1896–97 1899–1900, and 1902 were firmly correlated to El Niño warmings of the eastern Pacific. (The 1898 Yellow River flood, in addition, was probably a La Niña event.) Indeed, the last third of the nineteenth century, like the last third of the twentieth, represents an exceptional intensification of El Niño activity relative to the centuries-long mean.[29]

If, in the eyes of science, ENSO's messy fingerprints are all over the climate disasters of the Victorian period, historians have yet to make much of this discovery. In the last generation, however, they have generated a wealth of case-studies and monographs that immeasurably deepen our understanding of the impact of world market forces on non-European agriculturalists in the late nineteenth century. We now have a far better understanding of how sharecroppers in Ceará, cotton producers in Berar and poor peasants in western Shandong were linked to the world economy and why that made them more vulnerable to drought and flood. We also have magnificent analyses of larger pieces of the puzzle: the decline of the Qing granary and flood-control systems, the internal structure of India's cotton and wheat export sectors, the role of racism in regional development in nineteenth-century Brazil, and so on.

Part IV is an ambitious attempt to mine this vast literature for insights into the background forces that shaped vulnerability to famine and determined who, in the last instance, died. If the early narrative sections of Parts I and II introduced abrupt conjunctural economic factors (like the end of the cotton boom or world trade recession), these penultimate chapters are concerned with slower structural processes: the perverse logic of marketized subsistence, the consequences of colonial revenue settlements, the impact of the new Gold Standard, the decline of indigenous irrigation, informal colonialism in Brazil, and so on. Beginning with a chapter-length overview of the late Victorian economic order as a whole – and the strategic contributions of the Indian and Chinese peasantries, in particular, to maintaining British commercial hegemony – I offer critical summaries of recent work on late-nineteenth-century India, China and Brazil.

This is a "political ecology of famine" because it takes the viewpoint both of environmental history and Marxist political economy: an approach to the history of subsistence crisis pioneered by Michael Watts in his 1983 book, *Silent Violence: Food, Famine and Peasantry in Northern Nigeria*.[30] Although other umbrella terms and affiliations are possible, the fact that Watts and his co-thinkers label their ongoing work as "political ecology" persuades me to do the same, if only to express my indebtedness and solidarity. (Those familiar with Watts's book will easily recognize its influence in this work.)

Finally, I have tried to take on board David Arnold's indispensable emphasis on famines as "engines of historical transformation."[31] The great Victorian famines were forcing houses and accelerators of the very socio-economic forces that ensured their occurrence in the first place. A key thesis of this book is that what we today call the "third world" (a Cold War term)[32] is the outgrowth of income and wealth inequalities – the famous "development gap" – that were shaped most decisively in the last quarter of the nineteenth century, when the great non-European peasantries were initially integrated into the world economy. As other historians have recently pointed out, when the Bastille was being stormed, the vertical class divisions inside the world's major societies were *not* recapitulated as dramatic income differences *between* societies. The differences in living standards, say, between a French *sans-culotte* and Deccan farmer were relatively insignificant compared to the gulf that separated both from their ruling classes.[33] By the end of Victoria's reign, however, the inequality of nations was as profound as the inequality of classes. Humanity had been irrevocably divided. And the famed "prisoners of starvation," whom the *Internationale* urges to arise, were as much modern inventions of the late Victorian world as electric lights, Maxim guns and "scientific" racism.

# A Note on Definitions

The very words that rivet this book to the boilerplate of familiar ideology are, of course, the most dangerous. *Drought, famine* and other terms are like so many semantic time bombs waiting to go off. Better then to walk this minefield at the outset, detonating some of the more obvious booby traps, in the hope that it clears a path for the narrative that follows.

## El Niño

This is the least controversial but most confusing term. In scientific literature its usage slides back and forth, often without warning, between a series of sublated meanings nestled inside of each other like Russian dolls: (1) the weak counter-current that slightly raises sea temperatures off the coast of Ecuador and Peru every year near Christmas (hence El Niño, the Christ child); (2) the unusually large warmings that occur every three to seven years with sometimes catastrophic impacts on marine productivity (suppressed) and the Peruvian coastal desert (epic flooding); (3) the active ocean component of a vast, Pacific Basin–wide oscillation in air mass and ocean temperature known as the El Niño-Southern Oscillation (ENSO); (4) the warm phase of ENSO (the cold phase is known as La Niña); and (5) a metonym for ENSO itself.[1] In this book, El Niño will usually – but, alas, not always – refer to (4), the ENSO warm extreme, which is associated with drought in much of the monsoon tropics and northern China. ENSO, a clunky acronym, is the name of the Great White Whale, the "secret of the monsoons" itself. Part III tells its story.

## Drought

Drought is the recurrent duel between natural rainfall variability and agriculture's hydraulic defenses. It always has a manmade dimension and is never simply a natural disaster. Any drought with a significant agricultural impact is the product of two processes, operating at different temporalities. *Meteorological drought* is usually defined by the percentage shortfall in annual mean precipitation for a given locality or region. The definitions vary from country to country, and in relationship to socially defined "normal conditions." The present-day India Meteorological Department, for example, defines a 60 percent or greater deficiency in local mean rainfall as "severe drought," roughly equivalent to "monsoon failure." Yet what is critical from an agricultural standpoint is less the total amount of rainfall than its distribution relative to annual cycles. A well-distributed but subnormal rainfall may do little damage to crop yield, particularly in areas like the Indian Deccan or north China, where peasants cultivate millet and other drought-resistant crops, while a "normal" rainfall concentrated in the wrong months can lead to considerable crop loss. Historically, agricultural societies in areas of high rainfall variability were usually well-adapted to cope with severe single-year rain deficits; most, however, required massive inter-regional aid to survive two monsoon failures in a row.

The impact of deficient rainfall on food production, moreover, depends on how much stored water is available, whether it can be distributed to plots in a timely fashion, and, where water is a commodity, whether cultivators can afford to purchase it. *Hydrological drought* occurs when both natural (streams, lakes and aquifers) and artificial (reservoirs, wells, and canals) water-storage systems lack accessible supplies to save crops. It should be remembered, of course, that local water supply is often independent of local climate. The most advantageous situation occurs in regions like the Indo-Gangetic plain of northern India, where snow-fed rivers whose watersheds largely lie outside the drought zone can be tapped for irrigation.

Hydrological drought always has a social history. Artificial irrigation systems obviously depend upon sustained levels of social investment and labor upkeep, but even natural water-storage capacity can be dramatically affected by human practices that lead to deforestation and soil erosion. As we shall see, the most devastating nineteenth-century droughts were decisively preconditioned by landscape degradation, the neglect of traditional irrigation systems, the demobilization of communal labor, and/or the failure of the state to invest in water storage. This is why I agree with Rolando Garcia's assertion in *Nature Pleads Not Guilty* (a landmark study of the early 1970s Sahelian crisis) that "climatic facts are not facts in themselves; they assume importance only in relation to the restructuring of the environment within different systems of production." Garcia, after quoting Marx on the historical specificity of the "natural" conditions of production, poses a question that will be fundamental to discussion in this book: "to what degree did the colonial transformation of the system of production change the way in which climatic factors could exert their influence?"[2]

## Famine (Causality)

Whether or not crop failure leads to starvation, and who, in the event of famine, starves, depends on a host of nonlinear social factors. Simple FAD (food availability decline), as Nobel laureate Amartya Sen calls it, may directly lead to famine in isolated hunter-gatherer ecologies, but it is unlikely do so in any large-scale society. Although distant observers of the famines described in this book, including government ministers and great metropolitan papers, regularly described millions killed off by drought or crop failure, those on the scene always knew differently. From the 1860s, or even earlier, it was generally recognized in India, both by British administrators and Indian nationalists, that the famines were not food shortages per se, but complex economic crises induced by the market impacts of drought and crop failure.

The celebrated famine commissions were particularly emphatic in rejecting FAD as an explanation of mass mortality. Thus in the aftermath of the 1899–1902 catastrophe, the official *Report* on famine in the Bombay Presidency underlined that "supplies of food were at all times sufficient, and it cannot be too frequently repeated that severe privation was chiefly due to the dearth of employment in agriculture [arising from the drought]." Commissioners in neighboring Berar likewise concluded that "the famine was one of high prices rather than of scarcity of food." Chinese official discourse also treated famine as primarily a market perturbation, although giving considerable attention as well to the corruption of local granary officials and the delapidation of the transport infrastructure.[3]

In recent years, Amartya Sen and Meghnad Desai have meticulously formalized this Victorian common sense in the language of welfare economics. Famine in their view is a crisis of "exchange entitlements" (defined as "legal, economically operative rights of access to resources that give control of food" ) that may or may not have anything to do with crop yields. "Famine," emphasizes Sen, "is the characteristic of some people not having enough food to eat. It is not the characteristic of there not being enough food to eat."[4] In theoretical jargon, the "endowments" of different groups (ownership of land, labor, power and so on.) "map" to alternative "entitlement sets" of goods and services. People starve in a Senyan world when their endowments, for whatever reason, cannot command or be exchanged for minimal calories to subsist, or, alternately, when their entitlement mappings shift disastrously against them. Famine is thus a catastrophic social relation between unequally endowed groups that may be activated by war, depression or even something called "Development" as well as by extreme climate events. Most likely, of course, it is a conjuncture of different factors.

Critics have considerably sharpened the teeth of this model. David Arnold, for instance, has usefully warned against excessive demotion of environmental factors, especially the impacts of the nineteenth-century mega-droughts. He has also taxed Sen for ignoring mass extra-legal actions – riots, protests, rebellions – that constitute populist appropriations of entitlement.[5] Amarita Rangasami similarly has reminded us that famine "cannot be defined with reference to the victims of starvation alone" In her view (and mine), the great hungers have always been redistributive class struggles: "a process in which benefits accrue to one section of the community while losses flow to the other."[6]

Perhaps most incisively, Michael Watts, discounting any "generic theory" of such an "enormously complex social and biological phenomena," sees the exchange-entitlement model as merely a logical first step in building a fully historical account of famine in different social formations:[7]

> If famine is about the command over food, it is about power and politics broadly understood, which are embedded in a multiplicity of arenas from the domestic (patriarchal politics) to the nation / state (how ruling classes and subaltern groups

acquire and defend certain rights). In social systems dominated by capitalism, ownership through private property determines exchange entitlements, which is to say
that class and class struggle shape the genesis and the outcomes of the property–
hunger equation. At the same time capitalism has develped unevenly on a world
scale, with the result that there are national capitalisms (colored by differing con-
figurations of class and international geopolitics) which provide the building blocks
for distinguishing different species, and consequences, of subsistence crises. Actually existing socialisms have class and other interests, too, and perhaps other property rights consequent on political action and "socialistic" regimes of accumulation. The same can be said for pre-capitalisms for which the moral economy of the
poor may be constitutive of some important entitlement claims. In all such cases,
however, one needs to know how enforceable and legitimate are the legal and property relations which mediate entitlements and to recognize that all such rights are
negotiated and fought over. Such struggles are not peripheral to famine but strike
to its core.[8]

## Famine (Mortality)

"Who defines an event as a 'famine,'" writes Alexander de Waal, "is a question of
power relations within and between societies." He rejects the "Malthusian" idea
that mass starvation unto death is "a prerequisite for the definition of famine"
in favor of the broader spectrum of meanings, including hunger, destitution
and social breakdown, encompassed within traditional African understandings
of famine. Local people, like his Darfurian friends in the western Sudan, do not
build definitional firewalls between malnutrition and famine, poverty and starvation. Nor do they fathom the moral calculus of wealthy countries who rush aid to
certified famines but cooly ignore the chronic malnutrition responsible for half of
the infant morality on the planet. And they are rightly suspicious of a semantics
of famine that all too often renders "ordinary" rural poverty invisible.[9]

Thus, even while focusing on "famines that killed" (and killed on a gigantic
scale), we must acknowledge that famine is part of a continuum with the silent
violence of malnutrition that precedes and conditions it, and with the mortality
shadow of debilitation and disease that follows it. Each famine is a unique, historically specific epidemiological event, and despite the heroic efforts of demographers, famine and epidemic mortality are not epistemologically distinguish-
able. This was recognized by British medical authorities as far back as the 1866

famine in Orissa. "We think it quite impossible to distinguish between the mortality directly caused by starvation, and that due to disease.... In truth want and disease run so much into one another than no statistics and no observations would suffice to draw an accurate line."[10] "During the great famines," adds Klein, "the overwhelming majority of deaths resulted from the synergistic effect of extreme undernourishment on infection."[11]

But famine synergizes with disease in two different if mutually reinforcing modes. The "increase in mortality during the famine can occur either though an increase in susceptibility to potentially fatal diseases or through an increase in exposure to them or a combination of the two."[12] Malnutrition and immune-system suppression increase susceptibility while congested, unsanitary environments like refugee camps and poorhouses increase exposure and transmission. As we shall see, "famine camps were notorious centres of disease and may have killed with microbes as many lives as they saved with food."[13] Moreover, when basic sanitation and public health were so woefully neglected, modern infrastructures of commerce could become deadly vectors in their own right. India's "peculiar amalgam of modernization and underdevelopment" – a "modern transport system, huge grain trade, high human mobility (typical of advanced countries)" combined with "poverty, undernourishment, low immunities, insanitation and high exposure to infection (typical of some "underdeveloped' countries)" – promoted higher mortality than probably would have otherwise existed.[14]

## Holocaust (Picturing)

In her somberly measured reflections, *Reading the Holocaust,* Inga Glendinnen ventures this opinion about the slaughter of innocents: "If we grant that 'Holocaust,' the total consumption of offerings by fire, is sinisterly appropriate for the murder of those millions who found their only graves in the air, it is equally appropriate for the victims of Hiroshima, Nagasaki and Dresden."[15] Without using her capitalization (which implies too complete an equation between the Shoah and other carnages), it is the burden of this book to show that imperial policies towards starving "subjects" were often the exact moral equivalents of bombs dropped from 18,000 feet. The contemporary photographs used in this book are thus intended as accusations not illustrations.

PART I

# The Great Drought, 1876–1878

# One

# Victoria's Ghosts

The more one hears about this famine, the more
one feels that such a hideous record of human suffering
and destruction the world has never seen before.

– Florence Nightingale, 1877

"Here's the northeast monsoon at last," said Hon. Robert Ellis, C. B., junior
member of the Governor's Council, Madras, as a heavy shower of rain fell at
Coonoor, on a day towards the end of October 1876, when the members of the
Madras Government were returning from their summer sojourn on the hills.

"I am afraid that is not the monsoon," said the gentleman to whom the remark
was made.

"Not the monsoon?" rejoined Mr. Ellis. "Good God! It must be the monsoon.
If it is not, and if the monsoon does not come, there will be an awful famine."[1]

The British rulers of Madras had every reason to be apprehensive. The life-giving
southwest monsoon had already failed much of southern and central India the
previous summer. The Madras Observatory would record only 6.3 inches of precipitation for all of 1876 in contrast to the annual average of 27.6 inches during
the previous decade.[2] The fate of millions now hung on the timely arrival of
generous winter rains. Despite Ellis's warning, the governor of Madras, Richard

Grenville, the Duke of Buckingham and Chandos, who was a greenhorn to India and its discontents, sailed away on a leisurely tour of the Andaman Islands, Burma and Ceylon. When he finally reached Colombo, he found urgent cables detailing the grain riots sweeping the so-called Ceded Districts of Kurnool, Cuddapah and Bellary in the wake of another monsoon failure. Popular outbursts against impossibly high prices were likewise occurring in the Deccan districts of the neighboring Bombay Presidency, especially in Ahmednagar and Sholapur. Having tried to survive on roots while awaiting the rains, multitudes of peasants and laborers were now on the move, fleeing a slowly dying countryside.[3]

As the old-hands at Fort St. George undoubtedly realized, the semi-arid interior of India was primed for disaster. The worsening depression in world trade had been spreading misery and igniting discontent throughout cotton-exporting districts of the Deccan, where in any case forest enclosures and the displacement of *gram* by cotton had greatly reduced local food security. The traditional system of household and village grain reserves regulated by complex networks of patrimonial obligation had been largely supplanted since the Mutiny by merchant inventories and the cash nexus. Although rice and wheat production in the rest of India (which now included bonanzas of coarse rice from the recently conquered Irrawaddy delta) had been above average for the past three years, much of the surplus had been exported to England.[4] Londoners were in effect eating India's bread. "It seems an anomaly," wrote a troubled observer, "that, with her famines on hand, India is able to supply food for other parts of the world."[5]

There were other "anomalies." The newly constructed railroads, lauded as institutional safeguards against famine, were instead used by merchants to ship grain inventories from outlying drought-stricken districts to central depots for hoarding (as well as protection from rioters). Likewise the telegraph ensured that price hikes were coordinated in a thousand towns at once, regardless of local supply trends. Moreover, British antipathy to price control invited anyone who had the money to join in the frenzy of grain speculation. "Besides regular traders," a British official reported from Meerut in late 1876, "men of all sorts embarked in it who had or could raise any capital; jewelers and cloth dealers pledging their stocks, even their wives' jewels, to engage in business and import grain."[6] Buckingham, not a free-trade fundamentalist, was appalled by the speed with which modern markets accelerated rather than relieved the famine:

The rise [of prices] was so extraordinary, and the available supply, as compared with well-known requirements, so scanty that merchants and dealers, hopeful of enormous future gains, appeared determined to hold their stocks for some indefinite time and not to part with the article which was becoming of such unwonted value. It was apparent to the Government that facilities for moving grain by the rail were rapidly raising prices everywhere, and that the activity of apparent importation and railway transit, did not indicate any addition to the food stocks of the Presidency ... retail trade up-country was almost at standstill. Either prices were asked which were beyond the means of the multitude to pay, or shops remained entirely closed.[7]

As a result, food prices soared out of the reach of outcaste labourers, displaced weavers, sharecroppers and poor peasants. "The dearth," as *The Nineteenth Century* pointed out a few months later, "was one of money and of labour rather than of food."[8] The earlier optimism of mid-Victorian observers – Karl Marx as well as Lord Salisbury – about the velocity of economic transformation in India, especially the railroad revolution, had failed to adequately discount for the fiscal impact of such "modernization." The taxes that financed the railroads had also crushed the ryots. Their inability to purchase subsistence was further compounded by the depreciation of the rupee due to the new international Gold Standard (which India had not adopted), which steeply raised the cost of imports. Thanks to the price explosion, the poor began to starve to death even in well-watered districts like Thanjavur in Tamil Nadu, "reputed to be immune to food shortages."[9] Sepoys meanwhile encountered increasing difficulty in enforcing order in the panic-stricken bazaars and villages as famine engulfed the vast

### Table 1.1
### Indian Wheat Exports to the UK, 1875–78
(1000s of Quarters)

| | |
|---|---|
| 1875 | 308 |
| 1876 | 757 |
| 1877 | 1409 |
| 1878 | 420 |

Source: Cornelius Walford, *The Famines of the World,* London 1879, p. 127.

Deccan plateau. Roadblocks were hastily established to stem the flood of stick-thin country people into Bombay and Poona, while in Madras the police forcibly expelled some 25,000 famine refugees.[10]

## India's Nero

The central government under the leadership of Queen Victoria's favorite poet, Lord Lytton, vehemently opposed efforts by Buckingham and some of his district officers to stockpile grain or otherwise interfere with market forces. All through the autumn of 1876, while the vital *kharif* crop was withering in the fields of southern India, Lytton had been absorbed in organizing the immense Imperial Assemblage in Delhi to proclaim Victoria Empress of India (Kaiser-i-Hind). As *The Times*'s special correspondent described it, "The Viceroy seemed to have made the tales of Arabian fiction true ... nothing was too rich, nothing too costly." "Lytton put on a spectacle," adds a biographer of Lord Salisbury (the secretary of state for India), "which achieved the two criteria Salisbury had set him six months earlier, of being 'gaudy enough to impress the orientals' ... and furthermore a pageant which hid 'the nakedness of the sword on which we really rely.'"[11] Its "climacteric ceremonial" included a week-long feast for 68,000 officials, satraps and maharajas: the most colossal and expensive meal in world history.[12] An English journalist later estimated that 100,000 of the Queen-Empress's subjects starved to death in Madras and Mysore in the course of Lytton's spectacular *durbar*.[13] Indians in future generations justifiably would remember him as their Nero.[14]

Following this triumph, the viceroy seemed to regard the growing famine as a tiresome distraction from the Great Game of preempting Russia in Central Asia by fomenting war with the blameless Sher Ali, the Emir of Afghanistan. Lytton, according to Salisbury, was "burning with anxiety to distinguish himself in a great war."[15] Serendipitously for him, the Czar was on a collision course with Turkey in the Balkans, and Disraeli and Salisbury were eager to show the Union Jack on the Khyber Pass. Lytton's warrant, as he was constantly reminded by his chief budgetary adviser, Sir John Strachey, was to ensure that Indian, not English, taxpayers paid the costs of what Radical critics later denounced as "a war of deliberately planned aggression." The depreciation of the rupee made strict parsimony in the non-military budget even more urgent.[16]

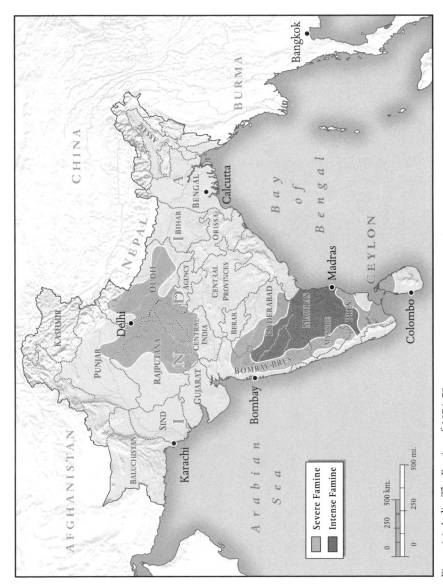

Figure 1.1  India: The Famine of 1876–78

Figure 1.2  The Poet as Viceroy: Lytton in Calcutta, 1877

The 44-year-old Lytton, the former minister to Lisbon, had replaced the Earl of Northbrook after the latter had honorably refused to acquiesce in Disraeli's machiavellian "forward" policy on the northwest frontier. He was a strange and troubling choice (actually, only fourth on Salisbury's short list) to exercise paramount authority over a starving subcontinent of 250 million people. A writer, seemingly admired only by Victoria, who wrote "vast, stale poems" and ponderous novels under the *nom de plume* of Owen Meredith, he had been accused of plagiarism by both Swinburne and his own father, Bulwer-Lytton (author of *The Last Days of Pompeii*).[17] Moreover, it was widely suspected that the new viceroy's judgement was addled by opium and incipient insanity. Since a nervous breakdown in 1868, Lytton had repeatedly exhibited wild swings between megalomania and self-lacerating despair.[18]

Although his possible psychosis ("Lytton's mind tends violently to exaggeration" complained Salisbury to Disraeli) was allowed free rein over famine policy, it became a cabinet scandal after he denounced his own government in October 1877 for "allegedly attempting to create an Anglo-Franco-Russian coalition against Germany." As one of Salisbury's biographers has emphasized, this was "about as absurd a contention as it was possible to make at the time, even from the distance of Simla," and it produced an explosion inside Whitehall. "Salisbury explained the Viceroy's ravings by admitting that he was 'a little mad'. It was known that both Lytton and his father had used opium, and when Derby read the 'inconceivable' memorandum, he concluded that Lytton was dangerous and should resign: 'When a man inherits insanity from one parent, and limitless conceit from the other, he has a ready-made excuse for almost any extravagance which he may commit.'"[19]

But in adopting a strict laissez-faire approach to famine, Lytton, demented or not, could claim to be extravagance's greatest enemy. He clearly conceived himself to be standing on the shoulders of giants, or, at least, the sacerdotal authority of Adam Smith, who a century earlier in *The Wealth of Nations* had asserted (*vis-à-vis* the terrible Bengal drought-famine of 1770) that "famine has never arisen from any other cause but the violence of government attempting, by improper means, to remedy the inconvenience of dearth."[20] Smith's injunction against state attempts to regulate the price of grain during famine had been taught for years in the East India Company's famous college at Haileybury.[21] Thus the viceroy was only repeating orthodox curriculum when he lectured Buckingham that high prices, by stimulating imports and limiting consumption, were the "natural saviours of the situation." He issued strict, "semi-theological" orders that "there is to be no interference of any kind on the part of Government with the object of reducing the price of food," and "in his letters home to the India Office and to politicians of both parties, he denounced 'humanitarian hysterics'."[22] "Let the British public foot the bill for its 'cheap sentiment,' if it wished to save life at a cost that would bankrupt India."[23] By official dictate, India like Ireland before it had become a Utilitarian laboratory where millions of lives were wagered against dogmatic faith in omnipotent markets overcoming the "inconvenience of dearth."[24] Grain merchants, in fact, preferred to export a record 6.4 million cwt.

of wheat to Europe in 1877–78 rather than relieve starvation in India.[25]

Lytton, to be fair, probably believed that he was in any case balancing budgets against lives that were already doomed or devalued of any civilized human quality. The grim doctrines of Thomas Malthus, former Chair of Political Economy at Haileybury, still held great sway over the white rajas. Although it was bad manners to openly air such opinions in front of the natives in Calcutta, Malthusian principles, updated by Social Darwinism, were regularly invoked to legitimize Indian famine policy at home in England. Lytton, who justified his stringencies to the Legislative Council in 1877 by arguing that the Indian population "has a tendency to increase more rapidly than the food it raises from the soil,"[26] most likely subscribed to the melancholy viewpoint expressed by Sir Evelyn Baring (afterwards Lord Cromer), the finance minister, in a later debate on the government's conduct during the 1876–79 catastrophe. "[E]very benevolent attempt made to mitigate the effects of famine and defective sanitation serves but to enhance the evils resulting from overpopulation."[27] In the same vein, an 1881 report "concluded that 80% of the famine mortality were drawn from the poorest 20% of the population, and if such deaths were prevented this stratum of the population would still be unable to adopt prudential restraint. Thus, if the government spent more of its revenue on famine relief, an even larger proportion of the population would become penurious."[28] As in Ireland thirty years before, those with the power to relieve famine convinced themselves that overly heroic exertions against implacable natural laws, whether of market prices or population growth, were worse than no effort at all.

His recent biographers claim that Salisbury, the gray eminence of Indian policy, was privately tormented by these Malthusian calculations. A decade earlier, during his first stint as secretary of state for India, he had followed the advice of the Council in Calcutta and refused to intervene in the early stages of a deadly famine in Orissa. "I did nothing for two months," he later confessed. "Before that time the monsoon had closed the ports of Orissa – help was impossible – and – it is said – a million people died. The Governments of India and Bengal had taken in effect no precautions whatever.... I never could feel that I was free from all blame for the result." Accordingly, he harbored a lifelong distrust of officials who "worshipped political economy as a sort of 'fetish'" as well as Englishmen in India who accepted "famine as a salutary cure for over-population."[29] Yet, whatever his private misgivings, Salisbury had urged appointment of the laissez-faire fanatic Lytton and publicly congratulated Disraeli for repudiating "the growing idea that England ought to pay tribute to India for having conquered her." Indeed, when his own advisers later protested the repeal of cotton duties in the face of the fiscal emergency of the famine, Salisbury denounced as a "species of International Communism" the idea "that a rich Britain should consent to penalize her trade for the sake of a poor India."[30]

Like other architects of the Victorian Raj, Salisbury was terrified of setting any precedent for the permanent maintenance of the Indian poor. As the *Calcutta Review* pointed out in 1877, "In India there is no legal provision made for the poor, either in British territory, or in the native states; [although] the need for it is said by medical men and others, to be exceedingly great."[31] Both Calcutta and London feared that "enthusiastic prodigality" like Buckingham's would become a trojan horse for an Indian Poor Law.[32] In its final report, the Famine Commission of 1878–80 approvingly underscored Lord Lytton's skinflint reasoning: "The doctrine that in time of famine the poor are entitled to demand relief ... would probably lead to the doctrine that they are entitled to such relief at all times, and thus the foundation would be laid of a system of general poor relief, which we cannot contemplate without serious apprehension...."[33] None of the principal players on either side of the House of Commons disagreed with the supreme principle that India was to be governed as a revenue plantation, not an almshouse.

## The 'Temple Wage'

Over the next year, the gathering horror of the drought-famine spread from the Madras Presidency through Mysore, the Bombay Deccan and eventually into the North Western Provinces. The crop losses in many districts of the Deccan plateau and Tamilnad plains (see Table 1.2) were nothing short of catastrophic. *Ryots* in district after district sold their "bullocks, field implements, the thatch of the roofs, the frames of their doors and windows" to survive the terrible first year of the drought. Without essential means of production, however, they were unable to take advantage of the little rain that fell in April–May 1877 to sow emergency crops of rape and *cumboo*. As a result they died in their myriads in August and September.[34]

Table 1.2

Madras Presidency: Chief Famine Districts, 1877

| District | Population (Millions) | Percentage of Crop Saved |
|---|---|---|
| Bellary | 1.68 | 6 |
| Kurnool | .98 | 6 |
| Cuddapah | 1.35 | 18 |
| Chingleput | 1.34 | 18 |
| Nellore | 1.38 | 25 |
| North Arcot | 2.02 | 25 |
| Coimbatore | 1.76 | 25 |
| Madura | 2.27 | 25 |
| Salem | 1.97 | 33 |
| Tinnevelly | 1.64 | 37 |

Source: From the report by Sir Richard Temple, in *Report of the Indian Famine Commission, 1878, Part 1, Famine Relief,* London 1880, p. 71.

Millions more had reached the stage of acute malnutrition, characterized by hunger edema and anemia, that modern health workers call skeletonization.[35] Village officers wrote to their superiors from Nellore and other ravaged districts of the Madras Deccan that the only well-fed part of the local population were the pariah dogs, "fat as sheep," that feasted on the bodies of dead children:

[A]fter a couple of minutes' search, I came upon two dogs worrying over the body of a girl about eight years old. They had newly attacked it, and had only torn one of the legs a little, but the corpse was so enormously bloated that it was only from the total length of the figure one could tell it was a child's. The sight and smell of the locality were so revolting, and the dogs so dangerous, that I did not stay to look for a second body; but I saw two skulls and a backbone which had been freshly picked.[36]

Officials, however, were not eager to share such horrors with the English or educated Indian publics, and the vernacular press charged that starvation deaths were being deliberately misreported as cholera or dysentery mortality in order to disguise the true magnitude of the famine.[37]

Conditions were equally desperate across the linguistic and administrative boundary in the Bombay Deccan. Almost two-thirds of the harvest was lost in

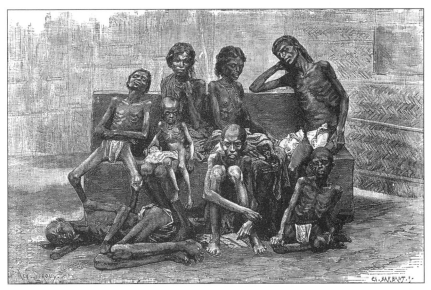

Figure 1.3  A Family in the Deccan, 1877

nine Maharashtran districts affecting 8 million people, with virtually no crop at
all in Sholapur and Kaladgi. The disaster befell a peasantry already ground down
by exorbitant taxation and extortionate debt. In the Ahmednagar region officials
reported that no less than three-fifths of the peasantry was "hopelessly indebted,"
while in Sholapur the district officer had warned his superiors in May 1875: "I
see no reason to doubt the fact stated to me by many apparently trustworthy witnesses and which my own personal observation confirms, that in many cases the
assessments are only paid by selling ornaments or cattle." (As Jairus Banaji comments, "A household without cattle was a household on the verge of extinction.")
Ahmednagar with Poona had been the center of the famous Deccan Riots in
May–June 1875, when ryots beat up moneylenders and destroyed debt records.[38]
    While British procrastination was sacrificing charity to their savage god, the
Invisible Hand, tens of thousands of these destitute villagers were voting with
their feet and fleeing to Hyderabad, where the Nazim was providing assistance to
famine victims. A large part of Sholapur was depopulated before British officials
managed to organize relief works. Then, as a horrified British journalist discov-

ered, they turned away anyone who was too starved to undertake hard coolie labor. But even "the labour test imposed upon the able-bodied," the correspondent noted, "is found to be too heavy for their famished frames; the wages paid are inadequately low; in many districts all who are willing to work do not find employment.... No arrangements have been made to preserve the cattle by providing fodder or pasture lands. No grain stores have been collected or charity houses opened for the infirm and the aged." The only recourse for the young, the infirm and the aged was therefore to attempt the long trek to Hyderabad – an ordeal that reportedly killed most of them.[39]

Widespread unemployment and the high price of grain, meanwhile, brought the spectre of hunger even into districts where rainfall had been adequate. As a result, several million emaciated laborers and poor peasants overwhelmed the relief works belatedly authorized by the Bombay and Madras governments. At the beginning of February, the lieutenant-governor of Bengal, Sir Richard Temple, was sent south as plenipotentiary Famine Delegate by Lytton to clamp down on the "out of control" expenditures that threatened the financing of the planned invasion of Afghanistan. Although the viceroy had also skirmished bitterly with Sir Philip Wodehouse, the governor of Bombay, over Calcutta's refusal to subsidize large-scale relief works during the fall of 1876, his greatest indignation was directed at Buckingham for making "public charity indiscriminate" in Bellary, Cuddapah and Kurnool, where one-quarter of the population was employed breaking stone or digging canals. [40]

Temple was a shrewd choice as Lytton's enforcer. Earlier, in 1873–74, he had followed Salisbury's urgings and dealt aggressively with a drought that severely damaged the harvest throughout most of Bengal and Bihar. Importing half a million tons of rice from Burma, he provided life-saving subsistence, both through relief works and a "gratuitous dole," which forestalled mass mortality. Indeed, the official record claimed only twenty-three starvation deaths. It was the only truly successful British relief effort in the nineteenth century and might have been celebrated as a template for dealing with future emergencies. Instead, Temple came under withering fire from London for the "extravagance" of allowing "the scale of wages paid at relief works to be determined by the daily food needs of the labourer and the prevailing food prices in the market rather than by the amount that the Government could afford to spend for the purpose."[41] In public, he was lambasted by *The Economist* for encouraging indolent Indians to believe that "it is the duty of the Government to keep them alive."[42] Senior civil servants, convinced (according to Lord Salisbury) that it was "a mistake to spend so much money to save a lot of black fellows," denounced the relief campaign as "pure Fourierism."[43] Temple's career was almost ruined.

In 1877 the thoroughly chastened lieutenant-governor, "burning to retrieve his reputation for extravagance in the last famine," had become the implacable instrument of Lytton's frugality. The viceroy boasted to the India Office that he could not have found "a man more likely, or better able to help us save money in famine management."[44] Indeed, *The Times* was soon marveling at the "pliability" of his character: "Sir Richard Temple, whether rightly or wrongly, has the reputation of having a mind so plastic and principles so facile that he can in a moment change front and adopt most contradictory lines of policy. His course in the famine districts certainly seems to bear this out, for he is even more strict than the Supreme Government in enforcing a policy which differs in every respect from that which he himself practised in Behar three years ago."[45]

Although Victoria in her message to the Imperial Assemblage had reassured Indians that their "happiness, prosperity and welfare" were the "present aims and objects of Our Empire,"[46] Temple's brief from the Council of India left no ambiguity about the government's true priorities: "The task of saving life irrespective of cost, is one which it is beyond our power to undertake. The embarrassment of debt and weight of taxation consequent on the expense thereby involved would soon become more fatal than the famine itself." Likewise, the viceroy insisted that Temple everywhere in Madras "tighten the reins." The famine campaign in Lytton's conception was a semi-military demonstration of Britain's necessary guardianship over a people unable to help themselves, not an opportunity for Indian initiative or self-organization.[47] If, as a modern authority on famine emphasizes, "emergency relief, like development aid, is only truly effective if the recipients have the power to determine what it is and how it is used," Temple's perverse task was to make relief as repugnant and ineffective as possible.[48] In zealously following his instructions to the letter, he became to Indian history what Charles Edward Trevelyan – permanent secretary to the Treasury during the Great Hunger (and, later, governor of Madras) – had become to Irish history: the personification of free market economics as a mask for colonial genocide.[49]

In a lightning tour of the famished countryside of the eastern Deccan, Temple purged a half million people from relief work and forced Madras to follow Bombay's precedent of requiring starving applicants to travel to dormitory camps outside their locality for coolie labor on railroad and canal projects. The deliberately cruel "distance test" refused work to able-bodied adults and older children within a ten-mile radius of their homes. Famished laborers were also prohibited from seeking relief until "it was certified that they had become indigent, destitute and capable of only a modicum of labour."[50] Digby later observed that Temple "went to Madras with the preconceived idea that the calamity had been exaggerated, that it was being inadequately met, and that, therefore, facts were, unconsciously may be, squared with this theory.... He expected to see a certain state of things, and he saw that – that and none other."[51]

In a self-proclaimed Benthamite "experiment" that eerily prefigured later Nazi research on minimal human subsistence diets in concentration camps, Temple cut rations for male coolies, whom he compared to "a school full of refractory children," down to one pound of rice per diem despite medical testimony that the ryots – once "strapping fine fellows" – were now "little more than animated skeletons ... utterly unfit for any work." (Noting that felons traditionally received two pounds of rice per day, one district official suggested that "it would be better to shoot down the wretches than to prolong their misery in the way proposed.")[52] The same reduced ration had been introduced previously by General Kennedy (another acerbic personality, "not personally popular even in his own department")[53] in the Bombay Deccan, and Madras's sanitary commissioner, Dr. Cornish, was "of the opinion that 'experiment' in that case [meant] only slow, but certain starvation." Apart from its sheer deficiency in energy, Cornish pointed out that the exclusive rice ration without the daily addition of protein-rich pulses (*dal*), fish or meat would lead to rapid degeneration.[54] Indeed, as the lieutenant-governor was undoubtedly aware, the Indian government had previously fixed the minimum shipboard diet of emigrant coolies "living in a state of quietude" at twenty ounces of rice plus one pound of dal, mutton, vegetables and condiment.[55] In the event, the "Temple wage," as it became known, provided less sustenance for hard labor than the diet inside the infamous Buchenwald concentration camp and less than half of the modern caloric standard recommended for adult males by the Indian government.

Table 1.3
The "Temple Wage" in Perspective

|  | Caloric Value | Activity Level |
|---|---|---|
| Basal metabolism (adult) | 1500 | No activity |
| Temple ration in Madras (1877 | 1627 | Heavy labor |
| Buchenwald ration (1944) | 1750 | Heavy labor |
| 7-year-old child, approved diet (1981) | 2050 | Normal activity |
| Minimum war ration, Japan (1945) | 2165 | Moderate activity |
| Indian adult, subsistence (1985) | 2400 | Moderate activity |
| Temple ration in Bengal (1874) | 2500 | Heavy labor |
| Survey of Bengal laborers (1862) | 2790 | Heavy labor |
| Indian male, approved diet (1981) | 3900 | Heavy labor |
| Voit-Atwater standard (1895) | 4200 | Heavy labor |

Source: Caloric value of Temple ration from Sumit Guha, *The Agrarian Economy of the Bombay Deccan, 1818–1941*, Delhi 1985, p. 186 fn35; Buchenwald ration from C. Richet, "Medicales sur le camp de Buchenwald en 1944–45," *Bulletin Academie Medicine* 129 (1945), pp. 377–88; recommended Indian adult subsistence diet from Asok Mitra, "The Nutrition Situation in India," in Margaret Biswas and Per Pinstrup-Andersen (eds.), *Nutrition and Development*, Oxford 1985, p. 149; basal metabolism from Philip Payne, "The Nature of Malnutrition," ibid., p. 7; child diet and recommended calories for Indian males performing heavy labor from C. Gapalan, "Undernutrition Measurement," in S. Osmani (ed.), *Nutrition and Poverty*, Oxford 1992, p. 2; Rev. James Long's 1862 study of Bengali diets in Greenough, *Prosperity and Misery in Modern Bengal*, Oxford 1982, p. 80 fn94; Voit-Atwater tables discussed in Elmer McCollom, *A History of Nutrition*, Boston 1958, pp. 191–2; and the Temple ration during the 1874 Bengal famine calculated on the basis of 1.5 pounds of rice per day with condiments and *dal* (see *Edinburgh Review*, July 1877).

Temple, who three years earlier had fixed the minimum ration during the Bengal famine at one and one-half pounds of rice plus dal, now publicly disdained the protests of Cornish and other medical officers. They erroneously, and "irresponsibly" in his view, elevated public health above public finance. "Everything," he lectured, "must be subordinated ... to the financial consideration of disbursing the smallest sum of money consistent with the preservation of human life."[56] He completed his cost-saving expedition to Madras by imposing the Anti-Charitable Contributions Act of 1877, which prohibited at the pain of imprisonment private relief donations that potentially interfered with the market-fixing of grain prices. He also stopped Buckingham from remitting onerous land taxes in the famine districts. In May, after Temple had reported back, the viceroy censured Madras officials for their "exaggerated impressions" of misery and "uncalled for relief."[57] Temple meanwhile proclaimed that he had put "the famine under control." (Digby sourly responded that "a famine can scarcely be said to be adequately controlled which leaves one-fourth of the people dead.")[58]

The militarization of relief, followed by the failure of the southwest monsoon and another doubling of grain prices in the six months from the middle of 1877, punctually produced lethal results.[59] Exactly as medical officials had warned, the "Temple wage" combined with heavy physical labor and dreadful sanitation turned the work camps into extermination camps. By the end of May horrified relief officials in Madras were reporting that more than half of the inmates were too weakened to carry out any physical labor whatsoever.[60] Most of them were dead by the beginning of the terrible summer of 1877. As Temple's most dogged critic, Dr. Cornish, pointed out, monthly mortality was now equivalent to an annual death rate of 94 percent. Post-mortem examinations, moreover, showed that the chief cause of death – "extreme wasting of tissue and destruction of the lining membrane of the lower bowel" – was textbook starvation, with full-grown men reduced to under sixty pounds in weight.[61] Mortality was similar in camps throughout the Bombay Deccan, where cholera, spread by polluted water and filth, accelerated the decimation. One official wrote that one relief road project "bore the appearance of a battlefield, its sides being strewn with the dead, the dying and those recently attacked."[62]

Jails ironically were the only exception to this institutional mortality pattern, and they were generally preferred by the poor to the disease-ridden relief camps. An American missionary described how a group of weavers begged him to have them arrested for nonfulfillment of a contract. "We are very sorry, sir, but we have eaten up all the money you gave us, and we have made no clothes. We are in a starving condition, and if you will only send us to jail we shall get something to eat." It was an eminently sensible request. "Prisoners were the best fed poor people in the country," and, accordingly, "the jails were filled to overflowing."[63]

During the Irish famine, Trevelyan had protested that the country's "greatest evil" was not hunger, but "the selfish, perverse and turbulent character of the people."[64] Similarly, Temple's ferocious response to reports of mass mortality in the camps was to blame the victims: "The infatuation of these poor people in respect to eating the bread of idleness; their dread of marching on command to any distance from home; their preference often for extreme privation rather than submission to even simple and reasonable orders, can be fully believed only by those who have seen or personally known these things."[65] Moreover, he claimed that the majority of the famine dead were not the cultivating yeomanry, "the bone and sinew of the country," but parasitic mendicants who essentially had committed suicide: "Nor will many be inclined to grieve much for the fate which they brought upon themselves, and which terminated lives of idleness and too often of crime."[66]

## The Relief Strike

These calumnies, of course, inflamed Indians of all classes. To the consternation of Temple and Lytton, the famished peasants in relief camps throughout the Bombay Deccan (where the sixteen-ounce ration had first been introduced) organized massive, Gandhi-like protests against the rice reduction and distance test. Temple added more than he realized to the imperial lexicon by calling it "passive resistance." The movement began in January 1877, when families on village relief refused orders to march to the new, militarized work camps where men were separated from their wives and children. They were subsequently joined by thousands more who left the camps in protest of the starvation wage and mistreatment by overseers.

> Temple estimated that between 12 January and 12 March, 102,000 people discharged themselves from Government employ. He thought he traced in their proceedings a sign of "some method and system." They imagined, by suddenly throwing themselves out of employ, they virtually offered a passive resistance to the orders of Government. They counted on exciting the compassion of the authorities and still more on arousing fears lest some accidents to human life should occur. They wandered about in bands and crowds seeking for sympathy.[67]

The "relief strike," as it was called, was sympathetically embraced by the Sarvajanik Sabha (Civic Association) in Poona, a moderate nationalist group composed of prominent local merchants, absentee landlords and professionals led

Figure 1.4  "Forsaken!": An Illustration from Digby's *History*

by Ganesh Joshi and Mahdev Govinda Ranade. (Temple cautioned Calcutta that the articulate Ranade might bid to become the "Deccan's Parnell".)[68] In widely publicized memorials to Governor Wodehouse and General Kennedy, the Sabha warned of the human catastrophe that British churlishness was ensuring. In addition to pointing out that the new ration was only half of the traditional penal standard and thus sure to doom "thousands by the slow torture of starvation," they focused attention on the group most ignored by district officers: the children of famine villages.

"It should be remembered," the Sabha wrote to Bombay, "that the same harsh policy which reduced the wages drove away the smaller children from the works, who, till then, had been receiving their small dole in return for their nominal labour. These children, though cast out by Government, will have a prior claim upon the affections of their parents, and many hundreds of poor fathers and mothers will stint themselves out of the pound allowed to support their children."[69] (An American missionary later pointed out that although a child could be fed for a pittance, "just for want of these two cents a day, hundreds and thousands of children wasted away and are no more.")[70]

With the support of the Sabha, the strike kindled the broadest demonstration of Indian anger since the Mutiny. "Meetings, immense as regards numbers, were held, speeches were made, resolutions were passed, and the telegraph wire called into requisition." Temple, in response, ordered Kennedy to "stand firm" against any concession to "combinations of workpeople formed with sinister or self-interested objects." The local relief officers, however, were unnerved, according to Digby, by the "obstinacy with which persons almost in a dying condition would go away anywhere rather than to a relief camp. They seem to have felt the repugnance to relief camps which respectable poor in England have to the Union Workhouses." Official morale seemed to be sapped by the dignity and courage of the protest. The viceroy, at any event, was convinced that a firmer hand was needed in Bombay, and at the end of April Wodehouse resigned and was replaced by Temple.[71]

In his original response to Disraeli's proposal to appoint him viceroy two years earlier, Lytton had protested his "absolute ignorance of every fact and question concerning India."[72] Now, after chastising both Buckingham and Wodehouse, he asserted virtual omniscience over life and death judgements affecting millions of Indians. The Indian press, however, was not as easily bridled or humiliated as the two Tory governors. Little newspapers that usually wasted newsprint with tedious social gossip and regimental sporting news were now conduits to the English public of shocking accounts of rebellion and starvation within the relief camps.[73] Dissident journalists like William Digby in Madras (who later published a two-volume critical history of the government's response to the famine) and the Bombay *Statesman*'s representative in the Deccan stirred troubling memories of the Irish famine as well as the Sepoy Mutiny. In England, moreover, a group of old Indian hands and Radical reformers, including William Wedderburn, Sir Arthur Cotton, John Bright, Henry Hyndman and Florence Nightingale, kept *The Times*'s letters column full of complaints about Calcutta's callous policies.

Although Lytton urged the India Office to hold fast against these "hysterics," the government was embarassed by the uproar.[74] Writing to Disraeli, the secretary of state for India, Lord Salisbury, expressed his own fear that the viceroy was "bearing too hard on the people."[75] With the prime minister's approval, Salisbury pulled on Lytton's reins in early May, advising him "not to place too much restriction on the discretion of the local government." In effect, while Disraeli defended Lytton against the Liberals in Parliament, the viceroy was ordered to give local officials the loopholes they needed to reduce mass mortality with higher rations and reduced workloads. This concession more or less tamed the Poona Sabha, whose own conservatives were wary of the explosive potential of the masses, but it was too little and too late to brake the slide into a terminal phase of starvation and epidemic disease. If rice harvests in Burma and Bengal in 1877 were normal, and overall grain inventories sufficed to service the export demand, it was no solace to the 36 million rural Indians whom Calcutta admitted in August 1877 were directly stalked by starvation. The weather remained relentless. After a brief flirtation with the monsoon in April, the skies cleared and temperatures sharply rose. In one of his economizing decrees the year before, Lytton had drastically cut back the budget for maintenance and repair of local water storage. The result, as Digby emphasized in his history of the famine, was that precious rainwater was simply "run to waste" in a needless "sacrifice of human lives." The furnace-hot winds that swept the Deccan added to the misery by evaporating what little moisture remained in the soil. The fields were baked to brick.[76]

As water supplies dried up or became polluted with human waste, cholera became the scythe that cut down hundreds of thousands of weakened, skeletal villagers. The same El Niño weather system that had brought the drought the previous year also warmed waters in the Bay of Bengal, promoting the phytoplankton blooms that are the nurseries of the cholera bacterium. A terrible cyclone, which drowned perhaps 150,000 Bengalis, brought the pandemic ashore,

Table 1.4
Sabha Estimates of Famine Mortality

| Taluks | Prefamine Population | Present Population | Decline |
|---|---|---|---|
| Madhee and Mohol | 24,581 | 15,778 | 36% |
| Indi | 39,950 | 20,905 | 48% |
| | Cattle Before Famine | Cattle Now | Decline |
| Madhee and Mohol | 16,561 | 5,470 | 67% |
| Indi | 35,747 | 5,644 | 84% |

Figure 1.5  Grain Stores in Madras, February 1877

"modern transport provided the invasion route for disease," and the fetid relief
camps became crucibles for "cholera's great synergism with malnutrition."[77]

Obdurate Bombay officials meanwhile continued to outrage Indians and incite
charges of a coverup in the press by refusing to publish any estimate of rural
mortality. Even Florence Nightingale was snubbed when she requested figures in
early 1878.[78] The Sabha accordingly decided to carry out its own census of people
and cattle in the fifty-four villages comprising three *taluks* of Sholapur district
in August 1877. "It perfected a network of school teachers, retired civil servants
and other throughout the dry districts, which gave it in some areas better data
faster than the government could produce." It was a trailblazing example of using
survey techniques and statistics against the empire.[79]

Buckingham, on the other hand, complied with public opinion and ordered
a rough census of famine deaths. Reports from the Madras districts indicated
that at least 1.5 million had already died in the Presidency. In the driest Deccan
districts like Bellary, one-quarter of the population perished, and in some taluks
with high percentages of landless laborers, more than one-third.[80] In Madras city,
overwhelmed by 100,000 drought refugees, famished peasants dropped dead in
front of the troops guarding pyramids of imported rice, while "on any day and
every day mothers might be seen in the streets ... offering children for sale."[81]

(The Madras Chamber of Commerce helpfully suggested that flogging posts be erected along the beach so that police could deter potential grain thieves.)[82] In the North Western Provinces, as we shall see, only desultory and punitive relief was organized, "with the result that in spite of the abundant winter crops and the restricted area affected, in nine months the mortality amounted to over a million."[83]

However, "the Malthusian overtones of famine policies and their disastrous consequences," Ira Klein argues, "were experienced most woefully in Mysore," where the British Commission of Regency later conceded that fully one-quarter of the population perished.[84] Frugality became criminal negligence as the chief commissioner, from "dread of spending the Mysore surplus," refused life-saving expenditure; and then, after his inaction had become a scandal, turned relief work into a sadistic regime of punishing the starving. "On the command of the Viceroy to develop a famine policy, he drew up a series of irrigation and other projects, most so far from the famine stricken tracts that emaciated victims had to walk a hundred miles or more to them."[85] Those who actually reached the camps found them fetid, disease-wracked boneyards where a majority of refugees quickly died. One official later recalled scenes out of Dante's *Inferno*:

> The dead and dying were lying about on all sides, cholera patients rolling about in the midst of persons free of the disease; for shelter some had crawled to the graves of an adjoining cemetery and had lain themselves down between two graves as support for their wearied limbs; the crows were hovering over bodies that still had a spark of life in them.... The place seemed tenanted by none but the dead and the dying. In a few minutes I picked up five bodies; one being that of an infant which its dying mother had firmly clasped, ignorant of the child being no more; the cholera patients were lying about unheeded by those around; some poor children were crying piteously for water within the hearing of the cooks, who never stirred to wet the lips of the poor things that were *in extremis*....[86]

By the summer of 1877, as the famine in Mysore approached its terrible apogee, social order was preserved only by terror. When desperate women and their hungry children, for example, attempted to steal from gardens or glean grain from fields, they were "branded, tortured, had their noses cut off, and were sometimes killed." Rural mobs, in turn, assaulted landowners and *patels*, pillaging their grain stores, even burning their families alive. In other instances, extremely rare in Indian history, hunger-crazed individuals resorted to cannibalism. "One madman dug up and devoured part of a cholera victim, while another killed his son and ate part of the boy."[87]

## Down from Olympus

Lytton was kept well-informed of such grisly details. From his hardminded perspective, however, the most serious escalation in the famine was the increasing burden on the Indian Treasury. The failure of the 1877 monsoon threatened to divert another £10 million for the salvation of what he viewed through his Malthusian spectacles as a largely redundant stratum of the population. Having bent his rules in May to accommodate London's anxieties, the viceroy felt confident enough in the summer to resume his campaign against profligate relief. In August 1877, shortly after the Great White Queen reassured the public that "no exertion will be wanting on the part of my Indian Government to mitigate this terrible calamity," Lytton finally came down from his seasonal headquarters in the Himalayas to spend a few days inspecting conditions in Madras.[88]

This was his first personal exposure to the terrible reality of the famine. A local English-language newspaper editorialized that after domiciling himself for so long in the distant comforts of Simla, "the Indian Olympus," where he displayed "merely the faintest idea of the extent of the calamity," Lytton would now have to confront inescapable truths. "There are, in the relief camps of Palaveram and Monegar Choultry, sights to be witnessed, which even we, who have become callous and hardened, cannot but look upon without a shudder; sights which we dare not describe, and which an artist could not paint. What the effect of these sights must have been on the sensitive and poetical mind of Lord Lytton, we pause to imagine."[89]

In addition to the hugely unpopular Temple wage, the British community in Madras was outraged by Lytton's public denunciation of their recent efforts to raise relief funds in England. With both grain prices and famine deaths (157,588 in August) soaring, but with his hands tied by the viceroy's various strictures and economies, the Duke of Buckingham had embraced the philanthropic appeal as a last-ditch hope. It remained to be seen whether Lytton and his "Supreme Government" (as it was called in those days) would yield to the overwhelming urgency of the crisis. "The Viceroy," editorialized the same paper, "has now the opportunity, literally speaking, of saving thousands of lives. Let him telegraph to England candidly, boldly, and fearlessly, the real facts of the case; he may, by this means, perhaps, remove the doubt now certainly engendered in the minds of people at home, as to the need of their charitable aid."[90]

In the event, the viceroy's "sensitive and poetical mind" was stubbornly unmoved by anything he experienced during his lightning tour of southern India. On the contrary, Lytton was convinced that Buckingham, like a fat squire in a Fielding novel, was allowing the lower orders to run riot in the relief camps. After briefly visiting one of the camps, Lytton sent a letter to his wife that bristled with patrician contempt both for Buckingham and the famished people of Madras. "You never saw such 'popular picnics' as they are. The people in them do no work of any kind, are bursting with fat, and naturally enjoy themselves thoroughly. The Duke visits these camps like a Buckingham squire would visit his model farm, taking the deepest interest in the growing fatness of his prize oxen and pigs.... But the terrible question is how the Madras Government is ever to get these demoralized masses on to really useful work."[91]

In a bitter conference in Madras, Lytton forced Buckingham to reaffirm his complete allegiance to the cardinal principles of famine policy – "the sufficiency of private trade" and "the necessity of non-interference with private trade" – and imposed his own man, Major-General Kennedy from Bombay, as Buckingham's "Personal Assistant." In practice, it was a coup d'etat that deposed Buckingham's Council and installed Kennedy as supremo for famine administration with orders to adhere to the strict letter of the Temple reforms.[92] Meanwhile, from the remote corners of the Deccan, missionaries reported more unspeakable scenes. "Recently, the corpse of a woman was carried along the road slung to a pole like an animal, with the face partly devoured by dogs. The other day, a famished crazy woman took a dead dog and ate it, near our bungalow." "This is not sensational writing," emphasized the Anglican correspondent. "The half of the horrors of this famine have not, cannot, be told. Men do not care to reproduce in writing scenes which have made their blood run cold."[93]

The Deccan's villages were also now rent by desperate internal struggles over the last hoarded supplies of grain. A social chain reaction set in as each class or caste attempted to save themselves at the expense of the groups below them. As David Arnold has shown, collectively structured, "moral-economic" *dacoities* (expropriations) against moneylenders and grain merchants tended to degenerate in the later stages of famine into inter-caste violence or even a Hobbesian war of ryot against ryot. "The longer famine persisted the less crime and acts of violence bore the mark of collective protest and appropriation, and the more they assumed the bitterness of personal anguish, desolation and despair."[94] Sharma agrees that the transition from communitarian action to intra-village violence followed a predictable pattern: "The change in the agricultural cycle had significant implications for forms of popular action and solidarities. The temporary class solidarities and collective popular action which had been witnessed during the failure of the *kharif* [crop] showed a declining tendency in the winter seasons. Standing *rabi* crops soon became the objects of plunder, more than granaries and storage pits of hoarders and banias. The zamindars had to guard their crops by employing *lathi*-wielding musclemen."[95]

Heavy rains in September and October finally eased the drought in southern India, but only at the price of a malaria epidemic that killed further hundreds of thousands of enfeebled peasants in the United Provinces as well as the Deccan. Modern research has shown that extreme drought, by decimating their chief predators, ensures an explosion in mosquito populations upon the first return of the monsoon. The ensuing spike in malaria cases, in turn, delays the resumption of normal agricultural practices.[96] But in 1878 there were other obstacles as well to planting a life-saving crop. The fodder famine had been so extreme that plough animals were virtually extinct in many localities. As *The Times*'s correspondent reported from the Madras Deccan in July, "To show how scarce the bullocks have become, I may mention, that in the Bellary district merchants send out their grain supplies to distant villages on carts drawn by men. The value of the labour of the human animal is so low that it is cheaper to employ half-a-dozen men to move a load of rice than a couple of bullocks. The men, at any rate, can be fed, whereas fodder for cattle employed on the roads is not to be had at any price."[97]

With their bullocks dead and their farm implements pawned, ryots had to scratch at the heavy Deccan soil with tree branches or yoke themselves or their wives to the remaining ploughs. Much of the seed grain distributed by relief committees was bad, while that which sprouted and pushed its way above the ground was instantly devoured by great plagues of locusts that, as in the Bible, were the camp followers of drought. "The solid earth," according to an American missionary, "seemed in motion, so great were the numbers of these insects; compounds and fields appeared as if they had been scorched with devastating fires after the pests had passed."[98] By early 1878 famine accompanied by cholera had returned to many districts, but relief grain stocks, in anticipation of a good harvest, were depleted and prices as high as ever. Digby tells a grim story about the distress that lingered through the spring: "Three women (sisters) had married three brothers, and they and their families all lived in one large house, in Hindu and patriarchal fashion. The whole household, on January 1, 1878, numbered forty-eight persons. Their crops failed, their money was gone, their credit was *nil*. They tried to live on seeds, leaves, etc. and, as a consequence, cholera attacked them, and thirty died from this disease. Fifteen others expired from what a relative called 'cold fever,' and in April only three persons remained."[99]

The final blow against the Deccan peasantry was a militarized campaign to collect the tax arrears accumulated during the drought. Although some Liberal critics, like *Indian Daily News* editor James Wilson in a speech in Sheffield in October 1877, warned the British public that "millions had died for the pretended axioms of political economy" and that the best famine prevention was "to relieve Indians of paying Britain's debt," there was remarkably little censure of the government's decision to pick the pockets of paupers.[100] In the Kurnool district of Madras, for example, "in 1879–80, coercive policies had to be employed for the recovery of as much as 78% of total collections." As D. Rajasekhar points out, the resulting auction of lands in arrears may have been a windfall for rich peasants and moneylenders, who had already profited from famine-induced sacrifice sales of cattle and land mortgages, but it crippled the recovery of an agrarian economy that traditionally depended upon the energy of (now ruined) smallholders to bring cultivable wastes under plough.[101]

## 'Multitudinous Murders'

The year 1878 also saw terrible, wanton mortality in northwestern India following the failure of the monsoon in the summer of 1877 and a retrenchment of dry weather in early 1878. Even more than in the south, however, drought was consciously made into famine by the decisions taken in palaces of rajas and viceroys. Thus in the remote and beautiful valleys of Kashmir, British officials blamed "the criminal apathy of the Maharaja and the greed of his officials, who bought up the stores of grain to sell at extravagant prices" for the starvation of a full third of the population. "Unless Sir Robert Egerton, then Lieutenant-Governor of the Punjab, had insisted on taking the transport and supply service out of the hands of the corrupt and incompetent Kashmir Government, the valley would have been depopulated."[102]

But with equal justice the same criminal charges could be (and were) lodged against the British administration in the North Western Provinces and Oud, as well as adjoining districts of the Punjab, where famine killed at least 1.25 million people in 1878–79. As Indian historians have emphasized, this staggering death toll was the foreseeable and avoidable result of deliberate policy choices. In contrast to the south, the northern harvests were abundant in 1874–76 and ordinarily would have provided ample reserves to deal with the kharif deficit in 1878. But subsistence farming in many parts of the North Western Provinces had been recently converted into a captive export sector to stabilize British grain prices. Poor harvests and high prices in England during 1876–77 generated a demand that absorbed most of the region's wheat surplus. Likewise, most of the provinces' cruder grain stocks like millet were commercially exported to the famine districts in Bombay and Madras Presidencies, leaving local peasants with no hedge against drought. The profits from grain exports, meanwhile, were pocketed by richer zamindars, moneylenders and grain merchants – not the direct producers.[103]

Still, early and energetic organization of relief and, above all, the deferment of collection of the land tax might have held mortality to a minimum. Indeed the province's executive, Sir George Couper, implored Lytton to remit that year's revenues. "The Lieutenant-Governor is well aware of the straits to which the Government of India is put at the present time for money, and it is with the utmost reluctance that he makes a report which must temporarily add to their burdens. *But he sees no other course to adopt*. If the village communities which form the great mass of our revenue payers be pressed now, they will *simply be ruined*."[104]

Lytton, however, was still bogged down in the logistics of his Afghanistan adventure and was again unswayed by images of destitute villages. He rejected Couper's appeal out of hand. The lieutenant-governor had none of Buckingham's stubborn, paternalist pity for the people, and, to the disgust of some of his own district officers ("a more suicidal policy I cannot conceive," complained

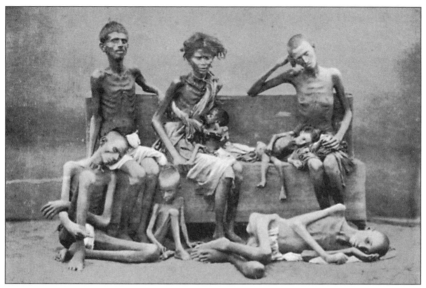

Figure 1.6  Famine Victims, 1877
The original caption of this missionary photograph reads, "Those who have got to this
stage rarely recover."

one), immediately and obsequiously vowed "to put the screw" upon the hard-hit
zamindars and their famished tenants. ("His Honour trusts that the realizations
will equal the expectations of the Governments of India, but if they are dis-
appointed, his Excellency the Viceroy ... may rest assured *that it will not be for
want of effort or inclination to put the necessary pressure on those who are liable for the
demand.*") He promptly ordered his district officers and engineers to "discourage
relief works in every possible way.... Mere distress is not a sufficient reason for
opening a relief work." The point was to force the peasants to give money to the
government, not the other way around.[105] When starving peasants fought back
(there were 150 grain riots in August and September of 1877 alone), Couper filled
the jails and prisons.[106]

As one dissident civil servant, Lt.-Col. Ronald Osborne, would later explain to
readers of *The Contemporary Review*, a murderous official deception was employed
to justify the collections and disguise the huge consequent casualties:

But the Government of India having decreed the collection of the land revenue, were now compelled to justify their rapacity, by pretending there was no famine calling for a remission. The dearth and the frightful mortality throughout the North-West Provinces were to be preserved as a State secret like the negotiations with Shere Ali [the emir of Afghanistan]....

During all that dreary winter famine was busy devouring its victims by thousands.... [I]n the desperate endeavor to keep their cattle alive, the wretched peasantry fed them on the straw which thatched their huts, and which provided them with bedding. The winter was abnormally severe, and without a roof above them or bedding beneath them, scantily clad and poorly fed, multitudes perished of cold. The dying and the dead were strewn along the cross-country roads. Scores of corpses were tumbled into old wells, because the deaths were too numerous for the miserable relatives to perform the usual funeral rites. Mothers sold their children for a single scanty meal. Husbands flung their wives into ponds, to escape the torment of seeing them perish by the lingering agonies of hunger. Amid these scenes of death the Government of India kept its serenity and cheerfulness unimpaired. The journals of the North-West were persuaded into silence. Strict orders were given to civilians under no circumstances to countenance the pretence of the natives that they were dying of hunger. One civilian, a Mr. MacMinn, unable to endure the misery around him, opened a relief work at his own expense. He was severely reprimanded, threatened with degradation, and ordered to close the work immediately.[107]

"Not a whisper" of this manmade disaster reached the public until a notable government critic, Robert Knight, publisher of the *Indian Economist and Statesman*, visited Agra in February 1878. "He was astonished to find all around the indications of appalling misery." His public revelations prompted a long, self-laudatory minute from Couper that was fulsomely endorsed by the viceroy. In his comment, Lytton blamed the horrendous mortality more on "the unwillingness of the people to leave their homes than by any want of forethought on the part of the local government in providing works where they might be relieved."[108] Knight replied, in turn, in an editorial that for the first time bluntly used the term "murder" to characterize official famine policy:

Do not accuse the *Statesman* of exaggerating matters. Accuse yourself. For long weary years have we demanded the suspension of these kists [land tax] when famine comes and in vain. With no poor law in the land, and the old policy once more set up of letting the people pull through or die, as they can, and with the vernacular press which alone witnesses the sufferings of the people silenced by a cruel necessity, we and our contemporaries must speak without reserve or be partakers in the guilt of multitudinous murders committed by men blinded to the real nature of what we are doing in the country.[109]

Indeed, "blind men" like Lytton and Temple were fortunate that they had to face only the wrath of newspaper editorials. The India of "supine sufferers" which they governed in 1877 was still traumatized by the savage terror that had followed the Mutiny twenty years earlier. Violent protest was everywhere deterred by memories of sepoys blown apart at the mouths of cannons and whole forests of peasants writhing at the noose. The exception was in Poona where Basudeo Balwant Phadke and his followers, inspired by still robust Maratha martial traditions, broke with the Sabha's moderation. "The destruction caused by the famine," Kavshalya Dublish explains, led Basudeo to "vow to destroy British power in India by means of an armed rebellion." Betrayed by a companion while organizing a raid on the treasury to buy arms, the "Maratha Robin Hood" was deported and died in prison – "the father of militant nationalism in India" – in 1883.[110] His abortive 1879 conspiracy stood in a similar relationship to the holocaust of 1876–78 as did the Young Ireland uprising of 1848 to the Great Hunger of 1846–47: which is to say, it was both postscript and prologue.

## Famine and Nationalism

No Englishman understood this point more clearly than Lytton's secretary of agriculture, Allan Octavian Hume. Odd man out in a Tory government that scorned Indian aspirations to self-government, Hume (whose father was a well-known Scottish Radical MP) was deeply sympathetic to the grievances of the Hindu and Muslim elites. Even more unusual, he had sensitive antennae tuned to the rumblings of revolutionary discontent among the poor. In the aftermath of Basudeo's plot, he "'became convinced," according to William Wedderburn, a leader of the parliamentary opposition on India, "that some definite action was called to counteract the growing unrest among the masses who suffered during the famine."[111] The first step was to resist the viceroy's punitive and incendiary scheme to foist the costs of famine relief entirely on the shoulders of the poor.

Originally advocated by Lord Northbrook, the idea of a "famine insurance fund" was revived in 1877 by Hamilton and Salisbury to pre-empt the Liberals from making the terrible mortality in India an issue in the next election. Lytton – aware that Radical members of the House of Commons favored financing the fund through a combination of wealth taxes and reductions in military expenditure – embraced the plan with the proviso that funding be entirely regressive, without harm to ruling classes or the army. He vehemently opposed a proposal from Hume, whom he forced to resign, that would have imposed a modest income tax "on the ground that it would affect the higher income groups, both European and Indian." His own preference was for a famine tax on potential famine victims (that is, a new land cess on the peasantry) – a measure that would have inflamed the entire country and was therefore rejected by Salisbury and the Council of India. As an alternative, Lytton and John Strachey drafted a scheme that was almost as regressive, reviving a hated license tax on petty traders (professionals were exempt) in tandem with brutal hikes in salt duties in Madras and Bombay (where the cost of salt was raised from 2 to 40 annas per maund).[112]

After the purge, Hume joined the small but influential chorus of opposition to Lytton that was led by Wedderburn, Cotton and Nightingale (whose campaign for Indian sanitary reform had been snubbed by the viceroy). Digby, the famine's chief chronicler, would also return to England in 1880 to champion Indian grievances in Liberal politics. In dozens of town meetings, as well as in the London press and the House of Commons, they argued that selfish and disastrous British policies like the salt tax, not nature, had paved the way for the Madras famine, and advocated a new policy based on reductions in ground rent and military expenditure, new spending on irrigation and public health, cheap credit through a system of rural banks, and a progressive famine fund. Nightingale was a particularly fiery campaigner against the salt tax, whose enforcement, she reminded audiences, had required the construction of a literal police state: "A tower commands the salt works, occupied by a policeman all day. Moats surround the works, patrolled by policemen all night; workmen are searched to prevent them from carrying off salt in their pockets...."[113]

The India opposition's emphasis on a "civilizing" (as Nightingale called it)[114] rather than "imperial" strategy in India corresponded closely with a parallel shift in the thinking of such Liberal pundits as John Stuart Mill, and converged with the platform of moderate nationalists like Dadabhai Naoroji and Romesh Chunder Dutt, who thought that Indian home rule within the Empire could best be achieved through collaboration with humanitarian English Liberals. Steeped in Millsian political economy, Naoroji and Dutt laid indigenous foundations for what a hundred years later would be called the "theory of underdevelopment" with their sophisticated critiques of Britain's "drain of wealth" from India. Although their most famous essays, Naoroji's *Poverty and Un-British Rule in India* (1901) and Dutt's *Famines in India* (1900) and his two-volume *Economic History of British India* (1902 and 1904), would be produced in the aftermath of the 1896–1902 holocaust, their basic polemical strategy – mowing down the British with their own statistics – was already discomforting Lytton and his council. Indeed on the eve of the famine in 1876, Naoroji had read his landmark paper, "The Poverty of India" (later reprinted as a pamphlet), to a crowded meeting of the Bombay Branch of the East India Association. The Parsi mathematician and former professor of Gujarati at University College London demolished the self-serving rhetoric about "free trade" that the government used to mask India's tributary relation to England. "With a pressure of taxation nearly double in proportion to that of England, from an income of one-fifteenth, and an exhaustive drain besides, we are asked to compete with England in free trade?" It was, he said, "a race between a starving, exhausted invalid, and a strongman with a horse to ride on."[115]

Such intellectually formidable critics were a major annoyance to Calcutta. Although the government was able to steamroll the passage of the license and salt taxes, Lytton was forced to reassure the Indian and English publics in his usual long-winded fashion of their benevolent purpose:

> The sole justification for the increase which has just been imposed upon the people of India, for the purpose of insuring this Empire against the worst calamities of a future famine ... is the pledge we have given that a sum not less than a million and half sterling ... shall be annually applied to it.... [T]he pledges which my financial colleague was authorized to give, on behalf of the Government, were explicit and full as regards these points. For these reasons, it is all the more binding on the honour of the Government to redeem to the uttermost, without evasion or delay, those pledges, for the adequate redemption of which the people of India have, and can have, no other guarantee than the good faith of their rulers.[116]

But the viceroy was lying through his elegant whiskers. Famine insurance was a cynical facade for raising taxes to redeem cotton duties and finance the invasion of Afghanistan. The truth can be found in Lytton's correspondence: "Lord Salisbury thinks that we are trying by our present measure to get more revenue than we absolutely need. And writing to you confidentially, I cannot deny that, in a certain sense and to a certain extent, this is quite true. But if we do not take advantage of the present situation ... for screwing up the revenue, we shall never be able to reform our tariff which grievously needs reform."[117]

Indeed, from 1877 to 1881, the "whole accumulated fund was used either to reduce cotton goods tariff or for the Afghan war." It did not take the Liberals long to expose such an egregious deceit, and during his famous Midlothian campaign in 1880 Gladstone repeatedly stirred the crowds against Tory perfidy. "Has the pledge been kept?" he thundered. "The taxation was levied. The pledge was given. The pledge has utterly been broken. The money has been used. It is gone. It has been spent upon the ruinous, unjust, destructive war in Afghanistan."[118]

The intrigues over the famine fund were paralleled by the government's manipulation of the royal commission to investigate the disaster. Although the "manoeuvres surrounding the creation of the Famine Commission were mainly controlled by the Strachey brothers," its impetus seems to have come directly from Salisbury, whose worries, in the face of a Liberal resurgence, were strictly partisan. "Strachey will also explain to you," he wrote Lytton in November 1877, "what I have talked a good deal to him about – the necessity of some commission on Famine measures in the future, in order to save ourselves from the Irrigation quacks. They will undoubtedly make a strong fight: for I observe that under the Presidency of Cotton, they have been beginning some sort of League ... for the Parliamentary campaign." It was suggested that the viceroy could steal his opponents' clothes through a harmless endorsement ("provided it could pay its way") of irrigation as a famine safeguard. The presidency of the commission was safely entrusted to Lt. General Sir Richard Strachey, who as member of the India Council and brother to Lytton's finance chief was unlikely to find fault with himself or his sibling. Convened in early 1878, the commission did not submit a report until June 1880.[119]

"The establishment of the Famine Commission," writes one historian, "was carried out as a political exercise to produce a favourable report, rather than as a measured response to one of the most significant problems of the Government of India. General Strachey protected his brother's policies...."[120] The whitewash,

however, was not unanimous. Two of the commissioners – the old India hand
James Caird and Madras civil servant H. Sullivan – dissented along lines similar
to Buckingham's policies in 1876–77. They urged the government to buy and
store grain in the most famine-prone districts, and in the future to relieve the
weak and infirm in their home villages. Both of these commonsense recommendations were subjected to scalding criticism by the majority who, instead, reaffirmed Lytton's policy of dormitory work camps and distance, task and wage
tests, supplemented as need be by poorhouses. Although the commission recognized that the "essential problem was shortage of work rather than food," the
majority clung to the Benthamite principle that relief should be bitterly punitive
in order to discourage dependence upon the government.[121]

The report, as intended, categorically absolved the government of any responsibility for the horrific mortality. As Carol Henderson emphasizes, "The 1878
Famine Commission set the tone for the [future] government response by asserting that the main cause of famine was drought 'leading to the failure of the food
crops on which the subsistence of the population depends.'"[122] In his 1886 critique of the commission, H. M. Hyndman caustically observed that famines "are
looked upon as due to 'natural laws,' over which human beings have no control
whatever. We attribute all suffering under native governments to native misrule;
our own errors we father on 'Nature'."[123] Naoroji likewise thought "how strange
it is that the British rulers do not see that after all they themselves are the main
cause of the destruction that ensues from droughts; that it is the drain of India's
wealth by them that lays at their own door the dreadful results of misery, starvation, and deaths of millions.... Why blame poor Nature when the fault lies at
your own door?"[124]

The report convinced a majority of Parliament (and some gullible modern
historians) that energetic measures were being taken to prevent future catastrophes. Just as misleading promises cloaked the misappropriation of the famine
fund, deliberate confusion seems to have been sown about the accomplishments
of the commission. Contrary to the popular belief that the commission had legis-
lated an obligatory "famine code," the report was surprisingly toothless and only
adumbrated "general principles" conforming to Utilitarian orthodoxy. "By the
mid-1880s, some four or five years after the Famine Report was published, most
of the provinces had famine codes but, apart from a reliance on public works for

famine relief and injunctions about interfering with the grain trade, they were not uniform."[125] Just as Calcutta had reserved in fine print the right to loot the famine fund ("there was no legal contract," Temple argued in 1890, "between the Government of India and the Indian people to the effect that the Fund should be exclusively devoted to famine purposes"), so too it refused to bind itself by code to "ill-directed and excessive distribution of charitable relief."[126]

Convinced, however, that such famines were not only inevitable but would bring revolution on the tide, Hume again took up agitation for a political safety-valve for Indian discontent. Fearing the rise of Maratha or Bengali counterparts to Ireland's violent republican brotherhoods, he proposed the pre-emptive organization of a moderate home-rule movement that could act as a unified interlocutor to a British Liberal government. The issue became urgent with the return of the Tories to rule in 1885, and Hume (with considerable sympathy from departing Liberal Viceroy Lord Ripon) engineered the foundation of the Indian National Congress in December with himself as general secretary. The mood of the delegates, writes McLane, "was somber and restrained. They gathered in the aftermath of a series of failures to obtain reforms. In the recent controversies over military expenditure, volunteering, impartial justice, and Indian admission to the civil services, nationalists had made few gains."[127]

Naoroji meanwhile went to England to run for Parliament in London – Wedderburn called it a "flanking movement" – with the aid of radical-Liberals and Michael Davitt's Irish National Land League. Although their friend H. M. Hyndman was already warning that "the time has gone for imploring, if it ever existed," Hume, Naoroji and the distinguished membership of the Congress were wagering India's future precisely on a principled appeal to English conscience.[128] As the violent reaction to Irish home rule over the next few years should have warned them, however, the age of Gladstone and J. S. Mill was giving way to jingoism and the New Imperialism. New famines, terrible beyond all apprehension, were already incubating in the loam of India's growing poverty.

# Two

# 'The Poor Eat Their Homes'

History contains no record of so terrible and distressing a state
of things, and if prompt measures of relief be not instituted
the whole region must become depopulated.
— Governor of Shanxi, 1877

India was not alone in its distress. Although their fate attracted surprisingly scant
attention in England, tens of thousands died from hunger and cholera in the
North-West Province of Ceylon, especially in Jafnapatam and Kadavely.[1] Comparable horrors, meanwhile, were reported from north China, Korea, southern
Java and Borneo, the Visayas, Egypt, Algeria, Morocco, Angola, South Africa and
northeast Brazil. Across the vast Indo-Pacific region, barometer readings were
"characterized by the most extreme departures from normal pressure … since
records began." ENSO's atmospheric half, the huge atmospheric see-saw of the
Southern Oscillation whose fulcrum was near the International Date Line in the
central Pacific, played havoc with meteorological records everywhere. In Santiago, Chile, standardized station pressure plummeted from near normal in August
1876 to the lowest ever recorded in September, while, conversely, in Djakarta
barometers began to soar in September, reaching an all-time height in August
1877 (3.7 standard deviations above the mean). "The spatial extent of the pressure
anomalies was vast, with records occurring in Lebanon, Australia and New Zealand." Likewise sea surface and nighttime marine air temperatures from October

1877 to March 1878 were the highest in history. The notoriously fickle East Asian Monsoon and the usually reliable Arabian Monsoon (whose rainfall over the watershed of the Blue Nile in the Ethiopian highlands becomes the annual Nile flood) disastrously failed to reach their normal latitudes. The apparent return to more normal conditions in late 1877 abruptly yielded to a secondary surge of El Niño conditions in early 1878 as pressure again plunged in Santiago and rose in Djakarta. In Brazil's Nordeste drought persisted well through the fall of 1879.[2]

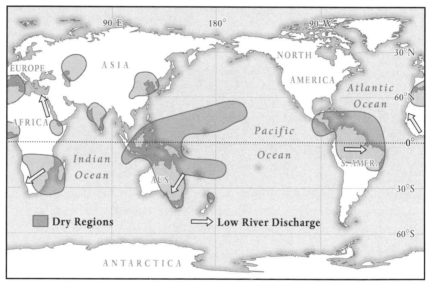

Figure 2.1  The Global Drought, 1876–78

The impact of El Niño drought was amplified by the worst global recession of the nineteenth century. "The intoxicating economic expansion of the Age of Capital," writes Eric Foner, "came to a wrenching halt in 1873." The puncture of a speculative bubble in American railroad stocks (symbolized by the collapse of New York's Jay Cooke and Company) rapidly became a worldwide crisis that "ushered in an entirely new business environment, one of cutthroat competition and a relentless downward price spiral."[3] The massacre of fictitious capital on Wall Street was punctually followed by the fall of real prices on Manchester's Cotton Exchange and soaring unemployment in the industrial centers of Pennsylvania, South Wales, Saxony and Piedmont. Deflation was soon a wolf at the door of tropical agriculturalists as well. The abrupt decline in metropolitan demand for key tropical and colonial products coincided with a vast increase in agricultural exports as railroads opened the American and Russian prairies and the Suez Canal shortened the distances between Europe, Asia and the Antipodes. The result everywhere was intensified competition and the plummeting of agricultural incomes. World market prices of cotton, rice, tobacco and sugar fell to their cost of production in many regions, or even below it.[4]

Millions of cultivators only recently incorporated into market networks or webs of world trade were thus whiplashed by long-distance economic perturbations whose origins were as mysterious as those of the weather. In western India, Algeria, Egypt (which plunged into bankruptcy in 1876), and northeast Brazil, as well as in Angola, Queensland, Fiji and Samoa, where Lancashire interests had orchestrated the conversion of vast acreages of subsistence agriculture to cotton production during the American Civil War, the boom had collapsed with the return of Southern cotton exports, stranding hundreds of thousands of small cultivators in poverty and debt (see Table 2.1).[5]

Table 2.1
The "Cotton Famine" and After
(Percentage of Raw Cotton Imports by the UK)

|      | USA | Egypt | Brazil | India |
|------|-----|-------|--------|-------|
| 1860 | 80  | 3     | 1      | 15    |
| 1865 | 19  | 21    | 6      | 50    |
| 1870 | 54  | 12    | 5      | 25    |

Source: Adapted from David Surdam, "King Cotton: Monarch or Pretender?", *Economic History Review* 61:1 (Feb. 1998), p. 123.

Tropical sugar producers in Brazil, the Philippines and the Dutch East Indies were likewise hammered by falling prices and the rising competition of European beet sugar, while Morocco's traditional exports of grain, wool and leather declined in the face of new competition from Australia and India following the opening of the Suez Canal. In the Cape, wheat farmers and wine growers, together with stockraisers, faced "the cold winds of free trade and indebtedness" as well as "the unbending orthodoxy of imperial finance in the shape of the Standard Bank."[6] Chinese tea producers likewise had to deal with the sudden rivalry of Assam and Ceylon, while Japan chipped away at China's monopoly on Asian silk exports. By 1875 agrarian unrest and rioting, on the largest scale since the great crisis of 1846–49, were spreading across the globe.

## I. China

The failure of the rains, two years in a row, throughout the basin of the Yellow River produced a drought-famine of extraordinary magnitude, overshadowing even the disaster in the Indian Deccan. Yet it took months for accurate reports to make their way to Beijing, and further long months for a sclerotic bureaucracy to organize relief campaigns for the five hardest hit provinces. Even then, rescue grain moved slowly, if at all, through a series of deadly transport bottlenecks. The Qing had refused to build railroads or telegraphs out of the rational fear that they would inevitably become weapons of foreign economic and ideological penetration.[7] As a result, a year or more elapsed before the first meager shipments of silver or grain arrived in many famine counties. Millions died in the meantime and large tracts of countryside were depopulated. Such immobility was construed by resident Westerners as the very essence of a stagnant civilization; in reality, it was a rupture with China's efficient famine relief campaigns of the eighteenth century or even the previous decade.

Drought was a grim finale to a quarter-century of extraordinary natural and social violence. Massive flooding in the 1850s had driven millions of peasants from their homes, many of them into the arms of the rebel armies – Taiping, Triad, Red Turban and Nian – that came within a hairsbreadth of destroying the Qing dynasty in the 1860s. The last insurgents (Muslim fundamentalists in Shaanxi and Gansu) were defeated only in 1872, and the accumulated economic damage since the founding of the Taiping Heavenly Kingdom of Great Peace in 1851 was colossal. During the brief interlude of Confucian reform – the so-called Tongzhi Restoration – that followed the defeat of the Taiping, there were several attempts to return to eighteenth-century state paternalism, most notably during the 1867–68 drought-famine in the Beijing region, which was energetically relieved with official soup kitchens and rice surpluses from the south.[8] But the Restoration's domestic phase was short-lived. Continuing and costly civil wars against Nian rebels in the north and Moslem insurrectionists in the northwest, followed by a major intervention in Central Asia, further drained the imperial budget and forced the Qing to slash nonmilitary expenditures. Beijing was also forced to resume the rampant sale of offices, a major source of the corruption that the Taiping had tried to extirpate.

The scale and intensity of the 1876–78 drought would have sorely tested the most scrupulous "Golden Age" administrations of the previous century. Now, thanks to epic grain fraud by hundreds of corrupt magistrates and their merchant conspirators, as well as the seasonally unnavigable condition of the Grand Canal, it quickly became a cataclysm. The small cultivator of north China has been famously described as "a man standing permanently up to his neck in water, so that even a ripple is sufficient to drown him."[9] But the drought that began in 1876 was a tsunami, not a ripple.

'TEN THOUSAND MEN HOLES'
The monsoon stalled over Guangdong and Fujian in the spring and summer of 1876, drowning those provinces in rain and flood, while all of northern China as far as the Korean border was parched by drought. Most of the summer and autumn harvests were totally lost. At the British Legation, Chinese Secretary W. Mayers carefully monitored the *Imperial Gazette* and reported back to the Foreign Office on the development of the ensuing famine. The first evidence of official concern with the failed summer monsoon was on 22 June 1876 when the five-year-old emperor, his father and uncle oversaw sacrifices and prayers for rain. The next day 100,000 taels were allocated for drought relief in Hebei, Shandong and Henan. Little else was noted until early October, when the governor of Shandong borrowed 30,000 taels for soup kitchens from his customs revenue, and then, shortly before Christmas, when Beijing suddenly diverted a large quantity of tribute grain. Any doubts about the gravity of the famine were removed at the beginning of winter, when tens of thousands of threadbare refugees suddenly appeared in the streets of Tianjin (Tientsin), Yantai (Chefoo), Zhengzhou (Chengchow) and even Shanghai.[10] The stories they told – which missionaries confirmed – were chilling.

In eastern Shandong, where three dry years had preceded the full-fledged drought of fall 1876, the desperate peasantry were reported to be eating their own homes:

Figure 2.2  Famine in China, 1876–78

In the summer the great cry of the mass of the people was for rain, rain. Now it is for very life. Having finished their corn, they eat grain-husks, potato stalks, and elm bark, buckwheat stalks, turnip leaves and grass seeds, which they gather in the fields and sieve the dust off. When these are exhausted, they pull down their houses, sell their timber, and it is reported everywhere that many eat the rotten kaoliang reeds (sorghum stalks) from the roof, and the dried leaves of which they usually burn for fuel … [then] they sell their clothes and children.[11]

With the onset of winter, "the caloric deficit was aggravated by the cold, since the price curve of fuels followed that of grain."[12] Peasants had no choice but to burn what was left of their homes for warmth. The famed American missionary Samuel Wells Williams was haunted for the rest of his life by the image of "people like spectres hovering over the ashes of their burnt houses, and making pyres for themselves out of the ruins of their temples."[13]

When there was nothing left to fuel a fire, those peasants who chose not to flee southward to the cities of Jiangsu resorted to the extraordinary stratagem of crowding together in giant underground pits. "In the eastern suburb of Ch'ing-chou," reported the Welsh missionary Timothy Richard, "four such pits were dug. In each pit as many as 240 people huddled for warmth. One-third of these succumbed within six weeks, leaving eagerly sought-after vacancies."[14] The British consul at Yantai wrote at the end of the winter about the collapse of relief efforts in the drought-stricken counties of Shandong. "The Government soup kitchens in I-tu Hsien still continue to deal out a scanty relief, but it is sad that their money is now exhausted and they will soon close.… [T]he Magistrate of that district has put out a Proclamation exhorting the wealthy to subscribe once more, but I fear with no effect. One can readily understand how powerless a district Magistrate is to cope with a gigantic evil like this."[15]

There is considerable debate amongst historians about the extent to which an explicit "moral economy," with ritualized traditions of protest and redistribution, operated during food scarcities in societies outside of Western Europe. Some of the strongest evidence comes from missionary accounts of the famine in Shandong, where peasant women organized highly theatricalized demonstrations, suggestive of customary precedents, against greedy gentry and dishonest magistrates. In one *hsien* (county), "a band of women marched to a rich man's house … took possession of it, cooked a meal there, and then marched to the next house for the next meal" and so on. In another locality, angry peasant women confronted a venal magistrate who had been pocketing relief funds from Beijing:

> One hundred women one day, each carrying her kitchen cleaver and board, went to the Yamen and sat down in the courtyard. The underlings asked them their business. They said they wished to speak to the magistrate…. As soon as he appeared, one of the women chosen as spokesman cried out, "The magistrate who steals the money of the poor instead of giving it when they are dying of starvation deserves to be chopped into pieces like this!" Then the hundred choppers beat a refrain on the boards, and all the women chanted in chorus: "He who steals the money of the poor deserves to be chopped into pieces like this!"[16]

Such militant self-organization, however, was generally only possible in the early phase of famine, before starvation began to dissolve the social fabric of the village and, eventually, of the extended family itself. By spring 1877 the drought-stricken hsien of Shandong were already partially depopulated by death and emigration. "At Chikien, a village of 200 families," wrote a missionary to the *Shanghai Courier,* "I found that thirty families had pulled down their houses to sell the timber and thatch for food; thirty families had gone away, and twenty individuals were dead from starvation. At Kiang-kia-low, with a population of thirty to forty families, forty-seven individuals had died of starvation. At Li-kai-chwang, out of 100 families, formerly well off, thirty persons were already dead of starvation. At Po-wang, out of sixty families forty persons were dead, and sixty gone away. At Masoong, out of forty families forty individuals had perished."[17] In a single hsien it was reported that more than 100,000 dependents were sold into servitude to contractors from the south, although the government later nullified all forced sales of women and children during the famine.[18] The Italian missionary Father di Marchi described the heartbreaking calculus of desperation that pitted family honor against survival in the stricken villages of Shandong. "In a village, entirely Pagan, where I went to distribute relief, all the women, except two very old ones, and all the children of both sexes had been sold." On the other hand, in another village that he visited, many of the families had committed suicide to "avoid the ignominy of begging."[19]

The provincial authorities seemed hopeless. They were far more efficient in

Figure 2.3 A Mother Selling Her Children to Buy Food, Chin-Kiang, 1877

executing famine-driven bandits by the thousands, usually by "slow, agonizing starvation in the 'sorrow cages,'" than in distributing relief in the countryside.[20] "According to Richard," reported *The Times*'s correspondent, "they have allotted only 43,000 taels (about £14,000) for the whole of these eight districts – a mere pittance for such a calamity."[21] Missionaries estimated that official relief efforts reached only 20 to 40 percent of the afflicted population in five provinces.[22] As Mayers in Beijing observed, the Empire was broke.[23] The revenue surplus accumulated since the end of the Taiping civil war had been expended on imperialist expansion in Central Asia or in building coastal forts and arsenals. The empire increasingly had to borrow from foreign powers at extortionate interest rates. The crucial customs revenue for 1877 and 1878, for example, was collateral for a 21 million tael loan, raised through the Hongkong and Shanghai Bank, that was used to pay off costs of the conquest of Xinjiang.[24] Left to fend for themselves, most of the provincial governments were already bankrupt by the beginning of the drought. As the imperial censors pointed out in an angry note in August 1877, what financial reserves remained were promptly looted by corrupt relief officials.[25] Nor were there any hidden resources in the countryside to compensate for official penury. On a local level when government assistance was desultory, peasants had traditionally relied on blood-oath fraternities (*baihui*) and mutual loan societies. During the terrible Shandong winter of 1876–77, however, village mutualism collapsed, bringing permanent discredit to the societies that failed to save their members.[26]

Not surprisingly some farmers preferred to fight for their survival. Far more than in caste-divided India, a proliferation of heterodox religious sects and underground anti-Qing traditions offered Chinese peasants a cultural matrix for organizing and legitimating agrarian insurrection. In southwestern Shandong, towards the end of the drought, "a certain Zhu Ahen-Guo, who made a living as a healer, claimed to be a descendant of the Ming ruling house and rose in rebellion.... Poor folks from the region rallied to his banner, and held out for almost a month before drenching rains came and his followers dispersed to return to their now cultivable fields."[27]

More commonly, entire villages fled towards the wealthy towns of the south. This organized system of village migration and collective begging was known as *t'ao-fang*, and was clearly distinguished in law and popular tolerance from ordinary (criminal) vagabondage.[28] Faced with the "threat of an aimlessly wandering peasantry, with all the consequences that this entailed," the government tried to channel and regiment migration with the help of the urban elites.[29] Although Beijing was surrounded by checkpoints during the famine, the wealthy gentry in the cities of Kiangsu were ordered to keep their gates open to honest refugees from the north. The people from Shandong were carefully registered at urban shelters and issued coupons for rice gruel, used clothing, even basic medical care. Later, after the drought abated, they were given travel stipends to return to their homes where magistrates often provided loans of seed and oxen to ensure resumption of the agricultural (and fiscal) cycle. But when, at times, the exodus from the north became too overwhelming or uncontrollable, as along the Shandong-Kiangsu border in 1877, the Qing had no qualms about sending in troops to turn back or even massacre the refugees.[30]

While the turmoil in Shandong was diverting official attention, famine was rapidly spreading throughout Shanxi and the greater part of Shaanxi, Hebei and Henan, as well as the northern counties of Hubei, Anhui and Jiangsu. In Hebei and Jiangsu, drought was accompanied, as it is so frequently, by devastating plagues of locusts. In total, more than 90 million people suffered from hunger in an area larger than France.[31] In Henan, where popular anti-Christian sentiment was legendary (missionaries called it "heartless Henan"), there were no permanent missionaries to chronicle the progress of the famine, but the governor told Beijing that more than half the harvest had been lost and that Kaifeng was overrun with 70,000 refugees.[32] Other vernacular accounts described cannibalism, brigandage and the death of more than a third of the population in the most afflicted counties.[33] In Lushan hsien, a renowned hearth of banditry and rebellion, the poor peasants and laborers who maintained the irrigation system (locally known as *tangjiang*) rose en masse. "In the face of recalcitrant landlords who were unwilling to provide relief, the *tangjiang* opened local granaries and distributed the grain to the poor. This act propelled other peasants to join the movement, and the numbers of participants reached tens of thousands. Only by calling up a large contingent of government troops could the riot be quelled."[34]

Likewise, it was almost a year before the foreign community had any appreciation of the magnitude of the famine in Shaanxi (Shensi). Provincial officials refused overtures of aid from the British Inland Mission, but allowed two representatives, F. Baller and George King, to make a brief visit.[35] The mortality in the forty counties that lined the great Wei River valley, the crucible of Han civilization, was staggering. "Human skeletons," recounted a later provincial history, "lay along roads. On the average a large county lost between 100,000 and 200,000 lives and even a small one lost some 50,000 or 60,000. The only possible way to dispose of dead bodies, was to dig huge holes, which today are still called, 'ten-thousand-men holes'; dead children were thrown into water wells."[36] Hunger-weakened farmers were often finished off by the packs of wolves – "gorged and stupid from the fulness of many ghastly meals" – that prowled the outskirts of villages and towns.[37]

## SHANXI: THE UNSPEAKABLE

But the famine's macabre climax was in neighboring Shanxi (Shansi), an impoverished, landlocked province as big as England and Wales with a population of 15 million. Drought had been entrenched here since 1875, but the province's densely populated southwestern prefectures had been temporarily able to mitigate food shortages with imports from the Wei Valley. The total crop failure in the latter was effectively a death sentence for hundreds of thousands of peasants in neighboring Shanxi.[38] Again the Qing bureaucracy responded with excruciating sluggishness. At the beginning of 1877, a censor complained about corruption in the administration of relief in Shanxi, and later Beijing issued a decree postponing the collection of land taxes. But it was only in March, a full year after the failure of the rains, that a sudden series of urgent appeals in the *Imperial Gazette* revealed that the granaries of southern Shanxi were empty and the peasants were now living off pellets of dirt or the corpses of their dead neighbors.[39] As Governor Li Hon-nien emphasized in his obituary-like report, entire social strata had been wiped out from the bottom up:

> The drought with which the province has been visited for several years in succession has resulted in a famine of an intensity and extent hitherto unheard of. As autumn advanced into the winter the number of those in need of relief increased daily, until at last they could be counted by millions. The lower classes were the first to be affected, and they soon disappeared or dispersed in search of subsistence elsewhere. Now the famine has attacked the well-to-do and the wealthy, who find themselves reduced to greater misery as each day goes by, and they, in their turn, are dying off or following those who have migrated elsewhere. In the earlier period of distress the living fed upon the bodies of the dead; next, the strong devoured the weak; and, now, the general destitution has arrived at such a climax that men devour those of their own flesh and blood.[40]

All of Beijing's belated efforts to move grain into the loess highlands had been frustrated by the breakdown of the transportation system. The condition of the Grand Canal, inland north China's all-important lifeline to the rice surpluses of the Yangzi Valley, was especially distressing. "The most extensive and important canal in the world," wrote a correspondent to the *New York Times*, "it is now for hundreds of miles unnavigable, its old channel grass-grown and incumbered with the rotting hulks of hundreds of the imperial junks which formerly brought their annual tribute of grain to the capital."[41] Rivers that once fed water to the canal had been cut off by the realigned Yellow River or silted-up through government neglect. As a result, water levels in the canal fell drastically with the onset of the drought, and only desultory efforts were made to dredge sections of the canal or,

Figure 2.4  Guguan Pass: "The way was marked by the carcasses of men and beasts."

alternately, to send grain in small flotillas up the drought-shallowed and treacher-ously silted Yellow River.[42]

With tribute rice shipments held up in the south, the government for the first time turned towards the wheat surpluses of Manchuria.[43] Although Manchurian farmers responded with huge shipments of grain, its progress towards the centers of mass starvation in Henan, Shaanxi and Shanxi was fatally impeded by a succession of transport bottlenecks. The first was in the port of Tianjin itself. As R. Forrest, the British consul in Tianjin and chairman of the Famine Relief Committee, complained:"In November 1877, this aspect of affairs was simply terrible.... Tientsin was inundated with supplies from every available port. The Bund was piled mountain high with grain, the Government storehouses were full. All possible means of transporting it were commandeered and the water-courses were crowded with boats, the roads were blocked with carts."[44] Other bottlenecks slowed the progress of the relief grain across the North China Plain despite warnings that the population of southern Shanxi "bids fair to become absolutely extinct."[45] The transport crisis reached a nightmarish crescendo in Guguan Pass, the narrow mountain gateway to southern Shanxi. Consul Forrest travelled up the 130-mile-long mountain trail to see the chaos for himself:

Frightful disorder reigns supreme ... filled with [an enormous traffic of] officials and traders all intent on getting their convoys over the pass. Fugitives, beggars and thieves absolutely swarmed ... camels, oxen, mules and donkeys ... were killed by the desperate people for the sake of their flesh (while the grain they were meant to be carrying into Shansi rotted and fed the rats of Tientsin). Night travelling was out of the question. The way was marked by the carcases of men and beasts, and the wolves, dogs and foxes soon put an end to the sufferings of any (sick) wretch who lay down ... in those terrible defiles.... No idea of employing the starving people in making new or improving the old roads ever presented itself to the authorities.... Gangs of desperadoes in the hills terrorised the travellers.... In the ruined houses the dead, the dying, and the living were found huddled together ... and the domes-tic dogs, driven by hunger to feast on the corpses everywhere to be found, were eagerly caught and devoured.... Women and girls were sold in troops to traffick-ers, who took the opportunity of making money in this abominable manner, and suicide was so common as hardly to excite attention.[46]

Figure 2.5  "Suicides in Consequence of the Famine"

Figure 2.6  "The Living Strive for the
Flesh of the Dead"

When Richard, dressed as a Chinese, crossed over the 4,000-foot-high escarp-
ment into Shanxi later that season, 1,000 people were starving to death every day,
and the representative of the Baptist Missionary Society, "aghast at the magnitude
of the catastrophe," thought he was witnessing a scene from the Book of Revelation. It had scarcely rained for three winters. Many county granaries had been
empty for years or had been looted by venal magistrates, while the provincial
government, crushed by the costs of the recent genocidal civil war between Muslims and Han, had no funds left to finance relief. Locust plagues, meanwhile, had
devoured every blade of grass that had escaped the drought, and the once fertile
countryside had been transformed into an ochre desert shrouded by howling dust
storms. "That people pull down their houses, sell their wives and daughters, eat
roots and carrion, clay and refuse is news which nobody wonders at.... If this
were not enough to move one's pity, the sight of men and women lying helpless
on the roadside, or of dead torn by hungry dogs and magpies, should do; and the
news which has reached us, within the last few days, of children being boiled and
eaten up, is so fearful as to make one shudder at the thought."[47]

Indeed, the correspondence of Qing officials confirms that "children abandoned by their parents ... were taken to secret locations, killed and consumed."[48]
Richard later discovered human meat being sold openly in the streets and heard
stories "of parents exchanging young children because they could not kill and
eat their own." Residents – who everywhere went armed with spears and swords
for self-protection – also "dare not go to the coal-pits for coal, so necessary for
warmth and cooking, for both mules and owners had disappeared, having been
eaten."[49] (Richard, on the other hand, was struck by "the absence of the robbery
of the rich" amongst so much death.)[50] The other European witness to the catastrophe, the Roman Catholic Bishop of Shanxi, confirmed Richard's most disturbing observations in a letter to the procurator of the Lazarist Fathers (later quoted
in *The Times*): "Previously, people had restricted themselves to cannibalizing the
dead; now they are killing the living for food. The husband devours his wife, the
parents eat their children or the children eat their parents: this is now the every-
day news."[51]

Almost two years after the drought-famine had begun, on 10 May 1878, the
British ambassador in Beijing reported to the foreign minister, Lord Salisbury,
that while recent rains had improved the situation in Hubei, there was little sign
of relief in Henan or Shanxi:

> The letters of the missionaries who remain there are merely stereotyped accounts
> of the same painful sights endlessly repeated. Every imaginable horror that famine
> can give rise to is said to have occurred on a large scale. One would prefer to hope
> that the extent of the disaster might be overestimated, if the numbers of destitute
> immigrants who may now be seen dying of want at the gates and in the streets of
> Peking itself, and the unusual prevalence of malignant fevers in the capital, did not
> bear witness to its reality. I heard yesterday, upon good authority, that as many as
> 7,000,000 persons in all are computed to have died in this famine. The Province of
> Shansi alone is said to have lost 5,000,000 of inhabitants in the last winter. If the
> drought should continue, it will not improbably become depopulated altogether.[52]

These reports of the horrors in Shanxi were eventually circulated around the
world by cable and later published at length in *China's Millions,* the famous British
missionary monthly. "Harrowing eye-witness accounts of famine conditions," its
editor Hudson Taylor wrote, "were needed to bring home to people's imagina-
tions what was happening." Shanxi particularly preoccupied Christians because

it was believed to be the epicenter of the opium evil, where the masses starved because "eight out of every ten smoked opium" and had abandoned the cultivation of grain. "See that poor wretch with the emaciated frame," editorialized Taylor, "he has parted with his land, his house, his furniture, his children's and his own clothing and bedding, and either sold his wife or hired her out for prostitution, and all for opium.... It is the source of poverty, wretchedness, disease, and misery, unparalleled in ... any other country."[53]

In London, meanwhile, a China Famine Relief Fund was organized by the Jardines, Mathesons, Reids, and other ancient pillars of the opium trade. Describing the catastrophe as "without parallel in the history of the world," the London committee circulated a booklet by a Chinese artist depicting grisly scenes of Henan peasants committing suicide or eating their dead neighbors.[54] Although relief of the Bulgarian victims of Turkish atrocities, followed by appeals to aid starving Madras, were more popular front-page philanthropies, supporters of the China missions acclaimed "famine relief as a heaven-sent opportunity to spread the gospel."[55] Here was an archimedean lever, it was believed, to open the "nine whole [northern] provinces where darkness reigns unbroken."[56] Indeed the General Missionary Conference in Shanghai in 1877 issued a famous call for "the Christian Church to evangelize China in the present generation," taking advantage of what Arthur Smith termed the "wonderful opening" of famine.[57] "The distribution of funds by brave and judicious men engaged in the [relief] work," added the British consul the same year, "will do more to open China to us than a dozen wars."[58] Guo Songtao, China's first minister to Britain, although repulsed by British gloating over their famine-generated "openings," found it politic to endorse the relief campaign.[59] (The famine-induced harvest of "rice Christians," as Guo Songtao probably expected, was short-lived, and missionaries were soon complaining about the recidivism of their converts. "The spiritual results of so much philanthropy in Shansi," wrote one around 1890, "have been very disappointing.... [A]fter thirteen years of work the Baptist Mission only numbered about thirty converts.")[60]

In the United States, the famous missionary and pioneer sinologist Samuel Wells Williams made a public appeal to Congress to return a portion of the indemnity extorted from China in 1859. Although "it seems to be nearly impossible to rescue those in Shansi," he wrote, "the famishing in and around Tsinan,

Schan Chau, The Chau, and Westerly can and ought to be accessible." A bill was accordingly drafted by a sympathetic congressman. But missionary humanitarianism and even American trade interests were overriden by the backlash of the Far West against the supposed "yellow peril" of immigrant labor. Starting in the sandlots of San Francisco in 1876, anti-Chinese violence had spread like a wildfire through the depressed towns and railroad camps of the Western states. In Congress, as a result, "the prejudice against the Chinese was too strong; Senator Hamlin reported the bill unfavorably, alleging that the starving would all be dead before the money could reach them in China."[61]

The other powers were as unrelenting as the United States in their collection of indemnities from starving China. Meanwhile, fragmentary reports began to reveal the famine's terrible toll in Shaanxi, Hebei and Henan, where, as we have seen, fierce anti-foreignism had discouraged missionary contact. It wasn't until early 1879, for example, that Europeans got a first-hand glimpse of conditions in Henan when W. Hillier, another British consul working on behalf of China Famine Relief, passed through the province en route to distribute 2,000 taels of silver in Shanxi. In south Henan the land had already returned to cultivation, and angry crowds, shouting insults and anti-foreign slogans, threatened Hillier in the streets; but in the north, where drought still reigned, living human beings remained an uncommon sight in a silent landscape:

> Many towns and villages were almost empty.... [We heard] nothing but the echo of our own footsteps as we hurried through ... cities of the dead. We had the curiosity to enter into one of these houses, but the sight that awaited us there gave us both so terrible a shock that we went into no more.... We gave up talking much about the things we had seen. The misery was too deep to be discussed. Only in some homes were the dead in coffins or bricked in by their families – to foil the certain alternative of being exhumed and eaten by starving neighbors.[62]

Recognizing that if relief grain could not get through to them, they must go to it, entire villages continued throughout the winter of 1878–79 to desert their homes in desperate migrations toward provincial capitals and, especially, the great entrepot of Tianjin. Unwittingly they were trading starvation for the deadly epidemics being incubated in fetid relief camps and shanty towns. "A hundred thousand refugees [mainly from Shaanxi] had flocked into Tianjin, finding shelter in 'hovels made of mud and millet stalks,' but typhus broke out and in the cold weather 400–600 died each night." Their plight was all the more pitiful because so many thousands of them were virtually naked, having sold their clothes long before for food.[63] This epidemic phase of the famine had a micro-biological momentum that extended mortality far beyond the spatial or social boundaries of starvation per se. Thus the typhus brought by famine refugees killed Europeans and Qing nobles as well as tens of thousands of plebeian city-dwellers in Beijing and Tianjin.[64] Likewise, cholera, incubated in the flood-stricken districts of Fujian in 1876, worked its way north through China's coastal cities until it finally arrived in southern Japan.[65]

Although the monsoon had finally returned to Shanxi in summer 1878, the resumption of normal agriculture, as in the Deccan, was incredibly difficult. Writing to the British ambassador, Timothy Richard explained that "in hundreds, or even thousands, of villages seven-tenths of the population are already dead," and that only 30 percent of the normal amount of grain had been sown.[66] Some peasants were afraid of the violence that might result if they revealed seed corn that they had secretly hidden; while others were simply too sick or weak to work. Those who did manage to sow a crop then faced the challenge of guarding it against their famished neighbors. And when crops were finally harvested again in 1879, "a new horror then claimed more victims. Among those who had survived to enjoy eating again 'a pestilence of dysentery beat out typhus as soon as the harvest was gathered, and the stomachs of the people were inflamed by too great indulgence in unaccustomed foods.' Fields of millet stood unharvested, sagged and decayed." In this way famine and its allied diseases continued to decimate parts of north China until the beginning of 1880 or even later.[67]

## II. Brazil

Meanwhile, half a globe away, the interior of Brazil's Nordeste baked under a relentless sun and cloudless sky. The *sertão* is a high, rolling plain broken by smooth-top tablelands and rocky monadnocks of decomposing granite. Rainfall is dramatically orchestrated by El Niño and few landscapes change their aspect so radically between seasons or wet and dry years. "Nature here rejoices," wrote Euclydes da Cunha in his epic *Os Sertões,* "in a play of antitheses."[68] When, after an arduous ride from the coastal Ceará capital of Fortaleza, the famed Harvard geologist Louis Agassiz and his wife first glimpsed the rainsoaked sertão in April 1868, they were flabbergasted by its lushness. Expecting a wasteland, they instead beheld a "verdant prairie ... beautifully green."[69] Yet when Herbert Smith, the "special famine correspondent" for *Scribner's Magazine*, looked down upon the Ceará interior a decade later, it was all antithesis: "a dry, cheerless desert, scorched with heat." As many as 500,000 sertanejos had just perished from hunger and smallpox.[70] (Da Cunha noted ghoulishly that under such conditions the bodies of dead men and horses were exquisitely mummified by the extreme aridity "without any unseemly decomposition.")[71]

The drought in the Nordeste began six months after the failure of the summer monsoon in India. (Indian droughts, as we shall see, tend to "lead" El Niño warmings of the tropical eastern Pacific by a season, while Brazilian *secas* "lag" by one, sometimes two seasons.) "Vague rumors of a drought," according to Smith, had first reached the coast in February 1877.[72] The unease was greatest in Ceará, where the previous year's harvest after scanty winter rains had been meager, but there was also concern about agricultural conditions in the high sertão of Paraiba, Pernambuco and Rio Grande do Norte. By March, the dreaded "drought winds" – the steady, dessicating northeasterlies – controlled the weather, and worried bishops ordered prayers *ad pretendam pluviam* in all the churches. "Most sertanejos," writes historian Roger Cunniff, "crossed the narrow line between hope for a belated winter and total despair during the first two weeks of April. Having already lost two plantings in the false winters of January and March, they fearfully refrained from casting what remained of their dwindling supplies when light rains appeared, lest they have nothing at all for the long treks which were already beginning, or to sustain themselves for the long months of drought most were now sure were upon them."[73]

Later, some savants would claim that the drought had been "due to the extreme deforestation which had been provoked by the increasing cultivation of cotton."[74] Certainly the collapse of the cotton boom had immiserated much of the backland population, and they now began to wander in search of work or subsistence of any kind. Some huddled around the handful of marginally prosperous market towns in the river valleys that drain the high sertão, while others, often in extended-family groups, migrated hundreds of kilometers. The *fazendeiros* (ranchers), for their part, ordered their *vaqueiros* to take part of the cattle

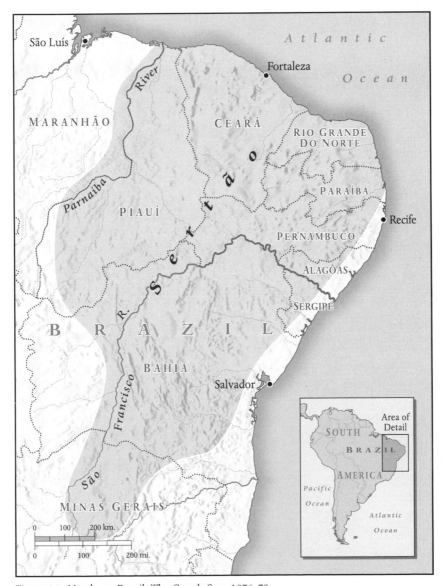

Figure 2.7  Northeast Brazil: The *Grande Seca*, 1876–78

to the more humid serras or across the sertão to Piauí, where the rains hadn't failed, while slaughtering the rest for hides and tallow. In some places, they shared this windfall of beef with the poor; in others, the poor simply took what they needed without permission. Sertanejos, "the most honest men in the world," began to rustle cattle, even pillage *fazendas*. In Quixeramobim, the poor briefly seized power, warning that "they do not have to die of hunger knowing that in the houses of the rich are money and food."[75]

## THE SCOURGED ONES

But charity and riot only postponed starvation until mid-summer. Then, according to Smith, "good men turned away and cried in their hearts to God." Even formerly well-off fazendeiros traded their slaves for grain and deserted their dying ranches for the towns.[76] The poor now foraged the skeletonal *caatinga* (thorn forest) for *xique-xique* cactus, the heart of the carnauba palm, even the roots of the *pao de moco*, ordinarily used by ranchers to poison anthills. ("The refugees, desperate from hunger after their long march, and not knowing the plant's toxic character, cooked and ate it. A few hours later, they were completely blind.")[77] In July and August, corpses began to appear by roadsides and abandoned homesteads; by September and October, dozens were dying daily and beriberi was rampant in the fetid refugee camps on the outskirts of towns like Acaracu, Ico and Telha. If the population of the sertão, especially in Ceará, were to survive in place until the winter, food had to be imported in massive quantity.[78]

The commercial grain trade was as hopelessly unequal to this task as in India or China. A handful of opportunist merchants gouged spectacular profits without relieving any of the hunger of the interior. "Small supplies of provision came in from other provinces and were sent to the interior towns on the backs of horses; but often the animals died on the way, or the caravans were robbed. In some places, where they had no horses, provisions were brought in on men's shoulders. The few baskets of mandioca-meal, obtained in this way, were retailed by the merchants at fabulous prices – frequently eight or ten times above the normal – so that only the rich could buy." Since most local governments, apart from the wealthy port of Recife, were already bankrupt before the onset of drought, responsibility for the emergency passed to the provincial presidents, some of whom, like the recently appointed president of Ceará, Caetano Estelita, were utterly unfamiliar with conditions in the backlands. Although the constitution of 1824 guaranteed subsistence as a right to every Brazilian citizen, the sertanejos had few advocates. British utilitarianism and social darwinism (above all, Herbert Spencer) had made rampant inroads in Liberal thinking, while the Conservatives followed a church hierarchy that preached that the drought "was God's punishment to Brazil for accepting the materialistic ways of the nineteenth century." ("Against God," thundered a Conservative leader during a legislative debate on famine relief, "there is no virtuous insurrection.")[79]

Precious months, as a result, were lost in abstract philosophical debates before the Conservative Estelita – shocked by the horde of indisputably famished sertanejos suddenly descending on Fortaleza – began to send aid into the interior. By this point, there was virtually no pasturage or water left for cargo horses so it had become impractical to ship food directly from the coast. (The *Cearense* reported cases of all the animals in relief pack trains dying in futile attempts to deliver food to Taua and other interior municipios.)[80] The president instead sent money, much of it raised by Cearán migrants in the rest of Brazil, to the besieged sertão municipalities. It made depressingly little impact on the massive subsistence crisis.

The last hope of preventing a fatal stampede toward the coast was truly heroic action by the minister for imperial affairs, Antonio da Costa Pinto. Since the imperial government was also laboring under a heavy deficit, Costa Pinto instead chose to play the role of Sir Richard Temple, turning mere disaster into catastrophe. He authorized limited food shipments to the Nordeste but otherwise took control of relief expenditure away from the formerly autonomous provincial presidents. Meanwhile, as legislators in Rio wasted June and early July debating farfetched schemes for developing the sertão, drought refugees were spilling out of the desertified interiors of Ceará and Pernambuco towards oases like the Cariri Valley in southeastern Ceará, Triunfo in Pernambuco and Acu in Rio Grande do Norte. Far from mitigating the crisis, Cunniff points out, this simply generalized the immiseration to areas where the rains had not failed:

> The masses of hungry people and cattle carried the destruction of the drought into regions that had escaped the meteorological effects. Triunfo complained that it had been converted into a "cattle ranch for the abuse of the poor by the rich." The roving cattle moved into the *agreste* regions "… smashing the cane, manioc and

other crops, and reducing to the last degree of misery and despair the class that lives exclusively from agricultural labor." Human refugees as well consumed and destroyed crops, quickly rendering the traditional agricultural hills and *brejos* nearly as desperate for food as the drought regions.[81]

In the Inhamuns sertão in southwestern Ceará, the leading oligarchs, the Feitosas, had temporarily quieted panic with food imports from unafflicted Piauí, while the provincial government provided some relief work for the poor. By June, however, even the well-to-do were ready to flee. "A prominent citizen of Saboeiro, Captain Salustio Ferrer, wrote on June 12 that migration was about the only course left open to most of the inhabitants of that municipio, since it was becoming increasingly difficult to find water. Many leaders of the community, he added, were forming a caravan to depart for Piaui in the following month. 'Grave must have been our sins,' Captain Ferrer wrote of the scca, 'to have deserved such horrible punishment.'" By mid-summer the region was almost deserted: only an estimated 10 percent of the population – some of them now *cangacerios* – grimly attempted to wait out the drought on their ruined farms and fazendas. "A large number," writes Billy Jaynes Chandler, "went to Piauí, particularly those who had some resources, while others sought refuge in Ipu, the Cariri and Fortaleza."[82]

As the population of the sertão now drew closer to the humid *zona de mata*, the sugar planters and urban merchants were forced to weigh difficult alternatives. The frightened elites vacillated over whether to divert the *retirantes* ("more wild beasts than rational human beings") to the labor-hungry Amazon, and thereby risk losing part of their surplus workforce, or allow them into the cities where, mixing with slaves and poor artisans, they might pose an insurrectionary threat. In Fortaleza, the pharmacist Rodolfo Theofilo kept a famous diary that chronicled the growing presence of desperate backlanders. "The sad procession," he wrote, "paraded along the streets of the capital at all hours.... Real animated skeletons, with skin blackened by the dust from the roads and stuck to their bones, held out their hands begging from everyone they met." A wave of looting and theft by the refugees was countered by bourgeois vigilantism and lynching that "went unpunished because the retirante was considered a leprous dog who was going to stain the land."[83]

Frightened by the strange army of ghostlike sertanejos, the Liberal opposition in Ceará reluctantly agreed to support a Conservative plan to ship the retirantes at imperial expense to the provinces of Amazonas and Para. Others were sent off to Recife, where they were loaded together with slaves on packets for trans-shipment to Rio and the labor-hungry southeast. Large landowners, however, expressed misgivings about such a massive exodus of workers, and Costa Pinto in Rio dragged his feet in remitting the promised subsidies. Grasping at an alternative policy to control an invasion that would eventually swell Fortaleza's population from 25,000 to 130,000, President Estelita "ordered rough shelters constructed for the hordes investing [the city] and a dole of both money and food allotted to those unable to work." Costa Pinto and his Conservative allies in Fortaleza, however, denounced this as a waste of money. Estelita, as a result, was replaced by a new, more conservative appointee, João Aguiar, who promptly discontinued the dole and public works. With Costa Pinto's support, he returned instead to the strategy of deporting the sertanejos to the rainforests. Although thousands were debarked, usually in overcrowded and squalid conditions, there was not enough coastal shipping to keep up with the influx of refugees into For-

Figure 2.8  Exodus from the Sertão

taleza and Recife. Meanwhile, on the rim of the sertão, a human dam was about to burst.[84]

## THE EXODUS TO THE COAST

By New Year's Day 1878 perhaps 50,000 had died in Ceará, several tens of thousands more in other provinces of the Northeast. For a long, terrible year, the majority of the sertão's people had clung to the land, waiting for the winter rains to work magic. In January it rained for a few days, raising spirits as well as a few blades of grass. Farmers scattered some of the seeds they had carefully guarded through months of hunger. But the skies cleared and the first planting shriveled. *Scribner's* correspondent Smith, who arrived at the end of the year, interviewed scores of survivors about what happened next.

> First of March, and no rains. Government aid almost withdrawn. No food left in the villages; no hope for the starving peasants. Then, as by one impulse, a wild panic caught them. Four hundred thousand, they deserted the sertão and rushed down to the coast. Oh! it was terrible, that mad flight. Over all the roads there came streams of fugitives, men and women and little children, naked, lean, famine-weak, dragging wearily across the plains, staining the rocky mountain-paths with their bleeding feet, begging, praying at every house for a morsel of food. They were famished when they started. Two, three, four days at times, they held their way; then the children lagged behind in weakness, calling vainly to their panic-wild fathers; then men and women sank and died on the stones. I have talked with men who came from the interior with the great exodus; they tell stories of suffering to wring one's heart; they tell of skeleton corpses unburied by the road-side, for a hundred thousand dead (some say a hundred and fifty thousand) were left by the way.[85]

The *retirada* to the coast overwhelmed provincial resources. In the drought-famine's epicenter, the state of Ceará, almost total social collapse had occurred by the spring of 1878. "The treasury was empty, commerce nonexistent, and over a hundred thousand refugees clogged the towns on and near the coast.... Outlaw bands roamed the backlands, threatening to displace completely the fragmented civil authority."[86] "It is horrible to see," wrote the future "saint of Joâseiro," the priest Cícero Romão Batista, "that the despair of hunger has led the indigent population to eat cows that have died of carbuncle, knowing, and saying, that they will soon die from eating them, and eating horses, dogs, cane already chewed by others, pieces of leather, and anything else they can find. It is horror upon horror!"[87] A trader told Smith "that a refugee asked permission to kill rats in his store, that he might eat them." Horrifying rumors of cannibalism were relayed as far as Rio by retirantes.[88]

After a starving mob looted the municipal market in Fortaleza, the middle classes locked themselves in their big houses. President Aguiar, who had compounded the chaos by cutting off relief, had fled the province in early February, and power finally passed from the defeated and bitterly divided Conservatives to the Liberal Party. Equally opposed to Estelita's dole, the Liberals extolled the example of the Lytton administration in India and proposed to restore order in Ceará with strictly "scientific British methods." Their approach, as Cunniff points out, had been eloquently outlined by the famous engineer and Liberal ideologue Andre Reboucas the previous October during a three-day debate at the Polytechnic Institute in Rio:

> Although he insisted that the government had a constitutional obligation to render relief to every citizen, he agreed with the rising sentiment that it should not be in the form of a dole. There was, he said, a lamentable Latin tendency to confuse relief with charity. Citing the "immortal" Richard Cobden ... he urged salaried employment on public works as the most efficient and morally appropriate remedy. He was guided by the example of the British government's handling of the severe drought in India, which had begun in 1876 and was still in progress, an account of which he had just read in the *Journal des Economistes*.[89]

"Motivated primarily by fears of revolution and epidemic," the new Liberal president of Ceará, José de Albuquerque, stepped up the shipments of labor-power to Amazonas and Para, in some cases allowing local elites to forcibly deport retirantes. "Consciously following the example of the British government in India, he ordered local relief committees to begin projects suitable to unskilled labor and to give relief only in exchange for labor." In Fortaleza, tens of thousands of retirantes were relocated to makeshift work camps outside the city, where they toiled in construction gangs of one hundred. Elsewhere, in Pernambuco as well as Ceará, the sertanejos provided labor armies for the railroads (most of them never completed) that the Liberals hoped to build with imperial support. Although the ration in the camps – "one-half kilogram of meat, one liter of manioc flour and one liter of a vegetable daily" – was a banquet compared to the

Temple wage, the living conditions were fully as deplorable as in the Deccan.[90] "The refugees," reported Smith, "were huddled together about Fortaleza and Aracaty, barely sheltered from the sun in huts of boughs or palm leaves. The camps were filthy to the last degree; no attempt was made to enforce sanitary rules."[91]

Before the famine, smallpox outbreaks had been confined to small scattered pockets of the sertão, and most of the population had lost the community resistance that comes from surviving regular exposure. Equally, for reasons that remain unclear, vaccination was uncommon in the rural Nordeste. As a result, the squalid work camps provided "virgin soil" for smallpox in the same way that the Indian camps had given full scope to murderous cholera outbreaks. "The greatest horror of the drought," smallpox, reached Ceará in the middle of 1878 after having ravaged the Paraiban capital of João Pessoa. Smith estimated that one-third of the population of Fortaleza died in the months of November and December 1878 alone; while Albuquerque testified that 100,000 had perished in Ceará by the end of 1879, including his own wife. "The Imperial government's only response to the emergency," says Cunniff, "was to send limited quantities of weak vaccine." Cearense refugees subsequently carried the epidemic as far afield as Belém and Rio de Janeiro.[92] A popular poet wrote of the despair of the retirantes trapped between starvation and disease:

> Let us march on and face
> Thirty thousand epidemics
> Cold, Dropsy,
> Which no one can escape.
> Those who go to the lowlands
> Die of the epidemic,
> Those who stay in the sertão
> Go hungry every day.[93]

Although the government ordered a cessation of all relief in June 1879 and thousands of retirantes were forcibly expelled from Recife, the great drought did not actually end until the beginning of March 1880, when the rains turned the sertão green for the first time in more than three years. With 80 percent of the herds destroyed, even fazendeiros were temporarily forced to scratch at the

Figure 2.9 *Retirantes*: Ceará, 1877

earth for their subsistence. Much of the sertão never completely recovered. Surveys by Cearense officials over the next decade revealed the profundity of the seca's impact. In Arneiros, the *vereadores* in 1881 "estimated that 90 per cent of the inhabitants left the municipio during the drought and that 50 per cent of those had not returned by August 1881, two winter seasons after it ended. In regard to the recovery of the cattle industry, the provincial president reported in 1887 that in a few areas herds were beginning to near their 1876 size. Within the Inhumans, there are many who believe that area never fully recovered from the drought of 1877–79, a result of the havoc wrought on fortunes and herds and the general feeling of demoralization which ensued. The Great Drought, it is said, cast a long shadow."[94]

Indeed, Gilberto Freire explains, the "apocalyptic double sevens [1877]" became the "dramatic synthesis" in Brazilian memory of the conjoined tragedies of drought and underdevelopment. Yet some sectors of the Nordeste's ruling class discovered that the "drought industry" was more profitable than the declining regional staples of sugar and cotton. This was certainly true for Singlehurst, Brocklehurst and Company, the British merchant house in Fortaleza, which supplied vast quantities of provisions to the government and transported thousands of retirantes to the Amazon on their coastal steamers. Likewise, big sugar planters profiteered from lucrative imperial grants for temporarily putting drought refugees to work. A precedent was thus set for allowing the *coroneis* (the landowners who dominated provincial and local politics in the Nordeste) to plunder disaster aid. "Development" became simply a euphemism for subsidizing a reactionary social order, and over the next century vast sums of "drought relief" disappeared into the sertão without leaving behind a single irrigation ditch or usable reservoir for its long-suffering population.[95]

The "double sevens," however, did spell the beginning of the end to slavery in Brazil. Land, cattle and free labor in the sertão became almost valueless commodities during the drought, leaving slaves, in keen demand by Paulista coffee planters, as the major fungible asset of the fazendeiros. Selling slaves to the south, like exporting free labor to the Amazon, generated obscene prosperity amid general catastrophe. "The Baron Ibiapaba, Joaquim da Cunha Freire, for example, profited greatly, being the principal exporter of human cargo from both Fortaleza and Mossoro. From Fortaleza alone, he was reputed to have sold at least fifteen thousand slaves south." This sudden revival on a grand scale of the slave trade, with all the brutal public spectacles that accompanied it, provoked enormous public resentment, particularly in Ceará where emancipation societies formed in virtually every town. Within six years, popular agitation had not only ended slavery in Ceará, the first province to do so, but sparked similar crusades across the Northeast. Four years later, in the final twilight of the old Empire, slavery was abolished throughout Brazil.[96]

# Three

# Gunboats and Messiahs

> Previously one laughed at the state of one's heart;
> now nothing at all elicits joy or laughter. It is said that
> people live on hope. I have no hope even of living.
> — Mirza Asadullah Khan Ghalib

India, China and Brazil accounted for the most massive mortality, but the world drought of the 1870s had profound and deadly impacts in at least a dozen other lands. Peasant producers, as we have seen, were already reeling from the impact of the trade depression, which deepened abruptly in 1877. Drought and famine gave foreign creditors, allied with indigenous moneylenders and compradores, new opportunities to tighten control over local rural economies through debt or outright expropriation. Pauperized countrysides likewise provided rich harvests of cheap plantation labor as well as missionary converts and orphans to be raised in the faith. And where native states retained their independence, the widespread subsistence crises in Asia and Africa invited a new wave of colonial expansion that was resisted in many cases by indigenous millenarianism. El Niño was thus followed by gunboats and messiahs as well as by famine and disease.

In the Korean case, the opportunist power was Japan. In a familiar pattern, the drought in north China extended latitudinally across the Yellow Sea into Korea's breadbasket Cholla region. The ensuing famine and peasant unrest coincided with the implementation of the "open door" treaty that Meiji Japan had extorted from Korea in 1876 and offered the Japanese a pretext for further prying open the Hermit Kingdom for economic exploitation. Thus Japanese envoy Hanabusa, meeting with wary Korean officials aboard a warship in November 1877, relentlessly lobbied them to accept a debt of relief. "After exchanging gifts they talked about the past year's drought. 'The Koreans said it was terrible and is equally bad this year.' Hanabusa asked if they would like to get some Japanese rice." The Koreans made a deliberately uninterpretable reply, but Hanabusa renewed his solicitations at a meeting in Seoul several weeks later. "Please send this message to your government.... Since coming into your country we have been entertained with many dishes by your government officials, and I thank you very much. But when I think of hungry people even this sweet food will not go into my stomach." When his hosts replied that Korea was "too small" to undertake the reciprocal obligation of supplying Japan with rice during a famine there, Hanabusa reassured them that such a situation would never arise. Within a decade, however, the commercial export of rice from southern Korea to Japan during a drought would become a revolutionary grievance amongst hungry peasants in the Cholla provinces.[1]

In Vietnam the coincidence of drought-famine and cholera was a bellows that fanned the embers of peasant anti-colonial resistance into millenarian revolt. With the killing in 1872 of Tran van Thanh, the leader of the populist Dao Lanh sect, the French believed they had pacified their new colony. "Unfortunately," as Reynaldo Ileto points out, "they had not reckoned on the popular belief in reincarnation." As the threat of famine spread panic through the countryside in 1877, another Dao Lanh apostle, Nam Thiep, announced that he was Tran's incarnation and "that the time had come to expel the French" (widely believed to be responsible for this conjugation of disasters). "Nam Thiep was able to unify the Dao Lanh groups and mount a rebellion in 1878. He announced that the Low Era was ending, and that the reign of the Emperor of Light ... was being established. Peasants armed with bamboo spears and amulets attacked French garrisons, only to be driven back decisively by rifle fire. But this did not faze Nam Thiep, who in 1879 proclaimed himself a living Buddha and built a new community on Elephant Mountain, in the region of the Seven Mountains."[2]

In the Dutch East Indies, meanwhile, drought ravaged fields and forests across two-thirds of the vast archipelago. Batavia (Jakarta), for example, reported less than one-third of its normal rainfall from May 1877 through February 1878 (a brief respite in the boreal spring was followed by six more dry months until January 1879).[3] Crop failure, exacerbated by coffee blight and other fungoid plant diseases, coincided with a costly rinderpest epidemic that decimated buffalo, pigs, even elephants.[4] And, as in the 1990s, El Niño was synonymous with vast, mysterious forest fires. Writing from the normally luxuriant Sundas, the British naturalist Henry Forbes described local foreboding as the landscape seemed to spontaneously ignite.

> The parched surface of the ground broke up into ravine-like cracks, which, extending from four to five feet in depth and two to three in breadth, destroyed great numbers of the forest-trees by encircling and snapping off their root. Shrubs and small trees in exposed places were simply burned up in broad patches.... Crops of all kinds failed, while devastating fires, whose origin could seldom be traced, were so frequent in the forest and in the great *alang-alang* fields, that the population lived in constant fear of their villages and even of their lives and stock. It was in vain that the natives, following their superstitious rites, carried their cats in procession, to the sound of gongs and the clattering of rice blocks, to the nearest streams to bathe and sprinkle them; the rain after such a ceremony ought to have come, but it did not.[5]

On Borneo/Kalimantan, according to Han Knapen, the drought was a godsend to the Dutch, long frustrated by their inability to subordinate the ruggedly independent Dayak communities that controlled vast tracts of valuable rainforest. Although the commercially sophisticated Dayaks grew or harvested commodities for the world market like rattan and *getah perca* (indispensable in undersea telegraph cables), they fiercely resisted sedentarization and plantation labor. At last in 1877, hunger gave the Dutch a means of coercion: "The rice barns were empty and famine was imminent. In order to obtain money to buy rice, only two options were left to the Dayak: either to collect more getah perca (of which the producing tree was already becoming extinct) or to sell one's labour to the Dutch, who had been eagerly looking for 'hands' for at least two centuries. Now ... the Dutch finally had the labour to dig a canal linking the Kahayan River with Banjarmasin and thereby to push the trade in forest products up to unprecedented levels. Even the most remote parts of Borneo were now becoming part of the global economy, exposing the local population both to new opportunities and to new risks."[6]

But the drought was most life-threatening in the overcrowded and geographically isolated Residency of Bagelen in south-central Java, where crop disease in 1875 had already depleted local grain reserves. The pressure of the so-called Cultivation System or *culturrstelsel*, which compelled villages to cultivate export crops for the benefit of the Netherlands at the expense of their own subsistence, was higher here, as measured by the proportion of acreage committed to exports, than anywhere else in Java.[7] Although in its death throes in 1877 – condemned as "an impediment to private enterprise" – the cultuurstelsel had been crucial to the Netherlands' great economic revival in the earlier Victorian period. Remittances forcibly extracted from the Javanese peasantry had at one point provided fully one-third of state revenues.[8] Conversely, the system's pressures on local producers during the episodically dry years from 1843 to 1849, vividly described in Multatuli's great anticolonial novel *Max Havelaar* (1860), had led to massive famine mortality and flight from the land. There was such distress that "in one regency the population fell from 336,000 to 120,000 and in another from 89,500 to 9000."[9]

Local officials in Bagelen, where cultuurstelsel methods still remained entrenched, feared that a disaster of similar magnitude was again at hand. When they attempted to buy rice to counter speculation, they were severely censured à la Lytton by the Council of the Dutch East Indies for abandoning free-market rectitude. Batavia also insisted that the famished peasantry punctually pay its annual land tax. Villagers were thus forced to sell their cattle and other possessions to the same merchants who hoarded the local grain supply. Again, as in south India, tens of thousands of them were cut down by cholera before they could die of starvation. This conveniently allowed the Dutch to claim that epidemic rather than famine was the cause of excessive local mortality.[10]

In the Philippines, the great drought struck hardest at the western Visayas, especially the island of Negros, where the explosive growth of sugar monoculture had displaced traditional food self-sufficiency. Just as the Philippines has been often described as a "Latin American social formation in East Asia," likewise the Occidental province of Negros, whose population skyrocketed from 18,805 in 1855 to 308,272 in 1898, came to replicate most of the exploitative and unsustainable characteristics of distant Caribbean sugar colonies. Former Spanish colonial officials and army officers, as well as wealthy mestizo merchants, used their political connections to wrest "through usury, terror, or purchase" vast tracts of land in Occidental's western plains from pioneering Panayan peasants who had first cleared the tropical forests in the 1850s. They were replaced first by immigrant sharecroppers, then by debt-bonded wage laborers.[11] As Violeta Lopez-Gonzaga has emphasized, sugar inexorably became an ecology of hunger:

> The widespread fencing of land and the emergence of the haciendas, landlords, and a landless proletariat, further led to rural indebtedness, widespread poverty, seasonal scarcity of food, and increasingly low level of nutrition and seriously adverse health conditions. Inevitably, such conditions led to high mortality rates which were the final result of a complex of factors ranging from hunger, natural calamities and epidemics, to the absence of health services. Outside sugar, trading was minimal and the prices of food commodities very high. With the limited development of infrastructure, traded food items hardly reached the interior areas which had been cleared of forest and the traditional subsistence patches of the natives or the small migrant farmers. The growing commitment of agriculture to sugarcane production made the emergent labouring class vulnerable to hunger with the onslaught of storm, drought or a plague of locusts. In fact, from the second half of the nineteenth century onward, the scourge of hunger frequently struck the people of Negros.[12]

Locust plagues, particularly devastating to rice crops, were the constant companion to the long drought from 1876 to 1878. In the absence of any organized relief effort by corrupt Spanish authorities, the astronomical rise in rice prices in conjunction with low sugar prices and high unemployment condemned large numbers of hacienda day-laborers and poor townspeople to starvation. Parish records suggest an island-wide excess mortality of at least 10 percent, with the rates rising as high as 50 percent in the town of Hinigaran and 30 percent in the town of Villadolid. As in India and Java, many of those who were weakened but not killed by the famine were subsequently picked off by cholera and malaria.[13]

Negros's neighbor island, Panay, the sacred capital of Visayan shamanism (the *babaylan*), also suffered massive mortality during the drought. Again, starvation was conditioned by recent a abrupt deterioration in economic autonomy and well-being. In the 1850s *sinamay* textiles sustained a rich trade that made Panay's principal port of Iloilo a "dynamic commercial entrepot ... second only to Manila in size and importance." Within twenty years, however, local textile production was destroyed and once-prosperous Panay weavers were *indio* peons on the sugar plantations of Negros. As Michael Billig explains, the process was expedited by an extraordinary representative of free trade imperialism:

> In 1855 Iloilo was officially opened to foreign commerce, and the next year the British sent a vice-consul, Nicholas Loney, to the city. Loney was to be the single most potent force in bringing down the Iloilo textile industry and building up the Negros sugar industry. Aside from being vice-consul, he was the commercial agent for British firms and an indefatigable purveyor of British goods. He pursued a local mission of substituting cheaper, machine-made British textiles for the locally made ones and encouraging the production of sugar as a profitable return cargo.... The fledgling sugar industry, unlike the older textile business, was thoroughly dependent on foreign capital. Loney lent as much P75,000 at a time at the low rate of 8 percent (compared to the 30–40 percent of the moneylenders) and he provided state-of-the-art milling equipment at cost, under the condition that the Loney & Ker Company be the sole purchaser of the produce.... [He] was ... remarkably successful in his mission. Iloilo's textile exports to Manila dwindled from 141,420 piezas in 1863, to 30,673 in 1864, to 12,700 in 1869, to 5,100 in 1873.[14]

Thus the ruined weaving villages of Panay, like their sister towns in Negros, had few resources to resist crop failure and price inflation. The records of the Augustinians, cited by Filomeno Aguilar, note the corpses strewn in the streets of San Joaquin in 1877, while "oral tradition among shamans of Panay recount 'three years' of drought and famine that ravaged this town and left people dying of starvation and thirst, as all the rivers and springs had dried up." As in Korea and Vietnam, famine produced a resurgence of folk messianism, in this case in magical rain-making competition with the Spanish friars.[15]

> According to the lore, people sought help from the parish priest, but he failed to induce rain. Desperate in his inability to alleviate the disaster, the curate advised the town [San Joaquin] leaders to call upon a *babaylan* known as Estrella Bangotbanwa, who ordered that seven black pigs be butchered, shaved, and covered with black cloth. She then took a black pig from the convent to the plaza, where she pressed its mouth to the ground until it gave a loud squeak. Suddenly, the sky turned dark and a heavy downpour followed.[16]

Aguilar explains how the supernatural impotence of the Spanish priests in face of the drought, together with the inability of officials to contain the cholera epidemic that followed in its wake, "inspired the shamans to mount direct challenges to a disintegrating colonial state, converting the whole of the Visayas into a theater of resistance." By the late 1880s, thousands of peasants and aborigines in both Panay and Negros (in a movement strikingly analogous to the millenarian refuges of Joāseiro and Canudos in contemporary northeast Brazil) had withdrawn into autonomous armed communities in the mountains led by prominent babaylans like Panay's Clara Tarrosa, "an eighty-year-old woman ... who claimed to be the 'Virgin Mary,'" or Negros's Ponciano Elopre, a transvestite miracleworker known as Dios Buhawi (the Waterspout God) for his/her skill in rainmaking. Despite brutal retaliations, including massacres and summary executions, Spanish power essentially collapsed in the island interiors, leaving the babaylons and their followers to confront the more ruthless, usurper colonialism of the Americans a decade later.[17]

The Kanaks of New Caledonia, also stirred to rebellion by El Niño drought and hunger, made a desperate bid in 1878 to liberate the interior of their island from French *colons* and penal *concessionaires*. The French invasion of New Caledonia in 1853 had been a singular catastrophe for Kanak society. "In less than two years," writes Myriam Dornoy, "... the local chiefly system was destroyed, and the Melanesians were dispossessed of nine-tenths of their best land and pushed into the mountainous interior. Assuming that the Melanesians would soon disappear, the French employed the policy they had used in Algeria – *refoulement* – which meant that Melanesians were regrouped arbitrarily and stationed on limited reserves which in fact were infringed on little by little, or were situated in infertile zones not favoured by the colons." This indigenous land shortage (the "basic factor in the great native insurrection in 1878") aggravated tribal conflict, as did the French practice of replacing village chiefs with their own sycophants. The "New Imperialists" of the Third Republic – intent on exorcising the national humiliation of 1871 through colonial conquest – continued the Second Empire's huge thefts of Kanak subsistence space. When the natives protested, the Republicans haughtily decreed that "the native is not the owner of the land, and when the French government appropriates land, it just takes back its own land."[18]

Ultimately, a "disastrous drought at the end of 1877" (New Caledonian agriculture, as we shall see in Chapter 8, is highly vulnerable to ENSO) combined with French arrogance generated a crisis that enabled Chief Atai in the La Foa Valley of central Grande Terre to bring together a coalition of previously hostile tribe.[19] (In a meeting with French Governor Olry, Atai had emptied two sacks at his feet: one full of soil, the other of pebbles. "Here is what we used to have," Atai explained, "and here is what you are leaving us!")[20] Kanak patience was pushed beyond all limits, as Martyn Lyons explains, by the drought-exacerbated deprecations of European cattle of precious yam and taro fields.

> The livestock problem had been severely aggravated in 1878 by the drought of the previous year. This meant that cattle and other livestock had to search even further afield than usual for adequate fodder, and the native plantations were very tempting targets for hunger-stricken animals. The territory between Noumea and Bouloupari was especially dry, and graziers were allowed to take their herds onto government property near Ourail, for a small fee. The cattle arrived there starving in an area of flourishing native fields, and set about systematically destroying them. *Colons* did all they could to avoid the capital expenditure involved in constructing effective enclosures. Their attitude was that if the Kanaks wanted proper protection, they should build their own. One Kanak replied to a stock-raiser who made such a suggestion: "When my taros go and eat up your cattle, then I'll put up a fence."[21]

Following the arrest of several traditional chiefs in June 1878, accumulated Kanak anger erupted in a succession of ferocious assaults on white homesteads and gendarme posts. Caught by complete surprise, 200 Europeans were killed and panic spread to Noumea where the settler mouthpiece *La Nouvelle Caledonie* called for a "war of extermination against all Melanesians."[22] With reinforcements from Indochina and the aid of Kanak mercenaries from coastal tribes, French *colonnes mobiles* under the celebrated Captain Riviere devastated much of the central region: burning "hundreds of villages," confiscating food stores, destroying irrigation systems, killing warriors on sight, and handing over their women as booty to the pro-French tribes. The charismatic Atai was killed in a surprise attack and his head with its mane of snow-white hair was sent to Paris to be scrutinized by savants. Although "the colonial regime had experienced a very severe shock, and had only reasserted its dominance with very great difficulty," the cost of defeat to the rebel Kanak tribes was truly staggering. In addition to thousands of casualties and the deportation of their surviving leaders, native New Caledonians were permanently uprooted from the rich west coast of Grande Terre in favor of plantations, ranches and penal colonies. (As Lyons points out, "the division between the mainly French west coast and mainly Kanak east coast persists today.")[23]

Among the eyewitnesses to the Kanak tragedy was a survivor of another defeated insurrection: Louise Michel, "the Red Virgin of Paris." Although some of Communards in penal exile on New Caledonia joined the race war against the Kanaks, Michel passionately supported the Kanak struggle for "liberty and dignity." She translated some of the haunting war chants of the rebel bard Andia (killed with Atai) and gave half of her famous red scarf ("the red scarf of the Commune that I had hidden from every search") to two native friends who joined the insurgents. As she explained in her *Memoirs*:

> The Kanakan Insurrection of 1878 failed. The strength and longing of human hearts was shown once again, but the whites shot down the rebels as we were mowed down in front of Bastion 37 and on the plains of Satory. When they sent the head of Atai to Paris, I wondered who the real headhunters were; as Henri Roche-fort had once written to me, "the Versailles government could give the natives lessons in cannibalism."[24]

## Drought and Imperial Design in Africa

In southern Africa, the great drought became the chief ally of Portuguese and British aggression against still independent African societies. The Angolan coast has famously erratic rainfall, especially in the environmentally unstable region around Luanda, but the drought that began in 1876 was exceptional both in its duration, lasting until the early 1880s, and its scale, affecting populations as far inland as the Huila highlands.[25] "The majority of inhabitants of this land are mummies rather than human beings," complained Luanda's medical officer in 1876. A year later it was noted that "the extreme weakness of African porters hired from the Golungo Alto district resulted in fourteen deaths during a four-day march to Massangano"; while throughout 1878 "five or six people a day were reported dying from starvation in Luanda."[26] As Jill Dias has shown, "the intensi-fication of external trade pressures and colonial intervention in Angola from the

1870s onwards both influenced the growing severity of famine and disease and was influenced by it."[27] Despite the world trade recession, Angola's export economy had found several profitable niches for rapid growth directly at the expense of African grazing and subsistence farming.

> A commercial "boom" in rubber and, to a lesser extent, in coffee, produced a fever of gathering and marketing these products among Africans in most parts of Angola. European trade and agriculture expanded within the colonial enclaves centered on Luanda, Benguela and Mossamedes. New pockets of white settlement and farmland sprang up in the Porto Amboim hinterland and the Huila highlands. The slave trade also increased as a result of the rapidly rising demand for labour by São Tomé planters eager to benefit from the island's cocoa "boom." Finally the initiation of a more vigorous programme of colonial expansion led to the beginnings of military occupation of Kongo, Luanda and the Ovimbundu highlands.[28]

During a previous severe drought in the late 1860s, the Portuguese themselves had been forced to retreat from plantations and forts in frontier regions like the edge of the Huila highlands. Now, with the emergence of drought- and-famine-related epidemics of smallpox, malaria, dysentery and sand jiggers, colonial troops made unprecedented headway against weakened populations in Kongo and to the east and south of Kwanza. Likewise, Dias adds, "The debilitating effects of hunger and disease in the decade of the 1870s may go far towards explaining why the social and political tensions generated by the spread of white plantations did not explode in revolt within the Portuguese enclave." Thereafter, the extension of the plantation system and the consolidation of colonial power in the Angolan interior were carefully synchronized to the sinister rhythm of drought and disease, as in 1886–87, 1890–91, 1898–99, 1911 and 1916.[29]

The drought was an even more important turning point in the highveld and its borderlands, where it sounded the deathknell of Xhosa, Zulu and even, temporarily, Boer independence. South Africa's seeming prosperity in the early 1870s, fueled by the diamond and wool booms, barely concealed the emergent ecological crisis as too many people and cattle competed for reliably watered grazing land. The relief of the veld with its innumerable rain shadows creates an intricate mosaic of rainfall variation as well as a complex schedule of ripening of pasturage: an environmental formula for interminable friction between pastoral communities. The ceaseless encroachment of Europeans upon the range resources of

African societies, whose populations were surging, generated, in Donald Morris's words, "an explosive situation which the next drought might spark off."[30] And the drought of 1876–79 was the most ruinous since the infamous arid spell of the early 1820s (probably arising out of back-to-back El Niño events) that had given the Zulu *Mfecane* – the violent redistribution of grazing territories and homelands under Shaka – its desperate energy.[31]

In the Eastern Cape and Natal, European stockraisers were battered by the simultaneous crash of wool export prices and the dying off of their herds. *Nature* recounted how in the Cape, "hitherto well-to-do colonists" had to go into "menial service in exchange for the barest necessities of life."[32] The Transvaal Boers, though less dependent upon world markets, were still hard hit by the conjuncture of drought, cattle disease and a growing shortage of land. For Africans, of course, climate shocks were magnified by their economic marginality. "Both Ciskei and Transkei," Morris writes, "were greatly overcrowded with Europeans, natives and cattle, and the land was overgrazed and failing. [The] ruinous drought had brought the frail native economy to the edge of collapse, and complaints of trespass and cattle theft were unending."[33] In Basutoland, "two-thirds of the crop failed and the number of men seeking work doubled in a year," while, further north, "the Pedi kingdom began to suffer from increased pressure on resources, the result of natural increase, the influx of refugees and recurrent drought."[34]

Nor was Zululand – the greatest surviving redoubt of African power – immune. "Despite the absence of European settlers," explains Donald Morris, "this kingdom suffered from the same land shortage as the other territories. Many of the well-watered sections were hilly and stony, other grassy slopes and elevated flats were infected with lung sickness and red-water fever had ravaged the Zulu herds after Cetshwayo's coronation, and the tsetse fly barred broad belts to settlement. Primitive agriculture made inefficient use of what remained, and the population of perhaps a third of a million Zulus was thickly clustered about such centers as the royal Kraal at Ulundi while other sections were deserted. The drought of 1877 and the winter months thus sent a wave of pressure surging against the fertile lands between the headwaters of the Buffalo and the Pongola Rivers, which had been a subject of dispute with the Transvaal since 1861."[35]

The drought crisis, which weakened both African and Afrikaans societies as well as increasing the tensions between them, was an undisguised blessing to imperial planners in London. Since 1875, Disraeli and his colonial secretary, Lord Carnarvon, had been committed to a "Confederation Scheme" that envisioned a single British hegemony over the southern cone of Africa. "Carnarvon's design," according to Cain and Hopkins, "was to turn central Africa and Mozambique into labour reserves for the mines and farms of the south."[36] The discovery of the great Kimberley diamond pipes had overnight made South Africa a major arena for capitalist investment, but the British were stymied by the lack of control over African labor, a problem that was considered insuperable as long as militarily independent African societies continued to exist on the periphery of the diamond fields.[37] Thus from his arrival in South Africa in March 1877, Carnarvon's special high commissioner Sir Bartle Frere (a former governor of Bombay) moved with extraordinary energy to impose British power on the drought-weakened Bantus and Boers alike.

Within a year he had raised the Union Jack over the Transvaal as well as ruthlessly crushed a last-ditch defense of Xhosa independence by Sarhili's Gcaleka in the Transkei: the ninth and last of the Cape–Xhosa wars. Cape troops in 1878 also put down a rebellion, "sharpened by drought," among the mixed race Griqua along the lower Orange River.[38] Frere's full attention then focused on a lightning campaign against Cetshwayo's Zulu kingdom. Although loyal allies of the British in their conflict with the Boer republics, the powerful Zulu kept a "spiritual fire" burning among Africans – "the vision of an armed and defiant black nation" – that Frere was determined to extinguish.[39]

In final talks before the British invasion, the anguished and betrayed Zulu monarch discerned a sinister connection between the high commissioner's perfidy and the drought that was devastating his herds:

"What have I done or said to the Great House of England? ... What have I done to the Great White Chief?"

"I feel the English Chiefs have stopped the rain, and the land is being destroyed."

"The English Chiefs are speaking. They have always told me that a kraal of blood cannot stand, and I wish to sit quietly, according to their orders, and cultivate the land. I do not know anything about war, and want the Great Chiefs to send me the rain."[40]

Carnarvon and Frere sent the British army instead. Arrogantly underestimating the military organization and valor of Cetshwayo's regiments, 1,600 crack British soldiers were annihilated at Isandhlwana in 1879. The Empire struck back, in turn, with a "systematic strategy of the burning of homes, the seizure of cattle in areas which the Zulus had not evacuated and ... the destruction of the economic foundations of Zululand." Indeed, Michael Lieven claims, "Genocide came close to being adopted as official policy."[41] Although the Zulu, overwhelmed as much by famine as by firepower, eventually surrendered in July 1879, the example of Isandhlwana, Britain's greatest military disaster since the charge of the Light Brigade, inspired both the Sotho and Pede to protracted resistance, and, even more ominously for Carnarvon's grand design, gave the Afrikaners under the tough leadership of Paul Kruger the military confidence to retrieve their independence at Majuba Hill in 1881 and assert control of the Rand's mineral wealth.

## North Africa's 'Open Tombs'

Disraeli's New Imperialism was more successful in Egypt, where the full human impact of the poor northeast African rains of autumn 1876 and the low Nile of 1877 was not felt until the beginning of 1878, when famine was receding in south Asia and north China. In one of the most dramatic Nile failures in half a millennium, the flood crest in 1877 had been six feet below average and more than one-third of the crop area could not be irrigated.[42] The drought struck a peasantry already reeling from collapsing export prices, high indebtedness, a rinderpest epidemic and overtaxation. Cotton prices, already depressed by the return of the American South to world trade, slumped further with the world trade depression.[43] After twenty years of being "an interest milk cow for European investors," the khedive was forced to default in 1876, surrendering control over revenues to a Franco-British Dual Control Commission. "Now the claims of European capital," wrote Rosa Luxemburg later, "became the pivot of economic life and the sole consideration of the financial system."[44] A system of Mixed Tribunals was established that allowed European creditors to directly attach the property of peasant smallholders, thus overriding the ancient Egyptian-Islamic tradition that tenancy was guaranteed for life. Under extreme European pressure, regiments of tax collectors, with moneylenders following them "like a vulture after a cow," imposed a reign of terror throughout the Nile Valley. Peasants who hid cattle or resisted the confiscation of their property were brutally flogged in front of their neighbors.[45]

Wilfred Blunt, traveling through Egypt on the eve of the famine, was shocked by the misery that the European creditors were creating in the countryside. "It was rare in those days to see a man in the fields with a turban on his head, or more than a shirt on his back.... The principal towns on market days were full of women selling their clothes and their silver ornaments to the Greek usurers, because the tax collectors were in their village, whip in hand."[46] The British consul in Cairo wrote to London that peasants were so desperate to escape the tax collector that they were simply giving their land away. "Many of the poorer classes of native, calculating that they could not obtain from the produce of the land sufficient to pay the increased demands, offered their lands gratis to any person who would relieve them of it and pay the newly imposed tax."[47]

Despite the failure of the Nile and widespread reports of starvation in the summer of 1878, tax collectors continued to mercilessly bastinado the peasantry. In Lower Egypt, where the drought "hurt peasants badly," widespread foreclosures transformed a stratum of smallholders into impoverished day laborers on the latifundia of Ottoman-Egyptian nobles.[48] *The Times* opined that boasts of triumphant revenue expeditions to the Delta "sound[ed] strangely by the side of the news that people are starving by the roadside, that great tracts of country are uncultivated, because of the physical burdens, and that the farmers have sold their cattle, the women their finery, and that the usurers are filling the mortgage offices with their bonds, and the courts with their suits of foreclosure."[49]

In Upper Egypt, where ecology confined farmers to a single annual crop, the confiscation of cattle, grain reserves, seed corn and agricultural tools in the wake of the drought was literally murderous. In early 1879, a special commissioner investigating famine conditions between Sohag and Girga "reported that the number who had died of starvation and as a result of the want of sufficient food was not less than ten thousand.... He added that all this was the direct result of poverty arising from over-taxation."[50] Alexander Baird, a frequent winter tourist who had been conscripted to help organize an impromptu British relief effort, confirmed the acuity of famine in the Girga area. "It is almost incredible the distances travelled by women and children, begging from village to village.... The poor were in some instances reduced to such extremities of hunger that they were driven to satisfy their cravings with the refuse and garbage of the street."[51]

Faced with death, or at least immiseration, some peasants revolted. "In late 1877 British sources in Aswan and Luxor underlined the hazards of traveling in Upper Egypt owing to peasant banditry, especially between Sohag and Girga." These were the phantoms that haunted the Grants' trip to Thebes. When Cairo sent 2,000 cavalry to quell the robberies, the outlaw farmers took to the hills where, according to Juan Cole, they unfurled a banner of social revolt. "It is hard to know how to think of the peasant brigandage of 1879 except as social banditry of the sort described by Eric Hobsbawm. The bandit gang operating between Sohag and Girga employed a rhetoric of social justice, vowing to unite those peasants oppressed by the state's overtaxation and brutal treatment of its subjects."[52]

In the Maghreb, meanwhile, Algeria's fields and vineyards simply burned up in the terrible heat of 1877. Half of the grain harvest was lost and famine was reported from Oran in the west to Constantine in the east.[53] The worst scenes were among the Constantinois, where drought and hunger persisted until early 1880, then resumed with the bad harvest of 1881. The Russian traveler Tchihatcheff, who passed through the Mila area, was horrified to find that "the poor population has been trying to survive for more than two months almost exclusively on boiled *kerioua* [a noxiously bitter wild arum]." Official attempts to minimize the famine were belied by the flood of skeletal refugees into the towns, and the governor-general was forced to ackowledge the gravity of the crisis in fall 1878, when it was reported in *Situations officielles* that "the tribes of Titteri (in the south of Medea and of Aumale), those of Bordj-Bou-Arreridj, of Hodna and of the region around Batna and Tebessa, were entirely without food."[54] But the disaster in the countryside was a windfall to the Marseille interests who controlled commerce in North African livestock products.

In the most drought-stricken regions, the harvest was utterly lost; elsewhere it was poor at best. The loss of seed ensured a poor yield the following year as well. Meanwhile, the lack of water and grass threatened to decimate the native herds; the interior tribes were forced to sell their animals to livestock dealers at dirt-cheap prices. Exports of sheep doubled while wheat and barley exports fell by half; likewise Algeria, which had exported 17,996 head of beef in the three years from 1874 to 1876, exported 143,198 head between 1877 and 1879. In order to avoid starvation, Algerians liquidated their only real wealth: their livestock.[55]

In his magisterial history of colonial Algeria, Charles-Robert Ageron has shown how the drought of 1877–81 battened upon and, in turn, accelerated the general tendency of indigenous pauperization. After the defeat of the Muqrani uprising of 1871–72, the Third Republic relentlessly extended the scope of *colon* capitalism through massive expropriations of communal land, enclosures of forests and pastures, persecution of transhumance, and the ratcheting up of land revenues. Indian tax extortion paled next to annual charges that sometimes confiscated more than a third of the market-value of native land.[56] In the Kabylia, angry poets sang that "the taxes rain upon us like repeated blows, the people have sold their fruit trees and even their clothes."[57] Environmental disaster simply shortened the distance to an "Irish solution" of a fully pauperized and conquered countryside. Some architects of French policy, quoted by Ageron, were keenly aware of the potentially revolutionary consequences of such complete dispossession of the native population. "The greatest danger for Algeria," wrote Burdeau during another hungry drought in 1891, "is the emergence of an indigent proletariat, an army of *déclassés* without hope or land, eager for brigandage and insurrection."[58]

In the end, Algerians could only be thankful that the drought-famine of 1877–81, unlike its terrible predecessor in 1867–68, failed to unleash massive epidemic mortality. There was no such succor across the Atlas, where both hunger and disease were as proportionately devastating as in the Deccan or the sertão. The ancient kingdom of Morocco was convulsed by its worst economic and environmental crisis in centuries: its countryside was turned into "an open tomb." Once again, drought pummeled a peasantry already brought to its knees by the world market. As Jean-Louis Miege has shown, the European demand for Moroccan grain and wool, which had fueled a sustained export boom beginning in the 1840s, collapsed during the 1870s in the face of lower-cost competition. By the fall of 1877, when drought began its seven-year-long siege of the countryside, the economy was already in steep decline, bled by a growing trade deficit, huge debt borrowed from England to pay war indemnities to Spain, and a depreciating currency that translated into runaway domestic inflation. Between 1875 and 1877 Moroccan real income fell by half while the relative burden of agricultural taxation grew ever more onerous. Farmers and herdsmen thus had to face the dry winter of 1877–78 (there was no rain at all in southern parts of the arable belt), and the great locust plague which followed, with much of their wealth already wiped out.[59]

By spring 1878, desperate *fellahin* were either eating their starving herds or selling them for a few days' supply of grain (cows for five francs, sheep for one). Miege estimates that 75 percent of the nation's livestock disappeared in this manner. Moreover, as grain prices soared, the poorest villagers were reduced to grubbing for roots; some even tried to subsist upon the poisonous *yernee*. There were other instances where formerly prosperous southern peasants traded their farms to merchants for a single bag of grain. The *makhzan's* efforts to prevent foreclosures and alienation of land were successfully opposed by the foreign diplomatic corps, who used their control over credit and relief supplies to demand strict adherence to "the principle of free trade."[60]

During the summer of 1878, as starvation became endemic, vast portions of the interior and south of Morocco were virtually depopulated as "hundreds of thousands of people bolted for the nearest port" and the security of imported grain supplies. As the worried Mogador correspondent of the *Jewish World* reported to his coreligionists in Britain:

> [T]he pauper population of Mogador, always disproportionately large, forming about one-third of its entire inhabitants, is being rapidly increased by numerous famished Jewish and Moorish families from the adjacent districts. It is a fearful sight to see some of them – mere living skeletons.... There is no business now doing, except in articles of food, and consequently the working classes have nothing to do. They are selling their clothes and furniture to obtain food.... If you could see the terrible scenes of misery – poor, starving mothers, breaking and pounding up bones they find in the streets, and giving them to their famished children – it would make your heart ache. Raise a few pounds if you can, and if you can do so lay it out in rice at the wholesale brokers, and have it shipped by the steamers leaving England.[61]

Six months later, American and German consuls reported "thousands dead by the roadsides," while the British consul, Sir John Drummond Hay, whose intelligence sources were unconsidered "unexcelled," wrote in April 1879 that "half the population of Sous and of Haha has died of starvation." The flight to the coast, as in India, China and Brazil, produced unsanitary concentrations of enfeebled people ripe for the spread of disease. Cholera, the universal scourge of famine refugees in this period, first appeared in Fez and Marknes at the end of July 1878. By September it was decimating inland cities as well as ports; in Marrakech an estimated 1 percent of the population was reported to be perishing daily. When the cholera epidemic finally subsided in December, its place was promptly taken by typhoid, which killed off the Italian and Portuguese consuls and a number of prominent European and Jewish merchants, as well as tens of thousands of weakened commoners.[54]

The crisis continued until the winter of 1879/80, when nearly normal rainfall allowed the resumption of agriculture after eighteen months of complete dependence on grain imports from Marseille and Gibraltar. Drought returned, however, in 1881 (an El Niño year) and worsened in 1882 when the south was again rainless while precipitation in the north was barely one-quarter of normal. The British consul, in a dismal repetition of his earlier reports, described "harvests completely lost, livestock dying and the famished population again reduced to eating poisonous roots." A second emptying-out of the mountains and countryside likewise produced a new epidemic crucible in the cities that was exploited this time by smallpox, which raged through 1883. However, Morocco's long ordeal by famine and disease, as Miege emphasizes, was not without "winners." "The crisis of 1878–1885 hastened the rise of the commercial and landed capitalism that dominated the future of the country.... The non-specialization of commerce permitted strong houses to switch from exports to imports of food. In the ports the famine created islands of prosperity." The "tremendous redistribution of property" likewise paved the way for famous comprador fortunes and allowed the foreign community to accumulate massive landholdings under fictive Moroccan ownership. It also inaugurated the era of Great Power rivalry, conducted with both loans and dreadnaughts, to turn Morocco's new economic dependence upon Europe into formal colonialism.[63]

## The Global Death Toll

Where populations escaped mass famine, drought still brought massive and sometimes irreversible economic distress. "Cape Colony, New Guinea, the Australian Colonies, the South Seas, and, it would appear, almost every known part of the southern hemisphere," observed the editors of *Nature* in March 1878, "have been suffering from a severe and protracted drought."[64] In New South

Wales, a quarter of the animals perished on the world's greatest sheep range.[65]All of Polynesia, meanwhile, experienced environmental turmoil. Hawaiian sugar plantations cobbled together makeshift irrigation to deal with the driest year (1877–78) of the nineteenth century, while drought forced desperate Gilbertese to hire themselves out as coolies on German-owned cotton plantations in Samoa, where missionaries in turn reported famine on outlying islands.[66] Drought in 1877 did huge economic damage throughout central Mexico, especially in Valley of Mexico itself, where the rains did not return until the summer of 1878.[67] In the circum-Mediterranean, finally, drought and famine were reported in Bosnia, as well as locusts, which also plagued farmers in Andalusia.[68]

But in the classic El Niño pattern, the climate system compensated deficit rainfall in one band of regions with surplus precipitation in another. Thus Tahiti was battered by a rare typhoon, while Northern California experienced its wettest winter in two centuries.[69] While Asia was starving, the United States was harvesting the greatest wheat crop in world history (400 million bushels), and in California's Central Valley worthless surplus wheat was burnt for fuel.[70] Meanwhile the heavy rains that inundated the southeastern United States may have contributed indirectly (through their impact on mosquito populations) to the infamous yellow fever epidemic of 1878, which ravaged cities from Louisville to New Orleans, killing tens of thousands.[71]

British and Irish farmers, already reeling from the impact of American imports and plunging prices for corn and cattle, lost one harvest after another to the cold wet summers of the late 1870s: perhaps the worst sequence since the early fourteenth century. Hundreds of thousands of laborers and marginal farmers were pushed off the land in the final extinction drama of the English yeomanry. In Ireland, the disastrous 1877–82 harvest cycle (coincident if not causally related to the El Niño droughts in the tropics) precipitated both a new wave of trans-Atlantic emigration and a decade-long agrarian revolt. Advised by the California radical prophet Henry George, Michael Davitt brilliantly channeled Irish rural distress into a "Land War" that shook the foundations of the economic as well as political Ascendancy.

Finally in coastal Peru, unprecedented rains, which continued intermittently for almost a decade, produced such an extraordinary transformation of the landscape that contemporaries believed they were witnessing either a mirage or a miracle. "The Sechura, a notoriously dry and barren desert region, became covered with trees and heavy vegetation, the likes of which were never seen before or afterward."[72] Although none of the contemporary articles or letters to *Nature* commented on this odd coincidence of epochal aridity and record rainfall in different parts of the Pacific Basin, scientists a century later would suddenly grasp that it was the crucial key to the mystery of the 1870s droughts.

The full measure of this global tragedy – *Nature* in 1878 called it "the most destructive drought the world has ever known" – can only be guessed at.[73] (Writing to a Russian correspondent about the British "bleeding" of India, Marx warned that "the famine years are pressing each other and *in dimensions* till now not yet suspected in Europe!")[74] In India, where 5.5 million to 12 million died despite modern railroads and millions of tons of grain in commercial circulation, embittered nationalist writers compared the callous policies followed by Calcutta to those emanating from Dublin Castle in 1846. The chief difference, as Indian National Congress leader Romesh Dutt later pointed out in his famous *Open Letters to Lord Curzon*, was that, instead of the 1 million Irish dead of 1846–49, "a population equal to the [whole] population of Ireland had disappeared under the desolating breath of the famine of 1877."[75]

The official British estimate of 5.5 million deaths was based on projections of "excess mortality" derived from test censuses in the Deccan and Mysore reported by the Famine Commission in 1880. It is undoubtedly too low, since it excluded any estimate of deaths in drought-afflicted native states like Hyderabad and the Central Province rajs. Nor, as Kohei Wakimura has pointed out, does it include the protracted famine mortality due to high food prices or the spike in malaria deaths (more than 3 million in 1878–79) among the immune-suppressed populations of the famine districts. "I think it likely," wrote a contemporary British official quoted by Wakimura, "that some portion of the excessive mortality, recorded during 1879, may have been due to this continuance of high prices. And especially I believe that many very poor people, who lived with difficulty during the last three years, had fallen into a low state of health which ... took away their power to recover from the attack of the fever disease prevailing so generally in the later months of the year."[76]

Adding princely India to British statistics but not counting the famine's "mortality shadow" in 1878–79, historical demographer Ira Klein concluded that at least 7.1 million had died. In his important 1984 study, Klein also compared ratios of relief to mortality (see Table 3.1). Despite Lytton's assertion that ryots were the recipients of promiscuous welfare, the vast majority of famine sufferers received no government aid whatsoever. "[A]ll over stricken India, relief reached only about a tenth of those whose lives were threatened seriously. In the parts of northern India where the crop was 'almost entirely lost' there were nearly eight famine-induced deaths for every person who received relief."[77]

Table 3.1

Parameters of the 1876–78 Famine in India

(Millions)

| Province | Affected Population | Average Number Receiving Relief | Deaths |
|---|---|---|---|
| Madras | 19.4 | .80 | 2.6 |
| Bombay | 10.0 | .30 | 1.2 |
| North Western | 18.4 | .06 | .4 |
| Mysore | 5.1 | .10 | .9 |
| Punjab | 3.5 | – | 1.7 |
| Hyderabad & Central Provinces | 1.9 | .04 | .3 |
| Total | 58.3 | 1.3 | 7.1 |

Source: Ira Klein, "When the Rains Failed," *IESHR* 21:2 (1984), pp. 199 and 209–11.

The 1878–80 Famine Commission statistics revealed a surprisingly perverse relationship between modernization and mortality that challenged British belief in "life-saving" railroads and markets. In both the Bombay and Madras Deccan, as Digby pointed out in an acerbic commentary, "the population decreased more rapidly [23%] where the districts were served by railways than where there were no railways [21%]. This is a protection against famine entirely in the wrong direction."[78] In a study of the Kurnool District, E. Rajasekhar came to a similar conclusion: "The population loss [1876–78] in areas well served with transport (such as Pattikonda) was high compared to irrigated areas (such as Sirvel and Nandyal) where though transport was ill-developed, better employment opportunities improved entitlement to food."[79] Likewise, as David Washbrook has shown in his study of Bellary, "The death-toll was heaviest in the most commercially-advanced taluks of the district (Adoni and Alur where nearly a third of the population was lost)."[80] In Madras, the mortality was overwhelmingly borne by the lower castes and the untouchables: the Boyas, Chenchus and Madas. Indeed, Rajasekhar estimates that fully half of the Madigas were wiped out in Kurnool.[81]

In the famine's epicenter in the Deccan districts of Madras Presidency, a fifth of the population perished and the demographic aftershocks, including a contraction in cultivated acreage, were felt for a generation. Rajasekhar argues that the higher mortality amongst men and boys – largely due to the Temple wage and epidemic conditions in the relief camps – left the next generation of peasants saddled with a higher, productivity-throttling ratio of dependents to producers. In Kurnool, for example, "the slow agrarian expansion in the district during the post-famine period is to be attributed not to the decline in the population per se but to changes in the age and sex composition of families of poor and small peasants, the disruption of their family life and the consequent general decline in the quality of their labour." Few of the famine survivors as a result were in any position to take advantage of the temporary recovery of agricultural prices.[74] Even as late as 1905, one settlement officer wrote, "The survivors among the ryots were impoverished, many doubtless had deteriorated physically. A new generation has grown up, but the memory of the Great Famine still lives and has increased the dull fatalism of the ryots."[75]

In addition to their hecatombs of dead, south Indians were also embittered by the exploitation of starvation to recruit huge armies of indentured coolies – over 480,000 from Madras alone between 1876 and 1879 – for semi-slave labor under brutal conditions on British plantations in Ceylon, Mauritius, Guyana and Natal.

Table 3.2
Demographic Change in Madras Famine Districts
(Percent)

|  | Bellary | Kurnool | Cuddapah |
|---|---|---|---|
| 1872–1881 | −20.34 | −25.80 | −17.03 |
| 1872–1901 | 3.89 | −4.63 | −4.41 |

Source: G. Rao and D. Rajasekhar, "Land Use Patterns and Agrarian Expansion in a Semi-Arid Region: Case of Rayalaseema in Andhra, 1886–1939," *Economic and Political Weekly* (25 June 1994), Table 3, p. A-83.

When Indian nationalists and English humanitarians pressed Lytton to oppose the export of coolies, he haughtily replied that the government was "purely neutral."[84] (During the next great drought-famine, in 1896–97, there would be similar forced migration from the Central Provinces to Assam tea plantations, and from Ganjam to Burma.)[85]

Table 3.3
China: Mortality Estimates

|  | W. W. Rockhill | A. P. Harper (1880) |
| --- | --- | --- |
| 1854–64 Taiping Rebellion | 20.0 million | 40 million |
| 1861–78 Muslim Rebellion | 1.0 million | 8 million |
| 1877–78 Famine | 9.5 million | 13 million |
| 1888 Yellow River floods | 2.0 million |  |
| 1892–94 Famine | 1.0 million |  |
| 1894–95 Muslim Rebellion | .25 million |  |
| Total | 33.7 million | 61 million |

Source: Hang-Wei He, *Drought in North China in the Early Guang Xu (1876–1879)* [in Chinese], Hong Kong 1980, p. 149.

1877 was China's driest year in two centuries, and official Chinese estimates of the death toll ranged as high as 20 million, nearly a fifth of the estimated population of north China.[86] As we have seen, the British legation in Beijing believed that 7 million had died through the winter of 1877. "The destruction as a whole," according to the 1879 *Report of the China Famine Relief Fund*, "is stated to be from nine and a half to thirteen millions," the estimate accepted by Lillian Li in her review of modern Chinese-language scholarship.[87] Hang-Wei He at Hong Kong University meanwhile has contrasted different contemporary estimates (see Table 3.3) of Taiping and famine deaths. Since overwhelmed officials were unable to keep accurate records or conduct sample censuses, it is hard to evaluate the discrepant figures in historical literature. If anything, there may be a bias toward underestimation, since the highest monthly death tolls, from a late-starting smallpox epidemic on top of malnutrition, dysentery and typhus, reportedly occurred in April and May 1879 after the famine was widely declared to have ended.[88]

The few local statistics available are extraordinary. The most reliable foreign estimates came from missionaries working in the famine epicenter of Shanxi, where Timothy Richards, who circulated questionnaires to local officials and Catholic priests, reported that one-third of the population in the north had died by 1879, and David Hill and Jasper McIlvaine estimated that a chilling three-quarters had perished in the southern counties.[89] Indeed, the famine in Taiyuan prefecture was almost an extinction event with only 5 percent of the population reported still alive in 1879. Despite heavy immigration from nearby provinces during the 1880s, Shanxi – decimated as if by modern nuclear war – did not regain its 1875 population until 1953.[90]

Table 3.4
Excess Mortality in Shanxi, 1877–79

| County | Prefamine Population | Famine Deaths | Percent Mortality |
|---|---|---|---|
| Tai Yuen | 1,000,000 | 950,000 | 95 |
| Huong Dong | 250,000 | 150,000 | 60 |
| Ping Lu | 145,000 | 110,000 | 76 |

Similarly, as Edmund Burke emphasizes, "The demographic consequences of the crisis of 1878–84 make it one of the capital events in the social history of modern Morocco."[91] Miege thinks that mortality in the ports was around 15 percent, but in much of the countryside it easily exceeded a quarter of the population. "In June 1879 the Italian consul at Tangiers estimated that a quarter of the Moroccan population had perished. This is the same percentage that Mathews presented in his report for 1878. Theodore de Cuevas, who through his many relatives in the north of the country had exceptional knowledge of local conditions, believed that one-third of the population of the Gharb was killed by the epidemic of 1878–79.[92]

Modern Brazilians still refer to the events of 1876–79 as simply the *Grande Seca*: "the greatest drama of human suffering in the nation's history."[93] Fully half of Ceará state perished and "the only transferable capital left by 1880 was in slaves."[94] "Of the dead in 1877–1879," says the Brazilian historian Edmar Morel, "it has been calculated that 150,000 died of outright starvation, 100,000 from fever and other diseases, 80,000 from smallpox and 180,000 from poisonous or otherwise harmful food."[95] It has also been characterized as "the most costly natural disaster in the history of the western hemisphere."[96]

Global mortality can only be estimated as a level of magnitude. Arup Maharatna in a recent systematic review of demographic debates and literature in both
India and China points to a combined Asian mortality range of between 20 million and 25 million famine-related deaths.[97] No greater precision seems possible.
What is certain is simply the staggering scale and worldwide synchronization of
starvation, unprecedented since the four horsemen of the apocalypse cut swathes
of famine, war, pestilence and death through Europe and China in the early fourteenth and mid seventeenth centuries.

PART II

# El Niño and the New Imperialism, 1888–1902

# Four

# The Government of Hell

Thousands of thatched-roof huts lament their empty
hearths; at each step, a cadaver, a skull, scattered bones
tell of the horror and the extent of the famine.
                                    – R. Anastase, Ethiopia in 1889

The Great Drought of the 1870s was merely Act One in a three-act world tragedy.
Millions more, likely tens of millions, would die during global El Niño droughts
in 1888–91 and especially in 1896–1902. There was first, however, a famous interlude of agricultural expansion and relative prosperity. The decade after the end
of famine in 1878–79 was characterized by well-distributed, plentiful rainfall and
abundant harvests in both hemispheres. It was the Age of Wheat.

The boom was propelled, in the first instance, by the climate crisis of the
late 1870s and the huge harvest shortfalls throughout the British Isles. "Land
under grain," writes Avner Offer of English agriculture after 1876, "contracted by
some two-thirds in thirty years, most of which reverted to rough pasture." The
resulting deficit "acted as a huge pump for the world's commerce." With British
demand for food imports soaring, massive amounts of London-generated capital
flowed into the railroads that opened up the American Great Plains, the Canadian Prairie, the Argentine pampas, and India's upper Gangetic plain. Maxim and
Gatling guns efficiently eradicated the last indigenous resistance to the incorpora-

tion of these great steppes into the world economy. By mid-decade, British red-coats had defeated Riel's utopian-socialist Northwest Rebellion in Saskatchewan and Manitoba, while the Argentine army crushed the last Indian resistance in the pampas. The grain trade under the leadership of great cartels like Bunge and Dreyfus for the first time achieved authentically global scope and integration. As thousands of square miles of virgin grassland were converted into wheat belts, the Liverpool Corn Trade Association and the Chicago Board of Trade (Wheat Exchange), with their new-fangled invention of "futures" trading, became the twin poles of a single world market in subsistence.[1]

In northern India, where railroads had recently integrated thousands of villages into international trade, these were the years of a fabled wheat export boom: a "golden age for rich peasants," if not for their poor neighbors.[2] Exporters and government officials pressed cultivators to take advantage of the good monsoons and expand wheat into areas where erratic rainfall or poor soil had previously favored only hardy millets or cattle. After the demographic catastrophe of the 1870s, officials were cheered by the population rebound of the 1880s; the Bombay government boasted that "only an utterly insignificant proportion of the population of this Presidency can be deemed [any longer] in danger of starvation."[3] In the irrigated valleys of the Tamilnad, agricultural prosperity, based on booming rice exports, produced the biggest decadal population surge (16.9 percent) of the nineteenth century.[4] A dramatic expansion of irrigation in the Irrawaddy delta likewise guaranteed rice supplies for peasants in Bengal and Java who were turning from subsistence farming to the cultivation of export crops like jute and sugarcane. The French meanwhile coerced additional rice exports from the Mekong Delta.

In North America, this was the decade of the "Great Dakota Boom" when "an unusual amount of moisture fell throughout much of the Great Plains," and what an earlier generation had seen as hopeless desert was now christened a "rain belt" by eager immigrants from northern Europe.[5] This was equally an era of wheat bonanzas and peasant expansion in the Russian steppe and the frontier farmlands of Manchuria. In Australia, meanwhile, former sheep walks were ploughed and planted in wheat varieties specially adapted to the antipodean climate. Everywhere, including the semi-arid margins of the Deccan, the *sertão* and the highveld, the wetter weather lured farmers.[6] There was widespread optimism, endorsed by leading scientists and agricultural experts, that "rain follows the plough" and that cultivation, especially by white pioneers, was permanently improving the climate.[7]

In fact, the weather "had not been cured, as the optimists claimed. It had only been in remission."[8] On five continents, Donald Meinig explains, this decade of "folk experimentation with the land" turned into one of the nineteenth century's greatest follies, resulting in "incalculable social and economic cost[s]."[9] As throughout history when intervals of above-average rainfall have allowed agriculture to expand beyond the ecological boundaries of its long-term sustainability, the inevitable manmade consequence was a drought cataclysm: as occurred in the Great Plains, India, Brazil, Russia, Korea, the Sudan and the Horn of Africa in 1888–89 and again in 1891, punctuated by extremely wet weather and flooding in many places in 1889–90. (Flooding and resulting famine had already claimed millions of lives in northern China in 1888.)

These extreme droughts and floods, we now know, correspond, although there is not necessarily a causal relation in each regional case, to powerful, clustered El Niño (1888–89 and 1891–92) and La Niña (1886–87 and 1889–90) perturbations in the eastern equatorial Pacific.[10] The new, globally integrated grain trade, moreover, ensured that climate shocks and corresponding harvest shortfalls were translated into price shocks that crossed the continents with the speed of a telegraph. A futures "corner" in Chicago or a drought in the Punjab could now starve (or enrich) people thousands of miles away. As the trend of US grain prices from 1891 onwards indicates, El Niño found a dramatic new "teleconnection" in the speculative price accelerator operated by the major boards of trade.[11]

## Drought Follows the Plow

In North America, it was the worst environmental crisis of the second half of the nineteenth century. "The wheat and land boom in Dakota," Gilbert Fite writes, "was really over by 1887, but if any life remained, it was destroyed by the terrible drought of 1889." All along the 100th meridian, from Manitoba to Texas, suddenly destitute "boomers" watched their crops wither and die under a scorching sun. Towns that once boasted of being future "Omahas" or "Topekas" lost most of their population or disappeared altogether. Hunger unexpectedly stalked the "world's breadbasket." "Conditions became so bad by the winter of 1889–1890 that many people were in dire want. In Miner County [South Dakota] where wheat and corn averaged between 2 and 3 bushels to the acre some 2500 individuals were reportedly threatened by death from starvation." Church groups that ordinarily sent contributions to relieve famine in Rajputana or Shandong mobilized instead to feed drought-stricken farm families in the Dakotas and western Kansas.[12] Across the southern border, most of Mexico (except for the Bajío) escaped hardship in 1888–89, but the strong La Niña of 1890 brought a drought – the most severe of the century – to much of the country that escalated the bitter struggle between *hacendados* and small farmers over water rights, especially in La Laguna and the North. It was a preview of the drought-fueled agrarian conflict that would help destroy the Porfiriato in 1910.[13]

In India, meanwhile, drought was severe in widely scattered parts of the subcontinent, although the total area affected was much smaller than in 1876. In Argul and the tributary states of Orissa, as well as in the neighboring Ganjam district in Madras Presidency, a failed monsoon and poor harvest were followed by a "price famine" – there was never really a true shortage of grain – that struck viciously at the pauper groups like the Pariahs, a tribal people who were prevented by new forest laws from "turning to jungle fruits and products on which they had customarily depended in the past in times of distress."[14] According to Digby, 155,000 died.[15] In 1891–92 – rated as a "very strong" El Niño year by modern meteorologists – there was a more general monsoon deficiency (ranging from 15 percent in Madras to 25 percent in Hyderabad) that affected almost every corner of India except the Central Provinces and the North Western Province. In Kurnool and Bellary (epicenters of the 1876 famine), "abnormal" deaths from hunger and the cholera that accompanied it were officially estimated at 45,000; about the same number died in several districts of Bengal and Bihar. Again the victims were the poorest of the poor.[16]

Cattle losses meanwhile through Rajputana were "enormous" and grain riots broke out in Ajmer. The Marwaris were forced to migrate en masse in search of subsistence for themselves and their animals.[17] In the neighboring Punjab, the 1891 drought was less devastating than the locust plague that it unleashed on crops in all of Peshawer, Derajat and Rawalpindi as well as some districts of Lahore. The natural destruction in turn was magnified by the operation of the world market. The Punjab had become an important shock-absorber for Britain and, to a lesser extent, continental Europe in face of poor harvests and higher prices in the US wheat belt. The coincidence of drought in North America and South Asia was particularly dangerous for poor Punjabis. Thus in spring 1891, as Navteg Singh explains:

> This enormous European demand for wheat at a higher price induced the export-ers not only to buy up old stocks largely, but also to make "forward" purchases of wheat to be supplied from the new crop at similar prices. Thus, an enormous amount of wheat was purchased at high price to be exported to Europe, resulting in a general depletion of stocks within the province. One European Company, namely, Messrs. Ralley Brothers & Co. purchased even the standing crops for the purposes of export to Europe. The local trader or *bania* as usual raised the prices of grains, thereby causing distress in almost all the districts of the Punjab.[18]

When villagers attempted to hold onto their grain, fearing that famine prices would soon exceed the export merchants' purchase price, they were in some cases beaten or coerced by agents of Ralley Brothers. On the other hand, as creditors foreclosed on farms, some smallholders chose pre-emptive violence over pauperization. A Rawalpindi paper, quoted by Singh, reported that "it has become a common practice with the *zamindars* to get rid of a creditor by murder-ing him if he presses for payments of debts." The "price famine" in the Punjab seemed to be leading to much larger clashes when heavy rainfall in October 1891 ended the drought. Although authorities learned little from the agricultural crisis of 1891, the explosive feedback between local crop conditions and world market forces was a disturbing preview of the future.[19] Census data later indicated an "excess mortality" of 3,120,000 in regions affected by the droughts of 1888–89 and 1891–92.[20] In his famous "bombshell circular" that winter, the Congress Par-ty's general secretary, Allan Octavian Hume, warned that British neglect was "pauperizing the people ... [and] preparing the way for one of the most terrible cataclysms in the history of the world." The "famine of the century" only five years down the road would tragically vindicate his prophecy.[21]

In China, where vast areas of the North had still not recovered from the 1877 catastrophe, the Yellow River had breached its new, hastily constructed dikes about twenty miles above Kaifeng and recaptured its old channel to the Yellow

Sea at the end of September 1887.[22] (The floods may have been the result of La Niña–generated rainfall anomalies, July 1886 through June 1887.)[23] Repair work was unfinished when the annual flood came earlier than usual in June 1888. According to an English civil engineer who visited the site at the end of the summer, "The breach through the dike was a full mile in width and the flood swept onward toward Hun-tze Lake and the Huai River, inundating a strip variously estimated at 20 to 50 miles in width, carrying away houses and villages and parts of walled cities." The correspondent for the *London Spectator,* struggling to convey the immensity of the disaster, picturesquely compared it to "five Danubes pouring from a height for two months on end" onto a "vast, open plain, flat as Salisbury Plain, but studded with 3000 villages, all swarming as English villages never swarm … a scene unrivaled since the Deluge." Contemporary accounts claimed that 7 million drowned or died in the ensuing famine in northern Henan and in Shandong that continued through 1889. A British consul later told the Manchester Geographical Society that "at least a million people were drowned, perhaps several millions."[24]

Korea's problem, meanwhile, was drought not flood, and the resulting food shortages were exacerbated by the export of rice under contract to Japan and the relentless fiscal pressure on the peasantry. The southern Cholla provinces – the peninsula's traditional granary but highly vulnerable to climate fluctuation – suffered especially from a "vicious circle" of rising and disproportionate revenue exactions. The region had long been a social tinderbox. "After the drought of 1888–89 in Cholla," Woo-keun Han explains, "the situation became really serious." Social banditry and violent protest became commonplace and eventually spread to other provinces:

> Farmers had turned bandit before in bad times, of course, but not to this extent. Well-armed and organized robber bands began to appear, with bases deep in the mountains, attacking shipments of tax grain and convoys of imported goods on their way to Seoul. Another result was a wave of local uprisings of various kinds, usually against corrupt officials. Miners revolted in Hamgyong and Kyongsang Provinces, and the fishermen of Cheju rebelled. There were peasant risings in almost every province, sometimes led by former officials or government slaves.[25]

The unrest in the countryside was aggravated by the growing visibility and arrogance of the foreign community. In addition to the scandal of food exports in the midst of drought and famine, fantastic rumors (common also in the Chinese countryside) circulated about ghoulish Western conspiracies. "Seeing that the Europeans had no cows yet drank milk from cans, [peasants] believed the story that the foreigners kidnaped women and cut off their breasts in order to obtain the condensed milk."[26] Like the White Lotus sects in China, the underground Tonghak ("Eastern Learning") Society – anti-Western and anti-Confucian – provided a millenarian framework for peasant resistance to intolerable taxation and foreign exploitation. In early 1894, demanding an end to rice exports to Japan and more equitable taxes, 100,000 peasant rebels under loose Tonghak leadership gained the upper hand over government troops in Cholla. Both China and Japan used the uprising as a pretext to send troops to Korea, precipitating the Sino-Japanese War, which the modernized Japanese military easily won. The tough Tonghak farmers, however, were more difficult to defeat, and even after a systematic extermination of their civilian base in Cholla province, embers of the revolt (regrouped in the Chondogyo or "Heavenly Way" movement) remained to trouble the Japanese for many years.[27]

In Russia, poor harvests during the dry years of 1888–90 were prelude to the catastrophic drought in spring and summer of 1891 that brought famine to the black soil provinces of the Volga valley as well as the Orenburg wheat-belt south of the Urals (epicenter of drought during the 1997–98 El Niño). Seventy percent of the rye crop, the chief subsistence of the muzhiks, was lost. As was so frequently the case in India, the tax collector had previously stripped peasant households of any savings in money or grain. Still staggering under the financial burden of their redemption payments from serfdom, peasants in 1891 also struggled to cope with the punitive tax offensive, launched in 1887 by finance minister Vyshnegradskii, that aimed to force them to export more grain. (*"Nedoedim no vyvezem* – We may not eat enough, but we will export" was the official slogan.) As a result, a majority of rural communes (*obshchinas*) were essentially insolvent, and "even before the disastrous harvest of 1891," writes Richard Robbins, "many of the signs associated with famine had begun to appear." Local priests, *zemstvo* physicians and visiting scientists had all warned of appalling poverty and widespread near-starvation.[28]

Now, in the grim winter of 1891–92, more than 12 million peasants, having already sold their cattle and horses, were forced to burn the thatched roofs of their huts for heat and bake almost nutrition-less "famine bread" from goose-foot and other wild herbs. Reports reached Moscow of "mothers attempting to murder their children in order to spare them the pain of hunger." Unlike British India a few years later, however, the government of the soon-to-be-assassinated Czar Alexander III was able to prevent outright starvation. Although there was widespread criticism of the incompetence of zemstvo institutions, the disorganization of public-works initiatives, and the additional financial burden of the loans forced on the peasantry, the official relief campaign succeeded in keeping the death rate in the affected provinces from increasing more than a single percentage point (from 3.76 percent in 1881–90 to 4.81 percent in 1892). By contrast, much vaunted British efforts during the famines of 1896–97 and 1899–1900 were accompanied by mortality spikes of 20 percent or higher. Most of the 400,000 to 600,000 victims in European Russia were killed by typhus and cholera spread by famine refugees rather than by starvation per se.[29]

In southern Africa the 1888–89 drought forced tens of thousands of farmers from their land, a tragedy that was welcomed as a godsend by European planters vexed by persistent labor shortages. Thus in 1889 John Peter Hornung wrote to his brother (the future bestselling author of *Raffles*) about the windfall of desperate drought refugees from outside the district that were allowing him to proceed on schedule with the poppy harvest on his new opium plantation in Mozambique. Hornung, a leading *narcotraficante* of late Victorian times, managed the so-called Mozambique Produce Company for Jardine Mathieson, the giant Hong Kong firm "whose existence was historically wedded to the sale of opium to the Chinese."[30]

Brazil's "Drought of the Two Eights" (1888), as it is still remembered in the Nordeste, began as early as January 1887, when sowing was delayed due to the failure of the rains.[31] Weak thunderstorms partially broke the drought, but it returned with a vengeance in 1888, then abated only to resume with new intensity in 1891. "The circumstances," writes one historian, "were not unlike those of the devastating years of 1877–1879." As crops failed and herds died, *sertanejos* again asked themselves, like the protagonist in the Graciliano Ramos novel, "could [they] go on living in a cemetery?"[32] In Ceará alone, 150,000 said no.[33]

While some headed directly for Fortaleza and hence Para and Amazonas, others clustered around interior river towns and oases. In one of these famine refuges, the small town of Joãseiro in Ceará's Cariri Valley, a small miracle took place whose full importance for the history of northeast Brazil would not become apparent until a second wave of drought, hunger and rebellion in the later 1890s. Maria de Araujo, a 28-year-old laundress and *beata* (lay nun) in the household of charismatic local priest Cícero Ramão Batista, was attending a special mass to invoke the power of the Sacred Heart of Jesus against the drought when her communion host suddenly turned the color of blood. For weeks, the transubstantiation repeated itself before ever growing crowds. Finally, on the feast day of the Precious Blood in July 1889, Monsignor Monteiro, Cícero's patron and another fiery millenialist, led a procession of 3,000 people to Joãseiro's little chapel of Our Lady of Sorrows:

> Before an overflowing assembly, Monteiro mounted the pulpit and delivered a sermon on the mystery of Christ's passion and death that reportedly brought tears to the eyes of his listeners; then he dramatically thrust aloft a fistful of altar linens which were visibly stained with blood; that blood, he declared, had issued from the host received by Maria de Araujo, and it was, according to the Rector, the very blood of Jesus Christ.[34]

## Ethiopia: The 'Cruel Days'

Meanwhile, in the ancient Christian kingdom of Ethiopia, desperate prayers went unanswered and there were no sudden miracles. Few regions have ever endured such a literally biblical declension of disaster – still known as the *Yakefu Qan* or "Cruel Days" – as did the Horn of Africa beginning in 1888.[35] The protracted drought that began in late 1888 and lasted until 1892 (almost certainly linked to the back-to-back El Niños) was accompanied by rinderpest, a cattle plague or murrain, that quickly killed off 90 percent of domestic and wild ruminants in the Horn of Africa before spreading south through the Rift Valley.[36] Five hundred years before, in the famine-stricken decades of the early fourteenth-century, rinderpest had wiped out much of the livestock base of feudal agriculture in Western Europe. The catastrophic symptoms of the epidemic closely resembled cholera in humans:

It was a terribly devastating disease, which ran its course in an infected animal over a period of a week or so. The animal initially manifests discharges around the nose, mouth, and eyes; these early symptoms (which sometimes are not conspicuous) are succeeded by astonishing stench, recurrent debilitating and explosive diarrhea (with subsequent dehydration), and, perhaps most arresting, tenesmus – the painful struggle of the beast to defecate even when nothing remains to be voided. Death is followed by very rapid putrefaction.[37]

The swiftness with which rinderpest decimated herds was indeed extraordinary. "Alaqa Lamma Haylu, a young man traveling through Gojjam at the time, recalled awakening from an intense fever and finding all the cattle dead."[38] European missionaries described herds of a thousand or more cattle reduced to one or two scrawny survivors. Emperor Menelik II was said to have lost 250,000 head. Without their sturdy plough oxen, highland farmers were reduced to scraping at the soil with sticks, while strictly pastoral people, like the Galla, were "utterly destroyed." The origins of the outbreak have been traced to infected cattle imported from India as part of the provision for an Italian army invading Eritrea under General San Marzano. "Many Ethiopians," writes Richard Pankhurst, who interviewed survivors of this period in the 1960s, "knowing of Italian ambitions in the country, believed that the disease had in fact been spread deliberately."[39]

Drought and the blast-furnace heat that accompanied it only intensified the deadly murrain. "Cattle and wildlife were concentrated at the few remaining waterholes, thus creating perfect conditions for the spread of the rinderpest virus."[40] At the same time, the scorched fields of the peasantry were overrun by successive invasions of caterpillars (army worms), locusts and rats. Contemporary accounts by European travelers and missionaries, surveyed by Pankhurst, emphasize the terrible swiftness with which verdant landscapes were transformed into bleak wastes. What had been "very beautiful fields of durra and barley, numerous herds of cattle, sheep and goats" were stripped down to skeletons of sand and rock: "absolutely a desert; no more inhabitants, no more cultivation, no more flocks."[41]

In Ethiopia's highlands, rinderpest and the other plagues struck at a society whose pillar was the ox. The farmers who struggled with the heavy, rocky soils of Wallo and Tigray were every bit as dependent upon their cattle as any pastoral people. "Evidence in written and oral form," explains James McCann, "plus contemporary studies of rural conditions in the area, indicate that for northern Wallo as a whole (and probably the entire northeast as well), the scarce unit of production was neither land nor labor but capital in the form of plow oxen. Far more than the acquisition of land – which was readily available to the vast majority of households – the breeding, buying, borrowing, and maintaining of oxen determined household strategies of land and labor allocation, affected cropping decisions, and cemented vertical patterns of dependency and stratification within the producing classes." Oxen, in other words, were simultaneously a means of production, store of wealth and symbol of social rank. Their decimation brought rapid social collapse.[42]

Without animal traction, moreover, the peasantry was unable to resume cultivation when the rains briefly returned in June 1889. Some farmers, to be sure, tried to work their fields with iron-tipped hoes, but the yields were only fractions of what they had produced two years earlier with plough oxen. Simultaneously at war with Sudanese Mahdists, Tigrean secessionists and (a little later) Italian invaders, Ethiopia had almost no wherewithal to import food. Although the new emperor, Menelik II (crowned in November 1889 after Emperor Yohannes was killed in battle with the Mahdists), promptly opened his granaries to his subjects and turned his soldiers to farming, the imperial supplies were quickly exhausted. When Menelik tried to import grain, "the caravans were pillaged going through Somali and Danakil country where the people were also starving."[43] The consequence was a radical shortage of food and livestock that threatened even the survival of the rich. Prices – to the extent that they retained any meaning – increased a hundredfold or more. Table 4.1 is constructed from contemporary

Table 4.1
Ethiopia: Famine and Price Ratios

|  | 1889 Price:Quantity | 1890 Price:Quantity |
|---|---|---|
| Wheat | 1:200 | 1:1.5 |
| Barley | 1:400 | 1:2 |
| Plough oxen | 2.4:1 | 80:1 |
| Cattle | 1:1 | 60:1 |

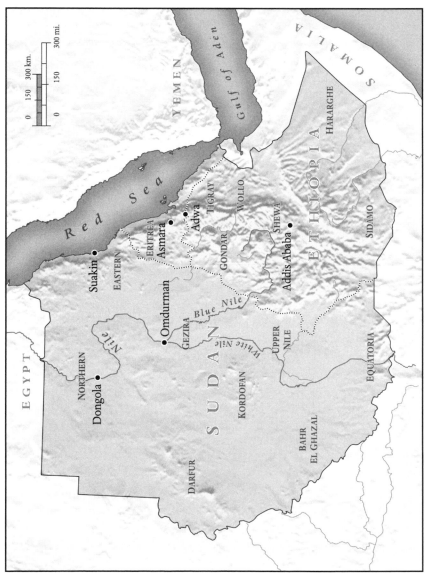

Figure 4.1 The Horn of Africa and Sudan

reports of the Russian explorer Mashkov and shows famine-driven inflation at its most extreme.[44]

Menelik's most recent biographer, Harold Marcus, emphasizes the fundamentally incomprehensible character of so many simultaneous disasters. "Populace, clergy, and *makwanent*," he writes, "were mystified and bewildered by the catastrophe engulfing them, and attributed their troubles to a lack of piety." Accordingly, Menelik (whom Marcus depicts as anything but a fatalist) issued a despairing proclamation at the end of July 1889 which blamed drought and plague on lack of prayer. "When the animal epidemic was starting, I made a proclamation, saying 'Pray to God.' The animals are … all dead … all this has happened because we have not prayed enough. Now the epidemic is turning to people and has begun to destroy them." Marcus asserts that "millions of people died" in the ensuing two years, and that the famine permanently reconfigured Ethiopia's regional hierarchy, shifting power from Yohannes' Tigreans to Menelik's Shewans. The once-powerful economies of Begemder (where an astounding 75 percent of the population was said to have perished or fled) and Gojjam were disabled, and the desperate efforts of Ras Alula – Menelik's chief competitor for the throne – to preserve Tigrean hegemony were undercut by lack of provisions.[45] "Feeding a small army even for a very short time was soon to become impossible in the shattered Tigre."[46]

When nobles and warriors went hungry, the rural poor of course died en masse. The French priest Coulbeaux, writing in March 1890 from Keren, reported that "everywhere I meet walking skeletons and even horrible corpses, half eaten by hyenas." A British consular agent on the Somali Coast complained of the "heart-rending cries and lamentations" of the starving that kept him awake each night. One Italian traveler described the great Tigran trade hub of Adwa as simply a "cemetery," while another found children frantically searching the dung of mules and camel for kernels of grain. "Horrified I turned away," he wrote, "only to see other boys whom the *zapte* [police] are driving away by force from the carcass of a horse, the stinking leftover of the hyenas, from this carcass they snatch, biting with their teeth at the entrails – the entrails because they are softer, softer because they are the most putrid." Famished people also "disputed the prey of vultures, hyenas, jackals, and pie-dogs," while others sold themselves to Muslim slave-dealers. Worst was the famine-induced insanity and cannibalism.

Ethiopian writers would terrify later generations with stories of mothers cooking and eating their children. Even in the extremes of starvation, however, Ethiopians retained a gallows sense of humor. A popular song, supposedly based on the true story of a man who killed and ate his spouse, was called "His Wife Gave Him Indigestion."[47]

Nature was perceived as radically disordered in other ways as well. One of the strangest and most horrifying aspects of the catastrophe was the utter boldness with which wild animals, crazed with hunger and thirst, attacked the weakened human population. "Contemporary accounts describe the country as swarming with animals and birds of prey who had lost all their fear. Old people of Tigray such as Abba Jerome and Wayzaro Sangal say it was common at night to hear the cry or groan *wasadanni* ('it is taking me away, away!') uttered by famine-enfeebled victims, often old men and women, as the hyenas carried them off to eat." From every corner of the country – the Shewan highlands, Karan, Harar, and so on – missionaries and local officials reported that the wild beasts "reigned supreme." In Begemder, for example, "lions, leopards, etc., have taken the upper hand and attack and eat human beings in broad daylight"; while at Burka, "leopards, jackals and lions attacked [the inhabitants] as far as their villages and ate large numbers of them."[48]

Human predation also increased. Ethiopia's feudal system, despite Menelik's energetic efforts, threatened to decompose into a Hobbesian war of the strong against the weak. Hunger became so acute that provincial governors and their warrior levies abandoned administrative responsibilities to forage as marauding bands. Pankhurst cites, for example, the case of Dajazmach Walda Gabreel, "the governor of the Charchar area, southwest of Harar, [who] had been obliged to abandon his province; in order to live he and his soldiers had gone to raid Arussi which was still well supplied with grain and had for that reason already been pillaged by the troops of Ras Makonnen [governor of Hararghe] and later by those of the incumbent governor Ras Darge."[49] Governor Makonnen, meanwhile, raided deep into the Ogaden, where he fortified water holes and garrisoned them with nomadic Somali allies (thus establishing an Ethiopian claim to the Ogaden that would be invoked in the bitter border war of 1977).[50] The Ethiopian invasion on top of the drought did vast damage to Somali society. An Englishman who visited the Ogaden a few years later "marched for over seven hours south across a desert that had once been covered with corn. Traces of irrigation were to be seen everywhere and many deserted villages. This was, ten years ago, the greatest grain-producing district in the country, the inhabitants supplying ... Somaliland with corn."[51]

A famished peasantry that was easy prey for hyenas and robbers, of course, was equally a lush target for epidemic disease. Dysentery, smallpox, typhus and influenza killed tens of thousands, while the great raiding parties sent by Menelik to the Ogaden to bring back cattle for his farmers also returned with cholera. It was conservatively estimated by Dr. R. Wurtz, a French physician who arrived in 1897 to conduct pioneering studies of the country's public health, that one-third of the population of Ethiopia, and perhaps of the entire Horn region, perished by 1892. Mortality, of course, was much higher in certain regions. In the pastoral Galla south, for example, Wurtz and other foreign observers estimated that somewhere between two-thirds and four-fifths of the population had disappeared. Vast tracts of once arable highlands, as well as semi-arid grassland, were desolate and abandoned.[52] Meanwhile, a second wave of drought (correlated to the powerful El Niño of 1891) revived famine and epidemic through 1892, just as Ethiopia was moving closer to all-out war with Italy.[53]

## Famine Defeats the Mahdists

The drought and low Nile of 1888 was equally devastating to the central and northern Sudan, where famine unhinged the great design of the Mahdists for a jihad against Egypt. In April 1887, the Mahdi's successor, the Khalifa Abdullahi, had sent messengers to Wadi Halfa in upper Egypt bearing letters "summoning the Khedive Muhammad Tawfiq, Queen Victoria, and Sultan 'Abd al-Hamid to submit to the Mahdia." When Buckingham Palace and the Sublime Porte refused, a large army was concentrated at Dongola in Nubia under the al-Nujumi, the most talented of the Mahdia's generals. Even before the failure of the annual flood, the thousands of warriors, their camp followers and horses had overwhelmed the scant food resources of the local riverine tribes, who became so starved, according to one account, that "they stole the Dervishes' sheepskins, on which they prayed, and ate them."[54] With grain suddenly scarce everywhere along the Nile, al-Nujumi was ordered to march on Egypt without waiting for reinforcements from the south. The Khalifa reassured his followers that the Egyptians would welcome them as liberators, and sent along a "final set of warnings to the khedive, Queen Victoria and the British agent in Cairo. Accompanying these were a number of documents proving the recent Mahdist victory over King John [Yohannes of Ethiopia]."[55]

But the hungry fellahin of upper Egypt, their own crops dying in the fields for lack of water, provided little succor to the Mahdist army whose advance on empty stomachs "was being made a terrible cost." Al-Nujumi's holy army was already half-dead from hunger went it finally collided with the well-fed Egyptian levies of General Grenfell at Tushki in August 1889. The annihilation of Mahdists on the battlefield was followed by a desperate exodus of the starving population of northern Sudan, who left a trail of skeletons along the sad road to Egypt.[56]

In the following year, famine – exploited with cruel genius by another British general, Kitchener – also wrecked Mahdist plans to overrun the Egyptian garrisons at Kossier and Suakin along the Red Sea. Previously, writes Holt, "trade with the local tribes was proceeding through Suakin and the import of grain was to some extent alleviating the hardships caused by the famines. The military authorities were strongly opposed to this policy, since it amounted to feeding the enemy. The political authorities thought differently, since it was desired to win over the support of tribes who were not fully committed to the Mahdia." In the event, Kitchener simply ignored his civilian superiors and cut off the food supply to eastern Sudan. The tribes starved and Kitchener won easy fame defeating the remnant of the jihad at Tukar in February 1890.[57]

In Darfur, a vast region the size of France in the western Sudan, the famine was also "possibly the worst ever," but Alexander De Waal principally blames civil war and Omdurman's grain requisitioning. "At one point there were more than 36,000 Mahdist troops in El Fahser, and when on campaign they 'ate, drank, wore or stole' everything there was. In western Darfur the armies are remembered as having 'eaten' the villages." The devastation was so complete that one of the rebel leaders referred to his country as simply "a heap of ruins."[58]

Meanwhile unspeakable scenes were being enacted in the great, bloated Mahdist capital. According to the captive Austrian priest Ohrwalder, "All the principal towns and villages on the Blue Nile as far south as Karkoj have been destroyed, such as Kemlin, Messalamieh, Wad Medina, Abu Haraz, Wad el Abbas and Rufaa; the inhabitants of all these towns, men, women, and children, under great fatigue, had come to Omdurman, where they sheltered in the north of the town near Khor Shambat."[59] They came believing that the Mahdia, which was importing grain from Fashoda in the south, would protect all equally against starvation. In fact, the Khalifa was transforming Omdurman into a murderous tribal dictatorship.

"The onset of the famine," Holt explains, "had occurred at a particularly critical time since it coincided with the migration of the Ta'aisha [the Khalifa's tribe] to Omdurman. The provisioning of their multitudes as they passed through Kordofan was a serious problem and when they reached Omdurman they were supplied with grain at preferential rates. The situation in Omdurman was aggravated by the influx of distressed provincials who fled from the famine in their villages only to starve in the capital." The military defeat of the Egyptian jihad was now redoubled by the moral defeat of Mahdists' claim to represent an incorruptible, egalitarian community of belief. When the courageous, non-Ta'aisha commissioner of the treasury, Ibrahim Muhammad 'Adlan, attempted to "shield the poor from the exactions required by the overgrown military caste," refusing to provision the Ta'aisha at all cost, he was promptly hung by the Khalifa. The Mahdia was becoming a "government of hell."[60]

Another of the Khalifa's prisoners, the Italian priest Rosignoli, recounted the gruesome and unequal struggle for survival in Omdurman in 1888–89:

> Omdurman became a stage on which horrible scenes took place. The Mahdists had insulted the besieged Egyptians in El Obeid for eating dogs, donkeys, leather and other filth. Now they were forced to go even further; they ate their own children.

> The rich were able to save themselves by buying up in time stocks of *dura,* but for the poor there was no escape. From 60 lire per ardeh the price rose to 250. The emaciated crowds with besotted eyes that I have seen in the streets of El Obeid during the siege, I saw once more in even greater numbers. There were large mobs searching for anything merely to prolong their lives. The streets were full of dead bodies and there was no one to throw the corpses into the Nile or even to take them to the area selected by the Khalifa to be the cemetery. Today there are piles of whitened bones being the remains of those who died during the famine. Hyenas finding such an abundance of food convened in large numbers and became so daring that they wandered through the streets of the city....

Children ran the risk of being kidnapped. One night we succeeded wrenching from the hands of a starving man, a boy who had raised the alarm by his desperate screams. On another occasion a girl ran to the *Mahkama* begging protection from her mother who had already devoured the smallest of her sons and had told the girl that this was to be her fate. The wretched woman was imprisoned and died insane a few days later. Mothers came to us offering their infants as their dried up breasts could offer them no substance. One day a woman came to Father Ohrwalder begging that he buy hers. He gave the woman some handfuls of *dura* and sent her away with God's blessings. The next day she reappeared with only two children, one having died of hunger. On the third day she was accompanied by one only. She was never seen again.[61]

Another witness, Rudolf von Slatin, who served the Khalifa in various capacities, wrote that "the majority of those who died belonged rather to the moving population than to the actual inhabitants of the town, for the latter had managed to secret a certain amount of grain and the different tribes invariably assisted each other."[62] Like Father Rosignoli, he titilated European readers with lurid accounts of darwinian spectacles in the streets of the Mahdi's starving capital:

One night – it was full moon – I was going home at about twelve o'clock, when, near the Beit el Amana (ammunition and arms stores), I saw something moving on the ground, and went near to see what it was. As I approached I saw three almost naked women, with their long tangled hair hanging about their shoulders; they were squatting round a quite young donkey, which was lying on the ground, and had probably strayed from its mother, or been stolen by them. They had torn open its body with their teeth, and were devouring its intestines, whilst the poor animal was still breathing. I shuddered at this terrible sight, whilst the poor women, infuriated by hunger, gazed at me like maniacs. The beggars by whom I was followed now fell upon them, and attempted to wrest from them their prey; and I fled from this uncanny spectacle.[63]

Conditions outside Omdurman in the Nilotic countryside, if contemporary witnesses are to be believed, were even more appalling. "I think the Jaalin," wrote von Slatin, "who are the most independent as well as the proudest tribe in the Sudan, suffered more severely than the rest; several fathers of families, seeing that escape from death was impossible, bricked up the doors of their houses, and, united with their children, patiently awaited death. I have no hesitation in saying that in this way entire villages died out." In addition, he added, "The Hassania,

Shukria, Aggalain, Hammada, and other tribes had completely died out, and the once thickly-populated country had become a desert waste."[64] Father Rosignoli likewise reckoned that the toll from famine and disease was nearly incalculable: "Many tribes have disappeared from the face of the Earth." Refugees told him terrifying stories, comparable to accounts from Ethiopia, of starving humans turned into the prey of wild animals. "Since the number of men formerly hunting them has diminished, the number of wild beasts has increased a hundred-fold. They have become so fearless that they enter villages in large numbers to devour the children and the sick, that is those unable to defend themselves against the horrible invaders."[65]

Comparable tales also were being told in the savannas of western Africa, where the drought-famine, as in the Sudan, was known as "Year Six" (*Sanat Sita*) because it began in the year 1306 (1888) of the Muslim calendar. According to Catherine Coquery-Vidrovitch, there was a great famine in Walata along the bend of the Niger River, in 1888–89 that took the lives of thousands of captives and slaves. Starvation was also reported in Katsina and Kano.[66] The major bloc of independent and militarily formidable societies remaining in Africa – the Muslim states of the Sahel/Sudan and the Christian Kingdom of Ethiopia – were suddenly rendered vulnerable by drought, famine and internal disorder. As the threat of Mahdist expansionism abated, the European powers grasped at the opportunity to turn the crisis to their own colonial advantage.

From their toehold on the Eritrean coast, the land-hungry Italians (encouraged by the British as a check on French ambitions in the Red Sea region) were the first to act. "The Colony of Eritrea," wrote a contemporary Italian commission, "is able to serve in the future as the vent of part of Italian emigration." Invoking "famine abandoned lands" as a pretext, they occupied Asmara in the summer of 1889 as staging area for the colonization of the drought-ravaged Eritrean highlands and the Tigray plateau. The rest of Ethiopia, meanwhile, was declared under the "protection" of Rome. (Menelik famously responded: "Ethiopia has need of no one; she stretches out her hands to God alone.")[67] Deprived by rinderpest of horses for his famous cavalry, and lacking provisions to sustain a large army on the march, Menelik (who had utilized Italian support to wrest his throne from the Tigreans) was initially forced to give way before the Italian columns. The fiery Empress Taitou, "who came close to accusing her husband of treason," exhorted him to defend Ethiopia's sovereignty at all costs.[68] With astonishing patience and skill (as well as French arms), he eventually rallied his stricken but valiant people to annihilate a large Italian expeditionary corps at Adwa on 1 March 1896. It was Europe's greatest defeat in Africa and the end of Prime Minister Francesco Crespi's dream of a "second Roman Empire" in the Land of the Queen of Sheba and Prester John.

## Fin de Siècle Apocalypse?

Ethiopians had little opportunity to celebrate, however. While Menelik's victorious army was marching back to Addis Ababa, drought was again – for the third time in less than a decade – fastening its grip on the Horn of Africa.[69] It was a global curse. "The period 1895–1902," Sir John Elliot told the British Association for the Advancement of Science in 1904, "was characterized by more or less persistent deficiency of rainfall over practically the whole Indo-oceanic area (including Abyssinia)."[70] More recently, a leading historian of the world grain trade has emphasized the extraordinary synchronization of crop failure across six continents:

[T]he years 1896 and 1897 were characterized by abnormally bad weather throughout widely dispersed wheat-producing areas. World yield per acre (12.1 bushels) for the 1897 crop remains the lowest ever recorded. Thus there was drought in 1896 in India, Australia, the winter-wheat belt of the United States, and North Africa, while locusts and late rains reduced Argentine yields. But weather was worse in 1897; the rainfall distribution in the principal wheat-producing areas was most abnormal. Drought occurred in India, Australia, southern Russia, Spain, and North Africa; France had excessive rain at seeding time. Heavy rains and storms during May and June reduced yields in the Danube Basin. Argentina had locusts, drought, frosts in November, and rains at harvest. In Canada there were summer frosts, late heavy rains, and even hail in some areas.... Of all the important exporters, only the United States had a good crop.[71]

Other cereals were equally affected, and a third wave of drought and famine, comparable in magnitude to the 1876–79 catastrophe, swept over India, northern China, Korea, Java, the Philippines, northeast Brazil, and southern and eastern Africa. Hunger also stalked the Upper Nile, where famished peasants ate dirt; southern Russia, where Tolstoy wrote about the despair of the muzhiks in the face of drought and oppression; Italy, where the soaring price of flour led to the century's bloodiest bread riots; and Australia, which lost half of its sheep in the worst drought in its modern history.[72] We now know that an extraordinary clustering of El Niño events – 1896/97, 1899/1900 and 1902 – was largely responsible for this global agricultural catastrophe. The wet intermission of 1898, perhaps the nineteenth century's most powerful La Niña, brought its own horror in the form of devastating floods in the basin of the Yellow River. Perhaps one quarter of the earth's population, mostly in what would become known as the "third world," was directly affected by ENSO-related dearth.

Indeed, the century's end became a radical point of division in the experience of humanity. For Europeans and their North American cousins, as David Landes has written, "the wheel turned" in 1896 and the depression that had started with the Panic of 1893 was replaced by a new boom. "As business improved, confidence returned – not the spotty, evanescent confidence of the brief booms that had punctuated the gloom of the preceding decades, but a general euphoria such as had not prevailed since ... the early 1870s. Everything seemed right again – in spite of rattlings of arms and monitory Marxist references to the 'last stage' of capitalism. In all of western Europe, these years [1896–1914] live on in memory as the good old days – the Edwardian era, *la belle epoque*."[73]

For most non-Europeans (Japanese and southern cone Latin Americans excepted), on the other hand, this was a new dark age of colonial war, indentured labor, concentration camps, genocide, forced migration, famine and disease. The epidemic-disease dimension of famine was much more lethal than in the 1870s. In Asia, for example, the new subsistence crises coincided with the Third Plague Pandemic that eventually killed more than 15 million people, while the rinderpest catastrophe (which also affected the East Indies) destroyed the economic foundations of traditional society throughout eastern and southern Africa. As health and longevity standards dramatically rose in the industrial cities of Europe and North America, they were collapsing throughout Africa and Asia. This vast human crisis, moreover, was aggressively exploited by the New Imperialism and its Christian counterpart. "Europeans," one African told a missionary, "track famine like a sky full of vultures."

As a result, the fin de siècle in the non-European world careened toward the apocalyptic, with an explosion of millenarian revelations, uprisings and messiahs. Everywhere desperate cultures set their calendars to End Time. Many Muslims, for example, believed that the conclusion of the thirteenth Koranic century (1785–1882) would be promptly followed by the end of the world.[74] In India it was widely expected that the month of Kartik in the Sambat year 1956 (November 1899) would "initiate an age of affliction and catastrophe for India and the world."[75] Similarly in north China, insurgent peasants embraced the White Lotus sect's prediction of an approaching world calamity, associated with the turning of a Buddhist *kalpa,* which "meant the elimination of existing society and the coming to power of the Eternal Mother."[76] Most Chinese also believed that the year 1900, because of "the fateful conjunction of an eighth intercalary month with the *gengzi* year of the lunar calendar" (the first since 1680), was destined to bring cataclysmic social disorder (which, of course, is what happened).[77] Throughout the sertão, moreover, dissident Sebastianist priests and lay *beatos* were identifying the new Brazilian Republic with the reign of the Anti-Christ and the advent of the Last Days.[78]

Not surprisingly, as Charles Ambler writes of Kenya in 1897, "people saw a connection between the disaster of drought, famine, and disease on the one hand, and the advance of European economic and political power on the other." Whether among the Ndebele insurgents of the Mwari cult in Zimbabwe, the Maji-Maji fighters (after 1904) in German East Africa, the Tawara followers of Kanowanga in Mozambique, the "Ethiopianist" churches in the Rand, the *conselheiristas* in northeast Brazil (victims of internal colonialism), the anti-French *phumibun* movement of Ong Man in Laos, the messianic Papa Isio guerrillas in Negros, the adherents of the Madhi (Kasan Mukmin) in Java, or the Boxers United in Righteousness outside the gates of Beijing – there was a pervasive belief that natural disaster was "the most immediate and punishing element of a larger social and cosmological crisis ... a terrible symbol of the advent of colonialism."[79] "It was an age of anxiety," John Lonsdale adds, "of sudden witchcraft panics, a time when the politics of survival seemed to demand desperate tyrannies."[80] Some Europeans, to be sure, were almost as apprehensive. If Kipling's verse exalted colonizing optimism and scientific racism, Conrad's troubling stories warned that Europe itself was being barbarized by its complicity in secret tropical holocausts. *La belle epoque,* in his view, was dangerously downriver of the Apocalypse.

# Five

# Skeletons at the Feast

> I am firmly convinced that in India we are working up to a hideous economical catastrophe, beside which the great Irish Famine of 1847 will seem mere child's play.
>
> — H. M. Hyndman, 1886

India's rulers, of course, had no premonition that Victoria's Diamond Jubilee (1897) would be celebrated in carnage: "the saddest year in its accumulation of calamities since the time that India passed from the hands of the East India Company to the Crown," as Romesh Chunder Dutt would later tell the Indian National Congress.[1] Instead, as the subcontinent anticipated the monsoon of 1896, there was smug confidence (the recent deaths in Orissa notwithstanding) that famine mortality on the scale of 1876 was no longer possible. Thanks to the 1880 report of Sir Richard Strachey's Commission, there were now regional famine codes that instructed the organization of local relief and provided new controls (registration within subdistrict "famine circles") over panic-driven population movements like those that had so alarmed the government twenty years earlier. Moreover, a Famine Relief and Insurance Fund had been established in 1878 to ensure that Calcutta could finance relief during major droughts and floods without fiscal risk to its other priorities, especially the permanent military campaign along its northwestern frontier.

In addition, wrote a contemporary economist, "the historic conditions controlling production and distribution ... had been revolutionised."[2] The integration of Burma's huge rice surpluses into the imperial system, along with the
10,000 miles of new railroad track (much of it financed by the Famine Fund),
were heralded as providing the rural population with a decisive margin of food
security.[3] "Famine in the original sense of the word, that is to say as a result of
a lack of food, has become impossible. In case of shortfalls, Burma feeds the
Punjab and the North Western Provinces or vice versa; Madras comes to the
aid of Bombay or the other way around."[4] As Lord Elgin reassured Queen Victoria: "The improvement of the means of communications particularly by railway
makes it possible to cope with scarcity now in a way that was out of the power of
the officers of former days."[5]

In the event, these improvements were all but meaningless. Even his worst
enemies marveled at Lord Elgin's singlemindedness in following Lytton's path to
exactly the same calamitous destination.[6] A severely deficient monsoon prevented
the sowing of the spring 1896 crop throughout the Punjab, North Western Provinces, Oudh, Bihar and the Madras Deccan. The failure of the rains was even
more devastating in the Central Provinces and eastern Rajputana (Rajasthan),
where three years of bad weather and poor harvests had already immiserated the
peasantry. Throughout India grain prices rose, then skyrocketed after the autumn
monsoon likewise failed. Grain reserves, especially in the wheat belt of northern
India, had been depleted by massive exports to make up the previous year's terrible harvest in England.[7] Meanwhile Elgin's "revolutionary" improvements in
distribution simply ensured that prices were as high in districts unaffected by the
drought (like the well-watered Godavari delta in Madras) as in those where most
of the crop had failed.[8]

The mere existence of railroads, moreover, could not bring grain into districts
where mass purchasing power was insufficient. British officials, with their doctrinaire faith in market rationality, were startled to see the price of millet and other
"poverty grains" surpass that of the milled wheat used in European bread.[9] As
for the vaunted Famine Fund, a substantial portion had been diverted against
the protests of Indians to pay for yet another vicious Afghan war. (At the inaugu-
ral meeting in London of a campaign for Indian famine relief in January 1897,
the socialist leader Henry Hyndman was pulled off the dais by police when he

proposed that "home charges for the current year should be suspended and the whole amount be devoted to expenditure on famine relief.")[10]

The government, moreover, had categorically discounted warnings from Indian nationalists as well as their own health officers about the ever-increasing population of poor people vulnerable to any sharp increase in food prices. Malnutrition, critics believed, had reached epic levels unprecedented in Indian history. The Dufferin Enquiry in 1887 had shown that "forty million of the poor go through life on insufficient food" and "half of our agricultural population never know from year's end to year's end what it is to have their hunger fully satisfied."[11] Five years later in his famous "bombshell" circular to the Indian National Congress, Allen Octavian Hume lamented that poverty was "swallowing up our lower classes like a rising swamp, it is deepening, widening, blackening.... "[12] William Wedderburn, John Bright's old friend and sometime leader of the Parliamentary Opposition on India, lobbied an apathetic House of Commons to undertake a major enquiry into Indian poverty before famine again decimated the subcontinent.[13] But the India Office in 1896 was no more eager than in 1876 to face the "nightmare" of poor relief in India. The *Spectator,* denouncing Hume, Wedderburn and the "baboos," warned its readers that "if India were as with England and had the same Poor-law, there would be eighty millions of paupers in receipt of relief."[14]

## 'Government Charnel Houses' (1896–97)

High prices, meanwhile, were rapidly turning drought into famine. Acute distress was already visible in the North Western and Central Provinces in August 1896; by October, the police were opening fire on grain looters in Bihar and the Bombay Deccan. The *New York Times* published a letter written in October from the American Board missionary R. Hume in Ahmednagar. Pointing out that the drought was much more widespread than in 1877, Hume despaired that "for two days my servants tried in vain to buy 50 cents' worth of grain for use." With "no more rain ... likely to fall for eight full months," the next possible harvest was nearly a year away, and thus Hume was not surprised at the desperation of his normally "quiet, orderly" neighbors.

> Already grain riots are common. Grain merchants will not sell grain, largely because they know the price will greatly increase, though even now prices are 300 per cent. above normal. So people break open grain shops and granaries, and threaten to kill the merchants if they interfere. They say: 'We shall have soon to die without grain. If you interfere with our getting your grain, and we kill you in the struggle, it will be all the same.' Similarly, these people say to the police and courts: 'Arrest us for stealing and support us in jail. There we shall not die from starvation.'[15]

At nearby Narsinghpur, the American missionary Margaret Denning described the heartrending ordeal of a Muslim smallholder who was forced to sell, first, his land, then his hut and finally his cooking utensils to provide food for his wife and two small children. Since "the government was doing nothing to relieve the poor," he gave his oldest child to the infidel missionaries in violation of his religion. "The man brought the boy to us, telling the child he could care for him no longer, although he had always hoped to send him to school, but that now he saw no way to save his life and educate him other than to give him away. The boy was not to think his father did not love him, and, if he lived and learned how to write, he was charged to write to his parents. The father bade him goodbye and, asking nothing for himself, went away." (Later the government begrudgingly opened a poorhouse in the vicinity, but the father, together with the child's mother and baby brother, perished under a squalid regime of poor sanitation, inadequate rations and hard labor.)[16]

Such stories were commonplace and they began to sow unease abroad. Sir Edwin Arnold was mobilized to reassure the Americans that "the British in India rule for the sake of the Indians first, and for revenue, reputation and power afterward."[17] But with *Spectator* and other prominent editorial pulpits chiding him for excessive parsimony, the viceroy – otherwise preoccupied with destroying rebel villages along the Afghan border – reluctantly agreed to open limited relief work in the most stricken districts. He remained stubbornly opposed, however, to private charity, including international missionary appeals, and bitterly condemned the press for their "exaggerations."[18] Like Lytton before him, Elgin foreclosed more liberal policies on a local or regional level. Thus the Bombay municipal committees were "banned to utilize their funds for running fair price shops," and the government of Bengal was forbidden to advance money to traders to import

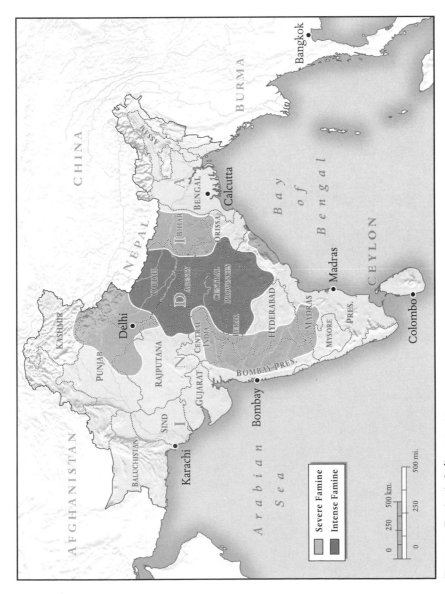

Figure 5.1 Famine in India, 1896–97

grain.[19] (Burma, as a result, exported its large rice surplus to Europe.)[20] Finally, "as his coffers were drained by war on the North Western Frontier, his government … reduced the contribution to the [Famine] Fund from Rs. 1.5 crores to Rs. 1 crore," in gross violation of previous official promises to Indians.[21]

Figure 5.2   "The prosperous appearance of the country…" Famine victims at Jubbulpur at the time of Lord Elgin's visit in 1897.

In early December Elgin passed through Jubbulpur in the Central Provinces, a town that would figure centrally in international debates over British famine policy. The drought here had been unbroken since the fall of 1895 and the monthly death rate had been over 10 percent since September. The government had previously refused desperate local appeals to open relief work or control the price of grain. But Elgin, like Temple and Lytton in Madras a generation before, was stonily unmoved by anything he saw. "I can only say that travelling during the last few days in Indore and Gowalior and now in these Provinces up to the gates of your city I have been struck by the prosperous appearance of the country even with the small amount of rain that has come lately." All India was outraged by this remark, based – one reporter claimed – on a quick glimpse from "the saloon window of the viceregal train."[22]

Convinced that Indians were natural shirkers and beggars, Elgin imported that old disciplinary cornerstone of utilitarianism, the poorhouse, to the subcontinent.[23] Designated for those too weak for heavy labor, the poor houses were despised by the peasantry who feared that "they would be converted to Christianity, or deported to places beyond the sea."[24] Confinement was especially unbearable to the tribal peoples, like the Gonds and Baigas, whom one missionary claimed "would sooner die in their homes or in their native jungle, than submit to the restraint of a government Poor House."[25] This was echoed by an English authority on the famine: "The hatred of the poorhouse has in many instances proved more strong than the fear of death."[26]

Although the British regarded this antipathy as irrational, a visiting American relief official was horrified by conditions inside the poorhouses, especially the diet. "The food was nothing but dry flour and some salt. An accustomed eye could at once see that THE GRAIN WAS ADULTERED WITH EARTH before it was ground into flour.... Alas! alas! for the poor who are obliged to eat the food given to them at the Poor Houses." Mennonite missionaries estimated that "perhaps about eight or ten annas or, at the most, a rupee per month is allowed for each person" by the government. (At 1899 exchange rates this was the equivalent of only 34 cents per month.)[27] As a result, one Mennonite wrote to Louis Klopsch, publisher of the *Christian Herald* in New York, "The death rate in this district which normally was under 50 in the thousand was forced by starvation up to the appalling figure of 627 in the thousand."[28]

The Americans accused the government of deliberately deceiving world opinion about conditions in the Indian countryside. "How many more might have been saved and be today happy and full of life and vigor if they could only have been reached in time will never be known. Perhaps the bleaching skulls on India's plains could give us some idea. But the long continued withholding of actual facts by the government and the consequent general ignorance of the true conditions of things must be looked upon as the cause of many thousands of deaths."[29] Such accusations were made all the more effective by the shocking photographs of famine conditions that were reprinted in newspapers around the world. (During the 1876–78 famine, dry plate photography had required professional skill with a cumbersome tripod-mounted field camera. The advent of the cheap, handheld Kodak Number One camera in 1888, however, turned virtually every missionary in India into a documentary photographer.)[30]

Rather than slowly die in the government charnel houses, peasants throughout the Central Provinces assaulted grain depots. The worst distrubances ironically occurred in Nagpur District, where the harvest was adequate but soaring market prices had nonetheless imposed starvation on Koshti caste weavers, immiserated by their losing competition against factory-made textiles. The local commissioner, Sir Andrew Fraser, arrogantly dismissed pleas to open relief works, and merchants outraged the public by selling adulterated grain at fantastic prices. After a series of violent clashes, the Lancashire Regiment had to be sent in to reinforce native infantry.[31] As James McLane points out, the rioting was incipient class war that did not spare the local leadership of the Indian National Congress: "In the Nagpur grain riots, the house of a leading Congressman, Gangadhar Madho Chitnavis, was singled out by a mob for looting and was saved by the intervention of sepoys. The rioters chose Chitnavis's house apparently because they believed, as a wealthy money-lender and landowner and president of the municipality, he could influence the price or supplies of grain."[32]

Similar conditions in the Bombay Presidency allowed the "Extremist leader" Bal Gangadhar Tilak to consolidate his takeover of the Poona Sarvajanik Sabha. Tilak, who had long urged the Congress to adopt the more militant agitational methods of the Irish, now played Michael Davitt in the Deccan, calling for popular resistance against tax collections.[33] (Davitt himself was meanwhile speaking alongside Naoroji and Eleanor Marx at protests against Elgin organized by Hyndman's Social Democratic Federation in London.)[34] Tilak's stirring invocations of the heroic Maratha past roused a martial populism in hungry villagers as they united once again, as in 1877, to oppose the hated revenue man. The British were unnerved. "The assistant collector of Poona district reported that 'not a *pie* of the revenue instalment' due on 10 December 1896 had been paid to the government." In the Kolaba district the collector was besieged by more than 4,000 ryots demanding remission of their taxes, and the *Times of India* trembled at the massive response of villagers to Tilak's organizers.[35] The tense political situation in western India was further inflamed by the draconian British response to the arrival of the Black Death from China.

The bubonic plague came to Bombay in summer 1896 probably as a stowaway on a ship from Hong Kong. At the time, some scientists theorized that drought, as previously in southern China, was a critical factor in driving plague-carrying rats into more intimate commensality with human victims.[36] Bombay, in any event, offered an ideal ecology for a pandemic: fetid, overcrowded slums (perhaps the densest in Asia) infested with a huge population of black rats. For years health officers had warned British administrators that their refusal to expend anything on slum sanitation was preparing the way for an "epidemic apocalypse."[37] Florence Nightingale, in addition, had repeatedly crusaded against the city's "phantasmagoria" of disease conditions, but the "European townspeople were united in blocking increased taxation to pay for new water and drainage schemes."[38]

The city's fabulous boom in the 1880s and 1890s moreover had been subsidized by the falling living and health standards of its vast majority: "The wages of unskilled laborers increased only five percent in 35 years while grain costs rose 50 percent and land values and rents tripled." The progressive immiseration of its working classes, Ira Klein argues, was the single most important factor in Bombay's "extraordinary, disproportionate blossoming of death near the turn of the century."[39] Despite several panic-stricken exoduses, the famine in Bombay's hinterlands left little option for the urban poor but to remain in their pestilential slums. Indeed, the drought inundated the city's environs with famished refugees from the Deccan: 300,000 of them in April, May and June of 1897 alone.[40] Starvation and cholera were promptly added to plague: eventually killing a fifth of the city's low-caste laborers.[41] Even more alarming to commercial elites, some foreign ports began to quarantine shipments of wheat from Bombay. There were fears that a general embargo might destroy western India's foreign commerce.

As the city's morale plummeted, the governor's Plague Committee, still ignorant of the plague's true vectors, launched an unprecedented war against the tenement neighborhoods that sheltered the pandemic. The resulting onslaught of fire, lime and carbolic acid utterly failed to stop the plague's advance (it simply drove rats into neighboring homes), but it did unhouse thousands. (In England, some of the press proposed the "radical purification" of burning the entire native city to the ground.)[42] While destroying peoples' homes and shops, however, the government did nothing to control the explosion in grain prices that was spreading starvation faster than plague. "Unrest in Bombay against continuing exports of foodgrains from the Presidency in the face of the serious famine" was thus combined with riots against the housing demolitions and the "kidnapping" of family members to the hated plague hospitals.[42]

Meanwhile railroad shipments of contaminated relief grain spread the plague with great efficiency across the Ghats into the arid and hungry Deccan. Modernization and immiseration were again a deadly combination:

> Even more important than travellers in bringing infectious rodent fleas to new locales was India's vast commerce, developed through the encouragement of free trade policies.... The transport of rice, bajri, wheat and other grains across the famine-stricken country in the late 1890s, a traffic meant to be life-giving, particularly helped disseminate plague amongst India's malnourished population. Grain was the favorite food of the black rat, while the great plague vector [the flea], 'bred best in the debris of cereal grains.' ... When these fleas arrived at new towns or villages they often carried plague bacilli with them, fastened on local black rats as new hosts, began epizootics and then transferred plague to humans as alternate hosts.[44]

Oblivious to native dignity, the subsequent eradication campaign in the Deccan was militarized under a special executive headed by a haughty racist, W. C. Rand. The new Epidemic Disease Act gave him powers to "detain and segregate plague suspects, to destroy property, inspect, disinfect, evacuate and even demolish dwellings suspected of harbouring the plague, to prohibit fairs and pilgrimages...."[45] Rand boasted that his measures "were perhaps the most drastic that had ever been taken to stamp out an epidemic."[46] As one Indian historian has written: "Rand had summoned British troops to his aid and had swept down on the slums like a proverbial wolf on the fold. Plucking out men, women and children from their homes, he burnt their belongings and desecrated their shrines. Suspected victims were forcibly evacuated, their families coming to hear of them only after they were dead."[47] The shocking contrast between the huge number of people detained, many of them apparently healthy, and the relatively few ever released alive from the plague camps played on Indians' worst apprehensions about British rule.[48] Rumors spread across the country that Indian patients were being murdered to extract a vital oil to be employed as a magic ointment by Europeans.[49]

Across India, meanwhile, there was growing outrage at the lavish preparations to celebrate the sixtieth anniversary of Queen Victoria's rule. "In the Lahore Town Hall, a group of Indian schoolboys broke up a meeting of leading English and Indian citizens by insisting that money be raised for famine orphans rather than

Figure 5.3 The Victoria Memorial Monument, Calcutta

for a memorial to Queen Victoria." But it was in famished and plague-infested Poona that imperial arrogance finally sparked what many feared to be the prelude to a second Mutiny. On 22 June two Indian patriots assassinated Rand and an underling as they were driving away from Diamond Jubilee fireworks at Government House. The murders were followed a month later by an unprecedented Muslim eruption in Calcutta after a court ordered the destruction of a neighborhood mosque. "For several days large groups ... roamed the steets, attacked isolated Europeans, and threatened to loot and burn factories. The disturbances were unusual in that the rioters singled out Europeans and ignored Hindus."[50]

The Poona assassinations nonetheless gave Elgin a welcome pretext to strike back against the Maharashtrian tax resistance movement as well as his critics in the vernacular press. Tilak, accused of being the "spiritual godfather of the Rand murders," and four newspaper editors were promptly charged under a new sedition law. "Magistrates were empowered to bind down editors of newspapers for good behaviour, and to send them to prison in default of security, without trial for any specific offence." Any native criticism of famine relief, as well as the anti-plague campaign, was effectively criminalized.[51]

Although the *Englishman* in Calcutta screamed that "India was on the verge of another Mutiny," authorities were in fact surprised by how "little observable" was any violent disorder in the wake of the devastating combination of plague and starvation – "a heavier burden ... than [the country] has known during the century."[52] Indeed, the chief preoccupation of the India Office, as revealed by recent studies of the official correspondence between London and Calcutta, was neither the holocaust in lives nor the threat of revolution, but that Indian disasters might "disturb the intricate system for the multilateral settlement of [Britain's] balance of payments, in which India played a large and vital part."[53] Hamilton and Elgin fretted that sales of Indian wheat, tea and jute would collapse in face of growing foreign fears about the plague and the proposed embargo of trade between India and Europe that the French were advocating. In a land where famished laborers were easily replaced, "The Secretary of State in London was telling the Viceroy that he was 'more concerned about plague than famine' because a 'market once lost, or even partially deserted, is not easily regained.' "[54]

## Suffer Little Children

> On the way back to the station, on the outskirts of the village,
> Dr. Ashe found the skeleton of a child, and brought away part of the
> bones of the head in his hankerchief, to preserve as a memento.
> – Rev. J. Scott

Famine mortality crested in March 1897. The next month Elgin himself conceded that 4.5 million poor people had perished. Behramji Malabari, the nationalist editor of the *Indian Spectator,* countered that the real number, plague victims included, was probably closer to 18 million.[55] At the same time, the *Missionary Review of the World,* which ordinarily praised British philanthropy, denounced the doublespeak by which the government had downplayed the severity of the crisis and sabotaged missionary efforts to organize prompt international relief. "When the pangs of hunger drive people in silent procession, living skeletons, to find food, dying by the way; the stronger getting a few grains, the feebler perishing, and children, an intolerable burden, are sold at from ten to thirty cents a piece, and when at best a heritage of orphaned children of tens of thousands must remain to the country – this is not 'impending' famine – it is grim, gaunt, awful famine itself."[56]

Meanwhile, the agrarian economy of northern India continued to unravel, and the famous jurist and national leader Mahdev Govinda Ranade complained that the "seven plagues which afflicted the land of the Pharaohs in old time were let loose upon us."[57] In the Punjab, where cattle powered wells and irrigation wheels, the decimation of animals was so great that the standing crops in the fields died because villagers could not lift water from their wells.[58] The most extreme distress, however, was still in the Central Provinces where, as the Indian National Congress charged and Lord Hamilton later conceded, revenue exactions had long threatened the subsistence of the poor. Prophetically, eight years earlier after a severe tax hike, 15,000 protesting peasants had confronted the chief commissioner in front of the Bilaspur railroad station. "Their cry was, *'bandobast se mar gaya'* – 'the settlement has killed us!' "[59]

The protestors' words came grimly true in the winter of 1896–97, when mortality soared in at least one district (Gantur) to an incredible 40 percent (200,000 out of 500,000 residents).[60] In his zeal to maintain fiscal pressure on the peasantry, the Central Provinces' governor-general took little account of the remarkable siege of natural disaster – three consecutive years of devastating rains, plant rust, caterpillar plagues and black blight – that preceded the drought. Despite the terrible velocity with which famine spread through an already prostrate countryside, Sir Charles Lyall followed Elgin's lead and downplayed the acuity of the famine. While allowing grain merchants to export the province's scarce reserves, he refused frenzied pleas to suspend revenue collections or provide village-centered relief as authorized in the famine code.[61] Destitute famine victims were instead herded into hastily improvised poorhouses that set new standards for administrative incompetence and corruption.

Reuter's "special famine commissioner," F. Merewether, shocked the British reading public with his exposé of suffering and neglect inside the poorhouses of Bilaspur and Jubbulpur. Although an ardent imperialist whose reports usually depicted heroic British district officers battling natural cataclysm and Hindu superstition, Merewether did not mince words about the atrocities that passed for relief in the Central Provinces:

[T]he actual inhabitants of Bilaspur were dying of starvation, while under the supposed aegis of the Government and within their very gates. I mentioned previously
that my opinion was that the famine in the Central Provinces was grossly misman-
aged. I collected tangible proofs of this daily, till I had to hand a mass of reliable
and irrefutable evidence, which showed only too clearly that the officials and those
responsible had not, and did not, fully recognized the gravity of the situation. With
reference to the poor-house, there can be no doubt that in addition to supineness
and mismanagement, there was decided fraud going on, and the poor hopeless and
helpless inmates were being condemned by a paternal Government to a slow, horrible, and lingering death by starvation.

I here came across the first specimens of "Famine Down," which is produced by
long-continued starvation. At certain stages of want a fine down of smooth hair
appears all over the bodies of the afflicted. It has a most curious look, and gives the
wearer a more simian look than ever.... There were more than a score of souls who
had reached this stage, and their bodies were covered from head to foot with the
soft-looking black fur.[62]

When Julian Hawthorne, son of the famous New England writer and *Cosmopolitan*'s special correspondent in India, reached Jubbulpur in April 1897, three
months after Merewether, conditions in the Central Provinces had grown even
more nightmarish. On the long, hot train ride up the Narmada Valley ("the great

Figure 5.4  The Central Provinces in 1897: A Young Famine Victim

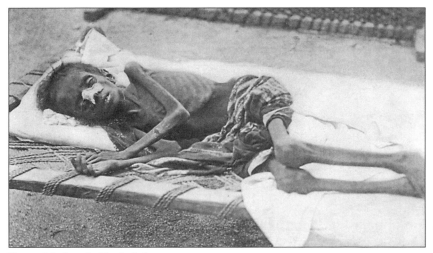

Figure 5.5  Attacked by Jackals

graveyard of India" according to American missionaries),[63] Hawthorne was horrified by the families of corpses seated in the shade of the occasional desert
trees. "There they squatted, all dead now, their flimsy garments fluttering around
them, except when jackals had pulled the skeletons apart, in the hopeless search
for marrow."[64] In Jubbulpur, he was escorted by the resident American missionary who took him first to the town market, where he was disgusted by the radical existential contrast between "bony remnants of human beings" begging for
kernels of grain and the plump, nonchalant prosperity of the local merchant
castes.[65]

The poorhouses, meanwhile, were converted cattle-pens terrorized by overseers who, as Merewether had accurately reported, systematically cheated their
doomed charges of their pathetic rations. "Emaciation" hardly described the condition of the "human skeletons" Hawthorne encountered:

> They showed us their bellies – a mere wrinkle of empty skin. Twenty per cent of
> them were blind; their very eyeballs were gone. The joints of their knees stood out
> between the thighs and shinbones as in any other skeleton; so did their elbows; their
> fleshless jaws and skulls were supported on necks like those of plucked chickens.
> Their bodies – they had none; only the framework was left.[66]

Figure 5.6 The British Self-Image: An Illustration from Kipling's "William the Conquerer."

Hawthorne's most haunting experience, however, was his visit to the children in the provincial orphanage in Jubbulpur. In imperial mythology, as enshrined in Kipling's famous short story "William the Conquerer" (published on the eve of the famine in 1896), British officials struggled heroically against all odds to save the smallest famine victims. The *Ladies Home Journal* (January 1896) version of Kipling's story had featured a famous woodcut by the American artist W. L. Taylor of a tall British officer walking slowly at the head of a flock of grateful, saved children. "Taylor accentuated the god-like bearing of Scott, as seen through the eyes of William [his love interest], standing at the entrance to her tent. The black cupids are there and a few capering goats ... " But as W. Aykroyd, a former Indian civil servant who in his youth had talked to the veterans of the 1896–97 famine, emphasizes, this idyllic scene was utterly fictional. "No particular attention was ... given to children in the famine relief operations."[67] Far more realistic than Scott's motherly compassion was the repugnance that Kipling's heroine William feels when, after dreaming "for the twentieth time of the god in the golden dust," she awakes to face "loathsome black children, scores of them wastrels picked up by the wayside, their bones almost breaking their skin, terrible and covered with sores."[68]

Hawthorne indeed discovered that "rescue" more often than not meant slow death in squalid, corruptly managed children's camps. After reminding American readers that "Indian children are normally active, intelligent and comely, with brilliant eyes, like jewels," he opens the door to the orphanage:

> One of the first objects I noticed on entering was a child of five, standing by itself near the middle of the enclosure. Its arms were not so large round as my thumb; its legs were scarcely larger; the pelvic bones were plainly shown; the ribs, back and front, started through the skin, like a wire cage. The eyes were fixed and unobservant; the expression of the little skull-face solemn, dreary and old. Will, impulse, and almost sensation, were destroyed in this tiny skeleton, which might have been a plump and happy baby. It seemed not to hear when addressed. I lifted it between my thumbs and forefingers; it did not weigh more than seven or eight pounds.

Beyond, in the orphanage yard, neglected children agonized in the last stages of starvation and disease. Hawthorne thought it obvious that the overseers, as in the adult poorhouses, were stealing grain for sale with little fear of punishment from their superiors:

> We went towards the sheds, where were those who were too enfeebled to stand or walk. A boy was squatting over an earthen saucer, into which he spate continually; he had the mouth disease; he could not articulate, but an exhausted moan came from him ever and anon. There was a great abscess on the back of his head. Another, in the final stage of dysentery, lay nearly dead in his own filth; he breathed, but had not strength to moan. There was one baby which seemed much better than the rest; it was tended by its own mother.... Now, this child was in no better condition than the rest of them when it came, but its mother's care had revived it. That meant, simply, that it had received its full allowance of the food which is supposed to be given to all alike. Why had the others – the full orphans – not received theirs?[69]

*Cosmopolitan* pointedly published photographs of famine victims from the Central Provinces next to an illustration of a great monument erected to Queen Victoria. Hawthorne, "on his way home from India," it editorialized, "heard it conservatively estimated in London that a total of more than one hundred millions of dollars would be expended, directly and indirectly, upon the Queen's

Figure 5.7 Aged by Hunger.
A fifteen-year-old girl.

Jubilee ceremonies."[70] But dying children in remote *taluks* were no more allowed to interrupt the gaiety of the Empress of India's Diamond Jubilee in June 1897 than they had her Great Durbar of twenty years before. Critics of Elgin were uncertain which was more scandalous: how much he had expended on the Diamond Jubilee extravaganza, or how little he had spent to combat the famine that affected 100 million Indians. When the government's actual relief expenditures were published a year later, they fell far below the per capita recommendations of the 1880 Famine Commission. As a new Famine Commission reported in 1898: "Our general conclusion is that, as compared with the past, a considerable degree of success as regards economy had been attained in the relief measures of the late famine."[71]

The relief works were quickly shut down with the return of the rains in 1898. Hundreds of thousands of destitute, landless people, without any means to take advantage of the monsoon, were pushed out of the camps and poorhouses. As a consequence, the momentum of famine and disease continued to generate a staggering 6.5 million excess deaths in 1898, making total mortality closer to 11 million than the 4.5 million earlier admitted by Elgin. Twelve to 16 million was the death toll commonly reported in the world press, which promptly nominated this the "famine of the century."[72] This dismal title, however, was almost immediately usurped by the even greater drought and deadlier famine of 1899–1902.

## Blue Skies of Famine (1899–1902)

In at least one part of India, however, 1899 is still remembered for the rain that never stopped falling. Indeed, Assam almost drowned in Noachian deluges; the 650 inches that fell in Chriapunji over the course of the year was a world record.

For the rest of India, Sir John Elliot, the director-general of observatories, predicted in May an unusually wet monsoon as well. The Simla social season, dominated by Lady Curzon, the Chicago heiress wife of the new Tory viceroy, began
with the usual whirlwind of parties, polo and white mischief. There was little discussion of the weather; certainly no apprehension that devastating back-to-back
drought was even possible. When the rains punctually commenced in June but
then suddenly stopped and did not return through July, Elliot reassured Curzon
that the monsoon would resume with heavy rain in August and September.[73] It
never did, and 1899 ended as the second-driest year (after 1877) in Indian history.[74]

Table 5.1
The Great Droughts Compared
(Percentage of Average Harvests)

|  | 1896–97 | 1899–1900 |
|---|---|---|
| Bombay Deccan | 34 | 12 |
| Karnatak | 25 | 16 |
| Gujarat | n.d. | 4 |

Source: Bombay Government, *Report on the Famine in the Bombay Presidency, 1899–1902,*
vol. 1, Bombay 1903, p. 114.

In the words of a modern researcher, who has reconstructed the synoptic patterns of the 1899 El Niño, the monsoons simply "jammed": "The rain-bearing
monsoon depressions, which usually enter India from the Bay of Bengal near
the Ganges Delta and then travel slowly west-northwestward across the country,
recurred in 1899 toward the north before reaching western India. Thus, the usual
two- to three-week cycles of Indian monsoon rains jammed. Instead of copious
rainfalls alternating with brief 'breaks' throughout the season, the western India
break which began in late June persisted for the rest of summer."[75] Indeed in
many parts of western and central India, the drought continued for three years,
until the rains of November–December 1902.[76]

"No such complete failure of the rains, after the first month of the monsoon,"
the glum imperial meteorologist told the viceroy, "is on record." In addition to
the traditional famine belts of the Deccan and Rajasthan, the new drought devastated crops in areas like Gujarat and Berar that were considered to be "particu-

larly free from apprehension of calamity of drought" (see Table 5.1). More than 420,000 square miles of farm land was transformed into "a vast, bare, brown, lonely desert." From Gujarat, a correspondent wrote to the *Times of India*:

> Were I an artist of the impressionist school and did I wish to represent the scene, I should dash in yellow grey, a long diminishing streak, which would be the road throwing up the heat that made the distance shimmering and indistinct; a great slash of reddy-brown on either side would indicate the land where the crops should be; and above all a liberal dash of blue from the horizon to the top of my canvas would be the sky. I do not think I ever hated blue before; but I do now.[77]

The famous French traveler Pierre Loti, en route from Pondicherry to Hyderabad, was also unnerved by the oppressive dome of silent sky, "limpid and blue as a great sapphire," that covered India like a bell-jar. He repeatedly resorted to the imagery of a landscape on fire as his train chugged across the scorched eastern Deccan:

> The dryness increases hourly as we penetrate further among the weary sameness of the plains. Rice patches, whose furrows can still be seen, have been destroyed as if by fire. The millet fields, which hold out longer, are for the most part yellow and hopelessly damaged.
>
> In those that are still alive, watchers – perched on platforms made of branches – are to be seen everywhere trying to scare away the rats and birds that would eat everything; poor humanity in the clutches of famine trying to guard a few ears of corn from the ravages of famished animals....
>
> The sun is setting, and Hyderabad is at last visible, very white amidst clouds of dust.... The river that flows in a large bed at the foot of the town is almost dried up.... Troops of elephants of the same grayish colour as the mud banks are slowly wandering along, trying futilely to bathe and drink.
>
> The day declines and the Eastern sky is lighted by a burning glow; the whiteness of the town fades slowly into an ashy blue, and huge bats commence to flit silently through the cloudless sky.[78]

Indians had never known such thirst. Peasants and district officers alike watched with fear as surface streams and canals suddenly dried up and wells "went blind." In the Bombay Deccan irrigation systems (113,000 acres irrigated in 1896) virtually collapsed (only 30,000 acres in 1900).[79] "The central horror of this famine," reported *Manchester Guardian* correspondent Vaughan Nash, "lies in the fact that the misery and torment of a water famine have to be endured together with a famine of food for people and fodder for beasts."[80] "Rivers, usually flowing full at this time," added an American missionary, "are dry beds of sand. Wells that have never before failed in the memory of anyone living have not a drop of water in them." For the first time in human recollection, the holy river Godavari simply disappeared into its sands.[81]

Rural India, moreover, was still economically prostrate from the 1896–97 disaster. Ryots could not afford to deepen their wells to reach lowered water-tables. "The people," wrote a Hyderabad Methodist, "had no reserves either of strength or grain to fall back on, the debts of the previous famine still hung around their necks, money was impossible to get, for lenders tightened their purse strings when they saw no chance of recovering their loans."[82] "Three years ago at the end of the famine," added another missionary from the Bombay Deccan, "there was less wretchedness and starvation than I saw here today at the beginning of the famine.... This famine is undoubtedly more severe in these parts than that of '76 or that of '96."[83] What surplus had been harvested in 1898 had been punctually confiscated by the moneylenders and tax-collectors. In the Punjab, for example, "the agreeable harvest of kharif of 1897 and rabi of 1898 had been largely drawn on to pay up arrears of government dues and to pay the banias for their overdrawn accounts of the famine years."[84]

Still, as the official *Report* on the 1899–1902 famine in the Bombay Presidency would emphasize, there was a surplus of grain in Bengal and Burma sufficient to compensate even such gigantic shortfalls in western and central India. The *Report* anticipated modern theories of famine as "entitlement crisis" by asserting that it was the regional deficiency of employment and income (which affected Bombay's working class as well as the rural population), not an all-India food shortage, that posed a mortal threat to so many millions.

> Owing to the excellent system of communications which now brings every portion of the Presidency into close connexion with the great market, the supplies of food were at all times sufficient, and it cannot be too frequently repeated that severe privation was chiefly due to the dearth of employment in agriculture and other industries, but the failure of the harvests caused loss of ordinary income in an enormous area and to an "unprecedented extent".... Even the skilled artisan felt the pinch of

high prices. Other classes too have suffered severely. The mill industry was much
hampered by short stocks and consequently high price of cotton, and several factories were obliged to work short hours: the result has been depression....[85]

Small landowners, in particular, were forced to beg relief work in unprecedented numbers. This contravened the official dogma (as Sir Richard Temple,
for instance, had explained it to the 1880 Famine Commission) that ryots were
self-sufficient and relief was primarily required to protect the "depressed classes
of village menials and itinerant tribes." By February 1900 *kunbis* comprised fully
half of the miserable armies breaking stone and digging canals in the Poona and
Ahmednagar districts. Moreover, the starvation of the peasantry led to an unprecedented wave of bankruptcy and land alienation. In a single year in the Maharashtran Deccan there was a mortgage or foreclosure for every seven rural inhabitants, a phenomenal index of the insecurity created by the double droughts.[86]

## 'A Truly Imperialist Viceroy'

The British reaction was again as inflexibly ideological as any fundamentalist
regime in history. Curzon, even more than Elgin, represented a hardened imperial policy that "believed that the government had gone as far as it should in meeting Indian desires for participation in the public service and legislatures." In a
preemptive strike against a future Home Rule movement along Irish lines, he
tightened press censorship, clamped down on education, restored aristocratic pre-
rogatives, snubbed the Congress, and, most dangerously, pitted Muslim against
Hindu.[87] He was likewise determined to prevent famine from being used as a
cause for reform. With hunger spreading on an unprecedented scale through
two-thirds of the subcontinent, he ordered his officials to publicly attribute the
crisis strictly to drought. When an incautious member of the Legislative Council in Calcutta, Donald Smeaton, raised the problem of over-taxation, he was (in
Boer War parlance) promptly "Stellenboshed."[88] Although Curzon's own appetite
for viceregal pomp and circumstance was notorious, he lectured starving villagers that "any Government which imperilled the financial position of India in the
interests of prodigal philanthropy would be open to serious criticism; but any
Government which by indiscriminate alms-giving weakened the fibre and demor-
alised the self-reliance of the population, would be guilty of a public crime."[89]

C. J. O'Donnell, a distinguished veteran of the Bengal civil service, sarcasti-

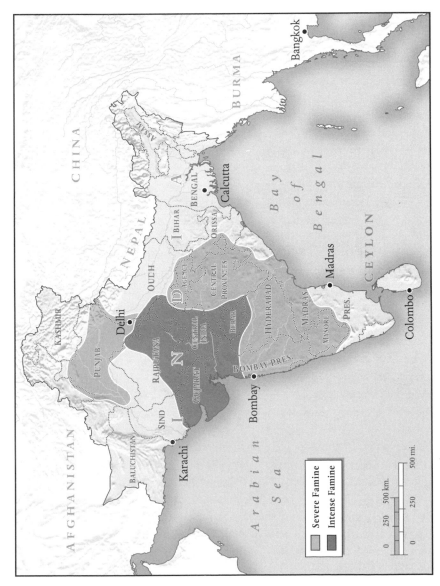

Figure 5.8  Famine in India, 1899–1902

cally commented, "With famine following famine in nearly every province of India, and desolating plague everywhere, who will deny that we have at last found a truly 'Imperialist' Viceroy?"[90] Just before New Year's, Curzon demonstrated his doctrinaire imperialism by cutting back rations that he characterized as "dangerously high" and stiffening relief eligibility by reinstating the despised Temple "tests." This led to a brief skirmish with local authorities, who worried that budgetary retrenchment in the face of such universal suffering might spark rebellion, but Curzon quickly imposed his will. In the Bombay Presidency alone, the government boasted that the tests had deterred 1 million people from relief.[91] Like Lytton twenty years before, Curzon would become the architect of a "brilliantly organized famine."

Curzon was responding to new stringencies dictated by the secretary of state for India, Lord George Hamilton. Financing of the Boer War trumped any "philanthropic romanticism" in India. Two years earlier, with the Northwest Frontier in upheaval, the secretary had in fact offered famine aid to Elgin, but now "Hamilton not only did not approach the Treasury for such a grant but also prevented Curzon from seeking it. The wars in China and South Africa made him more conscious of the Indian obligation with regard to the Imperial wars than of his responsibility to relieve the distress of the famine-stricken people." While refusing appeals to organize a famine charity in England, the secretary pressured Curzon to launch a War Fund in India so that its patriotic subjects could help defray Kitchener's expenses in the Transvaal. Though he did not interfere with the viceroy's plan to build a hugely ornate Victoria Memorial Monument in Calcutta, he urged the most ruthless Lyttonian vigilance in policing the relief works.[92]

Meanwhile, the English public's famed philanthropic instinct had dried up as completely as the Deccan's streams and wells. As Herbert Spencer warned of the "rebarbarization" of the English spirit by rampant jingoism, the popular press ignored the new Indian holocaust to focus almost exclusively on the unexpectedly difficult struggle to subdue the Boers.[93] "So far as the London Press and periodicals are concerned," complained a member of the Fabian Society, "India might almost have been non-existent."[94] A desultory Mansion House fund for Indian famine victims raised barely 7 percent of the Lord Mayor's parallel War Fund for South Africa.[95] "India," wrote an American missionary, "now would have to struggle alone, for the thoughts of every Englishman in the world were centered on South Africa."[96]

The most substantial international aid came not from London but from Topeka: 200,000 bags of grain "in solidarity with India's farmers" sent by Kansas Populists. (American relief organizers were incensed when British officials in Ajmir promptly taxed the shipment.)[97] There were also notable contributions from sympathetic Native American tribes and Black American church groups.[98] In Britain, where the old guard of Wedderburn, Naoroji and Dutt (now organized into the Indian Famine Union) were more isolated than ever, the only ray of hope was among the non-Fabian socialists (the Fabians by and large were staunch imperialists) and the left wing of the labor movement.[99] Indeed, Hyndman's feisty little Marxist party, the Social Democratic Federation, was the only British political organization which never wavered in its attention to India's famine victims. (Typical of the SDF's courageous anti-imperialism was the response of one Scottish branch to the otherwise delirious celebration of the British victory in South Africa in 1902: "While on all sides of the street the harlot, Capitalism, was decked in horrible array of all possible and impossible colours, there was projected from the windows of the SDF a transparency of five feet, giving the statistics of deaths in war, deaths in concentration camps, the numbers of paupers, the number of unemployed in Britain, the famine deaths in India, and the famine deaths, emigration and evictions in Ireland.")[100]

Meanwhile, Curzon continued to implement his "truly imperialist" policies for adjusting famine relief to stringencies of the Boer War finances. The *Guardian*'s Nash was revolted by the government's obsession with relief cheaters and their "buried hoards of grain and ornaments," which he believed were only "figments of the Secretariat's imagination." Writing from a drought-devastated corner of Gujarat where the population was "really and truly famine-stricken," he described the human consequences of the cruel distance and poverty tests used to discourage "unworthy" relief applicants:

Here, in Broach, where for some weeks the harshest treatment that I have seen in India was meted out, the state of the population beggars description. The "deterrent" element, on which the Bombay Government lay such stress, has had full play with a vengeance, but when the history of the famine comes to be summed up, I doubt if the result will be paraded as a success. The net effect of it on the works has been semi-starvation, sickness, and an appalling death rate, and in the villages, starvation on a wholesale scale amongst the people who were "deterred" by the harshness of the tests, from going upon the works.[101]

As Nash discovered in his visits to dozens of relief camps across northern India, inmates were treated with open contempt and denied resources – shelter, fuel, blankets and clothing – that the Famine Code had prescribed as essential to their survival. Moreover, a draconian system of measured labor and output, based on the British belief in the existence of organized shirking, kept nutrition below subsistence levels. Wages were paid in cash to gangs of thirty according to work quotas calibrated by what British administrators believed should be a strenuous nine-hour output by healthy adult males. Emaciated drought victims were, of course, seldom able to meet these unrealistic expectations, and, as a result, their wages were reduced according to the shortfall in their labor. For the weakest relief recipients in the Bombay Presidency, which again, as in 1877, set the standard for Benthamite severity, the wage was a "penal minimum" equivalent to fifteen ounces of food: less than the infamous Temple wage and only one-half the ration received by prison convicts. At a camp that Nash visited outside Poona, 1,100 inmates received the penal minimum; 900, the minimum; and only 180, a wage between the minimum and the maximum. "It should be explained," Nash told his readers, "that about a third of the recipients of the minimum and the penal minimum were children, and their wages in the case of the lowest class came to only 4.5 annas [43% of minimum] for the week. Seeing also that more than half the adults are women, I think it must be admitted that the punishment is indiscriminate as well as severe."[102]

Although relief officials angrily denied charges by Indian nationalists that they were wantonly starving drought refugees to death, Nash pointed to "the enormous death-rate at the camps where the penal minimum has become the prevailing standard."

> In any case, it is curious if the penal minimum to-day is working out so differently from the 1-lb. ration in the great famine of 1877. I described that ration in one of my letters as rather more generous than the one under discussion, and I am confirmed in this view by what I have learned since.

It is an ominous fact that whilst the minimum is being cut down by a quarter – a minimum which assumes that only 15 oz. of solid food a day will go into the stomach of the people who must work nine hours between the rising and setting of an Indian sun – cholera is on the march in Khandesh and God help if cholera attacks the famine camps.

It has been a race between cholera and starvation, a grand hunt of death with scores of thousands of the refugees at the famine camps for quarry. [103]

## The 'Song of Famine'

Not all the victims of Curzon's cost-cutting were in the countryside. Despite the immense grain stores piled up at the docks, the stringencies of relief in Bombay condemned thousands of refugees from the countryside to starve openly in the streets. Moreover, the unprecedented fall in well levels and watertables led to massive contamination of water supplies and the explosive spread of dysentery, diarrhea and, above all, cholera. From the middle of April 1900 cholera "swept like a destructive wave over the whole country," massacring city-dwellers and peasantry alike.[104] As Ira Klein writes, "Probably half of the increased mortality of 1896–1900 was famine-induced, and famine's influence certainly prevailed in the terrible year 1900, when recorded death-rates were 96.6 per mille."[105]

In the midst of this carnage, the viceroy, breaking precedent with previous governments, decided to deport refugees who had fled into British India from neighboring native states. Of an estimated 85 million drought victims, 43 million lived in native states and 42 million were under direct British administration.[106] As Curzon unquestionably understood, deportation was a virtual death sentence for hundreds of thousands of desperate people. The 688 native states, some of them literally microscopic, were puppet governments with dependent economies and subsidized rulers. If, in some notable instances, native princes (like the Maharajah of Kholapur or Prince Ranjitsinh of Jamnagar, the famous cricket hero) upheld more humanitarian, pre-British traditions of dignified relief and tax forgiveness, others – their power subvented by the Raj – simply turned their backs on their famished subjects.[107] The worst offenders included Indore, where the maharaja, a bottom-line man like Curzon, vetoed all relief expenditures, and Bundi, in southeast Rajputana, where the rajah let half his subjects starve to death. Conditions meanwhile in the sixty-four tiny statelets that comprised the Central India

Figure 5.9  Villagers, Rajputana 1899.

Agency were simply described as "unspeakable."[108]

Although nearly a million villagers eventually died in the native and British-administered sectors of Rajputana, grain traders earned immense profits as they shifted rice and millet stocks from the countryside to the cities. Foreign observers were shocked by the obscene contrast. An American missionary, for example, wrote of his repulsion at the sight of vast quantities of grain, imported by speculators, sitting on railroad sidings under armed guard. "At many of the railway stations I saw thousands of fat pigeons gorging themselves with grain from the loaded wagons on the siding, while apathetic native officials stood by and saw the precious food devoured in the sight of scores of miserable, famine-stricken villagers crying aloud for food."[109]

Similarly, Pierre Loti arrived in Rajputana ("a land of dead forests, dead jungles, dead everything") on a train pulling carloads of precious grain. His account is perhaps the most chilling memoir of conditions in 1899. At every station weary passengers heard the same terrible "song of famine." It was the wail of starving children:

At the first village at which we stop a sound is heard as soon as the wheels have ceased their noisy clanking – a peculiar sound that strikes a chill into us even before we have understood its nature. It is the beginning of that horrible song which we shall hear so frequently now that we have entered the land of famine. Nearly all the voices are those of children, and the sound has some resemblance to the uproar that is heard in the playground of a school, but there is an undefined note of something harsh and weak and shrill which fills us with pain.

Oh! look at the poor little things jostling there against the barrier, stretching out their withered hands towards us from the end of the bones which represent their arms. Every part of their meagre skeleton protrudes with shocking visibility through the brown skin that hangs in folds about them; their stomachs are so sunken that one might think that their bowels had been altogether removed. Flies swarm on their lips and eyes, drinking what moisture may still exude ...

"Maharajah! Maharajah!" all the little voices cry at once in a kind of quivering song. There are some who are barely five years old, and these, too, cry "Maharajah! Maharajah!" as they stretch their terribly wasted little hands through the barrier.[110]

If Loti was filled with admiration for the train's Indian passengers, crammed into the suffocating third- and fourth-class compartments, who unhesitatingly gave away their last copper coin or scrap of food, he loathed the official policy that made an unfettered grain market more sacred in principle than the lives of small children crying from hunger:

Even now there are four wagons of rice coupled to the train behind, and loads pass daily, but no one will give anything to the children, not even a handful, not even the few grains on which they might survive for a little while more. These wagons are reserved for the inhabitants of those towns where people still have money and can pay.[111]

For those without the price of a bowl of rice, a major alternative was to join the great exodus of famine victims from the desertified valleys of Rajputana (where a century later, the horror of 1899 remains "stored in the collective memory of folklore, sayings and songs")[112] to normally well-watered Gujarat in British India. As a missionary pointed out, it was an unwitting journey "from the frying pan to fire."[113] Undisturbed by drought or famine for three generations, Gandhi's home province had become the infernal core of the disaster in Bombay Presidency. Indeed, "Gujarat presented the picture of Ireland in 1844–45."[114]

## The Inferno in Gujarat

As elsewhere, El Niño worked in sinister partnership with the world market. The drought, which persisted until 1902 in Ahmedabad, Kaira and Panch Mahals, ravaged an agricultural economy already depressed by the global decline of the prices of cotton and cane sugar. It was made even more destructive by the plagues of locusts and rats (so numerous that "they disturb one's rest at night") that consumed what little grain farmers managed to coax to maturity with laboriously hand-toted water. Gujaratis, used to a dairy diet, watched in horror as first their cattle died and then as their lands, mainly loam soils dependent on constant manuring, became infertile.[115] An American missionary, writing to an old Princeton friend, described how a countryside, "once green as a park," had become "a blasted waste of barren stumps and burned fields.... Every leaf was torn from the trees long ago for the cattle, and now the trees themselves have been cut down for wood."[116]

Famine, moreover, crossed paths in Gujarat, as in the rest of India, with epidemics of both plague and cholera. By February 1900, there were so many cholera victims in Gujarat that local water supplies were being poisoned by the putrifying corpses. Several hospitals reported 90 percent mortality, and in one camp alone there were 3,000 deaths in four days.[117] Dr. Louis Klopsch of *The Christian Herald*, a veteran of famine relief expeditions to Russia, Armenia and Cuba, was "appalled at the shocking conditions" nonchalantly tolerated by British officials:

> The heat was intense; the thermometer indicated 108 degrees. A hot, blinding sand-storm filled our eyes and nostrils with microbe-laden dust, and the all-pervading stench from putrefying bodies, impregnated clothes, hair and skin. Cholera had broken out a short time before and 2400 famine sufferers had died within a few days and had been buried in shallow ground. Decomposition speedily set in and impregnated the ground with death-dealing malodor. There were no disinfectants, hence the awful, sickening, disease-spreading, suffocating stench.... Millions of flies were permitted undisturbed to pester the unhappy victims. One young woman who had lost every one dear to her, and had turned stark mad, sat at the door vacantly staring at the awful scenes around her. In the entire hospital I did not see a single decent garment. Rags, nothing but rags and dirt.[118]

Some formerly prosperous districts like Kaira lost almost a third of their population in less than two years.[119] In the Panch Mahals the 1900 death rate was a macabre 28.1 percent, and in Ahmedabad, 17 percent.[120] (As a result of such concentrations of high mortality, the 1911 census population of Gujarat would be significantly smaller than 1871's.)[121] The holocaust meanwhile began to unravel the tightly woven fabrics of family and religious life. Knowing the missionaries' hunger for young converts, some villagers resorted to selling their young children for a few days' supply of food. "Repeatedly parents have offered me their children for sale at a rupee each, or about thirty cents. And they love them as we love our children. Children are now being offered for sale as low as four cents each, for a measure of grain."[122]

Outcastes and tribals bore disproportionate shares of the suffering. The Dharalas of Kaira, as well as other poor shepherds and pastoralists in the Panch Mahals, faced the "insoluble" problem of "how to look after ... their cattle and at the same time labour on the relief works." As a result their mortality was appalling.[123] Likewise in the Surat district, where the overall death rate was only 2 percent, it was closer to 20 percent among the Chodhras. The survivors, having lost their land to unscrupulous moneylenders, were permanently reduced to extreme poverty.[124]

Even more dreadful was the death agony of thousands of Bhil tribals in eastern Gujarat. Forced out of their hills and forests by the unending drought, and fearful of the squalid relief camps, they clung wherever possible to the remaining sources of fresh water. An Englishwoman described her phantasmagoric encounter in early 1900 with a large group of Bhil refugees living in the open around a rapidly dessicating lake: "As the remainder of the water gradually evaporated in the fierce heat, the people were surprised to see the fish so close they could be caught by hand. For two or three whole nights the famished crowds seized, cooked, and devoured the fish as fast as they could." Then cholera struck and cut down people by the hundreds. "The air became laden with the stench of putrefying bodies. While riding over to the burning ground behind my bungalow to see that the bodies were being properly disposed of, I found that the bearers of the dead had themselves been struck down in front of the pyre."[125] Choksey estimates that fully a third of the Bhil population had perished by 1901.[126]

As elsewhere in India, British officials rated ethnicities like cattle, and vented

Figure 5.10  "The Gujarati is a soft man"

contempt against them even when they were dying in their multitudes. Asked to explain why mortality in Gujarat was so high, a veteran district officer is quoted in the official famine report:

> The Gujarati is a soft man, unused to privation, accustomed to earn his good food easily. In the hot weather he seldom worked at all and at no time did he form the habit of continuous labour. Large classes are believed by close observers to be constitutionally incapable of it. Very many even among the poorest had never taken a tool in hand in their lives. They lived by watching cattle and crops, by sitting in the fields to weed, by picking cotton, grain and fruit, and, as Mr. Gibb says, by pilfering.[127]

As famine waxed in intensity, the government in Bombay decided to milk this "soft man" and his family of their last reserves. "The revenue," it was announced, "must at all costs be gathered in" – a decision denounced by Nash as "picking the bones of the people."[128] When *patidar* farmers, ruined by the drought, combined to refuse a 24 percent increase in their tax payment, the collectors simply confiscated their land.[129] Officials in the Central Provinces (where 500,000 died in 1900 alone) were equally ruthless.[130] The corruption and incompetence of the

Provinces' poor houses contrasted with the efficiency of its militarized revenue campaign. "In the Narmada division, where famine was more intense, it [the government] employed more savage coercion than in the better year 1898–99. Rounding off a terrifying decade, officials claimed near full collections in most districts in 1900–01."[131]

No previous drought in Indian history had lasted for more than two years, so there was widespread expectation that normal monsoons would restore agriculture in 1902. In fact, "the season of 1901–02," the official Bombay famine *Report* explains, "was again disappointing. In Gujarat the summer rains began late and ceased early, and the winter rains failed almost entirely.... The damage done by shortage of rain was intensified by a severe plague of rats and locusts, grasshoppers, and other insects, which assailed parts of the Deccan and Karnatak and converted, in the case of some Gujarat districts, what would have been moderate scarcity into intense distress. In the Desert portion of Thar and Parkar there was an absolute failure of rain, and the crops were practically *nil*.... [I]n Gujarat at least, the distress was more intense in 1901–02 than in the preceding years."[132]

The Bombay authorities were forced to keep relief works open almost until Christmas 1902. As in 1877 and 1897, "the main peak in the famine death rate ... occurred relatively late," coinciding with the return of monsoon rains in August– September 1900 in the Central Provinces and a malaria epidemic that ravaged the weakened and immune-suppressed population.[133] The India Office, not counting malaria deaths, estimated famine mortality in British India 1899–1900 as 1.25 million, but Indian economists led by R. C. Dutt claimed that it "was actually three or four times this."[134] In a recent statistical reconstruction, demographer Arup Maharatna suggests a mortality range (not including 1901–02 victims ) of between 3 and 4.4 million, although Burton Stein believes the true figure was closer to 6.5 million and W. Arthur Lewis cites 10 million dead.[135] Certainly the uncounted dead in the native states and the heavy mortality through 1902 suggest a total comparable to that of the 1870s catastrophe, making nonsense of Curzon's claim that "there had never been a famine when the general mortality has been less, when the distress has been more amply or swiftly relieved.[136]

As in 1876–78, there were local concentrations of super-mortality. In scores of drought districts, at least 10 percent of the population perished; in Gujarat, the toll soared to a sixth of the population, perhaps even more.[137] The slaughter

Figure 5.11  Burning Plague Victims in Bombay, 1898.

of innocents was particularly appalling. Infant mortality in the Hissar district of the Punjab, according to Tim Dyson, was nearly 50 percent in 1899–1900, while in Berar half the deaths (some 8,000) on large relief works were children under the age of five – gruesome evidence of conditions like those denounced by Hawthorne at Jubbulpur in 1897.[138]

In 1901 *The Lancet* suggested that a conservative estimate of excess mortality in India in the previous decade (calculated from the 1901 Census after subtracting plague deaths) was 19 million.[139] As William Digby reminded English readers at the time, "This statement by what is probably the foremost medical journal in the world, means that the loss of life thus recorded represented 'the disappearance' of fully one-half a population as large as that of the United Kingdom."[140] A number of historians, including Kingsley Davis, Ira Klein and Pierre Le Roy, have accepted *The Lancet*'s figure as an order-of-magnitude approximation for the combined mortality of the 1896–1902 crisis.[141]

These great fin-de-siècle famines, followed by another El Niño–linked drought-famine in 1907–08 that Maharatna estimates took 2.1 to 3.2 million lives in the United Provinces, cast a long mortality shadow over the first decade of the twentieth century.[142] Their immune responses weakened by the long ordeal of hunger, the rural poor in western and northern India were mowed down in the millions by epidemic waves of malaria, tuberculosis and plague. The Black Death, spread by drought-induced rat migrations, entrenched itself in the former famine districts of the U.P. and the Punjab, where it had claimed 8 million further victims by 1914.[143]

The cumulative damage to the subcontinent's productive forces was colossal. "Almost all the progress made in agricultural development since 1880 was nullified during the famines."[144] Srivastava claims that 92 percent of plough cattle in the Punjab died in 1896–97; while in the Bombay Presidency (according to Tomlinson in the *New Cambridge History*) the herds did not regain their 1890s levels until the 1930s.[145] Partially as a result of this catastrophic shortfall of animal power, the net cropped area in both the Bombay Presidency and in the Central Provinces in 1900 had declined by 12 percent relative to 1890. In the most stricken districts the decrease in cultivation was 25 percent to 41 percent.[146]

The country's demographic engine likewise ground to a near halt. In the thirty years from 1891 to 1921, India's population barely grew from 282 million to 306 million – hardly a Malthusian boom.[147] Indeed, in many parts of India there had been a fifty-year standstill in population growth. Thus in Agra, Rohiklhand and Allahabad, among other localities, the 1921 population was less than that of 1872, while in Lucknow, Jhansi, Gujarat, most of the (former) United Provinces and the Native States, merely the same.[148] For India as a whole, only the 1880s had seen a relatively healthy ratio between birth and death rates.

And what lesson did the British draw from these catastrophes? The most comprehensive official survey, the *Report on the Famine in Bombay Presidency, 1899–1902*, conceded that much of the excess mortality might have been avoided by "widespread gratuitous [home] relief from the beginning," but insisted that "the cost could have been such as no country would bear or should be called upon to bear" (although both the Moguls and the Qing provided this form of relief during the eighteenth century). Likewise the principal finding of the *Report* of the 1901 [all-India] Famine Commission – despite the fact that barely a fifth of estimated famine victims received any British assistance whatsoever – was that "the relief distributed was excessive."[149]

# Six

# Millenarian Revolutions

In 1898 there will be many hats and few heads; in 1899 the
waters shall turn to blood, and the planet shall appear in the
east with the sun's rays, the bough shall find itself on the earth,
and the earth shall find itself in heaven. There shall be a great
rain of stars, and that will be the end of the world. In 1901 the
lights shall be put out.
                                        — Prophecies of Antonio Conselheiro

In the autumn of 1901, after a grueling overland journey of many weeks, Francis Nichols, special "famine commissioner" for New York's *The Christian Herald*,
arrived at the gates of Xian (Sian), the ancient capital of China. Renowned for his
"courageous and adventurous" reportage of the late war with Spain, Nichols had
been selected by Louis Klopsch, the *Herald*'s publisher, to carry cash aid (including a $100 contribution from recently assassinated President McKinley) directly
to the epicenter of a terrible drought-famine that was reported to be savaging the
loess provinces of Shaanxi and Shanxi.[1] He followed in the footsteps of the Dowager-Empress Tz'u-hsi and her court, who had fled to Xian in late 1900 after the
fall of Beijing to the International Expeditionary Force of eight foreign powers.
Although Nichols had been warned that Shaanxi was the citadel of anti-foreignism, and that vengeful Boxer remnants might be encountered en route, he was

determined to document the devastation of nearly three years of drought in the old Han heartland. Thanks to a pass from Prince Ching, the uncle of the new boy-emperor, he was in fact treated with scrupulous cordiality by local mandarins, who expedited his journey with fresh horses and armed escorts. They also warned him of the landscape of famine and death, too horrible to describe in words, that lay ahead. An estimated 30 percent of Shaanxi's population had perished, and some *hsien* (Kienchow, Pinchow and Yungshan, especially) were nearly depopulated.[2]

Indeed, the fabled valley of the Wei River seemed nearly as desolate as the Gobi. "Every quarter of a mile a mud village rose out of the white, treeless desert, which stretched away to the north, east, and west like a limitless ocean. The vast plain was silent. Along the old roads, all worn and sunken, we met no travellers. No farmers were in the fields. In some of the villages were groups of half-starved men and children, the only survivors of communities that had perished." The outskirts of Xian were honeycombed with thousands of "grim, blackened caves nearly all empty." During the terrible winter of 1900–01, an army of more than 300,000 starving refugees had been encamped outside the city walls. The provincial governor, frightened by bread riots and other omens of a peasant uprising, had locked the gates. Reduced to rags and without fuel for fires, the desperate refugees tried to escape the icy Siberian winds by burrowing deep into the loess embankments and hillsides. With the imperial granaries long emptied, this human rodent colony subsisted for a short time on coarse grass, weeds and roof thatch. Before long, however, the survivors were living off the bodies of the dead. "By-and-by human flesh began to be sold in the suburbs of Sian. At first the traffic was carried on clandestinely, but after a time a horrible kind of meat ball, made from the bodies of human beings who had died of hunger, became a staple article of food, that was sold for the equivalent of about four American cents a pound."[3]

## China: 'Bottling Up the Sky'

The festival of death and cannibalism outside the walls of Xian, related to Nichols by officials who had been powerless to relieve the calamity, was the macabre culmination of the crisis that had begun in 1897 with drought in north China and the German occupation of Jiaozhou Bay on the Shandong Peninsula.[4] For five years, northern China and Manchuria, along with Inner Mongolia, were overwhelmed both by foreign devils and natural disasters. Indeed the two curses were so closely aligned in time and space that they were understood by broad sections of the peasantry as a single, occult evil. Modern historians of the Boxer uprising, like Paul Esherick, Arthur Tiedemann and Paul Cohen, agree with contemporary missionary accounts that drought-famine was the bellows that transformed local sparks of anti-foreignism into a vast populist conflagration across north China. Ordinary people were convinced that the construction of so many arrogant foreign missions, churches and cathedrals had disrupted the *fengshui* or geomantic balance of nature, thus awakening the Earth Dragon and causing floods and drought.[5] As Boxer "big character" posters declaimed from the walls of Beijing: "No rain comes from Heaven. The earth is parched and dry. And all because the churches have bottled up the sky."[6]

The first phase of drought, which lasted from 1897 through summer 1898, caused acute distress in the western and southern counties of Shandong, where anti-foreign anger was already at a fever-pitch because of repeated German military interventions on behalf of Catholic missionaries.[7] As grain prices soared, banditry increased in tandem, and magistrates complained about the growing boldness of populist, heterodox sects. Although crop failure was considerably less devastating than in western India, the drought was immediately followed by a torrential monsoon in August that swelled the Yellow River to flood stage. On 8 August it broke through its banks first in Shouzhang, drowning 400 villages as its waters swept through Yuncheng to the Grand Canal; a second breach opened up southwest of Jinan, flooding another 1,500 villages. "Finally and most disastrously, the north bank broke at Dong'e, producing a vast lake extending through Chiping, where the 'Spirit Boxers' would soon be stirred to activity, and on to cover some 3000 square miles of farm land in northwest Shandong before it finally flowed to the sea."[8] The American consul at Chefoo reported that much of the province was now an Atlantis: "Hundreds of villages are submerged, cities surrounded by water, homes, furniture, clothing – in fact everything – is under water or destroyed."[9]

Millions fled, as best they could, the great inundation that covered vast sections of Henan as well as Shandong. Separate flooding created havoc in Hebei (Zhili), especially around Beijing. Myriads of villagers were stranded on dikes for

Figure 6.1  Flood Refugees in North China.

three months while waiting for the waters to recede. They tried to survive, with little success, on "a diet of willow leaves, wheat gleanings, and cottonseed mixed with chaff and pits."[10] American missionaries, appealing for aid in the winter of 1898–99, wrote that "the most conservative estimates place the number of starving at 2,000,000, and time and the increasing cold weather will undoubtedly greatly augment the distress." Without protection from the bitter Siberian winds, tens of thousands died of hunger, disease and cold. "Probably no place in the world," said the *New York Times,* "and probably not in this generation, has there been so much suffering as is now being endured in Shan Tung."[11]

The tragedy was made all the more bitter by the universal belief among the people that the disaster was man-made and avoidable. "Breaches of the Yellow River dikes had been occurring for several years as a consequence of embezzlement of flood control funds by officials of all ranks.... The censors in their impeachment memorials had reported this corrupt administration of the Yellow River Conservancy for many years."[12] The chief culprit, the pro-Catholic head of the Conservancy, had been dismissed for his venality, but was restored to power under pressure from the French. The hungry and half-drowned peasantry, according to Esherick, presumed that "this official, brought back at foreign insistence,

Figure 6.2  Boxer Rebels Practicing Archery, 1900.

was through his incompetence and corruption responsible for the great flood."[13] The foreign powers, meanwhile, seemed callously indifferent to the suffering in north China, ignoring desperate appeals for relief from missionaries and even, in some instances, their own local consuls. When Louis Klopsch of *The Christian Herald*, for example, begged US Secretary of State Hay for naval help to ferry grain to Shandong, he was brusquely turned away with the explanation that every available transport was needed for the invasion of the Philippines.[14]

Throughout 1898, moreover, the foreign menace seemed to grow day by day. While Beijing was distracted by the flood disaster and an accompanying cholera epidemic, London and Berlin negotiated the notorious Anglo-German Agreement, which acknowledged British hegemony in the lower Yangzi Valley in return for the recognition of a German sphere of influence in the north China plain. Japan, France and Russia immediately demanded comparable concessions. At the same time, Christian proselytism in China was intensifying so rapidly (a tripling of Protestant missionaries, for example, between 1890 and 1908) that it was widely perceived as a "religious invasion."[15] And, more subtly but no less alarmingly, centrifugal world market forces were becoming visible at the village level. Imported machine-spun cotton yarn from India wrecked havoc on the handicrafts of Shandong and other northern provinces, while the purchasing power of "cash" (China's popular copper coinage) plunged in tandem with China's worsening balance of trade. ("1900 saw ... the worst depreciation in the cash sector in the entire period 1890–1910.")[16] There was universal apprehension in north China that Qing sovereignty was being dismantled piecemeal, and with it the traditional rights and safeguards of the people including imperial commitments to flood control and famine relief. The esoteric doctrines of the Boxer movement were thus underlain by astute popular perceptions of imperialism. As the veteran missionary and pioneer sociologist of Chinese rural life, Arthur Smith, reminded British readers prone to dismiss the common people as ignorant and superstitious: "No shrewder people than the Chinese are to be found upon this planet – or perhaps any other."[17]

Disaster, moreover, had manufactured rebellion throughout Chinese history. When rivers broke their levies or changed their channels, a traditional adage warned that "the old died and the young became bandits."[18] Thus officials were hardly surprised when flood distress fused with perceptions of foreign conspiracy to produce a significant local uprising in the neighborhood of Wo Yang in northern Anhui as well as widespread violence in northern Jiangsu.[19] In the traditional bandit country of western Henan (especially Baofeng, Lushan and Linru counties) where "water works were in poor repair and thus unable to blunt the harshest effects of geography and climate," a Robin Hood army of 10,000 terrorized foreigners and Qing alike. As Elizabeth Perry has pointed out, these unusually disciplined brigands were scrupulously respectful of the poor and shared with them the impressive ransoms from missionary kidnappings. (A decade later, following a new round of natural disaster, the famous outlaw Bai Lang would assume command of these indomitable Henanese farmer-brigands.)[20]

More menacingly, the anti-Christian "Spirit Boxers" – direct progenitors of the 1899 "Boxers United in Righteousness" (*Yihetuan*) – began to spread like wildfire throughout the stricken districts of western Shandong, where the fall harvest had been drowned and the soil subsequently remained too wet to plant winter wheat. A martial arts movement of poor peasants, agricultural laborers and unemployed canal bargemen that combined the attributes of predatory social banditry with the defensive role of traditional village militias, the Spirit Boxers were quickly embroiled in escalating conflicts with both Christian villagers and local authori-

ties. The foreign powers exerted enormous pressure on the Qing court to exter-
minate the movement, and it might well have been contained in December 1898,
following the execution of the three principal leaders, if flooding had not been
punctually followed by renewed drought.[21]

The failure of the spring rains in 1899 was like throwing a match into a pool of
gasoline. "The drought was great and practically universal," wrote Arthur Smith.
"For the first time since the great famine in 1878 no winter wheat to speak of had
been planted in any part of northern China. Under the most favorable circumstances the spring rains are almost invariably insufficient, but that year they were
almost wholly lacking. The ground was baked so hard that no crops could be put
in."[22] Idled peasants and agricultural laborers by the tens of thousands flocked to
local boxing grounds where they imbibed the potent new doctrine of Boxer mili-
tancy combined with spirit possession and invulnerability rituals derived from the
underground White Lotus sect.[23]

Chiping hsien in western Shandong, which had been literally under water
during the floods and now was hammered by drought, was the reputed home
of "more than 800" of these boxing associations. "The weather in my region,"
wrote the local magistrate to Beijing, "has been exceptionally dry and the numbers of the poor have increased. When these poor people assemble they all claim
to be Boxers. The majority of these Boxers are poor people without any means of
livelihood." Later, after beheading some of the "Eighteen Chiefs" of the original
Yihetuan, another mandarin corroborated the plebeian, hunger-driven character
of the movement: "These Boxers are mostly homeless people.... Yan Shuqin and
'Little Pock-Mark' Gao, both of whom have already been executed, did not have
any property or other means; ... the twelve households connected with Xi De-
sheng, who also has been executed, altogether owned [a mere] 140 *mu* of land.
All of it was ordered confiscated and sold at auction."[24]

The government's inability, variously through insolvency or corruption, to
mount a credible relief effort, together with frequent refusal of the rich to
share food with the poor, only confirmed the core Boxer conviction that the
masses themselves must take responsibility for China's salvation. "A wide range
of sources," Cohen writes, "including gazetteers, diaries, official memorials, oral
history accounts, and the reports of foreigners, indicate a direct link between the
spread and intensification of the Boxer movement, beginning in late 1899, and

growing popular nervousness, anxiety, unemployment, and hunger occasioned
by drought." Tiedemann, another eminent historian of the uprising, agrees when
Cohen adds: "It was this factor [drought-famine], more than any other, in my
judgment, that accounted for the explosive growth both of the Boxer movement
and of popular support for it in the spring and summer of 1900."[25]

Joining the Boxers, moreover, was a sure way of filling one's belly. Everywhere
the movement was active it patriotically cajoled or, if necessary, simply expro-
priated surplus food from merchants and rich peasants. More violently, it seized
and divided the foodstocks of Christian villages and missions. *Wanguo gongbao*,
the missionary newspaper founded by Timothy Richard, warned that while the
"weak topple in the roadside ditches ... the stronger become outlaws [and] advocate dividing the wealth among rich and poor."[26] Indeed, most accounts agree,
the radical slogan "equal division of grain" was central to the explosive growth of
the Boxer uprising. Although some historians have claimed that this slogan only
meant to target Christians and foreigners, Qi Qizhang asserts that – at least by
1900 in Hebei – it included "wealthy households in general." He cites such official
notations as "they commanded the rich households to all give grain, but when
they didn't get what they wanted, they took it by force."[27] Likewise Presbyterian
missionaries reported in July 1899 that pro-Boxer peasants across north Anhui
were "looting the granaries of the wealthy."[28] There is little doubt, moreover, that
the ultimate endorsement of the insurgency by leading gentry and Qing nobles
was a systematic attempt to channel dangerous social anger in a purely patriotic,
non-revolutionary direction. Virtually certain defeat at the hands of the Great
Powers, in the eyes of veteran Manchu statesmen, seemed preferable to an apocalyptic class struggle. The Taiping, in the last instance, still cast the longest shadow
over the Forbidden City.

For the drought-victims themselves, however, the relevant memory was the
holocaust of 1877. The diary kept by Eva Price, a member of the large Oberlin
College contingent of missionaries who had been proselytizing in Shanxi since
1889, provides a vivid account of how folk memories of those millions of deaths
helped to fuel the uprising against a foreign menace indissolubly identified with
drought and famine. The catalytic roles of hunger, rumor and fear, alloyed with
resurgent elements of popular culture like the Boxer adoption of a pantheon
of animal gods from popular novels and operas, recall *le grand peur* of 1789,

famously analyzed by George Lefebvre, that propelled the French peasantry into a similarly desperate adventure.[29] Price's diary entries gain particular poignancy as she gradually realizes that her own fate, like that of her peasant neighbors, hinges upon the course of the drought.

Thus, from the last rains of September 1898 through the terrible starving spring of 1900, she charted the growing popular unease and the increase in anti-foreign insults and incidents. During the early summer of 1899, thunder frequently could be heard to the southwest, but the monsoons never crossed the mountains. "The south city gate has been closed again and the shopkeepers have built little altars outside their shops hoping the gods will honor their worship by sending rain. Everything is so dry and the dust is dreadful." In September the peasantry sowed their winter wheat crop as usual but the monsoon brought only "a little drizzle of rain but not enough to do any good." Over the next season the absence of a normal protective snow cover killed what little wheat actually germinated.[30]

Figure 6.3 Captured Boxer Rebel

As hunger spread, villagers began to make increasingly grim comparisons to 1877–79, when at least one-third of the province's population had perished. Rumors arrived of foreign plots and atrocities. "The most terrifying tale of all was one that asserted that foreign ships seized off the China coast were found to be carrying grisly cargoes of human eyes, blood, and female nipples."[31] (Cohen cites another widespread rumor that Christians were poisoning wells.)[32] By March 1900, Boxers were clandestinely organizing in Taiyuan, the provincial capital, under the tolerant eye of the new anti-foreign governor, Yu Sien. Two months later, as starvation became dramatically visible everywhere in Shanxi, villagers began to attack well-fed Chinese Christians and "foreign devils" at missions. Buddhist priests warned peasants that the drought would continue as long as Christians openly defiled Chinese traditions. The fearful Oberlin missionaries, in turn, held their own three-day-long prayer marathon for rain.[33]

In June, the monsoon rains began to break the drought in much of the north China plain, but the loess highlands of Shanxi and Shaanxi remained hot and arid. Rainmaking processions were transformed into ever larger and more militant patriotic demonstrations. Boxers now paraded openly under their slogan, "Support the Qing, Kill the Foreigners." Sometimes they chanted: "See the rain does not come / The sky is as brass / Foreign blood must be spilt / Or the season will pass."[34] On 28 June, Price wrote in her diary: "For months we have been anxious because of drought and feared the suffering that would probably come upon the people, not thinking it would be of any special meaning or menace to us. The past two months have marked such changes that we felt the pressure from lack of rain nearly as keenly as though starving."[35]

A few weeks later, after foreign attacks on the Taku forts, the dowager-empress declared war on Great Britain, Germany, France, the United States, Japan, Italy, Austria, Belgium, and Holland. "For forty years," she says, "I have lain on brushwood and eaten bitterness because of them." In response to her edict, Eva Price, her husband and forty-two other missionaries were promptly slaughtered by Yu Sien's bannermen.[36]

As oral histories gathered in the late 1940s and early 1960s by PRC historians have corroborated, the Boxer Uprising was an extraordinarily broad-based, popular movement. "Sympathy for the Boxer cause appeared almost universal in the villages of the north China plain," and "county after county reported boxing rounds as numerous as 'trees in a forest.'"[37] By contrast, last-minute Manchu support from the cabal around the dowager-empress was wavering and ineffective, while the commercial elites of the Yangzi delta, untouched by famine, acquiesced in foreign intervention with little risk of popular censure. In the end, the courage of the Boxers and Red Lanterns (their female counterparts), armed with little more than sticks and magic charms, was magnificent but of little avail in stationary battles against the combined forces of the Great Powers.

Figure 6.4 One of the Dead in North China

To the millions of deaths in north China from famine and epidemic between 1897 and 1901 were added hundreds of thousands of additional casualties from the exterminating armies of Field-Marshal Von Waldersee (personally ordered by the Kaiser to emulate the carnage of Attila) and the other foreign victors. Even the missionaries rescued by the relief forces were staggered by the scale and ferocity of the vengeance exacted against the Chinese civilian population. "It has seemed," complained Arthur Smith, "as if the foreign troops had come to northern China for the express purpose of committing within the shortest time as many violations as possible of the sixth, the seventh, and the eighth Commandments."[38]

Writing in *The Contemporary Review*, E. Dillon described the shoals of murdered Chinese floating in the Pei-ho River or washed in heaps upon islets and sandbars. One sight was particularly haunting:

Hard by a spot named Koh So, I saw two bodies on a low-lying ledge of the shore. Accustomed by this time to behold in the broad light of day some of the horrors which the soil of the graveyard hides from all living things but the worm, I should have glided carelessly past them but for the pathos of their story, which needed no articulate voice to tell. A father and his boy of eight had been shot down in the name of civilization while holding each other's hands and praying for mercy. And there they lay, hand still holding hand, while a brown dog was slowly eating one of the arms of the father.[39]

After recounting countless other atrocities committed by the allies, including rapes and murders of women and girls, Dillon presciently warned that the "'good work done' by the brave troops in China" had sown the seeds of nationalist revolution. "The policy of the powers is a sowing of the wind, and the harvest reaped will surely be the whirlwind. But that belongs to the 'music of the future.'"[40]

## Brazil: The Days of Judgement

Brazil's nineteenth century ended in a bloody sunset of drought, famine and genocidal state violence. Across widening regional and racial divides, the positivist Republic, established by coup in 1889 and dominated by Paulista elites, conducted a ruthless crusade against poor, drought-stricken but pious *sertanejos* in the Nordeste. The 1897 War of Canudos, which culminated in the destruction of the holy city of Canudos in the Bahian sertão and the massacre of tens of thousands of humble followers of Antonio Conselheiro, is one of the defining events in Brazil's modern history – the subject of Euclydes da Cunha's epic *Os Sertões* [1902]. Another famous backlands utopia led by a religious folk hero, Father Cícero Romão's city of Joãseiro in Ceará's Carirí Valley, narrowly escaped the fate of Canudos: it survived into the twentieth century only through shrewd compromises with local elites. If eschatological imminence (with the oligarchic Republic as the Anti-Christ) suffused both communities, each was also a pragmatic and successful adaptation to continuing environmental crisis and economic decline in the Nordeste. The roots of both movements, moreover, go back to the *Grande Seca* of 1876–78.

The sertão had long been a religious volcano. "Sebastianism," based on mystical belief in the return of the Portuguese monarch who had vanished fighting the Moors in 1578, was particularly widespread. The first massacre of millenarists occurred at Serra do Rodeador in the sertão of Pernambuco in 1819–20. "A prophet gathered together a group of followers to await King Sebastian, who was expected back at any moment to lead them on a crusade for the liberation of Jerusalem." Their roughshod utopia was instead destroyed by a nervous government who viewed the utopian-apocalyptic strand in folk Catholicism with the deepest suspicion.[41] The great droughts of the late nineteenth century, however, only further entrenched Sebastianist eschatology in popular culture. From the ranks of barefoot *beatos* and *beatas*, the famines of 1877 and 1889 mobilized fierce new visions of cataclysm followed by Christ's thousand-year kingdom.

Yet millenarianism in the sertão was also a practical social framework for coping with environmental instability. When foreign priests and missionaries fled the scorched sertão in the spring of 1877, the former-schoolteacher-turned-beato Conselheiro and the ordained priest Cícero stayed behind with their flocks, sermonizing apocalypse but practicing energetic self-help. The first acquired his reputation for holiness by repairing local churches and graveyards, while the second became locally famous for resettling starving drought refugees in the undeveloped but fertile lands of the Araripe Mountains. "When, during the terrible drought of 1877–79, [Cícero] dug wells, erected shelters and planted *mandioca* and *manicoba* for the refugees, the sertões rang with his praises."[42]

As we have seen, the oasis at Joãseiro again became a populist refuge during the scorching, cloudless year of 1888. Under Cícero's energetic direction, *flagelados* planted emergency crops of manioc, slaked their thirst in the perennial waters of the Cariri River, and prayed for rain. Maria de Araujo's *milagre* of the Precious Blood during the Holy Week of 1889 repeated itself for three years, drawing thousands more refugees and pilgrims to Joãseiro while opening a bitter breach between Cícero and a Romanizing church hierarchy – at war with Afro-Brazilian folk Catholicism – who refused to accept that a poor Black woman in the backlands could be the subject of such divine grace.

Drought abated in 1890 – thanks, many sertanejos believed, to the miracle at Joãseiro – but then returned with a vengeance in 1891, one of the most intense El Niño years in modern South American history. The subsequent bursting of the politically manipulated coffee investment bubble known as the *Encilhamento* plunged the Brazilian economy into deep crisis and incited runaway inflation even in advance of the world trade depression of 1893. The milreis lost fully half its value between 1892 and 1897, while the Republic, despite its modernizing pretensions, proved even less capable than the old Empire of providing any aid to the drought- and inflation-ravaged interior of the increasingly peripheralized Nordeste. Under the new federalism virtually all relief and public works were concentrated in the south, leaving the sertanejos at the mercy of corrupt and bankrupt

Figure 6.5  Antonio Conselheiro

state oligarchies.[43]

Simultaneously, there was greater population pressure than in 1877 on the overexploited but simultaneously underdeveloped resources of the sertão. Emancipation in 1888 freed slaves in the coastal plantation belt without providing them with land, tools or real means of independent survival. The decline in the export earnings of sugar at the same time depressed employment. Thousands drifted into the interior, where they joined the multitudes already scratching at the baked earth as sharecroppers, day-laborers or illegal squatters. Rural credit was nonexistent (London still firmly controlled Brazil's finances) and the sertão's reliable water resources were jealously monopolized by large landowners. Thus when drought resumed after 1888, there were few reserves to sustain the population on the land. As in 1877, the officials of Fortaleza, Salvador and the other ports were soon blockading roads against an overwhelming influx of famished refugees. Many sertanejos, however, chose a new survival option: they flocked to the "drought arks" being built by Cícero at Joãseiro, and, after 1892, by Conselheiro at Canudos.

Falsely portrayed by his enemies (and, more recently, by Mario Vargas Llosa) as a raving monster, Conselheiro preached a "dark, unforgiving Catholicism" that, as Robert Levine has shown, was not unorthodox by the traditional standards of the Nordeste. Unlike Cícero, he was not an impresario of miracles, nor did he encourage a cult around himself or perform sacraments. He may have been the sertão's Savonarola or Cotton Mather, but he was not its "messiah." His sermons were typically based on popular missionary tracts, focusing on penitential devotion to Our Lady of Sorrows. Even his interpretation of the recurrent droughts from 1889 on as harbingers of the end of the world was fully in accord with the passionate vision of much of the regular clergy in the Nordeste. On the other hand, when Conselheiro's fierce biblical rectitude crossed into the terrain of politics he was branded as a subversive. His "intense feelings about social justice," especially his opposition to slavery and the exploitation of the poor, led him to advocate nonviolent civic and religious disobedience. In the course of his two decades of spiritual peregrination he was repeatedly arrested, abused and deported by various local authorities – a persecution that only increased his sanctified stature among the sharecroppers and landless laborers of the sertão.[44]

During the 1888–91 drought, Conselheiro had settled followers on two abandoned fazendas north of Salvador. He also supported local market women in their struggle against new municipal taxes, condemning the Republic – which had replaced Christ with Comte – "for trying to deliver the people back into slavery." After an assassination attempt by the Bahian police in early 1893, he decided to move his rapidly growing congregation to the more remote locality of Canudos, 435 miles inland from Salvador. Here, in the center of the high sertão, was a ruined fazenda on fertile land, well defended by rugged mountains and watered by seasonal rivers and reliable springs. Within eighteen months Canudos had burgeoned into a self-sufficient, drought-resistant city of 35,000 people – "a mud-walled Jerusalem" in da Cunha's condescending phrase – that stunned visitors with its relative prosperity (river banks "planted in vegetables, corn, beans, watermelons, squash, cantaloupes, sugar cane, arrowroot, and potatoes") as well as its religious fervor. Although its population was a broad ethnic cross-section of the sertão, the community's civic and military leadership tended to be drawn from such previously outcast groups as the descendants of fugitive slaves, former *cangaceiros* (outlaws) and the remnants of the aboriginal Kiriri people, whose last two chiefs would die fighting to defend Canudos.[45]

For da Cunha and contemporary Brazilian intellectuals imbued with the arrogant liberalism of Comte and Spencer, this secession from Republican modernity could only be the "objectivization of a tremendous insanity." In fact, as Levine points out, "few joined Conselheiro capriciously or because they were seduced by a crazed magician." Instead, like Joãseiro, Canudos was a rational response to the relentless chaos of drought and depression. In the face of the inability of the state to develop, or even slow the decline, of the sertão, it exemplified the practicality of a self-organized, "socialist" alternative, even if its official ideology was Marian and monarchist. And, despite the calumnies of his enemies, Conselheiro did not regiment belief or impose a cult discipline. "Those who wanted to remained in constant touch with neighboring communities; they came and went at will. People visited Canudos, did their business, and left. Many *conselheiristas* worked outside the community every day. They were not prisoners. They came to Canudos to preserve their Catholicism, not to exchange it for a cult or deviant sect."[46]

As recent histories have emphasized, there was no "rebellion in the backlands" (the English title of da Cunha's account), only an attempt at peaceful withdrawal into millenarian autonomy. Like earlier *quilombos* (slave republics) in the Nordeste, however, Canudos's simple desire to be left alone in peace was perceived as a dire threat to social order. On the one hand, the holy city drained the surplus of cheap labor otherwise available to local oligarchs like the legal owner of Canudos, the Baron of Jeremoabo, Bahia's most powerful *fazendeiro*. On the other hand, Canudos signified successful resistance to the new order that the Paulista elites and their republican allies were attempting to impose across Brazil. Like Joãseiro, it also contradicted the church's project of subduing backlands Catholicism. As a result, Conselheiro's premature experiment in a "Christianity of the base" was denounced by Salvador's savants as "communism," by the ultramontane bishops as a "political religious sect," and by the federal government as "seditious monarchism." The Jeremoabos and other big landowners demanded Canudos's prompt destruction.[47]

Towards the end of 1896 – during the onset of a fierce new El Niño drought that lasted, with only brief respites, until 1907[48] – a battalion of Bahian troops, responding to landowners' demands for repression, opened fire on a peaceful procession of penitents. More than 150 were mowed down, but the enraged survivors – many of them tough *jaguncos* (cowboys) or former *cangaceiros* – drove off the troops with heavy casualties. As drought emptied the countryside, the *Canudenses* clung grimly, blunderbusses and knives in hand, to their new gardens and homes. While Conselheiro, seventy years old and in failing health, concentrated on the building of his dream church of Bom Jesus (later dynamited by the army), the actual defense of Canudos was organized by "the people's chieftain," João Abbade, the masterful commander of the Guarda Catolica.[49] In January 1897, he ambushed and routed a second expedition of more than 500 federal troops. As panic swept the coastal cities, a third expedition was prepared under the leadership of "the fearsome infantry commander" Antonio Moreira César. Advancing through an arid countryside made even more forlorn by the scorched-earth strategy of Abbade, César's large, well-armed force, equipped with brand-new Krupp cannons, launched a rash frontal assault on Canudos. It was a suicidal tactical decision reminiscent of Custer's foolish charge at the Little Big Horn:

> In the end, the very primitiveness of Canudos's construction aided in its defense. The settlement itself became a trap into which the arrogant invaders had been lured. Whole battalions were swallowed up in the mass of huts "as into some dark cave." The defenders ambushed the soldiers, using knives, rifles, scythes, cattle prods, and broken household furniture as weapons.[50]

César's supposedly crack troops were systematically annihilated by the Guarda Catolica. For the conselheiristas it was God's greatest miracle; for the federal government in Rio de Janeiro, an unendurable humiliation and challenge to the very legitimacy of the Republic. While balladeers in the sertão mocked the ghost of Moreira César ("Who killed you? It was a bullet from Canudos sent by the Conselheiro!"), a fourth expedition of overwhelming power – Brazil's greatest military exertion since the Paraguayan War – was painstakingly organized. Conscripts were told that they were marching off to "combat the forces of the devil."[51] The "final assault" began in July, but the Canudenses, well aware that this was a war of extermination, held out for three long months against modern artillery. "Canudos," da Cunha wrote, "did not surrender. The only case of its kind in history, it held out to the last man. Conquered inch by inch, in the literal meaning of the words, it fell on October 5, towards dusk – when its last defenders fell, dying, every man of them. There were only four of them left: an old man, two other full-grown men, and a child, facing a furiously raging army of five thousand men."[52] What had become the Europeanized Republic's race war against the "half-breed" followers of Conselheiro ended in an orgy of revenge.

> Some were shot when they could not keep up with the forced march. A pregnant woman whose labor pains had started was placed in an empty shack by the side of the road and abandoned. Soldiers killed children by smashing their skulls against trees.... Wounded *conselheirisas* were drawn and quartered or hacked to pieces limb

by limb. Their carcasses were doused with oil and burned – the same treatment as was given the surviving dwellings in Canudos. The army systematically eradicated the remaining traces of the holy city as if it had housed the devil incarnate.[53]

While Canudos was fighting for its life, Father Cícero was desperately refuting published reports that he was organizing an army of "Cearan fanatics" to come to its relief. Although the cannons were not yet pounding its homes to rubble, Joãseiro was also besieged by diverse enemies who equated its folk Catholicism (especially the growing numbers of apocalyptic beatos and beatas) with subversion in Bahia. In 1894, at the behest of the Brazilian hierarchy, the Inquisition in Rome had declared Joãseiro's "living saint" Maria de Araujo a fraud and suspended Cícero from sacramental office. Liberals equally looked for the "Conselheiro-like" glint of sedition in his eyes. But Father Cícero proved to be a wily politician (twenty years later, he would be acknowledged as the "most powerful figure in the Nordeste") who eschewed attacks on the status quo. In particular, he quelled fazendeiros' fears about disruptions in the labor market by contracting his followers to work on their estates. In contrast to Conselheiro's unyielding refusal to "render unto Caesar," Cícero "saved" Joãseiro by deutopianizing it: that is to say, by reintegrating it into traditional economic and political backwardness. As a result, Joãseiro (or Juarzeiro in modern spelling) a century later has shopping malls and slums, while Canudos remains a haunted ruin.[54]

In the end, however, neither the death of Conselheiro nor the opportunism of Cícero solved the labor problems of the regional elites. The El Niño–driven cycle of drought (1888–89, 1891, 1897–98, and 1899–1900) coupled with the declining earnings of all the Nordeste's traditional exports led to the gradual depopulation of parts of the sertão. The influx of the 1880s became the exodus of the 1890s. By 1900 at least 300,000 sertanejos had fled drought and repression for the gamble of a new life in the rubber forests of the Amazon.[55] As della Cava points out, the structural and environmental crisis of the Nordeste assumed its most extreme form in Antonio Conselheiro's home state of Ceará:

> Ample federal subsidies financed the outward passage to the Far North, while Ceará's state government collected a "head tax" for each able body that departed. Ironically the policy of substituting human exports, capable of remitting earnings home, for the export of raw materials soon resulted in the real crisis of the

Northeast.... Indeed, without cheap and abundant labor the traditional agriculture of the arid Northeast – cotton and cattle – was incapable of recovering in non-drought years and, in fact, was threatened with extinction.... Not even the collapse of the Brazilian rubber boom around 1913 alleviated the Northeastern labor shortage. It remained chronic until the early 1920s.[56]

## Colonial Asia: Starvation as Strategy

Throughout monsoon Asia, drought and crop failure interacted with increasing disease mortality, especially malaria in its most virulent strain. Rinderpest, as in Africa, ruined tens of thousands of small cultivators in southeast Asia whose major capital was their bullock or ox. Where small peasants and sharecroppers were conscripted into export commodity circuits, the world depression of 1893 had left a legacy of crushing debt, aggravated by the implacable revenue demands of the state. Everywhere, anticolonialism arrived as a watershed between religious millenarianism and modern nationalism. In some cases, like Korea and the Philippines, local messianism and revolutionary nationalism became complexly intertwined. So were environmental crisis and colonial exploitation.

Korea at the end of the Victorian era was still reeling from the terrible repression of the Tonghak Revolution by the Japanese in 1894–95. This undoubtedly explains why, despite the continuing erosion of national sovereignty and rural food security, there was no large-scale counterpart to the Boxers. The drought-famine of 1900–01 in southern Korea, however, did produce new seedlings of peasant self-organization and national resistance. In Cholla and Kyongsang, farmers, some of them Tonghak veterans, formed antilandlord groups known as *hwalpindang* ("help-the-poor party"), and on the famine-wracked island of Cheju, troops were dispatched to suppress antitax and anti-Christian riots.[57]

In the Dutch East Indies, meanwhile, there was widespread apprehension that the economic fabric of colonialism was beginning to unravel. The drought of 1896–97 was compounded by falling global commodity prices as well as diseases that attacked the sugar and coffee crops, making it impossible for planters to raise output. Rural per capita output and probably income stagnated between 1880 and 1900.[58] Liberal imperialism seemed to be on the verge of bankruptcy:

Prices were falling ... exports were almost stagnant, and imports were declining. The long-drawn [-out] Achin war was exhausting the country like a cancer; expenses were rising, revenue was falling, and attempts to raise new revenue were unproductive. Prospects were so bad that fewer Europeans sought a living in the Indies, and the population born in Europe fell from 14,316 in 1895 to 13,676 in 1905. Deputies heatedly discussed whether the situation was anxious, alarming, dangerous or critical, but all agreed that the patient was ill. Then in 1900–1 news of widespread crop failure and cattle disease aroused apprehensions of a general economic collapse.[59]

In Java, the greatest distress eventually centered on the Residency of Semarang, where in 1849–50 more than 80,000 peasants had died in a famine that contributed to the decline and fall of the *cultuurstelsel*.[60] From the end of 1899 or early 1900, and continuing through 1902, the region was again battered by drought and hunger as well as rinderpest and cholera. "The people," wrote local officials, "whose number had been decimated by the epidemic in several regions dared not leave their homes, and they abandoned even the fields."[61]

Once again the Dutch were faced with dramatic evidence that village subsistence was collapsing under the weight of the "corrupt exploitation of the peasant's labour power, the land rent and crop payment system, and the appropriation of peasant land."[62] Under indictment was the free-market system that Dutch Liberals had modeled on British India. Although its ideologues had claimed that piecemeal deregulation would lead to a better balance between export and subsistence sectors, the "Liberal period" (1877–1900) actually "represented a major intensification in the exploitation of Java's agricultural resources." Rice consumption per capita, as well as wages, fell significantly, while poor villagers became even more entrapped in debts to moneylenders and grain merchants.[63] It is not surprising, therefore, that colonial officials reacted to the Semarang famine in the true spirit of Sir Richard Temple: blaming the dying peasants for not being able to look after their own interests and concluding that more compulsion was required in the organization of rice cultivation.[64]

In the Netherlands, however, there was a backlash from socialist and Calvinist parties against the ruthless colonial policy exemplified in the official reaction to the Semarang famine. This led to a famous investigation into "the declining prosperity of the Javanese people," conducted from 1902 to 1905 and published in fourteen volumes in 1914, that finally forced the abandonment of a strictly laissez-faire colonial policy. The so-called "Ethical Policy," as crafted by Alexander Idenburg – variously, the minister of colonies and governor-general of Java – was supposedly based on a new trio of priorities: education, irrigation and emigration. The debate that produced the Ethical Policy has often been favorably contrasted to the obdurate conservatism of the Edwardian Raj. In practice, however, the reforms in Java went hand in hand with the military consolidation of Dutch power in the outer islands (the Dutch, like the Americans in Mindanao, were still mopping up local resistance in the Moluccas and New Guinea until the eve of the First World War.)[65] Moreover, "Ethics" did little to reduce the exploitation, or increase the food-security, of ordinary Javanese. Their real impact, rather, was to shift government investment toward the pacified outer islands in support of Royal Dutch Shell and other private interests who were exploiting lucrative oil and rubber bonanzas.[66]

In the Philippines, drought again brought famine to Negros's infamous sugar plantations in 1896–97, then returned to devastate agriculture on Luzon, Panay and other big islands from 1899 to 1903.[67] Climate stress was alloyed with warfare, poverty and ecological crisis. Thus the first phase of drought-famine coincided with a national uprising against the Spanish, while the second overlapped patriotic resistance to US recolonization. The independence movement itself, moreover, was spurred by the growing crisis of food security since mid-century, when Spain (prodded by Britain) had launched an ambitious campaign to develop exports and commercialize agriculture. Traditional forms of communal land ownership and subsistence-oriented production had been violently dismantled in favor of rice and sugar monocultures operated by pauperized smallholders and debt-shackled sharecroppers. (Spanish and mestizo *hacenderos,* like ubiquitous Chinese grain merchants and moneylenders, were merely links in a long chain of exploitation ultimately controlled by distant British and American trading companies.) Moreover, as the export boom generated a demand for new plantation land, Luzon's interior foothills were rapidly deforested, leading by the 1890s to the silting of river beds, more intense flooding, and gradual aridification of the lowlands.[68]

In addition, as Ken De Bevoise has shown, living standards and public health had been undermined by the ecological chain reaction set in motion by the arrival of the rinderpest virus in the late 1880s. "Arguably the single greatest

catastrophe in the nineteenth-century Philippines," rinderpest killed off most of
the draft animals on Luzon and forced farmers to drastically reduce the extent
of cultivation, aggravating malnutrition and debt. Meanwhile, "untilled land that
returned to scrub or vegetation provided favorable breeding conditions for both
locusts and anopheline mosquitos.... In lieu of its preferred blood meals [cattle],
*A. Minimus blaviorstris* increased its human-biting rate, setting off seasonal epidemics that made it difficult for the labor force to work even the reduced amount
of agricultural acreage." Thus debilitated by malaria and impoverished by the
loss of their cattle, Filipinos were then exposed to the microbial campfollowers
of the invading Spanish and US armies. The 122,000 American troops, especially,
brought a whole stream of diseases including hookworm as well as new lethal
strains of malaria, smallpox and venereal disease.[69]

The Americans, moreover, exceeded even the cruelest Spanish precedents
in manipulating disease and hunger as weapons against an insurgent but weakened population. Beginning with the outbreak of war in February 1899, military
authorities closed all the ports, disrupting the vital inter-island trade in foodstuffs
and preventing the migration of hungry laborers to food-surplus areas. Then,
as drought began to turn into famine in 1900, they authorized the systematic
destruction of rice stores and livestock in areas that continued to support guerrilla resistance. As historians would later point out, the ensuing campaign of
terror against the rural population, backed up by a pass system and population
"reconcentration," prefigured US strategy in Vietnam during the 1960s. "All palay,
rice, and storehouses clearly for use by enemy soldiers," writes De Bevoise, "were
to be destroyed. That plan would have caused hardship for the people even had
it been implemented as intended, since guerrillas and civilians often depended on
the same rice stockpiles, but the food-denial program got out of hand. Increasingly unsure who was enemy and who was friend, American soldiers on patrol
did not agonize over such distinctions. They shot and burned indiscriminately,
engaging in an orgy of destruction throughout the Philippines." As one soldier
wrote back home to Michigan: "We burned every house, destroyed every cara-
bao and other animals, all rice and other foods." As a result, "agricultural production was so generally crippled during the American war that food-surplus regions
hardly existed."[70]

As peasants began to die of hunger in the fall of 1900, American officers openly acknowledged in correspondence that starvation had become official military strategy. "The result is inevitable," wrote Colonel Dickman from Panay, "many people will starve to death before the end of six months."[71] On Samar, Brigadier General Jacob Smith ordered his men to turn the interior into a "howling wilderness."[72] Famine, in turn, paved the way for cholera (which especially favored the reconcentration camps), malaria, smallpox, typhoid, tuberculosis "and everything else that rode in war's train of evils." In such circumstances, of course, it was impossible to disentangle the victims of drought from the casualties of warfare, or to clearly distinguish famine from epidemic mortality. Nonetheless, De Bevoise concludes, "it appears that the American war contributed directly and indirectly to the loss of more than a million persons from a base population of about seven million." In comparative terms, this was comparable to mortality during the Irish famine of the 1840s.[73]

One of the most remarkable local rebellions during the Philippines' war for independence coincided with the ravages of drought and hunger on Negros. On the big sugar island anti-imperialism fused with stark class conflict between *hacenderos* and *pumuluyo* (the common people). The Negrense elites "to protect their interests against increasingly hungry and dissatisfied workers and peasants" ardently sided first with the Spanish, then with the American colonialists. They chose the Sugar Trust rather than Aguinaldo.[74] As arriving US military officals discovered, the protracted drought had made these social tensions volcanic. "The unusual dryness of the season," wrote the commanding officer of the Manapla and Victorias districts in June 1900, "has operated against the crops ... and has materially injured the sugarcane. On this account, many owners of haciendas have been forced to discharge part, if not all, of their laborers as they could not be fed. These laborers are now without means and work and the price of food is high."[75]

When the explosion came, it merged the grievances of unemployed sugar workers and marginalized peasants with those of aboriginal people displaced from their forests by land-hungry haciendas. The largest uprising was led by a Zapata-like plantation worker and *babaylan*, Dionisio Sigobela, more popularly known as Papa Isio, who conducted guerrilla warfare against the Guardia Civil, then the US Army, from his base on impenetrable Mt. Kanlaon. The restoration of food security and economic independence were principal goals of the struggle.

"Although Papa Isio's ideology fused animism with anti-Spanish nationalism," Alfred McCoy explains, "his movement remained a class, rather than racial war, waged by sugar workers determined to destroy the sugar plantations and return the island to peasant rice farming." In the district around La Carlota, Papa Isio's followers chased away planters, murdered those that resisted, and burned scores of haciendas. The rebellion was not finally defeated until 1908, "five years after the revolution had ended in most areas of the archipelago."[76]

## Africa: Europeans as Locusts

For most of Africa the 1875–1895 period, with the exceptions of the 1876–79 drought in South Africa and the 1889–91 catastrophe in Ethiopia and the Sudan, had been a period of better-than-average rainfall and ample pasturage, encouraging population growth, the formation of heavily nucleated settlements, and the cultivation of previously marginal soils. Ecological stability reduced the conflicts over grazing rights and water sources that traditionally provoked warfare between cattle-owning peoples. "A striking feature of many travellers' accounts of East and Central Africa in the nineteenth century is the evident agricultural prosperity of many – though not all – of its peoples and the great variety of produce grown, together with the volume of local, regional, and long-distance trade and the emergence of a wide range of entrepreneurs."[77] This is the social landscape that some historians have called "Merrie Africa."[78]

Then in 1896–97 the climate dramatically reversed itself. "A map of Africa illustrating the rainfall data for the period from 1870 to 1895 bears a healthy flush of plus signs ... but the map for the following twenty-five years is covered with minuses." Disasters "of biblical proportions" engulfed east and southeast Africa "just when Europe decided to take over the continent."[79] The unusual fin de siècle sequence of a very strong El Niño in 1896 punctually followed by a powerful La Niña event in 1898 and then the resumption of El Niño conditions in 1899 brought severe drought, first to southern, then to east Africa. The Portuguese reported drought and smallpox around Luanda in Angola in 1898. Drought also returned to the Sahel, and there is evidence of another famine (1900–1903) in the bend of the Niger River. Rainfall also faltered over the Ethiopian highlands, and the Nile flood in 1899 was the lowest since 1877–78.[80] Indeed, from the flanks of Mount Kenya to plateaux of Swaziland, millions of farmers and pastoralists struggled against crop failure and relentless onslaughts of rinderpest (which killed 95 percent of tropical Africa's cattle), smallpox, influenza, jiggers, tsetse flies, locusts and Europeans.[81]

The spirit-mediums of the Mwari cult at Great Zimbabwe told the Shona and Ndebele – whose lands and cattle had been recently stolen by Cecil Rhodes's British South Africa Company – that this chain of calamity would never be broken as long as the Europeans remained on their soil. ("Drought" and "disaster," significantly, are the same word in Shona: *shangwa*.) In his pioneering "Afrocentric" account of the 1896 risings in Matabeleland and Mashonaland, Terence Ranger stressed the striking similarity of the *mentalités* behind the Zimbabwean and Boxer revolts. Just as Boxer proclamations warned that "the Catholic and Protestant religions being insolent to the gods ... the rain clouds no longer visit us," so the divine Mwari, speaking through the mediums, told warriors: "These white men are your enemies. They killed your fathers, sent the locusts, this disease among the cattle, and bewitched the clouds so that we have no rain. Now you go and kill these white people and drive them out of our fathers' land and I will take away the cattle disease and the locusts and send you rain."[82] Despite incredible courage and early victories, both peoples were soon defeated, as much by *shangwa* and smallpox as by Rhodes's machine-gunners. Diehard bands of rebel warriors, sometimes finding game but mostly eating wild roots and the rotten skins of cattle killed by rinderpest, managed to hold out in the drought-stricken foothills until the summer of 1898.[83]

In central Kenya – where the 1897–99 drought is still recalled today as *Yua ya Ngomanisye*, "the famine that went everywhere" – the small, autonomous farming societies of the highland margin never rose in revolt against the British, but suffered social disintegration nonetheless. In some areas, the rains failed three years in a row and food reserves that might have arrested famine were depleted to feed railroad construction crews and Uganda-bound safaris. In addition, the bubonic plague, most likely brought from India with coolie labor, was the first passenger on the yet unfinished Uganda Railroad. As a result, according to a white settler, "the railway line was a mass of corpses."[84] Suffering was still intense when Halford Mackinder, the future apostle of imperialist geopolitics, passed down the line in July 1899, en route to a first ascent of Mount Kenya. Noting the "horrible evidence of the famine among the Wakamba," which had driven some men to raiding, he criticized the railroad police for indiscriminately burning villages in retaliation: "If food is destroyed the famine is made worse, and that is the prime cause of the raids." He also frowned at the Uganda Railroad's brutal expropriation of all the farmland in a two-mile corridor along its tracks.[85]

Mackinder and his companions, like European observers during the earlier Ethiopian drought, were stunned by the audacity with which drought-crazed lions and other large carnivores stalked men in broad daylight. Indeed, American missionaries in northern Uluwere were so mortified by the sudden aggressiveness of wildlife that they refused to leave their compound. "These are days," wrote one of them, "in which we are witnessing scenes almost too horrible to narrate." As famine victims weakened and collapsed by the roadside, for instance, they were promptly eaten alive by hyenas or had their eyes pecked out by vultures. Although the British eventually made desultory efforts to feed some of the surviving population, the losses were already enormous. In the single village in Kikuyuland where a famine census was undertaken, one-third of adult males had died by the end of 1899. Mortality amongst women and children may have been much higher.[86]

The same drought conditions also brought fearful famine to the Kikuyu and Kamba on the eastern side of the Rift Valley. Like the neighboring and purely pastoral Masai, these more sedentary peoples had already lost the greater part of their cattle wealth to rinderpest and livestock pleuro-pneumonia. Then, for the three years from 1896 to 1900, crop after crop withered in their fields. The coup de grace, as on the slopes of Mount Kenya, was smallpox, which "attacked the Kikuyu with particular virulence, especially in the more recently occupied southern tip of Kiambu."[87] In these densely populated areas, according to Marcia Wright, the mortality was an incredible 50 percent to 95 percent, and Kikuyu society tottered on the edge of complete disintegration.[88] At the climax of the famine in central Kenya, farmers' sons formed outlaw bands called *muthakethe*. "Ignoring the accepted strict limits on the use of violence, these bands preyed on the most vulnerable members of society, including children, the elderly, and the sick. Ranging out from makeshift bush camps, outlaw raiders attacked poorly defended herds and homesteads, seizing not only cattle and goats, but whatever food and property they could lay their hands on."[89]

"Any kind of concerted opposition to British control," however, "was out of the question." Using the hungry Masai as their mercenaries, the British were able to extend their new protectorate deep into Kikuyu and Kamba territory.[90] The Masai, of course, had their own grievances. They bitterly complained to Mackinder's party that British sponsorship of agriculturalists had intensified the famine by degrading the crucial watersheds and forests upon which their herds depended. "The Wakikuyu being under our protection are not now raided by the Masai. Therefore they have cleared much forest, and cultivated the virgin soil. The Masai are angry about this, because the rivers of the plain are in consequence liable to run dry, and there is no forest grass for their cattle in times of drought."[91]

The famine of 1898–1900, as Frederick Cooper has shown, also accelerated the decline of Arab and Swahili economic hegemony along the Kenyan coast. The decline in grain production, or its diversion to inland famine districts, weakened the plantation sector, while simultaneously the Mijikenda, who occupied the drought afflicted hinterland behind Malindi and Mombasa, encroached on coastal resources. "In the previous devastating famine in the hinterland in 1884, many children were pawned to coastal slaveowners, but this time Mijikenda came to the coast to obtain food through work, credit, charity, and helping themselves to land." The squatter agriculture of the Mijikenda quickly became a thorn in the side of British efforts to buttress traditional elites and land-titles. During another La Niña drought in 1914, the British moved savagely against a subgroup of Mijikenda squatters, the Giriama, killing 250 people and destroying 70 percent of their dwellings.[92]

The drought, in association with rinderpest, also devastated Uganda, where an estimated 40,000 people starved to death in Busoga and perhaps an equal number in Bunyoro, where colonial warfare had severely disrupted the economy. Moreover, a new scourge, sleeping sickness, followed hard on the heels of famine. "Whence it came is still a matter for speculation; but by 1902 deaths from sleeping sickness were being numbered in Buganda and Busoga in tens of thousands, and it was spreading to marginal areas elsewhere."[93] In central Africa, however, not every group suffered equal losses, nor did Europeans always gain the upper hand. The formidable Nandi people, for example, remained relatively immune from ecological disaster on their plateau between Lake Victoria and the Rift

Valley. Likewise, as rinderpest impoverished the Tutsi and made them more dependent upon the agricultural Iru, the centralized Kingdom of Rwanda waxed in strength.[94]

In Tanganyika the murderous drought of 1898–1900 (following locust famines in 1894–96) likewise combined with rinderpest and the colonial iron heel to threaten the very survival of peasant society. The introduction of monetary taxation in 1898, as elsewhere, was designed to hammer autonomous peasants into malleable wage-laborers on German plantations. When famished villages in the Nguu highlands refused to pay the new tax, German military patrols pillaged their grain stores and randomly murdered local people. Terrorized farmers were thus forced to sell their remaining grain reserves to coastal merchants and missionaries, who promptly hiked prices by 100 percent or more. A decade earlier, during the long "comet drought" of 1884–86, many highlanders had relied on grain supplied by patrons who, in turn, were enriched by the ivory trade. Now the Germans had gained control of the trade and replaced traditional chieftains with their own functionaries. With the destruction of village patrimonialism, the only option for villagers now reduced to "walking skeletons" was flight to the coastal towns or major inland administrative centers, where congestion favored smallpox epidemics that wiped out nearly half of the population. As ethno-historian James Giblin has shown in a remarkable case-study of the Uzigua region, this temporary abandonment of the countryside unleashed a nightmare biological chain-reaction. The collapse of vegetation control – the constant brush-clearing practiced by local farmers – allowed tsetse fly and tick-borne epizootics to take hold over a vast area of Tanganyika's lowlands, which they still rule more than a century later.[95]

In Mozambique, drought-driven peasant uprisings coalesced into a war of liberation that briefly threatened to push the colonialists into the sea. Insatiable demands for tax revenue and forced labor, as Vail and White point out, coincided with "a drought and a startling famine which exceeded all previous Portuguese experience."[96] "To Africans plagued by seasonal famines, taxation to be paid in agricultural produce intensified the problems of feeding their own families…. In the more arid regions, especially Tete district, the tax obligation threatened the health and well-being of the rural poulation."[97] In May 1897, Cambuemba led a broad anti-Portuguese coalition that burned plantations and disrupted river traffic in the lower Zambesi Valley. Simultaneously, spirit mediums roused the Tawara (Shona), who, in alliance with the Massangano and the Barue on the upper Zambesi, seized most of Tete and the northeastern frontier. "By 1901 the situation had become intolerable for the Europeans." Although the Barue were eventually crushed, the intensification of drought and cattle fever in 1903, as well as a major smallpox epidemic, renewed warnings from the famed medium Kanowanga that "both plagues would continue until the white men were driven from the ancestral homelands" of the Tawara in Tete and eastern Rhodesia. As earlier in Rhodesia, the ultimate defeat of the Shona Rebellion of 1904 was due to hunger and disease almost as much as to combined British and Portuguese military might.[98]

## Twentieth-Century Repercussions

This generation of disaster forever transfigured African society. Robin Palmer, in his major study of the roots of poverty in southern Africa, contrasts the dynamic village economies of the early 1890s with the "picture of widespread stagnation and decay" thirty years later: the decline in crop diversity and output, the cessation of inter-African trade, and the forced dependence on mine labor or urban migration. "By 1939 virtually all vestiges of African economic independence have been shattered, African cultivators have become tied to a world market over which they have no control, and a pattern of underdevelopment has been firmly established."[99] The colonial state, moreover, deeply entrenched itself in the social inequalities unleashed by drought-famine and epidemic disease. The "traditional" chiefs of the late colonial period were often little more than officially sanctioned vultures who had fattened themselves on communal disaster. "Even more striking [than missionary conversions]," writes Charles Ambler of Kenya after 1898, "was the way that the individuals whom the British recognized as 'chiefs' were able to accumulate power during the famine. Despite sometimes violent local hostility, a number of such men were able to expand substantially both their livestock herds and their circles of dependents and clients.... One woman from a poor background pointed to this process of accumulation with some bitterness: 'When the people who had gone away came back those rich who had remained tried to keep those returning from owning anything.'"[100]

The fin de siècle famines had comparable repercussions in the rest of the non-

Western world. In India, as we have seen, peasant indebtedness and land alienation soared and caste lines hardened during the long droughts. During famine
peasants were typically caught in a scissors between the falling value of their
assets and soaring food prices manipulated by middlemen who doubled as grain
merchants and usurers. In pre-British India, without an effective land market in
operation, the livelihood of the moneylenders had been tied to the survival of
the peasant household. However, "the decline in the solidarity of the village
community in the Deccan – partly connected with the decline in the social and
economic standing of the traditional officials such as the patels, desais and des-
mukhs – reduced the strength of the customary sanctions with which the villages
once could threaten the *vanias*."[101] After the British commodified property rights,
moreover, famine became a powerful opportunity for the accumulation of land
and servile labor. State enforcement of debt collection through the decisions of
distant and hostile courts amounted to (in Banaji's stinging phrase) "an arming
of the moneylenders."[102] The parasite, in effect, no longer needed to save its host.
Indeed, as Sumit Guha has shown in the case of the Bombay Deccan, middlemen
of all kinds, including rich peasants with a greater appetite for land than the mercantile castes, could now profit from the destruction of the independent cultivator. Rich peasants and roving cattle dealers also exploited hard times to buy cattle
cheap in drought-stricken regions and sell them dear in unaffected areas.[103]

There has been brisk debate, however, about how such famine-driven asset
redistribution affected agrarian class structures. Banaji, for instance, has argued
that famine "proletarianized" vast numbers of small cultivators in the Deccan,
while Arnold has retorted that real rural capitalism, based on the competitive capitalization of cultivation, was an illusion and that famine victims were only "semi-
proletarianized."[104] Likewise Charlesworth has pointed to the "vast increase in
tenancy in Bombay Presidency between 1880 and 1920," with the 1897–1902
Maharastran famines setting "the seal on the stratification process" by driving
the poor ryots to the wall "while a stratum of rich peasants consolidated their
newly 'dominant' position in village life."[105] (Indeed, Sir John Strachey took Social
Darwinist "hope and encouragement" from the fact that famine mortality in the
late 1890s spared rich peasants while decimating the poor.)[106] Sumit Guha, on
the other hand, claims that the social pyramid of the Bombay Deccan was "flat-
tened" not steepened since he believed that the famine had simultaneously killed

off poor laborers and impoverished more prosperous ryots.[107] Kaiwar stakes out
yet another position, arguing that "despite famines and epidemics there was a
remarkable continuity in the composition of both groups [rich and poor peas-
ants] in the years between the 1850s and 1947."[108]

China scholars have engaged in a symmetrical debate over famine, immiseration and stratification in the Yellow River plain. In his careful review of the village
social surveys undertaken in the 1930s and 1940s, Philip Huang has pointed to the
emergence of an aggressive stratum of "managerial" peasants, employing wage
labor and fully oriented to the market, who at least from the crisis of 1898–1900
had begun to exploit disasters as "business opportunities in rags." Yet, as Huang
persuasively argues, huge structural obstacles – including the lack of capital, the
centrifugal effects of partible inheritance, the decline of state investment in flood
control, and so on – prevented rich peasants from undertaking capitalist agriculture in any genuine sense. Capital–labor ratios did not increase, and there was
no competition-driven dynamic of investment in farm machinery, fertilizers, irrigation systems or new cultivation techniques.[109] Wealthier peasants simply took
advantage of a labor surplus to enlarge the scale of family cultivation. "There
was thus something of a stagnated equilibrium between managerial and family
farming. The most successful family peasants became managerial farmers, only
to slide back down into the small-peasant economy within a few generations."
The key structural trend, ratcheted upwards by drought, flood and famine, was
the growing percentage of the rural population that desperately sought wage-
labor to supplement the output from farms that were now too small to generate
subsistence. These "semi-proletarians" ranged from full-time day-laborers who
retained their own tiny plots to poor peasants who worked seasonally for their
"rich" neighbors.[110]

Huang thus joins with Indian historians like Arnold who see "semi-proletarianization" as the dominant structural outcome of the late-nineteenth-century
subsistence crises. "In using the term 'semi-proletarianization,' he explains, " I do
not mean to suggest that it was transitional to capitalism and complete proletarianization, as if those represented some inevitable stage of historical development
[as in Mao], but rather to characterize a process of social change distinctive of
a peasant society and economy under the combined pressures of social differentiation and intense population pressure, without the outlet and relief provided

by dynamic capitalist development."[111] (Tichelman makes a similar point about Indonesia in the late nineteenth century, where under the pressure of the colonial export regime "class differentiation in the village took not so much the form of proletarianization as of pauperization."[112]) Unlike Western Europe, which had such powerful urban growth-engines supercharged by the products and consumptions of wealthy colonies, Asia had neither burgeoning cities nor overseas colonies in which to exploit the labor of its supernumerary rural poor. The spectacular growth of entrepôt ports like Bombay and Shanghai was counterbalanced by the decline of interior cities like Lucknow and Xian. In relative terms, urban demography in India and north China (only 4.2 percent of the population) stood still (or even slightly declined) for the entire Victorian epoch.[113] Even the coolie trade – the estimated 37 million laborers sent abroad from India, China, Malaya and Java in the nineteenth and early twentieth centuries – did little to ease the crisis of undercapitalization in the Asian countryside.[114]

Did the tens of millions of peasants warehoused by the late-Victorian world economy in the purgatory of marginal petty-commodity production come to constitute a social force in their own right? Likewise, under what conditions did "semi-proletarianization," reproduced by famine and environmental instability, lead to new forms of protest and resistance? The clearest evidence of a juncture between the collective experience of nineteenth-century famine and twentieth-century revolutionary politics, as one might expect, comes from the insurrectionary seedbed of north China. In 1941–42 a Communist research team led by Chai Shufan carefully surveyed the impact of three generations of war and disaster on the regions of northern Shaanxi that had become the fortress of the Eighth Route Army after its famous 1937 Long March. Here the drought catastrophes of 1877 and 1900 had been repeated in the "Great Northwest Famine" of 1928–31 (3 million to 6 million dead), with each famine producing abrupt increases in poverty, landlessness and dependence on wage labor. (Landlordism, so central a peasant grievance in the Yangzi Valley and southern China,was a much more variable and locally specific issue than environmental insecurity in north China.) Pauline Keating summarizes the team's analysis of the "poverty trap that was making the poor poorer." It is a paradigmatic description – worth quoting at some length – of Huang's "semi-proletarian" condition:

Under-resourced families typically farmed the least fertile land and, not owning livestock, had to rely exclusively on nightsoil to manure their land. Both tenants and poor landowners often farmed several small plots and had to traipse distances of two or three kilometers between them. Like poor farmers all over China, they always had to look for supplementary employment, and their odd-jobbing during busy seasons was at the cost of their own crops. The 1942 survey team gave the example of a Suide county village in which 31 percent of all poor farmers hired themselves out at one time or another to other farmers each year, and another 31 percent hired out full-time.... The Communist survey team estimated that farming in the Suide-Mizhi counties provided full-time employment for less than half of the available workforce in 1942.[115]

Suide's most important and widespread sideline industry was cotton spinning and weaving. Cotton growing had once been well established in places east of the Wuding River, but under the warlords most farms were turned from cotton to opium poppies.... The radical reduction of cotton growing, combined with competition from foreign textiles and the collapse of trade during the civil war, all but destroyed the folk textile industry.... Still, because a strong spinning and weaving tradition lived on in Suide's peasant households, the Communists found it relatively easy to push forward a "mass movement" of spinning cooperatives here.[116]

As Keating explains, Mao's "Yenan Way," conceived in the historic epicenter of the great drought-famines, was a strategic response to a poor peasantry for whom the stabilization of the natural and social conditions of production, after so much chronic disaster and war, had become a revolutionary life-and-death issue.[117]

# PART III

# Decyphering ENSO

# Seven

# The Mystery of the Monsoons

Each veil lifted revealed a multitude of others. They perceived a chain of inter-locking and interdependent mysteries, the meteorological equivalent of DNA and the double helix.
— Alexander Frater, *Chasing the Monsoon*

The search for the cause of the global droughts of the 1870s and 1890s became an extraordinary scientific detective story. What we now understand as the El Niño-Southern Oscillation (ENSO) was the elusive great white whale of tropical meteorology for almost a century. Contemporary science, to be sure, believed it had harpooned the beast at first sight during the famines of 1876–78. But initial jubilation over the discovery of the sun's supposed control over monsoon rainfall and tropical drought soon turned into perplexity and frustration as celebrated sunspot correlations evaporated in a chaotic statistical fog. Heroic efforts in the early twentieth century – based on the premise that weather like geopolitics is organized by a few "strategic centers of action" – brought more order to meteorological data and disclosed the existence of a vast Indo-Pacific seesaw of air mass known as the Southern Oscillation (SO). But no sooner had Sir Gilbert Walker, the Captain Ahab of the Indian Meteorological Service, sighted the SO in the late 1920s than his research program was capsized by its own epistemological contradictions. After decades of demoralization, the hunt was finally revived and carried to a stunning conclusion in the 1960s by an aged Viking warrior of weather science, Jacob Bjerknes.

Before recounting this saga in some detail, it may be helpful to first put the monster itself into clearer view. For the nonscientific reader, especially, it is best to know something about the solution before we have even fully encountered the mystery. In the first iteration (which means robbed of all the complex beauty, beloved by geophysicists, of Kelvin waves and delayed-oscillators), the modern theory of ENSO might be summarized as follows:

World climate (the oceans, atmosphere and ice surfaces acting together) is driven by the excess of solar energy received in equatorial latitudes. Climate, indeed, is just the time-averaged precipitation and wind patterns created by the poleward redistribution of this energy.[1] But the tropical regions, where oceans and atmosphere are most tightly coupled, do not accumulate heat evenly. Tropical solar energy is moved by surface winds and ocean currents into several equatorial storage systems. The easterly trade winds, for instance, drive the warm surface waters of the equatorial Pacific westward. A "cold tongue" (the Pacific Dry Zone) forms off South America where cold water upwells to replace the stripped-away surface layer, while warm water pools around the "maritime continent" of Indonesia-Australia. This Warm Pool, with its atmospheric companion, the Indo-Australian Convergence Zone (IACZ), is the most powerful of the earth's regional heat engines (the others are the Amazon Basin and equatorial Africa) and sustains the largest organized system of deep convection: the transfer of energy from ocean to atmosphere through condensation and release of the latent heat of water vapor. Indeed, it can be imagined as a kind of cloud factory where the warmest surface waters on the globe daily manufacture untold thousands of towering cumulonimbus clouds.

The El Niño or warm phase of the ENSO occurs when the trade winds subside or reverse direction and the Warm Pool with its vast canopy of tropical thunderstorms moves eastward into the central Pacific, around the International Date Line. Correlatively, the normal "downhill" pressure gradient between the South Pacific High and the IACZ that drives the trade winds reverses itself. The sudden fall of barometers over the east-central Pacific (as measured in Papeete) and their simultaneous rise over the maritime continent (as measured in Darwin) is the "Southern Oscillation." Global wind circulation, meanwhile, reorganizes itself

# NON-EL NIÑO

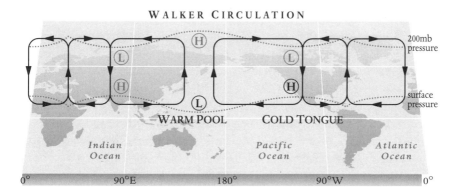

# EL NIÑO

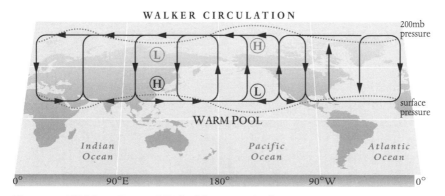

Figure 7.1  El Niño as Eastward Shift of the Warm Pool

around the IACZ's new location, massively shifting rainfall patterns throughout the tropics and parts of the higher latitudes. The jet streams are displaced equatorward, pushing weather systems into anomalous latitudes. The "El Niño" aspect of ENSO results from the subsequent warming of the Pacific off Ecuador and Peru due to the cessation of trade-wind-driven upwelling. Usually observed by fishermen near Christmas, hence El Niño or "Christ child." The central tropical Indian Ocean also catches a fever, which affects the strength and path of the monsoons. In big events, the normal geography of aridity and rainfall in the equatorial Pacific is reversed as thunderstorms flood the hyper-arid deserts of coastal Peru, while drought parches the usually humid jungles of Kalimantan and Papua. The monsoons fail to nourish agriculture in western India and southern Africa, while further afield drought holds northern China and northeast Brazil in its grip.[2]

The recognition that normal rainfall patterns over much of the globe change in response to these giant oscillations of ocean temperature and air pressure in the equatorial Pacific is the crux of ENSO theory. Like all profound insights in science, it is a deceptively simple idea achieved by an arduous and circuitous path. And because it touches on the wealth of empires and the subsistence of millions, the ENSO paradigm has a political as well as a scientific history.

## An Imperial Science

The foundations for tropical meteorology, as Richard Grove has shown, were laid during the great El Niño of 1790–91, which brought drought and famine to Madras and Bengal as well as disrupting agriculture in several of Britain's Caribbean colonies. For the first time, simultaneous meteorological measurements thousands of miles apart hinted that extreme weather might be linked across the tropics – an idea that would be only fully developed during the global drought of 1876–78. Moreover, the Indian famines spurred William Roxburgh, a young Edinburgh-trained physician and naturalist working for the East India Company, to explore the historical relationship between climate, food supply and famine in Madras. Although he discovered evidence of a comparable drought in 1685–87 (also most likely a very strong El Niño–driven drought), he attributed "the dreadful effects of which I have been constant eyewitness" less to any natural cycle than to the profound disturbances in land use arising from the East India Company's

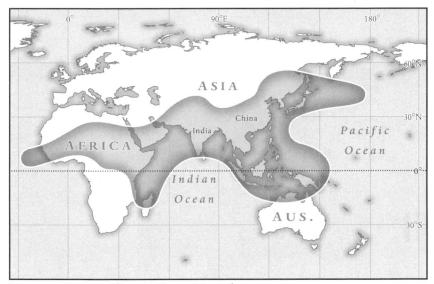

Figure 7.2  Monsoon Climates: Eastern Hemisphere

conquests. In contrast to later "climate-reductionists," Roxburgh was not afraid to impeach the Company for aggravating drought through profligate deforestation and intensifying famine through denial of ryots' permanent title to their land: a huge disincentive, in his view, to agricultural improvement and irrigation.[3]

When the monsoons again failed catastrophically in 1876, the British Empire had the operational rudiments of a world climate observation system linked by telegraph and undersea cables. In addition, the First International Meteorological Congress had just standardized the recording of weather data, making it easier to recognize and map large-scale events.[4] Henry Blanford, whose post as imperial meteorological reporter to the government of India had been established only the year before the drought (in a belated response to a chief recommendation of the 1866 Orissa Famine Commission), made urgent appeals for atmospheric pressure data from weather stations throughout the Empire as well as the rest of Eurasia and Oceana.[5] The extreme high pressure system associated with the new Madras drought was unprecedented in a half-century of Indian observations, and

Blanford was eager to establish its extent within the larger monsoon belt that dominates the eastern hemisphere tropics.

In the months that followed, as reports from Mauritius, Colombo, Singapore, Batavia, Australia and New Zealand were carefully analyzed, he was stunned by the nearly planetary scale and coherence of the event: "The condition of excessive pressure prevailed over not only the Indo-Malayan region and Eastern Australia, but also the greater part if not whole of Asia, probably the whole of Australia and the South Indian Ocean...." He also found evidence that "between Russia and Western Siberia on the one hand, and the Indo-Malayan region (perhaps including the Chinese region) on the other, there is a reciprocating and cyclical oscillation of atmospheric pressure."[6]

Blanford's research, published in tandem with the 1880 Famine Commission report, clearly established that a unitary climate event, like that vaguely glimpsed in 1791, was responsible for drought and crop failure in most of the Indo-Australasian region. Blanford surmised from Beijing observations that northern China also fell within the drought zone influenced by the high-pressure anomaly.[7] His hypothesis of a barometric see-saw regulating rainfall over a vast swathe of the globe, although erroneously located along a Russian–Indian axis, was a seminal idea that would contribute to the eventual discovery of the Southern Oscillation. (More generally, Blanford's dipole was one of the earliest suggestions of a"teleconnection": a persistent spatial structure of weather defined by two or more distinct and strongly coupled centers of action.)[8] Two key pieces of the monsoon puzzle – its planetary scale and its correlation to a gigantic air pressure oscillation – had suddenly fallen into place.

Yet advances like Blanford's in the quantitative analysis of monsoon climatology were purchased at the price of a narrowed and depoliticized scope of scientific inquiry. Until the Mutiny, the relationship of science to empire was still sufficiently protean that it was possible for savants like Roxburgh to boldly criticize ecological rapine and European exploitation – at least when it was embodied by private monopolies like the East India Company. As late as 1849, surgeon-naturalist successors to Roxburgh, like Edward Balfour in Madras, were still defending his view that famine was "a straightforward consequence of the onset of British colonial rule and revenue policies."[9] By 1876, however, when famine holocausts directly threatened the moral legitimations of empire, tropical science was rapidly being incorporated into colonial bureaucracies like Blanford's India Meteorological Department. Expanded resources for data collection and analysis were bought at the price of subservience to an ideology that contrasted British Progress to "tragic" Indian Nature.

From Lytton and Temple onward, as we have seen, official discourse about famine revolved around the zealously defended dogma that climate was its primary and inexorable cause. Or, as Lockyer and Hunter more poetically put it in 1877, "Indra and Vayu, the Watery Atmosphere and the Wind, are still the prime dispensers of weal or woe to the Indian races."[10] Roxburgh's sophisticated interest in the interaction of natural and social variables was no longer construed as science. Instead, meteorological research focused narrowly, if still heroically, on the search for the global mechanism responsible for synchronized drought across the tropics and parts of the extra-tropics. Having unlocked this secret, it was assumed that it would be possible to use precursory phenomena to predict the course of the monsoon in advance. This would be applied science, its sponsors claimed, of immense advantage to tropical imperialism. As *Nature* reminded readers during the 1899 drought-famine in India, "Rainfall is perhaps the most important element in the economy of nations."[11]

## Sunspots versus Socialists

In the decade after the great famine, the secret of the monsoon was widely believed to lie in the variable radiation of the sun. In 1852, the Swiss astronomer Rudolf Wolf had demonstrated the existence of an eleven-year sunspot cycle, and by the early 1870s a number of British scientists and scientific amateurs – Stewart at Kew Garden, Lockyer in Ceylon, Meldrum in Mauritius, Chambers, Hill and Hunter in India, and so on – were proposing sunspot correlations to the frequency of tropical cyclones and the behavior of the summer monsoon.[12] If the "dessicationist" theory that tied drought and crop failure to the "reckless destruction of [India's] trees and forests" retained some authority among colonial foresters and hydraulic engineers, solar theories otherwise held the high ground. (The dessicationist "Philindus," writing in a popular English magazine, however, poured scorn on tropical meteorologists for "wasting time in finding out when drought may exactly be expected rather than to set to work energetically in order to prevent the occurrence of any drought.")[13]

Famine was still ravaging India when Norman Lockyer and William Hunter informed readers of *The Nineteenth Century* (November 1877) that "a well marked coincidence exists between the eleven year's cycle of sun-spots and the rainfall at Bombay."[14] The next year Hunter published a widely applauded study, "The Cycle of Drought and Famine in Southern India," that purported to demonstrate a determinate relationship between sunspots and rainfall in Madras since 1813. Hunter also excited Lloyds' actuaries with an article correlating shipwrecks and sunspots based on an analysis of data in the firm's lossbooks.[15] If Hunter balked at including the temperate latitudes in the arena of solar-determined precipitation, the Mauritius-based observer C. Meldrum was convinced that mean rainfall in Edinburgh, Paris and New Bedford was even more strongly determined by sunspot periodicity than in Madras.[16]

The triumphant claims for a solar regulation of the monsoons encountered considerable skepticism from more cautious or statistically sophisticated researchers.[17] Blanford and his collaborator, the mathematician Douglas Archibald – supported by India's most eminent amateur meteorologist, Lt.-General Sir Richard Strachey – argued that any coincidence between the rainfall and sunspot cycles in tropical India involved a range of variation too small to generate crop failures like those of 1876–77.[18] But their reservations were overwhelmed by the general excitement in the international scientific community. The pages of *Nature,* edited by the sunspot enthusiast Norman Lockyer, were soon ablaze with claims and counter-claims about the influence of the Sun on tropical agriculture.[19] Even Blanford, who was highly skeptical of brazen claims that the solar cycle could predict famine, conceded that the mainspring in his own explanation of global drought – the cyclical oscillation – "appears to conform to the sun-spot period."[20]

Virtually everyone agreed, moreover, that drought obeyed a definite periodicity and was thus orchestrated by some common causality across at least the span of the Indian Ocean, if not the entire tropics. The temporal pattern of eastern Australian droughts had been recognized since 1835, and Meldrum purported to show a sunspot–Indian cyclone connection that affected Mauritius as well as southern India. "His results apparently were so convincing that, in the words of one of his admirers, 'the number of wrecks which came into the harbour ... and the number of cyclones observed in the Indian Ocean could enable anyone to determine the number of spots that were on the sun about that time.'"[21] "It would be a final link in this universal chain of evidence," wrote Archibald in 1878, "were we to find that the Cape had suffered drought either during the past or present year." Accordingly when reports of serious droughts in the Central and Eastern Districts of the Cape duly arrived in Calcutta, he declared that "this information therefore supplies the missing link."[22]

Meanwhile, some were wondering if droughts in the Western Hemisphere tropics might not also be determined by the same interactions. Brazilian scientists and engineers, convened in a series of extraordinary meetings at the Polytechnic Institute and later the National Society for Acclimation in Rio to discuss the causes of the Grande Seca, polarized into two acrimonious factions. The "meteorologists," led by Guilherme de Capanema (author of *Apontamentos sobre secas do Ceará*), and visiting professor Orville Derby enthusiastically embraced the sunspot theory.[23] Indeed, Derby excited the Indian meteorologists with a note in *Nature* summarizing the article he had published in *Diario Oficial do Brasil* in June 1878, which argued (after Hunter) that drought and flood records from Ceará strongly corresponded to sunspot fluctuations.[24] In contrast, the "rainmakers," including the most eminent Brazilian engineers of the day, attributed the droughts to deforestation and backward agricultural practices, which they blamed on the racial "primitiveness" of the *sertanejos*. In line with Liberal Party fantasies for the development of the Nordeste, they advocated a promethean program of giant dams, reservoirs and afforestation projects to "humidify" the climate. The two camps would continue to battle one another for the rest of the nineteenth century.[25]

Back in England, which was still in the grip of the Great Depression, the work of the colonial meteorologists captured broad public and parliamentary attention. As with Darwinism, a fundamental structure of natural history but with huge implications for contemporary humanity was deemed to have been uncovered. Here, the enthusiasts claimed, was a discovery that not only explained the origin of Indian famines, but also illuminated the hitherto secret engine of the business cycle: not the overaccumulation of capital relative to wages as Karl Marx had argued in a recent book, but the Sun. Thus, in a House of Commons debate in 1878, the renowned India-born scientist, political economist and Liberal MP Lyon Playfair triumphantly cited Meldrum's research as proof that "it was [now] established that famines in India came at periods when sunspots were not visible. Out of twenty-two great observatories of the world, it had been shown in eighteen that the mininum rainfall was at times when there were no spots on the Sun."[26]

Simultaneously, Sir Stanley Jevons, one of the founding fathers of mathematicized, neoclassical economics, was publishing a brace of famous articles on "Sunspots and Commercial Crises."[27] In 1875 he had excited the British Association's annual meeting with a pioneering paper on the role of solar variability (which he attributed to the gravitational configuration of the planets) in determining the price of grain.[28] Now he proposed a breathtaking theory that the Sun through its influence on Indian and Chinese agriculture drove the entire global business cycle.

Today seen as embarrassing curiosities in the great man's collected works, at the time of their writing these articles had a specific political urgency. Popular faith in free trade, Jevons warned, was being badly damaged by the recognition that "the slightest relapse of trade throws whole towns and classes of people into a state of destitution little short of famine."[29] His principal aim, according to Philip Mirowski, was to prove *contra* Marx and the socialists that global economic instability, as in the 1870s, was not a failure of capitalist institutions but was inexorably astronomical in origin. "All of Jevons's innovations in economics – his pioneering efforts in marginalist price theory, his work on the Coal Question, and his sunspot theory – may be understood as a unified response to the increasing skepticism about political economy in Britain.... [H]is project was to portray the market as a 'natural' process, so that doubts about its efficacy would be assuaged, or at the very least, countered by scientific discourse."[30]

Although Jevons's correlations between Wolf Zurich relative sunspot numbers and fourteen English commercial crises between 1700 and 1878 became a butt of humor even in his lifetime – including a "satirical statistical study showing that the periodicity of winning Oxbridge teams in collegiate boat races was the same as that of sunspots" – he stubbornly defended their statistical significance as the cornerstone of any scientific theory of the world economy.[31] Moreover, he argued that periodic booms and famines in India and China were the critical transmission belt (alternately of positive and negative feedback) between the Sun and British industry:

A wave of increased solar radiations favorably affects the meteorology of the tropical regions, so as to produce a succession of good crops in India, China, and other tropical and semi-tropical countries. After several years of prosperity the 600 or 800 millions of inhabitants buy our manufactures in unusual quantities; good trade in Lancashire and Yorkshire leads the manufacturers to push their existing means of production to the utmost and then to begin building new mills and factories. While a mania of active industry is thus set going in Western Europe, the solar radiation is slowly waning, so that just about the time when our manufacturers are prepared to turn out a greatly increased supply of goods, famines in India and China suddenly cut off the demand. [32]

Later, in a note to *The Times,* Jevons attempted to explain in more detail how solar variation acting upon the poverty of India could be the prime-mover of the prosperity of England. He boasted that historical grain price data from India, which supposedly reflected the sunspot cycle, was "the missing link." "The secret of good trade in Lancashire is the low price of rice and other grain in India." Although he admitted that "some may jest at the folly of those who theorize about such incongruous things as the cotton-gins of Manchester and the paddy-fields of Hindoostan," to those "who look a little below the surface the connexion was obvious":

Cheapness of food leaves the poor Hindoo *ryot* a small margin of earnings, which he can spend on new clothes; and a small margin multiplied by the vast population of British India, not to mention China, produces a marked change in the demand for Lancashire goods.... Let it be remembered, too, that because the impulse comes from India it does not follow that the extent of the commercial mania or crisis here is bounded by the variation of the Indian trade. The impulse from abroad is like the match which fires the inflammable spirits of the speculative classes. The history of many bubbles shows that there is no proportion between the stimulating cause and the height of folly to which the inflation of credit and prices may be carried. A mania is, in short, a kind of explosion of commercial folly followed by the natural collapse. [33]

Although Jevons died in 1882 while fast at work correlating new drought data from Brazil to buttress his theory, "cyclomania" (as Hoyt and Schatten have called it) continued to hold sway through the rest of the decade, and, indeed, to captivate eminent researchers well into the early twentieth century. [34] "Surely in meteorology, as in astronomy," the famous solar astronomer and editor of *Nature,* Sir Norman Lockyer, preached to eager Victorians, "the thing to hunt down is a cycle, and if that is not to be found in the temperate zone, then go to the frigid zones and look for it, or the torrid zones and look for it, and if found, then above all things, and in whatever manner, lay hold of it, study it, record it, and see what it means."[35] The sunspot cycle, in particular, seemed to be the big wheel that turned all the smaller wheels, regulating fluxes of rain and grain and thereby, as Jevons had shown, exchange rates and share prices. Political Economy was unmasked as a mere province of Solar Physics.

The most triumphal pronouncements came from the ebullient Lockyer, who believed that changes in sunspot spectra represented heat pulses that could be directly correlated with monsoonal rainfall. His research was sponsored by the Privy Council's Solar Physics Committee (including Sir Richard Strachey from the Indian government) and reflected Whitehall's keen interest in any influence upon imperial trade balances. As Lockyer reassured Lord Salisbury, "The riddle of the probable times of occurrence of Indian Famines has now been read, and they can be for the future accurately predicted, though not yet in various regions. The Nile River failures follow the same law."[36]

## Geopolitics and the Southern Oscillation

By the early 1890s, however, heroic solar correlation (if not Jevonsian economics) had begun to run afoul of its own burgeoning contradictions and inconsistencies. For every study that associated drought with sunspot maxima, there seemed to be another that correlated it with sunspot minima.[37] Lockyer's and Hunter's work had quietly sidestepped the embarrassing paradox, pointed out by Koppen as early as 1873, that "in the tropics, maximum temperature coincides more nearly with the minimum than with the maximum of sun-spots; preceding the former, however, by one to one and a half years."[38] As more sophisticated statistical tools became available, it became obvious that the algorithms used to detect these cycles could, in fact, find them in random data. Although Wolf's sunspot cycle was real enough, there was a creeping crisis of confidence in its presumed signature on Indian agriculture and Lancashire profits. The all-encompassing explanatory fabric that astronomers, meteorologists and neoclassical economists had woven in the late 1870s began to unravel.

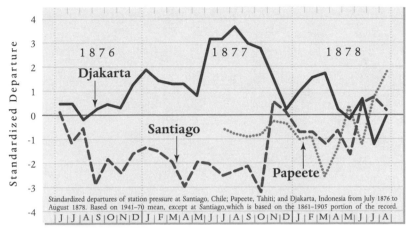

Figure 7.3  The Southern Oscillation

In the meantime, while others were still counting sunspots, Blanford had launched a pioneer investigation of snowfall in the Himalayas. He had been mandated by the 1877 Famine Commission to develop a method for forecasting drought and suspected that the Tibetan snowpack might be a more reliable precursor than the sun. Since the monsoons were driven by the differential heating/cooling of the mountains and Tibetan Plateau vis-à-vis the Indian Ocean, he proposed the logical hypothesis that the "varying extent and thickness of the Himalayan snows exercise a great and prolonged influence on the climatic conditions and weather of the plains of northwest India." In 1885 Blanford won accolades for successfully predicting deficient rains over western India as a result of a late and abnormally large spring snowfall in the western Himalayas. Building on this core technique of using one season's snowfall as an analogue for next season's rainfall, his successor Sir John Eliot added more variables, including Indian Ocean trade winds, Nile floods, and rainfall in South Africa and southern Australia. As we have seen, Eliot's growing confidence in his forecasting skill soon became tragic hubris: "The disastrously wrong forecasts preceding and during the terrible western Indian drought of 1899 threw the methods into disrepute."[39]

From the perspective of modern research, it is clear that Blanford and Eliot were correct in assuming that the Tibetan (or Eurasian) snow mass plays a fundamental role in conditioning the monsoon. (The Himalayas, as they recognized, also regulate the monsoon cycle orographically, lifting warm air flow from the south in the summer and blocking incursions of frigid Siberian air masses from the north in the winter.) But it is only half the story. Monsoon variability, we now understand, is an interaction between the weather of Eurasia and the dynamic convection systems of the tropical Pacific and Indian Oceans. In focusing on variable heat storage in the Himalayas, Blanford and Eliot (understandably) ignored clues that might have led them to the discovery of the great Indo-Pacific heat engine: ENSO.

Blanford had first glimpsed its power in the violent atmospheric oscillations that had accompanied the 1877 drought, and researchers in the 1890s were sighting it again. In the lead was Lockyer, the indefatigable solar cyclist, who had been convinced by his son James that analyses of the Indian meteorological record indicated that atmospheric pressure might be a better correlate to solar activity than rainfall. Examining global data, the Lockyers proposed that Blanford's seesaw was actually a conflation of two separate systems of atmospheric oscillation: one in phase with India, the other with Spain. As the elder Lockyer explained it: "If the effect of the sun was to create, say, a lower pressure at some point on the earth's surface, this would necessarily be balanced by higher pressure somewhere else. As the sun's effect varied, so the atmospheric pressure at these two poles would oscillate."[40]

The Lockyers ultimately failed to adduce compelling evidence for a statistical or causal linkage between solar cycles, Indian air pressure variations, and rainfall anomalies. But their emphasis on inter-hemispheric atmospheric oscillations, with possibly more than one frequency, provided a compelling framework for the next generation of research. By 1897, for example, the director of the Upsala Observatory, Hugo Hildebrandsson, had identified the inverse relationship between mean pressures in Iceland and the Azores – later dubbed the North Atlantic Oscillation – that plays such a large role in regulating rainfall and crop productivity in northwestern Europe. He also believed he had isolated a Siberian–Indian barometric see-saw as well as an oscillation that stretched across the Pacific between South America (Buenos Aires) and Australasia (Sydney).[41] For the first time, the Pacific Basin was identified as a principal "center of action" with influence on the monsoon: a decisive clue that was followed up, after the disgrace of Eliot, by his successor, the Cambridge senior math wrangler and physicist, Sir Gilbert Walker.

As Gisela Kutzbach has pointed out, Walker, an expert on electrodynamics and ballistics, was a newcomer to meteorology who "had to rely for the most part on his own resources."[42] He seems to have been inspired as much by contemporary geopolitics, the new "science of empire," as by geophysics. In an analogy with Alfred Mahon's famous dictum that modern world power depended upon the control of a handful of strategic choke-points of maritime commerce (Gibraltar, Singapore, etc.), Walker surmised that global agricultural production also depended upon a few "strategic points of world weather."[43] Reclaiming the bold optimism of the sunspot-chasers a generation earlier, he pursued a program of geo-historical reductionism whose goal had been adumbrated by Britain's chief geopolitician, Halford Mackinder (whom we last saw among the starving on the slopes of Mount Kenya), in a famous 1904 address on "The Geographical Pivot of History":

> In the present decade we are for the first time in a position to attempt, with some degree of completeness, a correlation between the larger geographical and the larger historical generalizations. For the first time we can perceive something of the real proportion of features and events on the stage of the whole world, and may seek a formula which shall express certain aspects, at any rate, of geographical causation in universal history.[44]

For Walker, the meteorological pivot of history – the secret of the monsoons, which regulated the lives of more than half the earth's population – was hidden in the pyramid of weather data that had accumulated since the observational revolution of the 1870s. To excavate it he proposed to radically increase the volume of computation. Today, of course, supercomputers crunch endless terabytes of weather observations, but Walker, a demon statistician, mobilized pharaonic levies of Indian clerks (a surplus of whom were made available during the First World War) to manually process worldwide pressure and rainfall data through his esoteric regression equations. The widespread drought and agricultural crisis of 1918 gave renewed urgency to these calculations. Yet, as Mark Cane has pointed out, this was little more than a huge scientific fishing expedition: "No conceptual framework supported the patterns he found; [his] methods were strictly empirical."[45] Although Walker speculated, as had Hildebrandsson earlier, that polar circulation might be a driving force of global pressure fluctuations, it was little more than a hunch.[46]

Nonetheless Walker's dogged super-empiricism eventually produced a rich harvest. After twenty years of patiently crunching numbers and expanding his data sets, the (after 1924, retired) director-general of observatories in India was able to present overwhelming evidence (following Hildebrandsson's pioneering work) for three coherent systems of intercontinental atmospheric oscillation:

> In 1924, Walker first used and defined the term Southern Oscillation (SO) as a "see-saw" in atmospheric pressure and rainfall at stations across the Indo-Pacific region, where increased (decreased) pressure in locations surrounding the Indian region (Cairo, north-west India, Darwin, Mauritius, south-eastern Australia and the Cape Colony) tended to be matched by decreased (increased) pressure over the Pacific region (San Francisco, Tokyo, Honolulu, Samoa and South America) and decreased (increased) rainfall over India and Java (including Australia and Abyssinia). The two other "oscillations" involved out-of-phase atmospheric pressure between the regions of the Azores and Iceland, named the North Atlantic Oscillation (NAO), and between Alaska and the Hawaiian Islands, termed the North Pacific Oscillation (NPO).[47]

This was a fundamental breakthrough: the global drought pattern first convincingly identified by Blanford in 1877–80 was now unequivocally related to the action of the great barometric see-saw over the equatorial Pacific Ocean. "It soon became apparent that the Southern Oscillation provided the most potential in terms of long-range forecasting [of the three oscillations], in that it displayed marked interannual variability in its lead and lag correlations with climatic conditions in each season over a large part of the earth's surface."[48] Walker clearly grasped that changes in the intensity and location of the great tropical convection cell (the Indo-Australian Convergence Zone) as reflected by the Southern Oscillation, would affect the summer monsoon over India, and in 1928 he proposed an additional link between the SO and drought-famines in northeast Brazil. There was growing confidence in the Indian government, as well as scientific circles, that Walker was breathtakingly close to his quarry.

But it ultimately eluded his grasp. In the absence of any theoretical model for understanding the teleconnections between strategic centers of weather action,

Walker was thrown back on an alchemy of formulae. Despite ever more baroque regressions, he could not discover an index or system of equations that would give even proximately reliable advance warnings of drought. Maddeningly, the monsoon consistently turned out to be a better predictor of the SO than vice versa. "Walker found that Indian summer rainfall, while weakly correlated with pressure variations some months earlier in locations as far away as South America, was more strongly correlated with subsequent events."[49] After the initial excitement generated by his pathbreaking papers in the 1920s, this "predicability barrier" (which continues to frustrate tropical meteorologists) was one of a number of difficulties that led to declining interest in the Southern Oscillation from the late 1930s through the early 1960s. "Of particular concern was the lack of any physical mechanisms that could explain pressure fluctuations such as the SO, NAO or NPO, let alone growing efforts to link numerous climatic patterns to lunar, solar and planetary influences. In addition, the correlations and algorithms described and used by Walker and others were often found to have diminished when the original data sets were extended as more data became available."[50] Indeed, no infinity of atmospheric data would have ever provided Walker with ultimate insight into the mechanism of the Southern Oscillation. The missing link to the problem of the monsoon, in fact, lay outside the boundaries of meteo-

---

### A Walker Formula

Southern Oscillation Index (December–February) = [Samoa pressure] + [North-east Australia rainfall (Derby and Halls Creek in Western Australia, 7 stations in north Australia, 20 throughout Queensland)] + 0.7 [Charleston pressure] + 0.7 [New Zealand temperature (Wellington, Dunedin)] + 0.7 [Java rainfall] + 0.7 [ Hawaii rainfall (12 stations)] + 0.7 [South Africa rainfall (15 stations, Johannesburg the most northern)] – [Darwin pressure] + [Manila pressure] – [Batavia pressure] – [South-west Canada temperature (Calgary, Edmonton, Prince Albert, Qu'Appelle, Winnipeg)] – [Samoa temperature] – 0.7 [Brisbane temperature] – 0.7 [Mauritius temperature] – 0.7 [South American rainfall (Rio de Janeiro and 2 stations south of it in Brazil; 3 in Paraguay, Montevideo; 15 in Argentina, of which Bahia Blanca is the southernmost)][51]

rology: in yet unsuspected large-scale temperature fluxes in the equatorial Pacific
Ocean.

## Bjerknes and the ENSO Paradigm

Forty years after Walker described the Southern Oscillation, Jacob Bjerknes at
UCLA began to look at the problem from an oceanographic as well as meteorological point of view. Bjerknes, then in his late sixties, was a legendary figure
who during the First World War, collaborating with his father, had revolutionized
meteorology with the modern "frontal" theory of how mid-latitude weather is
determined by the clash of polar and humid air masses (analogous in their view
to the collision of armies on the Western Front). Their "Bergen School" was the
fount both of physics-based dynamical meteorology and modern weather forecasting.[52] In the 1960s, moreover, Bjerknes was one of the relatively few meteorologists attentive to recent breakthroughs in understanding ocean heat circulation and internal wave behavior.

Building on the correlation discovered by the Dutch meteorologist Hendrik
Berlage in the 1950s between the time series of the SO index and sea surface
temperatures off Peru, and using International Geophysical Year (1957–58) data
that "provided, for the first time, observations of large-scale oceanic warming
extending across the equatorial Pacific beyond the dateline in association with
an El Niño event," Bjerknes argued that the SO and El Niño were the respective
atmospheric and oceanic expressions of solar energy cycling in powerful pulses
through a coupled ocean-atmosphere system.[53] (The term ENSO was first used
by Rasmusson and Carpenter in 1982 to characterize Bjerknes's unified interaction.)[54]

The Southern Oscillation, Bjerknes argued in his famous 1969 paper, resulted
from a "chain-reaction" exchange of energy between the ocean and atmosphere.
To begin with, the differential between the (low pressure) Warm Pool in the western equatorial Pacific and the (high pressure) Cold Tongue in the east forces relatively cold, dry air westward where it is heated and moistened over progressively
warmer water. This trade wind, part of which returns in the upper levels to sink
over the eastern Pacific (an equatorial circulation that Bjerknes named in honor
of Walker), pools more warm water in the west and thus reinforces the gradient
driving its flow. Or, in Bjerknes's own words, "an intensifying Walker Circula-

tion ... provides for an increase of the east–west temperature contrast that is the cause of the Walker Circulation in the first place."[55] This, of course, is a classical example of positive feedback and it also works in the opposite direction: should the easterly trade winds abate, the Warm Pool will move eastward, which, in turn, will further suppress the gradient. Sea temperatures in the central equatorial Pacific increase from the influx of warm surface water, while off the Ecuadorean/Peruvian coast the classical El Niño warming results from the suppression of wind-driven upwelling. Cold events, by contrast, involve an interactive intensification of the trade winds, warm pooling in the west and cold upwelling in the east. In either state of the Walker Circulation, in other words, there is a powerful feedback loop that accelerates movement towards the extreme points (El Niño and La Niña, respectively) of the cycle. The Southern Oscillation, moreover, is a real transfer of air mass (not just an epiphenomenon of surface pressure), via intensified or weakened Walker circulations, between the monsoon regions and the equatorial Pacific Ocean.[56]

The great perturbations in tropical weather, in other words, are self-generated and self-sustained: they do not require the intervention of sunspot cycles or other exogenous forcings. The essence of Bjerknes's model, explains George Philander, is that "changes in oceanic conditions are both the cause and the consequence of changes in atmospheric conditions." Anomalies of sea surface temperature cause the trade winds to strengthen or weaken and this in turn drives the ocean circulation changes that produce anomalous sea surface temperatures. "To ask why El Niño or La Niña occurs," continues Philander, "is equivalent to asking why a bell rings or a taut violin string vibrates. The Southern Oscillation is a natural mode of oscillation of the coupled ocean-atmosphere system: it is the music of the atmosphere and hydrosphere."[57]

Bjerknes's theory was stunningly bold but it left unsolved a key dynamic element of the problem. What forces or instigates the nonlinear transition from one state to another? And, similarly, how do El Niños terminate? As Bjerknes acknowledged in 1969, "Just how the turnabout between trends takes place is not yet quite clear. The study of a sequence of global meteorological maps during typical turnabouts may clarify part of the problem. An additional key to the problem may have to be developed by the science of dynamic oceanography."[58] In the event, the latter contribution was most crucial, and it was left to Klaus Wyrtki at

Figure 7.4
Key Stages in the Development of ENSO Theory

| | |
|---|---|
| 1. Recognizing global, synchronized drought | Roxburgh: 1790s<br>Blanford: 1880 |
| 2. Linking drought to interhemispheric<br>atmosphere"see-saw" | Blanford: 1880<br>Lockyer and Lockyer: 1900 |
| 3. Identifying the Southern Oscillation (SO) | Hildebrandsson: 1899<br>Walker: 1920s |
| 4. Unifying the SO and El Niño in a single model | Bjerknes: 1960s |
| 5. Recognizing La Niña (ENSO cold phase) | Philander: 1980s |
| 6. Mechanism for the phase transition | Wyrtki: 1980s |
| 7. Successful predictive model | Cane and Zebiak: 1986 |
| 8. Nature of interdecadal fluctuations | ?? |

the University of Hawai'i in the mid-1970s to rebuild Bjerknes's theory upon a more sophisticated foundation of ocean physics.

Wyrtki conceived of El Niños as turbulent "heat relaxation events" that arose in response to intensified trade winds and greater-than-average pooling of warm water in the western Pacific.[59] Like the rest of the world ocean, the Pacific is composed of two layers of fluid: a very deep cold layer and a shallow surface layer of warmer water.[60] The abrupt temperature transition between the two is known as the thermocline. The Warm Pool, as we have seen, is a trade-wind-driven pile-up of warm water (more than 100 meters deep) and consequent deepening of the thermocline at the western end of the Pacific Basin. Because it is unable to export all of its annual budget of solar energy, the Warm Pool functions like a planetary heat reservoir or "capacitor."[61] Small surface temperature increases over large ocean areas represent the storage of vast amounts of energy to potentially power weather systems.

The Warm Pool accumulates excess heat (as a deeper thermocline and higher sea level) until a trigger event, like a trade wind reversal, releases the stored solar energy in the form of a wavelike body of warm water (a "Kelvin wave") that sloshes eastward against South America. As the equatorial thermocline flattens, the disappearance of the normal east–west surface temperature gradient further weakens the trade winds. The slackening or cessation of the trade winds, in turn, simultaneously releases Warm Pool water eastward while allowing warm surface waters to accumulate off equatorial South America.[62] The complexity of causal feedbacks, of course, makes it difficult to disentangle the ultimate initiating factor.

The idea of westerly wind bursts across the International Date Line that trigger Kelvin waves in the thermocline was first introduced by Wrytki in 1975. Research in the mid-1990s, armed with data from the Tropical Ocean Global Atmosphere (TOGA) monitoring system, has tied these bursts to unusually strong instances of an intraseasonal (30- to 50-day) atmospheric fluctuation in the tropics known as Madden Julian Oscillation (MJO). The MJO interannually waxes and wanes in strength, with peaks in El Niño years. Researchers are uncertain whether these intensifications of the Madden-Julian are powered by rising sea surface temperature (and are thus predictable) or are simply stochastic.

Moreover, just as ENSO creates weather, it is in turn modified by weather. Although the heat reservoir model explains how El Niños in general evolve, "part of the reason for irregularity in the ENSO cycle in terms of frequency, duration and amplitude of warm and cold events may ... be attributed to the nonlinear interaction of higher frequency weather variability with lower frequency ocean-atmosphere dynamics."[63] On the timescale of El Niño events, weather (including the feedback effects of powerful storm systems and tropical cyclones) is statistically "noise." To make forecasters' lives more difficult, ENSO, like all nonlinear dynamic systems, also probably incorporates an important quotient of deterministic chaos.[64]

Wyrtki also clarified the physics of what happens when the Southern Oscillation dips far below the x-axis of the graph. As the system "relaxes" at the end of a warm event (often with the abrupt return of the trade winds and the explosive cooling of the eastern Pacific), it tends to overshoot its mean state. The El Niño phase is rapidly followed by its inverse mirror image: the cold phase that Princeton's George Philander labeled La Niña in a famous 1985 article. During a La Niña event, unusually strong (easterly) trade winds recharge the heat content of the Warm Pool while the IACZ retreats westward over Indonesia to the edge of the Indian Ocean. The extreme climate phenomena accompanying La Niña are opposite in sign but usually comparable in magnitude to those associated with El Niño, so that droughts are often followed by severe floods as in China in 1897–98 or 1997–98.[65]

Wyrtki's revision, of course, was not the end of debate about the dynamics of El Niño (fundamental aspects of which still elude researchers), but it does punctuate the passage from the heroic days of first capturing ENSO in the nets of analysis to an era of mature theory in which the construction of complex predictive models, using data from TOGA arrays in the equatorial Pacific, has become possible. In 1986 two oceanographers, Mark Cane and Stephen Zebiak, encapsulating Bjerknes's key variables in a simple atmosphere-ocean-coupled model, successfully forecast the 1986–87 El Niño. A decade later, several models (although not Cane and Zebiak's this time) correctly predicted the onset of the 1997–98 event, although its surprising intensity and spectacularly sudden ending (in May 1998) led some ENSO modelers to grade their efforts as "mediocre." Still, the basic physics underlying ENSO is now firmly understood. "El Niño–Southern Oscillation variability," declares a leading researcher, "is the first great coupled atmosphere-ocean-biota puzzle that humankind has solved."[66]

## Multidecadal Regimes?

Among the problems that remain, perhaps the highest priority is understanding the "complex symphony" of ENSO over time.[67] Paleoclimatologists and paleoceanographers are now beginning to make fundamental contributions to ENSO research. El Niños in modern times have a quasi-periodic frequency of two to seven years, but most researchers are convinced that this oscillation is nested within other cycles, powered by similar physics, with lower frequencies ranging from decades to millennia.[68] Since the compilation of the first ENSO chronologies in the 1970s, for instance, there has been intense curiosity about the weakening of El Niño from the early 1920s to the late 1950s in contrast to the strong cycles before and after. Figure 7.5, based on sea surface temperatures from the eastern Pacific since 1860, clearly shows a decline in both the frequency and inten-

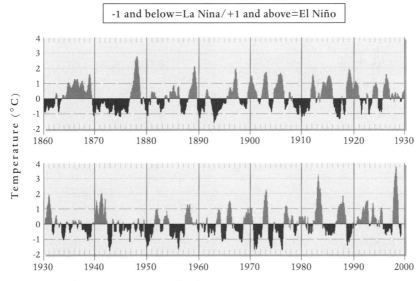

Figure 7.5    Changes in ENSO Amplitude

sity of warm events from 1925 until 1958 (or even 1972). There are also striking differences in the relative percentages of El Niños and La Niñas. Is this evidence that ENSO oscillates between high amplitude and low amplitude "regimes" on a multidecadal scale? If so, the implications for our understanding of agrarian history in the tropics and north China would be profound.

Some researchers think they can already glimpse the outlines of large-scale temporal structures. Rasmusson, Wang and Ropelewski, after crunching a mountain of historical data, believe that 31-year fluctuations in ENSO-cycle intensity "broadly correspond to changes in all-India monsoon-season rainfall variability, to the modulation of the intensity of drought episodes over the US Great Plains during the twentieth century, and, less clearly, to the century-scale variation in Sahel rainfall."[69] California tree rings and Andean ice cores, as well as instrumental rainfall records, provide additional evidence of changes in ENSO amplitude at a roughly similar frequency.[70] On the other hand, recent coral core data from eastern tropical Pacific, which extends ENSO event history back to 1600, indicates a strong variability in strength and coherence of the signal over 10–25 years.[71] The two sets of data may not be contradictory, since the first frequency might well be a harmonic composite of the second (the awkwardly named "quasi-bidecadal oscillation"). ENSO-cycle variability could even prove "fractal" across a spectrum of time scales.[72]

One explanation for regime variability is that ENSO is modulated by decade- to century-long changes in atmospheric and oceanic boundary conditions, especially in the mid-latitudes where ocean cycles tend to have longer periods. The North Pacific, in particular, has important sea temperature fluctuations at 25- to 40-year-long wavelengths that correspond to putative ENSO regimes or epochs.[73] All the more intriguing, then, that the central and eastern tropical Pacific abruptly warmed in 1976–77 in tandem with the cooling of the central and western North Pacific. This change of base state, which persisted until 1998, probably amplified the effects of succeeding El Niño events since they were piggybacking an increase in background sea surface temperature. (Conversely, the switch to a colder ocean probably intensified the 1999–2000 La Niña.)[74]

Some have attributed this change in ocean background state to anthropogenic warming, but others argue that it is the expression of a somewhat mysterious temperature flux known as the Pacific Decadal Oscillation (PDO). (Other reversals in its polarity may have occurred around 1925 and 1947.)[75] Aside from intensifying El Niños, it also seems to have significantly modified their behavior: "Before 1977, the warming along the Southern American coast led the warming in the central Pacific, whereas after 1977 the warm events first appeared in the central Pacific."[76]

Recent research, however, suggests that the PDO is only one of a quartet of major temperature-thermocline oscillations in the Pacific. If so, ENSO may be complexly interacting with an entire "cacophony of discordant cycles," including perhaps the epochal cycle in the Indian monsoon (described in the next chapter).[77] Untying this Gordian knot of phase-locked and resonating frequencies is, to say the least, a daunting challenge. "The interdecadal change in the strength of interannual variability associated with the ENSO," summarizes Xiao-Wei Quan, "is the result of interactions among climate oscillations in different regions that have different characteristic time scales. Particularly, the interaction between the multidecadal oscillation in the monsoon region and the North Pacific and the interdecadal oscillation in the tropical Pacific Ocean, and the interaction between the quasi 20-year oscillation in the Tropical Pacific and the quasi 25-to-40-year oscillation in the North Pacific and the 10-15 year oscillation in Monsoon region were of special importance."[78]

Climatologists have also been eager to discover whether large-scale global temperature oscillations operating at the even slower frequencies of centuries have modified ENSO. One of the most remarkable paleo-environmental discoveries of recent years has been the identification in Greenland ice cores (and subsequently in a variety of other natural archives) of a persistent millennial-scale fluctuation in Quaternary climates. Historical periods of global warming and cooling, like the "Mediaeval Climate Optimum" and its successor, the "Little Ice Age," have been unmasked as the muted Holocene expressions of the so-called "Dansgaard/Oeschger Oscillation." Yet so far researchers have had little luck establishing any statistically significant correlation between ENSO-cycle variability and millennial background climate.[79] On the other hand, there remain some intriguing "coincidences," such as the correspondence between the 1876–78 El Niño, which produced world record sea temperatures, and the generally recognized termination of the Little Ice Age circa 1880.

Hugely controversial has been the claim by some researchers that ENSO has been punctuated by chaotic flickering or temporary shutdowns. They have interpreted data from laminated lake sediments and western Pacific corals as proving that the ENSO cycle was somehow turned off during the early Holocene (between 5,000 and 12,000 years ago). It is unclear what might have been the "switch": possibly higher temperatures during the so-called Altithermal period or perhaps the changing strength of the seasonal cycle due to different orbital variables. Since there is unambiguous evidence of ENSO fluctuations during the glacial maximum (before 12,000 years ago), scientists are baffled by why El Niño would suddenly go AWOL.[80]

In addition to understanding its temporal patterns, researchers would also like to establish better parameters for the range of ENSO magnitudes. "Great" El Niños like 1876, 1982 and 1997, for all the global havoc they have caused, are not the top of the class. Paleoclimatologists in South America have found startling evidence of mega–El Niños like the mediaeval "Chimu flood" (circa 1100 CE) – "vastly more powerful than the most severe historical event" – associated with epic droughts and fires in the Amazon and biblical deluges in coastal Peru. Radioactive carbon-14 dating has placed these events, whose Eastern Hemisphere impacts have not yet been identified, at approximately 1,500, 1,000, 700 and 500 years before the present. Although rare, these 300- to 500-year events may have left indelible imprints in history.[81]

Finally, there is urgent concern to understand the relationship between ENSO and global warming. Some believe that the El Niño cycle has been speeding up and intensifying. In the historical ENSO record, for example, there have been only eight or nine "very strong" El Niños since 1728: an average of once every 42 years. Yet two of the three largest (1982–83 and 1997–98) have recently occurred within 14 years of one another. Even stranger was the persistent El Niño of 1990–95: the longest in the historical or, indeed, paleoclimatic records. Trenberth and Hoar, among others, have argued that "the prevailing warm condition during the 1990s is unique when compared with the remainder of the historical record, and is a result of anthropogenic global warming."[82] A popular hypothesis is that much of the additional heat trapped by greenhouse gases is stored in an expanded Warm Pool and deepened thermocline in the western tropical Pacific Ocean, then released in more frequent and larger El Niño events. An enhanced ENSO cycle, in other words, may be the principal modality through which global warming turns into weather.[83]

# Eight

# Climates of Hunger

> Where is the all-powerful white man today? He came,
> he ate, and he went. The important thing is to stay alive....
> If you survive, who knows? It may be your turn to eat tomor-
> row. Your son may bring home your share.
>
> —Chinua Achebe, *A Man of the People*

After the cycle of the seasons itself, ENSO is the most important source of global climate variability. No other interannual environmental perturbation has such amplitude or far-reaching impact, capable of bringing hardship to a quarter of the human race on five continents. Although certainly not the only harbinger of catastrophic drought or flood, it is the most frequent and thus far the most predictable.[1] Instructed by two great El Niños (1982 and 1997) in a single generation, social as well as environmental scientists are beginning to appreciate ENSO's impact on world history. In attempting to visualize El Niño historically, however, it is far easier to surmise its existence through teleconnected droughts and floods than to directly observe its feverlike outbreak in the eastern tropical Pacific. If its theater of influence includes the ancient, densely populated agrarian heartlands of Egypt, Ethiopia, India, Java, China and Peru, the region of its origination is a vast, obscure oceanic desert with scarcely a sprinkling of inhabited islands. With growing claims and counter-claims about El Niño's impact on civilization, how can we discern and authenticate its fingerprints in history?

## Teleconnection and Causality

Walker and his contemporaries sought the influence of the Southern Oscillation on rainfall in different regions of the globe without knowing what actually linked anomalies over such great distances. The physics underlying global drought were still a black box. Bjerknes, by contrast, was sure that ENSO pulses, originating in the ocean, were transmitted along the Equator by displacement of the Walker Circulation and broadcast to the extratropics by shifts in the alignment of semi-permanent high- and low-pressure systems. After earlier researchers, he called these disturbances "teleconnections." They are the coupling between ENSO in the tropical Pacific and the rest of the world climate system. As the Indo-Australian Convergence Zone (the convection system driven by the Warm Pool) moves into the central Pacific during an El Niño phase, for example, it shifts the position of the interhemispheric "wave train" of troughs and ridges as well as the weather patterns they organize. Storm paths are displaced and seasonal rainfall and aridity end up in unusual places for the time of year. Teleconnections are considered well established when regions show high probabilities of large, statistically significant signals during eastern equatorial Pacific warm events and equally large signals of the opposite sign during cold events.[2]

But ENSO is a complex quasi-periodicity (a "devil's staircase" in fractal terminology), not a clockwork cycle like sunspot fluctuations, and its geography is therefore subject to important reconfigurations over time. Teleconnections, for example, are simultaneously robust and delicate. ENSO can be analogized to a planetary game of musical chairs played with jet streams and semi-continent-sized air masses. But it is a game played more vigorously in some periods than in others. Teleconnections are strongly seasonal, but they also fluctuate over longer periods. There is persuasive evidence that the global power and organization of teleconnection patterns wax and wane according to strong/weak states of the underlying ENSO "regimes" that were discussed in the last chapter. Teleconnection fields were strongest and spatially extensive in 1879–1899 and again after 1963. The El Niño events of 1876–77, 1899–1900, 1972–3, 1982–83 and 1997–98 produced exceptionally coherent teleconnection patterns. Conversely, they were "weakened, fragmented and their spatial scales tended to be most contracted" between 1900 and 1963, especially during 1921–41.[3]

In addition, ENSO never exactly repeats itself: each El Niño is a distinctive, even eccentric, historical event. "Although there are often characteristics common to events, no two ENSO events are the same in terms of genesis, life cycle and cessation."[4] In the language of the earth sciences, El Niño may not be the best example of uniformitarianism. Researchers learned this the hard way. In the early 1980s, there was an ambitious attempt to define a "canonical ENSO event" based on a comparative analysis of all the El Niños since 1941. "However, no sooner had this model of ENSO become established than a massive El Niño event occurred in 1982–83 that provided the grounds for some serious reassessment of the canonical concept of the nature and structure of ENSO."[5] Analysis of 1997–98 El Niño – more extreme in ocean warming but shorter in duration than 1982–83 – will undoubtedly lead to further tinkering with the canonical model. The individual personalities – or what meteorologists like to call the "flavors" – of ENSO events in the Pacific are believed to arise principally from differences in internal ocean dynamics, especially the relative importance of advection (horizontal transport) or overturning in surface heating.

Moreover, because there is a "multiplicity of interaction modes" between ENSO, major circulation regimes and other periodic variabiles, the possible effects outside the tropical Pacific are quite complex.[6] Indeed the major ENSO teleconnections must be seen not as simple climate "switches" turned on and off every three to seven years, but as individual systems of selective interaction between the Southern Oscillation and other independent variables that can amplify or diminish its influence. ENSO is the enabling or necessary condition, but rarely by itself a sufficient cause. For example, El Niño warming contributed to the great 1993 flood in the upper Mississippi Valley by strengthening the subtropical jet stream and shifting storm tracks southward, but the extraordinary spring and summer rainfall required in addition a continuous supply of moisture provided by low-level flow from the Caribbean. The conjuncture of these two independently variable conditions was the true "cause" of the exceptional precipitation that, interacting with unwise floodplain land use, produced $35 billion in flood damages.[7]

Peter Webster and his colleagues, in a comprehensive review of ENSO-monsoon simulations, have usefully suggested a heuristic model for understanding

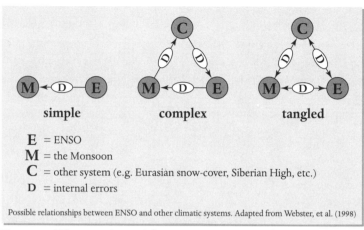

simple          complex          tangled

**E** = ENSO
**M** = the Monsoon
**C** = other system (e.g. Eurasian snow-cover, Siberian High, etc.)
**D** = internal errors

Possible relationships between ENSO and other climatic systems. Adapted from Webster, et al. (1998)

Figure 8.1  Teleconnection as Selective Interaction

the causal complexity of these teleconnections. In a simple system, an El Niño
(La Niña) impulse directly modifies another system, for example, the South Asian
or East Asian monsoon. A change in one circulation compels a change in the
other. "Relative to the growth of internal errors, the influence is linear and the
system highly predictable." Such simplicity in causation was the object of Walker's thirty-year quest, but nature is seldom so obliging. More likely is a complex
hierarchy where ENSO and the monsoon are linked through another variable like
Eurasian snowfall. "Within the complex hierarchy the monsoon may feed back
on the ENSO system through the third system or vice versa." Error growth can
easily become nonlinear, thus diminishing predictability. Least predictable would
be a tangled hierarchy where "each system interacts with the other, and the rout-
ing of the interaction is difficult to decipher." The South Asian monsoon, for
instance, might have important feedback effects on ENSO, perhaps even sometimes acting as the "detonator" of El Niño / warm phases. In such chaotic circumstances – with three or more variables free to blow their horns independently
– it is impossible to define which phenomenon is the "precursor" of the other,
and determinism is essentially lost. (Probabilistic prediction, however, may still be
possible, especially if one of the linkages is dominant over time.)[8]

In these entangled modes, ENSO impulses interact on longer time-scales with regional climate period-icities, which, depending on phase, can either amplify or decrease the signal from the Pacific. Even with the same tropical forcing, extratrop-ical responses can vary dramatically. Thus the strength of the ENSO tele-connection to the Indian monsoon depends upon interdecadal trends in Eurasian snow-cover, while the teleconnection to western North America is modulated by poorly understood 20- to 30-year oscilla-tions in the North Pacific.[9] Some cli-mate researchers, moreover, believe that "forecasts based on established [ENSO] teleconnections, even those considered highly statistically sig-nificant, could fail or even reverse sign in the future due to decadal time scale climate variability." The recent "decoupling" of ENSO and the Indian monsoon, as we shall see, is a dramatic case in point.[10]

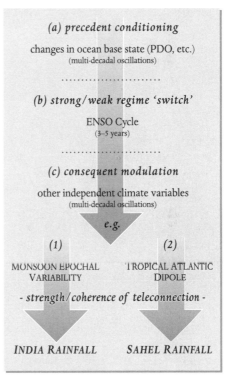

Figure 8.2 Two Modes of ENSO / Teleconnection Regulation

To summarize, then, the pattern and intensity of ENSO teleconnections are regulated over time in two different ways. On one hand, the amplitude of ENSO is conditioned by low-frequency variability in the background state of the tropi-cal Pacific (like the PDO and its unnamed sisters). "Strong" and "weak" ENSO regimes appear to follow one another at roughly 20- to 40-year periods. On the other hand (and independently of ENSO regime), the statistical significance of specific teleconnections seems to depend on whether the signal from the tropi-cal Pacific is in-phase or out-of-phase with other, slower oscillations. Thus, as we

Table 8.1

Teleconnections in Five Major El Niño Events

|  | 1877–78 | 1899–1900 | 1972–73 | 1982–83 | 1997–98 |
|---|---|---|---|---|---|
| India | D** | D* | D* | d | – |
| Indonesia | D | d (D1902) | D | D | D |
| Philippines | d | D | d | D** | d |
| Australia | D | D** | D | D | D |
| North China | D** | D* | D | d | d |
| Yangzi | F | – | – | F | F |
| South Africa | D | d | D | D | D |
| East Africa | f | D (1898 La Niña?) | – | – | – |
| Horn of Africa | d | d | D | D | D |
| Sahel | d | D | D** | D | – |
| [Mediterranean] | d | – | D** | d | – |
| [Russia] | d | – | D** | – | d |
| Nordeste | D | d | D | D | D |
| South Brazil | ? | ? | – | F | – |

D=intense drought; d=moderate drought; F=intense flooding; **=most severe in century; *=second
most severe. Brackets=possible teleconnection only.
Source: Collated from research in this book; Glantz, *Currents of Change*, pp. 65, 70–72.

shall see, monsoon epochs and tropical Atlantic dipoles modulate the impact of
ENSO events on rainfall in India and the Sahel, respectively. Figure 8.2 is a conceptual cartoon of these two different modes of modulation: one "precedent"
(or "upstream") and the other "consequent" (or "downstream") to ENSO heat-
storage release events.

More broadly, these manifold interactions and overdeterminations ensure a
distinctive global pattern during each event. It is extremely unlikely that all the
independent variables co-determining ENSO's regional impacts will ever line up
twice in the exactly the same way, although synchronicity and coherence are
increased by the power of the initial event (see Table 8.1). Finally, the further the
teleconnection is from the main theater of ENSO activity in the tropical Pacific,
the greater is the influence exercised by "weather-noise" (the feedback effect of
major storm systems) and natural chaotic variability.[11] Midlatitude climate with
its constant frontal clashes between polar and subtropical air masses is inherently

more turbulent and unpredictable than tropical climate. What meteorologists like to call the "signal/noise" ratio (the percentage of variation attributable to ENSO variability) correspondingly diminishes with distance from the equator.

To understand, therefore, how El Niño has helped to shape geographically specific "climates of hunger" in India, Indonesia, north China, southern Africa and northeast Brazil, we need to know something about these key non-ENSO variables. A survey of recent research on teleconnections – which also provides an opportunity to rediscuss some of the meteorology of the 1876–78 and 1896–1902 droughts – is followed by a brief overview of the archives and "proxies" used to establish ENSO chronologies. Needless to say, this account is self-consciously hostage to progress in a dynamic research arena, particularly as ENSO climatologies become more fine-tuned by season and subregion.

## Regional ENSO Climatologies

INDIA

"Unlike the West where the year is divided into four seasons, the Indian calendar consists of a triad: the Cold Season from October to December, the Hot Season from January to May and the Rains of the summer monsoon from June to September."[12] Drought in the subcontinent is a deficiency (delay, interruption, or early withdrawal) in the crucial summer monsoon, which provides 75 percent to 90 percent of rainfall for agriculture.[13] (Only coastal Tamil Nadu, among drought-prone regions, depends primarily on the October–December northeast monsoon.) "When the number of monsoon depressions or low pressure areas is normally low, and/or the monsoon trough lies close to the Himalayas for extended periods, there will be drought." The dry savannas and scrub forests of the Deccan Plateau in the rainshadow of the Western Ghats, along with the semi-arid plains of Rajasthan and the Punjab, are the regions most sensitive to ENSO-driven fluctuations in the monsoon, although, as the calamity of 1899–1902 revealed, more than two-thirds of India (all but the west coast and the northeast) is susceptible to drought at some time. Annual rainfall variability, less than 15 percent along the west coast and in Assam, rises to more than 40 percent in Rajasthan. According to modern estimates by the Ministry of Agriculture, 56 million hectares of farmland are subject to inadequate and highly variable rainfall.[14]

Famine can originate from floods (Bengal, 1883) or war (Bengal, 1943), but drought is the proximate cause of most Indian subsistence crises, and twenty-one out of twenty-six droughts since 1877 have been attributed to El Niños.[15] (Conversely, out of twenty-two El Niño years between 1870 and 1991, twenty were associated with Indian droughts or below-average rainfall.)[16] If ENSO events are thus "the strongest control governing the inter-annual behaviour of the Indian monsoon," there is also internal "epochal" variability in monsoon rainfall over India and Southeast Asia that is probably related to fluctuations in Eurasian snow-cover, especially on the Tibetan plateau, whose thermal properties determine monsoon intensity.[17] Monsoons, of course, are driven by the seasonal temperature/pressure gradients between land and ocean. An unusually large winter snow-cover over Tibet, as Blanford surmised in the early 1880s, will weaken the summer monsoon because there is decreased opportunity for protracted surface warming and accordingly less gradient to drive the air masses northward. Thus, high snow-cover (weak monsoon) will reinforce the effect of an El Niño event, while low snow-cover (strong monsoon) will tend to counteract it.[18] Meteorologists talk in terms of "constructive" and "destructive" interference patterns between the two phenomena. Indeed researchers at the Indian Institute of Tropical Meteorology have recently shown that the greatest modern droughts (1877, 1899, 1918 and 1972, in that order) have occurred when there was phase-locking between in intense El Niño and a below-normal rainfall epoch.[19]

On the other hand, powerful ENSO events can fail to produce serious droughts when the Indian rainfall oscillation is cresting in its above-normal mode. The situation since 1980, however, is "without precedent in the historical record." Recent Eurasian surface warming, and thus the thermal gradient driving the monsoon, is larger than in any previous era of the instrumental record. At the same time, the El Niño low-pressure center (the displaced Pacific Warm Pool) has moved further southeast during post-1980 events, consequently shifting monsoon-blocking subsidence (high pressure) in the Indian Ocean away from India toward Indonesia. As a result, India escaped widespread drought and confounded meteorological predictions during the great El Niños of 1982 and 1997. Researchers are now exploring the "intriguing possiblity that global warming has broken the link between ENSO and the [Indian] monsoon by preventing monsoon failure."[20] If so, it would be a singular silver lining in the present trend (also possibly driven by

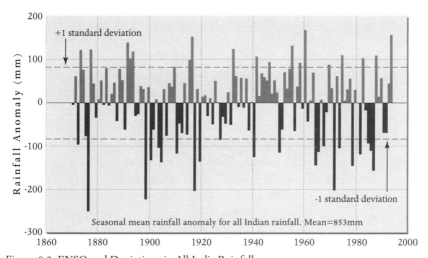

Figure 8.3 ENSO and Deviations in All-India Rainfall

Source: Julia Slingo, "The Indian Summer Monsoon," in Navarra (ed.), p. 107 (Fig. 5.4a).

anthropogenic warming) toward more frequent and destructive El Niños.

Figure 8.3 shows the annual deviations of all-India rainfall from the long-term mean (853 mm). Huge negative spikes correspond to the 1877, 1899, 1918 and 1973 El Niño droughts. The stable weather of the 1880s is clearly legible, as is, even more dramatically, the subdued El Niño cycle from 1922 to 1972. The final bars register the delinkage of Indian rainfall and ENSO in the 1990s. Such large-scale data, however, cannot reveal crucial regional variations. The devastating drought of 1896–97 in central India, for instance, is masked by positive rainfall anomalies elsewhere.

Indeed, as Ramasamy Suppiah demonstrated in a pathbreaking 1989 study of El Niño's impact on Sri Lanka, national climate statistics are artifacts that need to be resolved into finer-grained temporal and spatial patterns. Looking at ENSO influence from the perspective of Sri Lanka's constituent "rainfall fluctuation regions," with their distinct, orographically determined seasonal relationships to monsoon circulation, he discovered decisive correlations that are obscured at the national aggregate level. "Relationships are not clear in the first intermonsoon and northeast monsoon seasons if Sri Lanka is considered as a single unit. Yet the relationships are clear between the rainfall of the different regions and the seasonal Southern Oscillation Index." Although the overall effect of El Niño on Sri Lanka is increased rainfall, the regional patterns range from positive to negative depending on rainfall season and time-lagged correlation to the SO.[21] Suppiah provided a model, since widely emulated, for analyzing teleconnections at a subnational scale where ENSO impacts on agriculture are most clearly legible.

CHINA

Of the world's major grain belts and early seats of civilization, north China (the loess highlands and the deltaic plain of the Yellow River) is unique in the frequency of flood and especially drought disasters. With 45 percent of modern China's population, the provinces north of the Yangtze Valley, where rainfall variability can exceed 30 percent, account for only 18 percent of the country's surface run-off. The north, moreover, receives 70 percent of its mean annual rainfall of 21 inches during June, July and August.[22] The seasonal cycle "consists of a dry and windy spring, a hot dry summer with showers at long intervals, a very wet late autumn bringing two-thirds of the whole year's precipitation and causing great erosion if not serious floods, then finally a severe dry winter with wind-borne snow."[23] Wheat is harvested in June, and millet and *kaoliang* (a tall grain sorghum) in September. If the spring rains fail, there is a poor wheat crop; if the summer monsoon fails, however, there is no harvest for the entire year. Unfortunately, rainfall fluctuations are most common during June, "the critical month for the northern farmer." Over a modern period of fifty-five years, Beijing has had twenty-one Junes with deficient rainfall and five with virtually no rain at all.[24] Undependable rainfall, however, has to some extent been offset historically by irrigation, intense efforts at the conservation of soil moisture, and the marvelous qualities of the loess soil itself, which is unique in its perpetual fertility and capacity to retain moisture. ("With more adequate rainfall," observed an American expert in the 1930s, "it might form one of the most productive soils in the world.")[25]

The East Asian monsoon, like the ENSO cycle that modulates it, seems to fluctuate in a low-frequency pattern. The incidence of extreme climatic events for China as a whole during the late Victorian period 1870–1909 was only exceeded in the last half-millennium by the extraordinarily unstable period 1630–1669.[26] Other research confirms a dramatic "jump" around 1870, coincident with one of history's most catastrophic Yangtze floods, "from smaller [climate] variability to larger variability" and "from a state of few disasters to a state of frequent disasters."[27] This may have involved a transformation in the greater Asian monsoon from a "zonal" to "meridional" regime of circulation – changing again around 1900.[28]

Since the late nineteenth century there had been speculation about a possible atmospheric flywheel that might synchronize monsoon failures in the Yellow River basin with droughts in India and Java.[29] But it was not until what was officially labeled the "Great North China Drought of 1972" that a sustained research program, led by Wang Shao-wu at Beijing University, began to systematically explore linkages between the Southern Oscillation and the drought/flood history of north China.[30] These studies revealed "a longterm coupled oscillation between the equatorial eastern Pacific sea surface temperature [that is, the ENSO phase] and the location and intensity of the western Pacific subtropical high pressure system." When an El Niño event warms the eastern equatorial Pacific in winter, the subtropical high correspondingly intensifies and shifts westward the following summer. This blocks the monsoon from moving as far north as usual, resulting in decreased rainfall or drought in the Yellow River basin.[31] Typhoon landings in north China also decline in El Niño years.[32] A "dry area index" based on the percentage of weather stations in north China reporting drought shows a consistent correlation with ENSO warm phases since 1870, with the index highest in 1877, 1965 and 1972, followed by 1878, 1891, 1899, 1941, 1957 and 1982.[33] Ding Yihui has also pointed to an intriguing relationship between El Niño droughts in north China and cold injury to agriculture in Manchuria, Siberia, Korea and northern Japan.[34]

While La Niña teleconnections have not yet been as well studied as El Niño interactions, there is evidence that flooding of the Yellow River delta, as in 1888, 1898 and 1924, is synchronized to powerful cold phases.[35] Far better documented is the inverse precipitation relationship between north and south China during warm events. As the East Asian monsoon stalls over the middle and lower Yangzi Valley in the mature phase of an El Niño, it is very likely to cause severe flooding there and in southern China during the Mei-yu, the concentrated heavy rain period in June and July. Thus it is not surprising that China has so frequently experienced combinations of drought in the north and flooding in the south, or vice versa, depending on ENSO phase. During the spring and summer of 1876, while the monsoon had forsaken most of north China, the southern coastal provinces of Fujian and Guangdong were pounded by destructive torrential rains, and central Hunan, Jiangxi and Zhejiang were under flood waters.[36] Similarly, in their study of the post-1950 period Chenglan Bao and Yanzhen Xiang found that "all three extemely severe floodings (1954, 1991 and 1983) and all five severe floodings (1969, 1987, 1965 and 1957) in the Yangtse-Huaihe rivers took place during the summer of an El Niño year, or in the summer following."[37] (Yihui cautions, however, that El Niño's teleconnections to the climate of subtropical China are especially complex and produced contrasting anomalies in 1982/83 [cold and flooding] and 1986/87 [warm and drought].)[38]

Like their counterparts in India, leading researchers believe there is a multi-decadal pattern in northern China rainfall, although there is yet not enough data to convincingly tie this to low-frequency regime variations of ENSO.[39] One team from the Tokyo Metropolitan University claims to have uncovered a statistically dramatic transition in the "interdecadal drought/flood index in eastern China" – the biggest in several centuries – that coincides with the 1896 El Niño.[40] Others see a switch to more frequent and intense drought in northern China, coinciding with the circa-1976 regime shift in the Pacific.[41] Meanwhile, a still unexplored question is the historical relationship between ENSO periodicity and the Yellow River hydraulic cycle. The river's extraordinary rate of sedimentation (subject to human acceleration, as we shall see, through watershed deforestation) eventually elevates its bed too high above the north China plain to be confined by dikes and revetments. The history of each successive system of hydraulic control, therefore, has been a spiral of gradually increasing, then finally exploding costs, followed by catastrophic breakdown. It was a singular misfortune of the late Qing that an intensified El Niño regime in the last quarter of the nineteenth-century coincided with an advanced state of sedimentation and decay in the flood-control infrastructure.

Finally, there is controversy over the contribution of ENSO to the agricultural catastrophe of Mao's Great Leap Forward. The drought-famine of 1959–61, which killed 20 million peasants (the death toll officially admitted in 1980 by Hu Yaobang) was the most deadly of the twentieth century, perhaps of all time. Given the PRC's impressive commitments to food security and disaster mitigation in the early 1950s, as well as its dramatic success in raising average life expectancy, the scale of this holocaust is stupefying and, for many sympathizers with the Chinese Revolution, almost inexplicable. Certainly, the "strong" El Niño of 1957–59, which also produced a famous famine and nearly a million refugees in the Brazilian *sertão,* was the likely culprit responsible for the onset of drought in 1958–59, but recent interpretations radically disagree over the relative importance of climatic and political determinants. In *Hungry Ghosts,* a Robert Conquest–like exposé of Mao's orchestration of "the darkest moment in the long history of China," Jasper Becker fails to mention any natural context for the famine whatsoever, although Chinese meteorologists have characterized the drought, which affected one-third of the nation's cultivated acreage, as the most extreme of the twentieth century. For the first time in human memory, people could actually wade across the Yellow River.[42]

Taking a more sober approach, Y. Kueh (1998) has used impressive statistical modeling to show that "the weather was the main cause of the enormous grain-yield losses in 1960 and 1961," but that the communes could still have survived the crisis without mass mortality if Beijing had not stupidly reduced sown acreage in 1959 (to divert labor to public works and backyard steel-making) and criminally enforced confiscatory procurement quotas in 1959–60.[43] A hideous culpability (although not the conspiratorial malevolence that Becker alleges) thus falls upon the Maoist leadership. Although drought was again a proximate cause, the truly key variable was the absence of socialist democracy. As Amartya Sen has emphasized in a well-known contrast of postcolonial India and China, "The particular fact that China, despite its much greater achievements in reducing endemic deprivation, experienced a gigantic famine during 1958–61 ... had a good deal to do with the lack of press freedom and the absence of political opposition. The disastrous policies that had paved the way of the famine were not changed for three years as the famine raged on, and this was made possible by the near-total suppression of news about the famine and the total absence of media criticism of what was then happening in China."[44]

In the classical El Niño pattern, an anomalous high-pressure zone forms over Indonesia as the Pacific Warm Pool moves eastward towards the International Date Line. This can delay the onset of the western monsoon, especially in the central and eastern parts of the country, by more than a month. The Dutch meteorologist Hendrik Berlage, who resumed Sir Gilbert Walker's research on the Southern Oscillation, calculated in the 1950s that fully 93 percent of Javanese droughts during the colonial period had occurred in the course of these negative SO anomalies (El Niños). His findings have been corroborated by updated analyses of the instrumental record, as well as by tree ring series taken from teak that extend the ENSO correlations as far back as 1514.[45] Recent El Niño research has also revealed that "periodic long-term droughts and subsequent forest fires have been apparently been more frequent in Borneo than formerly realized. As in other humid tropical woodlands and societies, they have also been more critical to both social organization and local ecological processes."[46] The intensity of drought in the East Indies, however, does not always correlate with the magnitudes of Indian droughts or Peruvian El Niños. Thus the 1902 El Niño ("strong plus" as measured by Peruvian events) produced a much bigger rainfall deficit in both Indonesia and the Philippines than did the 1899 event ("very strong").[47]

Wetland rice production, which requires at least eight inches of rain per month, is highly sensitive to erratic or deficient rainfall. In areas where the precipitation regime is especially variable, like eastern Java, southeast Borneo, Sulawesi, Timor and Irian Jaya, cultivators had traditionally countered environmental uncertainty with agricultural diversity: using staggered plantings and varieties of rices.[48] In contrast, colonial monocultures with their simplification of crops and rotations increased vulnerability to drought.[49] Yet the complex island and mountain topography of Indonesia and "its puzzling variety of rainfall regimes" has always mitigated against drought-famines on the scale of India or China. General collapses of agricultural production are unlikely. Famines in the nineteenth century tended to be confined to those drought-stricken regions where the terrain dictated high transport costs and market prices for rice that were accordingly out of the reach of the poorest peasants. Since the 1960s, moreover, with more intensive multinational exploitation of Indonesia's hardwood resources, El Niño droughts have been associated with an increased frequency

Table 8.2
Indonesia: Most Severe Modern Droughts

| El Niño Year | Rainfall Anomaly (cm/month) |
|---|---|
| 1982 | −7.1 |
| 1902 | −7.02 |
| 1972 | −6.9 |
| 1914 | −6.5 |
| 1965 | −5.1 |
| 1930 | −3.9 |
| 1941 | −3.8 |
| 1905 | −3.6 |
| 1963* | −3.6 |
| 1923 | −3.4 |
| 1987 | −3.2 |
| 1899 | −2.6 |
| 1896 | −1.8 |

*Non–El Niño year.
Source: Assembled from International Research Institute for Climate Prediction data (iri.ucsed.edu/hot_Niño/impacts/indones/index.html).

of uncontrolled forest fires, like the vast conflagrations in East Kalimantan and North Borneo during 1982–83 and 1997.[50]

The rest of Southeast Asia, according to a recent study of historical rainfall records (excluding Indochina) by R. Kane, also experiences deficient rainfall or drought during strong El Niños, with the exception of the northwest Philippines, which is more strongly under the influence of the East Asian monsoon and thus tends towards flooding. The impact of ENSO perturbations, as in India, is modified by interdecadal fluctuations (probably due to Eurasian snow-cover trends) in the strength of the monsoon. Kane found that in Thailand these "epochs" average about thirty years, similar to India; while in more equatorial countries, like Singapore or Indonesia, they tend to be only a decade or so in duration.[51]

The ENSO signature is particularly vivid in Philippine history where it has often been associated with rural unrest and peasant revolution. Although there is no tradition of local reseach comparable to Berlage's Southern Oscillation time series for Indonesia, the teleconnection may be very robust (with a reversed signal in the case of northern Luzon). The International Research Institute for Climate Research data set, for example, shows a 95 percent correlation between El Niño events and below-average rainfall, with the most severe droughts in 1941, 1915,1902-03, 1983 and 1912. The period of national revolt and US colonial occupation, 1897–1915, was also the most environmentally turbulent in the last 200 years, with seven significant El Niño droughts as well as severe La Niña–related flooding in 1910.[52]

The commercially important plantation island of Negros has been especially vulnerable to the ENSO cycle, with eight of nine famines in the second half of the nineteenth century coinciding with El Niño events.[53] In the twentieth century, adds Lopez-Gonzaga, the conjugation of periodic drought and volatile sugar prices has produced so much hunger that Negros "became known world-wide as the Philippines' 'Ethiopia.'" Negros's rich tradition of messianic and class-based resistance movements, however, has ensured that deprivation did not go unchallenged. During the terrible 1982–83 El Niño drought, for example, thousands of unemployed Negrense sugarworkers flocked to the banner of the communist New People's Army. "By mid-1985, many of the haciendas and the upland settlements in the south-central towns of Negros were identified as NPA 'red liberated zones.'"[54]

Drought and flood disasters have also episodically sharpened agrarian discontent on other islands. The most recent crisis was in the winter of 1997–98 when 90 percent of the Philippines experienced moderate to extreme drought. Nearly a million people suffered the early stages of starvation as the impact of crop failure was magnified by the East Asian financial crisis.[55] The archipelago is also frequently in the direct path of typhoons spawned in abnormal numbers by the warming of the eastern equatorial Pacific. The typhoon rains and tropical storms that battered Luzon and Mindanao during the El Niño summer of 1972 have been described as "the worst natural disaster in Philippines history."[56]

AUSTRALIA AND OCEANIA

As we have seen, contemporary observers interpreted the synchronous droughts in Australia and India in 1877 as a correlation having almost oracular significance. Ten years later, in a review of historical data, Sir Charles Todd, government astronomer and meteorologist for South Australia, confirmed that the coincidence was indeed a fundamental meteorological relationship. "Comparing our records with those of India, I find a close correspondence or similarity of seasons with regard to the prevalence of drought, and there can be little or no doubt that severe droughts occur as a rule simultaneously over the two countries."[57] Modern research has shown, however, that while mean surface pressure and rainfall over most of Australia fluctuate with the Southern Oscillation, the correlation of drought with ENSO is strongest in New South Wales and northern Victoria, where tremendous losses were sustained by agriculture and the wool industry during the El Niño events of 1877, 1884, 1888, 1897, 1899, 1902, 1915, 1918 and 1958. At such times, vast areas become an antipodean Dust Bowl. "Not surprisingly," Ann Young explains, "the most severe wind erosion occurs during droughts. At the end of the 1895–1903 drought a huge series of dust storms engulfed Victoria and parts of New South Wales, Queensland and South Australia over a three-day period from 11 to 13 November 1903. Many places experienced gales of dust, fire balls, lightning, and darkness during the day that was so intense that the fowls roosted."[58] El Niño also orchestrates the fire cycle in the sclerophyll flora of eastern Australia, which episodically climaxes in great regional firestorms like the Ash Wednesday disaster of 16 February 1983.

The environmental history of Papua New Guinea/Irian Jaya is poorly understood, but El Niño droughts and La Niña floods are probably prime movers of episodic migration and intercultural violence. In 1997, for example, the combination of drought and killing frost (from colder temperatures during cloudless nights) forced tens of thousands of highland farmers to trek to the lowlands in a desperate search for food and water. The shortage of water also forced the huge gold mine at Porgera in the central highlands to shut down, and fires did terrible damage to forests on the western side of the island.[59]

ENSO is also the major control over rainfall in New Caledonia and, presumably, the rest of Melanesia. As the Warm Pool and its associated convergence zone move eastward, "there is a tendency for local colder than average sea surface temperature, for saltier than average sea surface salinity and consistent rainfall shortage." In strong El Niño years, riverflows decline by more than half (with disastrous impacts on taro irrigation systems), while during La Niña events they double. The La Niña effect is sometimes catastrophically reinforced by typhoons that track in the direction of New Caledonia during cold event years.[60]

As the most important variable in the ecological metabolism of the tropical Pacific, ENSO has also deeply shaped Polynesian history. In New Zealand, the north and east coasts of the country, including most of the urban population, are vulnerable to El Niño drought, while higher than average rainfall occurs along the west and south coasts of the South Island. All the island groups near the International Date Line, meanwhile, are subject to drastic rainfall variation as the Warm Pool shuttles back and forth in the course of the ENSO cycle. The Southern Oscillation likewise determines the geography of tropical cyclone activity in the Pacific and "island communities east of the Date Line [like Tahiti] experience high risk of damage during ENSO events."[61]

El Niño is the major control on agricultural output and water supply in the Hawaiian Islands. During warm events, the subtropical jet stream intensifies and moves southward, leaving Hawai'i on the anticyclonic side in a region of strong subsidence. The colder sea temperatures in the north-central Pacific likewise reduce evaporation and promote subsidence.[62] "Nearly all major statewide Hawaiian droughts have coincided with El Niño events," with the driest years in 1877, 1897, 1926 and 1919.[63] The recurrent droughts from 1982–83 onwards played a major role in the decline and eventual shutdown of most of the state's once dominant sugarcane industry.

Fijian agriculture – both the sugar industry and food crops like rice and *kava* – has likewise suffered severely from recent El Niños (as it did, presumably, in the nineteenth century). The 1997–98 drought was the worst in Fiji's modern history and led to the declaration of a state of emergency with 270,000 people at one point dependent on relief.[64] The drought crisis, which especially undermined indigenous subsistence agriculture, was probably a contributing factor to renewed ethnic tensions that led to the coup and hostage crisis in summer 2000.

SOUTH AMERICA

Brazil's Nordeste has long been a puzzle to climatologists. "Due to its geography (1 to 18 degrees South), one would expect a rainfall distribution typical of equatorial areas. However, the annual mean rainfall over this region, which is in the immediate vicinity of the largest tropical forest, the Amazon, is much smaller than the average equatorial rainfall." Although the *sertão* is certainly not the desert imagined by many urban Brazilians (the mean annual precipitation –

28 inches – is slightly more than that of Paris), very high rates of evapotranspira-
tion and soil dryness conspire against stable rainfed agriculture. Its semi-aridity,
most researchers now believe, is principally determined by the way the tip of the
Nordeste protrudes well into the influence of the stationary South Atlantic subtropical high.[65] ("This is the same stable air mass," Webb points out, "that provides the brilliant, transparent nights in the sertão. Many poems and songs have
been inspired by the 'luar do meu sertão.'")[66]

What has most decisively shaped the human ecologies of the sertão, however, is not the climate's mean trend but its extreme fluctuation. The core of the
sertão, for example, experiences rainfall variability in excess of 40 percent.[67] Even
compared to north China, this is an extraordinarily high quotient of environmental instability. Moreover, "even during a 'normal' year 80–90% of the rainfall is
concentrated during the wet season. The duration of the rainy season is fairly
constant but its starting point, which coincides roughly with sowing time in the
agricultural calendar, may vary by between fifty-five and eighty-five days.... The
reduction of total rainfall by one-third can have disastrous effects if the start of
the rainy season is delayed for long enough to make the crops fail." Sertanejos
believe that if the rains don't come by St. Joseph's Day, 19 March, a seca will surely
ensue. Erratic seasonal distribution, in other words, is just as much a problem as
an annual deficit in rainfall.[68]

Sir Gilbert Walker was convinced that the sertão's irregular rainfall resulted
from some influence exercised by the Southern Oscillation. He even proposed a
statistical formula in 1928 that tied the incidence of drought-famine in Ceará
to the phases of SO.[69] Subsequent research has elaborated Walker's insight in
terms of ENSO teleconnection theory. It works like this: rainfall in the northern
and central sertão is concentrated in the months (March–April) when the Intertropical Convergence Zone (ITCZ) in the Atlantic Ocean reaches its most south-
erly position. During strong El Niño phases, an anomalously strong Atlantic high
squats off the coast of Brazil and the ITCZ is blocked from moving southward
into its usual rainmaking position. One interpretation is that when the Warm
Pool/IACZ moves into the east-central Pacific it pushes the major equatorial
standing waves (troughs and ridges) eastward. The influence on the Nordeste's
rainfall, however, seems to be very sensitive to the exact timing of the onset
of the El Niño, and not all warm phases bring droughts.[70] Nonetheless, rainfall

records from Fortaleza (which date back to 1849) show that the ten driest January-to-July periods have all been synchronized to strong El Niños.[71] In addition, there seems to be a strong inverse relationship between El Niño (La Niña) drought (wet) incidents in the Nordeste/Amazonas and unusually wet (dry) episodes in southern Brazil that is analogous to the dipolar relationship between north China and the Yangzi Valley.[72]

Although the droughts of 1877–79 and 1888–91 were the most severe as measured at Fortaleza, recent data from the International Research Institute shows the 1896–97 drought, which accompanied the War of Canudos, was also exceptionally intense by twentieth-century standards (see Table 8.3). Moreover, general drought conditions persisted almost unbroken until 1907 and then, after a few humid years, resumed with the sharp El Niño spikes in 1915 and 1918 (respectively, the second and fourth most severe rainfall anomalies in the last century).[73] Indeed, the three decades from 1888 to 1918, as elsewhere, constitute an epoch of extraordinary environmental turmoil in the Nordeste.

El Niño droughts have also played destructive roles in the history of Andean and Amazonian cultures. As the research of C. Caviedes has shown, the phasing of droughts on the altiplano of Bolivia and Peru, as well as the outer Amazon Basin (centered around Manaus), is synchronized with ENSO. "Although the inter-annual precipitation variability in the Altiplano is not as large as in northern Peru, there are years when the winter dryness extends into spring and summer, thus producing droughts. It has been demonstrated that these droughts are especially pronounced during the years when northern Peru is struck by ENSO episodes."[74] Southern Peru's most severe modern droughts were in 1940–41 and 1956–58, with the later leading to near-famine and widespread agrarian unrest.[75]

In Amazonia, Caviedes has demonstrated that Manaus's rainfall is severely reduced by El Niño blocking of the Intertropical Convergence Zone.[76] ENSO, in fact, may be the chief climatic regulator of Amazon Basin ecology, producing the periodic droughts and accompanying wildfires (as in 1998) which are the major natural "disturbance regime." Even in the absence of fire, El Niño events, which lengthen the Amazon dry season, have stunning impacts on forest productivity and resultant carbon fluxes. A recent study of 1982–93 satellite data suggests that powerful warm events can temporarily transform the Amazon Basin from a major net $CO_2$ source to a net sink of comparable magnitude – a phenomenon

Table 8.3
Northern South America: Droughts and ENSO

| El Niño Year | Rainfall Anomaly (cm/month) |
| --- | --- |
| 1896 | −8.2 |
| 1915 | −3.3 |
| 1982 | −3.2 |
| 1918 | −3.2 |
| 1958 | −3.1 |
| 1905 | −2.1 |
| 1930 | −2.1 |
| 1902 | −2.0 |
| 1925 | −1.8 |
| 1972 | −1.7 |

Source: IRI, ibid.

with planetary biogeochemical implications.[77] Archaeologists, meanwhile, speculate that major discontinuities in cultural sequences throughout the Amazon, like counterpart sites in coastal Peru, probably correspond to El Niño catastrophes (drought in Amazonia, flooding in Peru). In the twentieth century, both the 1925–26 and 1982–83 El Niños were associated with severe droughts in Amazonia: during the former, forest fires raged uncontrolled for months, reputedly trapping and killing "thousands of rubber gatherers."[78]

When Amazonia, the Altiplano and the Nordeste are dry, most of the Southern Cone is anomalously wet. The great Paraná River basin, which encompasses 2.6 million square kilometers of Bolivia, Paraguay, Brazil and Argentina, typically experiences rainfall maxima during El Niños.[79] The 1982–83 event, for example, produced the Paraná's greatest historical flood with flows of almost Amazonian volume.[80] Across the Andes, central Chile is similarly inundated during most El Niño years. Researchers have shown how the wave train of troughs and ridges in the Southern Hemisphere, as in the Northern, is realigned by warm events; a blocking high over the Bellinghausen Sea usually leading to intensified winter storm systems over Chile's most populated provinces. It is an impressively consistent relationship, with twenty out of twenty-three of the wettest years in central Chile over the last century correlating to El Niños.[81]

NORTH AMERICA

During a canonical El Niño event, some of the warm water that piles up against the equatorial coastline of South America is driven far northward. (Technically, equatorial trapped Kelvin waves – the sloshing of the thermocline eastward – are transformed into coastal trapped Kelvin waves.) The subsequent warming and rise in sea level by as much as a foot of Mexico's Pacific coastal waters have profound meteorological effects. During the 1896 El Niño, for instance, central Mexico was gripped by severe drought while the north of the country experienced excessive precipitation, a pattern that was repeated during the very powerful 1982–83 event.[82] Again, in 1997–98, soaring ocean temperatures produced a crippling drought in the western parts of central Mexico. Hundreds of forest fires broke out and "covered the entire country with a thick layer of smoke that extended to the adjacent areas of the United States."[83] Under La Niña conditions, as in 1999–2000, the pattern reverses: unusually wet conditions in the Mesa Central contrast with severe droughts in Chihuahua (see Table 8.4 ) and states east of the continental divide of the Sierra Madre.

Table 8.4
Drought in 20th-Century Chihuahua

| Year | ENSO? |
| --- | --- |
| 1907–10* | La Niña (1907–10) |
| 1918–21 | ? (La Niña 1916–18/El Niño 1918–20) |
| 1929* | La Niña (1928–29) |
| 1934–35 | – |
| 1947–48 | El Niño? |
| 1950–51 | La Niña (1950–51) |
| 1953 | – |
| 1956 | La Niña (1955–56) |
| 1964 | La Niña (1964) |
| 1974 | La Niña (1973–75) |

*Extreme drought.
Source: Drought chronology from Luis Carlos Fierro; ENSO from NOAA and Allan, Lindesay and Parker.

Although local research is still in its relative infancy, it is clear that ENSO has been one of the major environmental forces shaping Mexican history. Indeed, the devastating drought from 1907 to 1911 (fusing with monetary and trade crises) that destabilized much of Mexico and helped precipitate the downfall of the Porfiriato coincided with the most protracted (four to five years) La Niña event of the last century.[84] Droughts, moreover, have been a major "push" factor in the modern fluxes of Mexican labor to Texas and California.[85]

North of the border, however, ENSO has conferred immense geopolitical power on US and Canadian grain surpluses. According to a 1997 study by researchers at the University of Illinois, the year preceding a warm event onset usually correlates with bumper crops in the US Midwest, while the El Niño year itself typically brings mild winters and early spring plantings.[86] A 1999 paper, more specifically focused on the cornbelt, also found a positive relationship between farm output and the ENSO warm phase.[87] American grain production, in other words, is typically in meteorological anti-phase with El Niño droughts and crop failures in India, north China and (most likely) the Russian chernozem belt. This potential to relieve the world's hunger during periods of synchronous global drought, as Kansas Populists realized in the 1890s, was also a partial solution to the problem of periodic overproduction in the Plains states. Later, Herbert Hoover showed how it could be elaborated into full-scale foreign policy of famine relief and food aid. Occasional flood damage in Southern California and the Gulf states during El Niño years is usually more than offset by enhanced bargaining power within world grain markets as well as by lower winter fuel bills and reduced hurricane damage. Stanley Changnon claims that the Midwest reaped almost $9 billion in net gains, and the United States as a whole more $14 billion, from the weather effects of the great 1997–98 El Niño.[88]

But ENSO's relative benign impact on the US GNP should not be taken for granted. In an important 1998 study, Cole and Cook find that ENSO's influence on the continental US moisture balance has a low-frequency pattern that corresponds to regime shifts in the Pacific, probably associated with the PDO. "Long ENSO records reveal decadal modulation of ENSO intensity [vis-à-vis US hydrology], with stronger variability in the early parts of this century, a general weakening around 1925, and stronger variability since about 1955." Stronger ENSO events, as theory would predict, produce more consistent teleconnection pat-

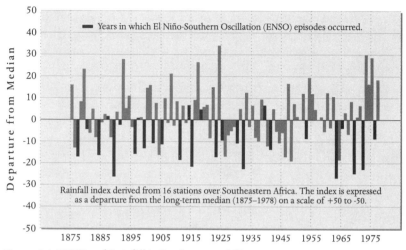

Figure 8.4  ENSO and Rainfall in Southeastern Africa

Source: From Eugene Rasmusson, "Global Climate Change and Variability: Effects on Drought and Desertification in Africa," in Michael Glantz (ed.), *Drought and Hunger in Africa: Denying Famine a Future*, Cambridge 1987, p. 10. I have interpreted two of Rasmusson's non-ENSO droughts as in fact El Niño–related (circa 1891 and 1915).

terns and greater penetration of moisture anomalies – drought (1988) or flooding (1993) – from the Southwest rim into the southern Great Plains and Midwest. In the case of the 1988 drought, farm output in the scorched southern plains declined by almost one-third.[89] New research also suggests a La Niña teleconnection that increases drought probabilities in the Midwest through a strengthening of the Mexican summer monsoon.[90]

SOUTHERN AFRICA

Catastrophic drought has been one of the principal axes of the history of southern Africa. The devastating aridity in Zimbabwe and much of South Africa since 1980, culminating in the 1991–92 drought (the worst this century) and an 82 percent decline in maize production, reminds us of what the protracted droughts of the 1820s, 1870s and late 1890s must have been like.[91] Dependent like northeast Brazil on the unreliable southern migration of the ITCZ, Natal, Zululand, the Transvaal, the Zambezi Valley and the low veld of southern Mozambique have

been accurately described as "kingdoms of uncertainty" where rulership was traditionally legitimated by rainmaking power and the relief of the poor during
droughts. Moreover, there is compelling, generally accepted evidence of strong
teleconnections between rainfall in southern Africa and ENSO.[92] A 1998 study
confirmed a correlation between the ten strongest twentieth-century El Niños
and rainfall over the entire southern half of Africa. The three major centers of
synchronized drought were eastern South Africa, southern Tanzania to northern Mozambique and, surprisingly, along the South Atlantic coast from Namibia
to Gabon.[93] As elsewhere in the tropics, the shifting IACZ rearranges ridges and
troughs, pushing the westerly jet stream equatorwards and weakening convection over southern Africa and sometimes the Horn of Africa, while typically
strengthening it over East Africa. The inverse pattern of exceptional convection in
the south, associated with strong La Niña events, can also be devastating to agriculture as the great flood of winter 2000 in Mozambique grimly demonstrated.

The impact of ENSO, however, is modulated by two other circulation regimes:
an eighteen- to twenty-year regional rainfall cycle (strongest in the northeast
of South Africa and parts of Zimbabwe) and the transequatorial phenomena
known as the Quasi-Biennial Oscillation, which involves reversals of stratospheric
winds.[94] The 1957–58 and 1977–78 El Niños, for example, had virtually no impact
on southern Africa. Nonetheless, it is estimated that at least 20 percent of summer
rainfall variance in southeastern Africa is "accounted for solely by the relationship
with the Southern Oscillation," and ENSO forecasts – which provide surprisingly
accurate predictions of maize yield in Zimbabwe up to a year in advance – are
now being used as an "early warning system" for millions of African farmers.[95]

THE HORN AND EAST AFRICA

ENSO impacts on the Horn and East Africa are less straightforward. In Ethiopia
there are three agricultural seasons: the main rainy season, *kremt* (June to September); the dry season, *bega* (October to January); and the season of small rains,
*belg* (February to May). Meteorological research, especially analyses of the fluctuations of the Nile flood, which originates in the Ethiopian Highlands, supports
a persistent teleconnection between Ethiopian weather and ENSO. However, the
outcomes for agriculture are highly variable since El Niño phases correlate both
to catastrophic failure of the *kremt* rains and to above-normal belg rainfall. In

## Table 8.5
### ENSO and Drought-Famine in Sudan and the Horn of Africa

| ENSO | Famine Years | Region |
|---|---|---|
| 1828 | 1828–29 | Shewa, Sudan |
| 1835 | **1835–37** | Ethiopia, Sudan |
| 1864 | 1864–66 | Tigray/Gondar |
| 1876 | 1876–78 | Tigray/Afar |
| 1889 | **1888–92** | Ethiopia, Sudan |
| 1896 | 1896 | Ethiopia |
| 1899 | 1899–1900 | Ethiopia, Darfur |
| 1912 | **1913–14** | N. Ethiopia, Sudan |
| 1918/19 | 1920–22 | Ethiopia |
| 1953 | 1953 | Tigray/Wallo |
| 1958 | **1958** | Tigray/Wallo |
| 1965 | 1964–66 | Tigray/Wallo |
| 1972/73 | **1973–74** | Tigray/Wallo, Sudan |
| 1982–83 | **1983–84** | Ethiopia, Sudan |
| 1987 | 1987–88 | Ethiopia |
| 1990–95 | 1990–94 | Ethiopia, Sudan |
| 1997/98 | 1997–98 | Ethiopia, Sudan |
| 1999–2000* | 1999–2000 | Ogadan/Somalia |

*La Niña. Largest crop failures are in bold.
Source: Based on chronologies in Joachim Von Braun, Tesfaye Teklu and Patrick Webb,
*Famine in Africa*, Baltimore 1998, pp. 36 and 39; and Workineh Degefu, "Some Aspects of
Meteorological Drought in Ethiopia," in Glantz, *Drought and Hunger in Africa*, pp. 29–31.

1997, for example, the rains largely failed during the kremt, but November, usually the driest month, was unusually wet.[96] Still, because the kremt is most critical
for agriculture and pastoralism, the impact is usually severe. Table 8.5 shows why
El Niño has become synonymous with hunger in northern Ethiopia, especially in
Wallo and Tigray which are in the rainshadow of the great highland massif.[97] On
the other hand, the autumn rainy season (the *Der*) of southern Ethiopia (Ogaden)
and Somalia, like the short rainy season in neighboring coastal East Africa, has a
positive linkage (greater than normal rainfall) to El Niño. Here drought-famine,
as in 1998–2000, occurs in the wake of protracted La Niñas.[98]

The Sudan and Upper Egypt, as we have seen, have tended to experience
famine in synchronization with the Horn. Nile flows, of course, are the addition

of seasonal rainfall over the Ethiopian Highlands, which supplies 80 percent of basin discharge via the annual flood of the Blue Nile, and the smaller but more regular outflow from the Great Lakes of central Africa via the White Nile. Within the vast Nile Basin as a whole it is estimated that as much as 40 percent of inter-annual rainfall variability is due to ENSO, but the two major watersheds, as one would expect from their different climatologies, react independently and asymmetrically to global forcings. Thus El Niño phases primarily affect the Blue Nile system, with Ethiopian droughts leading to 5 percent to 15 percent reductions in the total Basin water budget, while La Niña phases can produce spectacular 10 percent to 25 percent increases in precipitation over the White Nile catchment.[99]

Like Brazil's Nordeste, East Africa is surprisingly dry for its low latitude. "Undoubtedly the most impressive climatic anomaly in all of Africa," writes G. Trewartha, "is the widespread deficiency of rainfall in tropical East Africa."[100] The highlands of Madagascar intercept much of the moisture in the southeast trade winds, while the "rain-bearing equatorial trough passes the region rapidly, being hastened far to the north in the northern summer and far to the south in the southern summer."[101] According to Laban Ogallo and his colleagues at the University of Nairobi, an estimated 50 percent of East African rainfall variance is directly attributable to ENSO.[102] In Kenya, where the major growing season is March to June, the devastating rains of 1998 upheld the hypothesis that the same displacement of the ITCZ that produces drought in southeastern Africa brings extreme rainfall to eastern equatorial Africa. Conversely, historical rainfall data from the Kenyan coast, commencing in 1900, demonstrate a consistent relationship between La Niñas and dry anomalies. This suggests that the devastating Kenyan drought at the very end of the nineteenth century, which overlapped with El Niño droughts elsewhere, arose from the powerful La Niña event of 1898 that punctuated the El Niño pulses of 1896–97 and 1899–1900.[103] As the annual rainfall anomaly index for East Africa shows (see Figure 8.4), this event was extraordinary in magnitude.

Such broadbrush portraits, however, are locally modified by the region's Great Lakes and complex topography. Current research has thus adopted a methodology similar to the "rainfall fluctuation region" approach pioneered by Suppiah in his analysis of ENSO in Sri Lanka. Working from rainfall records in 136 stations throughout Kenya, Uganda and Tanzania, Ogallo and his colleagues have identi-

Table 8.6
ENSO and East African Droughts

| Year | ENSO | Departure from Average 1951–80 Rainfall |
|------|------|------------------------------------------|
| 1898 | La Niña | –50% |
| 1917 | La Niña | –30% |
| 1899[1] | – | –28% |
| 1921 | ? | –28% |
| 1892–93 | La Niña | –26% |
| 1990[2] | – | –25% |
| 1943/44 | La Niña | –23% |

1. Strong La Niña through first quarter 1899; El Niño in third quarter.
2. The 1989 La Niña persisted through winter 1990.
Source: Derived from Figure 5.6 in Mike Hulme, "Climate Change Within the Period of Meteorological Records," in Adams, Goudie and Orme, p. 96; and La Niña chronology in Allan, Lindesay and Parker, p. 137.

fied eight coherent subregions with distinct seasonal patterns of rainfall and correspondingly different interactions with ENSO. Under this higher magnification, East Africa in strong El Niño/La Niña years presents a variegated pattern of local drought amid generally abnormal regional rainfall (or vice versa). Thus during warm phases, when coastal rainfall is torrential, there is frequently a late onset to the March–May rains in the western highlands of Kenya, northwestern Kenya and northeastern Uganda, as well as significant deficiencies in summer rainfall over the central Rift Valley. "The suppression of this seasonal rainfall [in an otherwise 'wet' year] can have severe socio-economic impacts especially on agriculture. The June–September rainfall maintains the different growing stages of crops especially wheat planted by both large-scale farmers and small-scale peasant farmers."[104] Distinguishing between regions of Uganda with single and dual season rainfall zones, Phillips and McIntyre have similarly noted that El Niño events, which typically depress August but enhance November precipitation, can have very different impacts on agriculture in one part of the country from another.[105]

"Of ENSO-sensitive regions," caution Allan, Lindesay and Parker, "the Sahelian is perhaps one of the most complicated as it is also influenced markedly by multi-decadal fluctuations in the climate system, and thus ENSO impacts wax and wane over time."[106] In simple models, El Niño / La Niña events regulate rainfall in the Sahel by displacing the location and modulating the strength of the globe-spanning Walker Circulation discovered by Bjerknes. Shifts in the east–west Atlantic Walker cells force "anomalous subsiding/ascending vertical motions over western Africa." However, these zonal (east–west) anomalies are only part of the story. Equally or more important is the emergence of a powerful meridional (north–south) sea temperature gradient in the tropical Atlantic. "Dry years," writes Bette Otto-Bliesner, "are associated with El Niño conditions in the eastern tropical Pacific and a dipole pattern in the tropical Atlantic with positive anomalies south of 10 degrees North and negative anomalies north of 10 degrees North. The latter results in a weakening of the Atlantic Hadley cell [the major atmospheric circulation of heat from the equator to the mid-latitudes] and associated moisture flux into the Intertropical Convection Zone." This complex interaction between perpendicular circulations, moreover, takes place at differential speeds: "The tropical Atlantic dipole-Sahel precipitation connection is best defined on decadal time scales with Pacific SST anomalies playing a larger role on sub-decadal time scales."[107]

Conceptually we are on familiar ground, with the equatorial Atlantic dipole playing a comparable role to epochal variability in the Indian monsoon. Both modulate the impact of El Niño pulses on decadal scales. It is not surprising, therefore, that a sophisticated study of rainfall records for ten Sahelian stations (covering 1900–88) shows that the ENSO teleconnection (statistically most significant at Dakar and Kano) should fluctuate in intensity, almost vanishing, for instance, during the wet period of the 1950s and early 1960s.[108] North of the Sahara, meanwhile, ENSO dances with a different partner, the North Atlantic Oscillation (NAO) – the air-mass/pressure see-saw between Iceland and the Azores that was named by Walker in the 1920s. Although NAO, on the whole, exercises more control over Maghrebian precipitation, new research that correlates November–January sea surface temperature trends in the tropical Pacific with February–April precipitation over the arable valleys and plains of western

Morocco supports the likelihood that the terrible 1877–78 drought-famine was indeed part of the global El Niño configuration.[109]

As its celebrity increases, ENSO tempts historians and archaeologists as a deus ex machina, like the Victorian sunspot mania, that can be invoked to explain almost any drought or extreme weather pattern. Indeed, since ENSO is in a warm phase approximately 20 percent of the time, and because of the temporal "lead/lag" patterns in its teleconnections, nothing is easier than establishing a circumstantial correlation betwen a given historical event and an El Niño outbreak.[110] Accordingly, we should be deeply wary of claims about El Niño causality where the putative teleconnection is not solidly grounded in theory or supported by a robust time series.

One historian, for example, generated newspaper headlines across the world in 1997 with his "discovery" that El Niño had been "behind" the French Revolution (or at least the agricultural dearth that preceded it) and the Irish Potato Famine.[111] Certairly both events (unusually wet, cool summers ruinous of grain) coincided with contemporary El Niños, as did similar Irish and British crop failures in 1876–79, and thus may be legitimately treated as part of the same global agricultural conjuncture. But their meteorologies may have had only the most distant, if any, relationship. Despite vigorous investigation, there is yet little persuasive evidence of a significant ENSO teleconnection to Western European weather. Indeed a recent study found "no robust ENSO composite elements" out of thirty-four variables affecting Atlantic climate systems.[112]

Recent research, on the contrary, has shown that agricultural output in northwestern Europe is powerfully orchestrated by the North Atlantic Oscillation. The NAO is most likely the principal source of the cold, wet summers that are associated (rather than drought) with crop failure and famine in European history. There may well be, of course, some atmospheric flywheel (perhaps the enigmatic and encompassing "Arctic Oscillation") that meshes the NAO and ENSO into a single planetary system, but according to a 1998 review, "no study has so far defined a clear-cut association between the NAO and ENSO."[113] If the great El Niños of 1876-77 and 1982–83 were accompanied by a strengthened NAO that brought milder winters to Western Euope, other strong El Niños are perversely correlated with a weakened NAO and more severe winter weather.[114]

There is more evidence that the tropical Pacific exercises some influence over precipitation in the western Mediterranean (in tandem with NAO) and southern Russia. Ropelewski and Halpert in the late 1980s, for example, identified a positive SO relationship with summer rainfall in North Africa, the Mediterranean and the southeastern Iberian Peninusula. Their correlations, however, lacked a clear physical explanation and did not cast light on whether there was a teleconnection in other seasons.[115] In a 1998 study, Alfredo Rocha re-examined the Iberian data for the 1900–96 period. He found that El Niño was "associated with below-average spring and winter rainfall over the southeastern Iberian Peninsula, and above-average autmn rainfall in the Peninsula as a whole." The teleconnection, however, is "moody," having waxed and waned in strength over the course of the last century.[116]

Table 8.7
ENSO and Drought in the Volga Breadbasket

| Drought Crisis | ENSO Correlation |
| --- | --- |
| 1877 | 1876–77 El Niño |
| 1890–91 | 1888–90 La Niña / 1891 El Niño |
| 1896 | 1896–97 El Niño |
| 1905 | 1905 El Niño |
| 1911 | 1910 La Niña / 1911–12 El Niño |
| 1920–21 | 1918–19 El Niño |
| 1931 | 1930 El Niño |
| 1972 | 1971 La Niña / 1972 El Niño |
| 1982 | 1982–83 El Niño |
| 1997 | 1997 El Niño |

Source: See the description of the Volga drought-belt in Orlando Figes, *Peasant Russia, Civil War: The Volga Countryside in Revolution (1917–21)*, Oxford 1980, pp. 19–25. ENSO dates are from Quinn (1987) and Allan, Lindesay and Parker.

Any historian, meanwhile, must be considerably impressed by the synchronicity of drought and crop failure in south Russia (especially the Volga *gubernii* of Samara, Saratov, Simbrisk and Penza) with worldwide ENSO events. Yet this apparent teleconnection linking drought on the Volga steppe with warming/cooling in the eastern tropical Pacific should be treated with great caution. At this writing, there is no literature in English that illuminates a plausible mechanism or tests the statistical significance of these correlations. The seasonal fit between El Niño events and Volga droughts is not consistent, and in some cases (1891, 1911 and 1972) warm events follow so quickly on the heels of cold events as to blur which ENSO phase is being correlated. Moreover, the putative Volga teleconnection does not reproduce itself in larger geographical units of analysis. When Meshcherskaya and Blazhevich in a 1997 article, for example, divided the basic cereals-producing area of the former Soviet Union into European and Asian halves, the most significant pattern they discovered was a dipole where drought in the west is accompanied by normal or excessive moisture in the east, and vice versa. Although like most Russian researchers they did not specifically probe an ENSO connection, their century-long data on drought magnitude (measured by surface area affected) correlates primarily to a cold event chronology. Thus the four largest droughts in the Asian part of the grainbelt (1955, 1965, 1951 and 1931, in that rank order) occurred in the year following a La Niña, while three out of the four droughts in the European half (1981, 1936 and 1975, but not 1979) coincided with the year of Pacific cold events.[117] It is plausible, of course, that an El Niño–linked drought climatology is confined to the Volga with teleconnections of a different sign elsewhere, but nothing in the current scientific literature resolves the issue. Yet if ENSO's precise role in Russian weather is still a rich mystery, it remains of obvious geopolitical consequence that Volga grain shortfalls and famines have repeatedly aligned themselves, through whatever causality, with global El Niño droughts.

## An El Niño Chronology

Since Bjerknes's original synthesis of oceanic and atmospheric interaction, three principal databases have been used to reconstruct the chronology and magnitude of historical ENSO events. Australian meteorologists, first of all, have fine-tuned Walker's original Southern Oscillation Index ("normalized monthly mean Tahiti minus Darwin sea-level pressure anomalies") as far back as January 1876 and the onset of the great droughts. Researchers using the UK Meteorological Office's records ("the richest archive of meteorological observations in the world"), meanwhile, have compiled a series of sea surface temperatures from the east-central equatorial Pacific (the "Niño-3" region) from January 1871 to December 1994.[118] These pressure and temperature anomalies, in turn, have been interpreted and calibrated with the help of eyewitness accounts of El Niño events that the late William Quinn, an oceanographer at Oregon State University, spent decades excavating from South American archives as far back as the diaries of Pizarro's secretary, Francisco Xeres. Quinn used "canonical" El Niños – for example, 1877 and 1982 (very strong), 1972 (strong), and 1907 (moderate) – to scale

Table 8.8
Major ENSO Events Since 1780

| El Niño | Strength | Regions Affected by Drought/Famine |
|---|---|---|
| 1782–83 | s | China, India |
| 1790–93 | vs | India |
| 1803–04 | s+ | India, South Africa |
| 1824–25 | m+ | China, India, South Africa |
| 1828 | vs | South Africa |
| 1837 | m+ | China, India |
| 1844–46 | s | China, Brazil |
| 1867–70 | m+ | China, India |
| 1873–74 | m | India |
| 1876–78 | vs | China, India, South Africa, Egypt, Java, Brazil |
| 1887–89 | m+ | China, Ethiopia, Sudan, Sahel |
| 1891 | vs | China, India, Brazil |
| 1896–97 | m+ | India, Brazil |
| 1899–1900 | vs | China, India, South Africa |
| 1901–02 | m+ | China, South Africa |
| 1911–13 | s | China, India, Brazil |
| 1917–19 | s | China, India, Brazil, Morocco |
| 1925–26 | vs | China (floods), India |
| 1957–58 | s | China, Brazil |
| 1965–66 | s | China, India |
| 1972–73 | s | China, India, Ethiopia, Sahel, Brazil |
| 1982–83 | vs | China, India, Indonesia, South Africa |
| 1991–95 | s | South Africa, East Africa, Mexico |
| 1997–98 | vs | China (+ floods), Indonesia, Brazil |

Key: m=moderate; s=strong; vs=very strong.

magnitudes since 1525. He roughly gauged "very strong" events as corresponding to 7°–12°C anomalies in coastal sea surface temperatures, while "strong" events equalled 3°–5°C warmings, and "moderate," 2°–3°C. He supplemented his Peruvian and Chilean records with presumed ENSO proxies like Nilometer readings (the world's oldest instrumental record of climate variability), drought data from historical archives, and tree-ring chronologies from India, China and Java.[119] In Table 8.9, significant drought-famines since 1780 are correlated with the Quinn magnitudes of their corresponding El Niño events.

It should be re-emphasized, of course, that drought in some regions (like India) "leads" and in others (like north China and northeast Brazil) "lags", the canonical warming off the Peruvian coast, thus potentially stretching local duration of an ENSO event by a year on either side. Confidence that these droughts have high probabilities of ENSO causation thus requires a suite of diagnostic tests: First, a plausible temporal correlation with the Quinn series (the weakest and potentially most misleading test). Second, a theoretical model of teleconnection well-established in the scientific literature. Third, the "synchronicity test" as explained by Whetton and Rutherfurd (and alluded to in the previous chapter): "Although the rainfall of a region may show an ENSO signal, many extreme rainfall events in that region may not be associated with ENSO. However, where these extremes are also present in remote regions in a pattern characteristic of ENSO one can have increased confidence that they are ENSO-related."[120] Fourth, corroboration of these patterns by the "El Niño phase composites and impact maps" (based on gridded fields of filtered monthly mean sea level pressures and sea surface temperatures [SST], 1871–1994) recently published by Australian researchers.[121] In the absence of such reconstructed meteorologies, the evidence for the pre-1871 teleconnections is accordingly weaker.

Is there any structure in the Quinn chronology? The clustering of intense El Niño events and associated food crises again is suggestive of the existence of multidecadal "ENSO regimes." Thus from the American Revolution to the coronation of Queen Victoria, the ENSO cycle had a high amplitude and climate disasters were frequent. As African historians have already appreciated, there is a particularly robust El Niño signature in the drought-driven crisis in southern Bantu society in the early nineteenth century that culminated in the chaos of the Zulu *mfecane*.[122] The environmentally turbulent Age of Revolution was followed by a long generation of relative calm in the Indo-Pacific latitudes that corresponds to Hobsbawm's Age of Capital. Subsistence farmers, as well as colonialists, across the tropics took this as a norm warranting an expansion of cultivation and population. In the Bombay Deccan, for example, this "was overall a long period of relatively favourable conditions. Rainfall, despite the large annual variations, never failed seriously in a major region of the Presidency. This comparative climatic stability itself shaped patterns of farming and the judgements required about them. Poor quality land newly brought under the plough, for example, was not necessarily 'marginal' in the context of a series of good seasons."[123]

In the 1860s the ENSO cycle again intensified. The once-in-200-year global drought of 1876–77, however, is followed by a decade of mild, humid weather (1879–1888) that encourages a new wave of settlement in marginal belts and historical dust bowls. This expansion is halted almost universally by the thirty-five years of exceptional ENSO activity that begins in 1888–89. This period includes four "very strong" El Niños (1891, 1899, 1918 and 1925) and thirteen other moderate–strong El Niño years, along with nine La Niña years, including the very strong events of 1898 and 1917. This astonishingly high ENSO event frequency of 70 percent then abruptly declines to 39 percent between 1926 and 1971, with no "very strong" El Niños again until 1982.[124] Although this interregnum includes, of course, the contribution of the 1958 El Niño to the Great Leap Forward catastrophe, extreme climate events are otherwise relatively rare in most regions under strong ENSO influence. India, in particular, was granted an exemption from killing droughts for more than half a century.

The end of the twentieth century, by contrast, looks on first inspection like a photocopy of the late Victorian era. Both fin de siècle periods culminate in unusual "serial" El Niños 1896–97 / 1899–1902 and 1990–95 / 1997–98.[125] There are intriguing differences, however, that some researchers attribute to anthropogenic warming. In the late twentieth century, as we have seen, El Niños seem to have become uncoupled from the Indian monsoon. Some authorities also believe that the recent ENSO cycle has less impact on rainfall in the central US states than in the late Victorian period.[126]

Quinn and his colleagues recognized that this apparent succession of low- and high-intensity ENSO regimes superficially conforms to the controversial "Bruckner cycle": a long-debated 33- to 37-year oscillation in world rainfall records.

## Table 8.9
### Strongest La Niña Events
(Ranked by Rainfall Anomalies)

Indonesia: 1910, 1955, 1893, 1975, 1924, 1988, 1954
India: 1961, 1917, 1892, 1956, 1922, 1878, 1874, 1894, 1975
Queensland: 1974, 1976, 1917, 1901, 1894, 1910, 1904, 1968
East Africa: 1898, 1917, 1899, 1892, 1990, 1943
South Africa: 1976, 1974, 1917, 1955, 1916, 1909, 1893, 1894, 1939

Source: IRI data; and D. Mooly and J. Shukla, "Variability and Forecasting of the Summer Monsoon Rainfall over India," in C.-P. Chang and T. Krishnamurti (eds.), *Monsoon Meteorology*, Oxford 1987.

They cautioned, however, that the periodicity probably resulted from statistical smoothing and that "it is doubtful whether the Bruckner cycle has any reality."[127] If recent work on the PDO and other low-frequency background oscillations in the Pacific strengthens the case for nonstochastic ENSO periodicity, there is little consensus about the physics or even the frequency of presumed multidecadal ENSO regime shifts. Moreover there is considerable scientific unrest over the lacunae and inconsistencies in the documentation of historical ENSO events.

All published chronologies, like Table 8.9, are incomplete in crucial regards. First of all, they catalogue only El Niño phases. Although "there is good evidence that Cold Events may be as important as [Warm] Events in terms of associated midlatitude teleconnections," there has been far less research charting the history of La Niñas and their impact on ENSO-sensitive regions or attempting to estimate their relative magnitudes. Their importance is attested by disasters like the 1898 floods in the Yellow River plain or the 1988 drought in the Midwest that caused a 31 percent loss in US grain production. Table 8.9 shows the strongest instrumentally measured La Niñas in five major teleconnected regions. Noteworthy is the global coherence of the 1893–94 and 1917 events, as well as the strength in Indonesia of the 1910 La Niña, which we have previously associated with revolutionary drought in northern Mexico.

La Niñas are usually described as "mirror images" of El Niños, but this is not precisely true. Dying El Niños often turn into La Niñas, but the pattern is unpredictable and the ratio of warm to cold events has fluctuated dramatically over time. During the last quarter century, for example, El Niños have become more frequent while La Niñas have become rarer, a phenomena that some researchers attribute to global warming.[128] Likewise, while warm and cold phases have inverted equatorial Pacific sea temperature patterns, they are often less symmetrical in their far-flung effects. It has been suggested, for example, that in southern Africa La Niñas have a more robust and predictable relationship to heavy rains than do El Niños to droughts.[129]

Second, annual data "smear" or superimpose event durations that really should be dated seasonally or monthly. Because El Niños can so suddenly grow into La Niñas, they often overlap in the same calendar year, thus obviating efforts to make primitive year-to-event correlations without an understanding of the underlying teleconnection. Even more confusingly, some ENSO events in the historical record are of the "compound type": either an event that has gained a second wind after a temporary relaxation, or two events of different intensities separated by a short relaxation. As Quinn and Neal note (with some anxiety), "There may be an incomplete or staggered relaxation after a large anti–El Niño [La Niña] buildup; in some other cases there may be a secondary buildup to a higher level after an earlier premature relaxation; in still other cases there may just be two separate events with a one-year buildup between them" (like 1897/99).[130] Researchers, for example, are still debating whether there was a single El Niño of unprecedented duration between 1990 and 1995, or two successive warm events.

Third, Quinn primarily characterized El Niños in terms of phenomena observed along the Pacific coast of South America, but these magnitudes do not always correspond to the severity of the global ENSO field. The 1891 event, for example, was more powerful than the 1897 El Niño in South America, but the relative magnitudes were reversed in South Asia and China. Likewise the 1918–19 El Niño was only weak to moderate in Peru but very strong in India and Africa. As Enfield and Cid cautioned in 1991: "The anecdotal, impact-related methods of QNA [Quinn] are better suited to the identification of historical El Niño events than to the determination of their climatic intensity over a large geographic domain. Even if the QNA scheme classifies perfectly the climatic response of El Niño in Peru, it has no way of estimating conditions elsewhere in the Pacific. We know that the relationship between ENSO and its regional manifestations is not perfectly one-to-one. Hence, the QNA intensity scale is probably not an accurate characterization of the severity continuum of the broader ENSO melange."[131]

Finally, Quinn's "subjective" magnitudes also do not always agree with Southern Oscillation Index values, nor do all negative SO events produce classical South American El Niños. And there has been growing unease with the obvious circularity in using drought records (Quinn's analogues) to nail down El Niños, and then using the derived ENSO chronologies to establish causal correlations between the droughts and El Niño events. For these reasons, some leading researchers have recently advocated the abandonment of Quinn's heroic but outdated time series and index. "Regional statistics such as those derived from the Quinn et al. (1987) compilation of strong and very strong El Niño events in Peru," write Rasmusson, Wang and Ropelewski, "cannot be considered a reliable index of basin-scale ENSO-cycle variability."[132] There has been an energetic hunt for an improved ENSO "Richter scale." In the beginning, investigators concentrated on sea surface temperatures in the strategic zone of the eastern Pacific ("Niño-3"), where warm events are incubated, but the nonlinear relationship between ENSO intensity and duration (as well as between the SO and sea surface temperature) has favored multivariate indices that synthesize different event features. Harrison and Larkin, for example, offer what they call the "Bjerknes ENSO Index," summed from "very robust elements" (including zonal and meridional wind anomalies) composited from ten postwar El Niños.[133]

Unfortunately the instrumental record before 1957 is generally too poor to support such sophisticated indices. As a result, the modern El Niño chronology remains stratified into three classes of data: (1) recent events whose physics have been measured across a broad range of atmospheric and oceanographic variables; (2) events within the boundaries of instrumental times series (since 1875) where archival documentation is constrained by some understanding of associated sea surface pressure and temperature fields; and (3) pre-1875 events where Quinn's methodology, with all of its limitations, still remains the inevitable tool. Over the next decade, to be sure, paleoclimatologists are confident that high-resolution natural archives, like tree rings, isotope ratios in coral bands, and diatom abundances in varved seabed sediments, will permit reconstruction of an ENSO chronology for the entire Holocene. But these records are unlikely to offer much more than crude indices of magnitude.[134] Thus historical documentation of impacts will continue to be an integral and indispensable part of ENSO research.

# PART IV

# The Political Ecology of Famine

# Nine

# The Origins of the Third World

Emaciated people, disease, ribs showing, shriveled
bellies, corpses, children with fly-encircled eyes, with
swollen stomachs, children dying in the streets, rivers
choked with bodies, people; living, sleeping, lying,
dying on the streets in misery, beggary, squalor,
wretchedness, a mass of aboriginal humanity...
– Harold Isaacs

What historians, then, have so often dismissed as "climatic accidents" turn out
to be not so accidental after all.[1] Although its syncopations are complex and
quasi-periodic, ENSO has a coherent spatial and temporal logic. And, contrary to
Emmanuel Le Roy Ladurie's famous (Eurocentric?) conclusion in *Times of Feast,
Times of Famine* that climate change is a "slight, perhaps negligible" shaper of
human affairs, ENSO is an episodically potent force in the history of tropical
humanity.[2] If, as Raymond Williams once observed, "Nature contains, though
often unnoticed, an extraordinary amount of human history," we are now learning that the inverse is equally true: there is an extraordinary amount of hitherto
unnoticed environmental instability in modern history.[3] The power of ENSO
events indeed seems so overwhelming in some instances that it is tempting to
assert that great famines, like those of the 1870s and 1890s (or, more recently,

the Sahelian disaster of the 1970s), were "caused" by El Niño, or by El Niño acting upon traditional agrarian misery. This interpretation, of course, inadvertently echoes the official line of the British in Victorian India as recapitulated in every famine commission report and viceregal allocution: millions were killed by extreme weather, not imperialism.[4] Was this true?

## 'Bad Climate' versus 'Bad System'

At this point it would be immensely useful to have some strategy for sorting out what the Chinese pithily contrast as "bad climate" versus "bad system." Y. Kueh, as we have seen, has attempted to parameterize the respective influences of drought and policy upon agricultural output during the Great Leap Forward famine of 1958–61. The derivation of his "weather index," however, involved fifteen years of arduous research and the resolution of "a series of complicated methodological and technical problems" including a necessary comparative regression to the 1930s. Although his work is methodologically rich, his crucial indices depend upon comprehensive meteorological and econometric data that are simply not available for the nineteenth century. A direct statistical assault on the tangled causal web of the 1876–77 and 1896–1902 famines thus seems precluded.[5]

An alternative is to construct a "natural experiment." As Jared Diamond has advocated in a recent sermon to historians, such an experiment should compare systems "differing in the presence or absence (or in the strong or weak effect) of some putative causative factor."[6] We ideally need, in other words, an analogue for the late Victorian famines in which the natural parameters are constant but the social variables significantly differ. An excellent candidate for which we possess unusually detailed documentation is the El Niño event of 1743–44 (described as "exceptional" by Whetton and Rutherfurd) in its impact on the north China plain.[7] Although not as geographically far-reaching as the great ENSO droughts of 1876–78 or 1899–1900, it otherwise prefigured their intensities. The spring monsoon failed two years in a row, devastating winter wheat in Hebei (Zhili) and northern Shandong. Scorching winds withered crops and farmers dropped dead in their fields from sunstroke. Provincial grain supplies were utterly inadequate to the scale of need. Yet unlike the late nineteenth century, there was no mass mortality from either starvation or disease. Why not?

Pierre-Etienne Will has carefully reconstructed the fascinating history of the 1743–44 relief campaign from contemporary records. Under the skilled Confucian administration of Fang Guancheng, the agricultural and hydraulic expert who directed relief operations in Zhili, the renowned "ever-normal granaries" in each county immediately began to issue rations (without any labor test) to peasants in the officially designated disaster counties.[8] (Local gentry had already organized soup kitchens to ensure the survival of the poorest residents until state distributions began.) When local supplies proved insufficient, Guancheng shifted millet and rice from the great store of tribute grain at Tongcang at the terminus of the Grand Canal, then used the Canal to move vast quantities of rice from the south. Two million peasants were maintained for eight months, until the return of the monsoon made agriculture again possible. Ultimately 85 percent of the relief grain was borrowed from tribute depots or granaries outside the radius of the drought.[9]

As Will emphasizes, this was famine defense in depth, the "last word in technology at the time." No contemporary European society guaranteed subsistence as a human right to its peasantry (*ming-sheng* is the Chinese term), nor, as the Physiocrats later marveled, could any emulate "the perfect timing of [Guancheng's] operations: the action taken always kept up with developments and even anticipated them."[10] Indeed, while the Qing were honoring their social contract with the peasantry, contemporary Europeans were dying in the millions from famine and hunger-related diseases following arctic winters and summer droughts in 1740–43. "The mortality peak of the early 1740s," emphasizes an authority, "is an outstanding fact of European demographic history."[11] In Europe's Age of Reason, in other words, the "starving masses" were French, Irish and Calabrian, not Chinese.

Moreover "the intervention carried out in Zhili in 1743 and 1744 was not the only one of its kind in the eighteenth century, nor even the most extensive."[12] Indeed, as Table 9.1 indicates, the Yellow River flooding of the previous year (1742/43) involved much larger expenditures over a much broader region. (In addition to the ENSO-correlated droughts and floods shown in the table, Will has also documented seven other flood disasters that involved massive relief mobilization.) Although comparable figures are unavailable, Beijing also acted aggressively to aid Shandong officials in preventing famine during the series of El Niño

Table 9.1

ENSO Disasters Relieved by the Qing

|  | Quinn Intensity | Provinces | Amount of Relief |
| --- | --- | --- | --- |
| 1720/21 | Very strong | Shaanxi | Unknown |
| 1742/43 | (Flooding) | Jiangsu/Anhui | 17 million taels; 2.3 million shi |
| 1743/44 | Moderate+ | Hebei | .87 million taels; 1 million shi |
| 1778 | Strong | Henan | 1.6 million taels; .3 million shi |
| 1779/80 | La Niña | Henan | same |
| 1785 | ? | Henan | 2.8 million taels |

Source: Constructed from Table VII, Whetton and Rutherfurd, p. 244; Table 20, Will, *Bureaucracy and Famine*, pp. 298–9.

droughts that afflicted that province (and much of the tropics) between 1778 and 1787.[13] The contrast with the chaotic late-Qing relief efforts in 1877 and 1899 (or, for that matter, Mao's monstrous mishandling of the 1958–61 drought) could not be more striking. State capacity in eighteenth-century China, as Will and his collaborators emphasize, was deeply impressive: a cadre of skilled administrators and trouble-shooters, a unique national system of grain price stabilization, large crop surpluses, well-managed granaries storing more than a million bushels of grain in each of twelve provinces, and incomparable hydraulic infrastructures.[14]

The capstone of Golden Age food security was the invigilation of grain prices and supply trends by the emperor himself. Although ever-normal granaries were an ancient tradition, price monitoring was a chief innovation of the Qing. "Great care was exercised by the eighteenth-century Emperors in looking over the memorials and price lists in search of inconsistencies." On the fifth of every month *hsien* magistrates forwarded detailed price reports to the prefectures, who summarized them for the provincial governors who, in turn, reported their content in memorials to the central government.[15] Carefully studied and annotated by the emperors, these "vermillion rescripts" testify to an extraordinary engagement with the administration of food security and rural well-being. "In the 1720s and 1730s," R. Bin Wong writes, "the Yongzheng emperor personally scrutinized granary operations, as he did all other bureaucratic behavior; his intense interest in official efforts and his readiness to berate officials for what he considered failures partially explain the development of granary operations beyond the levels achieved in the late Kangxi period."[16] Yongzheng also severely sanctioned speculation by the "rich households [who] in their quest for profit habitually remove grain by the full thousand or full myriad bushels."[17]

His successor, Qianlong, ordered the prefects to send the county-level price reports directly to the Bureau of Revenue in Beijing so he could study them firsthand. The emperors' intense personal involvement ensured a high standard of accuracy in price reporting and, as Endymion Wilkinson demonstrates, frequently led to significant reform.[18] This was another *differentia specifica* of Qing absolutism. It is hard to imagine a Louis XVI spending his evenings scrupulously poring over the minutiae of grain prices from Limoges or the Auvergne, although the effort might have ultimately saved his head from the guillotine.

Nor can we easily picture a European monarch intimately involved in the esoteria of public works to the same degree that the Qing routinely immersed themselves in the details of the Grand Canal grain transport system. "The Manchu emperors," Jane Leonard points out, " had since the early reigns involved themselves deeply in Canal management, not just in broad questions of policy, but in the control and supervision of lower-level administrative tasks." When, for example, flooding in 1824 destroyed sections of the Grand Canal at the critical Huai–Yellow River junction, the Tao-kuang emperor personally assumed command of reconstruction efforts.[19]

In contrast, moreover, to later Western stereotypes of a passive Chinese state, government during the high Qing era was proactively involved in famine prevention through a broad program of investment in agricultural improvement, irrigation and waterborne transportation. As in other things, Joseph Needham points out, the eighteenth century was a golden age for theoretical and historical work on flood control and canal construction. Civil engineers were canonized and had temples erected in their honor.[20] Confucian activists like Guancheng, with a deep commitment to agricultural intensification, "tended to give top priority to investments in infrastructure and to consider the organization of food relief merely a makeshift." Guancheng also wrote a famous manual (the source of much of Will's account) that codified historically tested principles of disaster planning and relief managment: something else that has little precedent in backward European tradition.[21]

Finally, there is plentiful evidence that the northern China peasantry during the high Qing was more nutritionally self-reliant and less vulnerable to climate stress than their descendants a century later. In the eighteenth century, after the Kangxi emperor permanently froze land revenue at the 1712 level, China experienced "the mildest agrarian taxation it had ever known in the whole of its history."[22] Dwight Perkins estimates that the formal land tax was a mere 5 to 6 percent of the harvest and that a large portion was expended locally by hsien and provincial governments.[23] Likewise, the exchange ratio between silver and copper coinage, which turned so disastrously against the poor peasantry in the nineteenth century, was stabilized by the booming output of the Yunnan copper mines (replacing Japanese imports) and the great inflow of Mexican bullion earned by China's huge trade surplus.[24] Unlike their contemporary French counterparts, the farmers of the Yellow River plain (the vast majority of whom owned their land) were neither crushed by exorbitant taxes nor ground down by feudal rents. North China, in particular, was unprecedentedly prosperous by historical standards, and Will estimates that the percentage of the rural population ordinarily living near the edge of starvation – depending, for example, on husks and wild vegetables for a substantial part of their diet – was less than 2 percent.[25] As a result, epidemic disease, unlike in Europe, was held in check for most of the "Golden Age."[26]

Still, could even Fang Guancheng have coped with drought disasters engulfing the larger part of north China on the scale of 1876 or even 1899? It is important to weigh this question carefully, since drought-famines were more localized in the eighteenth century, and because the 1876 drought, as we have seen, may have been a 200-year or even 500-year frequency event. Moreover, the late Victorian droughts reached particular intensity in the loess highlands of Shanxi and Shaanxi, where transport costs were highest and bottlenecks unavoidable. It is reasonable, therefore, to concede that a drought of 1876 magnitude in 1743 would inevitably have involved tens, perhaps even hundreds, of thousands of deaths in more remote villages.

Such a drought, however, would have been unlikely, as in the late nineteenth century, to grow into a veritable holocaust that consumed the greater part of the populations of whole prefectures and counties. In contrast to the situation in 1876–77, when granaries were depleted or looted and prices soared out of control, eighteenth-century administrators could count on a large imperial budget surplus and well-stocked local granaries backed up by a huge surplus of rice in the south. Large stockpiles of tribute grain at strategic transportation nodes in Henan and along the Shanxi–Shaanxi border were specially designated for the relief of the loess provinces, and an abundance of water sources guaranteed the Grand Canal's navigability year-round.[27] Whereas in 1876 the Chinese state – enfeebled and demoralized after the failure of the Tongzhi Restoration's domestic reforms – was reduced to desultory cash relief augmented by private donations and humiliating foreign charity, in the eighteenth century it had both the technology and political will to shift grain massively between regions and, thus, relieve hunger on a larger scale than any previous polity in world history.[28]

### 'Laws of Leather' versus 'Laws of Iron'

What about famine in pre-British India? Again, there is little evidence that rural India had ever experienced subsistence crises on the scale of the Bengal catastrophe of 1770 under East India Company rule or the long siege by disease and hunger between 1875 and 1920 that slowed population growth almost to a standstill. The Moguls, to be sure, did not dispose of anything like the resources of the centralized Qing state at its eighteenth-century zenith, nor was their administrative history as well documented. As Sanjay Sharma has pointed out, "The problems of intervening in the complex network of caste-based local markets and transport bottlenecks rendered an effective state intervention quite difficult."[29]

On the other hand, benefiting perhaps from a milder ENSO cycle, Mogul India was generally free of famine until the 1770s. There is considerable evidence, moreover, that in pre-British India before the creation of a railroad-girded national market in grain, village-level food reserves were larger, patrimonial welfare more widespread, and grain prices in surplus areas better insulated against speculation.[30] (As we have seen, the perverse consequence of a unitary market was to export famine, via price inflation, to the rural poor in grain-surplus districts.) The British, of course, had a vested interest in claiming that they had liberated the populace from a dark age of Mogul despotism: "One of the foundations of Crown Rule was the belief that ... India's past was full of depravity."[31] But, as Bose and Jalal point out, "The picture of an emaciated and oppressed peasantry, mercilessly exploited by the emperor and his nobility, is being seriously altered in the light of new interpretations of the evidence."[32] Recent research by Ashok Desai indicates that "the mean standard of food consumption in Akbar's empire was appreciably higher than in the India of the early 1960s."[33]

The Mogul state, moreover, "regarded the protection of the peasant as an essential obligation," and there are numerous examples of humane if sporadic relief operations.[34] Like their Chinese contemporaries, the Mogul rulers Akbar, Shahjahan and Aurangzeb relied on a quartet of fundamental policies – embargos on food exports, antispeculative price regulation, tax relief and distribution of free food without a forced-labor counterpart – that were an anathema to later British Utilitarians.[35] They also zealously policed the grain trade in the public interest. As one horrified British writer discovered, these "oriental despots" punished traders who shortchanged peasants during famines by amputating an equivalent weight of merchant flesh.[36]

In contrast to the Raj's punitive taxation of irrigation and its neglect of traditional wells and reservoirs, the Moguls used tax subsidies to promote water conservation. As David Hardiman explains in the case of Gujarat: "Local officials had considerable discretion over tax assessment, and it seems to have been their practice to encourage well-construction by granting tax concessions. In the Ahmedabad region, for example, it was common to waive the tax on a 'rabi' crop raised through irrigation from a recently constructed well. The concession continued until the tax exemptions were held to have equalled the cost of construction."[37]

Occasionally, the British paid appropriate tribute to the policies of their "despotic" predecessors. The first Famine Commission Report in 1880, for example, cited Aurangzeb's extraordinary relief campaign during the (El Niño?) drought-famine of 1661: "The Emperor opened his treasury and granted money without stint. He gave every encouragement to the importation of corn and either sold it at reduced prices, or distributed it gratuitously amongst those who were too poor to pay. He also promptly acknowledged the necessity of remitting the rents of the cultivators and relieved them for the time being of other taxes. The vernacular chronicles of the period attribute the salvation of millions of lives and the preservation of many provinces to his strenuous exertions."[38]

Food security was also probably better in the Deccan during the period of Maratha rule. As Mountstuart Elphinstone admitted retrospectively after the British conquest, "The Mahratta country flourished, and the people seem to have been exempt from some of the evils which exist under our more perfect Government."[39] His contemporary, Sir John Malcolm, "claimed that between 1770 and

1820 there had been only three very bad seasons in the Maratha lands and, though some years had been 'indifferent,' none had been as 'bad as to occasion any particular distress.'"[40] D. E. U. Baker cites a later British administrative report from the Central Provinces that contrasted the desultory relief efforts of the East India Company during the droughts of the 1820s and 1830s ("a few thousand rupees") with the earlier and highly effective Maratha policy of forcing local elites to feed the poor ("enforced charity of hundreds of rich men").[41] Indeed the resilient Maratha social order was founded on a militarized free peasantry and "very few landless laborers existed." In contrast to the British-imposed *raiyatwari* system, occupancy rights in the Maratha Deccan were not tied to revenue payment, taxes varied according to the actual harvest, common lands and resources were accessible to the poor, and the rulers subsidized local irrigation improvements with cheap *taqavi* (or *tagai)* loans.[42] In addition, Elphinstone observed, the "sober, frugal, industrious" Maratha farmers lived in generally tolerant coexistence with the Bhils and other tribal peoples. Ecological and economic synergies balanced the diverse claims of plains agriculture, pastoralism and foothill swidden.[43]

In contrast to the rigidity and dogmatism of British land-and-revenue settlements, both the Moguls and Marathas flexibly tailored their rule to take account of the crucial ecological relationships and unpredictable climate fluctuations of the subcontinent's drought-prone regions. The Moguls had "laws of leather," wrote journalist Vaughan Nash during the famine of 1899, in contrast to the British "laws of iron."[44] Moreover, traditional Indian elites, like the great Bengali *zamindars,* seldom shared Utilitarian obsessions with welfare cheating and labor discipline. "Requiring the poor to work for relief, a practice begun in 1866 in Bengal under the influence of the Victorian Poor Law, was in flat contradiction to the Bengali premise that food should be given ungrudgingly, as a father gives food to his children."[45] Although the British insisted that they had rescued India from "timeless hunger," more than one official was jolted when Indian nationalists quoted from an 1878 study published in the prestigious *Journal of the Statistical Society* that contrasted thirty-one serious famines in 120 years of British rule against only seventeen recorded famines in the entire previous two millennia.[46]

India and China, in other words, did not enter modern history as the helpless "lands of famine" so universally enshrined in the Western imagination. Certainly the intensity of the ENSO cycle in the late nineteenth century, perhaps only equaled on three or four other occasions in the last millennium, must loom large in any explanation of the catastrophes of the 1870s and 1890s. But it is scarcely the only independent variable. Equal causal weight, or more, must be accorded to the growing social vulnerability to climate variability that became so evident in south Asia, north China, northeast Brazil and southern Africa in late Victorian times. As Michael Watts has eloquently argued in his history of the "silent violence" of drought-famine in colonial Nigeria: "Climate risk ... is not given by nature but ... by 'negotiated settlement' since each society has institutional, social, and technical means for coping with risk.... Famines [thus] are social crises that represent the failures of particular economic and political systems."[47]

## Perspectives on Vulnerability

Over the last generation, scholars have produced a bumper-crop of revealing social and economic histories of the regions teleconnected to ENSO's episodic disturbances. The thrust of this research has been to further demolish orientalist stereotypes of immutable poverty and overpopulation as the natural preconditions of the major nineteenth-century famines. There is persuasive evidence that peasants and farm laborers became dramatically more pregnable to natural disaster after 1850 as their local economies were violently incorporated into the world market. What colonial administrators and missionaries – even sometimes creole elites, as in Brazil – perceived as the persistence of ancient cycles of backwardness were typically modern structures of formal or informal imperialism.

From the perspective of political ecology, the vulnerability of tropical agriculturalists to extreme climate events after 1870 was magnified by simultaneous restructurings of household and village linkages to regional production systems, world commodity markets and the colonial (or dependent) state. "It is, of course, the constellation of these social relations," writes Watts, "which binds households together and project them into the marketplace, that determines the precise form of the household vulnerability. It is also these same social relations that have failed to stimulate or have actually prevented the development of the productive forces that might have lessened this vulnerability." Indeed, new social relations of production, in tandem with the New Imperialism, "not only altered the extent of hunger in a statistical sense but changed its very etiology."[48] Three points of articulation with larger socio-economic structures were especially decisive for rural subsistence in the late Victorian "proto-third world."

First, the forcible incorporation of smallholder production into commodity and financial circuits controlled from overseas tended to undermine traditional food security. Recent scholarship confirms that it was *subsistence adversity* (high taxes, chronic indebtedness, inadequate acreage, loss of subsidiary employment opportunities, enclosure of common resources, dissolution of patrimonial obligations, and so on), not entrepreneurial opportunity, that typically promoted the turn to cash-crop cultivation. Rural capital, in turn, tended to be parasitic rather than productivist as rich landowners redeployed fortunes that they built during export booms into usury, rack-renting and crop brokerage. "Marginal subsistence producers," Hans Medick points out, " ... did not benefit from the market under these circumstances; they were devoured by it."[49] Medick, writing about the analogous predicament of marginal smallholders in "proto-industrial" Europe, provides an exemplary description of the dilemma of millions of Indian and Chinese poor peasants in the late nineteenth century:

> For them [even] rising agrarian prices did not necessarily mean increasing incomes. Since their marginal productivity was low and production fluctuated, rising agrarian prices tended to be a source of indebtedness rather than affording them the opportunity to accumulate surpluses. The "anomaly of the agrarian markets" forced the marginal subsistence producers into an unequal exchange relationship through the market.... Instead of profiting from exchange, they were forced by the market into the progressive deterioration of their conditions of production, i.e. the loss of their property titles. Especially in years of bad harvests, and high prices, the petty producers were compelled to buy additional grain, and, worse, to go into debt. Then, in good harvest years when cereal prices were low, they found it hard to extricate themselves from the previously accumulated debts; owing to the low productivity of their holdings they could not produce sufficient quantities for sale.[50]

As a result, the position of small rural producers in the international economic hierarchy equated with downward mobility, or, at best, stagnation. There is consistent evidence from north China as well as India and northeast Brazil of falling household wealth and increased fragmentation or alienation of land. Whether farmers were directly engaged by foreign capital, like the Berari *khatedars* and Cearan *parceiros* who fed the mills of Lancashire during the Cotton Famine, or were simply producing for domestic markets subject to international competition like the cotton-spinning peasants of the Boxer hsiens in western Shandong, commercialization went hand in hand with pauperization without any silver lining of technical change or agrarian capitalism.

Second, the integration of millions of tropical cultivators into the world market during the late nineteenth century was accompanied by a dramatic deterioration in their terms of trade. Peasants' lack of market power vis-à-vis crop merchants and creditors was redoubled by their commodities' falling international purchasing power. The famous Kondratief downswing of 1873–1897 made dramatic geographical discriminations. As W. Arthur Lewis suggests, comparative productivity or transport costs alone cannot explain an emergent structure of global unequal exchange that valued the products of tropical agriculture so differently from those of temperate farming. "With the exception of sugar, all the commodities whose price was lower in 1913 than in 1883 were commodities produced almost wholly in the tropics. All the commodities whose prices rose over this thirty-year period were commodities in which the temperate countries produced a substantial part of total supplies. The fall in ocean freight rates affected tropical more than temperate prices, but this should not make a difference of more than five percentage points."[51]

Third, formal and informal Victorian imperialism, backed up by the supernational automatism of the Gold Standard, confiscated local fiscal autonomy and impeded state-level developmental responses – especially investments in water conservancy and irrigation – that might have reduced vulnerability to climate shocks. As Curzon once famously complained to the House of Lords, tariffs "were decided in London, not in India; in England's interests, not in India's."[52] Moreover, as we shall see in the next chapter, any grassroots benefit from British railroad and canal construction was largely canceled by official neglect of local irrigation and the brutal enclosures of forest and pasture resources. Export earnings, in other words, not only failed to return to smallholders as increments in household income, but also as usable social capital or state investment.

In China, the "normalization" of grain prices and the ecological stabilization of agriculture in the Yellow River plain were undermined by an interaction of endogenous crises and the loss of sovereignty over foreign trade in the aftermath of the two Opium Wars. As disconnected from world market perturbations as the starving loess provinces might have seemed in 1877, the catastrophic fate of their

populations was indirectly determined by Western intervention and the consequent decline in state capacity to ensure traditional welfare. Similarly the depletion of "ever-normal" granaries may have resulted from a vicious circle of multiple interacting causes over a fifty-year span, but the coup de grace was certainly
the structural recession and permanent fiscal crisis engineered by Palmerston's
aggressions against China in the 1850s. As foreign pressure intensified in later
decades, the embattled Qing, as Kenneth Pomeranz has shown, were forced to
abandon both their traditional mandates: abandoning both hydraulic control and
grain stockpiling in the Yellow River provinces in order to concentrate on defending their endangered commercial littoral.[53]

British control over Brazil's foreign debt and thus its fiscal capacity likewise
helps explain the failure of either the empire or its successor republic to launch
any antidrought developmental effort in the sertão. The zero-sum economic
conflicts between Brazil's rising and declining regions took place in a structural
context where London banks, above all the Rothschilds, ultimately owned the
money-supply. In common with the India and China, the inability to politically
regulate interaction with the world market at the very time when mass subsistence increasingly depended upon food entitlements acquired in international
trade became a sinister syllogism for famine. Moreover in the three cases of the
Deccan, the Yellow River basin and the Nordeste, former "core" regions of eighteenth-century subcontinental power systems were successively transformed into
famished peripheries of a London-centered world economy.

The elaboration of these theses, as always in geo-historical explanation, invites
closer analysis at different magnifications. Before considering case-studies of rural
immiseration in key regions devastated by the 1870s and 1890s El Niño events
or looking at the relationships among imperialism, state capacity and ecological
crisis at the village level, it is necessary to briefly discuss how the structural posi-
tions of Indians and Chinese (the big battalions of the future Third World) in the
world economy changed over the course of the nineteenth century. Understanding how tropical humanity lost so much economic ground to western Europeans after 1850 goes a long way toward explaining why famine was able to reap
such hecatombs in El Niño years. As a baseline for understanding the origins of
modern global inequality (and that is the key question), the herculean statistical
labors of Paul Bairoch and Angus Maddison over the last thirty years have been

complemented by recent comparative case-studies of European and Asian standards of living.

## The Defeat of Asia

Bairoch's famous claim, corroborated by Maddison, is that differences in income and wealth between the great civilizations of the eighteenth century were relatively slight: "It is very likely that, in the middle of the eighteenth century, the average standard of living in Europe was a little bit lower than that of the rest of the world."[54] When the *sans culottes* stormed the Bastille, the largest manufacturing districts in the world were still the Yangzi Delta and Bengal, with Lingan (modern Guangdong and Guangxi) and coastal Madras not far behind.[55] India alone produced one-quarter of world manufactures, and while its "pre-capitalist agrarian labour productivity was probably less than the Japanese-Chinese level, its commercial capital surpassed that of the Chinese."[56]

As Prasannan Parthasarathi has recently shown, the stereotype of the Indian laborer as a half-starved wretch in a loincloth collapses in the face of new data about comparative standards of living. "Indeed, there is compelling evidence that South Indian labourers had higher earnings than their British counterparts in the eighteenth century and lived lives of greater financial security." Because the productivity of land was higher in South India, weavers and other artisans enjoyed better diets than average Europeans. More importantly, their unemployment rates tended to be lower because they possessed superior rights of contract and exercised more economic power. But even outcaste agricultural labourers in Madras earned more in real terms than English farm laborers.[57] (By 1900, in contrast, Romesh Chunder Dutt estimated that the average British household income was 21 times higher.)[58]

New research by Chinese historians also challenges traditional conceptions of comparative economic growth. Referring to the pathbreaking work of Li Bozhong, Philip Huang notes that "the outstanding representative of this new academic tendency has even argued the overall economic development of the Yangzi Delta in the Qing exceeded that of 'early modern' England."[59] Similarly, Bin Wong has recently emphasized that the "specific conditions associated with European proto-industrialization – expansion of seasonal crafts, shrinking farm size, and good marketing systems – may have been even more widespread in

Table 9.2

Shares of World GDP

(Percent)

|         | 1700 | 1820 | 1890 | 1952 |
|---------|------|------|------|------|
| China   | 23.1 | 32.4 | 13.2 | 5.2  |
| India   | 22.6 | 15.7 | 11.0 | 3.8  |
| Europe  | 23.3 | 26.6 | 40.3 | 29.7 |

Source: Angus Maddison, *Chinese Economic Performance in the Long Run*, Paris 1998, p. 40.

China [and India] than in Europe."[60] "Basic functional literacy," adds F. Mote, "was more widespread than in Western countries at that time, including among women at all social levels."[61]

Moreover, in the recent forum "Re-thinking 18th Century China," Kenneth Pomeranz points to evidence that ordinary Chinese enjoyed a higher standard of consumption than eighteenth-century Europeans:

> Chinese life expectancy (and thus nutrition) was at roughly English levels (and so above Continental ones) even in the late 1700s. (Chinese fertility was actually lower than Europe's between 1550 and 1850, while its population grew faster; thus mortality must have been low.) Moreover, my estimates of "non-essential" consumption come out surprisingly high. Sugar consumption works out to between 4.3 and 5.0 pounds per capita ca. 1750 – and much higher in some regions – compared with barely 2 pounds per capita for Europe. China circa 1750 seems to have produced 6–8 lbs. of cotton cloth per capita; its richest area, the Yangzi Delta (population roughly 31 million), probably produced between 12 and 15 lbs. per capita. The UK, even in 1800, produced roughly 13 lbs. of cotton, linen and wool cloth combined per resident, and Continental output was probably below China's.[62]

Pomeranz has also calculated that "the Lower Yangzi appears to have produced roughly as much cotton cloth per capita in 1750 as the UK did cotton, wool, linen and silk cloth combined in 1800 – plus an enormous quantity of silk."[63] In addition, as Maddison demonstrates, the Chinese GDP in absolute terms grew faster than that of Europe throughout the eighteenth century, dramatically enlarging its share of world income by 1820.

The usual stereotype of nineteenth-century economic history is that Asia stood still while the Industrial Revolution propelled Britain, followed by the

United States and eventually the rest of Western Europe, down the path of high-speed GNP growth. In a superficial sense, of course, this is true, although the data gathered by Bairoch and Maddison show that Asia lost its preeminence in the world economy later than most of us perhaps imagine. The future Third World, dominated by the highly developed commercial and handicraft economies of India and China, surrendered ground very grudgingly until 1850 (when it still generated 65 percent of global GNP), but then declined with increasing rapidity through the rest of the nineteenth century (only 38 percent of world GNP in 1900 and 22 percent in 1960).[64]

Table 9.3
Shares of World Manufacturing Output, 1750–1900
(Percent)

|        | 1750 | 1800 | 1830 | 1860 | 1880 | 1900 |
|--------|------|------|------|------|------|------|
| Europe | 23.1 | 28.0 | 34.1 | 53.6 | 62.0 | 63.0 |
| UK     | 1.9  | 4.3  | 9.5  | 19.9 | 22.9 | 18.5 |
| Tropics| 76.8 | 71.2 | 63.3 | 39.2 | 23.3 | 13.4 |
| China  | 32.8 | 33.3 | 29.8 | 19.7 | 12.5 | 6.2  |
| India  | 24.5 | 19.7 | 17.6 | 8.6  | 2.8  | 1.7  |

Source: Derived from B. R. Tomlinson, "Economics: The Periphery," in Andrew Porter (ed.), *The Oxford History of the British Empire: The Nineteenth Century,* Oxford 1990, p. 69 (Table 3.8).

The deindustrialization of Asia via the substitution of Lancashire cotton imports for locally manufactured textiles reached its climax only in the decades after the construction of the Crystal Palace. "Until 1831," Albert Feuerwerker points out, "Britain purchased more 'nankeens' (cloth manufactured in Nanking and other places in the lower Yangzi region) each year than she sold British-manufactured cloth to China."[65] Britain exported 51 million yards of cloth to Asia in 1831; 995 million in 1871; 1413 million in 1879; and 2000 million in 1887.[66]

But why did Asia stand in place? The rote answer is because it was weighted down with the chains of tradition and Malthusian demography, although this did not prevent Qing China, whose rate of population increase was about the same as Europe's, from experiencing extraordinary economic growth throughout the eighteenth century. As Jack Goldstone recently argued, China's "stasis" is an "anachronistic illusion that come[s] from reading history backwards."[67] The

Table 9.4

Standing in Place: China vs. Europe

Dollars per Capita GDP/(Population in Millions)

| | Western Europe | | China | |
|---|---|---|---|---|
| 1400 | 430 | (43) | 500 | (74) |
| 1820 | 1034 | (122) | 500 | (342) |
| 1950 | 4902 | (412) | 454 | (547) |

Source: Lu Aiguo, *China and the Global Economy Since 1840*, Helsinki 2000, p. 56 (Table 4.1 as derived from Maddison).

relevant question is not so much why the Industrial Revolution occurred first in England, Scotland and Belgium, but why other advanced regions of the eighteenth-century world economy failed to adapt their handicraft manufactures to the new conditions of production and competition in the nineteenth century.

As Marx liked to point out, the Whig view of history deletes a great deal of very bloody business. The looms of India and China were defeated not so much by market competition as they were forcibly dismantled by war, invasion, opium and a Lancashire-imposed system of one-way tariffs. (Already by 1850, imposed Indian opium imports had siphoned 11 percent of China's money-supply and 13 percent of its silver stock out of the country.)[68] Whatever the internal brakes on rapid economic growth in Asia, Latin America or Africa, it is indisputable that from about 1780 or 1800 onward, every serious attempt by a non-Western society to move over into a fast lane of development or to regulate its terms of trade was met by a military as well as an economic response from London or a competing imperial capital. Japan, prodded by Perry's black ships, is the exception that proves the rule.

The use of force to configure a "liberal" world economy (as Marx and later Rosa Luxemburg argued) is what Pax Britannica was really about. Palmerston paved the way for Cobden. The Victorians, according to Brian Bond's calculations, resorted to gunboats on at least seventy-five different occasions.[69] The simultaneous British triumphs in the Mutiny and the "Arrow" War in 1858, along with Japan's yielding to Perry in the same year, were the epochal victories over Asian economic autonomy that made a Cobdenite world of free trade possible in the second half of the nineteenth century. (Thailand had already conceded a 3 percent tariff in 1855).[70] The Taiping Revolution – "more revolutionary in its aims than the Meiji Restoration, insisting on gender equality and democratizing literacy" – was a gigantic attempt to revise that verdict, and was, of course, defeated only thanks to the resources and mercenaries that Britain supplied to the embattled Qing.[71]

This is not to claim that the Industrial Revolution necessarily depended upon the colonial conquest or economic subjugation of Asia; on the contrary, the slave trade and the plantations of the New World were much more strategic streams of liquid capital and natural resources in boosting the industrial take-off in Britain, France and the United States. Although Ralph Davis has argued that the spoils of Plessy contributed decisively to the stability of the Georgian order in an age of revolution, the East India Company's turnover was small change compared to the great trans-Atlantic flow of goods and capital.[72] Only the Netherlands, it would appear, depended crucially upon Asian tribute – the profits of its brutal *culturrstelsel* – in financing its economic recovery and incipient industrialization between 1830 and 1850.

Paradoxically, monsoon Asia's most important "moment" in the Victorian world economy was not at the beginning of the epoch, but towards its end. "The full value of British rule, the return on political investments first made in the eighteenth century," write Cain and Hopkins in their influential history of British imperialism, "was not realised until the second half of the nineteenth century, when India became a vital market for Lancashire's cotton goods and when other specialised interests, such as jute manufacturers in Dundee and steel producers in Sheffield, also greatly increased their stake in the sub-continent."[73] The coerced levies of wealth from India and China were not essential to the rise of British hegemony, but they were absolutely crucial in postponing its decline.

## The Late Victorian World Economy

During the protracted period of stop-and-go growth from 1873 to 1896 (what economic historians misleadingly used to call the "Great Depression"), the rate of capital formation and the growth of productivity of both labor and capital in Britain began a dramatic slowdown.[74] She remained tied to old products and technologies while behind their tariff barriers Germany and the United States forged leadership in cutting-edge oil, chemical and electrical industries. Since British

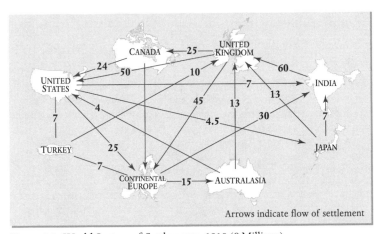

Figure 9.1  World System of Settlements, 1910 (£ Millions)

Source: S. Saul, *Studies in British Overseas Trade, 1870–1914*, Liverpool 1960, p. 58.

imports and overseas investment still dynamized local growth from Australia to Denmark, the potential "scissors" between UK productivity and consumption threatened the entire structure of world trade. It was in this conjuncture that the starving Indian and Chinese peasantries were wheeled in as unlikely saviors. For a generation they braced the entire system of international settlements, allowing England's continued financial supremacy to temporarily coexist with its relative industrial decline. As Giovanni Arrighi emphasizes, "The large surplus in the Indian balance of payments became the pivot of the enlarged reproduction of Britain's world-scale processes of capital accumulation and of the City's mastery of world finance."[75]

The operation of this crucial circuit was simple and ingenious. Britain earned huge annual surpluses in her transactions with India and China that allowed her to sustain equally large deficits with the United States, Germany and the white Dominions. True, Britain also enjoyed invisible earnings from shipping, insurance, banking and foreign investment, but without Asia, which generated 73 percent of British trade credit in 1910, Anthony Latham argues, Britain "presumably would have been forced to abandon free trade," while her trading partners would have been forced to slow their own rates of industrialization. The liberal world economy might otherwise have fragmented into autarkic trading blocs, as it did later during the 1930s:

> The United States and industrial Europe, in particular Germany, were able to con-
> tinue their policy of tariff protection only because of Britain's surplus with Asia.
> Without that Asian surplus, Britain would no longer have been able to subsidise
> their growth. So what emerges is that Asia in general, but India and China in par-
> ticular, far from being peripheral to the evolution of the international economy at
> this time, were in fact crucial. Without the surpluses which Britain was able to earn
> there, the whole pattern of international economic development would have been
> severely constrained.[76]

India, of course, was the greatest captive market in world history, rising from
third to first place among consumers of British exports in the quarter century
after 1870.[77] "British rulers," writes Marcello de Cecco in his study of the Victorian gold standard system, "deliberately prevented Indians from becoming skilled
mechanics, refused contracts to Indian firms which produced materials that
could be got from England, and generally hindered the formation of an autonomous industrial structure in India."[78] Thanks to a "government stores policy that
reserved most government purchases to British products and by the monopoly
of British agency houses in organizing the import-export trade," India was forced
to absorb Britain's surplus of increasingly obsolescent and noncompetitive industrial exports.[79] By 1910 this included two-fifths of the UK's finished cotton goods
and three-fifths of its exports of electrical products, railway equipment, books
and pharmaceuticals. As a result, observes de Cecco, Britain avoided "having to
restructure her industry and was able to invest her capital in the countries where
it gave the highest return." Thanks to India, "British financiers were not compelled to 'tie' their loans to British exports because the Imperial outlet was always
available for British products."[80]

The subcontinent was equally important to the rentier strata. The climate-det-
onated crisis of English agriculture in the late 1870s and the subsequent decline of
farm output produced a sharp fall in agricultural rents in England and Wales from
£53 million in 1876 to only £37 million in 1910.[81] Indian army and civil service
sinecures were accordingly famous for rescuing the fortunes of Britain's landed
aristocracy. But, as Cain and Hopkins have argued in making their case for a hegemonic "gentlemanly capitalism," even bigger spoils were returned to the middle

classes of London and the Home Counties as government-guaranteed interest on railroad debentures and Indian bonds. "This constituency of southern investors, and its institutional representatives in banking and shipping, fell in readily behind the flag of empire and gave full support to policies of free trade and sound money. If British rule in India was helpful to British industry, it was vital to British investment."[82] As Hobsbawm points out, "not even the free-traders wished to see this goldmine escape from British control."[83]

But how, in an age of famine, could the subcontinent afford to subsidize its conquerer's suddenly precarious commercial supremacy?[84] In a word, it couldn't, and India was forced-marched into the world market, as we shall see, by revenue and irrigation policies that compelled farmers to produce for foreign consumption at the price of their own food security. This export drive was the hallmark of the new public finance strategy introduced by James Wilson – founder of *The Economist* and finance member of the Council of India – in the first years of direct rule. The opening of the Suez Canal and the growth of steam shipping drastically reduced the transport costs of bulk commodity export from the subcontinent. As a result India's seaborne foreign trade increased more than eightfold between 1840 and 1886.[85] In addition to opium cultivation in Bengal, new export monocultures of indigo, cotton, wheat and rice supplanted millions of acres of subsistence crops. Part of this production, of course, was designed to assure low grain prices in the metropolis after the debacle of English agriculture in the 1870s. Between 1875 and 1900, years that included the worst famines in Indian history, annual grain exports increased from 3 million to 10 million tons: a quantity that, as Romesh Dutt pointed out, was equivalent to the annual nutrition of 25 million people. By the turn of the century, India was supplying nearly a fifth of Britain's wheat consumption as well as allowing London grain merchants to speculate during shortages on the Continent.[86]

But Indian agriculture's even more decisive contribution to the imperial system, from the East India Company's first illegal shipment of opium to Canton, was the income it earned in the rest of the Eastern Hemisphere. Especially in the 1880s and 1890s, the subcontinent's permanent trade and current account imbalances with Britain were financed by its trade surpluses of opium, rice and cotton thread vis-à-vis the rest of Asia. Indeed England's systematic exploitation of India depended in large part upon India's commercial exploitation of China.

This triangular trade between India, China and Britain had a strategic economic importance in the Victorian world system that transcended other far larger flows of commerce. If China generated only a tiny 1.3 percent of the total volume of world trade in the late nineteenth century, it was nonetheless immensely valuable to the British Empire, which monopolized fully 80 percent of China's foreign trade in the 1860s and 60 percent as late as 1899. (British firms, which controlled two-thirds of coastal shipping, also took an important slice of China's domestic commerce.)[87]

From the beginning of the nineteenth century, the East India Company had relied on opium exports from Bengal to Canton (which in 1832 earned a net profit "at least fourteen times the prime cost") to finance the growing deficits generated by its expensive military operations on the subcontinent. By forcibly enlarging the Chinese demand for the narcotic and, thus, the taxes collected on its export, the two Opium Wars (1839–42 and 1856–58) and the punitive Treaty of Tianjin (1858) revolutionized the revenue base of British India. "Opium," says John Wong, "serviced the cost of imperial expansion in India."[88] Opium shipments from India reached a peak of 87,000 chests in 1879, the biggest drug transaction in world history.[89]

This extraordinarily one-sided trade – in 1868 India supplied over 35 percent of China's imports but bought less than 1 percent of its exports – also subsidized the imports of US cotton that fueled the industrial revolution in Lancashire.[90] "The sale of Bengal opium to China," Latham explains, "was a great link in the chain of commerce with which Britain had surrounded the world. The chain worked like this: The United Kingdom paid the United States for cotton by bills upon the Bank of England. The Americans took some of those bills to Canton and swapped them for tea. The Chinese exchanged the bills for Indian opium. Some of the bills were remitted to England as profit; others were taken to India to buy additional commodities, as well as to furnish the money remittance of private fortunes in India and the funds for carrying on the Indian government at home."[91]

When, after 1880, the Chinese unofficially resorted to domestic cultivation of opium (an early example of "import-substitution") to reduce their trade deficit, British India found a lucrative new advantage in the export of factory-spun cotton yarn, which, as we shall see, had a devastating impact on Chinese folk textiles.

Moreover, in the later nineteenth century Britain herself started earning a substantial surplus in the China trade for the first time. The Second Opium War – or "Arrow" War – which increased British exports to China tenfold in a single decade was the turning point.[92] Britain's dominant role in Chinese foreign trade, built by Victorian *narcotraficantes* with gunboats, thus leveraged the whole free-trade imperium. "China," summarizes Latham, "directly through Britain and indirectly through India, enabled Britain to sustain her deficits with the United States and Europe on which those countries depended for export stimulus and, in the case of the United States, capital inflow to some degree."[93]

Moreover, China was forced at bayonet point to cede control over tariffs to the British inspector-general of the Imperial Maritime Customs Administration, a de facto imperial proconsul who "came to enjoy more influence with the Foreign Office than did the British Minister in Peking."[94] China's growing trade deficit became intractable by 1884. "Not a single year [in the rest of the nineteenth century] showed a surplus; the average annual deficit rose to 26.6 million taels – roughly about 10 percent of the yearly total trade, but over 20 percent of the annual imports or just under 30 percent of the annual exports."[95] Among its traditional monopolies, tea was undercut in the world market by Indian production while Japanese silk competed with the famous brands of southern China. Unlike India, China was unable to finance any of its "consistent and growing overall deficit" via trade surpluses with a third party, nor could it siphon compensatory incomes, like Britain, from its overseas colonies. As a result, the Qing became increasingly dependent upon foreign exchange remittances from 5 million Chinese emigrants in southeast Asia, Oceania, Peru, the Caribbean and the United States.[96] Although the government publicly expressed its disgust with the coolie trade, it had little alternative but to collaborate in its expansion. The so-called "yellow peril" that English writers would help to popularize was thus a direct consequence of Asia's increasing subsidization of faltering British hegemony. Emigrant Chinese plantation workers and railroad laborers, like Indian ryots, balanced England's accounts on their bent backs.

## Militarism and the Gold Standard

In addition to being at the losing end of the imperialism of free trade, the Indian and Chinese economies were also throttled by military expenditures and the Gold Standard. In the Victorian era, no other major countries were forced to devote such excessive portions of their national income to war. India, already saddled with a huge public debt that included reimbursing the stockholders of the East India Company and paying the costs of the 1857 revolt, also had to finance British military supremacy in Asia. In addition to incessant proxy warfare with Russia on the Afghan frontier, ordinary Indians also paid for such far-flung adventures of the Indian Army as the sacking of Beijing (1860), the invasion of Ethiopia (1868), the occupation of Egypt (1882), and the conquest of the Sudan (1896–98). As a result, military expenditures were never less than 25 percent (or 34 percent including police) of India's annual budget, and viceroys were constantly searching for creative ways to purloin monies for the army from other parts of the budget, even from the Famine Fund. Victorian England, on the other hand, never expended more than 3 percent of its net national product on its army and navy, a serendipitous situation that considerably diminished domestic tensions over imperialism.[97]

The Chinese case, of course, was even more extreme. From 1850 to 1873 China was aflame with social and ethnic conflict on a scale that utterly dwarfed the contemporary US War Between the States. As most historians have recognized, this carnage was largely rooted in the structural recession and increasing insecurity of existence that followed the First Opium War. The fiscal effects of epic civil war, in turn, were enormous.[98] The Taiping revolutionaries and their Triad allies for several years cut off Beijing from the revenues of half a dozen southern provinces. Nian rebels simultaneously disrupted administration in large parts of four northern provinces, while a Muslim revolt in Gansu and Shaanxi grew into a nightmarish and immensely expensive war of ethnic extermination. In the worst years, 75 percent of the imperial budget was expended on the maintenance of vast field armies (without, however, leading to real military modernization.)[99] The staggering costs of their survival forced the Qing, in Pomeranz's phrase, to "triage" state expenditure between regions. They ultimately chose to favor the coastal cities, where customs revenues were soaring but sovereignty was most under threat, over the vast subsistence economy of inland north China. As we shall see later, their abandonment of imperial mandates for flood control and canal navigation, essential to the ecological security of the Yellow River plain, had predictably catastrophic consequences when the ENSO cycle intensified in the later nineteenth century.

The two great nations of Asia were also victimized by the new international monetary system established in the 1870s. Although Britain adopted the Gold Standard in 1821, the rest of the world clung to either a silver standard or a bimetallic system. Supply and demand for both metals were relatively stable with only minor fluctuations in their exchange ratio. After defeating France in 1871, however, Germany shifted to gold and was soon followed by the United States, the rest of Europe and eventually Japan. Vast quantities of demonetarized silver flooded the world market, depreciating the currency of India and China, the major nations outside the hegemonic gold bloc. (India began to move to the Gold Standard after 1893.)

As John McGuire has shown, the London-based Chartered Bank of India, Australia and China, which financed much of the Indian trade, had the same kind of quasi-state influence over Indian monetary policy as the Manchester Chamber of Commerce enjoyed over Indian agriculture. Keeping the rupee tied to silver had obvious advantages for Britain, since the value of its exports (denominated in gold) to India increased in value while its imports (denominated in silver) declined in value. "From 1873 to 1895 the value of the rupee fell from an index value in gold of 100 to an index value of 64."[100] Since India's "home charges"– the annual payments to London for pensions, border wars, public debt, the secretary of state's office, and so on – were fixed in gold, the devaluation of the silver rupee cost Indians an additional £105 million between 1874 and 1894.[101]

Likewise it is estimated that the Gold Standard stole one-quarter of the purchasing power of the silver ornaments that constituted the savings of the common people.[102] While the gold-denominated export price of Indian grains remained stable to the benefit of British consumers, their domestic cost in rupees was sharply inflated to the detriment of the Indian poor.[103] As Sir William Wedderburn pointed out: "Indian peasants in general had three safeguards against famine: (a) domestic hoards of grain; (b) family ornaments; and (c) credit with the village moneylender, who was also the grain dealer. But towards the close of the nineteenth century all were lost by the peasants."[104]

Economic historians celebrate the irony of impoverished Indians providing a flow of cheap credit to Britain. While "at every harvest season," De Cecco writes, "Indian interest rates would shoot up to unbearable levels," British-owned Presidency banks "received deposits from the government and from other public bodies without paying on them one anna of interest." In addition, "The reserves on which the Indian monetary system was based provided a large *masse de manoeuvre* which British monetary authorities could use to supplement their own reserves and to keep London the centre of the international monetary system."[105] Krishnendu Ray expands this point: "By preventing India from transforming its annual surpluses into gold reserves the India Office contributed towards keeping British interest rates low. English banks were able to borrow from the India Office at 2 per cent and reinvest on the London market at 3 per cent."[106] Even more importantly, monetary policy was used, in Dieter Rothermund's phrase, "to flush out India's produce." Until fiscal exigencies forced a partial demonetarization of silver in 1893, inflation greatly abetted the British campaign to recruit peasants to the production of export crops like wheat, indigo, opium and jute that helped balance the Empire's accounts.

> At an earlier time the Dutch had adopted a deliberate method of extracting cash crops from Java by circulating a large amount of worthless copper coins. In India the British did not have to do this deliberately because by simply keeping the mints open to the free flow of depreciating silver they got practically the same result. The management of credit facilitated the extraction of cash crops. By advancing money to the peasants who grew cash crops for export the British and their agents preempted the productive capacity of India's agriculture. The area under cash crops expanded even at times when food grain for home consumption would have fetched a better price. What was grown for export has to be rated as a cash crop in this context. The depreciation of the currency and the preemption of the productive capacity of vast parts of the country combined so as to achieve the miracle that India could export produce at "stable" export prices even at a time when severe famines tormented the country. By absorbing silver and exporting wheat at the lowest price India served as the buffer at the base of the world economy of the late nineteenth century.[107]

In China's case, the shock of the Gold Standard in the late 1870s compounded the monetary chaos inherited from the civil wars of the 1850s and 1860s. Powerless to stop the drain of silver that the British had engineered with the imposition of the opium trade, the Qing had also lost control of their domestic copper supply in the 1860s when Muslim rebels seized the famous Yunnan mines. Accordingly, Beijing had to finance its struggle for survival by issuing worthless paper money and systematically reminting copper cash into higher denominations. The debasement of cash relative to silver created particular havoc in the Yellow River provinces where an estimated 99 percent of exchanges were in copper (versus only 30 percent in the Yangzi Delta).[108] Since land revenues were still assessed in silver, the continuing high price of the metal – as Mary Wright has emphasized – undercut the subsequent attempt of the Tongzhi restorationists in the late 1860s to reclaim the loyalty of the peasantry through an amelioration of the tax burden.[109]

The conversion of world trade to the universal Gold Standard aggravated both China's external and internal exchange crises. First of all, the international price of silver plummeted: "Within a generation, the tael had lost nearly two-thirds of its exchange value."[110] Some mercantile elites may have benefited from the advantage that cheaper international prices gave their exports, particularly tea and Shanghai cotton goods. But "imports from gold-standard countries became more expensive, which was particularly serious for railway development. Foreign investment in China was also discouraged, for fear of repayment in a depreciated standard."[111]

Yet precisely because China's growing commercial debt was financed by the outflow or "dehoarding" of silver, silver's internal value actually rose vis-à-vis the copper coinage that circulated in village economies. The country's shortage of gold in international trade (partly compensated, as we have seen, by the reluctant export of coolie labor) was mirrored by the continuing depreciation of cash, especially in the north. There the common people were also outraged that in order to pay their taxes they had to convert their copper to silver at much higher exchange rates than the privileged gentry. A principal grievance of the Taipings in 1851, monetary instability also helped fuel the Boxer Rebellion nearly a half century later.[112]

## The Myth of 'Malthusia'

Forcibly imposed trade deficits, export drives that diminished food security, over-taxation and predatory merchant capital, foreign control of key revenues and developmental resources, chronic imperial and civil warfare, a Gold Standard that picked the pockets of Asian peasants: these were key modalities through which the burden of "structural adjustment" in the late Victorian world economy was shifted from Europe and North America to agriculturalists in newly minted "peripheries." But surely we must also concede that demography – especially in India and China where partible systems of inheritance were the rule – played a major role in undermining food security in the nineteenth century.

Malthus is still a potent figure among at least the older generation of economic historians. Princeton's W. Arthur Lewis, one of the leading authorities on the nineteenth-century world economy, assumed as a matter of course in an influential 1978 study that the underlying cause of famine in Victorian India was not the "drain of wealth" to England as alleged by contemporary critics, but "a large population that continued to live at subsistence level on inadequately watered marginal lands, without a profitable cash crop."[113] Similarly, the historiography of late imperial China has been haunted by the spectre of "agricultural involution" and the so-called "high-level equilibrium trap" – both euphemisms for how the presumed population explosion of the eighteenth century squeezed arable land to the threshold of chronic famine.

Recent scholarship offers a more complex picture of the relationship between demography and subsistence in Asia. (Malthus is not an issue in the cases of Brazil and Africa where land/population ratios were high and labor shortages chronic until at least the middle of the twentieth century.) As Charlesworth points out, "It is indisputable that land was, in absolute terms, hardly under great pressure from population in the Deccan of the early British period." Through the 1840s, at least, "only about half of the cultivable land in most Deccan districts, according to formal British estimates, was being tilled."[114] Although population grew rapidly in the 1850s and 1860s, partly as a result of the cotton boom, the demographic momentum came to an abrupt halt with the catastrophe of 1876. In India as a whole during the half century between 1870 and 1920 there was only a single decade (1880s) of significant population growth. (South Asia's percentage of world population declined from 1750 to 1900 from 23 percent to 20 percent) while Europe was rising from 17 percent to 21 percent.[115]

Modern case-studies corroborate the position of nationalist critics of the Raj, like G. V. Josh in 1890, who argued that "the problem of India lies not so much in the fact of an alleged overpopulation as in the admitted and patent evil of under-production." (Josh estimated that fully half of the net savings of India was confiscated as revenue.)[116] If cultivators in the Deccan and other drought-prone regions were relentlessly pushed onto marginal lands where productivity was low and crop failures were inevitable, the culprit was less likely overpopulation than the "British land revenue system itself." This is certainly the finding of Bagchi, who, after a careful inquisition of colonial agricultural statistics, argues that the revenue collectors' inflexible claims on a high "average" harvest "compelled the peasants to cultivate marginal lands, and also forced them to 'mine' their land in a situation where most of them had few investible resources left to improve its productivity."[117]

Likewise contemporary scholars are dramatically revising the traditional image of late imperial China as a "demographic profligate": the hopeless "Malthusia" depicted by generations of economic theorists and demographers.[118] Until recently, most scholars have accepted fragmentary evidence for an eighteenth-century population explosion that doubled or even tripled China's 1700 population. Demographic reductionists, however, have always had difficulty explaining how population growth that was clearly so "Boserupian" in the eighteenth century (promoting a dynamic expansion of productive forces) could abruptly become so grimly Malthusian in the nineteenth (blocking all advances in productivity). (Esther Boserup, of course, inverted Malthus in a famous 1965 study to argue that population increase was really the motor, not the brake, of economic and social progress.)[119] Moreover, there is little evidence for any increase in demographic pressure after the end of the Qing Golden Age. As Maddison points out, China's population was no higher in 1890 than in 1820 while per capita income was significantly lower.[120]

Pomeranz, who has examined this issue in the context of north China, agrees that population pressures alone "do not explain why ecological problems greatly worsened after the mid-nineteenth century." His study area, the Huang-Yun (comprising parts of Shandong, Zhili and Henan around the intersection of the

Grand Canal and the Yellow River), "after the wars, floods and droughts of the 1850–80 period ... did not significantly exceed its 1840s population until after 1949"![121] Moreover, the vast human losses of the Taiping revolution created a demographic vacuum in the middle and lower Yangzi that was refilled after 1864 by millions of immigrants from congested provinces, including Honan and Kiangsu.[122] Thereafter famine and epidemic, followed by war and revolution, kept population growth in north China at a minimum until 1948.

Recently some experts on Qing China, led by Princeton's F. W. Mote and Martin Heijdra, have frontally challenged the orthodox view of a population doubling or even tripling during the eighteenth century. They advance compelling arguments for a late Ming population of 250 to 275 million, rather than the 150 million conventionally adopted as a baseline circa 1700 for Qing demography. This implies an annual growth rate of 0.3 percent (the same as India and less than the world average) rather than the 0.6 to 0.9 percent claimed in most histories.[123] Moderate, rather than exponential, population growth during the Golden Age would perforce revise neo-Malthusian explanations of China's subsequent nineteenth-century crises. As Mote carefully explains:

> A major implication of the proposed outline of Qing population growth is that it discredits what usually has been taken as the most significant demographic fact about Qing: the idea of a "population explosion" in the eighteenth century. That supposed phenomenon is given high explanatory value in relation to many social and political contexts. If, however, the population did *not* suddenly increase during that century, but started from a higher plateau and grew moderately, many social issues must then be otherwise explained. For example, calculations using those earlier population figures in conjunction with equally suspect Ming and Qing figures for land in cultivation show a disastrous fall in the ratio of cultivated land to consuming population; the implicit crisis in that ratio of productive land to population must be reexamined. Related views about the "optimum population" of China, perhaps in itself a suspect notion, also must be reconsidered....[124]

Rejecting demographic determinism, of course, does not mean that population regimes played no role in China's nineteenth-century crisis. On the contrary, it is clear that the very success of agricultural intensification in the Golden Age encouraged excessive subdivision of land in many regions as well as ecologically destructive reclamations of previously uncultivated highlands and wetlands.

Moreover, population growth often seems to have been concentrated in the poorest and most environmentally vulnerable areas. *Local* population–resource relationships will thus figure prominently in subsequent discussions of subsistence crisis and disaster vulnerability in north China. But population growth was hardly the self-acting, archimedean lever of history imagined by so many economic historians.

## The Irrigation Deficit

As Pomeranz points out, Europe faced even more severe demographic and ecological pressures at the beginning of the nineteenth century, but was able to resolve them with the help of New World natural resources, massive colonial emigration and, eventually, urban industrialization.[125] The relevant question, in other words, is less population pressure per se than why Western Europe was able to escape its incipient "high-level equilibrium trap" and Qing China wasn't.

In addition to the factors already highlighted, there is another variable that is frequently missing from historical discussions of "underdevelopment." If (according to Pomeranz) the chief "ecological bottleneck" to economic growth in Atlantic Europe at the beginning of the nineteenth century was the inelastic supply of fiber crops and timber, in both India and China it was water. As Patrick O'Brien observes, "up to half of the populations of Asia, Africa, and South America may have subsisted on land where water supply constituted the key constraint upon increasing agricultural output."[126] This was, of course, common sense to "Oriental despots," and a major achievement of the Qing Golden Age, as well as of the Mogul zenith, had been the high sustained levels of state and village-level investment in flood control and irrigation. As we shall see in detail, however, the nineteenth century was characterized by the near-collapse of hydraulic improvement.

"Traditional water-harvesting systems," emphasizes David Hardiman, "disintegrated and disappeared in large parts of India during the early colonial period [and] high rates of land-tax left no surplus for the effective maintenance of irrigation systems."[127] Despite the later development of the celebrated canal colonies of the Punjab, irrigation in British India lagged behind expansion of agriculture until Independence. In China, meanwhile, "irrigation, water storage and control, and grain storage facilities were not extended or improved beyond their eighteenth-century levels."[128] Indeed irrigated acreage shrank from its Qing high point of 29.4 percent of the arable in 1820 to only 18.5 percent of the arable in 1952. In Brazil's drought-stricken Nordeste, there was no state support whatsoever for irrigation.[129]

This *irrigation deficit* undergirded the Malthusian illusion of helpless "involution" in China and elsewhere. Whether as a result of population pressure or displacement by export crops, subsistence in all three lands was pushed onto drier, often less productive soils, highly vulnerable to ENSO cycles, without parallel improvements in irrigation, drainage or reforestation to ensure sustainability. Modern irrigation-based revolutions in agricultural productivity in northern India and north China (since 1960), as well as in the Nordeste (since 1980), only dramatize the centrality of water resources and the political capacities to ensure their development to any discussion of "carrying capacity" or "demographic ceilings."

More broadly, it is clear that any attempt to elucidate the social origins of late Victorian subsistence crises must integrally incorporate the relevant histories of common property resources (watersheds, aquifers, forests and pastures) and social overhead capital (irrigation and flood control systems, granaries, canals and roads). In the case-study chapters that follow, I argue that *ecological poverty* – defined as the depletion or loss of entitlement to the natural resource base of traditional agriculture – constituted a causal triangle with increasing *household poverty* and *state decapacitation* in explaining both the emergence of a "third world" and its vulnerability to extreme climate events.[130]

# Ten

# India: The Modernization of Poverty

> Let us go to the root of the matter. Let us, or those of us who can do so, mark the condition of the Indian cultivator in his home, and find out what causes impoverish him and make him unable to save. The reason is not a want of frugality, or of sobriety, or of prudence. The Indian peasant is the most sober, the most frugal, and the most prudent peasant on the face of the earth.
>
> – Romesh Chunder Dutt

If the history of British rule in India were to be condensed into a single fact, it is this: there was no increase in India's per capita income from 1757 to 1947.[1] Indeed, in the last half of the nineteenth century, income probably declined by more than 50 percent.[2] There was no economic development at all in the usual sense of the term. "Static overall yield figures," Tomlinson adds, "do not mean that output everywhere was stagnant, but rather that progressive forces were always cancelled out by regressive ones, and that periods of dynamism were interspersed with periods of enervation."[3] Celebrated cash-crop booms went hand in hand with declining agrarian productivity and food security. In much of the cotton-growing southern Deccan, for instance, per acre yields of food crops at the end of the Raj had fallen to only two-thirds to one-half the average level of 1870.[4] Moreover in the age of Kipling, that "glorious imperial half century" from 1872 to 1921, the life expectancy of ordinary Indians fell by a staggering 20 percent, a deterioration in human health probably without precedent in the subcontinent's long history of war and invasion.[5]

These dismal trends vindicate the often derided claim of nineteenth-century nationalists that British "Progress" was Indian ruin. Yet India's economic stagnation under the Raj has puzzling aspects. Where were the fruits of modernization, of the thousands of miles of railroad track and canal? And where were the profits of the great export booms that transformed the subcontinent's agriculture in the second half of the nineteenth century? Here, if anywhere in rural Asia, integration into the world market should have resulted in significant local increases in agricultural productivity and profitability. Apart from the plantation crops of tea and indigo, most export production – opium, wheat, rice and cotton – remained in native hands under a regime of modern property rights. British commissions and surveys, moreover, were forever applauding the saplings of Indian peasant capitalism.

Yet, as macroeconomic statistics demonstrate, such prosperity was usually ephemeral and quickly reabsorbed into the huge inertia of rural poverty. Peasant agriculture, even in the most dynamic cash crop sectors, remained radically undercapitalized. Only moneylenders, absentee landlords, urban merchants and a handful of indigenous industrialists seemed to have benefited consistently from India's renewed importance in world trade. "Modernization" and commercialization were accompanied by pauperization. Why this should be so is revealed by recent research (beginning with Laxman Satya's important case-study of Berar) on the cotton- and wheat-producing regions that were both dynamos of India's late-Victorian export economy and epicenters of mass mortality in the famines of the 1870s and 1890s.

## Cotton's Naked Misery

Prised away from Hyderabad in 1853, the Marathi province of Berar, together with the adjoining district of Nagpore, had been selected by the Cotton Supply Association – an arm of the Manchester Chamber of Commerce – as platforms for specialized cotton monoculture.[6] The Association wielded extraordinary power over the reshaping of the Indian economy in the wake of the Mutiny and the imposition of Free Trade. In the 1870s the "millocracy" (as Karl Marx called it) even won formal institutional recognition in the government of India with the appointment of Sir Louis Mallet – "a doctrinaire free trader who served as Cobden's assistant at the Board of Trade" – as permanent under-secretary at the Indian Office "to represent Lancashire's interests."[7] Indeed to ordinary Indians trying to decipher codes of power within the Raj, it sometimes seemed as if their real sovereigns ruled from Manchester's Royal Exchange rather than Buckingham Palace. "The most blatant example," Stanley Wolpert points out, "of such imperial favoritism occurred in 1879, when Viceroy Lytton actually overruled his entire council to accommodate Lancashire's lobby [the Association] by removing all import duties on British-made cotton, despite India's desperate need for more revenue in a year of widespread famine and tragic loss of life throughout Maharashtra."[8]

In the case of Berar, the Association encouraged the administrative dismantling of the *balutedari* system through which dominant local clans or castes had exercised managerial control over a complex network of social production including communal irrigation and cotton weaving. The essence of the old order was that the upper castes had claims on agricultural produce but did not own the land itself. After purging the "disloyal" leading families, the British spent seventeen years (1861–77) reorganizing the vast peasant universe of Berar (7,000 villages and 10.5 million acres of cultivatable land) into the so-called *khatedari* system. A varient of the *ryotwari* model that had been imposed on most of southern and western India, it was heralded as establishing the *khatedars* as sturdy Berari versions of the English yeomanry. In reality the government became the supreme landlord with peasant tenure, unlike Tudor England, strictly conditional upon punctual payment of revenue.

The complicated reciprocities of the old balutedari system, Satya explains, gave way to brutal and unilateral relations of exploitation. Diversity and mobility – "the characteristic feature[s] of precolonial Berar" – were replaced by coercive "standardization and sedentarization." The collection of taxes as well as the local marketing of the cotton crop ended up in the hands of moneylender/grain merchants who became the crucial intermediaries controlling almost all transactions between the village world, Calcutta and Manchester. Meanwhile punitive taxes on local woven goods and a flood of cheap English imports in the wake of the arrival of the Great India Peninsular Railway destroyed domestic manufacture and forced ruined artisans into the fields as propertyless laborers. The railroad inflicted the same fate on most of the *banjaras,* the colorful and ethnically diverse stratum of traditional porters and carters.[9]

From a British perspective, the reengineering of Berari society was a stunning success. By 1867 Berar alone was sending as much cotton to Manchester as all of Egypt, and cultivated acreage probably doubled by 1890.[10] But the khatedars and their tenants had no way to participate in the profits of the boom. Precisely as the Cotton Supply Association had intended, Beraris were captives of Lancashire's lopsided monopsony. As one agent of the Association explained in 1869, "Speaking generally, the cultivator who produces and sells the cotton cannot in any way regulate the market price. For this he is dependent on the home market and many causes which combine to raise and lower the price in Liverpool."[11] Berari cotton exports had been nurtured in the first place during the 1850s to buffer fluctuations in the premium American cotton supply and ensure price stability for Lancashire mills. "In short," Charlesworth explains, "British industry wanted Indian raw cotton as a sort of permanent twelfth man, always ready in the pavilion but only occasionally brought on to the field of play. This role hardly produced the consistency of demand necessary to promote a more extensive commercial agriculture."[12]

The khatedars, in other words, were a contingent workforce for the Association, which had no intention of ever allowing them to wield any autonomous bargaining power within the international cotton market. Instead, they were sucked into a vortex of high taxes, chronic debt and subsistence instability. The khatedars with more resources attempted to escape from the debt trap by becoming micro-exploiters themselves, and by the 1870s holdings were being fragmented into smaller parcels and worked by subtenants known as *bhagindars.* Satya estimates that the bhagindars paid rack-rents three- or four-fold greater than revenue demands imposed on the khatedars. By the great droughts of the 1890s, the stratum of authentically independent cultivators had been reduced to a minority, and at least 70 percent of the population were either impoverished bhagindars or landless laborers whose fates hung on the capricious dance of cotton prices in faraway exchanges.[13]

This layering of exploitation had a devastating impact on overall welfare in Berar. A society formerly celebrated for its rich cotton fabrics was virtually unclothed by poverty as per capita textile consumption plummeted in inverse ratio to soaring exports of raw cotton. "Most Berari children went naked, most Berari men were half-clad, and a majority of the Berari women clothed themselves in rags."[14] Although massive sums of capital were sunk into the Association's export infrastructure, including railroad spurs, cotton yards, and metalled feeder roads, none of it percolated to the village level where degraded sanitary conditions, especially the contamination of drinking water by human waste, spread cholera and gastrointestinal disease as well as tuberculosis. Similarly, local food security was eroded by the advance not only of cotton production (which doubled its acreage in the last quarter of the century) but of grain exports as well. During the famine of 1899–1900, when 143,000 Beraris died directly from starvation, the province exported not only tens of thousands of bales of cotton but an incredible 747,000 bushels of grain.[15] Despite heavy labor immigration into Berar in the 1890s, the population fell by 5 percent and "life expectation at birth" twice dipped into the 15 years range before finally falling to less than 10 years during the "extremely bad year" of 1900.[16]

Berar was not unique. Food security was also sacrificed to cotton export throughout the Deccan. Writing about the Bellary district, one of the epicenters of the 1877 Madras famine, David Washbrook observes that commercial cotton cultivation was "associated not with a broadening prosperity, but with a progressive crisis in agricultural production and social reproduction."[17] Although its heavy black volcanic soil was ideal for short staple cotton, Bellary was one of the driest cultivated districts in India and, without irrigation, a family required 15–20 acres of average-quality land to produce its subsistence (in millet) and pay taxes. By the 1870s, however, most ryots were lucky to farm 7 acres, and only an elite of several thousand rich *inamdars* (an emergent "magnate class" whom Washbrook argues were almost entirely "made" by the colonial state) could afford the heavy metal ploughs pulled by up to a dozen bullocks that were required for deep ploughing.[18] Before British direct rule, small farmers traditionally mitigated their harvest shortfalls with additional family income from stockraising and seasonal soldiering. Pax Victoria excluded the mercenary option while the expansion of commercial agriculture devoured pasture.[19]

Thus caught in a tightening vise between their undersized farms and rising debt, small producers made the apparently surprising choice of substituting cotton for millet, raising and selling the former in order to purchase the latter from grain merchants. Moreover they made the switch in face of declining or stagnant cotton prices. "In straightforward terms," Washbrook writes, "this 'decision' would seem to make no sense as a subsistence strategy. It meant producing a crop whose relative value against grain halved across this period. It also involved its producers in a three-sided structure of risk: from the climate, from the oscillation of grain prices and the oscillation in cotton prices which, being internationally determined, were scarcely calculable in Bellary itself."[20]

The decisive advantage of cotton – as we shall see again in the case of north China – was that "for land-short peasants, [its] higher returns per acre provided a better chance of approaching subsistence targets than did grain cultivation itself – even if, at 9.5 necessary acres, the majority of small farmers would still not have been able to quite reach it."[21] Cotton output was also more responsive to labor intensity than millet: desperate peasants (ignorant of marginal economics) could hope to increase their harvest incrementally by the application of massive quantities of unpaid family labor. But at all times, cotton-growing was a survival strategy wagered against the unknown variables of weather and the world market where the price of cotton from the US South generally determined demand for other varieties.

The peasantry's creditors, however, were eager to oblige the gamble. As small farmers – "more [in] response to economic adversity than to market opportunity" – turned towards cotton (which increased its percentage of the Deccan arable from 4 percent in the 1870s to nearly 12 percent in 1911),[22] the "magnates," who had dominated production during the bonanza years of the "cotton famine" in the 1860s, abandoned cotton cultivation. In a parodic rebuke to British hopes of an "improving yeomanry," they aggressively switched their assets in the opposite direction from that predicted by Ricardian theory: from cultivation to usury and cotton-factoring. As Washbrook points out, it was simply easier for them to expropriate the agrarian surplus through the credit system and the monopsony of the grain market than to bear the risks involved in the direct organization of production:

[T]he entire shift of cotton production from large to small farms can be seen as a mechanism whereby, through the application of usury and "service" capital, magnate-creditors sought to respond to the conditions of depression in the cotton market and to continue to squeeze a healthy profit out of the crop. By acting as its major financiers and advancing it the factors of production which it lacked, magnate farmers were able to draw returns from small farming's one supposed advantage – unpaid family labour. The family now laboured longer and harder and passed most of the profits of its work to the magnates in interest payments and rents. Not only did the new economic system "rationalize" the deployment of labor, most critically it cheapened it – in this case, literally, to the price of nothing.[23]

## The Wheat Boom's Hunger

The producing classes, to be sure, fared little better in the other leading sectors of Indian commercial agriculture. As D. E. U. Baker has shown in another revealing study, the famous wheat boom in the Central Provinces' Narmada Valley (today part of Madhya Pradesh) from 1861 to 1890, officially heralded as a reign of "almost unbroken agricultural prosperity," was in reality subsidized by destructive soil mining and crushing household debt. In the decade following the Mutiny, the "impetuous and authoritarian" administration of Sir Richard Temple had aggressively pushed landowners (*malguzars*) into commercial production of cotton and especially wheat.[24] Celebrated local handicrafts had been ruined by the cheap Lancashire cloth that flooded north-central India after the completion of the Bombay–Calcutta railroad, and farmers were encouraged to save themselves by using the railroad to export the soft wheat that British millers preferred. Bombay-based exporters and their local malguzar agents went door-to-door offering villagers cash advances if they would grow wheat rather than millet and gram.[25]

Narmada wheat, which began to reach Liverpool via the Suez Canal in 1871, arrived in English grain exchanges just in time to buffer the decline of Russian exports in the wake of the emancipation of the serfs (1873 was the last year that Russia was Britain's main grain supplier). It stabilized the price of flour in the season when other imported grains were scarce and provided a reserve for lucrative re-export during grain shortages on the Continent. Demand grew steadily through the good rainfall years of the 1880s, reaching a peak in 1890–91 after the disastrous crop failures in Russia. Proud British officials boasted that "the smallest cultivator can now sell his produce direct to the agent of a European firm at the

Figure 10.1   The Underside of the Wheat Boom

price current in the world's market."[26] Meanwhile "traders in grains speculated wildly" and land prices skyrocketed. In the main export districts, like Saugor, wheat occupied two-thirds of the acreage once devoted to subsistence grains.[27]

Behind the facade of prosperity, however, official policies had inexorably laid a "basis for an agrarian crisis between 1891 and 1901 that created famine, wrecked the wheat economy, and exposed the Central Provinces to bankruptcy."[28] Once again the inflexible revenue demands of the government drained capital from the countryside and put tenants at the mercy of a top stratum of malguzars who, no longer bound by any of the patrimonial obligations of the pre-British village system, ruthlessly combined the functions of moneylender and grain merchant. As smaller landowners defaulted, moreover, this elite acquired direct ownership of a vast swathe of the Narmada wheat belt. Baker estimates that "by 1889 more than half the malguzari area transferred in the Central Provinces since settlement had passed to moneylending castes, and 47 percent of the revenue on land sold since settlement was being paid by moneylenders."[29]

The wealth generated by usury and rackrenting was almost entirely parasitic, with negligible productive reinvestment in cattle, irrigation or farm equipment. Indeed, "absentee landlords did not normally visit their villages, and were thus not in touch with their tenants, who were no more important to them than the man who rented their shops in the bazaar."[30] As in Berar, fabled profits were accompanied by a progressive deterioration in the social condition of the direct producers. As early as Temple's commissionership there was concern over the depletion of local grain stocks by the high levels of exports and district officers reported growing immiseration among the tenantry.[31]

Even more than in the cotton districts, the Narmada wheat boom was built upon precarious climatic and ecological foundations. As T. Raghavan has emphasized, the soaring export demand of the 1880s had been accommodated by the expansion of cultivation into areas of inferior soil, traditionally devoted to hardy millets, where harvests were strictly dependent upon the unusual cycle of good monsoons from 1884 to 1894.[32] Moreover, commercialization was accompanied by ecological crisis as the railroad ravaged the forests of the Satpuras for lumber, and commercial wheat acreage absorbed pasture lands that traditionally fed Narmada's cattle. "By 1883–84 the price of grass had risen enormously" and bullocks were becoming too expensive for many cultivators to maintain. The subsequent manure shortage (aggravated by the rising cost of charcoal and the necessary resort to cattle droppings as fuel) increased the pace of soil exhaustion and further reduced productivity. Finally, using the excuses that Narmada was "not subject to famine" and that local topography made dams and canals too expensive to build, the government neglected irrigation works that might have safeguarded the rural population in the event of drought.[33]

Mass vulnerability to disaster as a result was becoming acute in 1887 when the government undertook a drastic resettlement of the Central Provinces' revenues.

Table 10.1
Wheat Exports from the Central Provinces
(Millions of Rupees)

| | |
|---|---|
| 1871–76 | 3.4 |
| 1876–81 | 7.2 |
| 1881–86 | 14.9 |
| 1886–91 | 16.6 |
| 1891–96 | 4.3 |

Source: From Haretty, *Imperialism and Free Trade*, p. 347 (Table 4).

Taxes (and, by automatic adjustment, rents) were reassessed on the basis of speculative land values inflated by the boom: in some cases this amounted to a 50 percent increase. Believing that "the brisk export trade would last forever," moneylenders accommodated the malguzars' pleas for more credit. Then, as Narmada exports reached an all-time height in 1891–92, their British buyers suddenly switched to more attractive sources: a deluge of cheap grain from the Argentine pampas together with high-quality wheat from the canal colonies of the Punjab and the western United Provinces. (Argentine wheat exports surged from 4.1 million bushels in 1889 to 28 million in the early 1890s.) The impact on local producers – especially the heavily indebted tenants cultivating inferior soils – was nothing short of catastrophic: by the eve of the great drought of 1896, Narmada's "export of wheat, gram and millets had become insignificant."[34] Saddled with huge debts, carrying the burden of exorbitant revenues, and now locked out of the world market, the peasantry of the Central Provinces was already in a free fall when the rains stopped. Just as the Berari cotton growers ended up naked, the famous wheat farmers of Narmada were living off imported millet and rice by the beginning of the twentieth century.

Famine, as Navtej Singh and others have shown, was also the underside of the export boom in the wheat-growing regions of northern India. Although the "irrigation revolution" in the Victorian Punjab (predecessor to the "green revolution" a century later) is usually cited as the Raj's most unqualified success in sponsoring indigenous agrarian capitalism, the reality was considerably grimmer.[35] Certainly some of the big landlords in the canal colonies spectacularly enriched themselves through the wheat exports, but their capital was quickly diverted into usury and grain-trading. "The object of the merchant-moneylender," points out Neeladri Bhattacharya in a discussion of debt in the Punjab countryside, "was not to earn interest as such, but to control prices of purchase and sale, and ensure regular channels for the supply and disposal of commodities."[36] Like the elite malguzars in Narmada, they discovered that it was more profitable to become *shahukars* or middlemen than to act the role of improving farmers as prescribed by British political economists. Meanwhile, the majority of small zamindars and their laborers faced radical new insecurity: "the commercialization of agriculture merely increased their indebtedness and consequent poverty."

They were generally indebted to the shahukars who compelled them to throw their produce at a low market price and thus acted as compulsory middlemen. In many cases, the shahukars financed the cultivation of these crops and carried them away from the zamindars' threshing floors as soon as the harvesting was done. The peasants were robbed not only because of low prices but of false weightments by these shahukar-traders. It may also be noted that the shahukars financed agriculture in order to have control on the process of fixation of prices of the agricultural commodities. The conditions in the south-east of the province were the worst because this area came under colonial control long back in 1809 and was comparatively more marked in drought and poverty environs.[37]

As in the Central Provinces, the cultivators who put bread on English tables could not guarantee their own families' subsistence. "The enormous [market] demands and the prospect of government purchases led to speculative hoarding, creating shortages and pushing prices to famine levels. Depletion of stocks as an outcome of exports increased the vulnerability of the exporting areas to famines both in normal times and harvest failures."[38]

Starvation also quickly followed on the heels of the celebrated indigo boom in Bihar. Here the reluctant peasantry was forcibly married to the world market, through the so-called *assamiwar* system, by British compulsion. "The planters were hated throughout eastern India because of their racial arrogance and their contempt for the law. They maintained small private armies of strong men, whom they would use to coerce the peasantry, forcing them to grow indigo."[39] As early as 1866, peasants in the drought-stricken rice lands had organized a common front against the indigo planters whom they blamed for displacing subsistence agriculture. "In short the paddy and bhit land in which the ryots had a right of cultivation have been converted into indigo lands. Thus there has been less grain producing land, a decrease in the quantity of grain has been the result which for the last few years has caused scarcity and famine, and thousands of human lives...." As an official report later corroborated, the 220,000 acres under indigo — a net loss of 150,000 acres of grain — in north Bihar represented the margin between survival and famine in a bad year "This also explains," Colin Fisher points out, "why the most spectacular indigo agitations occurred in rice growing lowlands like Bettiah, Sitamurhi, and Madhuban, areas which were peculiarly liable to famine."[40]

Nor, finally, did India's most notorious export crop – opium – guarantee full bellies to its producers. Any profit to the cultivator was again intercepted by khatadars who purchased the poppy harvest on behalf of the government (who "rarely made less than 100% net profit") at a fixed price, then loaned money for tax payments and household consumption at usurious rates.[41] Binay Chaudhuri summarizes the three evils which weighed on the Bengali peasantry: "the lowness of the price paid for crude opium; the increasing rigour of the Government in collecting arrears resulting from crop failures; [and] the uncontrolled exactions by the khatadars and zamindars." Although Bengal was spared the cataclysm of drought in 1876–77, the failure of the poppy crop in 1878 and the refusal of Calcutta to remit taxes nonetheless brought famine to many doorsteps.[42]

Peasants in other export sectors, including ground nuts, oilseeds and tobacco, could tell similar stories; only the special cases of jute cultivation in Bengal and some of the deltaic paddy-growing districts seemed to have offered small farmers any opportunity to exploit price trends or draw a profit from world markets.[43] Far more commonly, cash cropping, especially in the drier interior regions, went hand in hand with rural immiseration and the decline of food security. As Raghavan shows in another case-study of the Narmada Valley, financial entanglements in export markets tended to reinforce "'traditional' causes of peasant differentiation: rainfall, local price fluctuations, and the structure of landholding in terms of the quality of the soil held."[44]

The situation was little different with commodities primarily grown for the domestic market. Although native crude sugar (*gur*) was famously lucrative, small-scale cultivators in the eastern United Provinces were caught in a seasonal trap – a coincidence of labor and revenue demands – that forced them to hypothecate their crops (and potential profits from market fluctuations) to merchants and rich-peasant traders. "Far from leading to surplus accumulation, sugarcane cultivation in Gorakhpur [district] barely enabled the majority of the peasants to reproduce their conditions of economic existence on a year to year basis. It was the importance of sugarcane as a cash-raising and debt-servicing crop, rather than its value as a surplus accumulator, that imbued it with a special role in the small-peasant economy of Gorakhpur in the late nineteenth century."[45]

In the absence of urban employment alternatives or productivity-raising inputs to agriculture, cultivators across India were increasingly caught in a pincers between high land values and interest rates on one side, and low crop prices on the other. In his influential overview of the history of the Raj, Sumit Sarkar finds that the commercialization of Indian agriculture "emerges on analysis to have been often an artificial and forced process which led to differentiation without genuine growth.... [The] built-in tendency of the entire system [was] against significant advances in productive technology and organization."[46] Indeed, adds Bipan Chandra, the British merely "skimmed cash crops off the surface of an immobilized society."[47]

## The Colonial State

It was the state itself, as Naoroji and Dutt had argued in their pioneering critiques, that ultimately ensured that no productivity-raising benefit could flow from export booms to direct producers. On the expenditure side, a colonial budget largely financed by taxes on farm land returned less than 2 percent to agriculture and education, and barely 4 percent to public works of all kinds, while devoting a full third to the army and police.[48] "When all is said and done," observe two of the "new economic historians," "[British] India spent on public works at a lower rate than the underdeveloped countries, and at a level similar to the Princely States. Moreover, unlike the other sectors, where expenditures rose over time, in India they peaked in the early 1880s and declined thereafter." Compared to a progressive and independent Asian nation like Siam, which spent two shillings per capita on education, famine relief and public health, the Raj's investment in "human capital" (one penny per person or 4 percent of all expenditures) was a miserable pittance.[49] Even more to the point, Vasant Kaiwar cites what he considers to be the typical example of a village in the late nineteenth-century Bombay Deccan where the government collected nearly 19,000 rupees annually in taxes but returned only 2,000 rupees in expenditure, largely on official salaries and a rundown school.[50]

On the extractive side, Ricardian principles glossed the relentless fiscal erosion of producers' subsistence. In theory designed to transform ryots and zamindars into modernizing market-oriented farmers on the English model, the revenue settlements instead subjugated the peasantry to the local despotism of moneylenders and nouveaux riches landowners. "The gap between British legal theory and Indian local practice was immense."[51] By making the revenue demands too

Figure 10.2 "Gods in the Countryside"

high and inflexibly fixing them to the estimated average produce of the land with
scant regard for climate variation, the British "made it certain that a number of
the designated revenue-payers would lose their titles every year." "The creditor-
debtor relationship," Bagchi continues, "was easily transformed into one in which
the debtor delivered up whatever surplus produce he had to the creditor. The
creditor became his landlord, and de facto the master of his whole family."[52] British rule, which replaced traditional patrimonial obligations with the inflexible
enforcement of debt laws, provided massive institutional support for this systematic pillage of the direct producers. "The colonial state was fully aware," writes
Kaiwar, "that this kind of relationship was inimical to development, [but] did
little to bring capital into a productive relationship with landed property. The
colonial state [thus] came to resemble a classic agrarian bureaucracy rather than a
capitalist state."[53] Guilty post facto initiatives to prevent the total expropriation of
the peasantry (like the famous Deccan Act, which followed the anti-*bania* riots of
1875) typically went hand in hand with revenue settlements and court decisions
that bolstered the power of the very same creditors.

In the late-nineteenth-century Bombay Deccan, for example, the annual process of revenue collection began with the impounding of grain in village stockyards. In order to eat from their own harvest, the ryots had to immediately borrow money to pay off the taxes. Typically the moneylenders bought the crop at half of the current market value but lent money at a usorious 38 percent interest.[54] If the peasant was unable to promptly repay the principle, the exorbitant rates of interest ballooned to astronomical dimensions. "I remember one case which came before me," wrote a former district officer, "in which a cultivator was sued for 900 rupees, principal and interest, the original debt being only ten rupees worth of grain, borrowed a few years previously."[55]

When ryots balked at payment, Indian courts applied English civil law against them with the deadly efficiency of a Maxim gun. (Indeed, as Lytton's critic, Lt.-Col. Osborne, emphasized in 1879, British rule in India was "so hard and mechanical in its character" that "to the great mass of the people, the English official is simply an enigma ... a piece of machinery possessing powers to kill and tax and imprison.")[56] Lord Elgin's land transfer investigation in 1895 revealed that fully a fifth of the land in the Bombay Deccan was held by "non-agriculturalist moneylenders": both indigenous brahmins and Marwaris from Rajasthan.[57] As the Famine Commission of 1901 itself admitted, while the authors of the Bombay revenue system "expected the accumulation of agricultural capital," in operation "their plans did not promote thrift, nor did they conduce to the independence of the ryot. They looked for the capitalist cultivator; and [instead] we find the sowkar's serf."[58]

Mercantile exploitation of the small cultivator was a ubiquitous relation of production, and Baker's characterization of Tamilnadu undoubtedly can be applied to most of late-Victorian India: "Virtually everyone who realized a surplus from agriculture tried his hand at trade and moneylending, and thus there were many apprentice despots."[59] As we have seen, the moneylenders (at least 500,000 by the 1870s) and wealthy landowners were profoundly anti-developmental for eminently neoclassical reasons. As Washbrook points out, "It became progressively more 'economically rational' to sustain accumulation through coercion and the 'natural' decline in the share of the social product accorded to labour rather than to put valuable capital at risk by investment."[60] Likewise, Baker adds, "creditors gave out 'loans' in order to be able to secure dependents and it would have been foolish to make 'loans' which, by improving the productivity of the debtor's land, helped him to become more independent."[61]

Although the British regularly denounced the "parasitism" of the moneylenders and grain speculators, they were both father and mother to the system. The vast majority of smallholders could neither make production decisions independent of lenders nor take any advantage of market trends. "In these circumstances [not surprisingly] peasant agriculture had no chance of developing into capitalist farming."[62] As Kaiwar reminds us, it was not so much the rich peasant, zamindar or khatedar who failed to play the prescribed theoretical role of an "improving landlord" as the colonial state itself.[63]

## Victorian Enclosures

Village economy in India, as elsewhere in monsoonal Asia, augmented crops and handicrafts with stores of free goods from common lands: dry grass for fodder, shrub grass for rope, wood and dung for fuel, dung, leaves and forest debris for fertilizer, clay for plastering houses, and, above all, clean water. All classes utilized these common property resources, but for poorer households they constituted the very margin of survival. In an outstanding study of a contemporary Gujarati village struggling with seasonality and drought, Martha Chen has shown how decisive nonmarket resources and entitlements remain for laborers and small farmers. "Standard definitions of work, worker and income," she writes, "do not capture how poor households generate livelihoods." In the village of Maatisar (which she visited during the severe drought of 1985–87) fully 70 percent of the fuel and 55 percent of the fodder requirements of the poor are provided from free sources. The forest and pasture commons, which altogether generate thirty-five different useful products, "not only serve as a buffer against seasonal shortages, but also contribute to rural equity."[64]

The British consolidated their rule in India by transferring control of these strategic resources from the village community to the state. "Among all the interventions into village society that nurtured the Anglo-Indian empire," David Ludden argues, "dividing public from private land stands out as the most important."[65] Common lands – or "waste" in the symptomatic vocabulary of the Raj – were either transformed into taxable private property or state monopolies. Free goods, in consequence, became either commodities or contraband. Even cow dung was turned into a revenue source for Queen Victoria.[66]

As in Britain itself (so famously described by Marx in Volume One of *Capital*), the enclosure of common resources deeply undermined traditional household ecology. As angry Berar farmers told the Famine Commission in 1881: "The cultivator is now put to expenses which in former times he did not know.... He now pays more for his cattle than he did yore, and he can no longer fell a tree from any place he likes to provide him with a shaft for his plough, or a yoke for his oxen. He has now to practically expend coin where before he needed only to labour, and the grass with which he annually thatches his hut has now to be bought, not merely cut and carried as it used to be."[67]

Until 1870 all forests (20 percent of India's land area) had been communally managed; by the end of the decade, they were completely enclosed by armed agents of the state.[68] For plough agriculturalists the forests were not only essential for wood, but also for leaf manure and grass and leaf fodder.[69] Although the British had been concerned since the late eighteenth century that deforestation might be making the climate more arid, their overriding interest, as Hardiman reminds us, was "to assure a continuing supply of wood for imperial needs": shipbuilding, urban construction and, above all, the railroads which by the 1860s already consumed a million ties a year for track, as well as vast quantities of wood for fuel. The second Indian Forest Act of 1878 "allowed the authorities to take unoccupied or waste lands belonging to villages into the reserved forests, effectively depriving villagers throughout India of their common lands."[70] The consequence for millions of villagers was an acute wood famine. Indeed in Berar, lumber had become so scarce by the 1870s that khatedars ingeniously designed their carts and ploughs so they could be assembled from the same pieces of wood according to the season.[71]

The cash-crop boom greatly increased the demand for forest resources, yet, as Christopher Baker points out in his study of Tamilnad, the British "aimed to develop the remaining areas of major forest as economic resources in their own right, and thus tried to separate them off from the plains agrarian economy." This was the "great running sore of Madras administration," and "only the richer cultivators, the 'big men,' could afford to bribe the forest officials."[72] Although the government had looked the other way when the Madras Railways in the late 1860s had deforested the future famine districts of Salem, Cuddapah and North

Arcot, illegally cutting down hundreds of thousands of trees, the Forest Act of 1878 (crafted by B. Baden-Powell to remove all ambiguity about the "absolute proprietory right of the state") was ruthlessly wielded against the survival economy of the poor.[73]

Even in the midst of the most terrible famines, as in 1899, the foresters prevented local residents from gathering fodder for their dying cattle or firewood to heat their homes. Vaughan Nash, the *Guardian's* famine correspondent, castigated the forest guardians for the fodder famine that destroyed the Deccan's plough oxen and cattle. "The Forest Department has a pretty long queue of sins waiting at its door for the day of reckoning, and so have the Indian railway companies [who refused to haul fodder], and the two of them may now apportion the responsibility as best they may for the catastrophe which has robbed India of her cattle."[74]

The British also cut off communal access to grassland resources and dissolved the ancient ecological interdependence of pastoralists and farmers. While the fundamental agricultural division in China lies between the northern wheat belt and the southern rice lands, India is divided roughly along the eightieth meridian between the humid, rice-growing east and the dry western interior where wheat and millet are the staples. Here extensive agriculture, some of it shifting and semi-nomadic, interacted for centuries with a vast pastoral economy linked to Central Asia. Great margins of uncultivated grassland buffered intercultural contact and invited physical mobility. "The labour force moved constantly over short and long distance in the everyday conduct of subsistence, to work land, trade, fight, tend animals, flee drought, seek water, open and defend territory."[75] Far from a backland, Rajasthan and the western Deccan were the hearth of the warrior elites, both Hindu and Muslim, who created a series of formidable empires from the twelfth century onward. Indeed, Jos Gommans has recently claimed, "it was ... the inner frontier of the Arid Zone that molded South Asian history."[76]

After 1857, however, the British pursued a relentless campaign, especially in the Deccan, against nomads and shifting cultivators whom they labeled as "criminal tribes." Although the agroecology of the Deccan for centuries had been dependent upon the symbiosis of peasant and nomad, valley agriculture and hillslope pastoralism, the colonial state's voracious appetite for new revenue generated irresistible pressure on the ryots to convert "waste" into taxable agriculture. Punitive grazing taxes (which tripled between 1870 and 1920) drove pastoralists off the land, while cultivators were lured into the pastoral margins with special leases, even patelships.[77] "Landed tenures," Neeladri Bhattacharya writes, "provided the frame through which the pastoral tenurial structure was conceived. Within this regime of property, all rights to land were segregated, fragmented, classified and fixed. Within it the rights claimed by nomadic pastoralists appeared unintelligible and illegitimate."[78]

Radical changes in social relations were accompanied by equally sweeping ecological transformations. The traditional Deccan practices of extensive crop rotation and long fallow, which required large farm acreages and plentiful manuring, became difficult to maintain as the land became more congested and cattle less numerous. "More than any single asset, in the dry-crop regions of Bombay, the use of agricultural bullocks was vital to efficient farming operations." Between 1850 and 1930 the ratio of plough cattle to cultivated land in the Deccan steadily declined, making it almost impossible, according to Charlesworth, to raise per capita agricultural output.[79] At the same time, the quality of bullocks also deteriorated as expert nomad cattlebreeders were deliberately squeezed out of the economy.[80] Similarly, the government did little to sponsor the planting of drought-resistant fodder crops.[81] Kaiwar estimates that between 1843 and 1873 cattle numbers in the Deccan fell by almost 5 million. The 1876–78 drought killed off several million more, with cattle populations plummeting by nearly 60 percent in some districts.[82] After comparable destruction during the 1896–97 drought, "women were seen to be pulling the plough" in districts like Hissar in the southeast Punjab.[83]

The decline in labor productivity entailed by fewer and less powerful plough-cattle was matched by a corresponding fall in soil fertility because of the growing shortage of fertilizer. Irrigation water alone was of little value if the soil was depleted of nitrogen. Thus Indians, for the first time, had to confront the dilemma that had vexed the Chinese in the Yellow River plain for centuries: should scarce cattle dung be used as fertilizer or fuel? By the 1860s, moreover, cotton and other export crops were displacing cereal agriculture from the fertile soils of the Deccan valleys. In most cases the light soils converted from pasture could produce only one-third of the average *jowar* (millet) yield of the heavier,

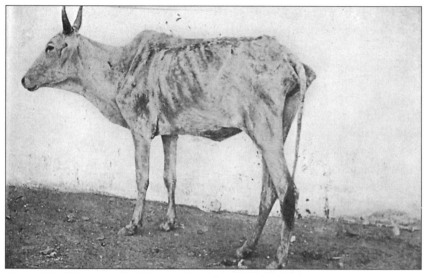

Figure 10.3  "Women pulled ploughs after the cattle died…"

valley soils. These poorer quality soils eroded rapidly and soon became useless for agriculture or even grazing. By the end of the colonial period, no less than 38 percent of the soil in the Deccan was estimated to be "highly eroded."[84] "Commercialised agriculture, in tandem with a largely subsistence-oriented cultivation of foodgrains," observes Kaiwar, "produced a particularly intensive regime of soil depletion and erosion."[85] Eroded soils, of course, retained less runoff and thus increased vulnerability to drought. It is not surprising, then, that food security was most tenuous in districts like Poona and Sholapur where the largest acreages of land formerly classified as "uncultivable" had been reclaimed for grain in compensation for cotton production on the good soils. Both districts were epicenters of famine and resistance in 1876 and again in 1899.[86]

In the cotton districts, overcultivation in the face of declining soil productivity was a structural problem over which peasants had scant control. "The poverty in Berar," Satya says, was "directly related to the fate of culturable waste lands under survey." Cotton cultivation is, of course, notorious all over the world for its rapid depletion of soil nutrients and its insatiable demand for virgin soil. Everywhere in the Deccan, moreover, cotton supplanted nitrogen-fixing legumes (like *gram*) in crop rotation, a strategy, dictated by revenue demands and debt, that maximized short-term income at the cost of longer-term soil fertility. The khatedar, crushed between growing debts and revenue obligations, had little choice, as one district official explained, except "to exhaust his land, by repeating his cotton crop too often or to grow it over too large a surface to the almost entire exclusion of cereals." As a result, cotton or displaced food grains took over not only pasture but even the traditional public spaces reserved for threshing and winnowing. Counting every square inch as potential tax base, the British privatized and auctioned off village common land. Villagers even had to beg government permission to build homes, which "was seldom given for the fear that the buildings cut into agricultural land and jeopardized the government revenue."[87]

Finally, in most of India water had always been a communally managed common resource. "Generally, there was no notion of selling titles to land and its water resources." In British common law as witlessly applied to India, however, water rights went along with land titles as private property. "In effect," as David Hardiman emphasizes, "this meant that only those who owned land had a right to the water on it. In this way, all those who did not hold colonial land-deeds were excluded from access to water ... [leading to] the collapse of traditional water management structures."[88] Tanks and wells were also privatized, with the consequence (as Satya points out in the case of Berar) that "for the first time ... water scarcity became a problem and this caused enormous hardship to the people and cattle alike."[89] The refusal of the state, in turn, to support local irrigation became a smoldering grievance, not only in Berar, but everywhere in interior India.

## The Decline of Indigenous Irrigation

British rule in India, according to Sir Richard and General Sir John Strachey, was the most extraordinary act of charity in world history. "India has obtained, to a degree unheard of and unthought of before, protection for life and property.... The country has been covered with roads, her almost impassable rivers have been bridged, 9000 miles of railway and 20,000 miles of telegraphs have been constructed.... [I]t is not the least remarkable part of the story that the accomplishment of all this work, and the expenditure of all this money, which have increased to an extent absolutely incalculable the wealth and comfort of the people of India, have added nothing to the actual burden of taxation."[90] Although he would have scoffed at the Stracheys' claims about Indians' "wealth and comfort," even Marx was impressed by the scale of railroad construction and the speed with which India was being integrated into the world economy.

For liberal and nationalist critics of the Raj, on the other hand, the railroads – a captive, publicly subsidized market for English steelmakers and locomotive builders – were the chief symbol of Calcutta's misplaced priorities. Public works in post-Mutiny India were driven first by the exigencies of military control and, second, by the demands of export agriculture.[91] On the eve of the 1876 famine, 29 percent of Indian public-works capital was invested in military installations in contrast to only 21 percent for irrigation, canals and drainage. ("Our soldiers' barracks," boasted the Stracheys, "are beyond comparison the finest in the world.")[92] The railroad system, meanwhile, consumed (to 1880) thirteen times as much investment as all hydraulic works. As the pro-irrigation lobby led by Sir Arthur Cotton and Florence Nightingale protested during the 1876–77 famine: "Now we have before our eyes the sad and humiliating scene of magnificent Works [railroads] that have cost poor India 160 millions, which are so utterly worthless in the respect of the first want of India, that millions are dying by the side of them."[93] (Gandhi, echoing this critique, would later denounce the railroads that "depleted the countryside of its [food] stocks and killed the handicrafts" as an underlying cause of famine.)[94]

The irrigationists eventually succeeded in lobbying Parliament to appoint a select committee to investigate their claims that the Indian government's exorbitant promotion of railroads was partially to blame for the recent famine, but the committee rejected their analysis as well as their proposal for a comprehensive canal system. Instead, the Secretary of State for India, Lord Salisbury, reaffirmed that railroads were the best safeguard against hunger and would continue to receive the lion's share of public investment. As a result, only about a fifth of public works expenditure in the 1880–95 period found its way to major irrigation projects, 90 percent of which were concentrated in the Punjab and the North-West Provinces (later, United Provinces), where canals watered commercial crops like cotton, opium, sugar cane and wheat and financial returns to the government were therefore highest.[95] As puny as they might have been in comparison to the vast capital sunk in the railroad network (only 11 percent of the cropped area of India was irrigated in 1921),[96] the canals that tapped the Ganges and Jumna Rivers to water the fertile soils of the Doab plain were nonetheless the pride of Victorian hydraulic engineering, a model for emulation in Australia, Palestine and the American West. They have also been the subject of much controversy amongst experts on Indian agricultural history.

For his part, Ian Stone has claimed that, despite some serious deficiencies, the canals brought relative prosperity and immeasurably greater food security to millions of northern farmers.[97] Elizabeth Whitcombe, on the other hand, has argued the canals which replaced well irrigation in the Doab were little short of an ecological disaster. They might have produced short-term bonanzas in wheat and cane, but at huge, unforeseen social costs. Without proper underground drainage, for example, the capillary action of irrigation brought toxic alkali salts to the surface, leading to such extensive saline efflorescence (locally called *reh*) that the superintendent of the Geological Survey warned in 1877 that once-fertile plains were on the verge of becoming a "howling wilderness." Indeed, fifteen years later, it was estimated that somewhere between 4,000 and 5,000 square miles of farmland – an immense area – was blighted by salinity "with 'valuable' crops isolated in clumps upon its surface."[98]

In addition, wherever flush irrigation was practiced side by side with traditional well irrigation, the new system undermined the old. In some places, rising water tables or lateral seepage from irrigated fields led to well collapses; in other cases, the water tables fell and wells became brackish and unpotable. As Stone concedes, peasants' efforts to save their wells from collapse by lining them with brick were opposed by landowners – many of them moneylenders – who feared any improvement that might make tenants more economically independent. "This was especially so in Bulandshahr, where the Settlement Officer noted that the proprietors 'not only failed to improve their property, but their policy had been directly and actively designed to prevent and obstruct improvements. It is almost universal practice for landlords to prevent their tenants from making masonry and half-masonry or, in extreme cases, earthen wells.'"[99]

Canal embankments, moreover, by blocking natural drainage and pooling water in swamps, created ideal breeding environments for anopheline mosquitos. The canal districts, consequently, became notorious for their extraordinary incidences of malaria, India's most deadly epidemic disease.[100] There is little doubt that death and debilitation were greatly abetted by the British reluctance to devote resources to rural public health and, after vector theory was firmly established, to mosquito eradication.[101]

Whitcombe's principal criticism, however, is that (contra Stone) export-oriented canal agriculture, by accelerating the marginalization of kharif crops, actually made producers more vulnerable to famine. "Generally speaking, canal irrigation did, and could do, little to decrease the ravages of scarcity by expanding the sources of staple food supply; indeed its effect seemed to be the reverse, to contract them – a process which tended to worsen with the stimulus of the export trade in grains, particularly wheat, beginning in the late 1870s."[102] Similarly, canal construction was based less on long-term developmental objectives like food security than upon expectations of quick returns from a state-controlled monopoly. "Canals may not protect against famines," Sir. Thomas Higham, chief irrigation engineer for the Punjab told the 1901 Irrigation Commission, "but they may give an enormous return on your money."[103]

"Revenues," declared an early government report, "should be the end and aim of all canal administration."[104] (In House of Commons hearings after the 1877 disaster, Sir Arthur Cotton complained that the secretary of state always treated the question of life-saving irrigation as if he "were a shopkeeper in London or a merchant in Manchester who was considering whether he should open another shop or another mercantile house.")[105] But, as Whitcombe emphasizes, "where works were most urgently required, viz. in the Central Provinces and in the Deccan tracts of Bombay and Madras, any expectation of profitability was frankly out of the question." The 420,000 square miles devastated by the 1899–1900 drought, mostly in the Bombay Presidency and the Central Provinces, contrasted with the less than 100,000 acres of canal-irrigated farmland in the same area.[106]

Farmers meanwhile railed against exorbitant water rates, and their protests were echoed by dissident members of the civil service. "There is nothing more urgently needed," wrote the veteran administrator C. J. O'Donnell, "than a scientific water supply in a country so often stricken by drought as India, but 'Imperialist' wisdom, lost in dreams of 'broadening the basis of taxation,' makes irrigation hateful to the very persons who ought to be most interested in its success."[107] The exorbitant revenue rate on irrigated land, ten to fifteen times the assessment of dry farmland, discouraged peasants from using irrigation for anything but cash crops.[108] Alternately, as Kaiwar points out, "villagers found it best to abandon the irrigated fields [altogether] and concentrate on lower-taxed unirrigated fields." As a result of perverse water-pricing disincentives, "there were in 1875, three major irrigation works [in the whole Bombay Deccan] capable of supplying water to 41,150 acres, but only 457 acres were actually being irrigated!"[109]

If, then, "even the best channel-watered villages had few signs of wealth," and "most of the people were forced to seek the moneylender's help and were in debt," the situation was much worse in British-ruled areas that still relied on traditional well and tank irrigation.[110] In stark contrast to the practice of the native states as well as the old Mogul tradition of subsidizing well construction, ryots in British India who sank wells at their own expense on their own land were punitively taxed 12 rupees per year.[111] Indeed, the British enthusiasm for revenue-generating irrigation in the Doab and the Punjab was counterbalanced by their disregard for the small-scale, peasant-managed irrigation systems that had been the hydraulic backbone of agriculture in western and southern India since the early medieval period.[112] The Raj, Hardiman observes, "placed a low value on any irrigation system which the peasantry themselves were responsible for."[113]

Yet modern studies of "industrial" versus "indigenous" irrigation in India and elsewhere in monsoon Asia have shown an inverse relationship between the scale of the system, on one hand, and productivity (output per unit of land over time) and efficiency (output per unit of energy), on the other. Indigenous irrigation systems, according to many modern developmental economists, avoid the problems of salinization and mosquito-borne disease associated with the big canal complexes and are generally "(1) more efficient in the use of energy, capital, and natural resources; (2) have more stable yields over the long term; and (3) are more equitable in terms of opportunities, benefits, and risks."[114] (Indeed, it was "minor irrigation" – especially deep tube wells – that "played a pivotal role in ushering the Green Revolution, particularly in Punjab, Haryana and Western U.P." in the mid-1960s.)[115]

Although such founts of ignorance about India as *The Times* sometimes portrayed native irrigation as nonexistent, British Army engineers generally marveled at the skill with which previous generations had configured water conservation to the needs of semi-arid India:[116]

In no other part of the world has so much been done by ancient native rulers for the development of the resources of the country. The further south one goes, and the further the old Hindoo polity was removed from the disturbing influence of foreign conquest, the more complete and elaborate was the system of agriculture and irrigation works connected with it.... Every available source of supply was utilised, and works in advance of supply have been executed, for tanks [reservoirs] have been very generally constructed, not only for general rainfall, but for exceptional rainfall.... Irrigation from rivers and channels, or by these and combined, was also carried on.[117]

The neglect of this magnificent legacy, moreover, was the subject of perennial complaint by both Indian and English critics of the government in Calcutta. As far back as 1785, Edmund Burke had indicted the East India Company for allowing native irrigation to fall into decay, thereby ensuring higher famine mortality during droughts. As Richard Grove has shown, Burke's line of criticism was expanded by William Roxburgh, the East India Company surgeon and pioneer tropical meteorologist who observed the Madras drought-famine of 1789–92 at close hand. In his official report on the famine, he praised precolonial irrigation systems and openly worried that India was becoming more arid and drought-prone as a result of their deterioration.[118] In the 1850s Cotton, perhaps the greatest connoisseur of indigenous engineering, resumed the critique of this "most unaccountable neglect." In up-country Salem district (an epicenter of mortality in 1877) he enumerated the scale of abandonment with characteristic precision: "8,864 wells, 218 dams, 164 small channels and 1017 small tanks." In Madras as a whole, he estimated that 1,262,906 acres of once-irrigated land had reverted into uncultivated waste.[119] In 1865 the Madras government rejected the advice of Cotton's friend William Wedderburn to continue "the system put into place by the native rulers in the Ceded Districts which granted a reduction in the land-tax rate to induce the ryots to undertake the repairs themselves."[120]

In the Bombay Deccan, meanwhile, a century of warfare had already done much damage to the tens of thousands of wells and tanks (small reservoirs), but British negligence was worse. As Bagchi has shown, the Bombay government completely abdicated public expenditure on irrigation during the first quarter century of direct rule.[121] In the famine year 1877–78, government loans for local irrigation improvements "hardly exceeded a thousand pounds for the whole Presidency of Bombay."[122] Radical MP Henry Fawcett complained in *The Times*:

"How is it that there are so many ruined tanks and disused canals in a country which has often to depend on them not only for the crops but for the cattle? A sad misgiving has often suggested itself that the former rulers of India, if not so great or so powerful, yet had more of that simple craft and homely benevolence which show themselves in storing the rain and diverting the torrent to the first necessities of man."[123]

On the eve of the great famine, the government's archives were bulging with ignored correspondence on the irrigation crisis. Some of the most knowledgeable observers, disagreeing with Cotton's emphasis on major projects, advocated the subsidization of traditional, bullock-powered well irrigation with its intensive focus on careful watering and manuring. In a prescient 1874 report, Sir Allan Octavian Hume (later the founder of the Indian National Congress) urged the government, as an alternative to costly canals that did not benefit poor peasants, to undertake a crash program of "innumerable small works, tanks and reservoirs ... as a reserve against drought."[124] But Calcutta ignored Hume's plan as well as all subsequent pleas (like H. M. Hyndman's and John Dacosta's in separate contemporary pamphlets) after the 1876–78 catastrophe to shift the focus from big canal projects to the repair of traditional wells and reservoirs.[125] It also disdained the appeals of Romesh Dutt and other moderate nationalists who wanted the newly established Famine Fund to support local irrigation: "During the period of 1877–78 to 1896–7 there is no evidence that such works were constructed out of that part of the Fund which was allocated for protective public works."[126]

Yet at the same time, as Baker points out in the case of Tamilnad, one commission after another churned out largely unimplemented schemes for repair of the rapidly deteriorating local irrigation infrastructure. "The commission that reported on the great famine of 1877–78 ... spent a lot of its time commenting on the urgent need for irrigation in the region, and particularly on the plains. It recommended a reform of the law on kudimaramat, and a concerted scheme to improve the condition of the tanks. The main result of this was the Tank Restoration Scheme. Although the Irrigation Commission in 1901–03 fulsomely approved the Scheme, and urged that it be intensified, it was never properly equipped with men and funds, was always vulnerable to government retrenchment, and had already been abolished and reconstituted twice by 1935."[127]

Conditions were no different in the Madras dry farming zones where, according to the research of Ludden, the decay of tank irrigation was well advanced by mid-century and hardly any new wells were dug between 1870 and 1900.[128] As *The Hindu* (Madras) editorialized during the 1900 drought: "The tanks and lakes to be found in the country are too few, and for want of occasional digging up and cleansing are often found silted up and too shallow to hold any large quantities of water. Nor is any attention paid to improving the facilities for gathering rain water falling over large areas of land into existing tanks and reservoirs. Owing to this state of things, the occurrence of famine in years when monsoons fail is almost inevitable."[129] Likewise, in the late Victorian Punjab, as Singh has shown, the neglect of small-scale irrigation improvements in the noncanal districts brought about increased dependence upon rainfall and thus greater vulnerability to drought.[130] And in Berar, Satya argues that the government's failure to keep up "the small-scale irrigation systems of dams and reservoirs traditionally constructed and maintained by local rulers, patrons and magnates" was a symptom of their larger unwillingness or inability to "coordinate the supply of public goods at the village level."[131]

The British constantly complained about the 'inertia' of India, but when it came to potentially life-saving local public works, they themselves were the embodiment of decisive inaction. This is anecdotally illustrated by one district officer's frustrated attempts over more than a decade to persuade his superiors to finance a small reservoir dam to check floods and store water for droughts:

> The engineering question was referred to the engineer at Bhaugulpore, an eminent authority on hydraulics, who began by picking to pieces the plans and calculations of my engineer, not an eminent authority; putting conundrums, calling for statistics, and demanding a thorough survey of the whole catchment basin. Years passed. He went away, leaving the question unsettled; and his successor refused to give an opinion until he had seen the place. He in his turn left, without having seen the site. The next man went to the spot without letting us know, and utterly condemned the project. I could not understand why, and persuaded him to go again with me. I walked him all over my site, and he then said he must have been shown the wrong place. This was quite a good project. He promised to put his revised opinion on record, but retired from the service soon after without doing so. About this time I came to the conclusion that the next famine would be on us before I should have dragged an opinion on my pattern from our professional experts, and I reluctantly abandoned this form of relief work....[132]

In addition to their failure to finance the upkeep or expansion of small-scale irrigation, the British also typically destroyed the social mechanisms that had allowed villages to undertake irrigation works by themselves. "Settling the land revenue with individual ryots," Kaiwar emphasizes, "broke down the supra-individual authority needed to direct the working of the co-operative system that provided the structural underpinning for building and maintaining the bandharas and regulating water use. In this way, the British methods of taxing agriculture supervened to create a system in which an absolute decline in the technical base of agriculture (e.g., cattle, fodder, manure, tools, and so on) went hand in hand with ecological breakdown (e.g., soil erosion, nutrient depletion, falling or polluted water tables, waterlogging, and so on)."[133]

Indeed, the sahibs themselves often conceded that the devaluation of communal institutions had been a disaster. "In the name of liberty," Nash told readers of the *Manchester Guardian,* "we have made the individual a bond slave; and we have destroyed the corporate life – that seemingly imperishable thing which the bloody tumults of Mogul and Mahratta left untouched, and which neither famine nor pestilence disturbed."[134] Unlike the rice-growing deltas of Bengal and eastern India, where colonialism forged alliances with zamindars to jointly exploit agricultural labor, British rule in the dry lands led to the displacement of traditional warrior elites and the rapid disintegration of communitarian institutions. In the Bombay Deccan, Kaiwar adds, "within a half a century of the British conquest the village communities were divested of their cohesion and vitality, and they were fragmented into discrete, indeed, antagonistic social groups which had formerly enjoyed an intimate relationship of interdependence."[135] Likewise in the districts of the Madras Deccan, the "development of private property rights and the dissolution of landowning collectivities ... destroyed the investment capacity of mirasidar assemblies altogether."[136] "British rule, in various ways, emancipated local political chiefs and big men from the obligation to invest in community resources and public institutions such as tank systems. The shortfall was not made good by the government's own public works."[137]

As David Hardiman suggests, British policies, however Smithian in intention, were usually Hobbesian in practice. In the case of Gujarat, which he cites, the new property forms freed village caste-elites from traditional reciprocities and encouraged them to exploit irrigation resources to their selfish advantage. "This two-fold process created a situation in which dominant communities exchanged water amongst themselves on strictly controlled terms, and supplied water to subordinate groups in highly exploitative ways, normally involving sharecropping arrangements."[138] The entitlement to water thus openly became a relation of inequality and a means of exploitation.

# Eleven

# China: Mandates Revoked

When the wealthy vie with each other in splendor and
display while the poor squeeze each other to death; when
the poor do not enjoy a moment's rest while the rich are
comfortable; when poor lose more and more while the rich
keep piling up treasures ... all of this will finally congeal in
an ominous vapor which will fill the space between heaven
and earth with its darkness.

– Gong Zizhen

The kaleidoscopic variation of rural social patterns in Victorian India was only
partly mirrored in late imperial China. Amid vast ecological and cultural diversity there was also a fundamental geo-economic polarity that had no real counterpart in the subcontinent. The reality of "two Chinas" predated the Cold War
by almost a millennium. Every foreign traveler in Qing China was struck by the
dramatic contrasts between the bustling mercantilism of the Yangzi Valley and
the seemingly frozen subsistence economy of the Yellow River basin.

The silk and cotton monocultures of the lower Yangzi, supported by rice
imports from the middle river provinces, generated impressive prosperity during
the Qing Golden Age of the eighteenth century at the cost of deepening social
divisions between absentee landlords, leaseholding tenants, and landless semi-

proletarians. The great recession of the nineteenth century, induced by opium imports, silver outflows and ecological decline, culminated in the anti-Confucian Taiping Revolution, whose millenarian, leveling impulses threatened landlord as well as mandarin power. The immense destruction of the Taiping wars, especially in the middle Yangzi, sapped decades of economic growth and bankrupted the Qings, while leaving intact the hegemony of the lower Yangzi merchant elites and the European allies upon whom they increasingly depended.

North China, by contrast, was a world apart. The largest economy of independent peasants on earth, its historical gentry had been decimated, first by the Mongol invasions, and then by the rebellions that had brought the Ming to power. The Qing, in turn, supported smallholder agriculture as the preferred fiscal base for their centralized state while freeing the peasantry from the heavy burdens of forced labor imposed by the Ming. In contrast to the later fiasco of the *ryotwari* system in British India, Qing policies – like the freezing of corvee revenues in 1713 and state-insured protection against drought and flood, as well as the appreciation of copper currency in the mid-1700s – greatly benefited the freehold peasant majority. As even Wittfogel in his famous disquisition on "Oriental despotism" was forced to concede, peasant landownership in northern China was a massive historical fact.[1]

Landlordism, of course, was far from extinct, but it remained a subordinate relation of production in the Yellow River provinces, preponderant only in pockets or within the periphery of cities.[2] In contrast to the late-nineteenth-century Yangzi delta, where Philip Huang estimates that 45 to 100 percent of the cultivated land (depending on the *hsien*) was leased from landlords, only 18 percent of the cropland in the Yellow River plain was rented.[3] In Shaanxi or Hebei at the end of the Qing dynasty four out of every five males worked primarily on their own family farm; in the southern province of Jiangxi, on the other hand, the ratio of tenants to freeholders was exactly the inverse.[4] Instead of urban absentees, "managerial farmers," employing hired hands in addition to family labor, tended to be the agricultural elite in the north. (At the time of the Boxer Rebellion only 4.2 percent of the northern population lived in large cities, one of the lowest rates of urbanization in the world.)[5] Because wealthier peasants supported larger households, however, per capita income differentials tended to be small, while diet (40 percent sweet potatoes, 31 percent vegetables and 28 percent grain), as

Sidney Gamble discovered in his famous 1920s study of Ting hsien in Hebei, dif-fered little except in quantity between most rural income groups.[6]

Although these farms are often described as the first shoots of rural capi-talism, Huang has shown that northern managerial farms "resembled capitalist enterprises only in their use of wage labor: they clearly failed to generate any real advances in labor productivity, whether through economies of scale, increased capital use, or technological improvement." Likewise, the elite kinship networks so central to the highly commercialized economies of the lower Yangzi or the Pearl River deltas were peripheral in the more egalitarian north.

Huang argues that the harsher northern environment and relatively greater frequency of natural disasters were crucial factors in differentiating its social structures and land-tenure patterns from the south.[7] In a climate zone where, as we have seen, annual rainfall variability exceeded 30 percent and irrigation was the exception rather than the rule, average rates of return on agriculture were generally too marginal to attract substantial merchant capital. But the environ-mental instability of agriculture was counterbalanced by the deeply anchored monolithic character of the smallholder social order supported by a towering imperial state.[8]

If to most foreigners the cultural and ecological landscapes of the north epito-mized China's inability to modernize, to others they represented the very essence of China's epochal achievement as a civilization. Francis Nichols, the American journalist who, as we saw earlier, traveled to Zian in 1901 to report on famine relief and the Boxer aftermath for the *Christian Herald*, discovered Jeffersonian as well as Confucian virtues in the Shaanxi yeomanry. Although the peasants were poor, "there is a complete absence of that condition that we call 'poverty.' … By Shensi roadsides one finds some professional beggars, most of whom are opium-victims, but here are very few 'unemployed,' except as the result of a universal calamity like a famine or a flood. Shensi farms seldom contain more than 3 or 4 acres, but they often remain in the possession of one family for generations. No one ever seems to desire more land or hold it solely for the purpose of selling it again." Moreover, Nichols discovered that Qing despotism, supposedly embodied in the mandarin suppression of all free speech, was belied by a rambunctious civil culture of irreverent political gossip and scalding public criticism.[9]

In "hidden Shensi," where he temporarily swelled the foreign population,

Nichols was overwhelmed by the cultural and agronomic continuity of contemporary peasant life with ancient Han civilization. As a courageous critic of
imperialist calumnies against the Chinese, he is easily forgiven for romanticizing
peasant traditionalism as well as for failing to recognize the changed relations
of production that were partly responsible for hideous starvation during the
1899–1901 drought. Everywhere in Shaanxi, the declining economic and ecological viability of smallholder agriculture over the course of the nineteenth century
was expressed by increased peasant dependence upon cash crops like opium and
cotton. Nichols's admirable farmers were almost universally entrapped in a hopeless system of petty commodity production on subliminal plots that annually
wagered household survival on fickle market prices and rainfall patterns. At the
same time, vital rural handicrafts were under siege from manufactured imports.
Although the only indications of overseas trade (as opposed to traditional inter-
Asian trade) that Nichols could find in the markets of Zian were imported cotton
thread and some cotton fabrics (marked "Fall River, Massachusetts"), these were
potent enough symbols of the destabilizing impact of the world market upon
inland China.[10]

## The Commercialization of Subsistence

The so-called "single whip" reforms under Zhang Juzheng in the late sixteenth
century, which transmuted corvées and revenues-in-kind into cash taxes, had
inexorably monetarized subsistence production. As immigration and high fertility rates supported by Qing antifamine policies began to rebuild populations in
the provinces devastated by late Ming warfare (especially Henan, Shaanxi and
Shanxi, where as much as one-third of the cultivated land had been depopulated) to their historical maximums, the customs of partible inheritance generated growing pressure on farmland.[11] In the absence of the European alternatives
of rapidly growing cities and overseas colonies to absorb supernumery agricultural labor, Qing China struggled to sustain its standard of living within traditional parameters of land use and agricultural technique.

    Initially, there was stunning success. In her recent study of Shaanxi's densely
populated Wei River Valley – the site of terrible mortality in 1877–78 and again
in 1899–1901 – Laura Murray confirms the role of new world crops (especially
sweet potatoes and maize) and marginal land reclamation in accommodating

population growth at constant levels of per capita output through the mid eighteenth century. By the 1780s, however, the Wei Valley peasantry was caught in what Murray (borrowing from Mark Elvin) characterizes as a "high-level equilibrium trap" in which increasing labor inputs realized diminishing returns in crop yield. With average cultivated land per capita reduced to three-quarters of an acre, even the most intense efforts by Wei farmers could barely produce the caloric minimum of grain to maintain their continued labor. In this context, cash crops' higher value per unit of land made them irresistibly attractive to the poorest strata of the peasantry.[12]

Commercialization on these terms was usually more "a gamble for survival" than an exercise in optimal resource utilization, and cash crops were immediately sold to purchase food and pay taxes, not used to accumulate capital or land. As Murray emphasizes, "land use tended to shift from grain crops to cash crops when population density reached the point that average holdings were too small to supply adequate subsistence grains.... Many families [were only] able to survive on plots too small for subsistence farming because of the higher value of cash crops. Most counties with a high level of commercialization also had grain deficits, and their residents depended on complex trade networks."[13]

The Wei Valley case was probably typical of the logic of subsistence cash-cropping throughout north China. "From their differing perspectives, Chao Kang, Philip Huang, and Ramon Myers have all shown that faced with diminishing farm size, the vast majority of peasants were able to sustain their livelihoods only by the ability to intensify, to turn to subsidiary occupations, and to switch to cash crops."[14] Huang, in particular, cautions against the common assumption of development theorists that such peasants, simply because of their dependence on commodity networks, were suddenly transformed into the competitive, incipient capitalist subjects of neoclassical economics. "This kind of market involvement should not be mistaken for entrepreneurial marketing, nor should such peasant behavior be mistaken for profit-maximizing rationality. Theirs was the rationality of survival, not of profit maximization." Moreover, Huang offers a useful distinction between the "survival-driven commercialization" so common in north China and the "extraction-driven commercialization" in the more class-stratified Yangzi Delta, where peasants were forced into the market primarily to earn rent payments to landlords and interest payments to moneylenders.[15]

North China peasants, within the limits of a relatively uniform ecology, embraced several alternative systems of cash crop subsistence. Throughout the Yellow River plain, for example, villages commonly sold wheat to the cities or distilleries (like those around Linqing on the Grand Canal) and used the cash to buy coarse grains – millet, sorghum and buckwheat – for their own diet. Likewise in Shandong, along the route of the Jiaozhou–Jinan railroad, tobacco monoculture supplanted grain production on much of the best farmland. Peanuts were commercially important by the eve of the Boxer uprising in southern Hebei as well as in the semi-arid foothills just north of the Great Wall.[16]

Opium cultivation, meanwhile, was a primitive form of import substitution, embraced, despite its theoretical illegality, by magistrates and merchants throughout northwest and southwest China. In Shanxi the governor had sponsored opium cultivation as early as 1852 in a desperate attempt to bolster revenues and peasant incomes. Poppies quickly supplanted so much grain acreage that missionaries, like the American Presbyterian Dr. Elkins, blamed the extreme famine mortality of 1877–78 on the opium boom.[17] In the Wei Valley, opium got a later start, becoming a major commercial crop only after 1870, when fiscally strapped county governments began to encourage its export to other parts of northern China. Once established, however, its growth was dramatic. By 1890, opium had become the livelihood of a majority of the peasantry in the eastern counties of the valley.[18]

For marginal peasants everywhere in China, however, the most important cash crop was cotton. It had two principal virtues. In the first place, there was huge, relatively stable internal demand. Second, peasants could add value by processing cotton as spun yarn and woven fabric. Moreover, from the merchant standpoint, rural surplus labor was more rationally exploited at home than in the workshop. "Once the marginal product of labor fell below the subsistence wage," Madeleine Zelin explains, "it became more economical for merchants to contract or purchase goods from household producers than to produce them themselves using hired labor. Surplus labor was thus retained at home, where the peasant and his family, wishing to garner whatever they could from their residual productivity, were willing to work for less than subsistence wages. The system was possible because the equipment needed to produce yarn, cloth, and other handicraft items was relatively cheap, and problems of marketing were solved by the dense

Figure 11.1 Home Cotton Spinning
Spinning cotton yarn was often the margin of survival on undersized farm plots.

network of rural markets in place by the early Qing."[19]

Originally, the north China plain had been simply a periphery to the lower Yangzi textile revolution, exchanging raw cotton for cotton cloth. The northern winters, however, gave peasant households a long slack time in which they could concentrate on spinning and weaving for household use and sale. In Arthur Smith's famous account of *Village Life in China* (1899), the Shandong-based missionary marveled at the grim dedication of north China's peasants-cum-handloom weavers: "In some regions every family owns a loom (one of the clumsy machines exiled from the West a century ago) and it is not uncommon for the members of a family to take turns, the husband weaving until midnight, when the wife takes up the task till daylight (often in cellars two-thirds underground, damp, unventilated, and unwholesome)."[20]

As in pre-industrial Europe, a vast system of cotton handicrafts emerged, centered on the Yellow River Delta, which, in turn, stimulated the further conversion of cereal acreage to cotton in counties as far away as the loess plateaux. Simultaneously, new world crops like maize and sweet potatoes, which demanded less labor for higher yields, allowed producers to devote more land and labor to all phases of cotton production. Thus by the middle of the eighteenth century, north China was second only to the lower Yangzi in cotton cultivation, which "replacing grain, occupied an estimated 20–30% of all agricultural land."[21] It was not rare to find counties near river or canal transport, as in southern and central Hebei, where 80 to 90 percent of the population derived its principal subsistence from trading cotton cloth (sold as far away as Korea) for millet. Indeed for poorer peasants forced to lease land, "there was often no choice at all: once rental terms on land that could grow cotton came to be set according to the market potential of that crop, no tenant could really afford to grow cereals."[22]

In good years, therefore, cash cropping allowed basically "sub-subsistence" farms to survive in great numbers. Although cotton required twice as much labor per *mu* as sorghum or millet, this was not a problem in an "involuted" economy where labor was abundant and land was scarce. But cotton cultivation in north China "cut both ways," as Huang has emphasized in his study of the Hebei–northwest Shandong region. "The smallholder found that, though his returns became higher, so too did his expenses. The risks from natural or man-made disaster were thus correspondingly greater." Whereas millet and sorghum depend upon the late summer monsoon, cotton requires ample rainfall or irrigation in the spring: "a relatively dry season at best, with only 10–15 percent of the total annual precipitation." To the extent that households derived increasing subsistence from the sale of cotton or cotton handicrafts, their survival was mortgaged more precariously than before against ENSO fluctuations. "Drought in the spring could bring total disaster to a household completely dependent on cotton."[23]

The boom–bust cycle of cotton production also reinforced social stratification, enlarging the ranks of poor peasants or laborers dependent upon seasonal or permanent wage labor. Since partible inheritance dissolved most village-level concentrations of wealth after a generation or two, the growth of a rich peasant class in north China in the Victorian era was less dramatic than the accumulation of mendicancy and instability below. Unlike the Yangzi Delta, agrarian immiseration in the North was not counterbalanced by the consolidation of big mercantile or agrarian capital. In drought-ravaged northern Shaanxi, where survivors of the Long March would regroup in 1935, "it could be said that socioeconomic differences within the region were really a matter of varying depths of poverty."[24] Reliance on the market only exacerbated the radical nakedness of these pauper layers in face of the threats of drought and flood. Huang cites the apprehensions of a mid-nineteenth-century magistrate in a Shandong county where most of the sown land was dedicated to cotton. "The rich do not store grain, and the poor rely entirely on hiring out and the board that comes with wage labour. Once confronted with natural disaster and bad harvests, they are at a complete loss."[25]

Micro-commercialization in addition added new exposures to such man-made disasters (often interacting with the natural) as commodity cycles, price inflation and monetary speculation. The diversion of so much cultivable acreage from grain production made tens of millions of formerly autonomous peasants directly dependent upon the grain trade and the price ratio between cash crops and subsistence cereals. Folk textiles, meanwhile, faced the competition after 1880 of factory-produced imports from India and Japan. Handspun yarn declined from 98 percent of China's consumption in 1876 to little more than 40 percent in 1900, and cotton merchants were transformed from peddlers of domestic production into salesmen of foreign yarn. India's export to Asia, principally China, meanwhile increased from 21.3 million pounds in 1878 to nearly 300 million pounds in 1905.[26] The most spectacular surge in yarn imports – 40 percent in value in a single year – occurred, ominously enough, between 1898 and 1899.[27]

"A peasant spinner," Huang emphasizes, "simply could not overcome the overwhelming advantage of a technology by which, according to one estimate, he could be outproduced by as much as 8,000 percent by a worker using a power spindle. The result was a product so cheap it sometimes sold close to the cost of raw cotton."[28] It was not surprising that rural Chinese were baffled by the origin of such cheap thread. Thus a Shaanxi spinner whom Francis Nichols interviewed in 1901 "accounted for [the cheapness of American cotton thread] by the theory that the United States was an island not far from China. When I told him that the country from which the thread came was 18,000 *li* from the plain of Sian, he shook his head dubiously. 'The thread would cost more,' he said, 'if it had to be brought such a long distance.'"[29] Although handloom weaving, which benefited from better factory-made yarn, would struggle on against machine competition for another generation, the collapse of cotton spinning in the 1890s had profound repercussions for the poorest strata of north China peasants.

Esherick in his study of the social origins of the Boxer movement, as we have seen, argues that western Shandong became the seedbed of revolt in the late 1890s precisely because of its combined vulnerability to natural disaster and foreign textile imports. The changed course of the Yellow River after 1855 and the consequent silting up of the Grand Canal, combined with an increased frequency of flood and drought, had made the depressed regions along the Shandong–Hebei and Shandong–Jiangsu–Henan borders ever more dependent on cotton handicrafts for sheer survival. "Too isolated and too lacking in alternative resources to enjoy any of the stimulative effects that the treaty port economies sometimes generated in their more immediate hinterlands," western Shandong was economically devastated in the 1890s by the loss of its traditional markets to factory-made Indian cotton yarn and cloth.[30] The imports were the dragons' teeth, sown by the world market, that eventually grew into peasant insurrection.

## Depletion of the Granaries

The commercialization of subsistence in north China was only weakly supported by long-distance grain trading. The raw cotton and cotton handicrafts, wheat, tobacco and opium grown by poor peasants were principally exchanged within "cellular" local markets usually coinciding with county boundaries or, more rarely, with the north China regional system.[31] There was an insufficient two-way flow of goods between the periodically grain-deficit north and the surplus-producing Yangzi Valley to protect against harvest shortfalls on a large scale. As late as 1900, the inter-regional trade of farm products was only 7 percent of total empire-wide production.[32] Regular long-distance grain trading was confined to east–west corridors within southern China – for example, from Sichuan and Hunan down the Yangzi River, or from Guangxi to Guangdong – where economic specialization was most developed. By contrast, the flow of grain from south to north, frequently against the gravity of market prices, required the heavy lifting of the imperial tribute system. Ironically, as northern peasants increasingly staked their survival on cash crops, they became, if anything, more dependent on the state's capacity to ensure the inter-regional redistribution of grain outside of market mechanisms. And this depended, in the first place, on the empire's fiscal health.[33]

    "The eighteenth century," Susan Naquin and Evelyn Rawski emphasize, "was a period of surplus revenues for the Qing state: bulging treasuries and a fat Privy Purse, the product not only of peace and prosperity but also of the successful tightening of control over tax remittances from the provinces under Yongzheng [emperor]."³⁴ On the eve of the French Revolution, the Qing treasury still had a surplus of 70 million taels, but this was rapidly expended in costly military campaigns or squandered by corrupt courtiers. By the time that the Jiaqing emperor took the throne in 1796, the Golden Age had ended and fiscal crisis was becoming chronic. The turning point was a millenarian peasant uprising in the disaster-prone border region of western Shandong ("repeatedly afflicted by either drought or flooding of the Huai and Yellow Rivers").³⁵ The ensuing decade-long war (1796–1804) against the White Lotus rebels – "the first major human calamity (renhuo) in about 120 years" – sapped both the treasury and tribute grain reserves.³⁶ "The food supply priorities of the state shifted to provisioning large numbers of troops": a diversion that would become almost total during the later Taiping, Nian and Muslim civil wars.³⁷

Immensely costly flood catastrophes, which had no equivalent in the eighteenth century, also conspired to push the late Qing state deep into insolvency. There were no less than seventeen consecutive years of flooding between 1839 and the final Yellow River cataclysm of 1855.³⁸ "The cost to the state in social disruption, lost agricultural income, and relief and repair funds was immense. Combined with the expense of the Opium War and the state's already weakened fiscal conditions, these floods left the state treasury barren."³⁹ Even greater calamities, of course, followed in the 1850s when the rain-swollen Yellow River hijacked the course of the Daqing River (one of its ancestral channels) to switch deltas from the Yellow Sea to the Gulf of Bohai just as the Taiping revolution was cutting off Beijing's all-important revenues and grain tributes from the Yangzi Valley.

The Qing fiscal system, as we saw earlier, was additionally undermined by price inflation rooted in China's opium-generated trade deficits as well as the exchange perturbations that followed the Great Powers' adoption of the Gold Standard in the 1870s. Despite desperate efforts to insulate taxes from monetary erosion by maintaining a favorable copper/silver ratio, Wang Yeh-chien has estimated that the real value of land revenues declined by almost two-thirds from the Golden Age of the 1750s to the Boxer uprising. From the mid nineteenth century the Qing had mixed success in using commercial taxes, special surcharges and customs revenue to arrest the erosion of their traditional agrarian tax-base. Their increasing reliance on tax farmers to collect old and new revenues only increased the illegal "leakage." At the end of day, however, the fiscal crisis came to weigh most heavily upon provincial and county governments, which depended even more than Beijing on land revenue yet were increasingly expected to shoulder additional responsibilities for self-defense, flood control, irrigation and famine relief.[40]

Fiscal crisis directly translated into reduced administrative capacity and indirectly into diminished peasant food security, at least in areas poorly served by the inter-regional rice trade. The ever-normal and charity granary systems which stored as much as 48 million *shih* of reserve rice, wheat and millet in the high Qing were rapidly depleted.[41] "Even in the early eighteenth century, when the population of China was not much more than half of its 1840 (or 1930) level, this amount probably represented little more than 3 or 4 per cent of the nation's grain output."[42] Will cites an edict of 1799 complaining that only one-quarter of the ever-normal granaries had stored their full quotas.[43] Reduced to these levels, the imperial granaries were no longer able to act as an economic flywheel "normalizing" grain prices. By the 1820s, according to R. Bin Wong, the empire-wide grain reserves had fallen below 30 million shih; by the 1850s, they were under 20 million.[44] Twenty years later, at the onset of famine in 1876, there was probably less than 10 million shih left in the entire system.[45]

At a local level, this was often equivalent to complete collapse. Even in the Golden Age, the ever normal mechanism of restocking granaries with autumn purchases had broken down in much of the northwest. Granaries in Shaanxi and Gansu were forced to distribute grain more frequently than they could afford by their own account, and the ensuring deficit had to be financed by Beijing.[46] From the calamitous watershed of the White Lotus Rebellion, the regional disequilibrium between annual harvest and minimum consumption was exacerbated by a vicious circle of declining agricultural productivity, ethno-religious warfare and government insolvency.[47] Gentry-managed community and charity granaries, which took up some of the burden of food security elsewhere (Hunan and Sichuan, for example), were ineffective in braking the decline of state granaries in the impoverished loess areas. As a result, granary inventories in some counties of Shaanxi had fallen to less than 10 percent of their quotas by the early 1870s.[48] On the eve of the great drought, in other words, northwest China was ripe for catastrophe.

The empire-wide rundown in ever-normal granary inventories was also accompanied by an increasing diversion of tribute grain flows from the inland north China plain. Although, as Dwight Perkins points out, the "amount of grain going north to Peking was trivial in comparison to total national output (0.2–0.3 per cent)," it represented about 15 percent of the revenues of the central government, and, as we saw in the case of the 1743 drought, constituted a strategic famine reserve close at hand in north China. Most of the tribute was supplied by four provinces (Jiangsu, Jiangxi, Anhui and northern Zhejiang), and there was intense lobbying by the Jiangnan elites to substitute the maritime route for the Grand Canal. "Beginning in the 1870s, the coastal steamer rapidly replaced grain-tribute junks on the Grand Canal. By the 1890s, the only substantial amounts of grain carried by canal junk were the shipments of millet from Shantung." Beijing's port of Tianjin (Tientsin) boomed as a result, while the older Canal entrepôts with their large workforces of bargemen and laborers (key constituencies of the Boxer uprising) declined into permanent depression.[49] Although the imperial granaries at Tongzhou, near Beijing, were still theoretically available for relief campaigns, Will shows that by the end of the Jiaqing reign in 1820 tribute grain had ceased to play a major role in combating famine.[50]

As the state infrastructure deteriorated, the Empire increasingly relied on a combination of cash handouts and local philanthropy to relieve famines. In 1831, the Daoguang emperor, noting "the wretched condition" of the imperial granaries, "remarked that 'for this reason, when a province is hit by calamity, [the local authorities] rarely ask that [the victims] be aided with ever-normal grain; in general, they content themselves with applying for silver from the provincial treasury and converting it into copper cash to be distributed [to the population].'"[51] Although the Tongzhi reformers temporarily returned to a vigorous hands-on approach to famine relief when the region around the capital was successively baked by drought and drowned by flood in 1867–68, it was a last hurrah for Confucian statecraft in the heroic mode of Fang Guancheng. Henceforth Beijing's principal response to weather disasters was the tardy donation of cash. As we have seen in the accounts of the 1877 and 1899 famines, the resort to monetary relief had fatal flaws.[52]

The market, for example, was frequently unable to accommodate emergency demand. Either the explosion in grain prices quickly exceeded the minimal sur-

vival value of cash relief, or, as in the extreme case of Shanxi, there was simply
not enough grain locally available at any price. Attempts to purchase and transport large amounts of grain at one time into the loess highlands only produced
catastrophic traffic pile-ups like that at Guguan Pass in 1877. Unlike the Yangzi
Valley, where water transport of rice remained cheap and efficient, grain commerce in the drier northern provinces, especially during droughts, suffered from
the paucity of navigable waterways. In John Lossing Buck's epic study, *Land Utilization in China*, only two out of fifty-one northern villages had access to water
transport in contrast to twenty-three out of eighty in the south.[53] From the perspective of a society dependent on commercial grain for survival during famine,
overland transport was staggeringly expensive and inefficient. Summarizing the
Royal Asiatic Society's extensive 1893–94 investigations of inland communications in China, T. Kingsmill marveled that a civilization so brilliant in its development of water transport could entirely abdicate road construction. "Probably no
country in the world," he wrote, "has paid so little attention to roads," especially
in the north where "neglect culminates."[54]

Table 11.1
Transport in the North China Plain: Comparative Efficiency

|  | Tonnage | Cost Index |
|---|---|---|
| River junks | 40–100 tons | 1.0 |
| Carts | 1 ton | 3.3 |
| Pack mules | .125 ton | 8.2 |
| Coolies | .09 ton | 8.6 |

Source: Data from George Cressey, *China's Geographic Foundations*, New York 1934, p.
179.

Mary Wright long ago suggested that deliberate neglect of inland arteries of
transport was rational policy from Beijing's point of view. State-power in imperial
China was frequently equated with immobilization of the peasantry and their iso-
lation from disruptive ideological or economic influences. The Qing, in this interpretation, were no more eager to encourage the peasantry to move around the
country than they were to invite foreign powers to use railroads to bring troops
and cheap factory goods into the interior. Even the reformers of the 1860s "were
interested in improved communications only in so far as they might affect mari-

time defense and the food supply of the capital."[55] This neglect, however, would over time grow into a principal popular grievance. The Communists in Shaanbei and other northern base areas in the late 1930s won great popularity for making road-building a top priority of their rural reconstruction program.[56]

## Corruption and Devolution

The monetarization of relief also made it even easier for venal officials to pilfer funds. The rampant practice in the nineteenth century of selling local offices to generate relief funds dramatically expanded the number of lower-level fiscal predators. The ever-normal granaries and the grain-tribute administration were especially lush targets for corrupt officials in the Rasputin-like mold of Heshen, the notorious late-eighteenth-century minister of revenue with whom the Qian-long emperor probably had a homosexual liaison. As Will points out, everyone in late Qing China, from the emperor to secret societies, believed that honesty and efficiency in local government had declined dramatically from the 1790s:

> As early as 1801, the year the Jiaqing emperor closely supervised the special mea-sures carried out in Zhili in the wake of severe flooding, he was struck by the troubling thought that the skyrocketing cost of relief in other provinces was per-haps better explained by the profits made by the "clerks and runners" than by the number of ruined peasants pure and simple; and later in the reign, various memo-rials spoke of the extortions exacted by investigators and subbureaucrats, unau-thorized deductions from provincial funds, registers of disaster victims drawn up without verification of any kind, distribution centers established with attention to actual needs, gruel containing sand, fraudulent exchange rates in converting silver to copper, and other abuses.[57]

By the coronation of the unhappy Xiangong emperor a half century later, these abuses, seemingly magnified by the Qings' inability to defend Chinese sovereignty, had become core revolutionary grievances. As prolonged drought turned into famine through much of Guangxi and Guangdong in 1848–49, "cor-rupt local magistrates connived with local grain merchants to manipulate distri-butions from the local granaries so as to drive the already exorbitant rice price higher."[58] When, ultimately, rice became "as high as the price of pearls," starv-ing peasants attempted to open granaries and were slaughtered by the magis-

trates' troops. As a direct result, countless thousands flocked to the angry millenarian banner of "God's Chinese Son," Hong Xiuquan. Later, in the summer
of 1852, when the Taiping kings paused in Daozhou (southern Hunan) to issue
their famous proclamations against the Qing, they accused their rulers of "withholding public relief from victims of flood, famine and other natural calamities in
order to decrease the Chinese population."⁵⁹ The benevolent eighteenth-century
welfare state of the Yongzheng emperor was not even a distant memory. "When-
ever floods and droughts occur, [the Manchus] do not show the slightest compassion; they sit and watch the starving people wander by until the bleached bones
grow like wild weeds."⁶⁰

The Tongzhi Restoration did little to restore popular confidence in local government's ability to provide protection against disaster. Despite the reformers'
rhetorical exaltation of the social compact between the Qing and the peasantry,
one of their most significant initiatives (in the name of rewarding the loyal elites
who had fought the Taiping) was a vast sale of Confucian merit that increased
the caste of degree-holders from 1.1 million to 1.45 million.⁶¹ The venal appetite
of this enlarged gentry explains why peasants were groaning under new fiscal
oppressions while Beijing was simultaneously complaining that it was broke.
Granary administration, in particular, was treated as a spoils system by local col-
lusions of corrupt officials and grain merchants. By 1893, when the first Western
study of Chinese finances was completed, more than half of the north's tribute
grain was estimated as lost to pilferage.

> The officials in charge of the granaries juggle with the rice, and every few years
> a great scandal occurs; old and decayed rice is paid out in the place of new rice,
> weights and measures are falsified, the Manchu soldiery are found to be selling their
> nominal rights for what they will fetch, and to be actually buying eatable rice in the
> market, and so on. Peking, in short, is like a filthy colony of rats, each official living
> in a hole of his own, and preying, when he can and where he can, upon the public
> storehouse.⁶²

Although honest local officials still struggled heroically to restock the granaries,
their efforts were everywhere undercut by corrupt subordinates. Murray cites
the example of a magistrate in Shaanxi's Han-ch'eng county – which in the early
1890s had not yet recovered from the 1877–78 disaster – who conscientiously

bought up grain surpluses during good years to fill twenty local granaries. When drought destroyed the harvest in 1900, he turned confidently to his reserves only to find that the granary administrators had secretly sold off two-thirds of the inventory.[63] As a result, the county was almost depopulated by famine. (When the empress-mother arrived in Zian at the end of the famine, she ordered a thorough review of the famine-relief accounts "that ended in cutting off the heads of three of the most prominent mandarins of the province.")[64]

In face of such obdurate corruption and overwhelmed by fiscal exigencies, the imperial government disengaged itself even further from direct administration of food security. As Mary Rankin, Mark Elvin and others have emphasized, the formidable state capacities of the eighteenth century were gradually devolved to the non-office-holding gentry during the long nineteenth-century siege by imperialism and domestic rebellion. Nouveaux riches merchants and landowners increasingly coordinated tax collection, local law-and-order, flood control and famine relief. When the resources of the locally managed *zhenju* (relief bureaus) and their privately stocked charity granaries were inadequate to the task, the late Qing state turned to the wealthy Jiangnan elites, who donated rice and cash, provided assistance with transportation, and opened their city gates to famine refugees from the north. But this makeshift system, which failed so catastrophically in 1877 and 1899, was never a real alternative to the vertically integrated state infrastructure of the previous century with its abilities to maintain local ever-normal granaries as well as to carry out the inter-regional transfers that "alone made large-scale and long-lasting famine relief possible."[65]

The reconstruction of the granary system and restoration of peasant food security, accordingly, became central demands of all anti-Qing revolutionaries. Long before Mao's "Yenan Way," the Taipings in their utopian manifesto, *The Land System of the Heavenly Dynasty*, had envisioned a more directly "communist" system for redistributing the entire agricultural surplus through new state granaries.

All land under heaven will be cultivated in common by all who live under heaven.... [The produce from] all land under heaven will circulate to equalize abundance and scarcity. The produce of one locality where the harvest is good will be transported to give relief to another place where famine occurs.... At harvest time the *liang-*

*ssu-ma* [headmen of twenty-five households] will supervise the *wu-chang* [headmen of five households] and will, after deducting [quantities of grain] sufficient for food for each of the persons belonging to the twenty-five households until the next harvest, [collect] the surplus and send it to the state granaries.[66]

## Paying the Bill for the Golden Age

North China's history has been shaped by its paradoxical position within the larger spatial economy of the Empire: economically peripheral, it remained the administrative core. The geographical separation of economic and political power in China – equivalent to the distance between London and Berlin – has been unique for a land-based state. Since the early Sung Dynasty, the greater part of the economic surplus had been produced in the lower Yangzi Valley, but the largest center of surplus consumption usually has been in the north (Chang'an, Dadu, Kaifeng and Beijing) on the edge of the steppe, close to the nomadic sources of Jurchen, Mongol and Manchu military hegemony.

The extraordinary transportation infrastructure – comprising the Grand Canal, its feeder waterways and storage depots – used to move surplus wealth from south to north also made it possible for the Qings to ecologically stabilize northern agriculture with vital imports of rice, fuel, timber and stone. In the mid eighteenth century, as we have seen, the imperial bureaucracy could mobilize famine relief more effectively than any European polity. Yet a century later, Beijing seemed almost powerless to intervene in one of the most deadly chain reactions of civil war, foreign intervention, climate disaster, disease and famine in history. This collapse in state capacity to control the natural as well as social environments has long vexed historians of modern China. "Why did ecological degradation," asks Kenneth Pomeranz in a recent forum, "which up until the mid-eighteenth century was arguably under better control than in Europe or Japan assume crisis proportions thereafter?"[67]

Recent scholarship suggests the necessary distinction between two discrete, if ultimately convergent, environmental crises, developing at separate tempos and levels in the social formation. In the first case, peasant land clearances in the mountainous watersheds of the Yellow, Wei and Huai Rivers accelerated the erosion cycle with inevitably devastating consequences for the plains below. In the second case, the mid-Victorian fiscal crisis of the Qing state, which coincided with skyrocketing costs of flood control arising from increased sedimentation, led to the gradual devolution of hydraulic management to a pauperized peasantry and unwilling gentry. North Chinese agriculture was thus exposed to the most severe climate stress in 200 years (the extreme ENSO cycles of the 1870s and 1890s) precisely when the state was in full retreat from its traditional ecological mandates.

The Qing Golden Age in the eighteenth century, Robert Marks reminds us, was based on a "massive remaking" of Chinese environmental space. Population growth under a system of partible inheritance between 1750 and 1850, at least partly induced by the rising "protoindustrial" demand for family labor in rural handicraft production, put increasing stress on agro-ecological carrying capacity. Unlike Europe, this population explosion was not absorbed through the parallel growth of urban centers or emigration to overseas colonies. Indeed, according to Maddison, "by 1820 the Chinese degree of urbanisation was not much greater than it had been a thousand years earlier," and actually declined from the early Qing (6.8 percent of population) to the late Qing (5.9 percent).[68] As in India, the long economic recession in the first half of the nineteenth century – due in China's case to the negative balance of trade and silver outflows caused by opium imports – caused widespread urban unemployment and pushed many workers into the countryside.[69]

Instead, the eighteenth-century population boom (estimates, as we have seen, range wildly from a 33 percent to a 200 percent increase) was largely accommodated by ecologically unsustainable settlement in formerly uncultivated mountains, foothills and wet lowlands. Peasant pioneers and improving landowners brought nearly 25,000 square kilometers of new land under the plough during the eighteenth century – most of it hilly or periodically inundated. The immediate advantages were great.[70] Legendary profits were made clear-cutting the forests that still protected the watersheds of China's great rivers. Worrisome congestion in the fertile valleys and plains was temporarily relieved by mass emigration into foothill and mountain peripheries where New World crops like maize and sweet potatoes allowed cultivators to wrest a living from sandy, unfertilized soils previously regarded as untillable. At the same time, land-hungry peasants and urban speculators built dikes to reclaim hundreds of thousands of acres of rich marsh and bottom land for commercial agriculture.

By the last quarter of the eighteenth century, however, the marginal returns from forestry and land conversion were near the vanishing point. Manchuria aside, Rhoads Murphey estimates that Chinese forests "were already largely gone by 1820, almost wholly by 1860."[71] Too many peasants clung to eroding hillsides or struggled to drain malarial wetlands. Overflow basins that managed flood waters, as well as reservoirs that stored water for irrigation in dry spells, had been ill-advisedly turned into fields, with predictably disastrous results.[72] Thus the great clearances that had subsidized the Golden Age became root causes of intractable ecological crisis during the century that followed. This previously little-understood environmental history of Qing population growth has been admirably explored in recent case-studies of the Pearl River watershed (Marks) and the Dongting Lake region in the middle Yangzi Valley (Perdue). In both regions, the early windfalls of virgin soil cultivation were inevitably followed by environmental degradation and increased vulnerability to natural hazards. Nature collected the bill for eighteenth-century prosperity in deferred payments of drought, flood and famine.[73]

## The Denudation of North China

The greatest downstream tragedies, however, took place in the system of the Yellow River and its major tributaries. Shaanxi's Wei River Valley, studied by several authors, is a sobering example. At the end of the Ming Dynasty, the foothills of the Chinling Mountains, which formed the valley's southern border, were still heavily wooded. During the early and mid-Qing, however, huge "timber factories" mobilizing armies of 3,000 to 5,000 woodcutters and laborers systematically denuded the forests. Subsequently, thousands of poor peasants from congested counties as far away as Szechwan and Hupei were officially encouraged by tax exemptions and other subsidies to emigrate to the region. (Edward Vermeer stresses the perverse role of Qing tax policies that often rewarded the exploitation of marginal lands while penalizing farmers for improvements on existing, high-quality plots.)[74] New World crops allowed cultivation on soils that were "too sandy, too acidic, too infertile and drought-prone to have supported settled populations in any numbers in the past."[75] Maize and potatoes, especially, could be cultivated on sloping, unterraced hillsides with thin soil layers otherwise unsuitable for rice or wheat. However, the price of this cheap subsistence was increased erosion that eventually became catastrophic.

Within a few generations, geomorphological forces had crossed a dynamic threshold and gullies grew with alarming speed, deepening sometimes by several hundred feet within the span of a single human lifetime. "By the mid-nineteenth century," writes Murray, "the mountains became barren and the rivers were blocked up."[76] The first modern European visitors, like Baron von Richthofen in 1870, gave vivid accounts of the silting up of the famous Qing irrigation systems, particularly the magnificent complex that had made the Wei plain a hearth of civilization. Similarly, many of the areas in the loess country that Marco Polo had praised for verdancy and the abundance of mulberry trees had become treeless near-deserts by Victorian times.[77] Although foreigners often confused modern and ancient decay (serious hydraulic deterioration in the Wei Valley dated back to Tang times), the nineteenth century administered the environmental coup de grace.

For peasants, meanwhile, the easy living of early pioneer days became an increasingly grim battle for survival on eroding islands of semi-arable soil. "On the lower slopes, by the later nineteenth century, there had been up to a century of maize cultivation with only limited fertilizer; yields began to fall drastically. Potato crops began to suffer seriously from disease.... Yields were unstable; the price of food began to rise, doubling in the nineteenth century, owing to the increasing population and static or declining supplies."[78] Eventually many mountain farmers were unable to produce their own family subsistence, so they turned to fruit trees as a cash crop. "This specialization," Murray explains, "was regarded by the authors of the local history as particularly precarious, because the profit of the entire year depended on a single harvest. Many of the fruit growers were extremely poor, lacking even adequate food and clothing."[79]

The mid-century civil wars completed the denudation of China's surviving forested watersheds:

> Accounts of the time ... repeatedly mention wanton destruction of forests by the Taipings, and equally massive assaults by the Imperial forces in their effort to deny shelter to the rebels. The major weapon seems to have been fire. There are descriptions of former forests which by the 1860s consisted only of blackened stumps over hundreds of square miles. All of this activity was concentrated in the remaining

Figure 11.2  Hillside Farms in Shaanxi
As farming deforested hillsides the erosion rate  increased exponentially.

area within, or around the edges of, the major center of population in China proper
which still had some vestigial forest cover. The mountainous far west was unaffected, but forests there were of little use to the rest of China, where the vast majority of the people lived. Those forests were in turn heavily exploited in the course of
the great Muslim rebellions and their suppression, concentrated in Yunnan and in
Shensi-Kansu, between 1855 and 1878.[80]

Depopulation and ecological devastation was perhaps most extreme in Shaanxi,
where genocidal ethnic warfare killed or displaced an estimated 90 percent of the
Muslim population and left much of the province outside the Wei Valley a wilderness for the Chinese Communists to resettle a full half-century later. As Pauline
Keating points out, the financially strapped Qing "invested only in the pacifica-
tion of Shaanxi, not its reconstruction."

In the absence of both an official resettlement strategy and a sustained program of infrastructural repair and development, local economic systems disintegrated. Whole villages were deserted, the distances between settlements became longer, transport routes fell into disrepair (a process made swifter by the rapid erosion of earthen constructions in loess country), and market centers and trading networks disappeared. Water wells, irrigation and drainage systems, cropland embankments, granaries, and pathways were not maintained.[81]

The same dismal sequence, if less apocalyptically, was repeated everywhere throughout the foothills and loess plateaux of northwest China. "It seemed as if humans had set out to reduce their original environment to only two types of land: carefully maintained, productive, private farmland, and ruthlessly exploited, unproductive, common wasteland."[82] Nor was deforestation, as an account from turn-of-the-century Shandong makes clear, the last stage in the economic exploitation of the foothills and mountains. "All the boys of the village big enough to walk and carry a basket are sent out over the hillsides to collect grass, twigs, and any kind of herbage that can be used as fodder or fuel. Each boy carries an iron grubbing hook, and thus equipped he clambers up the slopes, working away at this task with cheerful energy. Through the industry of this army of human locusts the mountains are denuded of herbage and even roots often grubbed up."[83] The stubble that remained on the slopes was burnt to provide fertilizing ash run-off for fields downhill.[84]

As the last local sources of firewood were exhausted, a fuel and lumber famine began to undermine agriculture throughout north China. Despite vast, although poorly mined, coal deposits in Shandong and Shanxi, the rural poor could seldom afford coal, and the breakdown of the Grand Canal system, to be discussed in a moment, inflated its price as well as that of imported wood from central China. Cheap Manchurian timber was available in the coastal cities, but was generally not imported into the interior.[85] "Demand for construction material," wrote an American authority on Chinese forestry in the 1920s, "has been reduced to supply, until in northern Shensi about the only articles of wood within a house are chopsticks, and only the door and the paper window lattice of the house are of wood."[86] Likewise in southwest Shandong, Pomeranz estimates that the fuel supply per peasant household at the time of the Boxer upheaval was barely a quarter of what was traditionally held to be the subsistence minimum. Scarce

Figure 11.3  A Silted-up Channel in the Wei Valley.

cattle dung, therefore, had to be burnt for heat and less fertilizer was applied to the soil.[87] Alternatively, more intensive efforts had to be made gathering residual vegetation from the hillsides, thus ensuring their complete denudation.[88]

As in India, deforestation enhanced the frequency of hydrological drought by lowering water tables, increasing runoff, and ruining irrigation systems and reservoirs with sedimentation.[89] Fatalistic peasants, all too conscious that they were involuntary actors in a vicious circle of poverty and environmental destruction, quoted Mencius to each other: "mountains empty – rivers gorged." The acceleration of the erosion cycle became nearly exponential. The American forestry expert W. C. Lowdermilk estimated in 1930 that slope denudation in Shanxi and Shandong in the previous century or so had "increased superficial runoff fifty-fold." But the "rate of erosion is increased from one hundred to several thousand-fold."[90] As a result, visitors frequently encountered deforestation's ubiquitous monuments: great stone bridges completely mired in sediment:

> Their arches were partially or entirely blocked by silt, although they had been designed originally to accommodate a deeper, more regular flow of water. One

might in fact have derived a round measure of the chronology of deforestation and siltation in many areas by fixing the date of the bridges (many of them as old as Ming, some more recent) as an indication of the time when the streams were less silt-laden and comparing this with the depth and apparent recency of deposition since.[91]

Traveling in 1923 through northern Shaanxi, the future redoubt of Mao's Long Marchers, Lowdermilk was stunned by the extent to which overcultivation had eroded the landscape into badlands. As soil exhaustion in the eighteenth century led to the substitution of pasturage for agriculture, shepherds began to systematically burn off shrub cover to open land for grass. "The result was that 50% of the groundspace in the region was occupied by erosion gullies, some several hundred feet deep."[92]

Erosion on this scale led to radical changes in the composition of the sediment load carried downstream. For millennia, the Yellow River and its tributaries had conveyed rich loess silt to replenish and fertilize the north China plain. By the nineteenth century, however, accelerated erosion had removed the deep loess cover in many parts of the watershed and the highlands were beginning to erode bedrock and sand instead. As early as 1810, Shaanxi officials were already worried about the vast quantities of sand and gravel that were annually washed from the deforested hillsides, clogging up irrigation ditches and canals in the valleys below. ("People suffer greatly because of this!")[93] By the end of the century, flood-deposited sand was smothering some of the best cropland in north China.

Finally, the denudation of the mountains and hills directly affected the water supply available during droughts in the plains below. "In addition to erosion and flooding," Murphey explains, "deforestation had the predictable effect of lowering the water table, especially critical in north China with its heavy dependence on shallow traditional wells, which increasingly ran dry. Without adequate cover, especially on slopes, to retain and absorb rainfall, ground water reserves were not recharged as they should be by slow release and seepage."[94] In a fuel-famished economy that lacked cheap energy sources (even bullocks) for running hydraulic pumps, the lowering of the water tables below the reach of manually operated windlasses or level poles was a constant and sometimes deadly frustration. Drought-stricken peasants knew that there was plenty of water underneath their fields but had no means to pump it to the surface. It was not until after Liberation that suitably deep wells with electric pumps revolutionized farming in the north China plain.

## The Crisis of River Conservancy

Sedimentation in the Yellow River Delta is a problem in hydraulic control that dwarfs the challenge of all other civilized rivers except perhaps the modern Mississippi. Twentieth-century measurements show that each cubic meter of river water carries an astonishing hundred pounds of silt in suspension. "Approximately one and one-half billion tons of loess are eroded annually in the Yellow River basin. Half of that amount settles out of suspension as the river slows down across the floodplain, and half of it is carried to the sea."[95] (Alternately, before construction of the post-Liberation upstream dam system, the Yellow had a 40 percent silt content at flood stage.)[96] Deposited on the nearly flat north China plain, the sediment will either force the river into chaotic and rapidly changing meanders like a great writhing snake or, if the channel is constricted by human engineering, will lead to the rapid buildup of the riverbed high above the plain.[97] Although the mandarin engineers of the Yellow River Conservancy developed extraordinary expertise in using the diked power of the river to scour deeper and faster channels, sedimentation eventually overcame their most ingenious efforts at streamlining the flow.

There were, in fact, two warring schools about how to tame the Yellow River. One school of river managers wanted to confine the river between high, narrowly spaced levees to maximize its channel-deepening power and emancipate more floodplain for tillage, while the other advocated lower levees set five to ten kilometers apart. "These two strategies," Charles Greer writes, "represent more than different technical approaches to controlling the river. Their roots lie in different philosophical outlooks. Needham associates the construction of close, strong dikes with a Confucianist tendency to curb nature, analogous to the reliance by this school of thought on strict ethical codes for shaping human behavior. He associates widely separated, low levees with the Taoist approach of letting nature follow its own course."[98] Even the Taoists, however, were ultimately forced to respond to the rising bed with higher levees and revetments, as well as more cutoffs, overflow basins, drainage canals and polders.

This inexorable construction program in turn required a growing army of hired labor (the Qing had abolished the Mings' hated corvée), specialist river troops and their overseers. Thus the hydraulic evolution of the river produced a corresponding expansion in the scale, complexity and financial burden of its Conservancy. Soaring costs were aggravated by "excessive bureaucratization" and rampant corruption (especially in the procurement of the sorghum stalks used in revetments) that ultimately sped the system toward collapse.[99] The rising river bed also generated bitter social conflict everywhere along the Yellow's course. "Newer, higher dikes," Vermeer writes, "diverted the flood problem to less well protected flood-prone areas. The city walls might offer protection for county capitals, but the countryside was left to its own devices." Likewise the widespread conversion, usually illegal, of polders and reservoirs to fields increased the river's pressure against its levees and exacerbated the chance of a catastrophic breach.[100]

Inevitably, despite the most arduous efforts of the Conservancy's hydraulic experts, the defenses would fail after an unusually heavy summer monsoon, most likely in a major La Niña year. Angry brown waters would engulf hundreds, even thousands of villages, as in 1898 on the eve of the Boxer Rebellion. More than 1,500 such floods have been recorded since the time of the Han: they are north China's "ordinary" disasters and a major cause of its chronic peasant unrest. Every few centuries, however, cumulative sedimentation, modulated by human action (including both flood control and war), would so reshape the topography of the plain that the river would break free into a completely different channel. Thus eight times in written history the Yellow River has radically switched its path to the sea, moving hundreds of miles from the Yellow Sea to the Gulf of Bohai and back again.[101] These epochal changes of channel, by regionally redistributing the costs of flood control, have had complex political repercussions: indeed, have determined the fate of dynasties.

In 1800, the Yellow River flood-control system, redesigned by the great engineer Pan Jixun between 1577 and 1589, was more than 200 years old. As Randall Dodgen points out, the river "had gone longer without a change of course, but it had never been held in one course for so long by dint of human labor and engineering."[102] It was the singular misfortune of the Qings that this inescapable hydraulic cycle, which in its final stages entailed almost geometrical increases in the costs of dike construction, reached its crisis point in coincidence with eco-

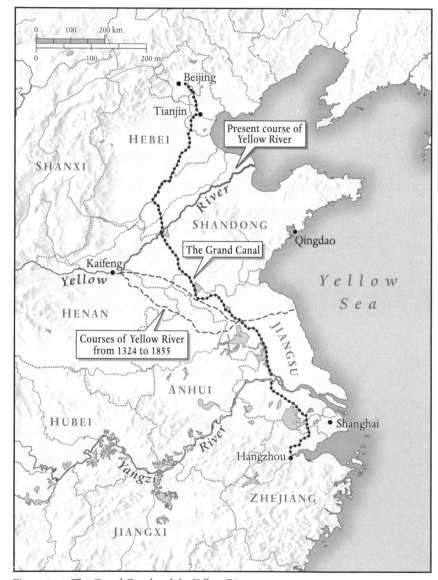

Figure 11.4 The Grand Canal and the Yellow River

nomic recession and the most destructive civil war in history. Already by the early nineteenth century, more than 10 percent of the Imperial budget was devoted to increasingly desperate efforts to control the path of the Yellow River, "an expense totally without parallel in the eighteenth century."[103] Thereafter, as we saw in Chapter 9, the Qing treasury was rapidly emptied by the forced outflow of silver to purchase opium from British India, the depletion of the Yunnan copper mines, the costs of the Opium Wars, and, finally, the Taiping catastrophe, which cut off tribute from the middle Yangzi provinces for almost a decade.

As early as 1837, Conservancy officials had warned Beijing that, despite huge expenditures on reinforcement, many of the dikes in Henan were too weak to withstand high water. In the event, the three successive floods of 1841–43, coincident with the First Opium War, dealt crippling blows to the Qing's simultaneous effort to contain both imperialism and the river. As Dodgen points out, "the cost to the state in social disruption, lost agricultural income, and relief and repair funds was immense. Combined with the expense of the Opium War and the state's already weakened fiscal condition, these floods left the state treasury barren."[104] For another decade, during the last years of the Daoguang emperor, troops and engineers gamely struggled to restore control over a river seemingly becoming wilder each year. "It was not until a second series of floods took place in 1851, 1852 and 1853 that the Qing's commitment to Yellow River conservancy began to waver. Concerned with the growing scope of the Taiping Rebellion, the state slowed the pace of repairs and redirected funds to the struggle against the rebels."[105]

While Beijing was thus diverted, the Yellow in 1855 broke free of its old channel, hijacked the course of the Daqing River, and poured downgrade through Honan and Shandong, drowning hundreds of thousands of peasants and millions of acres of fertile farmland. Flood refugees, ruined farmers and displaced transportation workers, in turn, swelled the ranks of the Nian rebels and local "Turban bandits" who controlled a vast swathe of territory from the Huai River to the new course of the Yellow. (Most of the Nian, Jonathan Spence points out, were "poor peasants or ex-peasants struggling to survive in a bleak environment of worked-out soil, harsh winters, and unstable river systems subject to appalling floods.")[106] The alliance of the Taiping and Nian in the aftermath of the channel-switching catastrophe might have doomed the Qing had not a simultaneous civil

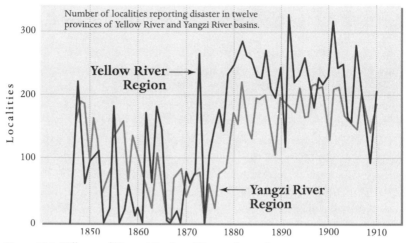

Figure 11.5  Yellow and Yangtzi Regions Disaster Reporting

Source: B. Stavis, "Ending Famines in China," in Garcia and Escudero, p. 117.

war amongst the Taiping leaders in Nanking fatally splintered the Kingdom of
Heavenly Peace.

Fighting desperately for its survival on multiple fronts, meanwhile, the Empire
was powerless to control nature in the Yellow River plain. Only after the defeat
of the Taipings in 1865 could Beijing focus again on the complex, almost overwhelming, problem of the unleashed Yellow River. Arguing that neglect of the
hydraulic infrastructure had been a principal cause of the Taiping and Nian
revolts, the Qing hero Zeng Guofan made "repair of old waterworks and the
construction of new and improved systems ... a cardinal point in Restoration
planning." His expensive schemes for forcing the Yellow back into its old channel and for developing new irrigation in eastern Hebei, however, collided with
other equally ambitious plans for military modernization and the reconquest of
Central Asia. The Manchu generals, not surprisingly, were a more powerful lobby
than millions of ruined peasants in Shandong and Hebei. Even established water
agencies, like the General Office for the Control of the Huai, "unable to compete
with the armies for funds," were forced to close up shop, and thus "water control
continued to be dealt with in piecemeal fashion."[107]

The resulting decline in hydraulic control after 1870, in the Yangzi as well as the Yellow River basins, has been graphically depicted by B. Stavis as a sudden spike in locally reported disasters (see Figure 11.5).

## Abdicating Hydraulic Control

The Tongzhi Restoration's failure to resolve the flood control crisis ignited an epic battle between regional elites. The wealthy Jiangan gentry, for their part, were delighted by the northern migration of the Yellow River, which relieved them of their traditional burden in taxes, labor duties, flood relief and periodic flood damage. On the other side, local gentry in western Shandong faced ruin: by the early 1880s the channel had grown high above the plain and flooding had become chaotic and almost impossible to contain. Then "in 1886–87, it briefly appeared that the river gods had come to Shandong's aid as the Yellow broke its banks in Henan and returned to a southern course. Shandong peasants were said to have resisted government requisitions of millet stalks to repair the break, while Shandong officials lobbied Beijing to let the river resume its old course. But the province's political weight was no match for that of Jiangnan and its powerful governor-general.... After a year's respite, the breach was repaired and the river returned to continue its devastation of northwest Shandong."[108]

This *political* decision to keep flood waters channeled through the north China plain, Esherick points out, reflected the emergent control of the rich coastal cities over inter-regional resource flows. It was also a decisive step in the long campaign by the Jiangnan commercial elites to shift the transport of Beijing's annual grain tribute from the Grand Canal to coastal shipping.[109] Indeed one of the major consequences of the Yellow River's change of channel was to cut off the clear waters of the Wen River that fed the Grand Canal and kept critical sections navigable during El Niño droughts. Periodic attempts to use the Yellow River to replenish the Canal were no solution since its waters deposited too much silt. As a result, traffic along the Canal began its steep decline, with only the smallest boats able to proceed along the stretches vulnerable to drought.[110] As we have seen, the resulting bottleneck was fatal to relief efforts during the 1876–78 drought-famine. In the 1890s the water-starved northern sections of the Canal were abandoned, and in 1901 the grain tribute was formally consigned to coastal shipping and the new railroad between Tianjin and Beijing. The decline of the Canal redounded to the great profit of the two British-owned steamship lines – the Ewo (Jardine Matheson & Co.) and Taikoo (Butterfield & Swire) – who from the 1870s dominated the maritime transport of rice, cotton and other staples.[111] (Japan, by contrast, banned foreign flags from its coastal trade.)

This abdication of hydraulic control in inland north China was perhaps the most portentous consequence of the growing imperialist pressure on the Qing. "The foreign onslaught," writes Pomeranz, "destroyed basic principles of Ming-Qing statecraft, particularly a commitment to social reproduction that had often required rich areas to subsidize the infrastructure of poorer ones. Instead foreign pressures helped impart a quasi-mercantilist logic to the actions of a state that was struggling to survive. Resources had to be used where they did the most to protect China's autonomy from direct intervention or the consequences of foreign debt or both." In effect, Beijing resorted to "regional triage" by abandoning the costly upkeep of the Yellow River dikes and the Grand Canal in order to concentrate on creating new armies, coastal arsenals and flood-control works around the mouth of the Yellow River "where major floods seemed likely to provide excuses for further foreign encroachment." Whereas in the eighteenth century Qing policies had served to reduce regional inequalities, using tribute grain as a tool to regulate the flow of resources within the Empire, the decision to place all bets on the coastal-oriented economy exploded regional differentials. The Yangzi landlords, coastal merchants and British shipping interests profited directly from this neomercantilist orientation, while the inland North now became peripheralized in every sense.[112]

Except in the Tianjin-Beijing region, which was now provisioned by sea, the ruin of the Grand Canal system grievously undermined food security in the north, especially in the event of drought-famines, which tended to be longer in duration and larger in area than flood-famines. It also wrecked the economies of the famous canal towns and grain depots. From the jobless ranks of former boatmen and Canal laborers the Boxers recruited some of their most militant leaders and fighters; as did the Communist Party in the 1930s and 1940s from their descendants.[113]

Moreover without the Canal to transport timber and stone, it became increasingly difficult to keep the Yellow River within its embankments. "Lacking stone, brick, or often even wood, dike builders used various inferior materials. The most common was *gaoliang* (a type of sorghum) stalks.... At best, they might last three years; one to two years was common, and improperly cut stalks, lacking the plant's roots, would decay in months."[114] In 1891 Beijing disbanded most of the specialized battalions of "river troops" (*ying*) who maintained the dikes and devolved responsibility for flood control, like famine relief, to the impoverished counties of the plain. Within a generation, fully one-fifth of the region's net income and an equivalent proportion of its labor-time were consumed in Sisyphean efforts to defend agriculture against almost annual flood destruction.[115]

This unraveling of centralized hydraulic control had repercussions at every level of environmental management. In contrast to India, where the traditional hydraulic infrastructure in dry regions consisted of free-standing improvements (wells, ditches and tanks) that seldom depended upon a massive central project, public works in north China functioned only as an integrated and coordinated hierarchy. Flood control, canal management and local irrigation were largely inseparable. *Shuili* ("water benefits") or village-level irrigation farming, as well as local drainage, depended upon the *hegong* ("riverworks"): regional networks of dikes, levees and master canals. A hegong system like the Yellow River Conservancy may have been designed for flood control rather than irrigation (diversion of water from the raised river channel was outlawed because of the danger of breaching the dikes), but its reliable operation was the prerequisite for stable agriculture of any kind. "Until the main drainage arteries are made effective," wrote the American agricultural expert Loessing Buck in 1938, "local drainage systems will be of limited value."[116] Poor water management, in turn, exacerbated the problem of land scarcity. Marshes formed where the Yellow River dikes bisected local streams, and vast sections of valuable cropland were lost to waterlogging, salinization and sand sedimentation.

Finally, as in India, "small irrigation" lost much of its state sponsorship during the recessions and fiscal retrenchments of the nineteenth century. On a macro-scale, Maddison calculates an absolute decline in irrigated cropland from 21.7 million hectares (or 29.4 percent of arable) in 1820 to 20 million hectares (18.5 percent) in 1952.[117] On a regional scale, studies of Shaanxi's Wei Valley contrast the attention given to irrigation under the early Qing to its political neglect in the nineteenth century. Thus in the aftermath of the drought of 1690–92, a famous mandarin, Wang Hsin-Ching, published a treatise on famine administration in the Wei Valley urging the government to help peasants tap plentiful groundwa-

ter reservoirs. Given the region's unreliable transport links with the surplus-producing provinces, Wang advocated well-digging and self-sufficiency as the "only
'solid and reliable' plan for preventing future drought-famines."[118] Later agricultural reformers in the loess region echoed Wang's recommendations about peasant-managed irrigation while specifically warning against large-scale, centrally
managed projects that encouraged official corruption, pitted upstream against
downstream villages, and were ultimately unsustainable. There is considerable
evidence, moreover, that Shaanxi's eighteenth-century governors authorized significant investment in wells, irrigation and drainage under the direct supervision
of energetic hsien magistrates.[119] The result in many cases was a 200 percent to
300 percent increase in the output of grain and cotton.[120]

In the tumult of the nineteenth century, irrigation subsidies were more or less
abandoned. The predictable consequences were a sharp decline in agricultural
productivity and a concomitant increase in vulnerability to drought and flood.
Murray points to Ching-yang, traditionally the richest county in the entire Wei
Valley, where "agriculture was crippled" by the late nineteenth century as a result
of the deterioration of the irrigation system. "A similarly depressing scene was
revealed in the 1882 history of Hua-chou, located in the southeastern sector of
the valley, where neglect of water control was also blamed for the decline of local
agriculture. Not only had the irrigation ditches often become useless, but the
natural waterways had silted up, and flooding along the riverbanks had destroyed
much of the county's best farmland."[121] Neglect of irrigation (only 6.8 percent
of cultivated acreage in north China in 1932) continued through the Republican
period. The famous Mass Education Movement study (1926–33) of Ting Hsien
in Hebei concluded that 30,000 additional small wells were needed in this single
county to fully realize its agricultural potential.[122]

The failure of successive warlord, Guomindang and Japanese occupation governments to improve local irrigation, like their similar inability to tame the
Yellow River, became powerful factors in rallying the northern peasantry behind
the program of the Communist Party. After Liberation (and despite the costs
of the Korean intervention), water conservancy was duly accorded the highest
priority in successive agricultural plans, and, according to E. Vermeer, "during
1946–1954 the State funds expended on anti-flood work on the Yellow River
constituted 22-fold the total invested during the period 1914–1932." Dam con-

struction and dike repair in the 1950s was followed in the early 1970s by a pump-well revolution in the north China plain which (measured from 1949) increased pump horsepower 400-fold and quadrupled the irrigated acreage along the Yellow River.[123] Irrigation, in tandem with the expansion of the chemical fertilizer industry, was the most important productive force unleashed by China's agrarian reforms just as it was the principal engine powering India's contemporaneous "Green Revolution."

Yet real environmental stability in north China has proven elusive. Modern hydraulic control has been achieved in the style of the Colorado Basin or Soviet Central Asia: at the cost of enormous wastage without systematic efforts at recycling. Indeed, by the 1990s, the profligate water-use made possible by reservoirs and electric pumps had both dried up the lower Yellow River (which now fails to reach the Bohai Sea most of the year) and lowered the water table 60 meters in the Beijing region. The northern water shortage, according to experts, is "without a doubt the country's most serious ecological problem," a direct threat to further breakneck economic expansion. The recent intensification of the ENSO cycle only magnifies the danger of growth-choking drought. Accordingly, Beijing has opted for the ultimate "Confucian fix": a vast scheme to divert northward millions of acre-feet from the headwaters of the Yangzi, and possibly from the upper reaches of the Mekong and Irrawaddy. Even more than the controversial Three Gorges Dam on the Yangzi, such diversions are fraught with unpredictable environmental and geopolitical hazards.[124]

# Twelve

# Brazil: Race and Capital in the Nordeste

Definition of "drought": "a strategic element in the process of accumulation by large rural production units in the Northeast."

– G. Dias

Nineteenth-century Brazil, also a subcontinent much visited by El Niño, shared two other things in common with contemporary India. First, while nominally independent, its economy, especially in the Nordeste, was so dominated by English investors and creditors that it has become the classic example of an "informal colony" in modern literature on economic dependency.[1] Second, economic development on a national scale ground to a halt during the second half of the nineteenth century with no appreciable increase in per capita income or productivity. While per capita GDP soared by 600 percent between 1800 and 1913 in the United States and even 150 percent in Mexico, there was zero growth in Brazil. A fabulous coffee boom in the São Paulo region was counterbalanced by the equally spectacular economic retrogression of the Nordeste.[2] As in the case of the Deccan, a formerly core region was transformed into a periphery of hunger. Even the *zona da mata*, the Nordeste's lush littoral, suffered a drastic decline in nutrition as real wages plunged 60 percent from 1870 to 1890.[3] Whereas in India, however, increasing vulnerability to famine went hand in hand with notable infrastructural modernization in the late nineteenth century, the modern history of the *sertão* is striking for the absence of any significant state developmental role until the 1960s and the threat of revolution.

## Informal Colonialism and State Capacity

British commercial and financial hegemony in Brazil had ancient roots in Portugal's vassalage to London during the seventeenth and eighteenth centuries. When the Bragança monarchy was relocated under "tremendous British pressure" to Brazil in 1808, the immediate payoff was a commercial treaty that gave British imports preference over those from Portugal. Then in 1827 Emperor Dom Pedro, in return for British recognition of his slave empire, codified dependency in one of the most inequitable trade agreements in history: a nonreciprocal treaty that limited taxes on British imports to 15 percent ad valorum while allowing the British to impose 300 percent tariffs on Brazilian coffee. The Commercial Treaty, according to Cain and Hopkins, transformed Brazil into a "virtual British protectorate."[4] Although the United States made substantial commercial inroads during the 1850s, the Civil War cotton boom re-established British preeminence. On the eve of the Grande Seca, Britain supplied 51 percent of Brazil's imports and consumed 37 percent of its exports.[5]

But the deepest level of British hegemony was financial. Chronic trade deficits were repeatedly financed by punitive British loans whose interest payments generated permanent budget deficits which, in turn, were financed by yet more foreign bonds.[6] "The London Rothschilds were the empire's exclusive bond-raising agents, the leading exporters and importers were all British, and all the early railroads were British owned or financed. The largest British bank, the London and Brazilian, had considerably greater financial resources than the semi-official Bank of Brazil."[7] The domestic banking system was stunted and undeveloped. As late as 1888, thirteen of the twenty Brazilian provinces had no local banks at all, and the total capital of the entire national system was only 48 million. The state bank largely confined itself to the conservative management of the money supply in the interest of its British creditors.[8]

Domestic capital formation as a consequence was severely bridled. "The foreign banks were notorious ... [for] their reluctance to make long-term loans to agriculture or domestic concerns."[9] Commerce, in turn, was skewed toward foreign middlemen and British imports, above all in the Nordeste. In 1890s Bahia, for example, only one of eleven licensed exporters was Bahian; and twenty-four of sixty-four import houses specialized in imported British textiles.[10] Foreign capital, moreover, vigilantly policed the growth of any saplings of competitive, indigenous industrialism like that imagined in the utopian *literatura do Norte* of Franklin Tavora. ("If capital and credit were mobilized, if agriculture, industrial and artistic markets were put in place, we would see at every turn a Manchester or a New York....")[11] When local entrepreneurs occasionally tried to increase value-added income by setting up cotton-related manufactures, British exporters punctually retaliated. Warren Dean cites the telling example of a sewing thread mill in Alagoas that was purchased by an English firm for the sole purpose of dismantling it and dumping the machinery into the São Francisco River.[12]

Despite its elites' vast aspirations to a modernizing tropical empire, the developmental autonomy of the Brazilian state was thus circumscribed by foreign debt, a primitive banking system and the volatility of its export income. Leff argues that in land-rich Brazil, as contrasted to India and Japan, there was "little pressure of population on land," thus "Ricardian rent, the basis for land taxation, was small." The Empire, as well as the conservative Republic that succeeded it in 1889, relied on export taxes for revenue, but "until the end of the nineteenth century, the volume and growth of Brazil's foreign trade were too small to permit a high level of government expenditure."[13] In the 1890s, as coffee prices stalled then fell, debt service soared to half the federal budget.[14] As drought and famine again desolated the Nordeste, the Republic was hard-pressed even to pay for the bullets to kill Conselheiro's followers.

The adoption of the international Gold Standard during the 1870s "automated," as it were, Brazil's unequal exchange relationships. Although Rio might balk at British attempts to steer its foreign policy, London retained through the early 1900s quasi-veto power over major capital flows within the Brazilian economy. When some Brazilians protested the draconian terms of the Funding Loan of 1898, which confiscated the entirety of customs revenue for debt repayment, they were forceably reminded that dreadnaughts were the City's debt collectors of last resort. "Lord Rothschild, anticipating that the resolve of the recipients might weaken, took care to point out, in a manner which was unauthorised but managed to sound authoritative, that the alternative, repudiation, would involve not only 'the complete loss of the country's credit' but might also 'greatly affect Brazil's sovereignty, provoking complaints that could arrive at the extreme of foreign intervention.'"[15]

Informal colonialism, however, did not affect Brazil's regions equally. If the northeastern sugar fazendas were the very paradigm of dependence upon British capital, the southern coffee industry was relatively more independent. "The paulistic market," Ruthanne Deutsch points out, "was never the private sphere of influence of a single country or a single financial combine."[16] First linked to the coast by railroad in 1872, the fertile São Paulo region was supplying half of the world's coffee by the 1890s. An informal pact between the Republican parties of São Paulo and Minas Gerais after the overthrow of the Empire in 1889 "guaranteed these two states control of the economic policy of the central government," supplanting the old landowning elites of Rio who had been the chief beneficiaries of the Empire. The new dispensation was sweetened, however, by an elaborate system of bribes and concessions that buttressed the local power of the *coroneis* in the smaller states.[17]

Despite its nationalist rhetoric, the "Revolution of 1889–91," as Dean emphasizes, did nothing to address export dependency or the financial dominance of the City of London. Indeed, with the consolidation of Paulista power, Brazil became a monoculture. "It is remarkable that Brazil, a country of immense territory and varied resources, participated in world trade essentially as a planter of a single crop: coffee."[18] The developmental ambitions of the new Republic, moreover, were almost entirely concentrated on railroad construction in the dynamic coffee-growing core. "National integration" meant little more than the Paulistas in Congress occasionally scratching the backs of other oligarchs. Unlike Victorian India with its impressive railroads and inter-regional grain trade, Brazil until the early twentieth century remained an "archipelago" of distinctive economies separated by dauntingly high internal costs of transportation. Indeed, "class interests were so disparate as to raise serious questions concerning the validity of using the nation as a unit of analysis."[19]

The rise of the coffee states inevitably accelerated the decline of the northern sugar littoral. Contemporary Brazilians are used to thinking of their country

Table 12.1

Unequal Regional Development

(Per Capita Product)

|  | 1872 | 1900 | Change |
|---|---|---|---|
| Ceará | £2.2 | £0.8 | −275% |
| Rio Grande do Norte | £0.4 | £0.2 | −100% |
| Bahia | £4.0 | £3.9 | −3% |
| São Paulo | £3.1 | £15.7 | +506% |

Source: Mircea Buescu, "Regional Inequalities in Brazil During the Second Half of the Nineteenth Century," in Barioch and Levy-Leboyer, p. 352.

as "Belindia: Belgium in the south, India in the north," but as Deutsch shows, "around 1870, the quality of life and the level of economic development in the Nordeste rivaled, if it did not surpass, that of the Southeast."[20] This quickly changed, however, as real per capita income in the once economically dominant north fell by 30 percent (to 1913) in tandem with the collapse of its chief exports. Sugar and cotton, which in 1822 comprised 49 percent of Brazil's export income, contributed barely 3 percent in 1913 against the 60 percent represented by coffee.[21] Meanwhile, local markets were supplanted by warehouses at railroad hubs and town life atrophied. The rapid urbanization of the southeast after 1880 contrasted with relative deurbanization in the north. [22]

The dismal decade of the 1890s, which combined drought with the international deflation of commodity prices and a national financial panic, was particularly devastating in the Nordeste. By 1897, for example, the transport price of sugar exceeded the selling price offered by brokers, and numerous plantations and *usinas* (sugar refineries) went belly up.[23] ("Only southern Bahia's cacao region avoided the overall economic decline of the 1890s, chiefly because prices for cacao on the world market rose during this period and planters were able to profit from cheaper labor costs because of an influx of migrants driven from the sertão by drought.")[24]

## Eugenics and Economic Involution

As Leff has pointed out, it is not immediately obvious why the late-nineteenth-century Nordeste should have undergone such extraordinary economic devolution. Certainly other primary producers made up for falling export prices with higher productivity and increased output. "In view of the rapid growth of world demand for cotton and sugar during the nineteenth century, Brazil's failure to expand its exports of these products much more vigorously seems astonishing." His own explanation hinges on the exchange-rate consequences of Brazilian coffee's dominant position in the world market. Under the gold standard system, strong coffee earnings led to the automatic appreciation of the milreis, which in turn raised northern sugar and cotton prices to uncompetitive levels. The Nordeste's biggest problem, in this view, was its monetary integation with the rest of Brazil. "The coffee-dominated exchange rate," writes Leff, "squeezed factor returns and priced ever-larger quantities of the northeast's sugar and cotton out of the world market."[25]

The decline of export competitiveness brutally pruned the foliage of the Nordeste's class structure. If successive southern-dominated governments assuaged the great northern oligarchs with regular political kickbacks (often in the guise of "drought aid"), more modest fazendeiros were left to the mercy of market forces. From about 1875, control over production began to pass into the hands of the owners (often foreign or foreign-born) of modernized usinas. "The capability of the usinas to handle a greater load of cane called for further monopolistic consolidation of land resources; in the wake of this process, small and middle landowners became uprooted."[26] The fate of ex-slaves, of course, was unimaginably more difficult in an economic system that no longer required the same huge levies of labor-power. As the Nordeste's economy slumped into a coma, supernumerary labor was either pushed into the sertão's "black, barren fields of hunger" (Tavora) or induced to gamble with disease and exploitation in the rubber forests of Amazonas.

What did *not* happen in the last quarter of the nineteenth century was what neoclassical theory would have predicted as an automatic reflex: the emigration of northern labor to southeastern growth poles. Instead, beginning in the late Empire, national and local governments began to heavily subsidize mass immigration from Italy, Germany and Portugal. Even the elites of the Nordeste fervidly embraced "Europeanization." An extraordinary example was Bahia during the terrible "Two Eights" drought-famine of 1888–89. While state authorities were roadblocking *retirantes'* route to the cities and forcibly interning them by the thousands in camps, they continued efforts to lure European immigrants with expensive subsidies (few were tempted).[27] Southeastern coffee planters, for their part, wanted only "white" overseas laborers after Emancipation, and soon made this federal policy in the new Republic. (The racial preference was later amended to include Japanese as well as southern Europeans.) "Why were the coffee planters in the southeast more willing to finance immigration from Europe than from the northeast?" Leff believes that "part of the answer may have been the prevalent racial attitudes on the part of the coffee planters, which led them to prefer European to mulatto workers," while Deutsch points to "cultural biases on the part of Southeastern planters against native Brazilian workers."[28]

Both understate racism as public policy. Gerald Greenfield has shown how Liberal discourse about drought and development in the late 1870s revolved around urban perceptions of the "dark, primitive world of the hinterland" and "retirante inferiority and aversion to labor."[29] "To the extent that Brazil during the latter portion of the nineteenth century embraced the tenets of positivism, enlightenment notions of progress, and the concomitant scientific racism of thinkers like Buckle and Spencer, the backlanders became not merely curiosities from a bygone age, but detriments to the nation's progress. Evolving institutions of national culture, largely based in Rio and revealing marked influence from Western Europe and the United States, stressed the nation's great potential while lamenting the inadequacies, intellectual as well as moral, of much of the nation's population."[30] The Brazilian Republic, moreover, was probably the first government anywhere explicitly committed to large-scale "positive Eugenics." Leading fin-de-siècle savants like the Bahian scientist Nina Rodrigues corroborated fears that "race mixing was responsible for all social deviance such as banditry, religious heresy, and the like."[31] Whereas mass European immigration into the United States in the 1890s was conceived as simply providing human fuel for the economy, Brazil's elites also wanted to use immigration to radically transform the nation's racial physiognomy. They were obsessed with "de-Africanizing" and "whitening" Brazil.

The War of Canudos, as we have seen, became a macabre racial allegory driven by elite fears of the northern poor whom they denigrated as *caboclos*: a racial caste strongly marked by admixture of Indian ancestry with Portuguese and African. The demonized figure of Antonio Conselheiro was frequently invoked to justify the urgency of Europeanization. ("Always insecure over the rest of Brazil's whispers that Bahia's leading families had intermixed so much with the *gente de cor* during the heyday of slavery, the Bahians seized the conflict as a way to demonstrate their commitment to continued progress on the European model.")[32] In this way, European immigration became the deliberate substitute for either developing the sertão and/or letting the northern poor move southwards.

As a result, scientific racism helped create the mother of all dual labor markets. "The highly elastic supply of labor from overseas meant that output could expand at a rapid pace in Brazil's advanced sector without raising the wages of workers in the rest of the economy."[33] By 1889 the British consul in Pernambuco reported to London "that labor there was cheaper than anywhere in the world except in Asia."[34] As Celso Furtado famously argued, the Nordeste, following the pattern of previous export booms and busts in Brazilian history, regressed on a diet of super-cheap labor. As in Victorian India or late Qing China, the glut of labor-power created massive disincentives to productivity-raising capital investment (the usinas being a partial exception). "This economic 'involution,' as Furtado called it, was the opposite of development because each historical export boom until coffee (brazilwood, sugar, gold, and contemporaneous with coffee, rubber) led to retrogression, not to sustained growth."[35]

## Ecological Decline

Since the emergence of the great *fazendas de gado* in the late seventeenth century, the ecology and economy of the sertão repeatedly have been reshaped by El Niño droughts. The "Leather Age" of the eighteenth century, when fazendeiros made legendary fortunes selling their longhorned cattle and *carne do Ceará* (dried beef) to coastal sugar plantations and the gold mines of Minas Gerais, was brought to an end by the terrible drought of 1791–93, which decimated the semi-wild herds. Some of the big fazendeiros clung to their feudal domains, while others moved to the coast and became absentee landlords, but even more let their cattle ranges be broken up into impoverished shards.[36] The ecology of the sertão was ill-suited to the pressures of many small, marginal ranches. "As a matter of fact," Kenneth Webb has argued, "the sertão is not really very good for cattle," but was adapted to this use when the herds were forced out of the zona da mata by the sugar boom. The productivity of the sertão with its scant forage was notoriously low.

"The carrying capacity of the land was determined not by how many head of cattle were supported by one hectare of *caatinga,* but rather how many hectares of land were required by one beef critter."[37] A typical ranch of 1,000 hectares, for example, might sustain only 50 scrawny cattle; and even the biggest fazendas (10,000 hectares or more) rarely pastured herds larger than 1,000.[38]

In the early nineteenth century, large numbers of subsistence farmers and laborers as well as fugitive slaves, mostly from the adjacent *agreste* of Pernambuco or Bahia, began to move into the sertão for the first time. "Agriculture required little or no investment," writes Chandler in her study of the Cearán sertão of Inhamuns, "and although it was even more susceptible to the disastrous effects of droughts than cattle, recovery was much easier."[39] The vast northeast interior became a frontier safety valve for the social contradictions of the coastal slave economy. "The sertão absorbed the surplus population of the zona da mata during the stagnant periods of the sugar industry, and benefited from the labors and energies of those who, for economic, psychological, or whatever reason, could not integrate themselves into the famous *casa grande e senzala* sugar culture."[40] Between 1822 and 1850, the Empire officially supported this immigration by recognizing homestead claims on land formerly belonging to the sertão's fast-disappearing indigenous peoples.

As the greatest twentieth-century authority on Nordeste agriculture, Jose Guimaraes Duque, has emphasized, most of the new settlers brought labor-intensive, midlatitude farming techniques ill-suited to the dry tropical climate and infertile soils of the sertão.[41] This 650,000-square-kilometer region – Euclydes da Cunha pointedly named his famous book *Os Sertões* rather than *O Sertão* – encompasses a stunning variety of landscapes and local climates. But only the fertile bottomlands along the rivers corresponded to the immigrants' experience and these were monopolized by the cattle fazendas, their orchards and loyal tenants. So the newcomers moved into the humid *serras* (uplands). These hilly soils gave good harvests for a year or two, but quickly lost their fertility. After tragic trial and error, they eventually adapted a semi-nomadic swidden style of agriculture: two years of cultivation followed by eight years of fallow and cattle-grazing.[42] But population pressure eventually forced thousands into the dry sertão or caatinga – characterized by shallow rocky soils and spiny cacti – where ownership was unestablished or where they squatted at the pleasure of the big fazendeiros whose gunmen might remove them at will.[43]

After the termination of legal squatting in 1850, most new immigrants to the sertão simply became *parceiros* (sharecroppers) on fazenda land. Although the backlands were still popularly identified with the picturesque figure of the free-ranging *vaqueiro,* the great majority of the population by midcentury were threadbare subsistence farmers, parceiros or migratory *agregados* (day-laborers). "In the mid-nineteenth century," estimates Levine, "certainly less than 5% and probably less than 1% of the rural population owned land."[44] These poor *sertanejos,* unlike the slaves of the zona de mata, were nominally free men, but access to land and water was as tenuous as the life of a laborer confronted by the *capangas* of an angry landowner. The most powerful fazendeiro in each rural municipio typically held the rank of "coronel" in the old imperial Guardia Nacional, and the system of boss-controlled voting and elite violence, which originated in the coastal sugar plantations then spread to the fazendas, became known as *coronelismo.* It was the "essential partner to economic exploitation, allowing landlords to squeeze the maximum possible surplus from their work-force, eliciting submissiveness and crushing any resistance or attempts to challenge their monopoly over the land."[45] As Hamilton Monteiro has emphasized, high levels of routine violence – whether between squatters and fazendeiros or between competing elite *parentelas* – organized and directed the relations of production in the Victorian sertão.[46]

The slow deterioration of the landscape under the pressure of overgrazing – visible since the late eighteenth century – was accelerated by the slash-and-burn agriculture of the rural poor who cultivated maize, beans and manioc. "In the caatinga especially, impermeable, crystalline rock formations are common, which slope towards the rivers, facilitating rapid run-off, soil erosion, silting up of rivers and evaporation."[47] Poverty became synonymous with the lack of water and clear title to the land. A small number of big fazendas, the enduring centers of oligarchical power, monopolized the perennial water sources and were usually well protected from drought, but the rest of the population in the *semi-arido* was pitifully dependent upon the erratic rainfall. Every year the sertanejo made a desperate wager with a devil we know as El Niño.

The lives of all the dwellers of the backlands were inescapably linked to the fluctuations of the seasons, but none so closely, hence so vulnerable, as the small subsistence farmer. In November and December he would burn off the dry stalks remaining from the previous season, preparing to plant his beans, corn, and manioc in the ashes of the previous crop; if the land had yielded poorly the past year, he might move to a new location. When the first rains arrived, usually in January, he would plant his seeds and hope for their continuance.

In seasons of relatively light rainfall, those able to plant in the *baixos* [pockets of rich soil in streambeds] were better off than those on the higher ground, but they ran the risk of losing their crops to flash floods which might sweep down the creekbeds without warning with heavy local showers upstream. If heavy showers came before the seedlings had taken firm hold, they would be washed out; frequently, plants sprouted only to wither as the rains stopped. In such cases, the farmer would plant again, and if necessary, a third or fourth time. Exhibiting astonishing tenacity and patience, he would plant time and time again, reserving only a minimal stock of seed for food until the harvest.

At intervals, the rain would fail completely, or hold off so long as to make a successful harvest impossible. Only then would the stubborn backlands farmers leave their homes and move toward the better-watered hills, the coast, or, as a last resort, to the towns and cities like "… so many errant ants hunting food wherever they could find it, crossing and recrossing the roads and on them meeting others in similar condition." In the towns they would seek work, or failing that, surrender their pride and beg, but only until such time as they could safely return to their plots of ground.[48]

The drought-famine of 1825, which killed 30,000 in Ceará alone, exposed the full ecological precariousness of the sertão's hybrid cattle and subsistence farming economy in the absence of systems of water storage and irrigation.[49] It caused "such widespread mortality and human dislocation," according to Cunniff, "as to alter radically the settlement and economic patterns of the region." In effect, it revealed that the biological endowments of the sertão were being dangerously mined out. "Cattle were grazed beyond the areas of natural pasture, into the previously shunned arid land and onto the wooded hills, where they came into conflict with the similarly expanding agriculture of the slopes." What cattle on the overstocked ranges did not eat up was quickly stripped away as firewood or fodder by squatters. The infinite network of cattle trails worn into the sterile, friable soil accelerated erosion. In the classic pattern, as the sparsely wooded hillsides were denuded, runoff increased while water tables and springflows declined. It was evident both to the sertanejos themselves as well as the occasional foreign visitor that they were desertifying parts of the backlands and probably altering the climate as well. Some dreamed of a vast irrigation network of wells, dams and reservoirs; others envisioned reforestation "as the route back to the mythical once-verdant sertão."[50]

But there was no source of investment to stabilize or reverse the sertão's ecological decline. The backward cattle industry, little changed since the seventeenth century, supported the autocratic power of the local coroneis but failed to generate an accumulable surplus for irrigation works had such inclinations towards improvement existed amongst the sertão's oligarchs. Even on the great fazendas, hydraulic engineering consisted simply of shallow wells (cacimbas) in creek beds that were dug by hand every May as the surface waters dried up. The few small reservoirs actually built during the nineteenth century were so unusual as to become objects of local awe.[51]

As discussed earlier, the capacity of any layer of government to sponsor irrigation works was constrained by what might be called "triple peripheralization": the underdevelopment of the Brazilian financial system vis-à-vis British capital; the Nordeste's declining economic and political position vis-à-vis Sao Paulo; and the sertão's marginality within state politics vis-à-vis the plantation elites of the coast. Politicians endlessly proposed irrigation schemes, but none were built. Ironically, the State's impotence to develop the sertão was inverted by the littoral elite into the racist caricature of the indolent, backward sertanejo.

## The Cotton Boom

The socio-ecological crisis in the backlands was temporarily hidden from view (as in India and Egypt) by the cotton boom that accompanied the US Civil War. The abdication of the irrigation debate, as Cunniff points out, had ultimately fatal consequences. "Ironically, the most prosperous period in the history of the sertão was to compound the errors and continue the trends of the previous years; the relative affluence of the 1860s was in large part responsible for the horrors of the 1870s."[52] A drought-resistant variety of arboreal cotton was introduced in the sertão and exports to English textile mills from the port of Recife increased from 165,265 kilos in 1845 to nearly 8 million kilos in 1871.[53] Prices almost doubled from 885 reis in 1861 to 1,600 reis in 1863, and "the cotton boom at its zenith

BRAZIL: RACE AND CAPITAL IN THE NORDESTE

Table 12.2
Rise and Fall of the Sertão Cotton Boom

|  | Pernambuco | | Ceará | |
|---|---|---|---|---|
|  | Kilos Exported | Price | Kilos Exported | |
| 1860 | 1.3 million | – | 0.8 million | – |
| 1862 | 2.8 million | – | 0.7 million | – |
| 1864 | 8.4 million | 1.00 | 1.0 million | 1.00 |
| 1866 | 18.2 million | .62 | 2.1 million | .74 |
| 1869 | 15.2 million | .71 | – | .49 |
| 1871 | 16.8 million | – | 7.3 million | .35 |
| 1873 | 15.2 million | .47 | 5.1 million | .35 |
| 1875 | 11.1 million | .35 | 5.8 million | – |
| 1877 | 2.6 million | – | 0.6 million | .24 |

Price: 1864=1.00
Source: Adapted from data in Cunniff, Table II-1, p. 81 and Johnson, *Sharecroppers of the Sertão*, Table 1, p. 20.

reached into nearly every corner of the sertão."[54] The mirage of prosperity was reinforced by the remarkable absence of drought between 1845 and 1869.

But high cotton prices were only a magnet that attracted yet more "landless, directionless subsistence farmers" to the backlands. The labor required during the short vegetative cycle of cotton did not amortize the annual subsistence cost of slaves, so it was usually cultivated by free labor.[55] "Although it is evident that some larger landholders turned to cotton, it was essentially the crop of the poor, who had no previous agricultural investment to hinder their plunge into its culture." As workers deserted the plantations of Pernambuco for the cotton frontier of Ceará's Cariri valley, the sugar barons complained bitterly about the growing labor shortage.[56] By 1876 the poorest stratum of the sertão social order, the landless *agregados*, comprised fully 40 percent of the population of Ceará (epicenter of the 1877 drought).[57]

Although it should have been evident after Appomattox that high-quality US cotton would soon flood the world market, the Cotton Supply Association of Manchester, whose overriding interest (as we saw in Berar) was a permanently overstocked buyer's market in raw cotton, fiercely lobbied Brazilians to bring even more acreage under cultivation. Before long, however, the return of short-staple Southern cotton drove down the price of the varieties that Manchester had promoted so zealously in Egypt, India and Brazil. Desperate sertanejos tried to compensate by producing yet more cotton. But as cotton patches blossomed in the most remote corners of the sertão, the producers were caught in a vise between falling world market prices and high, rigid costs of overland transport to the nearest river ports. Unlike India, the Nordeste lacked a railroad infrastructure, and unlike China, which also suffered from transportation bottlenecks, it lacked a huge domestic market to encourage value-added cotton handicrafts. The only hope for saving the sertão's cotton industry was a crash program of railroad and road construction in the interior. As Cunniff explains, the imperial government toyed in the late 1860s with a plan to build a railroad from Ceará's capital of Fortaleza to the major cotton center of Uruburetama, but the project was abandoned in 1868 after the completion of a only few kilometers of track. As with irrigation, there was neither state capacity nor obvious foreign interest to take up the challenge of developing the sertão.[58]

By 1869, when a new drought devastated subsistence crops in many parts of the backlands, the same British cotton buyers who had orchestrated the boom a decade before were rejecting the Nordeste's "inferior," "poorly processed" cotton shipments. The sertanejos – once again pariahs – had nowhere to turn. "From subsistence farmers and herdsmen, a large proportion of backlanders had been converted into the marginal commercial farmers and agricultural laborers existing in an extremely precarious economic state, more vulnerable than ever to sudden crisis by virtue of the fact that their traditional ties to the large landholders had been greatly weakened or broken."[59] As in north China, the commercialization of agriculture in the sertão had less to do with seedlings of rural capitalism than with increased social and ecological marginality.

To make matters worse, the overextension of cotton cultivation during the 1860s had been matched by the expansion of the cattle population: from 1.2 million in Ceará in 1860 to 2 million in 1876. Like the pauper cotton-growers, the fazendeiros had recklessly increased the size of their herds, despite legislation attempting to stabilize land/cattle ratios, to compensate for falling beef and leather prices. Soil degradation and erosion were accelerated. Moreover the combined pressure of cotton and cattle on the soil left less room for traditional subsistence crops, and Cunniff finds indications that the Nordeste "was entering a period of famine even before the great drought devastated the area." The epidemiological evidence includes the appearance of beriberi in Ceará and Paraiba in 1872 – attributed to the sertanejos' increasing dependence on cheap, poorly milled rice imported from India – as well as outbreaks of smallpox, cholera and yellow fever.[60]

The international shockwaves from the collapse of the US railroad boom, which inaugurated the depression of 1873–79, reached the sertão in 1874. "The most drastic deflation in the memory of man," it depressed even further the prices of the agricultural exports that were now the faltering livelihood of agregados as well as fazendeiros. The small trickle of domestic credit, inadequate even in boom times, dried up completely. "By the end of the year the majority of banks [in the Nordeste] suspended loans. In 1875 the Banco Maua begged for a moratorium, while the Banco National stopped payments and the director of the Banco Alemão committed suicide. There was no way to control the ensuing panic."[61]

The provincial governments, meanwhile, were wrestling with public debts they could no longer finance. At the edge of default, several provinces, led by Pernambuco, imposed onerous taxes on foodstuffs sold at regional fairs. This despised legislation fatefully coincided with simultaneous efforts by the imperial government to introduce the metric system and reinforce conscription (a measure that was widely feared as an attempt to "enslave" freedmen). The resulting explosion was known as the Quebraquilos ("smashing the kilos") revolt. Throughout the agreste and sertão regions of Paraiba, Pernambuco, Rio Grande do Norte and Alagoas, armed crowds systematically destroyed decimal weights and measures and burned tax records.[62] The revolt was finally crushed by imperial troops, forcing many rebellious sertanejos to flee into the hills where they became *cangaceiros* preying on the fazendas and towns.[63] Thus, on the eve of the Grande Seca, local government in the Nordeste was bankrupt, malnutrition and beriberi were widespread, rioting had broken out in some of the towns, the poor were pillaging fazendas, and banditry was the only growth sector in the economy.

## The Irrigation Charade

Large northern landowners, needless to say, welcomed the emergence of this overstocked labor-supply without realizing that they were, in effect, embracing their own underdevelopment. Indeed, as we have seen, they protested violently against anything, like Conselheiro's saintly and autarchic city of Canudos, that appeared to threaten their abundance of labor. Elsewhere such a surfeit of immiseration might have produced a social revolution, but the northeastern littoral had the vastness of the sertão as a social safety-valve. Indeed, from the 1870s onward, the Nordeste was effectively capitalized on the fluxes of labor between the backlands and the coast. Potentially explosive accumulations of poor and unemployed laborers in the littoral were diverted into the subsistence economy of the sertão, then periodically regurgitated towards the coast by drought. The sertão, in effect, provided welfare for the poor, while drought guaranteed that desperate laborers would always be available to depress wages on the coast. Even in the Ceará sertão, virtually depopulated by the great secas of the 1870s and 1890s, local oligarchs as we have seen were able to find profit as labor contractors for Pará and Amazonas.

Thus while the coroneis had the most avid interest in "drought relief" (which they largely intercepted), they were little disposed toward any real development or ecological stabilization of the sertão. The all-out national mobilization to destroy Canudos was in stark contrast to official apathy over the fate of sertanejos in the four successive El Niño droughts between 1888 and 1902. The great domestic debate of the 1890s, symptomatically, was not over arrresting the decline of the Nordeste, but between Paulistas who urged more state spending in the southeast and the opposition, which wanted to bolster Brazil's international credit after the milreis lost half of its value to runaway inflation between 1892 and 1897. The Rothschilds rescued the government in 1898 with a £10 million loan in return for a surcharge on import duties and a deflationary budget that left no spare change for public works.[64]

The economic and political hegemonies, respectively, of the British and the Paulistas, plus the northeastern oligarchs' deepening investment in their own underdevelopment, thus explains much of the structural context of the century-long burlesque of "irrigating the sertão." In the wake of successive El Niños, national commissions and visiting foreign irrigation experts drew up sweeping, never-implemented plans for stabilizing agriculture and human settlement in the backlands. The few hydraulic projects that were actually built, beginning with the Acude Quixada reservoir in Ceará in 1899, "stored water which benefited large landowners and protected their cattle by providing pasture and watering facilities but ... left most of the low-income agricultural population untouched."[65] Only 500 hectares of the sertão had actually been irrigated by 1941, and twenty-seven years later, when a military dictatorship worried about possible Guevarist *focos* in the Nordeste hired Israeli consultants to conduct the first comprehensive irrigation survey, conditions of life for millions of drought-stricken and immiserated sertanejos were little different from the days when Conselheiro and Cícero first preached Apocalypse on the backroads of Ceará. [66]

# Glossary

| | |
|---|---|
| agregado | Tenant or tolerated squatter (literally, one who lives by favor on another's land); same as *morador*. |
| agreste | Intermediate zone between the drought-stricken sertão and humid coastal zona de mata. |
| bajra | Pearl millet: extremely drought resistant and more nutritious than higher-status grains. |
| bania | Moneylender (and usually trader). |
| beata(o) | Lay ascetic. |
| caatinga | Thorny scrub forest. |
| caboclo | Mixed-race person. |
| cangaceiro | Outlaw. |
| cash | Bronze coin (1/1000th of a tael). |
| coronel | Rural political boss (plural: *coroneis*). |
| culturrstelsel | "Culture system": obligatory regime of agricultural export production in Netherlands East Indies. |
| dacoit | Robbery/expropriation. |
| Deccan | Peninusular interior of India south of the Narmada River; also the volcanic Deccan Plateau. |
| durbar | State meeting of officials. |
| Encilhamento | Speculative bubble in the early Brazilian Republic. |

| | |
|---|---|
| ENSO | El Niño-Southern Oscillation. |
| fazenda | Cattle ranch (in the Nordeste). |
| fazendeiro | Rancher (*hacendado*). |
| fellah | Peasant (plural *fellahin*). |
| flagelado | "Ccourged one" (drought victim). |
| gente de cor | People of color. |
| gram | Pulse grown during *rabi*. |
| hsien | Chinese county. |
| ITCZ | Intertropical Convergence Zone (of trade winds). |
| jagunco | Pejorative term for herdsmen of the sertão/follower of Conselheiro. |
| jawar | *Sorghum vulgare.* |
| khatedar | Equivalent of *ryot* in Berar. |
| kaoliang | All-purpose sorghum: milled for grain while stalks used in construction. |
| kharif | Growing season of crops harvested in the autumn. |
| lakh | 100,000. |
| makhzan | Government/royal power (Morocco). |
| malguzar | Landowner, often with tenants (India's Central Provinces). |
| mandioca | Cassava (the root is poisonous unless carefully prepared). |
| maund | Unit of weight (82 lbs.). |
| milreis | Nineteenth-century Brazilian currenc. |
| MSLP | Mean Sea Level Pressure . |
| mu | One-sixth of an acre (China). |
| NAO | North Atlantic Oscillation. |
| Nian rebellion | Vast peasant uprising north of the Huai River (1851–68) led by Zhang Luoxing and defeated by U.S. Grant's host, Li Hongzhan. |
| Nordeste | Eight states of the Brazilian northeast whose vast interior is the sertão. |
| parceiro | Sharecropper. |
| rabi | Growing season of crops harvested in the spring. |
| retirante | Refugee (Brazil). |
| ryot | Peasant (Deccan). |

| | |
|---|---|
| ryotwari | System by which each peasant is assessed separately for revenue. |
| sabha | Association. |
| seca | Drought. |
| sertão | Backland region of Brazil's Nordeste. |
| sertanejo | Resident of the sertão. |
| shi | Measure of grain: about 176 pounds in weight. |
| SOI | Southern Oscillation Index. |
| sowcar | Moneylender (also *sahukar*). |
| SPCZ | South Pacific Convergence Zone. |
| SST | Sea surface temperature. |
| takavi | State-backed agricultural loan (also *taqavi* and *tagai*). |
| tael | Chinese ounce of silver; nineteenth-century monetary unit. |
| taluk | Indian revenue division. |
| talukdar | Large landowner. |
| teleconnection | Correlation between widely separated climate events. |
| thermocline | The sharp temperature gradient separating warm surface layer of ocean from deeper cold water. |
| Warm Pool | Trade Wind–driven pooling of very warm surface water in the western Pacific (Indonesia and Queensland); it drives earth's largest tropical convection system; both migrate towards the International Date Line during El Niño events. |
| vaqueiro | Cowboy (in Brazil's Nordeste). |
| zamindar | Property-holder under permanent settlement (Bengal). |
| zemstvo | Provincial and county council. |
| zona de mata | Well-watered zone of sugar cultivation on the coast of the Nordeste. |

# Notes

## Notes to the Preface

The epigraph is from John Hidore, *Global Environmental Change: Its Nature and Impact,* Upper Saddle River, N.J. 1996, p. 96.

1. William McFeely, *Grant: A Biography,* New York 1981, pp. 453, 457–60 and 471.
2. Ibid., pp. 458–71.
3. John Russell Young, *Around the World with General Grant,* subscription edn. (American News Company in 20 parts), New York 1878–79, pp. 242 and 246.
4. Ibid., pp. 266–7 and 274.
5. Ibid., pp. 278 and 284–5.
6. Ibid., p. 622.
7. Ibid., p. 624.
8. "On this occasion 'our distinguished guest,' the double Ex-President of the 'Great Western Republic,' who got as drunk as a fiddle, showed he could also be as profligate as a lord. He fumbled Mrs. A., kissed the shrieking Miss B. – pinched the plump Mrs. C. black and blue – and ran at Miss D. intent to ravish her. Finally, after throwing all the … female guests into hysterics by generally behaving like a must elephant, the noble beast was captured by main force and carried (quatre pattes dans l'air) by six sailors … which relieved India of his distinguished presence. The marine officer … reports that, when deposited in the public saloon cabin, where Mrs. G. was awaiting him … this remarkable man satiated there and then his baffled lust on the unresisting body of his legitimate spouse, and copiously vomited during the operation. If you have seen Mrs. Grant you will not think this incredible" (Lytton quoted in McFeely, p. 473).
9. Adam Badeau, *Grant in Peace,* Hartford 1887, pp. 310–11.
10. Quoted in McFeely, p. 474.
11. Young, p. 414.
12. Hang-Wei He, *Drought in Northern China in the Early Guang Xu (1876–1879),* Hong

Kong 1980, pp. 36–7 (in Chinese).

13. Quoted in McFeely, p. 557 fn43.

14. J. T. Headley, *The Travels of General Grant,* Philadelphia 1881, p. 444.

15. William Digby, *"Prosperous" British India: A Revelation from Official Records,* London 1901, p. 118.

16. Ibid., p. 122.

17. Alfred Russel Wallace, *The Wonderful Century: Its Successes and Its Failures,* London 1898, p. 341.

18. David Landes, *The Wealth and Poverty of Nations,* New York 1998, p. 437.

19. W. Arthur Lewis, *Growth and Fluctuations, 1870–1913,* London 1978, pp. 29, 187 and 215 especially.

20. Karl Polanyi, *The Great Transformation,* Boston 1944, p. 160.

21. Ibid., pp. 159–60.

22. Slavoj Zizek, *The Spectre Is Still Roaming Around! An Introduction to the 150th Anniversary Edition of the Communist Manifesto,* Zagreb 1998, p. 17.

23. Rosa Luxemburg, *The Accumulation of Capital,* trans. Agnes Schwarzchild, London 1951 [1913], pp. 370–71.

24. Bertolt Brecht, *Poems 1913–1956,* London 1976, p. 204.

25. See Chapter 7.

26. Jill Dias, "Famine and Disease in the History of Angola, c. 1830–1930," *Journal of African History* 22 (1981).

27. P. Wright, *An Index of the Southern Oscillation,* University of East Anglia, Climate Research Unit Publication, Norwich 1975; and William Quinn et al., "Historical Trends and Statistics of the Southern Oscillation, El Niño, and Indonesian Droughts," *Fish. Bull.* 76 (1978).

28. George Kiladis and Henry Diaz, "An Analysis of the 1877–78 ENSO Episode and Comparison with 1982–83," *Monthly Weather Review* 114 (June 1986). Although they "resist the temptation to compare the 'intensity'" of the two events, they point out that the 1876–78 event lasted longer and was associated with sea-level pressure anomalies across a larger area of the tropics (p. 1046).

29. Peter Whetton and Ian Rutherfurd, "Historical ENSO Teleconnections in the Eastern Hemisphere," *Climatic Change* 28 (1994), p. 243.

30. Michael Watts, *Silent Violence: Food, Famine and Peasantry in Northern Nigeria,* Berkeley 1983.

31. David Arnold, *Famine: Social Crisis and Historical Change,* London 1988.

32. Alfred Sauvy, "Trois mondes, une planete," *L'Observateur* 118 (14 Aug. 1952), p. 5.

33. See the discussion in Chapter 9; also the much-awaited study by Kenneth Pomeranz, *The Great Divergence: China, Europe, and the Making of the Modern World Economy,* Princeton, N.J. 2000, which appeared while this book was in proof.

## Notes on Definitions

1. See Kevin Trenbeth, "General Characteristics of El Niño-Southern Oscillation," in M. Glantz, R. Katz, and N. Nichols (eds.), *Teleconnections Linking Worldwide Climate Anomalies,*

Cambridge 1991, pp. 13–42.

2. Rolando Garcia, *Drought and Man: The 1972 Case History, vol. 1, Nature Pleads Not Guilty,* Oxford 1981, p. 157.

3. *Report on the Famine in the Bombay Presidency, 1899-1902, vol. 1,* Bombay 1903, p. 3; and J. A. Crawford, *Report on the Famine in the Hyderabad Assigned Districts in the Years 1899 and 1900,* Nagpur 1901, p. 2. On China, see Pierre-Etienne Will, *Bureaucracy and Famine in Eighteenth-Century China,* Stanford, Calif. 1990.

4. Amartya Sen, *Poverty and Famines: An Essay on Entitlement and Deprivation,* Oxford 1984, p. 1. Also Meghnad Desai, "The Economics of Famine," in G. Harrison (ed.), *Famine,* Oxford 1988.

5. Arnold, pp. 44–5 and 85.

6. Amarita Rangasami, "'Failure of Exchange Entitlements' Theory of Famine: A Response," in *Economic and Political Weekly* 20:41 (12 Oct. 1985), p. 178.

7. Michael Watts, "Drought, Environment and Food Supply," in Michael Glantz (ed.), *Drought and Hunger in Africa: Denying Famine a Future,* Cambridge 1987, p. 205.

8. Michael Watts,"Heart of Darkness" in Stephen Reyna (ed.), *The Political Economy of African Famine,* New York 1991, p. 44.

9. Alexander De Waal, *Famine That Kills: Darfur, Sudan, 1984-1985,* Oxford 1989, pp. 6 and 10.

10. *Report of the Commissioners Appointed to Enquire into the Famine in Bengal and Orissa 1866, vol. 1,* Calcutta 1867, p. 24.

11. Klein, "Plague, Polity and Popular Unrest," p. 731.

12. Maharatna, pp. 7–8.

13. David Washbrook, "The Commercialization of Agriculture in Colonial India: Production, Subsistence and Reproduction in the 'Dry South,' c. 1870–1930," *Modern Asian Studies* 28:1 (1994), p. 151.

14. Klein, p. 735.

15. Inga Glendinnen, *Reading the Holocaust,* Cambridge 1999, p. 14.

## Notes to Chapter 1

1. William Digby, *The Famine Campaign in Southern India: 1876–1878,* 2 vols., London 1900, p. 505; references are to vol. 1 unless otherwise noted.

2. "Philindus," "Famines and Floods in India," *Macmillan's Magazine,* Jan. 1878, pp. 244–5.

3. Digby, pp. 7 and 13.

4. British Parliamentary Papers, *Report of the Indian Famine Commission,* part 1, *Famine Relief,* cd. 2591, London 1880, p. 191. On the revolutionary role of Burmese rice surpluses in the imperial economy, see Cheng Siok-hwa, *The Rice Industry of Burma, 1852–1940,* Kuala Lumpur 1968.

5. Cornelius Walford, *The Famines of the World,* London 1879, p. 126.

6. Meerut district officer quoted in Elizabeth Whitcombe, *Agrarian Conditions in Northern India,* vol. 1 of *The United Provinces Under British Rule, 1860–1900,* Berkeley 1972, p. 195.

7. Letter from Madras Government to Government of India, 30 Nov. 1876, quoted in

B. Bhatia, *Famines in India, 1850–1945*, Bombay 1963, p. 94.

8. *The Nineteenth Century*, Sept. 1877, p. 177.

9. Christophe Guilmoto, "Towards a New Demographic Equilibrium: The Inception of Demographic Transition in South India," *The Indian Economic and Social History Review* (hence, *IESHR*) 29:3 (1992), p. 258.

10. Digby, pp. 38 and 361.

11. Andrew Roberts, *Salisbury: Victorian Titan*, London 1999, p. 215.

12. *The Times*, 9 Jan. 1877; Aurelia Harlan, *Owen Meredith*, New York 1946, pp. 218–20; and Bernard Cohn, "Representing Authority in Victorian India," in Eric Hobsbawm and Terence Ranger, eds., *The Invention of Tradition*, Cambridge 1983, pp. 179–208.

13. Digby, vol. 1, p. 46.

14. R. Neelankanteswara Rao, *Famines and Relief Administration: A Case Study of Coastal Andhra, 1858–1901*, New Delhi 1997, p. 120.

15. Roberts, p. 218.

16. For Lytton as a war hawk within Disraeli's government, see R. Ensor, *England: 1870–1914*, Oxford 1936, p. 62; and Lt.-Col. R. Osborne, "India Under Lord Lytton," *Contemporary Review*, Dec. 1879, p. 555 (Liberal view). On the effects of the Gold Standard on Indian finances, see Lance Brennan, "The Development of the Indian Famine Codes," in Wolf Tietze, ed., *Famine as a Geographical Phenomenon*, Dordrecht 1984, pp. 94 and 97.

17. "Swinburne called Lytton's poem 'Lucille' an 'infamous imposture' in that the plot, characters, situations, and even minute descriptions were borrowed from George Sand's novel *Lavinia*. The accusation of plagiarism was also made by Lytton's father" (John Lowe Duthie, "Lord Lytton and the Second Afghan War: A Psychohistorical Study," *Victorian Studies* [Summer 1984], p. 471).

18. Janet Oppenheim, *"Shattered Nerves": Doctors, Patients and Depression in Victorian England*, Oxford 1991, pp. 173–4.

19. Roberts, p. 220.

20. Adam Smith, *An Inquiry into the Nature and Causes of the Wealth of Nations* (1776), fifth edn., London 1930, pp. 27–8.

21. S. Ambirajan, *Classical Political Economy and British Policy in India*, Cambridge 1978, p. 63.

22. Osborne, p. 553; Hari Srivastava, *The History of Indian Famines*, Agra 1968, p. 131; Digby, pp. 50–51; and David Steele, *Lord Salisbury: A Political Biography*, London 1999, p. 98. Compare also to Bentham: "*Laissez faire*, in short, should be the general practice: every departure, unless required by some great good, is a certain evil." In a notable dissent from ultra-orthodoxy, however, John Stuart Mill criticized the policy of absolute nonintervention when large numbers of lives were at stake: "Direct measures at the cost of the state, to procure food from a distance are expedient when, from peculiar reason, the thing is not likely to be done by private speculation" (quoted in Rao, pp. 250).

23. Steele, p. 98 (it is unclear whether this is a direct quotation or paraphrase from a letter from Lytton to Sir John Strachey, Oct. 1877).

24. Angus Maddison, *Moghul Class Structure and Economic Growth: India and Pakistan Since the Moghuls*, New York 1971, p. 40.

25. Derived from Bhatia, Table 5, p. 38.

26. Quoted in John Caldwell, "Malthus and the Less Developed World: The Pivotal Role of India," *Population and Development Review* 24:4 (Dec. 1998), p. 683.

27. From *Parliamentary Papers*, 1881, 68, "Famine Commission – Financial Statement," quoted in Sheldon Watts, *Epidemics and History: Disease, Power and Imperialism*, New Haven, Conn. 1997, p. 203.

28. Caldwell, p. 683.

29. Quoted in Roberts, pp. 85–6.

30. Quoted in Steele, pp. 95 and 102.

31. "General Tremenheere on Missions," *Calcutta Review* 128 (1877), p. 278.

32. Salisbury in Steele, p. 98.

33. Government of India, *Report of the Indian Famine Commission, 1878*, Part I, Famine Relief, London 1880, p. 59.

34. Digby, pp. 173-4

35. K. Suresh Singh, *The Indian Famine 1967*, New Delhi 1975, p. 242.

36. Digby, p. 105.

37. Ibid., pp. 103–4.

38. "Famine and Debt in India," *The Nineteenth Century*, Sept. 1877, p. 184; and Jairus Banaji, "Capitalist Domination and the Small Peasantry: The Deccan Districts in the Late Nineteenth Century," in Gyan Prakash, ed., *The World of the Rural Labourer in Colonial India*, Delhi 1992, p. 124.

39. Correspondent for the *Calcutta Statesman* quoted in Digby, pp. 276–81.

40. Digby, pp. 46–7 and 265; and Bhatia, pp. 94–5. For the quarrel between Lytton and Wodehouse, see *The Times*, 5 Feb. 1877.

41. Bhatia, pp. 85–7.

42. *The Economist* 32 (July 1874), p. 802.

43. See Ambirajan, p. 92.

44. Quoted in ibid., p. 96.

45. *The Times*, 5 Feb. 1877.

46. Copy of Victoria's telegram to the Imperial Assemblage, 1 Jan. 1877, in Huntington Library (San Marino), Grenville Papers (Stowe Collection), 3rd Duke of Buckingham and Chandos, STG India, box 2 (file 7).

47. Secretary of State for India quoted in A. Loveday, *The History and Economics of Indian Famines*, London 1914, p. 57.

48. De Waal, p. 32.

49. "Although no one person can be blamed for the deficiencies of the relief policies, Trevelyan perhaps more than any other individual represented a system of response which increasingly was a mixture of minimal relief, punitive qualifying criteria, and social reform" (Christine Kinealy, *This Great Calamity: The Irish Famine, 1845–52*, Dublin 1994, pp. 349–50).

50. Cf. Rao, p. 118, and Currie, p. 47.

51. Digby, p. 52.

52. Ibid., pp. 85 and 135.

53. Anonymous, "The Indian Famine: How Dealt with in Western India," *Westminster Review*, Jan. 1878, p. 145.

54. Quoted in "Indian Famines," *Edinburgh Review*, July 1877, p. 80. Of all common cereals, rice is the most incomplete in amino acids. See discussion of rural diet and protein deficiencies in Paul Greenough, *Prosperity and Misery in Modern Bengal*, Oxford 1982, p. 70 passim.

55. S. Partridge, medical inspector of emigrants, in *Indian Economist*, 15 Oct. 1870, p. 45 (cited in Dadabhai Naoroji, *Poverty and Un-British Rule in India*, London 1901, p. 25).

56. Quoted in "The Indian Famine: How Dealt with in Western India," p. 145. Cornish hoisted Temple by his own petard by publishing in parallel columns Temple's contrasting views on nutrition requirements in the 1874 and 1876 famines – see his account in *The Times*, 18 May 1877.

57 Digby, pp. 55, 74–5, 85, 113, and 135; and Bhatia, p. 96. For Temple's point of view, see *The Story of My Life*, vol. 1, London 1896, esp. 289–94.

58. Digby, vol. 2, pp. 247 and 252.

59. Kohei Wakimura, "Famines, Epidemics and Mortality in Northern India, 1870–1921," in Tim Dyson (ed.), *India's Historical Demography: Studies in Famine, Disease and Society*, London 1989, pp. 285–6 (on grain prices).

60. *The Times*, 9 July 1877.

61. Digby, vol. 2, pp. 203–4.

62. Digby, p. 26.

63. Rev. A. Rowe, *Every-Day Life in India*, New York 1881, pp. 347–8.

64. Quoted in Kerby Miller, *Emigrants and Exiles: Ireland and the Irish Exodus to North America*, New York 1985, p. 283.

65. Rowe, pp. 204 and 372–3.

66. Quoted in "The Indian Famine: How Dealt with in Western India," p. 153.

67. Digby, p. 340.

68. S. Mehrotra, "The Poona Sarvajanik Sabha: The Early Phase (1870–1880)," *IESHR* 3 (Sept.1969), pp. 305 and 310.

69. Quoted in Digby, pp. 341–2. Lytton's granite face towards India's starving children in these months – like Temple's repudiation of his own "excessive charity" in 1874 – perhaps needs to be seen in a tormented psychological context: perhaps his father's (Bulwer Lytton's) cruel attacks on his "unmanly repining" after the death of his little son in 1871 (Harlan, p. 205).

70. Rowe, p. 345.

71. Digby, p. 283.

72. Harlan, p. 214.

73. "The Sabha humbly submits that no small portion of the success [in restoring rations and reducing deaths] is due to the attitude of complaint and watchfulness taken up by the native and European press...." Letter to Temple, 16 May 1877, quoted in Digby, p. 355.

74. Lytton in a letter to Sir Louis Mallet (11 Jan. 1877), quoted in Ambirajan, p. 93.

75. Quoted in Brennan, p. 97.

76. Digby, pp. 148–50 and 361–2.

77. Ira Klein, "Imperialism, Ecology and Disease: Cholera in India, 1850–1950," *IESHR* 31:4 (1994), pp. 495 and 507; David Arnold, "Cholera Mortality in British India, 1817–1947" in Dyson, p. 270; and Rita Colwell, "Global Climate and Infectious Disease: The Cholera

Paradigm," *Science* 274 (20 Dec. 1996), p. 2030.

78. Cecil Woodham-Smith, *Florence Nightingale: 1820–1910*, New York 1983, p. 338.

79. Digby, pp. 361–5; and Richard Tucker, "Forest Management and Imperial Politics: Thana District, Bombay, 1823–1887," *IESHR* 16:3 (1979), p. 288 (quote).

80. Washbrook, "The Commercialization of Agriculture in Colonial India," *Modern Asian Studies* 28:1 (1994), p. 131; and W. Francis, *Bellary District*, Madras 1904, p. 135.

81. Digby, vol. 2, p. 148.

82. Kate Currie, "British Colonial Policy and Famines: Some Effects and Implications of 'Free Trade' in the Bombay, Bengal and Madras Presidencies, 1860–1900," *South Asia* 14:2 (1991), p. 43.

83. Loveday, p. 60.

84. Cf. Ira Klein, "When the Rains Failed: Famine, Relief, and Mortality in British India," *IESHR* 21:2 (1984), p. 195; and Charles Elliot, *Report on the History of the Mysore Famine of 1876–1878*, pp. xx–xxix.

85. Klein, p. 195.

86. Elliot, p. 42.

87. Klein, pp. 196–7.

88. Victoria's speech in *The Economist*, 18 Aug. 1877.

89. A clipping from August 1877 in Grenville Papers, STG India, outsized box (file 5).

90. Ibid.

91. Mary Lutyens, *The Lyttons in India*, London 1979, pp. 111–12. The Madras Government, on the other hand, described its relief workers as "an industrious, hardworking set, fully alive to the grave situation they were in, and grateful for the work provided for them" (*Report on the Buckingham Canal [Koitadatam] Division During the Madras Famine*, Box 2[a], Grenville Papers, STG India).

92. Digby, pp. 206–23.

93. Rev. J. Chandler quoted in Digby, vol. 2, p. 148.

94. David Arnold, "Famine in Peasant Consciousness and Peasant Action: Madras, 1876–78," *Subaltern Studies* 3 (1984), pp. 86–7 and 93; and "Dacoity and Rural Crime in Madras, 1860–1940," *The Journal of Peasant Studies*, p. 163.

95. Sharma, p. 359.

96. Neville Nicholls, "Complex Climate-Human-Ecosystem Interactions in the 1877 El Niño," *Abstracts*, Second International Climate and History Conference, Norwich 1998, pp. 65–6; and J. Mayer, "Coping with Famine," *Foreign Affairs* 53:1 (Oct. 1974), p. 101.

97. *The Times*, 9 July 1877.

98. Digby, p. 241.

99. Ibid., pp. 243–4.

100. Reprinted as James Wilson, *The Government of India in Relation to Famines and Commerce*, London 1878, pp. 9 and 13.

101. D. Rajasekhar, "Famines and Peasant Mobility: Changing Agrarian Structure in Kurnool District of Andhra, 1870–1900," *IESHR* 28:2 (1991), pp. 143 (quote), 144 and 150.

102. This is the hardly unbiased recollection of a relief official, Lepel Griffin, told to *Harper's Weekly* many years later during the famine of 1896 ("Indian Famine," 7 Nov. 1896, pp. 489–90).

103. Bhatia, pp. 98–101.

104. Quoted in Osborne, p. 563 (his emphasis).

105. Ibid., pp. 563–7.

106. Wakimura, p. 286.

107. Osborne, p. 564.

108. Ibid., pp. 553 and 565.

109. Digby singles out Knight's *Statesman* for praise for sending a correspondent to spend six months reporting from the famine districts of Bombay, Madras and Mysore (Digby, p. 22). The *Statesman's* scathing editorials and similarly critical letters from missionaries were published in pamphlet form as *Sir George Couper and the Famine in North Western Provinces* (Calcutta 1878). This excerpt is from Bhatia, p. 100.

110. Cf. Kaushalya Devi Dublish, *Revolutionaries and Their Activities in Northern India*, Delhi 1982, pp. 3–4; and Mehrotra, pp. 310–11.

111. John McLane, *Indian Nationalism and the Early Congress*, Princeton, N.J. 1977, p. 45. On widespread British anxiety that the 1876–77 famine might lead to "revolution," see Ems Namboordiripad, *A History of the Indian Freedom Struggle*, Trivandrum 1986, p. 136.

112. Premansukumar Bandyopadhyay, *Indian Famine and Agrarian Problems*, Calcutta pp. 97–103.

113. Nightingale, quoted in *The Ninetenth Century*, 8 Sept. 1878.

114. F. B. Smith, *Florence Nightingale*, London 1982, p. 146.

115. "When I wrote these notes in 1873, or read them in 1876, I little dreamt that they would so soon obtain such terrible confirmation as the present deplorable famines have given them" (D. Naoroji, *Poverty and Un-British Rule in India*, London 1901, pp. 60 and 141); and R. Masani, *Dadabhai Naoroji: The Grand Old Man of India*, London 1939, p. 192.

116. Quoted in Osborne, p. 568.

117. Bandyopadhyay, p. 104.

118. Ibid., pp. 106 (Gladstone) and 113 (funds spent).

119. Brennan, p. 98.

120. Ibid., p. 108.

121. Ibid., pp. 103–7.

122. Carol Henderson, "Life in the Land of Death: Famine and Drought in Arid Western Rajasthan," Ph.D. diss., Columbia University 1989, p. 66.

123. H. M. Hyndman, *The Bankruptcy of India*, London 1886, p. 26.

124. Naoroji, pp. 212 and 216.

125. Brennan, p. 107.

126. Bandyopadhyay, p. 109; and 1880 Report quoted in *Report of the Indian Famine Commission, 1901*, Calcutta 1901, p. 2.

127. McLane, p. 49.

128. Masani, p. 295.

## Notes to Chapter 2

The statement by the governor of Shanxi appeared in the *Imperial Gazette* (15 March), translated in *The Times* (London), 21 June 1877.

1. Cf. *L'Exploration* [Paris] 6 (1877), p. 43; and K. De Silva, *A History of Sri Lanka*, Berkeley 1981, p. 308.

2. George Kiladis and Henry Diaz, "An Analysis of the 1877–78 ENSO Episode and Comparison with 1982–83," *Monthly Weather Review* 114 (1986), pp. 1035 (quote), 1037–9 and 1046.

3. Eric Foner, *Reconstruction: America's Unfinished Revolution, 1863–1877*, New York 1988, pp. 512–13. "1873 is a great economic divide. It was the peak of the trading boom of the mid-nineteenth century" (Derek Beales, *From Castlereagh to Gladstone, 1815–1885*, New York 1969, p. 232).

4. Eric Hobsbawm, *The Age of Capital 1848–1875*, London 1975, p. 46.

5. The extensive plantation economy of Oceania, usually associated with copra and sugar, actually started with the cotton boom of the 1860s. See the preface in Brij Lal, Doug Munro and Edward Beechert, *Plantation Workers: Resistance and Accommodation*, Honolulu 1993, pp. 3–4.

6. P. Cain and A. Hopkins, *British Imperialism: Innovation and Expansion, 1688–1914*, London 1993, p. 371.

7. *The Times* (21 June 1877) blamed the famine on the refusal of the Qing to allow European investors to build a mainline railroad into interior northern China.

8. On the 1867–68 famine in Hebei (Xhili), see Mary Wright, *The Last Stand of Chinese Conservatism: The T'ung-Chih Restoration, 1862–1874*, Stanford, Calif. 1957, p. 135.

9. R. H. Tawney, *Land and Labour in China*, London 1932, p. 77.

10. UK, Foreign Office, *Parliamentary Papers*, China No. 2 (1878), pp. 1–2.

11. Rev. Timothy Richard, quoted in Paul Bohr, *Famine in China and the Missionary*, Cambridge, Mass. 1972, p. 14.

12. Will, *Bureaucracy and Famine*, p. 36.

13. Frederick Williams, *The Life and Letters of Samuel Wells Williams*, New York 1889, p. 432.

14. Bohr, p. 15.

15. *Parl. Papers*, No. 2, p. 3.

16. Richard, pp. 98 and 117.

17. Cited in the *Pall Mall Gazette*, 1 May 1877.

18. Bohr, p. 15; and Timothy Richard, *Forty-Five Years in China* (third edn.), New York 1916, p. 119.

19. Quoted in *Parl. Papers*, No. 2, p. 11.

20. Bohr, pp. 60–63 and 218.

21. *Times* (London), 1 May 1877.

22. Bohr, pp. 35–41 and 227.

23. *Parl. Papers*, No. 2, p. 6.

24. Srinivas Wagel, *Finance in China*, Shanghai 1914, p. 23.

25. *Parl. Papers*, No. 2, p. 6.

26. Arthur Smith, *Village Life in China*, Boston 1970 [1899], p. 116. See also Kamal Sheel, *Peasant Society and Marxist Intellectuals in China*, Princeton, N.J. 1989, p. 12.

27. Joseph Esherick, *The Origins of the Boxer Uprising*, Berkeley 1987, p. 101.

28. David Faure, "Local Political Disturbances in Kiangsu Province, China: 1870–1911,"

Ph.D. diss., Princeton, N.J. 1975, pp. 162–3.

29. Will, p. 49.

30. Faure, pp. 162–5, 275 and 468.

31. John Hidore, *Global Environmental Change*, Upper Saddle River, N.J. 1996, p. 96.

32. *Parl. Papers*, No. 2, p. 6. Two members of the China Inland Mission had attempted to found a mission in Henan in 1875 but were quickly driven out. With enormous difficulty a foothold was finally achieved in Chowkiakow in 1884, but missionaries had little success and most were forced to flee during the uprising in 1900 (Marshall Broomhall [ed.], *The Chinese Empire: A General and Missionary Survey*, London 1907, pp. 159–61).

33. Resumes in *L'Exploration* [Paris] 6 (1878), pp. 172 and 416.

34. Elizabeth Perry, "Social Banditry Revisited: The Case of Bai Lang, a Chinese Brigand," *Modern China* 9:3 (July 1983), p. 362.

35. Milton Stauffer, *The Christian Occupation of China*, Shanghai 1922, p. 211.

36. In Ping-ti Ho, *Studies on the Population of China, 1366–1953*, Cambridge, Mass. 1959, p. 232.

37. S. Wells Williams, *The Middle Kingdom*, vol. 2, New York 1883, p. 736.

38. On Shanxi's dependence on Wei Valley surpluses, see Helen Dunstan, *Conflicting Counsels to Confuse the Age: A Documentary History of Political Economy in Qing China, 1644–1840*, Ann Arbor 1996, pp 250–51.

39. *Parl. Papers*, No. 2, pp. 5–7.

40. *Gazette* (15 March), translated in *The Times*, 21 June 1877.

41. *New York Times*, 24 February 1878.

42. Harold Hinton, *The Grain Tribute System of China (1845–1911)*, Cambridge, Mass. 1956, pp. 42–3.

43. *Parl. Papers*, No. 6 (1878), p. 2.

44. Bohr, p. 43.

45. *The Times* (London), 21 June 1877.

46. A. Broomhall, *Hudson Taylor and China's Open Century: Book Seven (It Is Not Death to Die!)*, London 1989, pp. 170 and 467 ff 13. See also Adrian Bennett, *Missionary Journalist in China: Young J. Allen and His Magazines, 1860–1883*, Athens, Ga. 1983, p. 174.

47. Bohr, pp. 16–21.

48. Hang-Wei He, *Drought in North China in the Early Guangxu (1876–1879)* [in Chinese], Hong Kong 1980, p. 15.

49. William Soothill, *Timothy Richard of China*, London 1924, p. 102.

50. Richard, p. 130.

51. Syndicated to the *New York Times*, 6 July 1878.

52. *Parl. Papers*, No. 6, p. 1.

53. A. Broomhall, *China's Open Century: Book Seven*, pp. 111 and 163.

54. James Legge (trans.), *The Famine in China. Pictures Illustrating the Terrible Famine in Honan That Might Draw Tears from Iron. Extracts from a Translation of the Chinese Texts*, London 1878 (Trinity College Library [Dublin] pamphlet collection).

55. Lillian Li, "Introduction: Food, Famine, and the Chinese State," *Journal of Asian Studies*, 41:4 (Aug. 1982), p. 700.

56. *Records of the General Conference of the Protestant Missionaries of China* (Shanghai, 10–24

May 1877), Shanghai 1878, p. 446.

57.  A. Broomhall, *China's Open Century, Book Seven*, p. 115; and Arthur Smith, *The Uplift of China* (revised edn.), New York 1912, p. 175.

58.  Arnold, *Famine*, p. 137.

59.  Rudolf Wagner, "The *Shenbao* in Crisis: The International Environment and the Conflict Between Guo Songtao and the *Shenbao*," *Late Imperial China* 20:1 (June 1999), p. 117.

60.  Quoted in B. MacGillivray, *A Century of Protestant Missions in China*, Shanghai 1907, pp. 78–9.

61.  Williams, p. 433.

62.  Ibid., p. 184.

63.  A. Broomhall, *China's Open Century: Book Six*, pp. 169 and 246.

64.  Ibid., pp. 176–7

65.  *Parl. Papers*, No. 2, p. 7.

66.  A. Broomhall, *China's Open Century: Book Six*, p. 169.

67.  Ibid., pp. 175 and 181.

68.  Euclydes da Cunha, *Rebellion in the Backlands (Os Sertões)*, trans. Samuel Putnam, Chicago 1944, p. 41.

69.  Professor and Mrs. Louis Agassiz, *A Journey to Brazil*, Boston 1869, p. 459.

70.  Herbert Smith, *Brazil: The Amazon and the Coast*, New York 1879, p. 400.

71.  Da Cunha, p. 24.

72.  Ibid., p 410

73.  Roger Cunniff, "The Great Drought: Northeast Brazil, 1877–1880," Ph.D. diss., University of Texas, Austin 1970, p. 128.

74  Pierre Denis, *Brazil*, London 1911, p. 330.

75.  Ibid., p. 129.

76.  Smith, pp. 411–13.

77.  Rodolfo Theofilo, *Historia da seca do Ceará, 1877–1880*, Rio de Janeiro 1922, p. 120.

78.  Smith, ibid.

79.  Cunniff, pp. 248–50.

80.  Account of 11 November 1877 cited in Billy Jaynes Chandler, *The Feitosas and the Sertão dos Inhamuns*, Gainesville, Fla. 1972, p. 162,

81.  Cunniff, pp. 152–3.

82.  Chandler, pp. 160–61.

83.  Rodolfo Theofilo, quoted by Anthony Hall in *Drought and Irrigation in North-East Brazil*, Cambridge 1978, p. 5.

84.  Gerald Greenfield, "Migrant Behavior and Elite Attitudes: Brazil's Great Drought, 1877–1879," *The Americas* 43:1 (July 1986) p. 73; and Cunniff, ibid.

85.  Smith, pp. 415–6.

86.  Cunniff, p. 163.

87.  Father Cícero Romão Baptista describing conditions in Ceará's Cariri Valley (ibid., p. 202).

88.  Smith, p. 417.

89.  Cunniff, pp. 166 and 192.

90.  Ibid., pp. 206–11 and 242.

91. Smith, p. 419.

92. Cunniff, pp. 212–13; Smith, pp. 419–35; Kempton Webb, *The Changing Face of Northeast Brazil*, New York 1974, pp. 30–32; and Hall, p. 5.

93. Nicanor Nascimento quoted in Josué de Castro, *Death in the Northeast*, New York 1969, pp. 51–2.

94. Chandler, pp. 164–5.

95. Cunniff, p. 299

96. Ibid., pp. 292–3.

## Notes to Chapter 3

The quote from Mirza Asadullah Khan Ghalib appears in Sugata Bose and Ayesha Jalal, *Modern South Asia*, Delhi 1999, p. 43.

1. Hilary Conroy, *The Japanese Seizure of Korea: 1868–1910*, Philadelphia 1974, pp. 90–91. See also Han Woo-Keun, *The History of Korea*, Seoul 1970, p. 403.

2. Reynaldo Ileto, "Religion and Anti-colonial Movements," in Nicholas Tarling (ed.), *The Cambridge History of Southeast Asia*, vol. 2, Cambridge 1992, pp. 220–21.

3. Kiladis and Diaz, p. 1038.

4. Han Knapen, "Epidemics, Droughts, and Other Uncertainties on Southeast Borneo During the Eighteenth and Nineteenth Centuries," in Peter Boomgaard, Freek Colombijn, and David Henley, *Paper Landscapes: Explorations in the Environmental History of Indonesia*, Leiden 1997, p. 140.

5. Henry Forbes, "Through Bantam and the Preanger Regencies in the Eighties," reprinted in Pieter Honig and Frans Verdoorn (eds.), *Science and Scientists in the Netherlands Indies*, New York 1945, pp. 112–13.

6. Knapen, p. 144.

7. W. Hugenholz, "Famine and Food Supply in Java, 1830–1914," in C. Bayle and D. Kolff (eds.), *Two Colonial Empires*, Dordrecht 1986, pp. 169–71.

8. M. Ricklefs, *A History of Modern Indonesia Since c. 1300*, 2nd edn., Stanford, Calif. 1993, pp. 121–23; C. Faseur, "Purse or Principle: Dutch Colonial Policy in the 1860s and the Decline of the Cultivation System," *Modern Asian Studies* 25:1 (1991), p. 34.

9. J. Furnivall, *Netherlands India: A Study of Political Economy*, Cambridge 1944, pp. 138 and 162. For a synthesis of current research on the *cultuurstelsel*, see R. Elson, *Village Java under the Cultivation System, 1830–1870*, Sydney 1994.

10. Hugenholz, ibid.

11. Alfred McCoy, "Sugar Barons: Formation of a Native Planter Class in the Colonial Philippines," *The Journal of Peasant Studies*, 19:3/4 (April/July 1992), pp. 109–14.

12. Violeta Lopez-Gonzaga, "Landlessness, Insurgency and Food Crisis in Negros Island," in *Famine and Society*, p. 111.

13. Angel Martinez Duesta, *History of Negros*, Manila 1980, pp. 253, 259–61, 378–9, 400, and 412–13.

14. Michael Billig, "The Rationality of Growing Sugar in Negros," *Philippine Studies* 40 (1992), pp. 156–7.

15. Filomeno Aguilar, *Clash of Spirits: The History of Power and Sugar Planter Hegemony on a Visayan Island*, Honolulu 1998, p. 166.

16. Ibid.

17. Ibid., pp. 166–70.

18. Myriam Dornoy, *Politics in New Caledonia*, Sydney 1984, pp. 19, 24–5 and 26.

19. Linda Latham, "Revolt Re-examined: The 1878 Insurrection in New Caledonia," *Journal of Pacific History* 10:3 (1975), p. 62.

20. Martyn Lyons, *The Totem and the Tricolour*, Kensington, NSW 1986, p. 61.

21. Ibid.

22. Latham, p. 49.

23. Lyons, pp. 58–65.

24. Louise Michel, *The Red Virgin: Memoirs of Louise Michel*, Birmingham 1981, p. 114.

25. Sharon Nicholson, "Environmental Change Within the Historical Period," in J. Adams, A. Goudie and A. Orme, *The Physical Geography of* Africa, Oxford 1996, pp. 75 and 79; and Jill Dias, "Famine and Disease in the History of Angola, c. 1830–1930," *Journal of African History* 22 (1981), pp. 366–7.

26. Dias, p. 368.

27. Ibid., p. 366.

28. Ibid.

29. Ibid., pp. 368–9.

30. Donald Morris, *The Washing of Spears*, London 1966, p. 267.

31. See Charles Ballard, "Drought and Economic Distress: South Africa in the 1800s," *Journal of Interdisciplinary History*, 17:2 (Autumn 1986), pp. 359–78.

32. *Nature*, 28 March 1878, p. 436.

33. Morris, p. 254.

34. Shula Marks, "Southern Africa, 1867–1886," in Roland Oliver and G. Sanderson (eds.), *The Cambridge History of Africa*, vol. 6, Cambridge 1985, pp. 381 and 387.

35. Morris, p. 267.

36. Cain and Hopkins, p. 372.

37. On the centrality of the labor-supply question to British strategy, see Marks, p. 380; and Jeff Guy, *The Destruction of the Zulu Kingdom*, London 1979, p. 45.

38. T. Davenport, *South Africa: A Modern History*, 4th edn., Toronto 1991, p. 128.

39. Morris, p. 286.

40. Guy, p. 49.

41. Michael Lieven, "'Butchering the Brutes All Over the Place': Total War and Massacre in Zululand, 1879," *History* 84:276 (Oct. 1999), pp. 621 and 630.

42. Karl Butzer, "History of Nile Flows," in P. Howell and J. Allan (eds.), *The Nile: Sharing a Scarce Resource*, Cambridge 1994, p. 105.

43. *The Times* (London), 2 Jan. 1878.

44. Luxemburg, p. 437. Luxemburg devoted most of a chapter to debt imperialism and the ensuing famine in Egypt (pp. 429–39).

45. Lady Gordon quoted in Roger Owen, *The Middle East in the World Economy, 1800–1914*, 2nd edn., London 1993, p. 142.

46. Wilfred Blunt, *Secret History of the British Occupation of Egypt*, New York 1922, pp.

8–9.

47. Roger Owen, *Cotton and the Egyptian Economy: 1820–1914*, Oxford 1969, p. 147.

48. Juan Cole, *Colonialism and Revolution in the Middle East: Social and Cultural Origins of Egypt's 'Urabi Movement*, Princeton, N.J. 1993, pp. 87–8.

49. Cited in Theodore Rothstein, *Egypt's Ruin*, London 1910, pp. 69–70.

50. Cole, ibid.

51. Quoted in the Earl of Cromer, *Modern Egypt*, vol. 1, London 1908, p. 35.

52. Cole, pp. 87–8. See also Allan Richards, "Primitive Accumulation in Egypt, 1798–1882," *Review* 1:2 (Fall 1977), pp. 46–48.

53. "The Winter of 1876–7 in Algiers," *Symons' Monthly Meteorological Magazine*, October 1877, pp. 132–3.

54. Charles-Robert Ageron, *Les Algeriens musulmans et la France (1871–1919)*, vol. 1, Paris 1968, pp. 380–81.

55. Ibid., pp. 378–9.

56. Ageron, *Histoire de l'Algerie contemporaine*, vol. 2, Paris 1979, p. 202.

57. Julia Clancy-Smith, *Rebel and Saint: Muslim Notables, Populist Protest, Colonial Encounters*, Berkeley 1994, p. 224.

58. Ageron, *Histoire*, pp. 201–2, 211 and 220.

59. Jean-Louis Miege, *Le Maroc et l'Europe (1830–1894)*, vol. 3, Paris 1962, pp. 383–4, 403, 419 and 441. On the monetarization of agrarian taxation, see Edmund Burke III, *Prelude to Protectorate in Morocco, Precolonial Protest and Resistance, 1860–1912*, Chicago 1976, p. 22.

60. Miege, pp. 382–3, 390 and 398.

61. Quoted in Cornelius Walford, *The Famines of the World*, London 1879, p. 19.

62. Miege, pp. 385–8 and 393.

63. Ibid., pp. 395–7, 450–53 and 458.

64. *Nature*, 28 March 1878, p. 436.

65. Walford, p. 49.

66. Letter to *Nature*, 4 April 1878; Doug Munro and Stewart Firth, "Samoan Plantations: The Gilbertese Laborers' Experience, 1867–1896," in Lal, et al. (eds.), *Plantation Workers: Resistance and Accommodation*, Honolulu 1993, p. 111; and Kiladis and Diaz, p. 1040.

67. Enrique Florescano and Susan Swan, *Breve historia de la sequia en Mexico*, Xalapa (Ver.) 1995, p. 57.

68. Walford, p. 70.

69. Kiladis and Diaz, p. 1042. It was the second wettest winter in San Francisco, the first elsewhere in Northern California.

70. Walford (1879), p. 299.

71. H. Diaz, "A Possible Link of the 1877–78 Major El Niño Episode and a Yellow Fever Outbreak in the Southern United States," *Abstracts*, Second International Climate and History Conference, University of East Anglia, Norwich 1998.

72. W. Quinn and V. Neal, "The Historical Record of El Niño Events," in R. Bradley and P. Jones (eds.), *Climate Since AD 1500*, London 1992, p. 638.

73. *Nature* (1878), p. 447.

74. Marx to N. F. Danielson (19 February 1881) in *Karl Marx and Friedrich Engels on Colonialism*, Moscow n.d., p. 337.

75. Romesh Chunder Dutt, *Open Letters to Lord Curzon*, Calcutta 1904, pp. 3–4.

76. Kohei Wakimura, "Famines, Epidemics and Mortality in Northern India, 1870–1921," in Tim Dyson (ed.), *India's Historical Demography*, London 1989, pp. 288–90.

77. Klein, "When the Rains Failed," pp . 199 and 210.

78. William Digby, "Famine Prevention Studies," in Lady Hope, *General Sir Arthur Cotton: His Life and Work*, London 1900, pp. 362–3.

79. Rajasekhar, "Famines and Peasant Mobility," p. 132.

80. Washbrook, p. 141.

81. Rajasekhar, p. 134.

82. Ibid., pp. 142 and 150 (quote).

83. Rao and Rajasekhar, p. A-82.

84. Figures from Hugh Tinker, *A New System of Slavery: The Export of Indian Labour Overseas, 1830–1920*, Oxford 1974, pp. 49 and 305.

85. Srivastava, p. 226.

86. Zhang Jiacheng, Zhang Xiangong and Xu Siejiang, "Droughts and Floods in China During the Recent 500 Years," in Jiacheng (ed.), *The Reconstruction of Climate in China for Historical Times*, Beijing 1988, p. 46 (driest year); Hang-Wei He, pp. 36–7 (quote); Will, *Bureaucracy and Famine*, p. 30 ("the worst drought in North China's premodern history was undoubtedly that of 1876–79"); A. Broomhall, *China's Open Century, Book Six*, p. 466 fn44 (official estimate); and Cahill, p. 7. Susan Cotts Wakins and Jane Menken estimate that 12 percent of the population died in five northern provinces ("Famines in Historical Perspective," *Population and Development Review* 11:4 (Dec. 1985), p. 651.)

87. *Report of the China Famine Relief Fund*, Shanghai 1879, p. 7; and Lillian Li, "Introduction: Food, Famine, and the Chinese State," *Journal of Asian Studies*, 41:4 (Aug. 1982), p. 687. This is the same range of mortality earlier quoted by Tawney in his famous study (p. 76).

88. This is based on articles in *China's Millions* used by A. Broomhall, *China's Open Century, Book Six*, p. 181.

89. Ibid., p. 181; Soothill, p. 101. Richard, it should be noted, believed that the death toll throughout nine affected provinces was somewhere between 15 and 20 million (Soothill, p. 103).

90. Arnold, p. 21.

81. Burke, p. 23.

92. Miege, p. 443.

93. Luis Felipe de Alencastro (ed.), *Historia da vida privada no Brasil: Imperio*, São Paulo, 1997, p. 312.

94. Seymour Drescher, "Brazilian Abolition in Comparative Perspective," in Rebecca Scott, et al. (eds.), *Abolition of Slavery in Brazil*, Durham, N.C. 1988, p. 32.

95. Quoted in de Castro, p. 53.

96. Cunniff, p. 283.

97. Arup Maharatna, *The Demography of Famines: An Indian Historical Pespective*, Delhi 1996.

## Notes to Chapter 4

R. Anatase quoted in Harold Marcus, *The Life and Times of Menelik II*, Oxford 1975, pp. 136–7.

1. Cf. Avner Offer, *The First World War: An Agrarian Interpretation*, Oxford 1989, pp 85, 89; Dan Morgan, *Merchants of Grain*, New York 1979, esp. pp. 32–6; and Carl Solberg, *The Prairies and the Pampas: Agrarian Policy in Canada and Argentina, 1880–1930*, Stanford, Calif. 1987, esp. p. 36.
2. Eric Stokes, *The Peasant and the Raj*, Cambridge 1978, p. 275.
3. Quoted in Neil Charlesworth, "Rich Peasants and Poor Peasants in Late Nineteenth-Century Maharashtra," in Dewey and Hopkins (eds.), p. 108.
4. Christopher Baker, *An Indian Rural Economy, 1880–1955: The Tamilnad Countryside*, Bombay 1984, p. 135.
5. Gilbert Fite, *The Farmers' Frontier, 1865–1900*, New York 1966, p. 96.
6. The Nordeste was an exception: the improvement in weather could not make up for the decline in the earnings of sugar and cotton. Recession on the coast, moreover, turned into depression in the hinterlands. "In the sertão, even formerly independent cowherds reverted to marginal activities, selling goat hides and working for pitiful wages on the ranches of large landowners. Bankrupt agriculturalists sold or abandoned their land and moved to cities" (Levine, p. 37).
7. See Donald Meinig's brilliant studies of bonanza wheat belts and rainfall modification theories, "The Evolution of Understanding and Environment: Climate and Wheat Culture in the Columbia Plateau," *Yearbook of the Association of Pacific Coast Geographers* 16 (1954); and *On the Margins of the Good Earth: The South Australian Wheat Frontier, 1869–1884*, Chicago 1962. (It should be noted that South Australia's climatic boom–bust cycle was in antiphase to most other regions, with humid years in the late 1870s and severe drought in the early 1880s. Unlike eastern Australia, its weather has little correlation with ENSO.)
8. Jonathan Raban, *Bad Land: An American Romance*, New York 1996, p. 208. He refers to the drought of 1917–20 that broke the wartime wheat boom in eastern Montana.
9. Meinig, *On the Margins*, p. 207.
10. See "Filtered Normalised Monthly Anomalies of MSLP and SST Since 1871," in Rob Allan, Janette Lindesay and David Parker, *El Niño Southern Oscillation and Climate Variability*, Collingwood, Vic. 1996, pp. 188–201.
11. Peak grain prices in the pre-Depression United States (which reflect global, not just local, harvest conditions) – e.g., 1891–92, 1897–98, 1908–09, 1914–19 and 1924–25 – correlated to observed El Niño events (price trend from Wilfred Malenbaum, *The World Wheat Economy, 1885–1939*, Cambridge, Mass. 1953, p. 29).
12. Fite, pp. 108–9 and 126–7. Drought in 1892–93 again produced great distress throughout the Great Plains. The famous hunger-fighter Louis Klopsch, the publisher of New York's *The Christian Herald*, reported incredulously from Nebraska that "there was really a famine in one of the richest agricultural regions of the United States" and that thousands faced death from cold or starvation unless they received immediate relief (quoted in Charles Pepper, *Life-Work of Louis Klopsch: Romance of a Modern Knight of Mercy*, New York

1910, pp. 245–6).

13. Florescano and Swan, pp. 57 and 113–14.

14. Bhatia, pp. 168–9.

15. Digby, *Prosperous British India*, London 1901, p. 129.

16. Bhatia, pp. 172–8.

17. Carol Henderson, "Life in the Land of Death: Famine and Drought in Arid Western Rajasthan," Ph.D. diss., Columbia University 1989, p. 42.

18. Navtej Singh, *Starvation and Colonialism: A Study of Famines in the Nineteenth Century British Punjab, 1858–1901*, New Delhi 1996, pp. 89–91.

19. Ibid.

20. Digby considered this an accurate estimate of total famine mortality (*"Prosperous" British India*, p. 129).

21. "Hume to Every Member of the Congress Party" (16 Feb. 1892, quoted in Edward Moulton, "Allan O. Hume and the Indian National Congress: A Reassessment," in Jim Masselos (ed.), *Struggling and Ruling: The Indian National Congress 1885–1985*, New Delhi 1987, p. 11.

22. For an 1888 account of depopulation in Shaanxi, see George Jamieson, "Tenure of Land in China and the Condition of the Rural Population," *Journal of the China Branch of the Royal Asiatic Society* (for 1888), Shanghai 1889, p. 91.

23. Allan, Lindesay and Parker, pp. 188–91.

24. Cf., T. L. Bullock (consul at Chefoo), "The Geography of China," *The Journal of the Manchester Geographical Society*, 14:4–6 (April–June 1896), p. 129; John Freeman, "Flood Problems in China," *Proceedings, American Society of Civil Engineers*, May 1922, pp. 1113 and 1137–8; Alvyn Austin, *Saving China: Canadian Missionaries in the Middle Kingdom*, Toronto 1986, pp. 36–8; A. Broomhall, *China's Open Century: Book Seven*, pp. 97–8; *Spectator* syndicated in *New York Times*, 5 March 1888; and C. Vorosmarty, et al., "Drainage Basins, River Systems, and Anthropogenic Change: The Chinese Example," in James Galloway and Jerry Melillo, *Asian Change in the Context of Global Climate Change*, Cambridge 1998, p. 212.

25. Han Woo-Keou, *History of Korea*, p. 404.

26. George Lensen, *Balance of Intrigue: International Rivalry in Korea and Manchuria, 1884–1899*, vol. 1, Tallahassee 1982, p. 118.

27. Han Woo-Keou, pp. 404–13.

28. Richard Robbins, Jr., *Famine in Russia: 1891–1892*, New York 1975, pp. 6–10.

29. Ibid., pp. 12–13 and 170–71.

30. Leroy Vail and Landeg White, *Capitalism and Colonialism in Mozambique: A Study of Quelimane District*, Minneapolis 1980, pp. 100–101.

31. Denis, p. 351.

32. Graciliano Ramos, *Barren Lives*, Austin, Tex. 1971, p. 121.

33. Arthur Dias, *The Brazil of Today*, Nivelles 1903, pp. 249–50.

34. Ralph Della Cava, *Miracle at Joaseiro*, New York 1970, p. 31.

35. James McCann, *People of the Plow: An Agricultural History of Ethiopia, 1800–1900*, Madison, Wis. 1995, p. 89.

36. Richard Pankhurst, *The History of Famine and Epidemics in Ethiopia Prior to the Twenti-*

*eth Century*, Addis Ababa 1986, pp. 62–3.

37. William Jordan, *The Great Famine: Northern Europe in the Early Fourteenth Century*, Princeton, N.J. 1996, p. 36.

38. McCann, p. 89.

39. Pankhurst, pp. 59 and 91–2.

40. Holger Weiss, "'Dying Cattle': Some Remarks on the Impact of Cattle Epizootics in the Central Sudan During the Nineteenth Century," *African Economic History* 26 (1998), p. 182.

41. Richard Pankhurst, *Economic History of Ethiopia, 1800–1935*, Addis Ababa 1968, pp. 216–20.

42. James McCann, *From Poverty to Famine in Northeast Ethiopia: A Rural History, 1900–1935*, Philadelphia 1987, pp. 73–4.

43. Chris Prouty, *Empress Taytu and Menelik II*, London 1986, p. 101.

44. Pankhurst, *The History of Famine*, pp. 71–2 and 100.

45. Marcus, *Menelik II*, pp. 135, 139 and 143 fn2.

46. Haggai Erlich, *Ethiopia and Eritrea During the Scramble for Africa: A Political Biography of Ras Alula, 1875–1897*, East Lansing 1982, p. 141.

47. Pankhurst, *History of Famine*, pp. 74–85 and 96; and *Economic History*, pp. 216–20. McCann (*People of the Plow*) questions accounts of cannibalism, "since no such practices have been reported from recent famines of equal or greater severity" (p. 90).

48. Pankhurst, *The History of Famine*, pp. 87–8.

49. Ibid., p. 91.

50. Harold Marcus, *A History of Ethiopia*, Berkeley 1994, p. 94.

51. A. Donaldson Smith, "Expedition through Somaliland to Lake Rudolf," *Geographical Journal* 8 (1896), p. 127.

52. Pankhurst, *The History of Famine*, pp. 86–9, 105.

53. Marcus, p. 143.

54. Father Joseph Ohrwalder (edited by F. Wingate), *Ten Years' Captivity in the Mahdi's Camp*, London 1897, p. 283.

55. P. Holt, *The Mahdist State in the Sudan: 1881–1898*, Oxford 1958, pp. 157–60.

56. Ibid., pp. 160 and 165–7.

57. Ibid., pp. 171–3. See also Augustus Wylde, *Modern Abyssinia*, London 1901, p. 106.

58. Alexander De Waal, *Famine that Kills: Darfur, Sudan, 1984–1985*, Oxford 1989, pp. 63–4.

59. Ohrwalder, p. 306.

60. Holt, pp. 174–5.

61. C. Rosignoli, "Omdurman during the Mahdiya," *Sudan Notes and Records* 48, Khartoum 1967, p. 43.

62. Rudolf Slatin Pasha, *Fire and Sword in the Sudan*, London 1897, p. 274.

63. Ibid., p. 273.

64. Ibid., pp. 274–5.

65. Rosignoli, *Sudan Notes*, p. 42.

66. Catherine Coquery-Vidrovitch, "Ecologie et historie en Afrique noire," *Histoire, economie et société* 16:3 (1997), p. 501;

67. Richard Pankhurst, *The Ethiopians*, Oxford 1998, pp. 183–9.

68. Marcus, pp. 92–3.

69. On the 1896 drought-famine in Ethiopia, see Coquery-Vidrovitch, p. 503. For a recent overview of Ethiopian climate history, see Maria Machado, Alfredo Perez-Gonzalez and Gerardo Benito, "Paleoenvironmental Changes During the Last 4000 years in the Tigray, Northern Ethiopia," *Quaternary Research* 49 (1998), pp. 312–21.

70. Sir John Elliot, "Address to the Sub-section Cosmical Physics," reprinted in *Symon's Meteorological Magazine* 465 (Oct. 1904), p. 147.

71. Malenbaum, pp. 178–9.

72. For a discussion of drought and dearth in Upper Egypt and the Sudan, see A. Milne, "The Dry Summer on the Upper Nile," *Scottish Geographical Magazine* 16 (1900), pp. 89–91. Tolstoy's observations on the agrarian crisis that began with the 1896–97 crop failures ("La Famine en Russie en 1898") was published in *La Revue socialiste* (Paris), 1898, pp. 129–42. In Milan, the army massacred 80 bread rioters on 8 May 1898 (see Offer, p. 220).

73. David Landes, *The Unbound Prometheus: Technological Change and Industrial Development in Western Europe from 1750 to the Present*, Cambridge 1969, p. 231.

74. Elizabeth Isichei, *A History of African Societies to 1870*, Cambridge 1997, p. 293.

75. David Arnold, "Touching the Body: Perspectives on the Indian Plague, 1896–1900," *Subaltern Studies* 5 (1987), p. 74.

76. Esherick, p. 300; and David Little, *Understanding Peasant China*, New Haven, Conn. 1989, pp. 152–3 (quote).

77. Arthur Smith, *China in Convulsion*, vol. 1, Edinburgh 1901, p. 219; and A. Broomhall, *China's Open Century, Book Seven*, p. 306.

78. Della Cava, p. 55.

79. Charles Ambler, *Kenyan Communities in the Age of Imperialism*, New Haven, Conn. 1988, p. 3.

80. John Lonsdale, "The European Scramble and Conquest in African History," in Oliver and Sanderson, p. 692.

## Notes to Chapter 5

The quote appears in H. M. Hyndman, *The Bankruptcy of India*, London 1886, p. vi.

1. "Presidential Address at Lucknow Congress," (Dec. 1899) in Romesh Chunder Dutt, *Romesh Chunder Dutt*, New Delhi 1968, p. 202.

2. Loveday, p. 65.

3. Michelle McAlpin, "Price Movements and Fluctuations in Economic Activity (1860–1947), in Dharma Kumar (ed.), *Cambridge Economic History of India*, Cambridge 1983, pp. 886–8. See also Sir John Strachey, *India*, London 1894, pp. 184–5.

4. Augustin Filon, "L'Inde d'aujourd'hui d'apres les ecrivains indiens: I. La Situation economique et la vie publique," *Revue des deux mondes*, Nov.–Dec. 1899, p. 381.

5. Rashmi Pande, *The Viceroyalty of Lord Elgin II*, Patna 1986, p. 131.

6. Premansukumar Bandyopadhyay, *Indian Famine and Agrarian Problems*, Calcutta, p. 231.

7. The steep decline of British agriculture is vividly illustrated by the contrast between the harvest of 80 million bushels in 1884 and the meager 37 million bushels harvested in 1895 (Marcello de Cecco, *The International Gold Standard: Money and Empire*, New York 1984, p. 25).

8. Thus in an October 1896 letter the collector of Godavari complained that despite a bountiful local harvest, grain prices "depend almost entirely on the condition in other parts of India" (quoted in A. Satyananarayana, "Expansion of Commodity Production and Agrarian Market," in Ludden [1994], p. 207). Satyananarayana provides a useful overview of the complex debate on the degree of integration and automatic price movement in local, national and international markets by the late nineteenth century.

9. G. Chesney, "Famine and Controversy," *The Nineteenth Century*, March 1902, pp. 479 (preexisting drought in Central Provinces and Rajputana) and 481 (price of millet).

10. *The Times*, 18 Jan. 1897.

11. Quoted in B. Bhatia, "The 'Entitlement Approach' to Famine Analysis," in G. Harrison (ed.), *Famine*, Oxford 1988, pp. 39–40.

12. Moulton, p. 17.

13. Bandyopadhyay, p. 140.

14. *Spectator*, 30 Jan. 1897.

15. "From Ahmednagar," 16 Oct., in *New York Times*, 22 Nov. 1896.

16. Margaret Denning, *Mosaics from India*, Chicago 1902, pp. 168–9.

17. "Sir Edwin Arnold on the Famine in India," reprinted from the *North American Review* (March 1897) in the *Review of Reviews*, April 1897, p. 459.

18. "Pestilence and Famine in India," *Spectator*, 16 Jan. 1897, p. 81.

19. S. N. Kulkarni, *Famines, Droughts and Scarcities in India (Relief Measures and Policies)*, Allahabad 1990, p. 16; and Hari Srivastava, *The History of Indian Famines*, Agra 1968, pp. 205 and 226; Bandyopadhyay, pp. 14–16.

20. Bandyopadhyay, ibid.

21. Ibid., p. 231.

22. Ibid., p. 39.

23. As Currie points out, most of the apparatus of the New Poor Law of 1834 was imported into India, except "under normal conditions, there was no commitment to the maintenance of the 'deserving' poor" (p. 49) .

24. Singh, p. 110.

25. George Lambert, *India, The Horror-Stricken Empire*, Elkhart, Ind. 1898, p. 144.

26. Loveday, pp. 88–9.

27. Lambert, pp. 99–100.

28. Pepper, p. 59.

29. Ibid., pp. 318–19.

30. G. Thomas, *History of Photography in India, 1840–1980*, Pondicherry 1981, p. 28. For a British howl of protest against "misleading" famine photographs, see J. Rees, "Fighting the Famine in India," *The Nineteenth Century*, March 1897, pp. 358–61.

31. Sir Andrew Fraser, *Among Rajas and Ryots,* London 1911, pp. 111–25.

32. John McLane, *Indian Nationalism and the Early Congress*, Princeton, N.J. 1977, p. 71.

33. On Tilak and the Irish, see H. Brasted, "Irish Models and the Indian National Con-

gress, 1870–1922," in Masselos, pp. 31–2.

34.  E. Pratt, "India and Her Friends," *Westminster Review*, June 1897, p. 647.

35.  McLane, p. 29.

36.  H. Birdwood, "The Recent Epidemics of Plague in Bombay," *Journal of the Manchester Geographical Society*, 1898, pp. 141–3. See also Alok Sheel, "Bubonic plague in south Bihar: Gaya and Shahabad districts, 1900–1924," *IESHR*, 35:4 (1998), pp. 426–7.

37.  Rajnarayan Chandavarkar, "Plague Panic and Epidemic Politics in India, 1896–1914," in Terence Ranger and Paul Slack (eds.), *Epidemics and Ideas*, Cambridge 1992, p. 213.

38.  F. B. Smith, *Florence Nightingale*, London 1982, p. 125.

39.  Ira Klein, "Urban Development and Death: Bombay City, 1870–1914," *Modern Asian Studies* 20:4 (1986), p. 748.

40.  Radhika Famasubban and Nigel Crook, "Spatial Patterns of Health and Morality," in Sujata Patel and Alice Thorner (eds.), *Bombay: Metaphor for Modern India*, pp. 148–51.

41.  Klein, p. 734.

42.  See the *Spectator*, 16 January 1897, p. 81.

43.  On unrest over grain prices, see Kulkarni, p. 16; on rioting, David Arnold, *Colonizing the Body: State Medicine and Epidemic Disease in Nineteenth-Century India*, Berkeley 1993, pp. 214 and 230.

44.  Ira Klein, "Plague, Policy and Popular Unrest in British India," *Modern Asian Studies*, 22:4 (1988), p. 737.

45.  Arnold, p 204.

46.  Chandavarkar, p. 207.

47.  Nayana Goradia, *Lord Curzon: The Last of the British Moghuls*, Delhi 1993, p. 123.

48.  "Four of every five patients who entered Bombay hospitals perished there," Klein, "Plague, Policy and Popular Unrest," p. 742.

49.  Arnold,"Touching the Body," p. 71.

50.  McLane, p. 30.

51.  Cf. D. Tahmankar, *Lokamanya Tilak*, London 1956, p. 68 passim; N. Kelkar, *Life and Times of Lokamanya Tilak*, Delhi, p. 338 passim; Richard Cashman, *The Myth of the Lokamanya*, Berkeley, pp. 123–50; and Romesh Chunder Dutt, *The Economic History of India in the Victorian Age*, 2nd edn., London 1906, p. 456 (quote).

52.  I. Catanach, "Plague and the Indian Village, 1896–1914," in Peter Robb (ed.), *Rural India: Land, Power and Society Under British Rule*, London 1983, pp. 218 and 227.

53.  Chandavarkar, p. 210.

54.  Catanach, ibid.

55.  *India in 1897*, quoted in Filon, p. 381. In his study of the history of famine in a poor district of Bihar, K. Suresh Singh observes that although "the [1896–97] famine was the most lethal in Palamau's recorded history ... officially it was reported that 'no deaths were caused by starvation'" (*The Indian Famine 1967*, New Delhi 1975, p. 32).

56.  "The Famine in India," *Missionary Review of the World*, April 1897, p. 286.

57.  He judged 1897, not 1857 or 1877, to be India's "most calamitous year of the century"; see Ramabai Ranade (ed.), *Miscellaneous Writings of the Late Hon'ble Mr. Justice M.G. Ranade*, Delhi 1992 (reprint), p. 180.

58.  Singh, *Starvation and Colonialism*, pp. 98–9.

59. Dutt, pp. 219–22 (Indian National Congress); *Famine and Agrarian Problems,* pp. 193 (Bilaspur) and 227 (Hamilton in House of Commons).

60. This claim (supposedly based on testimony by Sir Charles Lyall in 1898) was made by "E. C." in "The Indian Famine," *Westminster Review* 155:2 (1901), p. 135.

61. D. E. U. Baker, *Colonialism in an Indian Hinterland: The Central Provinces, 1820–1920,* Delhi 1993, pp. 174, 194 and 202.

62. F. Merewether, *A Tour Through the Famine Districts of India,* London 1898, pp. 129–30. Merewether's account of the Jubbulpur poorhouse was scoffed at by J. Rees in *The Nineteenth Century* (March 1897), who claimed that conditions were not radically different than in Limehouse or Mile End. "If the misery and destitution of London itself were collected within a ring fence, it is doubtful if a visitor from the east would think it other than a sad spectacle" (p. 359).

63. See Pepper, p. 78.

64. *The Memoirs of Julian Hawthorne,* ed. Edith Hawthorne, New York 1938, p. 295.

65. Julian Hawthorne, "India Starving," *Cosmopolitan* 23:4 (August 1897), pp. 379–82

66. Ibid. Dr. Louis Klopsch of the *Christian Herald* penned equally shocking accounts from the Ahmedabad poorhouse where prostrate victims were left out in the open, to be eaten by flies in the 110-degree heat. "On inquiring why these people were exposed to the relentless rays of the sun without shelter or shade, I was told that they had been brought in from the neighboring villages on carts and were to remain under observation for twenty-four hours in order to determine whether symptoms of contagious disease developed. They had come in during the afternoon, they had lain there for three or four hours, they were to remain there all night and to stay there all the next forenoon. Possibly the evening of the next day they would be admitted to the inhospitable shelter of the Ahmedabad poor-house. Myriads of flies were feasting on each individual bundle, and the eyelids, mouths, nostrils and ears were all besieged with battalions of flies gorging themselves on the helpless victims of the India famine." Klopsch found the "indescribable misery" of the small children almost "unbearable" to relate (quoted in Pepper, pp. 79–80).

67. W. Aykroyd, *The Conquest of Famine,* London 1974, pp. 64–7.

68. Rudyard Kipling, "William the Conqueror," in *The Day's Work,* London 1898, p. 203.

69. Ibid., pp. 380–81.

70. Caption on photographs, inside front cover, *Cosmopolitan* 23:3 (July 1897).

71. Bandyopadhyay, p. 51.

72. For example, *Harper's Weekly* in 1900 claimed: "The famine of 1877 killed some ten million beings; that of 1897, about sixteen millions; whilst the present one will probably break the record with twenty million" (p. 350). See also Digby, *"Prosperous" British India,* p. 129.

73. C. Ramage, *The Great Indian Drought of 1899,* Boulder 1977, pp. 1–3. Ramage is a world authority on the Indian monsoon.

74. See D. Mooley and B. Parthasarathy, "Fluctuations in All-India Summer Monsoon Rainfall During 1871–1978,"*Climate Change* 6 (1984), pp. 287–301.

75. Ramage, p. 6.

76. Bombay Government, *Report on the Famine in the Bombay Presidency, 1899–1902,* vol.

1, Bombay 1903, p. 114.

77. Ramage, p. 4.

78. Pierre Loti, *India*, English translation by George Inman, London 1995, pp. 145–6.

79. Bombay, *Report*, vol. 1, p. 3.

80. Vaughan Nash, *The Great Famine and Its Causes*, London 1900, p. 12.

81. Scott, pp. 142–3.

82. Frederick Lamb, *The Gospel and the Mala: The Story of the Hyderabad Wesleyan Mission*, Mysore 1913, p. 49.

83. Scott, pp. 31–2.

84. Singh, pp. 113–18.

85. Bombay, *Report*, vol. 1, pp. 3 and 83 (artisans and mill workers).

86. Charlesworth, "Rich Peasants and Poor Peasants," pp. 110–11.

87. McLane, pp. 26–7.

88. C. J. O'Donnell, *The Failure of Lord Curzon*, London 1903, pp. 37–41.

89. Quoted in C. Ramage, p. 5.

90. O'Donnell, p. xviii.

91. Nash, p. 171.

92. Bandyopadhyay, pp. 63–7 and 226.

93. Bernard Semmel, *The Liberal Ideal and the Demons of Empire*, Baltimore 1993, p. 109. "Never since the Crimean War, never perhaps since the death of Castlereagh in 1822," wrote Dutt, "has Imperialism been so rampant in England, never have the higher instincts of humanity and justice, of respect towards rival nations, and fairness towards subject nations, been at a lower ebb" (quoted in Romesh Chunder Dutt, *Romesh Chunder Dutt*, New Delhi 1968, p. 63).

94. S. Thorburn, *Problems of Indian Poverty*, Fabian Tract No. 110, London, March 1902, p. 226 (he is writing about 1899–1901).

95. See figures in *The Times* (London), 17 Feb. 1900.

96. Scott, p. 153.

97. Ibid.

98. Eddy, p. 25.

99. On Naoroji's and Dutt's disenchantment with British Liberalism and the former's turn towards the Socialists, see Masani, pp. 201, 400–402 and 432; Dutt, pp. 62–3 and 79; and J. K. Gupta, *Life and Work of Romesh Chunder Dutta, CIE*, Calcutta 1911 (reprinted Delhi 1986), pp. 240–44, 318–19 and especially 458. On demoralization and lack of direction within the Indian National Congress during the famines, see McLane, pp. 130–31. On British Christian socialists and imperialism, see Peter d'A. Jones, *The Christian Socialist Revival 1877–1914*, Princeton, N.J., esp. pp. 198–205; and on Fabian imperialism, see Francis Lee, *Fabianism and Colonialism: The Life and Political Thought of Lord Sydney Olivier*, London 1988.

100. Raymond Challinor, *The Origins of British Bolshevism*, London 1977, p. 15 (Falkirk SDF). At the 1904 Amsterdam Congress of the Socialist International, which branded "Great Britain with the mark of shame for its treatment of India," a thousand delegates (including Hyndman, Jaurès, Luxemburg and Lenin) stood in silence in commemoration of the Indian famine dead, then gave Naoroji a rapturous applause when he declared that

the liberation of India from hunger and the drain of wealth "rests in the hands of the working classes. Working men constitute the immense majority of the people of India, and they appeal to the workmen of the whole world, and ask for their help and sympathy" (Masani, pp. 431–2).

101. Nash, pp. 179–80.
102. Ibid., pp. 19–33.
103. Ibid., pp. 19, 173 and 181.
104. Bombay, *Report*, vol. 1, p. 91
105. Klein, p. 752.
106. Ibid., p. 54.
107. On Kholapur, see Merewether, pp. 27–8.
108. Goradia, pp. 71–4 and 146.
109. Scott, pp. 113–14.
110. Loti, pp. 171–2.
111. Ibid., p. 172.
112. Kuldeep Mathur and Niraja Jayal, *Drought, Policy and Politics*, New Delhi 1993, p. 63.
113. Scott, p. 107.
114. "The outturn of crops which was in the previous year 27,710,258 Indian maunds fell in 1899–1900 to 1,174,923 Indian maunds" (R. Choksey, *Economic Life in the Bombay Gujarat [1800–1939]*, Bombay 1968, p. 171).
115. Ibid; and Scott, pp. 107–8. Choksey estimates that about half of the cattle (or 800,000 head) in Gujarat perished (p. 176).
116. Sherwood Eddy, *India Awakening*, New York 1911, p. 24.
117. Scott, ibid.
118. Quoted in Pepper, pp. 82–3.
119. Vasant Kaiwar, "The Colonial State, Capital and the Peasantry in Bombay Presidency," *Modern Asian Studies*, 28:4 (1994), p. 813.
120. Bombay, *Report*, p. 100.
121. Choksey, p. 44.
122. Eddy, ibid.
123. Klein, "When the Rains Failed," p. 205.
124. J. Coe, "Congress and the Tribals in Surat District in the 1920s," in Masselos, pp. 60–62.
125. "A lady writing from Ahmedabad," quoted in ibid., p. 36.
126. Choksey, p. 44.
127. Bombay, *Report*, p. 95.
128. Nash, pp. 9–10.
129. David Hardiman, "The Crisis of Lesser Patidars: Peasant Agitations in Kheda District, Gujarat, 1917–34," in D. Low (ed.), *Congress and the Raj*, London 1977, pp. 55–6.
130. Baker, p. 231.
131. Ibid., p. 198.
132. Bombay, *Report*, pp. 5–6.
133. Tim Dyson, "On the Demography of South Asian Famines – Part 1," *Population Studies* 45 (1991), pp. 16 and 22.

134. Dutt, *Romesh Chunder Dutt*, p. 252.

135. Arup Maharatna, *The Demography of Famines: An Indian Historical Perspective*, Delhi 1996, p. 15 (Table 1.1); Stein, "The Making of Agrarian Policy in India," p. 18; and Lewis , p. 173.

136. Speech to the Legislative Council, Simla, 19 Oct. 1900 (in Curzon, *Lord Curzon in India: Being a Selection of His Speeches...*, London 1906, p. 394.

137. Bombay, *Report*, p. 103.

138. Tim Dyson, "Indian Historical Demography: Developments and Prospects," in Dyson (ed.), *India's Historical Demography: Studies in Famine, Disease and Society*, London 1989, p. 5; and J. A. Crawford, *Report on the Famine in the Hyderabad Assigned Districts in the Years 1899 and 1900*, vol. 1, Nagpur 1901, p. 8.

139. *The Lancet*, 16 May 1901.

140. Digby, *"Prosperou" British India*, pp. 137–9.

141. Klein, "When the Rains Failed," p. 186 (on Davis); and Pierre Le Roy, *Le Faim dans le monde*, Paris 1994, p. 16.

142. Maharatna, pp. 15 and 63–7.

143. Chandavarkar, p. 203.

144. Srivastava, p. 269.

145. Ibid., p. 219; and B. Tomlinson, *The Economy of Modern India, 1860–1970* (*The New Cambridge History of India*, 3:3), Cambridge 1993, p. 83.

146. Bandyopadhyay, pp. 192 and 200.

147. Sumit Sarkar, *Modern India: 1885–1947*, Madras 1983, p. 36.

148. Wakimura, p. 301; and Choksey, p. 44.

149. *Report of the Indian Famine Commission, 1901*, Calcutta 1901, p. 7; Klein, "When the Rains Failed," p. 204 fn33.

## Notes to Chapter 6

The epigraph appears in Euclydes da Cunha, *Rebellion in the Backlands* (*Os Sertões*), trans. Samuel Putnam, Chicago 1944, p. 133.

1. Pepper, *Life-Work of Louis Klopsch*, p. 172.

2. Francis Nichols, *Through Hidden Shensi*, New York 1902, pp. 2–9; Marshall Broomhall, *The Chinese Empire: A General and Missionary Survey*, London (China Inland Mission) 1907, p. 206 (mortality figures).

3. Broomhall, pp. 228–35 and 242. Arthur Tiedemann draws attention to comparable suffering in northern Anhui. "A Jesuit priest at Mengcheng observed, for example, that so many people were dying in the city that the naked dead and dying had to be dumped outside the city walls to be devoured by hungry dogs" ("Boxers, Christians and the Culture of Violence in North China," *Journal of Peasant Studies* 25:4 [July 1899], p. 156).

4. According to Wilkinson (Table 3, p. 144) 75 of 90 Shenxi districts reported crop disaster in 1898. The drought continued through 1900 (67 districts) and was punctually followed by war and brigandage affecting agriculture in 68 districts.

5. On the centrality of *fengshui* doctrines to the popular Chinese interpretation of the

crisis, see Smith, vol. 1, p. 57.

6. Esherick, p. 299.

7. Tiedemann (p. 159) cites the *North-China Herald* on "a general crop failure in the wheat-exporting area of northwestern Shandong" previous to the inundation.

8. Ibid., pp. 175–7.

9. Quoted in Pepper, p. 164.

10. Paul Cohen, *History in Three Keys: The Boxers as Event, Experience, and Myth*, New York 1997, p. 69.

11. *New York Times*, 25 March 1899.

12. Lu Yao, "The Origins of the Boxers," *Chinese Studies in History*, 20:3–4 (1987), p. 54.

13. Esherick, pp. 179–80.

14. Pepper, pp. 164–5. A year later, however, the navy did provide Klopsch with a transport, the *Quito*, to carry 5,000 tons of Kansas relief grain to India.

15. Harlan Beach, "The History of Christian Missions in China," in G. Blakeslee (ed.), *China and the Far East*, New York 1910, p. 274.

16. Endymion Wilkinson, "Studies in Chinese Price History," Ph.D. diss., Princeton University 1970, p. 52.

17. Smith, vol. 2, p. 573.

18. S. Teng, *The Nien Army and Their Guerrilla Warfare, 1851–1868*, Paris 1961, p. 127.

19. Smith, vol. 1, pp. 155–6.

20. Elizabeth Perry, "Social Banditry Revisited: The Case of Bai Lang, a Chinese Brigand," *Modern China* 9:3 (July 1983), pp. 361, 366 and 369.

21. Esherick, pp. 174, 223 and 281–2.

22. Smith, p. 219.

23. Ibid., p. 244.

24. Lu, p.52.

25. Cohen, pp. 35, 77–82 (first quote) and p. 95 (second quote); Tiedemann, p. 156.

26. Lu, p. 55.

27. Qi Aizhang, "Stages in the Development of the Boxer Movement and Their Characteristics," *Chinese Studies in History* 20:3–4 (1987), p. 115. In the same issue, Liao Yizhong ("Special Features of the Boxer Movement") denies the existence of any "anti-feudal" dimension, although his citations are from Shandong, not Hebei (pp. 186–7).

28. Broomhall, vol. 7, p. 374.

29. Georges Lefebvre, *The Great Fear of 1789: Rural Panic in Revolutionary France*, New York 1973.

30. Eva Price, *China Journal, 1889–1900: An American Missionary Family During the Boxer Rebellion*, New York 1989, pp. 199 and 203–4. See also Sarah Alice (Troyer) Young, letter from Shanxi (2 Dec. 1899) in coll. 542, box 1, folder 7, Billy Graham Center.

31. Price, pp. 204 and 222.

32. Cohen, p. 172. For similar populist, anti-foreign reactions to the drought in the Beijing region, see E. Ruoff (ed.), *Death Throes of a Dynasty: Letters and Diaries of Charles and Bessie Ewing, Missionaries to China*, Kent, Ohio 1990, p. 68 (letters of Sept. and Oct. 1899).

33. Price, pp. 191–4, 199 and 209.

34. Archibald Glover, *A Thousand Miles of Miracle in China*, London 1904, pp. 6, 85, 195

and 244 (song).

35. Price, p. 224.

36. Austin, p. 75.

37. Esherick, pp. xv–xvi, 282 and 291–2.

38. Smith, vol. 2, p. 716. The Japanese, in contrast to the barbarities of their armies in China in the 1930s, were the honorable exception, and were praised by all independent observers for their humane and respectful treatment of Chinese civilians.

39. E.J. Dillon, "The Chinese Wolf and the European Lamb," excerpted in the *New York Times*, 27 Jan. 1901.

40. Ibid.

41. Joseph Page, *The Revolution That Never Was: Northeast Brazil, 1955–1964*, New York 1972, pp. 26–7.

42. Vera Kelsey, *Seven Keys to Brazil*, New York 1941, p. 172.

43. Robert Levine, *Vale of Tears: Revisiting the Canudos Massacre in Northeastern Brazil, 1893–1897*, Berkeley 1992, pp. 34–8.

44. Levine, pp.193–203 and 229.

45. Ibid., pp. 139, 151 and 159–61.

46. Ibid., pp. 132–3 and 229–31.

47. Ibid., pp 142–6.

48. On the drought in 1898 and 1900, see Charles Wagley, *An Introduction to Brazil*, London 1971, p. 41. According to historical statistics from the International Research Institute for Climate Prediction (University of California, San Diego), the 1897–98 drought in the Nordeste had a rainfall anomaly of –8.15 cm/month. In the following century, the next most severe drought (1915) measured –3.3 cm/month. Moreover, all years from 1897 through 1906 were in the driest historical tercile and had rainfall anomalies of at least –1.4 cm/month. (database at iri.ucsd.edu/hot_nino/impacts/ ns_amer/index).

49. Levine, pp. 164–5.

50. Ibid., p. 177.

51. Ibid., p. 178.

52. Da Cunha, p. 475.

53. Levine, p. 190.

54. Della Cava, ibid.

55. Levine, p. 148.

56. Della Cava, p. 89.

57. C. Kim and Han-Kyo Kim, *Korea and the Politics of Imperialism, 1876–1910*, Berkeley 1967, pp. 116–17.

58. Pierre van der Eng, "The Real Domestic Product of Indonesia, 1880–1989," *Explorations in Economic History* 1992, pp. 355 and 358.

59. Furnivall, p. 232.

60. See R. Elson, "The Famine in Demak and Grobogan in 1849–50; Its Causes and Circumstances," *Review of Indonesian and Malaysian Affairs* 19:1 (1985).

61. Hugenholz, pp. 178–9

62. R. Elson, "From 'States' to State: The Changing Regime of Peasant Export Production in Mid-Nineteenth Century Java," in J. Lindblad (ed.), *Historical Foundations of a*

*National Economy in Indonesia, 1890s–1990s*, Amsterdam 1996, p. 128.

63. Ricklefs, pp. 124–5.

64. Hugenholz, ibid.

65. H. Dick, "The Emergence of a National Economy, 1808–1990s," in Linblad, p. 36.

66. Ricklefs, pp. 151–3.

67. Martinez Duesta, p. 260.

68. Ken De Bevoise, *Agents of Apocalypse: Epidemic Disease in the Colonial Philippines*, Princeton, N.J. 1995, pp. 60–62 and 447.

69. Ibid., pp. 41–2 and 158–60.

70. Ibid., pp 63–6, 177 and 181–2.

71. Ibid., p. 65.

72. Brian Linn, *Guardians of Empire: The US Army and the Pacific, 1902–1940*, Chapel Hill, N.C. 1997, p. 14.

73. De Bevoise, pp. 13 and 65; see also Matthew Smallman-Raynor and Andrew Cliff, "The Philippines Insurrection and the 1902–04 Cholera Epidemic: Part I – Epidemiological Diffusion Processes in War," *Journal of Historical Geography* 24:1 (1998), pp. 69–89.

74. Billig, p. 159.

75. Violeta Lopez-Gonzaga and Michelle Decena, "Negros in Transition: 1899–1905," *Philippine Studies* 38 (1990), p. 112.

76. McCoy, pp. 120–22.

77. Robin Palmer, "The Agricultural History of Rhodesia," in Palmer and Parsons, p. 223.

78. S. Nicholson, "The Historical Climatology of Africa," in Wigley , pp. 262–3.

79. John Reader, *Africa: A Biography of the Continent*, New York 1998, p. 587.

80. Coquery-Vidrovitch, pp. 495 and 502; A. Milne, "The Dry Summer on the Upper Nile," *Scottish Geographical Magazine* 16 (1899), pp. 89–90; and Quinn, "A Study of Southern Oscillation–Related Climatic Activity," p. 144.

81. On the drought-famine in Swaziland in 1896–97, see Neil Parsons and Robin Palmer, "Introduction: Historical Background," in Palmer and Parsons (eds.), *The Roots of Rural Poverty in Central and Southern Africa*, Berkeley 1977, p. 17.

82. T. O. Ranger, *Revolt in Southern Rhodesia, 1896–7*, London 1967, p. 148.

83. John Iliffe, *Famine in Zimbabwe*, pp. 21–30.

84. Charles Ambler, *The Great Famine in Central Kenya 1897–1900*, Nairobi 1977, pp. 122–8 and 143. (On the plague and the railroad, see Peter Curson and Kevin McCracken, *Plague in Sidney: The Anatomy of an Epidemic*, Kensington, p. 31.)

85. H.J. Mackinder, *The First Ascent of Mount Kenya*, ed. K. Michael Barbour, London 1991, pp. 82–5. This account was never published in the author's lifetime, its editor explains, to prevent disclosure of an atrocity: eight of the expedition's Swahili porters were executed at Mackinder's order (pp. 22–3).

86. Ambler, ibid.

87. D. Low, "British East Africa: The Establishment of British Rule, 1895–1912," in Vincent Harlow et al. (eds.), *History of East Africa*, vol. 2, Oxford 1965, pp. 4–5.

88. Marcia Wright, "East Africa, 1870–1905," in Oliver and Sanderson, p. 576.

89. Isichei, p. 454; and Ambler, p. 146.

90. Low, pp. 16–17.

91. Mackinder, p. 99.

92. Frederick Cooper, *From Slaves to Squatters: Plantation Labor and Agriculture in Zanzibar and Coastal Kenya, 1890–1925*, New Haven, Conn. 1980, pp. 59–60 and 220–22.

93. Low, pp. 110–11.

94. Ibid., p. 111; and Wright, p. 576–7.

95. James Giblin, *The Politics of Environmental Control in Northeastern Tanzania, 1840–1940*, Philadelphia 1992, pp. 90–91, 114–15, and 124–7

96. Leroy Vail and Landeg White, *Capitalism and Colonialism in Mozambique: A Study of Quelimane District*, Minneapolis 1980, pp.

97. Allen and Barbara Isaacman, *The Tradition of Resistance in Mozambique: The Zambesi Valley 1850–1921*, Berkeley 1976, p. 115.

98. Ibid., pp. 134–42.

99. Palmer, ibid.

100. Ambler, p. 149.

101. Tomlinson, p. 195.

102. Jairus Banaji, "Capitalist Domination and the Small Peasantry: The Deccan Districts in the Late 19th Century," in Gyan Prakash (ed.), *The World of the Rural Labourer in Colonial India*, Delhi 1994, p. 123.

103. Sumit Guha, *The Agrarian Economy of the Bombay Deccan*, p. 192.

104. Banaji, pp. 123–4; Arnold, "Famine in Peasant Consciousness," p. 42.

105. Charlesworth, *Peasants and Imperial Rule: Agriculture and Agrarian Society in the Bombay Presidency, 1850–1935*, Cambridge 1985, pp. 109–10.

106. Sir John Strachey, *India: Its Administration and Progress*, London 1911, p. 249.

107. Guha, pp. 149–58.

108. Vasant Kaiwar, "The Colonial State, Capital and the Peasantry in Bombay Presidency," *Modern Asian Studies* 28:4 (1994), p. 822.

109. Philip Huang, *The Peasant Economy and Social Change in North China*, Stanford, Calif. 1985, pp. 85–105.

110. Philip Huang, *The Peasant Family and Rural Development in the Yangzi Delta, 1350–1988*, Stanford, Calif. 1990, p. 71.

111. Huang, *Peasant Economy*, p. 17.

112. Fritjof Tichelman, *The Social Evolution of Indonesia*, The Hague 1980, p. 33.

113. D. R. Gadgil, *The Industrial Evolution of India in Recent Times, 1860–1939*, Delhi 1971, p. 180; and Daniel Little, *Understanding Peasant China*, New Haven, Conn. 1989, p. 92.

114. Jan Breman and E. Valentine Daniel, "Conclusion: the Making of a Coolie," in Daniel, Bernstein and Brass (eds.), *Plantations, Proletarians and Peasants in Colonial Asia*, London 1992, p. 290.

115. Pauline Keating, *Two Revolutions: Village Reconstruction and the Cooperative Movement in Northern Shaanxi, 1934–1945*, Stanford, Calif. 1997, pp. 27–8.

116. Ibid., p. 33.

117. Ibid., pp. 10–13, 23 and 30. Between 1920 and 1936 18,350,000 people were officially estimated to have died of famine in China, mostly in the north (E. Vermeer, *Water Conservancy and Irrigation in China*, The Hague 1977, p. 32).

## Notes to Chapter 7

The quote is from Frater, *Chasing the Monsoon*, New York 1991, p. 190.

1. "Climate" and "weather" differ not only in time-scale (mean versus individual value), but also in causal level. As Kevin Trenberth has pointed out, "Climate variation results from the interactions between the atmosphere and the other spheres (hydrosphere, cryosphere, biosphere, etc.) in the Earth system. Weather variations occur from instabilities within the atmosphere itself and are much more short-lived" (see ENSO Colloquium, July 1997, at www.dir.ucar.edu/esig/enso).

2. Why not, then, an Atlantic "El Niño" as well? The trade winds also pool warm water off Brazil and leave a cold tongue off Africa, but the Atlantic Ocean apparently does not provide a wide enough basin for ENSO-scale fluctuations to initiate or become a self-sustaining system. See F. Jin, "Tropical Ocean-Atmosphere Interaction, the Pacific Cold Tongue, and the ENSO," *Science* 274 (4 Oct. 1996), pp. 77–8.

3. Richard Grove, "The East India Company, the Raj and the El Niño: The Critical Role Played by Colonial Scientists in Establishing the Mechanisms of Global Climate Teleconnections, 1770–1930," in Richard Grove, Vinita Damodaran, and Satpal Sangwan, *Nature and the Orient: The Environmental History of South and Southeast Asia*, Delhi 1998, pp. 301–23.

4. Frederik Nebeker, *Calculating the Weather: Meteorology in the 20th Century*, San Diego 1995, p. 12. By 1880 there were 121 meteorological stations in India including Burma and Ceylon (*Nature*, 23 August 1883, p. 406).

5. Blanford virtually founded modern monsoon meteorology, and his 1877 book, *The Indian Meteorologist's Vade-Mecum*, "became the most widely used textbook on tropical meteorology for the rest of the century" (see Gisela Kutzbach, "Concepts of Monsoon Physics in Historical Perspective," in Jay Fein and Pamela Stephens [eds.], *Monsoons*, New York 1987, p. 181).

6. "On the Barometric See-Saw Between Russia and India in the Sun-Spot Cycle," *Nature*, 18 March 1880, p. 477. See also his *Report on the Meteorology of India in 1878*, Calcutta 1880.

7. On China, see "On the Barometric See-Saw," p. 480.

8. The first use of the term *teleconnection* was apparently A. Angstroem, "Teleconnections of Climate Changes in Present Time," *Geogr. Ann.* 17 (1935), pp. 242–58.

9. Richard Grove, *Green Imperialism: Colonial Expansion, Tropical Island Edens and the Origins of Environmentalism, 1600–1860*, Cambridge 1995, p. 446.

10. J. Norman Lockyer and W. Hunter, "Sun-Spots and Famines," *The Nineteenth Century*, Nov. 1877, p. 601.

11. *Nature*, 17 Aug. 1899, p. 374.

12. Douglas Hoyt and Kenneth Schatten, *The Role of the Sun in Climate Change*, Oxford 1997, pp. 36 and 144–5.

13. For a dessicationist perspective – influenced by Marsh's *The Earth as Modified by Human Action* – on the famine of 1876, see "Philindus," "Famines and Floods in India," *Macmillan's Magazine*, Feb. 1878 (quote from p. 256).

14. Lockyer and Hunter, p. 599.
15. See the discussion by Lloyd's expert Henry Jeula in Cornelius Walford's *The Famines of the World: Past and Present,* London 1879, pp. 94–6.
16. Meldrum also virtually accused Hunter of plagiarizing his 1875 research on Madras rainfall; see "Sun-Spots and Rainfall," *Nature,* 4 April 1878, pp. 448–50. Hunter's earlier reservations about a sunspot signature in higher latitude rainfall can be found in "Rainfall in the Temperate Zone in Connection with the Sun-Spot Cycle," *Nature,* 22 Nov. 1877, pp. 59–61.
17. See, for example, the richly sardonic critique of Hunter's speculations by Richard Proctor: "Sun-Spot, Storm, and Famine," *Gentleman's Magazine,* Dec. 1877, pp. 705–6.
18. E. Archibald, "W. W. Hunter: The Cycle of Drought and Famine in Southern India," *Calcutta Review* 131 (1878), p. 129; and for an account of Strachey's paper "On the Alleged Correspondence of the Rainfall at Madras with the Sun-spot Period, and on the True Criterion of Periodicity in a Series of Variable Quantities," read before the Royal Society in May 1877, see letter of B. Stewart to W. S. Jevons, 5 June 1877, in *Papers and Correspondence of William Stanley Jevons,* vol. 4, ed. R. Collison Black, London 1977, p. 203.
19. See C. Meldrum, "Sun-Spots and Rainfall," 4 April 1878, pp. 448–50; E. Archibald, "Indian Rainfall," 25 April 1878, p. 505; and S. Hill, "Indian Rainfall," 20 June 1878, p. 193.
20. Blanford, "On the Barometric See-Saw," pp. 477–8.
21. Kutzbach, p. 199.
22. Archibald, pp. 148–9.
23. Cunniff, p. 195. Cunniff points out, however, that Tomas Pompeu, an ardent "rainmaker" and author of *Memoria sobre a clima e seccas do Ceará* (1878), had been "the first Brazilian to correlate sunspots and droughts" (ibid.).
24. "The Rainfall of Brazil and the Sun-Spots," *Nature,* 8 Aug. 1878, p. 384; and Joaquim Alves, *Historia das secas (Seculos XVII a XIX),* Fortaleza 1953, p. 123.
25. Cunniff, pp. 183–9.
26. Hoyt and Schatten, p. 163.
27. "The Periodicity of Commercial Crises and Its Physical Explanation," *Journal of the Statistical and Social Inquiry Society of Ireland* 7 (1878); "Commercial Crises and Sun-Spots I," *Nature,* 14 Nov. 1878; and "Commercial Crises and Sun-Spots II," *Nature,* 24 April 1879.
28. Walford, pp. 292–3.
29. W. Jevons, "Economic Policy," in R. Smyth (ed.), *Essays in Economic Method,* London 1962, p. 26.
30. Philip Mirowski, "Macroeconomic Instability and the 'Natural' Processes in Early Neoclassical Economics," *Journal of Economic History* 44:2 (June 1984), p. 346.
31. Ibid., p. 349. In an earlier letter to his brother, Jevons admitted that "my theory of crises has the appearance of being a little too ingenious ... but I have great confidence in its substantial truth" (14 Nov. 1878 in *Papers and Correspondence,* vol. 4, p. 293).
32. Letter to *The Times,* published 17 Jan. 1879, ibid., vol. 5, pp. 10–11.
33. Letter to *The Times,* published 19 April 1879, ibid., vol. 5, pp. 44–8.
34. On Jevons's interest in Brazilian secas, see his letter to his brother, 18 June 1879, vol. 5, p. 65. While she never saw sunspots, Rosa Luxemburg in *The Accumulation of Capital* (1913) accepted part of Jevons's argument, agreeing that "periodical famines in India ...

recurring at intervals of ten or eleven years, were ... among the causes of periodical crises in England," p. 286).

35. Quoted in Proctor, p. 701.

36. Ibid., p. 165.

37. Indeed, the indefatigable Archibald, after a quarter-century's statistical labor, claimed that droughts in southern India followed minima, while those in the north coincided with maxima: a decidedly confusing (or, as he put it, "spasmodic") conclusion (*Nature*, 2 Aug. 1900, p. 335).

38. Quoted in Kutzbach, p. 200.

39. Colin Ramage, *Monsoon Meteorology*, New York 1971, p. 239.

40. A. Meadows, *Science and Controversy: A Biography of Sir Norman Lockyer*, Cambridge, Mass. 1972, pp. 284–6.

41. Cf. report on Hildebrandsson's recent papers in *Nature*, 17 Aug. 1899; and Allan, Lindesay and Parker, p. 12.

42. Kutzbach, p. 202. See, for example, Gilbert Walker, *Outlines of the Theory of Electromagnetism*, Cambridge 1910.

43. Ibid., p. 203 (the analogy to geopolitics is mine).

44. Halford Mackinder, "The Geographical Pivot of History," *Geographical Journal* 23 (1904), p. 422.

45. Mark Cane, "El Niño," *Ann. Rev. Earth Planet. Sci.* 14 (1986), p. 44. On the other hand, contemporary geodesists – like John Hayford in America – had achieved spectacular results (the figure of the earth) through massive computations where the "sheer bulk of information" was most important. (See the discussion of turn-of-the-century geodesy in Naomi Oreskes, *The Rejection of Continental Drift: Theory and Method in American Earth Science*, New York 1999, pp. 234–5.)

46. Donald Mock, "The Southern Oscillation: Historical Origins," NOAA (www.ced.noaa.gov/-dm/pubs/mock81).

47. Allan, Lindesay and Parker, p. 13. Walker's concept of the SO was partly anticipated by C. Brooks and H. Braby's 1921 article "The Clash of the Trades in the Pacific" (*Q. J. R. Meteorol. Soc.* 47, pp. 1–13).

48. Peter Webster and Song Yang, "Monsoon and ENSO: Selectively Interactive Systems," *Q. J. R. Meteorol. Soc.* 118 (1992), p. 878.

49. Ibid.

50. Ibid., p. 17.

51. Allan, Lindesay, and Parker, p. 14.

52. See the brief history of the Bergen School in Nebeker, pp. 49–57 and 84–6.

53. H. Berlage, "Fluctuations of the General Atmospheric Circulation of More Than One Year: Their Nature and Prognostic Value," *K. Ned. Meteorol. Inst. Meded. Verh.* 69 (1957); and Allan, Lindesay and Parker, p. 5 (quote). An even earlier precursor of Bjerknes's focus on ocean–atmosphere interaction was J. B. Leighly's "Marquesan Meteorology" (*Univ. Calif. Publ. Geogr.* 6:4 [1933], pp. 147–72), although as J. Wallace et al. note, "The lack of citations of this remarkable paper indicates that it had little or no impact on the field at the time" (J. Wallace et al., "On the Structure and Evolution of ENSO-Related Climate Variability in the Tropical Pacific: Lessons from TOGA," *Journal of Geophysical Research* 103:C7

[29 June 1998], p. 14,242).

54. E. Rasmusson and T. Carpenter, "Variations in Tropical Sea Surface Temperature and Surface Wind Fields Associated with the Southern Oscillation/El Niño," *Mon. Wea. Rev.* 110 (1982), pp. 354–84.

55. J. Bjerknes, "Atmospheric Teleconnections from the Equatorial Pacific," *Mon. Wea. Rev.* 97 (1969), p. 170.

56. Thomas Levenson argues that John Leighy, studying the weather of the Marquesas Islands in 1933, had glimpsed this complex wind/sea surface temperature interaction in microcosm, but his work was not resurrected until 1978, a decade after Bjerknes's breakthrough (*Ice Time: Climate, Science and Life on Earth*, New York 1989, pp. 70, 72).

57. George Philander, "Learning from El Niño," *Weather* 53:9 (Sept. 1998), p. 273.

58. Bjerknes, ibid.

59. K. Wyrtki, "El Niño: The Dynamic Response of the Equatorial Pacific Ocean to Atmospheric Forcing," *Journal of Physical Oceanography* 5, pp. 572–84; and "The Response of Sea Surface Topography to the 1976 El Niño," *Journal of Physical Oceanography* 9, pp. 1223–31. Also see the characterization of Wyrtki's contribution in Allan, Lindesay and Parker, pp. 19 and 24–5.

60. There is also a deep ocean transfer of heat through thermohaline convection – the famous "conveyor belt" – driven by subduction of water masses in the Nordic Sea and Antarctica, but it works very slowly on wavelengths of decades or more. It constitutes the long-term memory of the coupled atmosphere–ocean system.

61. On the "capacitor" analogy, cf. Joel Gunn, "Introduction," special issue of *Human Ecology* (22:1 [1994]) on global climate change, p. 11; and Peter Webster and Timothy Palmer, "The Past and the Future of El Niño," *Nature* 390 (11 Dec. 1997), p. 562.

62. There is considerable debate about which is the more important control over the ENSO cycle: heat storage in the Warm Pool or the internal wave dynamics of the Pacific. The latter is given priority in the famous "dampened oscillator" or "delayed action oscillator" model of ENSO developed by P. Schopf and M. Suarez in 1988 ("Vacillations in a Coupled Ocean–Atmosphere Model," *J. Atmos. Sci.* 45 , pp. 549–66). Their revision of Wyrtki was a response to the puzzling absence of a "canonical" buildup of sea level and sea surface temperature in the western Pacific before the massive 1982–83 El Niño.

63. Michael McPhaden, "Genesis and Evolution of the 1997–98 El Niño," *Science* 283 (12 Feb. 1999), p. 953.

64. See G. Kiladis, G. Meehl and K. Weickmann, "The Large-Scale Circulation Associated with Westerly Wind Bursts and Deep Convection over the Western Equatorial Pacific," *J. Geophys. Res.* 99 (1994), pp. 18527–44.

65. S. G. Philander, "El Niño and La Niña," *J. Atmos. Sci.* 42 (1985), pp. 451–9.

66. Richard Barber in Michael Glantz, *Currents of Change: El Niño's Impact on Climate and Society,* Cambridge 1996, p. 167.

67. Richard Kerr, "Big El Niños Ride the Back of Slower Climate Change," *Science* 283 (19 Feb. 1999), p. 1108.

68. For the most sweeping case for El Niño–like forcing of world climate on nested timescales from the seasonal to the orbital, see Mark Cane and Amy Clement, "A Role for the Tropical Pacific Coupled Ocean–Atmosphere System on Milankovitch and Millennial

Timescales: Parts I & II," in Peter Clark, Robert Webb and Lloyd Keigwin (eds.), *Mechanisms of Global Climate Change at Millennial Time Scales*, Washington, D.C. 1999.

69. Eugene Rasmusson, Xueliang Wang and Chester Ropelewski, "Secular Variability of the ENSO Cycle," Natural Research Council, *Natural Climate Variability on Decade-to-Century Time Scales*, Washington, D.C. 1995, pp. 458 and 469.

70. Henry Diaz and Roger Pulwarty, "An Analysis of the Time Scales of Variability in Centuries-Long ENSO-Sensitive Records in the Last 1000 Years," abstract, NOAA El Niño website; and Xiao-Wei Quan, "Interannual Variability Associated with ENSO: Seasonal Dependence and Interdecadal Change," Ph.D. diss., University of Colorado, Boulder 1998, p. 105.

71. Webster et al., "Monsoon Predictability and Prediction," *Journal of Geophysical Research* 103: C7 (29 June 1998), p. 14,457. See also C. Folland et al., "Large Scale Modes of Ocean Surface Temperature Since the Late Nineteenth Century," in Navarra (ed.).

72. For a sense of what a devilish business periodizing low-frequency ENSO variations has turned out to be, see Rasmusson, Wang and Ropelewski, "Secular Variability of the ENSO Cycle," pp. 458–69.

73. See the discussion in Chapter 3, Xiao-Wei Quan, pp. 89–137.

74. Richard Kerr, "In North American Climate: A More Local Control," *Science* 283 (19 Feb. 1999), p. 1109.

75. See N. Mantua, "A Pacific Interdecadal Climate Oscillation with Impacts on Salmon Production," *Bulletin of the American Meteorological Society* 78:6 (June 1997), pp. 1069–79.

76. Ben Kirtman and Paul Schopf, "Decadal Variability in ENSO Predictability and Prediction," *Journal of Climate* 11 (Nov. 1998), p. 2805.

77. Cf. Kerr, ibid. (quote); and Xiao-Wei Quan, p. 106.

78. Xiao-Wei Quan, pp. 109–10.

79. Although their cause is not yet known, compelling evidence that Dansgaard/Oeschger cycles have regulated climate instabilities in the Holocene as well as throughout the Quaternary is presented in Gerard Bond et al., "A Pervasive Millennial-Scale Cycle in North Atlantic Holocene and Glacial Climates," *Science*, 278 (14 Nov. 1997), pp. 1257–66.

80. Cf. Richard Kerr, "El Niño Grew Strong as Cultures Were Born"; and Donald Rodbell et al., "A 15,000-Year Record of El Niño–Driven Alluviation in Southwestern Ecuador," *Science* 283 (22 Jan. 1999).

81. Betty Meggers, "Archeological Evidence for the Impact of Mega-Niño Events on Amazonia During the Past Two Millennia," *Climatic Change* 28 (1994), p. 328–9.

82. Cf., Kirtman and Schopf, p. 2805 (quote); and K. Trenberth and T. Hoar, "El Niño and Climate Change," *Geophys. Res. Lett.* 24 (1997), pp. 3057–60.

83. *Summary Report*, NOAA/CIRES La Niña Summit, July 1998, p. 14.

### Notes to Chapter 8

The quote is from Achebe, *A Man of the People*, New York 1966, pp. 161–2.

1. It is important to note that the famous protracted droughts of the 1930s in the US Great Plains, Australia and southern Africa occurred during one of the weakest periods of

ENSO activity in the last 150 years.

2. Kiladis and Diaz, p. 1071.

3. Allan, Lindesay and Parker, p. 77.

4. Ibid., pp. 25–6.

5. Ibid.

6. Peter Webster, "The Variable and Interactive Monsoon," in Fein and Stephens, p. 305.

7. David Rodenhuis, "The Weather That Led to the Flood," in Stanley Changnon (ed.), *The Great Flood of 1993*, Boulder, Colo. 1996, pp. 44–5.

8. P. Webster et al., "Monsoons: Processes, predictability, and the prospects for prediction," *Journal of Geophysical Research* 103:C7 (19 June 1998), p. 14,459.

9. Alexander Gershunov, Tim Barnett and Daniel Cayan, "North Pacific Interdecadal Oscillation Seen as Factor in ENSO-Related North American Climate Anomalies," *EOS* 80:3 (19 Jan. 1998), pp. 25 and 29–30.

10. *Summary Report*, La Niña Summit, p. 10.

11. Kevin Trenberth, "The Different Flavors of La Niña," La Niña Summit, 1998, p. 2.

12. Greg O'Hare, "The Indian Monsoon, Part Two: The Rains," *Geography* 82:4 (1997), p. 335.

13. Seasonal distribution is everything. For example, the cyclone of 18–20 May 1877 dumped 20 inches of rain – half a year's precipitation – over Madras in three days during the height of the Great Drought. As Digby points out,"it did more harm than good" and the drought continued for six months more (Digby, *The Famine Campaign*, vol. 1, pp. 148–9).

14. K. Rao, *India's Water Wealth*, Delhi 1975, pp. 10 and 16.

15. J. Ju and J. Slingo, "The Asian Summer Monsoon and ENSO," *Q. J. R. Meteorol. Soc.* 121 (1995), pp. 1133–68. "Displacement of the IACZ into the Pacific results in the establishment of a separate convection zone over southeast Asia during Monsoon season. This draws air from a much reduced area compared to a normal Monsoon, because of the adjustment of the tropospheric circulation to competition from the central Pacific convergence. Weak Monsoon rainfall, and drought in extreme cases, is the result."

16. Webster et al., p. 14,476 (text differs from Table 2).

17. O'Hare, p. 349. See also Peter Webster and Song Yang, "Monsoon and ENSO: Selectively Interactive Systems," *Q. J. R. Meteorol. Soc.* 118 (1992), pp. 877–926; and Madhav Khandekar, "El Niño/Southern Oscillation, Indian Monsoon and World Grain Yields – A Synthesis," in M. El Sabh et al. (eds.), *Land-Based and Marine Hazards*, Kluwer 1996, pp. 79–95. Equatorial stratospheric wind oscillation may be a third independent variable interacting with ENSO and Eurasian snow cover. (See Khandekar, "Comments on 'Space–Time Structure of Monsoon Interannual Variability,'" in *Journal of Climate* 11 (Nov. 1998), pp. 3057–9.)

18. Buwen Dong and Paul Valdes, "Modelling the Asian Summer Monsoon Rainfall and Eurasian Winter/Spring Snow Mass," *Q. J. R. Meteorol. Soc.* 124 (1998), pp. 2567–9.

19. R. Kripalani and A. Kulkarni, "Climatic Impact of El Niño/La Niña on the Indian Monsoon: A New Perspective," *Weather* 52:2 (1997), p. 45.

20. K. Krishna Kumar, Balaji Rajagopalan and Mark Cane, "On the Weakening Relation-

ship Between the Indian Monsoon and ENSO," *Science* 284 (25 June 1999), pp. 2156–9. See also H. Annamalai and Julia Slingo, "The Asian Summer Monsoon, 1997," *Weather* 53:9 (Sept. 1998), pp. 285–6.

21. Ramasamy Suppiah, "Relationships Between the Southern Oscillation and the Rainfall of Sri Lanka," *International Journal of Climatology* 9 (1989).

22. Y. Kueh, *Agricultural Instability in China, 1931–1991*, Oxford 1998, p. 29.

23. Needham, p. 246.

24. Keith Buchanan, *The Transformation of the Chinese Earth*, London 1970, p. 80; Walter Mallory, *China: Land of Famine*, New York 1926, p. 43.

25. George Cressey, *China's Geographic Foundations: A Survey of the Land and Its People*, New York 1934, pp. 84–5.

26. The occurrence of several severe El Niños in the mid seventeenth century raises the possibility that the extraordinary agricultural crisis of the late Ming dynasty – seven years of drought followed by nine years of flooding – was ENSO-related: 1640 was the driest year in the last five hundred (cf. Zhang Jiacheng [ed.], *The Reconstruction of Climate in China for Historical Times*, Beijing 1988, p. 45; Manfred Domros and Peng Gongbing, *The Climate of China*, Berlin 1988, p. 198; and Jiacheng Zhang and Zhiguang Lin, *Climate of China*, Shanghai 1992, p. 330).

27. Ye Zongwei and Wang Cun, "Climatic Jumps in the Flood/Drought Historical Chronology of Central China," *Climate Dynamics* 6 (1992), p. 158.

28. Ding Yihui, *Monsoons over China*, Dordrecht 1996, p. 290–92.

29. A pioneering consideration of SO's possible role in drought and flood was Tu Chang-Wang, "China Weather and the World Oscillation," in Academia Sinica, *Collected Scientific Papers: Meteorology 1919–1949*, Beijing 1954.

30. Shao-Wu in Glantz, *Currents of Change*, p. 173; as well as Kueh, pp. 159–61.

31. Wei-Chyung Wang and Kerang Li, "Precipitation Fluctuation over a Semiarid Region in Northern China and the Relationship with El Niño/Southern Oscillation," *Journal of Climate* (July 1990), p. 769.

32. Wang Shao-wu, "La Niña and Its Impact on China's Climate," La Niña Summit, 1998, p. 1.

33. Wang and Li, p. 777.

34. Ding Yihui, pp. 273, 285.

35. See the La Niña impact map for 1898 in Allan, Lindesay and Parker, p. 139.

36. For weather conditions in 1876, cf. Broomhall, p. 166; and *Parl. Papers*, China No. 2 (1878), p. 1.

37. Chenglan Bao and Yanzhen Xiang, "Relationship Between El Niño Event and Atmospheric Circulation, Typhoon Activity and Flooding," in W. Kyle and C. Chang (eds.), *Proceedings*, Second International Conference on East Asia and Western Pacific Meteorology and Climate (Hong Kong, Sept. 1992), Singapore 1993, p. 239.

38. Yihui, pp. 286–7.

39. PRC, National Environmental Protection Bureau, *The Yellow River Runs Dry and Its Sustainable Development* (in Chinese), Beijing 1997: cited in Z. Yang et al., " Yellow River's Water and Sediment Discharge Decreasing Steadily," *EOS* 79:48 (1 Dec. 1998), p. 592.

40. Zhenhao Bao et al., "Drought/Flood Variations in Eastern China During the Colder

(1610–1719) and Warmer (1880–1989) Periods and Their Relations with the Southern Oscillation," *Geographical Reports of Tokyo Metropolitan University* 33 (1998), p. 10.

41. Hengyi Weng et al., "Multi–Scale Summer Rainfall Variability Over China," *Journal of the Meteorological Society of Japan* 77:4 (1999), pp. 845–57.

42. Cf. Jasper Becker, *Hungry Ghosts: Mao's Secret Famine*, New York 1996; and Philip Short, *Mao: A Life*, London 1999, pp. 504–10 (on the severity of the drought). There is no necessary discrepancy between the characterization of the 1958 drought as the most severe *throughout* China and the study (cited in fn 35) that finds other droughts in *north* China to have been more extreme.

43. Y. Kueh, *Agricultural Instability in China, 1931–1991*, Oxford 1998. See also Penny Kane, *Famine in China, 1959–61: Demographic and Social Implications*, London 1988.

44. Jean Dreze and Amarya Sen, "Introduction," in Dreze, Sen and Hussain, *The Political Economy of Hunger: Selected Essays*, Oxford 1995, pp. 18–19.

45. J. Murphy and P. Whetton, "A Re-analysis of a Tree Ring Chronology from Java," *Proceedings of the Koninklijke Nederlandse Akademic van Weterschappen* B92:3 (1989), pp. 241–57.

46. Christine Padoch and Nancy Peluso (ed.), *Borneo in Transition: People, Forests, Conservation, and Development*, Oxford 1996, p. 3. See also H. Brookfield, L. Potter and Y. Byron, *In Place of the Forest: Environmental and Socio–Economic Transformation in Borneo and the Eastern Malay Peninsula*, Tokyo 1995.

47. See rainfall anomaly tables for Indonesia and the Philippines since 1896, International Research Institute for Climate Prediction, UCSD (iri.ucsd.edu/hot_Niño/impacts).

48. US Naval Intelligence Division, *Netherlands East Indies*, Vol. 1, Geographical Handbook Series, Washington D.C. 1944, p. 338. On a drought belt in eastern Java and southernmost New Guinea, see Glenn Trewartha, *The Earth's Problem Climates*, Madison, Wis. pp. 202–3.

49. Knapen, pp. 126–7.

50. Jean-Paul Malingreau, "The 1982–83 Drought in Indonesia: Assessment and Monitoring," in Michael Glantz, Ricard Katz, and Maria Krenz (eds.), *Climate Crisis: The Societal Impacts Associated with the 1982–83 Worldwide Climate Anomalies*, New York 1987, pp. 11–18; and Eric Hackert and Stefan Hastenrath, "Mechanisms of Java Rainfall Anomalies," *Monthly Weather Review* 114 (April 1986), p. 746.

51. R. Kane, "El Niño Timings and Rainfall Extremes in India, Southeast Asia and China," *International Journal of Climatology* 19 (1999), pp. 653–72.

52. See the webpage iripred.ido.columbia.edu/research/ENSO/tables/phil 1.html.

53. Famine chronology from Martinez Duesta, p. 260 (my correlation to ENSO).

54. Lopez-Gonzaga, pp. 113–15.

55. Data from Relief Web (www.reliefweb.int), 3 Aug. 1998.

56. See the chart in Glantz, Katz and Krenz, pp. 90–91.

57. Quoted in Allan, Lindesay and Parker, p. 9.

58. Ann Young, *Environmental Change in Australia Since 1788*, Melbourne 1996.

59. Ian Anderson, "Parched Papua Prays for Rain," *New Scientist*, 20 Sept. 1997, p. 18.

60. Jean Nicet and Thierry Delcroix, "ENSO-related Precipitation Changes in New Caledonia, Southwestern Tropical Pacific: 1969–98," *Monthly Weather Review* 8:2 (August 2000),

pp. 3001–6.

61. Andrew Sturman and Nigel Tapper, *The Weather and Climate of Australia and New Zealand*, Melbourne 1996, pp. 367–70.

62. Pao-Shin Chu, "Hawaiian Drought and the Southern Oscillation," *Inter. J. Climatol.* 9 (1989), p. 628.

63. Thomas Schroeder, "Climate Controls," in Marie Sanderson (ed.), *Climate and Weather in Hawaii*, Honolulu 1993, p. 17.

64. "Summary of Drought Around the World, August–September 1998," National Drought Mitigation Center.

65. Antonio Moura and Jagadish Shukla, "On the Dynamics of Droughts in Northeast Brazil: Observations, Theory and Numerical Experiments with a General Circulation Model," *Journal of the Atmospheric Sciences* 34 (December 1981), pp. 2653 (quote) and 2654.

66. Webb, p. 44.

67. Vernon Kousky, "Frontal Influences on Northeast Brazil," *Monthly Weather Review* 107 (1979), pp. 1140–53.

68. Hall, pp. 16–17.

69. Gilbert Walker, "Ceará (Brazil) Famines and the General Air Movement," *Beitr. z. Phys. der freien Atmosphare* 14 (1928), pp. 88–93.

70. Cf. José Gasques and Antonio Magalhaes, "Climate Anomalies and Their Impacts in Brazil During the 1982–83 ENSO Event," in Glantz, Katz and Krenz, pp. 31–2; and Pao–Shin Chu, "Brazil's Climate Anomalies and ENSO," in Michael Glantz, Richard Katz, and Neville Nicholls (eds.), *Teleconnections Linking Worldwide Climate Anomalies*, Cambridge 1991, pp. 56–61.

71. Cf. Rodolfo Teofilo, *A Seca de 1915*, Forteleza 1980, 129–31; and Kiladis and Diaz, pp. 1038–40.

72. Pao–Shin Chu, pp. 64–5.

73. See Kiladis and Diaz, ibid.; and data at iri.ucsd.edu/hot_Niño/impacts/ns_amer/index.html.

74. C. Caviedes, "The Effects of Enso Events in Some Key Regions of the South American Continent," in Stanley Gregory (ed.), *Recent Climate Change*, London 1988, pp. 252–3 and 264.

75. Carlos Malpica, *Cronica del Hambre en el Peru*, Lima 1966, pp. 161–3.

76. Caviedes, ibid.

77. Gregory Asner, Alan Townsend and Bobby Braswell, "Satellite Observation of El Niño Effects on Amazon Forest Phenology and Productivity," *Geophysical Research Letters* 27:7 (1 April 2000), p. 981.

78. Betty Meggers, "Archeological Evidence for the Impact of Mega-Niño Events on Amazonia During the Past Two Millennia," *Climatic Change* 28 (1994), p. 330.

79. Allan, Lindesay and Parker, p. 65.

80. Miguel Gonzalez, "Probable Response of the Paraná River Delta (Argentina) to Future Warmth and Rising Sea Level," *J. Coast. Res. Spec. Issue* 17 (1995), pp. 219–20.

81. José Rutllant and Humberto Fuenzalida, "Synoptic Aspects of the Central Chile Rainfall Variability Associated with the Southern Oscillation," *International Journal of Cli-*

*matology* 11 (1991), pp. 63 and 65.

82. For the 1896 drought, see Antonio del Bajio, *Crisis alimentarias y subsistencias populares en Mexico*, vol. 1, Mexico, D.F. 1987, p. 162.

83. A. Filonov and I. Tereshchenko, "El Niño 1997–98 Monitoring in Mixed Layer at the Pacific Ocean near Mexico's West Coast," *Geophysical Research Letters* 27:5 (1 March 2000), p. 705.

84. During the drought corn prices soared 130 percent while minimum agricultural wages fell 28 percent (Moises Gonzalez Navarro, *Cinco crisis mexicanas*, Mexico, D.F. 1999, p. 19). See also Florescano and Swan, *Breve historia*, pp. 124–6 and 161; del Bajio, pp. 166–71; and Friedrich Katz, *The Life and Times of Pancho Villa*, Stanford, Calif. 1998, pp. 48–50.

85. Gonzalez, p. 31.

86. See Midwestern Climate Center (Champaign, Ill.), "El Niño and the Midwest" (http://mcc.sws.uiuc. edu/elNiño.html).

87. Jennifer Phillips, et al., "The Role of ENSO in Determining Climate and Maize Yield Variability in the US Cornbelt," *International Journal of Climatology* 19 (1999), pp. 877–88.

88. Stanley Changnon, "Impacts of El Niño's Weather," in Changnon (ed.), *El Niño 1997–1998: The Climate Event of the Century*, Oxford 2000, pp. 151, 165.

89. Julia Cole and Edward Cook, "The Changing Relationship Between Enso Variability and Moisture Balance in the Continental United States," *Geophysical Research Letters* 25:24 (15 Dec. 1998), pp. 4529–32.

90. Research in progress reported by Arthur Douglas, Creighton University (www.ncdc. noaa.gov/ogp/papers/douglas.html).

91. Cf. Charlotte Benson, "Drought and the Zimbabwe Economy: 1980–93," p. 246; and Bill Kinsey, "Dancing with El Niño," pp. 276–7, both in Helen O'Neill and John Toye (eds.), *A World Without Famine?*, New York 1998.

92. J. Lindesay and C. Vogel, "Historical Evidence for Southern Oscillation–Southern African Rainfall Relationships," *International Journal of Climatology* 10 (1990), p. 679; and Mark Cane, Gidon Eshel and R. Buckland, "Forecasting Zimbabwean Maize Yield Using Eastern Equatorial Pacific Sea Surface Temperature," *Nature* 370 (21 July 1994), pp. 204–5.

93. Vincent Moron and M. Neil Ward, "ENSO Teleconnections with Climate Variability in the European and African Sectors," *Weather* 53:9 (Sept. 1998), p. 288.

94. S. Mason and M. Jury, "Climatic Variability and Change over Southern Africa: A Reflection on Underlying Processes," *Progress in Physical Geography* 21:1 (1997), pp. 23–50.

95. Lindesay and Vogel, ibid.; and Cane, Eshel and Buckland, p. 204.

96. Tsegay Wolde-Georgis, "The Impact of Cold Events on Ethiopia," La Niña Summit, 1998, pp. 1–2. See also Y. Seleshi and G. Demaree, "Rainfall Variability in the Ethiopian and Eritrean Highlands and Its Links with the Southern Oscillation Index," *Journal of Biogeography* 22 (1985); and Tesfaye Hale, "Causes and Characteristics of Drought in Ethiopia," *Ethiopian Journal of Agricultural Sciences* 10:1–2 (1988).

97. Based on Coquery-Vidrovitch, p. 503; and Glantz, Katz and Krenz, "Appendix: Climate Impact Maps," pp. 81–105.

98. Cf. P. Hutchinson, "The Southern Oscillation and Prediction of 'Der' Season Rainfall

in Somalia, *Journal of Climate* 5 (May 1992), p. 525; and Gerard Beltrando, "Interannual Variability of Rainfall in the Eastern Horn of Africa and Indicators of Atmospheric Circulation," *International Journal of Climatology* 13 (1993), pp. 533 and 543.

99. M. Hulme, "Global Climate Change and the Nile Basin," in P. Howell and J. Allan (eds.), *The Nile: Sharing a Scarce Resource*, Cambridge 1994, p. 148.

100. G. Trewartha, *The Earth's Problem Climates*, Madison, Wis. 1981, p. 134.

101. A. Gouldie, "Climate: Past and Present," in W. Adams, A. Goudie and A. Orme (eds.), *The Physical Geography of Africa*, Oxford 1996, p. 38.

102. Matayo Indeje, Frederick Semazzi and Laban Ogallo, "ENSO Signals in East African Rainfall Seasons," *International Journal of Climatology* 20 (2000), p. 20.

103. Cf. G. Farmer, "Rainfall Data Bases and Seasonal Forecasting in Eastern Africa" in Gregory, pp. 197–9; and Peter Usher, "Kenya and ENSO: An Observation and La Niña Prediction," La Niña Summit, 1998.

104. Indeje, Semazzi and Ogallo, pp. 30 and 44–5.

105. Jennifer Phillips and Beverly McIntyre, "ENSO and Interannual Rainfall Variability in Uganda: Implications for Agricultural Management," *International Journal of Climatology* 20 (2000), p. 171–82.

106. Allan, Lindesay and Parker, p. 22.

107. Bette Otto-Bliesner, "El Niño/La Niña and Sahel Precipitation During the Middle Holocene," *Geophysical Research Letters* 26:1 (1 Jan. 1999), pp. 87–8.

108. Abdel Kader Ali, "El Niño Events and Rainfall Variations in the Sahel Region of Africa," *Bulletin of the Egyptian Geographical Society* 70 (1997), pp. 77 (see Fig. 3) and 81–3.

109. M. Neil Ward et al., "Climate Variability in Northern Africa: Understanding Droughts in the Sahel and the Mahgreb," in Navarra (ed.), p. 138.

110. According to the Center for Ocean-Atmosphere Prediction Studies, ENSO (1944–96) was in a warm phase 21 percent of the time; cold phase, 28 percent; and neutral phase, 51 percent; see the COAPS website. A 1950–1997 timeframe, however, gives warm phase, 31 percent; cold phase, 23 percent; and neutral, 46 percent (NCAR News–La Niña website).

111. Cf. "History's Favorite Hitman," *Hong Kong Standard,* 22 May 1998; and "El Niño," *The Irish Times,* 28 May 1998.

112. D. Harrison and N. Larkin, "El Niño-Southern Oscillation Sea Surface Temperature and Wind Anomalies, 1946–1993," *Reviews of Geophysics* 36:3 (Aug. 1998), p. 391. For an opposing view, however, see B. Dong et al., "Predictable Winter Climate in the North Atlantic Sector During the 1997–1999 ENSO Cycle," *Geophysical Research Letters* 27:7 (1 April 2000), pp. 985–8.

113. Moron and Ward, p. 289.

114. Kiladis and Diaz, pp. 1041–2.

115. M. Halpert and C. Ropelewski, "Surface Temperature Patterns Associated with the Southern Oscillation," *Journal of Climate* 5 (1992). See also X. Rodo, E. Baert and F. Comin, "Variations in Seasonal Rainfall in Southern Europe During the Present Century: Relationships with NAO and ENSO," *Climate Dynamics* 13 (1997).

116. Alfredo Rocha, "Low-Frequency Variability of Seasonal Rainfall over the Iberian Peninsula and ENSO," *International Journal of Climatology* 19 (1999), p. 889.

117. A. Meshcherskaya and V. Blazhevich, "The Drought and Excessive Moisture Indices

in a Historical Perspective in the Principal Grain-Producing Regions of the Former Soviet Union," *Journal of Climate* 10 (Oct.1997), pp. 2670–82.

118. Trevor Davies, "Guest Editorial – Hubert Lamb," *Weather* 53:7 (July 1998) p. 199. These data sets recently have been used to generate a landmark atlas (Allan, Lindesay and Parker, 1996) of the global oceanic and atmospheric patterns accompanying ENSO warm and cold phases since 1871.

119. Cf. William Quinn, "A Study of Southern Oscillation–Related Climatic Activity for AD 622–1900, Incorporating Nile River Flood Data," in Henry Diaz and Vera Markgraf (eds.), *El Niño: Historical and Paleoclimatic Aspects of the Southern Oscillation*, Cambridge 1992; and Quinn, Victor Neal and Santiago Antunez de Mayolo, "El Niño Occurrences over the Past Four and a Half Centuries," *Journal of Geophysical Research* 92:C13 (15 Dec. 1987), p. 14,454.

120. Whetton and Rutherfurd, p. 225.

121. See discussion of data sources in Allan, Lindesay and Parker, pp. 59–60.

122. Charles Ballard, "Drought and Economic Distress: South Africa in the 1800s," *Journal of Interdisciplinary History* 17:2 (Autumn 1986), pp. 359–78.

123. Charlesworth, *Peasants and Imperial Rule*, p. 76.

124. My rough annual ratios would, of course, be better expressed as seasonal ratios.

125. On modification of ENSO cycle by changes in Pacific Ocean circulation, see Robert Dunbar et al., "PEP-1 Contributions to Increased Understanding of Past Variability in Enso and Its Teleconnections," poster session *Abstracts*, IGBP PAGES Open Sciences Meeting, "Past Global Changes and Their Significance for the Future," London, 20–23 April 1998; and for a discussion of a shortened, intensifed ENSO, see Tahl Kestin et al., 'Time-Frequency Variability of ENSO and Stochastic Simulations," *Journal of Climate* 11 (Sept. 1998), pp. 2260–61.

126. "Simultaneous correlation between ENSO and the monsoon is very robust over the past 140 years. The sole exception, the drop during the recent decades, obviously is of great interest, and perhaps a cause for concern": K. Kumar et al., "Epochal Changes in Indian Monsoon–ENSO Precursors," *Geophysical Research Letters* 26:1 (1 Jan. 1999), p. 78. "Before 1900, the ENSO influence on US moisture balance was more extensive than in later periods": Julia Cole and Edward Cook, "The Changing Relationship Between ENSO Variability and Moisture Balance in the Continental United States," *Geophysical Research Letters* 25:24 (15 Dec. 1998), p. 4530.

127. Quinn et al, "El Niño Occurrences," p. 14,459.

128. D. Rind, "Complexity and Climate," *Science* 284 (2 April 1999), p. 106.

129. Brent Yarnal and George Kiladis, "Tropical Teleconnections Associated with El Niño/Southern Oscillation (ENSO) events," *Progress in Physical Geography* 9 (1985), pp. 541 and 544.

130. Quinn and Neal, p. 627.

131. David Engield and Luis Cid, "Low-Frequency Changes in El Niño-Southern Oscillation," *Journal of Climate* 4 (Dec. 1991), p. 1139.

132. Eugene Rasmusson, Xueliang Wang and Chester Ropelewski, "Secular Variability of the ENSO Cycle," in National Research Council, *Natural Climate Variability on Decade-to-Century Time Scales*, Washington, D.C. 1995, pp. 458–70.

133. D. Harrison and N. Larkin, "El Niño-Southern Oscillation Sea Surface Temperature and Wind Anomalies, 1946–1993," *Reviews of Geophysics* 36:3 (Aug. 1998), pp. 386–91.

134. T. Baumgartner et al., "The Recording of Interannual Climatic Change by High–Resolution Natural Systems: Tree-Rings, Coral Bands, Glacial Ice Layers, and Marine Varves," *Geophysical Monograph* 55 (1989), pp. 1–14.

## Notes to Chapter 9

The epigraph is from Isaacs, *Scratches on Our Minds: American Images of China and India*, New York 1958, p. 273.

1. For a typically cavalier view, see Roland Lardinois, "Famine, Epidemics and Mortality in South India: A Reappraisal of the Demographic Crisis of 1876–1878," *Economic and Political Weekly* 20:111 (16 March 1985), p. 454.

2. Emmanuel Le Roy Ladurie, *Tmes of Feast, Times of Famine: A History of Climate Since the Year 1000*, Garden City, N.Y. 1971, p. 119.

3. Raymond Williams, *Problems in Materialism and Culture*, London 1980, p. 67.

4. When it served their interests, of course, the British could switch epistemologies. In the case of late-nineteenth-century China, for example, the British and their allies primarily blamed Qing corruption, not drought, for the millions of famine deaths.

5. Kueh, pp. 4–5.

6. Jared Diamond, *Guns, Germs, and Steel: The Fates of Human Societies*, New York 1997, pp. 424–5.

7. Re 1743–44: "another exceptional period in the eastern hemisphere, which corresponds with QN El Niño of 1744, although conditions were more markedly dry in the east in 1743" (Whetton and Rutherfurd, pp. 243–6).

8. "The first Qing emperor envisioned ever–normal granaries in county seats, charity granaries in major towns, and community granaries in the countryside. Ever–normal granaries were to be managed by members of the magistrate's staff, who were directed to sell, lend, or give away grain in the spring and to make purchases, collect loans, and solicit contributions in the autumn" (Pierre-Etienne Will and R. Bin Wong [with James Lee, Jean Oi and Peter Perdue], *Nourish the People: The State Civilian Granary System in China, 1650–1850*, Ann Arbor, Mich. 1981, p. 19).

9. Will, *Bureaucracy and Famine*, Chapters 7 and 8.

10. Ibid., pp. 86 and 189.

11. John Post, *Food Shortage, Climatic Variability, and Epidemic Disease in Preindustrial Europe: The Mortality Peak in the Early 1740s*, Ithaca, N.Y. 1985, p. 30.

12. Will, p. 270.

13. Jean Oi and Pierre-Etienne Will, "North China: Shandong During the Qianlong Period," in Will and Wong, pp. 369–70. ENSO correlations based on Quinn chronology.

14. "Introduction," in Will and Wong, p. 21. China's roads, on the other hand, remained miserable, and were a major obstacle to market integration as well as famine relief.

15. Wilkinson, pp. 122–9.

16. R. Bin Wong, "Decline and Its Opposition, 1781–1850," in Will and Wong, p. 76.

17. Helen Dunstan, *Conflicting Counsels to Confuse the Age: A Documentary Study of Political Economy in Qing China, 1644–1840*, Ann Arbor, Mich. 1996, p. 251.

18. Wilkinson, pp. 122–9. See also Will, "The Control Structure," in Will and Wong, pp. 220–21.

19. Jane Leonard, "'Controlling from Afar': Open Communications and the Tao-Kuang Emperor's Control of Grand Canal–Grain Transport Management, 1824–26," *Modern Asian Studies* 22:4 (1988), p. 666.

20. Joseph Needham, *Science and Civilization in China*, vol. 4, Cambridge 1971, p. 326.

21. Will, p. 257.

22. Jacques Gernet, *A History of Chinese Civilization*, 2nd edn., Cambridge 1996, p. 468.

23. Dwight Perkins, *Agricultural Development in China, 1368–1968*, Chicago 1969, p. 176.

24. Endymion Wilkinson, "Studies in Chinese Price History," Ph.D. diss., Princeton University 1970, p. 31.

25. Will, p. 32.

26. J. A. G. Roberts, *A Concise History of China*, Cambridge, Mass. 1990, p. 173.

27. On the special tribute granaries at Luoyang and Shanzhou organized during the Kangxi reign, see Will and Wong, pp. 32 and 301.

28. Food security in the mid eighteenth century may have consumed 10 percent of annual Qing revenue. As Wong emphasizes, "For a state to spend such sums for this purpose on a regular basis for well over a century is likely unique in the early modern world" ("Qing Granaries and Late Imperial History," in Will and Wong, p. 477).

29. Sanjay Sharma, "The 1837–38 Famine in U.P.: Some Dimensions of Popular Action," *IESHR* 30:3 (1993), p. 359.

30. Bhatia, p. 9.

31. Darren Zook, "Developing India: The History of an Idea in the Southern Countryside, 1860–1990," Ph.D. diss., University of California, Berkeley 1998, p. 158. The Raj was built upon mythology and hallucination. As Zook points out, the British universally attributed the ruins scattered through the Indian countryside to the decadence of native civilizations, when, in fact, many were direct memorials to the violence of British conquest (p. 157).

32. Sugata Bose and Ayesha Jalal, *Modern South Asia*, Delhi 1999, p. 43.

33. Ashok Desai, "Population and Standards of Living in Akbar's Time," *IESHR* 9:1 (1972), p. 61.

34. Chetan Singh, "Forests, Pastoralists and Agrarian Society in Mughal India," in David Arnold and Raachandra Guha (eds.), *Nature, Culture, Imperialism: Essays on the Environmental History of South Asia*, Delhi 1996, p. 22.

35. Habibul Kondker, "Famine Policies in Pre-British India and the Question of Moral Economy," *South Asia* 9:1 (June 1986), pp. 25–40; and Kuldeep Mathur and Niraja Jayal, *Drought, Policy and Politics*, New Delhi 1993, p. 27. Unfortunately, contemporary discussion of famine history before 1763 has been contaminated by Hindu-versus-Muslim bickering. See, for example, the apparent anti-Muslim bias in Mushtag Kaw, "Famines in Kashmir, 1586–1819: The Policy of the Mughal and Afghan Rulers," *IESHR* 33:1 (1996), pp. 59–70.

36. C. Blair, *Indian Famines*, London 1874, pp. 8–10.

37. David Hardiman, "Well Irrigation in Gujarat: Systems of Use, Hierarchies of Con-

trol," *Economic and Political Weekly*, 20 June 1998, p. 1537.

38. Commission quoted in W. R. Aykroyd, *The Conquest of Famine*, London 1974, p. 51. See also John Richards, *The Mughal Empire* (*The New Cambridge History of India*, 1:5), Cambridge 1993, p. 163.

39. Bagchi, pp. 11–12 and 27.

40. J. Malcolm, *A Memoir of Central India*, vol. 1, London 1931, p. 7, quoted in D. E. U. Baker, *Colonialism in an Indian Hinterland: The Central Provinces, 1820–1920*, Delhi 1993, p. 28.

41. Baker, p. 52.

42. J. Richards and Michelle McAlpin, "Cotton Cultivating and Land Clearing in the Bombay Deccan and Karnatak: 1818–1920," in Richard Tucker and J. Richards (eds.), *Global Deforestation and the Nineteenth-Century World Economy*, Durham 1983, pp. 71 and 74.

43. Ibid.

44. Nash, p. 92.

45. Greenough, *Prosperity and Misery*, p. 59.

46. C. Walford, "The Famines of the World: Past and Present," *Journal of the Statistical Society* 41:13 (1878), pp. 434–42. I cite Walford elsewhere from the expanded 1879 book version of this article.

47. Michael Watts, *Silent Violence: Food, Famine and Peasantry in Northern Nigeria*, Berkeley 1983, pp. 462–3. This "negotiation," of course, is two-sided and must include climate shock as an independent variable.

48. Watts, pp. 267 and 464.

49. Hans Medick, "The Proto-Industrial Family Economy and the Structures and Functions of Population Development under the Proto-Industrial System," in P. Kriedte et al. (eds.), *Industrialization Before Industrialization*, Cambridge 1981, p. 45.

50. Ibid., pp. 44–5.

51. Lewis, *Growth and Fluctuations*, p. 189.

52. Cited in Clive Dewey, "The End of the Imperialism of Free Trade," p. 35.

53. Kenneth Pomeranz, *The Making of a Hinterland: State, Society, and Economy in Inland North China, 1853–1937*, Berkeley 1993.

54. Paul Bairoch, "The Main Trends in National Economic Disparities Since the Industrial Revolution," in Paul Bairoch and Maurice Levy-Leboyer (eds.), *Disparities in Economic Development Since the Industrial Revolution*, London 1981, p. 7.

55. Paul Bairoch, "International Industrialization Levels from 1750–1980," in *Journal of European Economic History* 11 (1982), p. 107.

56. Fritjof Tichelman, *The Social Evolution of Indonesia*, The Hague 1980, p. 30.

57. Prasannan Parthasarathi, "Rethinking Wages and Competitiveness in Eighteenth-Century Britain and South India," *Past and Present* 158 (Feb. 1998), pp. 82–7 and 105–6.

58. Dutt, cited in Eddy, p. 21.

59. Philip Huang, *The Peasant Family and Rural Development in the Yangzi Delta, 1350–1988*, Stanford, Calif. 1990.

60. Wong, p. 38.

61. F. W. Mote, *Imperial China, 900–1800*, Cambridge, Mass. 1999, p. 941.

62. Kenneth Pomeranz, "A High Standard of Living and Its Implications," contribution to "E. H. R. Forum: Re-thinking 18th Century China," Internet, 19 Nov. 1997.

63. Pomeranz, "Two Worlds of Trade, Two Worlds of Empire: European State-Making and Industrialization in a Chinese Mirror," in David Smith et al., *States and Sovereignty in the Global Economy*, London 1999, p. 78 (my emphasis).

64. See S. Patel, "The Economic Distance Between Nations: Its Origin, Measurement and Outlook, *Economic Journal*, March 1964. (There is some discrepancy between his figures for the aggregate non-European world and the later estimates of Bairoch and Maddison.)

65. Albert Feuerwerker, *The Chinese Economy, 1870–1949*, Ann Arbor, Mich. 1995, pp. 32–3.

66. Paul Bairoch, "Geographical Structure and Trade Balance of European Foreign Trade, from 1800–1970," *Journal of European Economic History* 3:3 (Winter 1978), p. 565. Ch'en cites 1866 as the beginning of the serious penetration of imported textiles into China (p. 64).

67. Jack Goldstone, "Review of David Landes, *The Wealth and Poverty of Nations*," *Journal of World History* 2:1 (Spring 2000), p. 109.

68. Carl Trocki, *Opium, Empire and the Global Political Economy*, London 1999, p. 98.

69. Brian Bond, *Victorian Military Campaigns*, London 1967, pp. 309–11.

70. See O'Rourke and Williamson, pp. 53–4.

71. Historians traditionally contrast the Meiji and Tonzhang restorations, but as Goldstone suggests, the more significant comparison is between the Taipings and Japan. "What if China's old imperial regime, like Japan's, had collapsed in the mid nineteenth century, and not fifty years later, what then? What if the equivalent of Chiang Kai-shek's new model army had begun formation in the 1860s and not the 1920s? Would Japan still have been able to colonize Korea and Taiwan? What would have been the Asian superpower?" (Goldstone, ibid.).

72. "India wealth supplied the funds that bought the national debt back from the Dutch and others, first temporarily in the interval of peace between 1763 and 1774, and finally after 1783, leaving Britain nearly free from overseas indebtedness when it came to face the great French wars from 1793" (Ralph Davis, *The Industrial Revolution and British Overseas Trade*, Leicester 1979, pp. 55–6).

73. P. Cain and A. Hopkins, *British Imperialism: Innovation and Expansion, 1688–1914*, London 1993, p. 334.

74. For a recent review, see Young Goo-Park, "Depression and Capital Formation: The UK and Germany, 1873–96," *Journal of European Economic History* 26:3 (Winter 1997), especially pp. 511 and 516.

75. Giovanni Arrighi, *The Long Twentieth Century: Money, Power and the Origins of Our Times*, London 1994, p. 263.

76. A. Latham, *The International Economy and the Undeveloped World, 1865–1914*, London 1978, p. 70. Latham, it should be noted, is notoriously apologistic for British colonialism in India, arguing that the subcontinent's "relatively low growth overall is due largely to climatic factors, not to any deleterious effect of British colonial policy" (See A. Latham, "Asian Stagnation: Real or Relative?", in Derek Aldcroft and Ross Catterall (eds.), *Rich*

*Nations – Poor Nations: The Long-Run Perspective*, Cheltenham 1996, p. 109).

77. Robin Moore, "Imperial India, 1858–1914," in Andrew Porter (ed.), *The Oxford History of the British Empire: The Nineteenth Century*, Oxford 1999, p. 441.

78. Marcello de Cecco, *The International Gold Standard: Money and Empire*, New York 1984, p. 30.

79. Ravi Palat, et al., "Incorporation of South Asia," p. 185. According to these authors, the apparent exceptions to Indian deindustrialization in fact proved the rule: cotton spinning was integral to the production of an export surplus from the China trade while jute manufacture was an "island of British capital ... initiated, organized, and controlled by British civil servants and merchants" (p. 186).

80. Ibid., pp. 37–8.

81. J. Stamp, *British Incomes and Property*, London 1916, p. 36.

82. Cain and Hopkins, pp. 338–9.

83. Eric Hobsbawm, *Industry and Empire: An Economic History of Britain Since 1750*, London 1968, p. 123.

84. The same question, of course, could be asked of Indonesia, which in the late nineteenth century generated almost 9 percent of the Dutch national domestic product. See Angus Maddison, "Dutch Income in and from Indonesia, 1700–1938," *Modern Asian Studies* 23:4 (1989), p. 647.

85. Eric Stokes, "The First Century of British Colonial Rule in India: Social Revolution or Social Stagnation?" *Past and Present* 58 (Feb. 1873), p. 151.

86. Dietmar Rothermund, *An Economic History of India*, New York 1988, p. 36; Dutt, *Open Letters*, p. 48.

87. Lu Aiguo, *China and the Global Economy Since 1840*, Helsinki 2000, pp. 34, 37 and 39 (Table 2.4).

88. J.W. Wong, *Deadly Dreams: Opium and the Arrow War (1856–1860) in China*, Cambridge 1998, pp. 390 and 396. The British tea imports from China, which opium also financed, were the source of the lucrative tea duty that by mid-century almost compensated for the cost of the Royal Navy (pp. 350–55).

89. Lu Aiguo, p. 36.

90. Latham, *The International Economy*, p. 90. India (including Burma) also earned important income from rice exports to the Dutch East Indies.

91. Ibid., pp. 409–10. See also M. Greenberg, *British Trade and the Opening of China*, Cambridge 1951, p. 15.

92. Latham, pp. 453–4.

93. Ibid., pp. 81–90. After Japan's victory in 1895, however, its textile exports began to crowd India and Britain out of the Chinese market (p. 90).

94. Cain and Hopkins, p. 425.

95. Jerome Ch'en, *State Economic Polices of the Ch'ing Government, 1840–1895*, New York 1980, p. 116.

96. Latham, ibid.

97. John Hobson, "The Military-Extraction Gap and the Wary Titan: The Fiscal Sociology of British Defense Policy, 1870–1913," *Journal of European Economic History* 22:3 (Winter 1993), p. 480.

98. Historians have yet to address Chi-ming Hou's complaint in 1963 that "no serious studies have ever been made of the effects of such wars on the Chinese economy" ("Some Reflections on the Economic History of Modern China, 1840–1949," *Journal of Economic History* 23:4 [Dec. 1963], p. 603).

99. Bohr, p. 24.

100. Michelle McAlpin, "Price Movements and Fluctuations in Economic Activity," in Dumar (ed.), *Cambridge Economic History of India*, p. 890.

101. John McGuire, "The World Economy, the Colonial State, and the Establishment of the Indian National Congress," in I. Shepperson and Colin Simons (eds.), *The Indian National Congress and the Political Economy of India, 1885–1985*, Avebury 1988, p. 51.

102. Nash, p. 88.

103. McAlpin, "Price Movements," ibid.

104. Bandyopadhyay, *Indian Famine*, p. 130.

105. De Cecco, pp. 62 and 74. "[Indians] considered fiscal pressure to be unduly high, in view of the fact that the Indian government's budget was every year in surplus and the country had a trade surplus year after year; in addition to which the government had a substantial credit balance" (p. 74).

106. Krishnendu Ray, "Crises, Crashes and Speculation," *Economic and Political Weekly* (30 July 1994), pp. 92–3. By 1913 the Government of India's account in London was £136 million (ibid.).

107. Dieter Rothermund, "The Monetary Policy of British Imperialism," *IESHR* 7 (1970), pp. 98–9.

108. Wilkinson, pp. 34, 41–3, 52.

109. Wright, *The Last Stand of Chinese Conservatism*, p. 166.

110. Ch'en, p. 120.

111. Aiguo, p. 48.

112. Wilkinson, pp. 34, 41–3, 52.

113. Lewis, p. 216.

114. Charlesworth, pp. 13 and 22.

115. Tomlinson, "Economics: The Periphery," p. 68 (Table 3.7).

116. Quoted in Bipan Chandra, "Colonial India: British versus Indian Views of Development," *Review* 14:1 (Winter 1991), p. 102.

117. Bagchi, p. 27.

118. William Lavely and R. Bin Wong, "Revising the Malthusian Narrative: The Comparative Study of Population Dynamics in Late Imperial China," *Journal of Asian Studies* 57:3 (Aug. 1998), pp. 714–48.

119. Esther Boserup, *The Conditions of Agricultural Growth: The Economics of Agrarian Change Under Population Pressure*, Chicago 1967.

120. Angus Maddison, *Chinese Economic Peformance in the Long Run*, Paris 1998, p. 39. See also Zhang Kaimin, "The Evolution of Modern Chinese Society from the Perspective of Population Changes, 1840–1949," in Frederic Wakeman and Wang Xi (eds.), *China's Quest for Modernization: A Historical Perspective*, Berkeley 1997.

121. Pomeranz, p. 121.

122. Gernet, p. 560.

123. Martin Heijdra, "The Socio-Economic Development of Ming Rural China (1368–1644)," Ph.D. diss., Princeton University 1994, pp. 50–56; and Mote, pp. 903–6.
124. Mote, p. 906.
125. Pomeranz, "Two Worlds of Trade," pp. 81–3.
126. Patrick O'Brien, "Intercontinental Trade and Third World Development," *Journal of World History* (Spring 1997), p. 91.
127. Hardiman, "Well Irrigation in Gujarat," p. 1533. He is characterizing the conclusions of Anil Agarwal and Sunita Narain (*Dying Wisdom: Rise, Fall and Potential of India's Traditional Water Harvesting Systems*, Delhi 1997).
128. Feuerwerker, p. 21.
129. Maddison, *Chinese Economic Performance*, p. 30.
130. As the geographer Joshua Muldavin has emphasized, economic and ecological poverty are not equivalent: Households with identical levels of economic poverty can have extremely different levels of vulnerability to climatic instability or disaster ("Village Strategies for Maintaining Socio–Ecological Security in the post-Mao Era," unpublished paper, UCLA Department of Geography, 1998).

## Notes to Chapter 10

The quotation in the epigraph is from Romesh Chunder Dutt, *Open Letters to Lord Curzon*, Calcutta 1904, p. 27.

1. Maddison, *Chinese Economic Performance*, p. 67. Revisionist attempts to claim an increase in per capita income in Victorian India despite an undeniable collapse in life expectancy are dealt with, rather devastatingly, by Irfan Habib in "Studying a Colonial Economy — Without Perceiving Colonialism," *Modern Asian Studies* 19:3 (1985), pp. 368–74.
2. H. M. Hyndman, *The Awakening of Asia*, London 1919, p. 22.
3. B. Tomlinson, *The Economy of Modern India, 1860–1970*, Cambridge 1993, p. 31.
4. Sumit Guha, "Introduction," in Guha (ed.), *Growth, Stagnation or Decline? Agricultural Productivity in British India*, Delhi 1992, pp. 45–6.
5. Kingsley Davis, *Population of India and Pakistan*, Princeton, N.J. 1951, p. 8. Measured from the "good decade" of the 1880s to 1911–21, Irfan Habib (Table 2, p. 373) finds that male life expectatancy declined by 22 percent.
6. Laxman Satya, "Cotton and Famine in Berar, 1850–1900," Ph.D. diss., Tufts University 1994, pp. 50 and 155. See also Peter Harnetty, *Imperialism and Free Trade: Lancashire and India in the Mid-Nineteenth Century*, Vancouver 1972.
7. Dewey, "The End of the Imperialism of Free Trade," p. 51.
8. Stanley Wolpert, *A New History of India*, Oxford 1989, p. 248.
9. Satya, pp. 21–7, 36–7, 50–51, 72, 155, 162, 188–90 and 333; and "Introduction" to book version (*Cotton and Famine in Berar, 1850–1900*, Delhi 1997), p. 25.
10. Satya, p. 182 (export); and Vasant Kaiwar, "Nature, Property and Polity in Colonial Bombay," *Journal of Peasant Studies* 27:2 (Jan. 2000), p. 7 (acreage).
11. Satya, p. 182.

12. Charlesworth, p. 81.

13. Satya, pp. 68 and 298.

14. Ibid., p. 200.

15. Ibid., pp. 148, 281–2 and 296.

16. Tim Dyson, "The Historical Demography of Berar, 1881–1980," in Dyson (ed.), *India's Historical Demography: Studies in Famine, Disease and Society*, London 1989, pp. 181–2.

17. David Washbrook, "The Commercialization of Agriculture in Colonial India: Production, Subsistence and Reproduction in the 'Dry South,' c. 1870–1930," *Modern Asian Studies* 28:1 (1994), p. 131.

18. Ibid., pp. 137 and 161. In another article, Washbrook claims that the average cultivator had only half the dry land acreage needed for subsistence ("Economic Development and Social Stratification in Rural Madras: The 'Dry Region' 1878–1929" in Dewey and Hopkins [eds.], pp. 70–72).

19. David Washbrook, *The Emergence of Provincial Politics: The Madras Presidency, 1870–1920*, Cambridge 1976, p. 69.

20. Washbrook, "Commercialization of Agriculture," p. 145.

21. Ibid., p. 146.

22. Richards and McAlpin, p. 83

23. Washbrook, "Commercialization of Agriculture," p. 153.

24. As elsewhere in India, British land settlements in the 1860s had transformed the conditional tenure of Mogul or (in this case) Maratha tax farmers into a simulacrum of an English squirearchy. The ranks of the *malguzars,* however, were severely pruned in the terrible repression that followed 1857. Rebel leaders were shot from cannon, hanged or, in one case, even crucified by vengeful British officers. See D. E. U. Baker, pp. 101–6.

25. On the credit system and merchant hypothecation of harvests, see T. Raghavan, "Malguzars and Peasants: The Narmada Valley, 1860–1920," in David Ludden (ed.), *Agricultural Production and Indian History*, Delhi 1994, pp. 309 and 339–40.

26. Baker, p. 124

27. Peter Harnetty, "Crop Trends in the Central Provinces of India, 1861–1921," *Modern Asian Studies* 11:3 (1977), p. 347.

28. Baker, p. 106.

29. Ibid., p. 147.

30. Ibid., p. 151.

31. Ibid., pp. 129 and 150.

32. Raghavan, p. 311.

33. Ibid., pp. 137–41.

34. Ibid., pp. 182–3; Solberg, *The Prairies and the Pampas*, p. 36 (Table 3.3).

35. Singh, *Starvation and Colonialism*, p. 220.

36. Neeladri Bhattacharya, "Lenders and Debtors: Punjab Countryside, 1880–1940" in Bose (ed.), *Credit, Markets and the Agrarian Economy*, p. 200.

37. Singh, *Starvation and Colonialism*, p. 220.

38. Ibid., p. 221.

39. Hardiman, "Introduction," pp. 13–14.

40. Colin Fisher, "Planters and Peasants: The Ecological Context of Agrarian Unrest on the Indigo Plantations of North Bihar, 1820–1920," in Clive Dewey and A. Hopkins (eds.), *The Imperial Impact: Studies in the Economic History of Africa and India*, London 1978, pp. 125–31.

41. Carl Trocki, *Opium, Empire and the Global Political Economy*, London 1999, p. 67.

42. Binay Chaudhuri, "Growth of Commercial Agriculture," *IESHR* 7:2 (1970), pp. 231, 246–9.

43. Ibid., p. 251. On sugar, see Shahid Amin, *Sugar and Sugarcane in Gorakhpur: An Inquiry into Peasant Production for Capitalist Enterprise in Colonial India*, Delhi 1983.

44. Raghavan, p. 336.

45. Shahid Amin, "Small Peasant Commodity Production and Rural Indebtedness: The Culture of Sugarcane in Eastern U.P., c. 1880–1920" in Sugata Bose (ed.), *Credit, Markets and the Agrarian Economy of Colonial India*, Delhi 1994, p. 124.

46. Sarkar, pp. 30–31.

47. Bipan Chandra quoted in D. Rothermund, *Phases of Indian Nationalism*, Bombay 1970, p. 264 fn19.

48. Burton Stein, *A History of India*, London 1998, p. 263.

49. Lance Davis and Robert Huttenback, *Mammon and the Pursuit of Empire: The Economics of British Imperialism*, Cambridge 1988, pp. 101 (quote) and 135.

50. Vasant Kaiwar, "The Colonial State, Capital and the Peasantry in Bombay Presidency," *Modern Asian Studies* 28:4 (1994), p. 800.

51. David Washbrook, "Economic Development and Social Stratification," p. 69.

52. Bagchi, pp. 6 and 38.

53. Kaiwar, p. 793.

54. Guha, pp. 27 and 70.

55. Scott, p. 21.

56. Osborne, p. 554.

57. Charlesworth, pp. 193–5.

58. Quoted in ibid., p. 40.

59. C. Baker, "The Markets," in Sugata Bose (ed.), *Credit, Markets and the Agrarian Economy of Colonial India*, Delhi 1994, p. 192.

60. David Washbrook, "Progress and Problems: South Asian Economic and Social History, c. 1720–1860," *Modern Asian Studies* 22:1 (1988), p. 90.

61. Christopher Baker, *An Indian Rural Economy, 1880–1955: The Tamilnad Countryside*, Bombay 1984, p. 156.

62. B. Chaudhuri, "Agrarian Relations in Bengal: 1859–1885," in N. Sinha (ed.), *The History of Bengal (1757–1905)*, Calcutta 1967, pp. 318–20.

63. Kaiwar, p. 800.

64. Martha Chen, *Coping with Seasonality and Drought*, Delhi 1991, p. 119.

65. David Ludden, *Peasant History in South India*, Princeton, N.J. 1985, p. 122.

66. Chetan Singh, p. 44.

67. Satya, p. 299.

68. Atuluri Murali, "Whose Trees? Forest Practices and Local Communities in Andhra, 1600–1922," p. 100.

69. Madhav Gadgil and Ramachandra Guha, "State Forestry and Social Conflict in British India," in Hardiman (ed.), *Peasant Resistance*, p. 275.

70. Hardiman, "Introduction," pp. 47–8.

71. Satya, p. 120.

72. Baker, pp. 157 and 161.

73. V. Saravanan, "Commercialisation of Forests, Environmental Negligence and Alienation of Tribal Rights in Madras Presidency, 1792–1882," *IESHR* 35:2 (1998), p. 139; and Ramachandra Guha, "An Early Environmental Debate: The Making of the 1878 Forest Act," *IESHR* 27:1 (1990), p. 67.

74. Nash, pp. 21, 125 and 164–5.

75. Ludden, "Introduction," pp. 23–4.

76. Jos Gommans, "The Silent Frontier of South Asia, c. AD 1000–1800," *Journal of World History*, 9:1 (1998), p. 17.

77. Ludden, "Introduction," pp. 23–4.

78. Neeladri Bhattacharya, "Pastoralists in a Colonial World," p. 70.

79. Charlesworth, pp. 77 and 295.

80. Sumit Guha, pp. 58–61, 65–6.

81. Bandyopadhyay, p. 163.

82. Kaiwar, p. 57.

83. Bhattacharya, p. 65.

84. Ibid., pp. 56–7,

85. Kaiwar, "Nature, Property and Polity," p. 14.

86. Sumit Guha, pp. 83 and 121–3. See also H. Mann, *A Study of Rainfall in the Bombay Deccan, 1865–1938*, Bombay 1955.

87. Satya, pp. 72, 116 and 122.

88. Hardiman, "Well Irrigation in Gujarat," p. 1534.

89. Satya, ibid.

90. *The Finances and Public Works of India* (pp. 7–8), quoted in Elizabeth Whitcombe, *Agrarian Conditions in Northern India*, vol. 1, *The United Provinces Under British Rule, 1860–1900*, Berkeley, Calif. 1972, p. 2.

91. Under Company rule, of course, infrastructural investment had been infamously nugatory. Thus John Bright once demonstated in Parliament that the Corporation of Manchester spent more on public works in 1856 than the East India Company had expended on all of India during the preceding fourteen years (cited in Lady Hope, p. 258).

92. Elizabeth Whitcombe, "Irrigation," in Dharma Kumar (ed.), *The Cambridge Economic History of India, Volume Two: 1757–c. 1970*, Cambridge 1983, p. 703.

93. General Sir Arthur Cotton, *The Madras Famine*, London 1877, p. 5. See also Florence Nightingale, letter to the *Illustrated News*, 29 June 1877.

94. "Discussion with Woodrow Wyatt," *The Collected Works of Mahatma Gandhi*, vol. 83 (no. 473, 13 April 1946), Ahmedabad 1981, pp. 404–5.

95. S. Sharma, "Irrigation," in V. Singh, *Economic History of India: 1857–1956*, Bombay 1966, pp. 165; and Whitcombe, "Irrigation," pp. 678, 703–7.

96. *Famine and Agrarian Problems*, p. 232.

97. Ian Stone, *Canal Irrigation in British India*, Cambridge 1984.

98. Whitcombe, *Agrarian Conditions*, p. 11.

99. Quoted in Stone, p. 88.

100. Ibid., p. 154; and Whitcombe, *Agrarian Conditions*, p. 81.

101. Tomlinson, p. 76.

102. Whitcombe, *Agrarian Conditions*, pp. xi and 75.

103. Quoted in Whitcombe, "The Environmental Costs of Irrigation in British India: Waterlogging, Salinity, Malaria," p. 247.

104. *Papers on the Revenue Returns of the Canals of the North-Western Provinces* (1865), quoted in Stone, p. 75.

105. Ibid., p. 260.

106. Whitcombe, "Irrigation," pp. 716–17 and 720 (quote).

107. C. J. O'Donnell, *The Failure of Lord Curzon*, London 1903, p. 99.

108. Ludden, "Introduction," pp. 104 and 146.

109. Kaiwar, "Nature, Property and Polity," pp. 23 and 25.

110. The *Nasik Gazetteer*, 1883, quoted in Kaiwar, ibid.

111. Hyndman, *The Bankruptcy of India*, p. 128.

112. See Ranabir Chakravarti, "The Creation and Expansion of Settlements and Management of Hydraulic Resources in Ancient India," in Grove, Damodaran and Sangwan, pp. 87–105.

113. Hardiman, "Small–Dam Systems of the Sahyadris," p. 204.

114. Jonathan Mabry and David Cleveland, "The Relevance of Indigenous Irrigation," in Mabry (ed.), *Canals and Communities: Small-Scale Irrigation Systems*, Tucson, Ariz. 1996, pp. 227–8 (quote) and 236 (efficiency).

115. M. Quraishi, *Drought Strategy*, Delhi 1989, p. 42. On the other hand, private exploitation of underground water resources since the 1960s has led to a profligate drawing down of the water table and a wholly avoidable water crisis.

116. "But for their listless acceptance of the worst miseries in the hand of fate, India would ages ago have been fertilized by a system of irrigation, and saved almost from the possiblity of Famine. The Natives are one of the most improvident as well as helpless races on earth" (*The Times*, 23 Jan. 1877).

117. Col. J. Anderson of the Madras Engineers quoted in "Philindus," "Famines and Floods in India," *Macmillan's Magazine*, Jan. 1878, p. 237.

118. Grove, pp. 134–5.

119. Lady Hope, p. 194. See also G. Rao, "Canal Irrigation and Agrarian Change in Colonial Andhra: A Study of Godavri District, c. 1850–1890," *IESHR* 25:1 (1988).

120. Quoted in Zook, pp. 163–4.

121. Bagchi, pp. 28–9.

122. William Wedderburn, *Agricultural Banks for India*, p. 27.

123. Fawcettt in *The Times* quoted in George Chesney, "Indian Famines," *The Nineteenth Century*, Nov. 1877, p. 618.

124. Berar, p. 197.

125. H. M. Hyndman, *The Indian Famine*, London 1877, p. 12; and John Dacosta, *Facts and Fallacies Regarding Irrigation as a Prevention of Famine in India*, London 1878, pp. 2–4. Simi-

lar arguments are advanced in "A Journalist," *The Great Lesson of the Indian Famine*, London 1877 (pamphlet collection, Trinity College Library, Dublin).
126.  Bandyopadhyay, p. 115.
127.  Baker, p. 472.
128.  Ludden, *Peasant History*, p. 146 (see Table 5).
129.  *The Hindu* (Madras), 10 May 1900.
130.  Navtej Singh, *Starvation and Colonialism: A Study of Famines in the Nineteenth Century British Punjab, 1858–1901*, New Delhi 1996, p. 8.
131.  Satya, p. 85.
132.  R. Carstairs, *The Little World of an Indian District Officer*, London 1912, pp. 364–5.
133.  Kaiwar, "Nature, Property and Polity," p. 23.
134.  Nash, p. 2.
135.  Ravinder Kumar, *Western India in the Nineteenth Century*, London 1968, p. 325.
136.  Ludden, "Introduction," pp. 104 and 146.
137.  David Mosse, "Colonial and Contemporary Ideologies of 'Community Management': The Case of Tank Irrigation Development in South India," *Modern Asian Studies* 33:2 (1999), p. 315.
138.  Hardiman, "Well Irrigation in Gujarat," p. 1541.

## Notes to Chapter 11

The epigraph is from Wolfgang Bauer, *China and the Search for Happiness*, New York 1976, p. 257.

1.  Karl Wittfogel, *Oriental Despotism: A Comparative Study of Total Power*, New Haven, Conn. 1957, p. 290.
2.  Susan Naquin and Evelyn Rawski, *Chinese Society in the Eighteenth Century*, New Haven, Conn. 1987, pp. 22, 146 and 219; and Will, *Bureaucracy and Famine*, pp. 64–5.
3.  Huang, *Peasant Family*, p. 42 (also pp. 74–6).
4.  Kamal Sheel, *Peasant Society and Marxist Intellectuals in China*, Princeton, N.J. 1989, p. 94.
5.  Little, *Understanding Peasant China*, p. 92.
6.  Sidney Gamble, *Ting Hsien: A North China Rural Community*, New York 1954, pp. 52, 64 and 110.
7.  Huang, *Peasant Family*, p. 5.
8.  Huang, *Peasant Economy*, pp. 102–6 and 152.
9.  Nichols, pp. 128–9.
10.  Ibid., pp. 248–50.
11.  Huang, *Peasant Economy*, p. 115.
12.  Laura Murray, "New World Food Crops in China: Farms, Food and Families in the Wei River Valley, 1650–1910," Ph.D. diss., University of Pennsylvania, 1985, pp. 43–4.
13.  Ibid., pp. 45, 68, 82 and 138.
14.  Madeleine Zelin, "Modernization and the Structure of the Chinese Economy in the Nineteenth and Twentieth Centuries," in Frederic Wakeman and Wang Xi (eds.), *China's*

*Quest for Modernization: A Historical Perspective*, Berkeley 1997, p. 93.

15. Huang, *Peasant Family*, pp. 102–6.
16. Huang, *Peasant Economy*, p. 124; and Will, pp. 178 and 180–81.
17. Dr. J. Edkins, *Opium: Historical Note on the Poppy in China*, Shanghai 1898, p. 66.
18. Murray, pp. 74–5 and 79.
19. Zelin, p. 108.
20. Arthur Smith, *Village Life in China* (1899), Boston 1970 (reprint), pp. 210–11.
21. Naquin and Rawski, p. 143.
22. Huang, *Peasant Economy*, pp. 7 and 118–19.
23. Ibid., p. 60.
24. Pauline Keating, *Two Revolutions: Village Reconstruction and the Cooperative Movement in Northern Shaanxi, 1934–1945*, Stanford, Calif. 1997, p. 15.
25. Huang, *Peasant Economy*, pp.107–8 and 114.
26. Kamal Sheel, *Peasant Society and Marxist Intellectuals in China*, Princeton, N.J. 1989, pp. 54–7; and K. Chaudhuri, "Foreign Trade and Balance of Payments," in Dharma Kumar (ed.), *The Cambridge Economic History of India, Volume 2*, Cambridge 1983, p. 853.
27. Calculated from Table 7 in Albert Feuerwerker, *The Chinese Economy, ca. 1870–1911*, Michigan Papers in Chinese Studies, Ann Arbor, Mich. 1969.
28. Huang, *Peasant Economy*, p. 132.
29. Nichols, p. 248.
30. Esherick, pp. 72–3.
31. Wilkinson, pp. 198–9.
32. Perkins, *Agricultural Development in China, 1368–1968*, Chicago 1969, pp. 119 and 136.
33. On long-distance commercial flows, see R. Bin Wong, "Food Riots in the Qing Dynasty," *Journal of Asian Studies* 41:4 (Aug. 1982), pp. 768–9.
34. Naquin and Rawski, p. 219.
35. Esherick, p. 40.
36. Will, p. 291.
37. "Decline and Its Opposition," in Will and Wong, p. 91.
38. Manfred Domros and Peng Gongbing, *The Climate of China*, Berlin 1988, p. 198.
39. Randall Dodgen, "Hydraulic Evolution and Dynastic Decline: The Yellow River Conservancy, 1796–1855," *Late Imperial China* 12:2 (Dec. 1991), pp. 51 and 55–6.
40. Wang Yeh-chien, *Land Taxation in Imperial China, 1750–1911*, Cambridge, Mass. 1973, pp. 113, 121 and 125–6.
41. Kung-Chuan Hsiao, *Rural China: Imperial Control in the Nineteenth Century*, Seattle 1960, p. 146.
42. Perkins, p. 164. (As explained in Chapter 9, however, the population in 1700 may have been much higher than Perkins assumes.)
43. Will, p. 276.
44. Wong, p. 783.
45. Perkins, p. 164.
46. R. Bin Wong, "The Grand Structure, 1736–1780," in Will and Wong, pp. 60–61.
47. On the crisis in Shaanxi's granaries, see "Decline and Its Opposition," ibid., p. 78.
48. Hsiao, p. 154.

49. Perkins , pp. 150–51.

50. Will, p. 289.

51. Will, pp. 276–7.

52. There were exceptions, of course, as in Gansu in 1810 where "the large sum of one million taels was allotted for a comprehensive and apparently successful effort to reach the stricken population" (Will, p. 296).

53. *Land Utilization in China: Statistics*, Nanking 1937, p. 344, Table 2.

54. T. Kingsmill, "Inland Communications in China," *Journal of the China Branch of the Royal Asiatic Society* (for the year 1895–96), Shanghai 1899, pp. 3 and 147.

55. Wright, p. 175 (also pp. 176–80).

56. Keating, p. 25.

57. Ibid., p. 314. "Corruption had always been a way of life in China, but in the nineteenth century it reached unprecedented proportions, not to be exceeded until the first half of the twentieth century" (Victor Lippit, "The Development of Underdevelopment in China," in Philip Huang (ed.), *The Development of Underdevelopment in China: A Symposium*, White Plains, N.Y. 1980, p. 67).

58. Jonathan Spence, *God's Chinese Son: The Taiping Heavenly Kingdom of Hong Xiuquan*, New York 1996, p. 158.

59. Jen Yu-wen, *The Taiping Revolutionary Movement*, New Haven, Conn. 1973, pp. 54 and 94. "Toleration of corrupt and rapacious officials" and the "selling of offices through bribes" were another two of the "ten major crimes" of the Qing (p. 94).

60. Spence, p. 161.

61. Roberts, pp. 181–2.

62. E. Parker, "The Financial Capacity of China," *Journal of the China Branch of the Royal Asiatic Society* (1893–1894), Shanghai 1898, pp. 97–8.

63. Murray, p. 270.

64. Nichols, p. 235.

65. Murray, pp. 315 and 318.

66. Ibid., p. 183.

67. Kenneth Pomeranz, EH.NET Forum: "Rethinking 18th-Century China," Internet, 16 Dec. 1997.

68. Maddison, pp. 34–5.

69. Hans Van De Ven, "Recent Studies of Modern Chinese History," *Modern Asian Studies*, 30:2 (1996), p. 241.

70. Robert Marks, *Tigers, Rice, Silk, and Silt: Environment and Economy in Late Imperial South China*, Cambridge 1998, pp. 277 and 307.

71. Rhoads Murphey, "Deforestation in Modern China," in Richard Tucker and J. F. Richards (eds.), *Global Deforestation and the Nineteenth-Century World Economy*, Durham 1983, p. 111. He cautions, however, that "it is not known, or discoverable by any means, what China's forest cover was at any point in the nineteenth century, or the extent of net depletion in the course of that century" (p. 114).

72. Anne Osborne, "The Local Politics of Land Reclamation in the Lower Yangtzi Highlands," *Late Imperial China* 15:1 (June 1994), p. 2.

73. Marks, ibid.; and Peter Perdue, *Exhausting the Earth*, Cambridge, Mass. 1987.

74. Eduard Vermeer, "Population and Ecology along the Frontier in Qing China," in Elvin and Liu, pp. 249–51 and 261. Since Qing tax rates were essentially capped, the easiest way to increase land revenues was by encouraging the expansion of land area under cultivation.

75. Anne Osborne, "Barren Mountains, Raging Rivers: The Ecological Effects of Changing Landuse on the Lower Yangzi Periphery in Late Imperial China," Ph.D. diss., Columbia University 1989, p. 158.

76. Murray, p. 278.

77. Von Richtofen's letters to the *North China Herald* (1870–72) are discussed in W. Lowdermilk, "Forestry in Denuded China," *Annals of the American Academy* 15 (Nov. 1930), pp. 137–8.

78. Frank Leeming, *The Changing Geography of China*, Oxford 1993, p. 50.

79. Murray, p. 69.

80. Murphey, p. 119.

81. Keating, pp. 23–4.

82. Vermeer, p. 235.

83. Eliot Blackwelder, "A Country That Has Used Up Its Trees," *The Outlook* 82 (24 March 1906), pp. 693–700.

84. Murphey, p. 116.

85. Lowdermilk, p. 137.

86. Ibid., p. 139.

87. Pomeranz, p. 124.

88. On this process in Shandong and Liaotung, see Cressey, pp. 208–9.

89. Will, p. 129.

90. Lowdermilk, pp. 130 (proverb) and 140 (erosion rate).

91. Murphey, pp. 126–7.

92. W. Lowdermilk, "A Forester's Search for Forests in China," *American Forests and Forest Life* 31 (July 1925), p. 239.

93. Vermeer, pp. 273–4.

94. Murphey, p. 125.

95. Charles Greer, *Water Management in the Yellow River Basin of China*, Austin, Tex. 1979, p. 18.

96. Murphey, pp. 124–5.

97. Greer, p. 33.

98. Ibid. The struggle to control the Mississippi in the late nineteenth and early twentieth centuries produced its own version of warring hydraulic schools with the Army Corps as unconscious Confucians and civilian engineers like Charles Ellet and James Eads as spontaneous Taoists. See the fascinating account (pp. 19–93) in John Barry, *Rising Tide*, New York 1997.

99. Randall Dodgen, "Hydraulic Evolution," pp. 36 fn1 and 50–51. In a significant dissent from the mainstream of late Imperial historians, Dodgen argues that the "crisis of the Yellow River control system was the product of riparian realities, and was not primarily determined by Qing institutional vitality or decline" (p. 59).

100. Vermeer, p. 265.

101. Mark Elvin and Su Ninghu, "Action at a Distance: The Influence of the Yellow River on Hangzhou Bay Since A.D. 1000," in Mark Elvin and Liu Ts'ui-jung (eds.), *Sediments of Time: Environment and Society in Chinese History*, Cambridge 1998, pp. 344–407.
102. Randall Dodgen, "Controlling the Dragon: Confucian Engineers and the Yellow River in the Late Daoguang, 1835–1850," Ph.D. diss., Yale Univesity 1989, p. 40.
103. Will, p. 292; also Naquin and Rawski, p. 24.
104. Dodgen, "Hydraulic Evolution," p. 55.
105. Ibid., p. 56.
106. Jonathan Spence, *The Search for Modern China*, New York 1990, p. 185; and Teng, p. 40.
107. Wright, pp. 161–3.
108. Esherick, pp. 14–15.
109. Ibid.
110. Pomeranz, *The Making of a Hinterland*, p. 179.
111. Jurgen Osterhammel, "Britain and China," in Andrew Porter (ed.), *The Oxford History of the British Empire: The Nineteenth Century*, Oxford 1999, p. 160.
112. Ibid., pp. 3, 15–16, 131 and 157–60.
113. Esherick, p. 292.
114. Pomeranz, p. 183.
115. Ibid., p. 16.
116. Buck quoted in Kueh, p. 117.
117. Maddison, p. 30.
118. Murray, pp. 128 and 266.
119. Naquin and Rawski, p. 24.
120. Modern studies of the impact of irrigation in Shaanxi cited in E. Vermeer, *Water Conservancy and Irrigation in China*, The Hague 1977, p. 182.
121. Murray, pp. 276–7.
122. Vermeer, p. 172 fn26; and Sidney Gamble, *Ting Hsien*, p. 235.
123. Vermeer, pp. 7, 182, 187 and 288–9 (quote).
124. James Kynge, "Yellow River Brings Further Sorrow to Chinese People," *Financial Times*, 7 Jan. 2000.

## Notes to Chapter 12

The definition in the epigraph is from G. Dia et al., "Drought as a Social Phenomenon in Northeastern Brazil," in Rolando Garcia and José Escudero, *Drought and Man, Volume 3: The Roots of Catastrophe*, Oxford 1986, p. 106.

1. Cf. Bradford Burns, *A History of Brazil*, Berkeley, Calif. 1970, p. 102; Andre Gunder Frank, *Capitalism and Underdevelopment in Latin America: Historical Studies of Chile and Brazil*, New York 1967, pp. 162–4; and Emilia Viotta da Costa, *The Brazilian Empire: Myths and Histories*, Chapel Hill, N.C. 1985, pp. 21–4.
2. Nathaniel Leff, "Economic Development in Brazil, 1822–1923," in Stephen Haber (ed.), *How Latin America Fell Behind*, Stanford, Calif. 1997, pp. 1, 35; and Warren Dean,

"The Brazilian Economy, 1870–1930," in Leslie Bethall (ed.), *The Cambridge History of Latin America*, vol. 5 (1870–1930), Cambridge 1986, p. 685.

3. Jaime Reis, "Hunger in the Northeast: Some Historical Aspects," in Simon Mitchell (ed.), *The Logic of Poverty: The Case of the Brazilian Northeast*, London 1981, pp. 50–52.

4. Cain and Hopkins, p. 298.

5. Stephen Haber and Herbert Klein, "Hunger in the Northeast: Some Historical Aspects," in Haber (ed.), p. 251; and Alan Manchester, *British Preeminence in Brazil: Its Rise and Decline*, Chapel Hill, N.C., pp. 337–40.

6. Bertha Becker and Claudio Egler, *Brazil: A New Regional Power in the World-Economy*, Cambridge 1992, p. 32.

7. Dean, p. 708.

8. Stephen Haber, "Financial Markets and Industrial Developments," in Haber (ed.), p. 151.

9. Ruthanne Deutsch, "Bridging the Archipelago: Cities and Regional Economies in Brazil, 1870–1920," Ph.D. diss., Yale University 1994, p. 190.

10. Levine, *Vale of Tears*, p. 55.

11. Quoted in David Jordan, *New World Regionalism*, Toronto 1994, p. 35.

12. Dean, p. 708.

13. Leff, p. 53–4.

14. Cain and Hopkins, p. 303.

15. Ibid., pp. 303–4.

16. Deutsch, p. 167.

17. Dean, p. 723; and Winston Fritsch, *External Constraints on Economic Policy in Brazil, 1889–1930*, London 1988, p. 3.

18. Dean, p. 696.

19. Nathaniel Leff, *Underdevelopment and Development in Brazil*, vol. 1, London 1982, p. 7.

20. Deutsch, pp. 3–5. In Jeffrey Williamson's well-known 1960s study of regional inequality in twenty-four major countries, the polarization between Brazil's Northeast and its Center-South was the most extreme. (See the discussion in "Regional Inequality and the Process of National Development: A Description of the Patterns," in L. Needleman (ed.), *Regional Analysis: Selected Readings*, Baltimore 1968, pp. 110–15.)

21. Leff, "Economic Development," p. 35.

22. Deutsch, p. 86.

23. Leff, "Economic Development," p. 35.

24. Levine, p. 55.

25. Leff, "Economic Development," pp. 27, 35–6.

26. Eul-Soo Pang, *PCCLAS Proceedings* 8 (1981–82), p. 2.

27. Levine, p. 49.

28. Leff, "Economic Development," p. 39; and Deutsch, p. 163.

29. Gerald Greenfield, "The Great Drought and Imperial Discourse in Imperial Brazil," *Hispanic American Historical Review* 72:3 (1992), pp. 385 and 396.

30. Greenfield, "Migrant Behavior and Elite Attitudes," p. 83.

31. Eul-Soo Pang, *Bahia in the First Brazilian Republic*, Gainesville, Fla. 1979, p. 62.

32. Ibid., p. 56.

33. Leff, "Economic Development," p. 39.

34. J. Galloway, "The Last Years of Slavery on the Sugar Plantations of Northeast Brazil," *Hispanic American Historical Review* 51 (Nov. 1971), fn54.

35. Quoted in Joseph Love, *Crafting the Third World: Theorizing Underdevelopment in Rumania and Brazil*, Stanford, Calif. 1996, p. 163.

36. Sir Richard Burton, visiting the sertão in 1867, described one vast fazenda that used to run 66 kilometers along the São Francisco river divided into scores of impoverished and failing ranches (Hall, *Drought and Irrigation*, p. 33).

37. Webb, pp. 68, 81. In the twentieth century, palma, a spineless cactus, would be adopted as a forage crop ideally suited to the aridity of the sertão (pp. 84–5).

38. Chandler, *The Feitosas*, pp. 129–30.

39. Ibid., p. 137.

40. Webb, p. 115.

41. Webb summarizes Guimaraes Duque's landmark study, *Solo e agua no poligono das secas* (1949), pp. 85–8.

42. Allen Johnson, *Sharecroppers of the Sertão: Economics and Dependence on a Brazilian Plantation*, Stanford, Calif. 1971, pp. 17, 47–8.

43. Cunniff, pp. 14–15, 25 and 28–9.

44. Levine, p. 43.

45. Cunniff, p. 37.

46. Hamilton de Mattos Monteiro, *Crise agaria e luta de classes: o Nordeste brasileiro entre 1850 e 1889*, Brasilia 1980, pp. 157–63.

47. Hall, p. 17.

48. Cunniff, pp. 33–4.

49. Hall, p. 3.

50. Cunniff, pp. 55, 61; Webb, pp. 112–13.

51. Chandler, pp. 131–2.

52. Cunniff, pp. 65–6.

53. Hall, p. 4.

54. Cunniff, p. 80.

55. Webb, p. 116.

56. Ibid., p. 83.

57. Hall, p. 36.

58. Cunniff, 87–93.

59. Ibid., p. 96.

60. Cunniff, 104–6

61. Monteiro, p. 47.

62. Ibid., pp. 129–33 and 191–3.

63. Cunniff, p. 102.

64. Dean, p. 690.

65. Hall, p. 5.

66. "… one indication of how little times have changed lies in the reports of root poisoning suffered by the desperately hungry in 1970, reminiscent of the graphic accounts given by Theophilo a century earlier" (Hall, p. 12).

# Index